World of Warcraft®
Programming

World of Warcraft® Programming

Programming

A Guide and Reference for Creating WoW Addons

James Whitehead II
Bryan McLemore
Matthew Orlando

Wiley Publishing, Inc.

World of Warcraft® Programming: A Guide and Reference for Creating WoW Addons

Published by
Wiley Publishing, Inc.
10475 Crosspoint Boulevard
Indianapolis, IN 46256
www.wiley.com

Copyright © 2008 by Wiley Publishing, Inc., Indianapolis, Indiana
Published simultaneously in Canada

ISBN: 978-0-470-22981-1

Manufactured in the United States of America

10 9 8 7 6 5 4 3 2 1

For general information on our other products and services or to obtain technical support, please contact our Customer Care Department within the U.S. at (800) 762-2974, outside the U.S. at (317) 572-3993 or fax (317) 572-4002.

Library of Congress Cataloging-in-Publication Data
Whitehead, James, II, 1979-
  World of Warcraft programming : a guide and reference for creating WoW addons / James Whitehead II, Bryan McLemore, Matthew Orlando.
      p. cm.
  Includes index.
  ISBN 978-0-470-22981-1 (paper/website)
  1. Computer games--Programming. 2. World of Warcraft. I. McLemore, Bryan, 1982- II. Orlando, Matthew, 1982- III. Title.
  QA76.76.C672W55 2008
  794.8'1526--dc22
                        2008004978

For the World of Warcraft User Interface Community

About the Authors

James Whitehead II is the author of a number of popular addons for World of Warcraft such as PerfectRaid, Clique, LightHeaded, TomTom, and many other small addons available at www.wowinterface.com. He has been an active member of both the WoW UI and the Lua communities since the World of Warcraft Beta began and has been writing addons since. When he actually has time to play the game, you can find him playing one of his many characters on the Stormrage (US) server, or feverishly leveling his characters on Ravencrest (EU).

Jim is a graduate of Syracuse University where he completed both his BSc and MSc in computer science. He is currently pursuing his DPhil in computer science at the University of Oxford, where he is also the teaching assistant for the Computing Laboratory. In his spare time, he enjoys rowing competitively for Worcester College and stabbing his friends in the back playing Munchkin.

Bryan McLemore has been a member of the UI community since early 2005. After creating KC_AutoRepair, he went on to co-found the Ace Project and WowAce.com as Kaelten alongside Brent Miller (Turan in the UI community). Following Brent's official departure from WoW, Bryan found himself having to devote more and more time to WowAce and less to his addons; however, he refuses to give up on OneBag and KC_Items. When he actually manages to spend time playing World of Warcraft, he plays one of his many alts on the US server Whisperwind.

In the remainder of his free time, he is leading the development of Ace3 and working on plans for his addons, along with a few websites he would like to see developed. Bryan recently started a full-time career in web development and system administration when he moved to California with his wife and daughter. They currently live in San Francisco.

Matthew Orlando is the author of numerous addons for World of Warcraft, including BuyEmAll, CogsBar, and MacroTalk. He has been programming for 13 years and has been active in the addon community since early 2006. In addition to his extensive experience with Lua and the World of Warcraft API, he maintains "Cogwheel's Complete Macro Guide," the definitive source for information on writing macros for WoW.

Matthew currently resides in Sebastopol, California, with his wife, Juliella; their dog, Ari; and two cats, Ryo-ohki and Zoe. He works for Kistler Vineyards where his duties range from customer service and data entry to database programming and website development, and he plans to begin law school in mid-2008.

Credits

Executive Editor
Chris Webb

Development Editor
Maryann Steinhart

Contributing Author
Dan Fernandez

Technical Editors
Rick Roe
Stephen Luster
James Carrothers
André Ericsson
Daniel Gilbert
Hendrik Leppkes
Antonio Lobato
Matt Richard
Esteban Santana Santana

Production Editor
Martine Dardignac

Copy Editor
Marcia Ellett, Cate Caffrey,
Foxxe Editorial Services

Editorial Manager
Mary Beth Wakefield

Production Manager
Tim Tate

**Vice President and Executive
Group Publisher**
Richard Swadley

**Vice President and Executive
Publisher**
Joseph B. Wikert

Project Coordinator, Cover
Lynsey Stanford

Compositor
Craig Woods,
Happenstance Type-O-Rama

Proofreader
Sossity Smith

Indexer
Johnna VanHoose Dinse

Cover Image
Front cover art: Lar Desouza (based on
the characters of Looking For Group)
Back cover art © Dorling
Kindersley/Getty Images

Contents

Introduction

Since World of Warcraft (WoW) was released on November 23, 2004, it has quickly grown to be one of the most popular video games ever created. Currently boasting more than nine million subscribers, it seems that everyone knows *someone* who plays. World of Warcraft is an extremely immersive environment that allows you to customize your character, explore new worlds, and group with friends without requiring an enormous time commitment. Some players spend 4 to 6 hours a night raiding with their guilds trying to defeat the latest and greatest monster. Others prefer player-to-player combat, spending time in the Arena or Battlegrounds trying to improve their standing. Some players just enjoy playing the game when they have spare time with a group of friends. World of Warcraft has something to offer each of these players, and that's probably one of the primary reasons for its success.

One aspect of the game that reaches each of these play styles is user interface customization in the form of *addons*. For those players who are technically inclined or simply can't accept things being anything less than perfect, Blizzard has opened up its user interface to allow players to customize and change its overall functionality. Addons can be as simple as changing the colors of health bars or adding a new slash command to do random emotes, or as complex as providing a full-scale networked calendar that allows guilds to organize and synchronize events. Beyond opening up this world of customization, Blizzard continues to provide enhancements and support for the user interface community in a way that no other game developer has done.

The user interface community has grown immensely over the past few years, and shows no signs of stopping. This book was written to give the reader the tools necessary to create custom modifications to the World of Warcraft user interface, including an introduction to the languages, terminology, and structure of addon creation. There are thousands of addons out there waiting to be written, and this book provides you with the skills necessary to realize them.

Whom This Book Is For

This book is designed to be useful to the novice addon user who wants to learn how to tweak existing addons, to the budding addon authors looking to add more exciting features to their repertoire, and to the advanced addon developer as a reference to the extremely complex WoW UI system. The only assumptions made throughout the book are that the reader is familiar with World of Warcraft and has an interest in programming. Readers who have had exposure to programming languages in any form will find many of the concepts presented to be familiar.

The reader with little to no prior programming experience should initially focus on the first section of the book, which teaches Lua, the programming language that is used to write addons. Although readers with no programming experience will learn enough to create and modify addons, they may want to pursue more general programming lessons from another source to supplement the material presented.

For readers with prior programming experience, the first few chapters will be very easy. The examples can be used to pick up the basic rules of the Lua programming language rather quickly. If the reader is already familiar with high-level scripting languages such as Python, he can easily skim the first few chapters and move right into the second section, which covers the basics of addon creation itself. These chapters detail how the WoW addon system works for the author, and leads users through writing their first addon.

Addon authors may want to skip directly to the third section of the book. Its chapters introduce specific concepts and walk through the creation of working example addons that use the concepts. Some of the more difficult systems (such as tooltips, dropdown menus, and state headers) are explored in depth.

In addition, the fourth section of the book contains an extremely comprehensive reference to the WoW API, including events and widgets.

How This Book Is Organized

This book is divided into four parts that introduce increasingly complex topics to the reader.

Part I is an introduction to Lua and XML, bringing the user up to speed with the languages needed to create addons.

Part II discusses the anatomy of an addon and the basics behind event-driven programming in World of Warcraft. In this part the reader creates his/her first addon and becomes familiar with the WoW API.

Part III of the book guides the reader through some of the more advanced topics by creating a number of addons from start to finish.

Finally, Part IV is a comprehensive reference to the entire API, including functions, widgets, events, and secure templates.

What's on the Web Site

Every few months, Blizzard releases a new patch for World of Warcraft that may intro-duce new content, fix existing bugs, or even drastically change game mechanics. As a result, the material covered in this book will change from time to time. To help combat this problem, the authors have created a companion website for the book at `http://wowprogramming.com`. While we do not expect sweeping changes to the core concepts, the details of any specific changes will be listed on the website, including information about how those changes affect the material in this book. Besides serving as a glorified errata repository, the website also has online versions of all the references included in the book.

From Here

The World of Warcraft user interface community is a very exciting place with endless possibilities for customization and realization of ideas. World of Warcraft is a fun game in its own right; the capability to use it as a development platform for addons that can help users and enhance their game experience is an extra bonus that each of us can enjoy. So Enjoy!

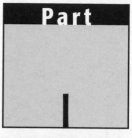

Part

I

Learning to Program

Programming for World of Warcraft

James Whitehead II

World of Warcraft (WoW) was released in November 2004 and has quickly become the model for Massively Multiplayer Online Role Playing Games (MMORPG). Providing an intuitive user interface and a low barrier to success, more than ten million users currently play the game with their friends, co-workers, and family. WoW provides something for the players who spend six hours a night with their guilds, the cubicle warriors who play for half an hour a day on their lunch breaks, and a large range in between.

Beyond the gameplay itself, a meta-game has formed around customizing the user interface and writing elaborate macros for the game. Blizzard provides an extremely powerful system for creating third-party addons, and programmers have been taking advantage of the open system since the beta test for the game. This book is designed to teach you how to create these custom addons.

Customizing the User Interface

The World of Warcraft game client consists of two major parts: the game world and the user interface. The game world is the three-dimensional world in which your character resides. This includes the buildings and terrain, other players, and interactive objects such as herbs, mining veins, and signposts. The game world also includes the character names that are displayed above other players. These elements are not accessible through the scripting interface and cannot be modified.

3

The user interface comprises the other elements of the game client, including the action buttons, unit frames, maps, and options windows. Addons are written to add to or modify existing elements to add functionality, or show information in a different way.

How Do Addons Work?

An addon is simply a folder that resides in your World of Warcraft directory, consisting of text files, images, sounds, and fonts. These addons are loaded by the client and run within its scripting system. This definition of addons does not include any third-party executables that are run outside the game (these sorts of programs are prohibited by WoW's terms of services). Addons use only the scripting interface that is provided to developers, and are run by the game itself.

The average addon consists of several individual components that work together to create a final product, including:

- A table of contents file to identify the addon and its components
- Media files, such as graphics and sounds
- Lua scripts that define the behavior of the addon
- XML files that define the visual elements (frames) of your addon

The first part of this book takes you through each of these components, giving you the tools and skills you will need to write addons effectively.

What Can Addons Do?

As a general rule, addons are allowed to display any information available to the game client to enable the user to make well-informed decisions. They can visually alter the user interface in many ways, although there are limitations on how they can change the behavior of that interface.

Prior to the release of the Burning Crusade expansion pack, there were several addons that Blizzard deemed against the spirit of the game. These addons were later disabled with changes to the way they interact with the game client. The following actions are unavailable to addons:

- Automatic character movement
- Automatic target selection
- Automatic selection and use of spells or items
- Real-time communication with external programs

In addition, addons are unable to provide a way for Horde to speak with Alliance, or vice versa. This is prohibited through the World of Warcraft "Terms of Use" (http://www.worldofwarcraft.com/legal/termsofuse.html).

Getting Started with Lua

The Lua programming language was designed and implemented at the Pontifical Catholic University of Rio de Janeiro in Brazil. Lua is a powerful, lightweight, embedded scripting language that is used in several large software projects, including WoW.

The first five chapters of this book introduce you to the Lua programming language through a series of interactive examples. While these examples should be easy to understand without you needing to run them, we strongly encourage you to download a Lua interpreter so you can run through the examples on your own. In addition, an interpreter allows you to easily explore the language to increase your overall understanding of concepts.

There are three easy ways to obtain a Lua interpreter:

1. Download WowLua, an addon the authors have written that gives you an interactive Lua interpreter within World of Warcraft.

2. Visit the book's website at `http://wowprogramming.com/utils/weblua` to use an interactive Lua interpreter within your web browser.

3. Download a Lua interpreter onto your computer, so it can be run locally without access to the Internet or WoW.

Downloading and Installing WowLua

For the purposes of this book, we have created a version of the Lua interpreter that runs as an addon within World of Warcraft. This is the simplest way to install a Lua interpreter for anyone with experience using addons. It also has the advantage of letting you work within the game, allowing you to test your work on-the-fly, experiment with the default UI and other addons, and still be able to chat with your friends and guild.

Navigate to `http://wowprogramming.com/addons/wowlua` and click the download link to get the latest version of the WowLua addon. This will download a .zip file to your computer. Once you save the file, you can extract it using your favorite compression utility or by double-clicking it on a standard Windows XP or Mac OS X machine. A single folder called `WowLua` will be extracted. Place the folder in the `Interface\AddOns` folder underneath your World of Warcraft installation.

You can verify that the addon is installed properly by clicking the Addons button in the bottom-left corner of your character selection screen. You should see the addon listed in a fashion similar to that shown in Figure 1-1.

Figure 1-1: WowLua in the addon listing

Select a character and log in to the game. Type either /lua or /wowlua into the chat box to open the WowLua window (see Figure 1-2). You can close the window by clicking the X button in the top-right corner, or by pressing the Esc key.

Figure 1-2: WowLua interactive interpreter

Using Lua on the Web

For those people who don't want to run these examples within WoW and have access to an Internet connection, we've created a simple webpage that serves as a Lua interpreter over the web, called WebLua. Simply browse to http://wowprogramming.com/ utils/weblua to begin.

Downloading and Installing a Lua Interpreter

If you prefer to download an interpreter so you can work offline, downloadable packages are available for both Microsoft Windows and Mac OS X.

Microsoft Windows

The interpreter for Microsoft Windows can be downloaded at http://wowprogramming .com/downloads/lua/windows. The package doesn't require any installation; you can simply place it anywhere that is convenient for you. Extract the ZIP file to a new folder and place it where you can easily find it again.

To launch the Lua interpreter, go to the files you've extracted and double-click the icon for the interpreter. This opens a window that looks something like that shown in Figure 1-3. You can also create a shortcut to this file from which you can launch the interpreter.

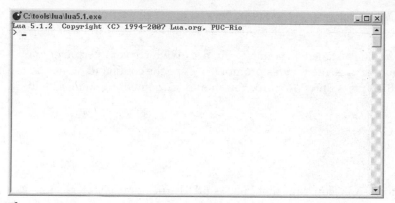

Figure 1-3: Lua running on Microsoft Windows

Mac OS X

A Lua interpreter for Mac OS X can be found at `http://wowprogramming.com/downloads/lua/macosx`. The download is a standard disk image that can be mounted on your system. To mount it, navigate to the disk image and double-click it. From the new volume, simply copy the Lua interpreter application somewhere on your machine that you will remember (the Applications folder may be a good location).

To launch the Lua interpreter, navigate to the file you downloaded and extracted, and double-click the icon. A window similar to that shown in Figure 1-4 should appear. There is no setup program to run and the application can be run from anywhere.

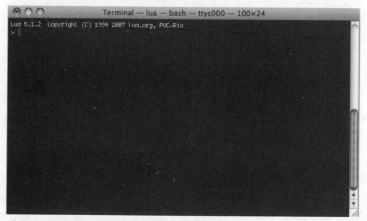

Figure 1-4: Lua running on Mac OS X

Exploring Your Lua Interpreter

Now that you have Lua installed on your system, fire up whichever interpreter you've chosen. You should be presented with a prompt (>). Type the command `print("Hello Azeroth!")` and then press Enter (Return). You should see something similar to this in your window:

```
> print("Hello Azeroth!")
Hello Azeroth!
>
```

You've just successfully run your first Lua script! The next few chapters show you what exactly this command does, but the simple test shows you have the basics you need to run everything presented in Part I of this book.

# CHAPTER 2

Exploring Lua Basics

James Whitehead II

The Lua programming language is relatively small so you may find similarities to other languages you already know. Lua is most often compared to Python because both are relatively easy for a non-programmer to use when compared to languages such as C or Java. Many different languages have served as inspiration for the design and evolution of Lua, including Lisp, Scheme, Pascal, and C.

This chapter serves as a general introduction to the Lua programming language. If you have prior experience with Lua or have extensive experience using other programming languages, you may want to skim this chapter and run through some of the interactive exercises.

ON THE WEB You can read more about the Lua programming language at www.lua.org. The website contains a large amount of reference material, including an online version of *Programming in Lua*, a book entirely about the Lua programming language.

Using the Lua Interpreter

You'll use the interactive Lua interpreter you installed in Chapter 1 for all of the examples and exercises in this chapter. When you launch your interpreter for the first time, you are greeted with something similar to the following:

```
Lua 5.1.1  Copyright © 1994-2007 Lua.org, PUC-Rio>
```

The first line contains the version string of the particular Lua interpreter you are using. Because World of Warcraft uses a slightly modified version of Lua 5.1, it is best to use an interpreter with a minimum version of 5.1. If you are using the WowLua addon that was introduced in Chapter 1, you are already using the correct version, so the version prompt is not displayed. The second line of output is the prompt, where you can type commands to be run.

Running Commands

The Lua interpreter is interactive, enabling you to input commands and receive a response, like a conversation between two friends. You will receive instant feedback with any errors in your code, allowing you to tinker with the language to see how it works.

Type the following command at the prompt (you only need to type the part after the >):

```
> print("Hello Azeroth!")
```

You should see the following output:

```
Hello Azeroth!
>
```

This simple command takes the text string `"Hello Azeroth!"` and sends it to the function `print()`, which outputs the string to your window. You'll examine the nitty-gritty details of what this actually means later in this chapter.

NOTE For the purposes of this chapter, consider a function to be a process that you can give information, and have it complete some task. In this case, you feed a string to the function, which prints it to the output window.

Understanding Error Messages

Inevitably, you will make a typo and get an error from Lua when running a command. The error messages are usually human-readable and will tell you where the problem occurred. Type the following command at the prompt (note that you're intentionally misspelling the word `print`):

```
> prnit("Hello Azeroth!")
```

The response, a typical error message in Lua, is similar to this:

```
stdin:1: attempt to call global 'prnit' (a nil value)
stack traceback:
        stdin:1: in main chunk
        [C]: ?
>
```

The first line gives you the error message and the line number on which the error occurred. In this case, Lua says that you tried to call a global `'prnit'`, which is a nil value. In layman's terms, it means you tried to call a function that doesn't exist.

The rest of the error message is called a stack traceback, which tells you where the error occurred. This will be useful when you begin calling functions from other functions.

Using History to Make Changes

Depending on the Lua interpreter you are using, you may be able to view recent command-line history (the last few commands you've given the interpreter) by pressing the Up and Down arrow keys. Test this now by pressing the Up key on your keyboard while in your Lua interpreter. (This always works in WowLua, but may not work correctly if you are using a standalone version of Lua.)

If it worked correctly, you should see the last line you typed (`prnit("Hello Azeroth!")`) and your cursor should be at the end of the line. If it didn't work, you may instead see something similar to the following:

```
> ^[[A
```

That simply means your specific interpreter doesn't handle history. While you may find this inconvenient at times, it certainly shouldn't hamper your capability to run through the examples correctly.

Quitting the Interpreter

When you are done running code in the interpreter, in most cases, you can simply close the window. However, if you started the interpreter from a command line and want to return to it, you can use one of the following methods, depending on your operating system.

Microsoft Windows

On a Microsoft Windows system, Lua can be closed by pressing Ctrl +Z. This inserts the following into your interpreter:

```
> ^Z
```

In Windows this inserts a special character that means end-of-file, and it causes the interpreter to quit. You can also press Ctrl+C to outright kill your session.

Mac OS X

Mac OS X is a UNIX-based system, so the end-of-file character is different from that of the Windows systems. At your prompt, press Ctrl+D to insert the end-of-file character and end the session immediately. You can also use Ctrl+C to kill the session.

Working with Numbers

Almost every language has a way to calculate numeric values, and Lua is no different. Type the following into your interpreter:

```
> print(2 + 2)
```

As expected, you will see 4 as the response followed by another prompt. Although it may not be the most convenient calculator, the interpreter does enable you to perform calculations in your programs.

Basic Arithmetic Operations

Table 2-1 shows Lua's basic arithmetic operators. You can use any of them to compute a value.

Table 2-1 Valid Arithmetic Operators

OPERATION	IN LUA	EXAMPLE
Addition	+	> print(4 + 4) 8
Subtraction	–	> print(6 - 10) -4
Multiplication	*	> print(13 * 13) 169
Division	/	> print(10 / 2) 5
Exponentiation	^	> print(13 ^ 2) 169
Modulo	%	> print(8 % 3) 1
Unary Negation	–	> print(- (4 + 4)) -8

The Modulo operator is new to Lua 5.1.

In addition to these operators, you can use parentheses to group expressions together to make more complex expressions. Consider the following example:

```
> print(2 * (1 + 2 + 3) ^ 3)
432
```

If you run this command with no parentheses in the expression itself, you get an entirely different answer:

```
> print(2 * 1 + 2 + 3 ^ 3)
31
```

Parentheses are used to make an expression explicit and ensure that it is evaluated properly. In the second case, the exponentiation operator is processed first, followed by the multiplication operator and then the addition operator, giving you the equivalent formula:

```
> print(2 + 2 + 27)
```

When in doubt, make your math explicit so it is easier to read when review is needed in the future.

Scientific Notation

Occasionally, you'll encounter an extremely large number such as 10,000,000,000,000,000 (10^{15}). Rather than type it out each time with zeroes or use parentheses to make sure it's being calculated correctly inside another formula, you can use scientific notation. Lua may automatically display large numbers using scientific notation if printing them would be unwieldy. Run the following commands:

```
>print(10 ^ 15)
1e+015
>print(10 ^ -15)
1e-015
```

As you can see, Lua converts the numbers to scientific notation for the purpose of printing them. Conveniently, you can also write numbers in this fashion, which takes the first number and multiplies it by 10 raised to the second number (the e in between can be capitalized or lowercase.) For example:

```
> print(1.23456e5)
123456
> print(1.23456 * (10 ^ 5))
123456
> print(1234e-4)
0.1234
> print(1234 * (10 ^ -4))
0.1234
```

You may not encounter numbers in scientific notation often, but understanding the output when Lua sends it back to you is important.

Hexadecimal Notation

Lua can natively convert a number in hexadecimal notation to the decimal value. You can use this as a quick hex-to-decimal conversion, or you may actually have a need to use hexadecimal notation in your systems. Lua expects a zero, followed by the letter x, followed by a string of valid hex digits (0-F).

```
> print(0x1)
1
> print(0xF)
15
> print(0x10)
16
> print(0x10a4)
4260
```

When writing code, you can refer to numbers in this format and Lua will convert them properly. As you can see from these examples, however, Lua only responds in decimal or scientific notation, regardless of how the numbers were input.

```
> print(2 * 0xF)
30
> print(0x10 ^ 2)
256
```

Understanding Floating Point

Every number in a standard Lua system is represented internally as a floating point number. For average use this won't make a difference, but it can have some odd implications. Here's a simple (but confusing) example, which uses some concepts that you won't examine until later in this section of the book:

```
> pointTwo = 1.2 - 1.0
> print(pointTwo < 0.2)
true
> print(pointTwo)
0.2
```

The number 0.2 cannot be accurately represented as a floating point number, so the programming language must do a bit of rounding when calculating the value, and then again when printing it. The floating point numbers can accurately represent any integer from 10^-37 through 10^37, so you shouldn't encounter many of these problems. This rounding can, however, serve as a source of calculation error when working with the real numbers.

ON THE WEB   Much information regarding floating point numbers and the implications of the format exists out there on the Web. The following resources are all extremely helpful if you're interested in exploring the topic further:

```
wikipedia.org/wiki/Floating_point
docs.sun.com/source/806-3568/ncg_goldberg.html
lua-users.org/wiki/FloatingPoint
```

Understanding Values and Variables

Like most other languages, Lua makes a distinction between values (such as the string `"Hello"` and the number `14`) and variables (or references). Understanding the underlying types of values and the distinction between a value and a variable can be helpful while programming.

Exploring Values and Their Types

A value is the actual thing that is used, such as the number `17`, or the string `"Hello"`. The number `14` is a different value from the number `27`, but they are both number values. The string `"Hello"` is a value, but it is a different type of value than the two numbers. (There's nothing tricky or complex that you need to understand about values, I promise!)

There are eight primitive types in the Lua programming language and every value you encounter will have one of them. You've already seen two different types, number and string. The line between a string and number can occasionally get blurry, such as drawing the distinction between the string `"4"` and the number `4`, but they remain discrete types.

Primitive Types

Table 2-2 describes Lua's primitive types. Every value ends up being one of these types, regardless of where it's encountered in the language.

Table 2-2 Lua's Primitive Types

TYPE	DESCRIPTION
number	All numbers (include hexadecimal numbers and those using scientific notation) have this type. **Examples:** `1`, `7313`, `1e5`, `0xFFF1a`
string	A sequence of characters. **Examples:** `"Hello"`, `"Test String"`.
Boolean	The values `true` and `false` are of the Boolean type.

Continued

Table 2-2 *(continued)*

TYPE	DESCRIPTION
function	A function is a collection of statements that can be called, and will be introduced in Chapter 3.
table	A table is a mix between a traditional hash table (dictionary) and arrays.
nil	The value `nil` is of the special type `nil`.
thread	A value of the thread type is a coroutine (limited lightweight thread) that can be used for asynchronous computation.
userdata	Userdata is traditionally a wrapper around some data structure defined in the host language (usually C).

Each of these types will be encountered through the course of your work, so you should be aware of them.

Using the type() Function

Within Lua you can use the `type()` function to determine the type of a given value, which gives you flexibility when it comes to validation and verification in your programs. Type the following into your Lua interpreter:

```
> print(type(5))
number
```

What you've done here is call the `type()` function with a value of 5, and call the `print()` function with that result (you'll explore functions further in Chapter 3). The output shows that the type of the value 5 is `number`, as you'd expect. Here are some other examples:

```
> print(type("Hello Azeroth!"))
string
> print(type(2 * (1 + 2 + 3) ^ 3))
number
> print(prnit)
nil
```

In the third example note the misspelling of the variable `prnit`. As you saw earlier in this chapter, that is a `nil` value, so the type function returns `nil` as expected. You can always use the `type()` function to find out which type your value is.

Using Variables

A *variable* can be seen as a temporary name for a specific Lua value, with the caveat that the same value may have multiple names. An example here will be more telling than words, so type the following into your interpreter (it may not have output after each line, so just move on to the next line):

```
> x = 4
> y = 2
> print(x + y)
6
```

In this example, you take the name x and bind it to the value 4; and bind the name y to the value 2. You then call the print function, and instead of using the numbers 4 and 2, you use the names x and y.

Valid Variable Names

A variable's name or *identifier* has to start with a letter or an underscore character. The name cannot contain anything other than letters, numbers, or the underscore character. In addition, it can't be any of the keywords that are reserved by Lua: and, break, do, else, elseif, false, for, function, if, in, local, nil, not, or, repeat, return, then, true, until, and while. A variable name is also case-sensitive, so the character a is different from the character A, meaning that the following are all different identifiers:

- MyVariable
- myVariable
- myvariable

Assigning Variables

Use the assignment operator = to bind a value to a variable name, with the variable name on the left and the value on the right. Try the following examples in your Lua interpreter:

```
> foo = 14
> print(foo)
14
> foo = "Hello!"
> print(foo)
Hello!
```

The first example binds the value 14 to the identifier foo, and you can print and use that variable instead of the value itself. The second binds the value "Hello" to the identifier, changing what the variable refers to.

Variables can be used on the right-hand side of an assignment operator as well, and what happens in those situations is different depending on the context. Try the following in your interpreter:

```
> x = 4
> y = x
> print(y)
```

```
4
> x = 3
> print(y)
4
```

The first line simply binds the value 4 to the identifier x. The second line, however, assigns the value of identifier x to identifier y. This means quite literally that both x and y are names for the same value (the number 4). As a result, when you run x = 3, you simply change that binding, leaving y intact.

TIP The distinction between *values* and *variables* can be confusing, especially when working through more advanced topics. Use the Lua interpreter as a tool to explore the rules and better understand what's happening.

Assigning Multiple Variables

There are occasions where you will be assigning more than one variable at a time, and a convenient short form makes this easier. Run the following example:

```
> x,y = 3,5
> print(x * y)
15
```

The assignment operator allows a list of variables on the left side and a list of values on the right side. That'll be a bit more useful when you get into functions and return values. If there are more variables on the left hand side than there are values on the right hand side, the remaining variables will be set to nil.

Comparing Values

In many cases, you will need to compare different values to see how they are related. There are several comparison operators (listed in Table 2-3) that can be used.

Table 2-3 Comparison Operators

COMPARISON OPERATOR	EQUIVALENT LUA OPERATOR
equality	==
less than	<
greater than	>
less than, or equal	<=
greater than, or equal	>=
not equal	~=

These operate exactly as you'd expect, but you can play in the Lua interpreter to better understand them. When you print the result of a comparison, it will be of the Boolean type (that is, `true` or `false`).

```
> print(1 == 1)
true
> print(1 < 3)
true
> print(1 > 3)
false
> print(2 <= 2)
true
> print(1 >= 3)
false
> print(1 ~= 3)
true
```

The equality operators (`==` and `~=`) can be used to compare any two values, but the `<`, `>`, `<=`, and `>=` operators can only be used with values of the same type, such as when comparing number to number or string to string; otherwise you will get an error as follows:

```
> print(1 < "Hello")
stdin:1: attempt to compare number with string
stack traceback:
        stdin:1: in main chunk
        [C]: ?
```

In other words, while the `==` and `~=` operators work for all values, the less than/greater than (`<` and `>`) family of operators is only defined for numbers, as string values.

Working with Strings

You've already been introduced to the `string` type, and you've used it to print `"Hello Azeroth!"` in the interpreter. Now you'll examine strings in a bit more detail.

Comparing Strings

The less than (`<`) and greater than (`>`) operators can be used on strings, but the result depends on the way your system internally sorts the different characters. For single character comparisons, the operator compares the two characters' order in the character set; for multiple character strings, it compares the order of the first two differing characters. For example:

```
> print("a" < "b")
true
> print("d" >= "c")
true
```

```
> print("abcd" < "abce")
true
> print("a" < "A")
false
> print("abcd" < "abcde")
true
> print("rests" < "test")
true
```

You may be surprised by the output from the fourth example. In the standard Lua character set, uppercase English letters precede lowercase letters, so the string `"a"` is actually greater than the string `"A"`. In the fifth example, the strings are identical until the first string runs out of characters. At this point, Lua sees that the second string still has the letter `"e"` and returns that the second is greater. However, in the final example, even though the first string is longer than the second one, the letter `"r"` is less than the letter `"t"`, so the whole string `"rests"` is less than `"test"`.

Concatenating Multiple Strings

Strings in Lua are immutable, which means they cannot be changed without creating an entirely new string. To add to a string, you use the special concatenation operator (..), which enables you to take two strings and fuse them together to make a new, larger string. Here are a couple of examples:

```
> x = "Hello"
> y = "Azeroth"
> print(x .. y)
HelloAzeroth
> foo = "a" .. "b" .. "c" .. "d" .. "e"
> print(foo)
abcde
```

Converting Numbers to Strings

As you can imagine, there are times you will need to convert from numbers to strings and, in most cases, Lua handles this for you. Try the following:

```
> print("Number: " .. 4)
Number 4
```

Lua automatically converts the number 4 to a string, and it's added to the string `"Number: "`. If you need to explicitly convert a number to a string, you can use the `tostring()` function, as in the following example:

```
> x = 17
> foo = tostring(x)
> print(type(foo))
string
```

The `tostring()` function takes whatever it is given (in this case a number) and turns it into a string value.

Converting Strings to Numbers

Conversely, you may have a string of digits that you'd like to convert to a number. Lua's built-in `tonumber()` function takes a value and turns it into a number. If the digits can't be converted (such as when the string doesn't contain a number), the function returns the value `nil`. Here are some examples:

```
> x = tonumber("1234")
> print(type(x))
number
> print(x)
1234

> x = tonumber("1e3")
> print(type(x))
number
> print(x)
1000
```

Here the strings are converted into numbers, and the results are printed to the screen. The `tonumber()` function has a few more tricks up its sleeve that you can explore in Chapter 7.

Quoting Strings

So far, you've used double quotes to create strings, but there are several ways to construct a string for use in Lua. When programming, it is considered proper style to use the same type of quote character (as described in the following sections) unless you have a specific reason for needing to use a different type. This helps other people read your code without confusion.

Single Quote (')

You can use the single quote mark (') — also called a tick or tick mark — to create a string, and this is standard convention. Nothing really special happens here unless you need to include a tick mark within your string. Look at the following examples:

```
> x = 'Hello'
> print(type(x))
string

> x = 'Isn't it nice?'
stdin:1: '=' expected near 'it'
```

The first example works correctly and creates a new string with the text Hello inside.

The second example throws an error that we should explore a bit more. What Lua sees here is an identifier (x), the assignment operator (=), and a string ('Isn'). Because Lua doesn't require any whitespace between most operations, it immediately starts the next part of the expression, which begins with the identifier t. The next thing the interpreter sees is another identifier called it, and doesn't know what to do with it. In this case, it infers that you meant to use the assignment operator and errors out with this suggestion.

You can get around this by *escaping* the tick mark that is inside the string to tell Lua that it's part of the string instead of the end of it. Here's an example:

```
> x = 'Isn\'t it nice?'
> print(type(x))
string
```

You'll tackle the details of string escaping shortly.

Double Quote (")

The double quote (") can be used the same way as the single quote, with the same caveat of needing to escape embedded quote characters. Here are some examples:

```
> x = "Hello"
> print(type(x))
string

> x = "Isn't it nice?"
> print(type(x))
string

> x = "I play the game, "World of Warcraft""
stdin:1: '=' expected near 'of'
```

The second works because the tick mark isn't being used to delimit the quote, but the inner quote in the third example needs to be escaped with a backslash.

```
> x = "I play the game, \"World of Warcraft\""
> print(type(x))
string
```

Bracket Quote ([[ ]])

Lua has the concept of a long quote that enables you to include multiple lines and internal quote characters. These quotes begin with the open bracket character ([), have any number of equal signs (=), including 0, and then another open bracket ([). The string closes only when it finds the opposite combination (close brace, equal signs, close brace). While this may seem overly complex, it enables you to tailor-make your quote start/end for the contents inside. Consider the following example:

```
> x = [[This is a long string, and I can include ' and "]]
> print(x)
This is a long string, and I can include ' and "
```

This includes no equal signs, which is the typical case. You could instead include any number of them, if you needed to use the string `"]]"` somewhere in your larger string, as in this example:

```
> x = [==[This is a long string, and I can include ]], ', and "]==]
> print(x)
This is a long string, and I can include ]], ', and "
```

You may not find yourself using the `[[Some String]]` syntax often, but it can be useful when the string spans multiple lines, or includes quote characters.

Escaping Special Characters

Beyond the ' and " characters, there are other characters that aren't necessarily typeable but need to be included in a string. Try to make a multiline string and see what happens:

```
> x = "First line
>> Second line"
stdin:1: unfinished string near '"First line'
```

Two things happen here: First, the prompt changes to two >> signs instead of the normal one. This typically means you have an unfinished block and the interpreter is waiting for you to finish the expression. Second, you get an error about an unfinished string. This is a peculiarity in the Lua interpreter, because nothing you can type on the second line will allow you to complete the expression.

You get around this by using \n, an escaped character that means new-line. Type the following:

```
> x = "First line\nSecond line"
> print(x)
First line
Second line
```

When constructing a string, you can include any of the escape sequences listed in Table 2-4. Not all entries will have effect when printed inside World of Warcraft, but you should be aware of what valid sequences exist because you may find them in pre-existing strings.

Table 2-4 String Escape Sequences

SEQUENCE	DESCRIPTION
\a	audible bell
\b	backspace
\f	form feed
\n	newline
\r	carriage return
\t	horizontal tab
\v	vertical tab
\\	backslash
\"	double quote
\'	single quote
\xxx	ASCII character ddd

In World of Warcraft, you typically only encounter \n, \\, \", \', and \xxx, because the output widgets in World of Warcraft don't support the others.

NOTE More often than not, you will find escape codes used in localization strings for addons. Some locales contain characters that aren't type-able on all keyboards, so they are inserted using the \xxx syntax. In the deDE localization for World of Warcraft, the word Hunter is "J\195\164ger", which is typically displayed as Jäger. Localization is discussed further in Chapter 9.

Getting a String's Length

There are two ways to obtain the length of a specific string: using the # operator or using the string.len() function. The length of a string is often used when validating or parsing strings.

Using the # operator before a string value returns the length as a number, as shown in the following example:

```
> print(#"Hello")
5

> foo = "This is a test string"
> print(#foo)
21
```

You can use the built-in function `string.len()` to accomplish the same feat. The period in between `string` and `len` means that this specific function is a part of the string namespace (which you'll learn more about in Chapter 4). Type the following into your interpreter:

```
> foo = "This is a test string"
> print(string.len(foo))
21
```

It returns the same value as the `#` operator because they both use the same underlying method to calculate the length.

Boolean Values and Operators

The `boolean` type is relatively simple and only has two possible values — `true` or `false` — but as with many things in programming, there's more than meets the eye. Three logical operators can be applied to Boolean values: `and`, `or`, and `not`.

Using the and Operator

The `and` operator is true when both of its arguments are true, and false when either of them is false or doesn't have a value. Examples help make this clearer:

```
> print(true and true)
true
> print(true and false)
false
> print(false and false)
false
> print(false and true)
false
```

This operator has one peculiarity that you might run into, illustrated by the following example:

```
> print(true and 4)
4
> print(true and "Hello")
Hello
```

Lua only evaluates as much of the expression as necessary (referred to as short-circuit evaluation). If the first argument is `true`, it simply returns the second argument, because the expression `true and value` evaluates to `true` if and only if `value` itself would evaluate to `true`.

Using the or Operator

The or operator is true any time either of its arguments is true. Again, a simple set of examples should make this clear, because there are only two possible truth values:

```
> print(true or true)
true
> print(true or false)
true
> print(false or false)
false
> print(false or true)
true
```

This operator has a lower precedence than the and operator, so make sure you are using it correctly, and include parenthesis when necessary. For example:

```
> print(false and false or true)
true
> print(true and false or false)
false
```

In the first example, even though false and false turns out to be false, it is part of a larger or statement, so the whole expression evaluates to true. This isn't Lua being confusing; it's the underlying Boolean logic at play.

HINT You can use the behavior of the and **and** or **operators to shorten some of your expressions if you remember how they are evaluated. These operators allow you to make the equivalent of the a ? b : c statement in C, using Lua. You will encounter more useful examples of this later, but here's a small example:**

```
> print(true and "Hello")
Hello
> print(false and "Hello" or "Azeroth!")
Azeroth!
```

Negation Using the not Operator

Simply enough, if you need to turn one Boolean value into the other, toggling it, you can use the not operator:

```
> print(not true)
false
> print(not false)
true
> print(not 4)
false
> print(not "Hello")
false
```

Again, because any value in Lua that is not `false` or `nil` evaluates to `true`, you can even negate those values.

Understanding the nil Value

Earlier in this chapter, you encountered the following error message:

```
stdin:1: attempt to call global 'prnit' (a nil value)
```

`nil` is a special thing that means lack of value in Lua. This is most often seen when working with variables and tables (which you will learn about in Chapter 5). Type the following into your interpreter:

```
> print(SomeEmptyVariable)
nil
> print(type(SomeEmptyVariable))
nil
```

Because you have not bound the variable `SomeEmptyVariable` to anything yet, it holds the special value `nil`, which is of type `nil`. You can use this knowledge to check if a variable is currently un-set, as in the following example:

```
> print(SomeEmptyVariable == nil)
true
> print(type(SomeEmptyVariable) == "nil")
true
```

You can check to see if a value is equivalent to nil, using the `==` operator. You can also check the type of the value, to see if that is `nil`. Be sure to note the difference between the value `nil`, and the string `"nil"`, since the `type()` function always returns a string.

Exploring Scope

So far, each and every variable you have declared has been a *global* variable, meaning it is accessible to all other parts of your program. There is another type of variable, which is called *local*, in that its visibility to the rest of the program is limited in some way. To fully understand the difference between global and local variables you need to understand the scope (or visibility rules) of blocks and chunks.

Blocks

The best way to illustrate a block is with an example, so type the following into your Lua interpreter:

```
> do
>> local i = 10
```

```
>> print("Inside: " .. i)
>> end
Inside: 10
```

Apart from the new keywords do, end, and local, you're simply assigning the value 10 to the variable i, and printing that out as part of a string. In this case, the do keyword tells the interpreter to begin a block, and the end keyword shows where the block ends. Now run the following code:

```
> print(i)
nil
```

By declaring the variable i as local, you've limited its scope to the current block, that is, all the variables within the do and end keywords. You can access this variable as much as you like within those boundaries, but outside that it's as if the variable doesn't exist.

In addition to manually creating blocks using do and end, certain Lua constructs such as for loops, while loops, and function definitions implicitly begin a new block. You will learn more about these constructs in Chapter 3.

BEST PRACTICE In World of Warcraft, your addons will be competing with any number of other addons that may use global variables. As a result, it is considered good practice to use local variables in many cases.

Chunks

Earlier in this chapter, you received a stack traceback with an error, and it may have referenced the main *chunk*. In Lua, a chunk is either the file being executed, or the string that is being run. Variables are also limited in scope to their specific chunk. This means a local variable declared at the top of one file won't be accessible in another file (they are different chunks).

In the Lua interpreter, each individual line you type is its own chunk, unless you wrap it in a block (such as the preceding do … end block). For this reason, the following code will not work:

```
> local i = 10
> print(i)
nil
```

This is just a peculiarity of the way the Lua interpreter works. To get around this, you can use do … end to wrap multiple lines of code.

```
> do
>> local i = 10
>> print(i)
> end
10
```

Scope and visibility will be more important when you start working with functions in Chapter 3, but it is important to understand the implication that almost all variables are global, unless specified otherwise.

Summary

This chapter gave you a very broad introduction to fundamental concepts central to the Lua programming language, including variables, values, types, operators, and scope. Chapters 3 through 6 will give you a more in-depth introduction to specific aspects of the language, as it relates to World of Warcraft. The Lua programming language is used extensively outside WoW and there are a number of good reference books on the language as a whole.

# CHAPTER 3

Basic Functions and Control Structures

James Whitehead II

In Chapter 2, you explored the basics of the Lua programming language using the `print()` and `type()` functions, without fully understanding what a function is. In addition, basic control structures such as loops and conditionals haven't been introduced yet.

The first part of this chapter explains the concept of functions and guides you through creating several of your own. The second half introduces the basic looping and conditional statements.

Using Functions

A function is a portion of a program that can be used to simplify repeated tasks or perform complex calculations. When a function is called it may be passed several *arguments*, that is, data that the function can use for the duration of its execution. When a function completes, it can *return* any number of values to the calling portion of the program.

Creating a Function

The function keyword can be used to create a new function, which can then be stored in a variable or called directly. A basic function declaration looks like this (type this into your Lua interpreter):

```
> hello = function()
>> print("Hello World!")
>> end
```

The function constructor begins where you type `function()` and continues to the matching end keyword, with the code between the delimiters making up the body of the function. The Lua interpreter recognizes the new block of code and indents the prompt to show you're continuing the same section of code (until you type the final `end`.) In this case, a function is created that takes no arguments (more on this in the next section) and prints the string `"Hello World"` before ending. The resulting function value is then assigned to the variable `hello`.

Now, instead of typing `print("Hello World")` every time you want to print that string, you can simply type `hello()` to call the new function. This is an extremely simple example, but you'll use the full power of functions as you move through the examples in this chapter.

Local Functions

The function constructor returns a new Lua value, so it can be assigned to a local variable the same as any other value. This can be useful when defining functions that are called within your addons, but need not be exposed for other addons to call. Local variables are difficult to explore in the Lua interpreter because each line of code is in its own scope, but you may find the technique of using local functions useful when working through the rest of this book.

SYNTACTIC SUGAR

Lua provides a different way to define functions that is more conventional and may be easier to read. Examine the following function definition:

```
function hello()
   print("Hello World!")
end
```

When the Lua interpreter encounters this definition, it is converted into the definition used in the previous section:

```
hello = function()
   print("Hello World!")
end
```

That is to say, the two definitions end up running the same code in the interpreter. Functions defined in this manner can be made local by adding the keyword `local` before the function constructor, such as:

```
local function hello()
   print("Hello World")
end
```

When the `local` keyword is used, it is converted to roughly the following version:

```
local hello = function()
   print("Hello World")
end
```

Function Arguments and Returns

When a function is called, it can be passed any number of arguments to be used in its calculations. In addition, a function may return any number of values when it completes. This allows for the creation of dynamic functions that can operate on values that are passed into the function, rather than some static formula or process.

Simple and repetitive tasks such as converting degrees Celcius to degrees Fahrenheit can easily be made into functions that use arguments and return values.

Converting Celsius to Fahrenheit

The conversion formula given for temperature conversion is "Multiply the temperature in degrees Fahrenheit by 1.8 and add 32 to the result."Instead of answering this with simple math, a function can be written that takes a value as an argument and returns the converted value as the answer. Type the following into your Lua interpreter:

```
> convert_c2f = function(celsius)
>> local converted = (celsius * 1.8) + 32
>> return converted
>> end
```

Here, a function is created with a single argument, which is named celsius. The first line of the new function calculates the converted value and the second line returns it. To see how this works, type the following:

```
> print(convert_c2f(0))
32
> print(convert_c2f(-40))
-40
```

When the new function is called, the first argument passed to it (the number 0) is assigned to a local variable named celsius (this corresponds to the name given in the function *declaration*). This allows the function to define the formula for conversion without needing to know the number we're converting.

Empty Arguments

Try the following in your interpreter:

```
> print(convert_c2f())
stdin:2: attempt to perform arithmetic on local 'celsius' (a nil value)
stack traceback:
        stdin:2: in function 'convert_c2f'
        stdin:1: in main chunk
        [C]: ?
```

When no value is passed as an argument, the argument gets the value of nil. Because the first line of the `convert_c2f` function tries to multiply `celsius` by `1.8`, it errors out, as `nil` can't be part of an arithmetic expression. A similar error will occur if you pass other non-number values into this function.

No Return Values Not each function you encounter will have a return statement since not every single function needs to return a value. The `hello()` function defined earlier in this chapter is one such example.

Functions as Lua Values

Each function in Lua is just a plain Lua value of the type `function`. These values can be compared (using `==` and `~=`), bound to variable names, passed to functions, returned from functions, and used as keys in tables (tables will be explored in Chapter 4). A Lua value that is treated in this way is called a *first-class object*, and a language that supports functions in this way is said to have *first-class functions*.

Run the following in your interpreter:

```
> hello = function() print("Hello World!") end
```

This creates a new function called `hello`. This value can now be compared in the same way you'd compare any other Lua value.

```
> print(hello == hello)
true
> hello2 = hello
> print(hello2 == hello)
true
> hello2 = function() print("Hello World!") end
> print(hello2 == hello)
false
```

In the preceding example, a new function is created and bound to `hello2`. Even though the new function has the exact same definition and body, it is actually a different distinct function.

Making Decisions with the if Statement

The if statement serves as the basis for decision making in Lua, and it supports simple conditionals as well as more complex statements. The syntax of the most basic `if` statement looks like this:

```
if <boolean expression> then
  -- do something
end
```

Simple Conditionals

An `if` statement can be used to execute a block of code conditionally when the boolean expression evaluates to true. A simple example will help make this clearer:

```
function conditional_test(num)
  print("You input: " .. num)
  if (num == 7) then
    print("You found the magic number!")
  end
end
```

This example function prints whatever number it gets passed, but if the number 7 is passed, it will print a special message. Input this function into your interpreter, and then test it with the following:

```
> conditional_test(3)
You input: 3
> conditional_test(7)
You input: 7
You found the magic number!
> conditional_test(13)
You input: 13
```

As with other arithmetic and boolean expressions, the parenthesis around the conditional are not strictly necessary, but they can certainly make code easier to read.

Complex Expressions

Every boolean condition in an if statement can be a simple test (such as `num == 7`) or a more complex expression that evaluates to some boolean value. This allows you to combine multiple conditions using the logical operators (`and`, `or`) into a single condition. The following are all valid conditions:

- `name`
- `type(name) == "string"`
- `(not anonymous_flag) and type(name) == "string")`

The first example simply checks to see that the variable `name` is anything other than `nil` or `false`. The second example checks to verify that the type of the variable `name` is `"string"`, and the final example checks to see that the variable `anonymous_flag` is either `false` or `nil`, and the type of the `name` variable is `"string"`.

Extended Conditionals

An extended form of the `if` statement allows multiple decisions along with default decisions. The full syntax for the `if` statement is:

```
if <boolean expression> then
  -- if part
```

```
elseif <boolean expression> then
  -- elseif part
elseif <boolean expression> then
  -- another elseif part
else
  -- else part
end
```

When the interpreter runs this expression, it checks each boolean expression in order, stopping at the first expression that evaluates to true and running that portion of the code. If none of the expressions are true, then the code in the else section is run. Not every if statement will include elseif or else options, but they are always available if you need them.

Displaying a Personalized Greeting Redux

Conditionals can be used for verifying the arguments for a function. For example, consider a function that takes a name (or nil) and prints a personalized greeting. Define this function in your Lua interpreter:

```
function greeting(name)
  if (type(name) == "string") then
    print("Hello " .. name)
  elseif (type(name) == "nil") then
    print("Hello friend")
  else
    error("Invalid name was entered")
  end
end
```

The first condition checks to see if the name argument is a string, in which case it generates and prints a custom greeting. If the name argument is nil, meaning nothing was passed into the function, then it will print the generic string "Hello friend". Finally, if neither of the previous conditions match, the function triggers a custom error message using the error() function. Test this new function in your interpreter:

```
> greeting("Frank")
Hello Frank
> greeting()
Hello friend
> greeting(13)
stdin:7: Invalid name was entered
stack traceback:
        [C]: in function 'error'
        stdin:7: in function 'greeting'
        stdin:1: in main chunk
        [C]: ?
```

When the `error()` function is called, Lua provides the error message supplied along with a stack traceback. In this case, you can see that the error was triggered from the `greeting()` function, which was called from the *main chunk*.

The preceding `greeting()` function could have been written without using the elseif statement, by using nested if statements, as follows:

```
function greeting(name)
  if (type(name) == "string") then
    print("Hello " .. name)
  else
    if (type(name) == "nil") then
      print("Hello friend")
    else
      error("Invalid name was entered")
    end
  end
end
```

This nested style is useful in certain situations when you have multiple `if` conditions but also need to have an `else` portion for each of them. In general, you should use whatever style you consider to be more readable for the given situation.

Repeating Actions with the while Statement

Computers are often used to repeat tasks or simplify complex calculations that would otherwise require manual repetition. Lua provides the `while` statement, which will repeat a block of code as long as a specified condition is met. The `while` statement's syntax is:

```
while <boolean expression> do
  -- body
end
```

The boolean expression is evaluated on each and every repetition of the loop, and as soon as it no longer evaluates to true the loop will exit.

Computing Factorials

The process of computing a number's factorial is a good example of something that is easily automated. A factorial is computed by taking all numbers from 1 to the given number and multiplying them together. Thus, 3 factorial is `1 * 2 * 3`. If a function `factorial()` is defined, then we can simply type

```
> print(factorial(9))
```

instead of

```
> print(9 * 8 * 7 * 6 * 5 * 4 * 3 * 2 * 1)
```

Define this function now by typing the following definition into your interpreter:

```
function factorial(num)
  local total = 1
  while (num > 1) do
    print("total: ".. total .. " num: " .. num)
    total = total * num
    num = num - 1
  end
  return total
end
```

This function includes a `print()` statement that will help us see what the function does on each iteration of the loop. Before using this code in an addon, you would want to remove that line from the function. For now, test this in your Lua interpreter:

```
> print(factorial(5))
total: 1 num: 5
total: 5 num: 4
total: 20 num: 3
total: 60 num: 2
120
```

You can see each step of the loop and how the value is being calculated. Using debug statements like this can be really handy when writing code, but you have to remember to remove them before you release the code.

TIP The condition of a `while` statement is checked prior to running the loop, and again on each subsequent run of the loop. This means if the condition is never met, the body of the `while` loop is never executed, and Lua just skips past it.

Differences Between while and repeat

The `repeat/until` loop is a variant of the `while` loop that has the following form:

```
repeat
  -- body
until <boolean expression>
```

The primary difference between the `while/do` loop and a `repeat/until` loop is that the condition of a repeat loop is checked at the *end* of the computation, so the loop of the body is always executed at least once. Here's how you'd define a new factorial function using this construct:

```
function factorial2(num)
  local total = 1
```

```
  repeat
    total = total * num
    num = num - 1
  until (num < 1)
  return total
end
```

You can verify the results of this function by testing it with a few different values:

```
> print(factorial2(1))
1
> print(factorial2(2))
2
> print(factorial2(3))
6
> print(factorial2(5))
120
```

If you happened to test these two functions with some unexpected value, such as -3, you should see a difference between the results:

```
> print(factorial(-3))
1
> print(factorial2(-3))
-3
```

When running `factorial()`, the `num` variable is already less than 1, so the `while` body never runs; it simply returns the default value of 1. When `factorial2()` is called, the body of the loop happens once, which causes the different return value of -3.

Looping with the Numeric for Statement

As the preceding factorial function demonstrated, many loops begin at a simple integer value and then either increment or decrement to some predefined limit. In the case of `factorial(9)`, the loop starts at 9 and continues until it reaches 1. Rather than managing this sort of loop yourself, the `for` statement provides an easy way to write these loops:

```
for variablename=start_value, end_value, step_value do
  -- body
end
```

Table 3-1 explains the different arguments that must be supplied to the `for` statement.

Table 3-1 Arguments for Numeric for Loop

ARGUMENT	DESCRIPTION
variablename	A valid variable identifier, the counter variable
start_value	A number, the initial value of variablename
end_value	A number, the end value of the loop
step_value	The number by which to increment the counter after each loop

The following are examples of simple for loops:

```
> for i=1, 3, 1 do
>> print(i)
>> end
1
2
3
> for i=3, 1, -1 do
>> print(i)
>> end
3
2
1
```

These two loops translate to the following code blocks using while loops:

```
do
  local i = 1
  while (i <= 3) do
    print(i)
    i = i + 1
  end
end
```

and

```
do
  local i = 3
  while (i >= 1) do
    print(i)
    i = i - 1
  end
end
```

When the step value in a `for` loop is not provided, Lua assumes a value of 1 for the loop. The earlier 1, 2, 3 example can thus be written as follows:

```
for i=1, 3 do
  print(i)
end
```

Computing Factorials

The `for` loop can be used to make the `factorial()` function even more clear. Type the following definition into your interpreter:

```
function factorial3(num)
  local total = 1
  for i=1, num do
    total = total * i
  end
  return total
end
```

Rather than manually writing the terminal condition for the `while` or `repeat` loop, you can just provide the `for` statement with a start value, and an upper bound. In this case, we can use the variable `num`, which is evaluated correctly when the function is run.

Evaluation of Loop Conditions

In a `for` loop, the `end_value`, and `step_value` are both calculated once, at the start of the loop. As a result, variables and expressions can be used for these values. These values cannot be changed mid-loop; they will have already been calculated. Consider the following example:

```
> upper = 3
> for i=1, upper do
>> print(i)
>> upper = upper + 1
>> end
1
2
3
```

This example doesn't loop forever because of the way loop conditions are evaluated (being calculated once).

Variable Scope in for Loops

When writing a `for` loop, it is important to remember that the counter variable name you supply will automatically be made local to that block and won't be accessible outside that level:

```
> i = 15
> for i=1,3 do print(i) end
1
2
3
> print(i)
15
```

If, for some reason, you need to save the control variable's value, you can declare a local variable just prior to the `for` loop, where you can save the number you need, as in the following example:

```
upper = 10
do
  local max
  for i=1,upper do
    max = i
  end
  print(max)
end
```

When the loop terminates, `max` will be `10`, which was the last value of the control variable.

Summary

This chapter introduced you to functions and showed you two different methods to create functions, using the `foo = function() end` syntax as well as the function `foo() end` syntactic sugar. Conditionals and control structures were introduced, enabling you to easily repeat computations. The next chapter explores advanced techniques using functions and control structures.

# CHAPTER 4

Working with Tables

James Whitehead II

Storing data in variables is handy when working on simple programs, but larger projects require an easier way to store data. Consider a simple address book program that allows you to electronically store contact information. Using variables, this may look something like this:

```
alice_name = "Alice Applebaum"
alice_phone = "+1-212 555-1434"
alice_address1 = "114 Auburn Street"
alice_address2 = "Apt 14"
alice_city = "Atlanta"
alice_state = "GA"
```

As you can see, using this method for more than a few simple entries would be completely unwieldy. Adding a new entry requires you to create a new variable name and enter each of the details in a new variable. Computers are all about automating processes, so there has to be a better way to deal with this.

Storing Data Using Tables

You may be familiar with tables or some analogous object from other programming languages (arrays, dictionaries, hash tables). In Lua, tables are objects that can be used to store other (usually related) values.

To understand how to use tables, it's important to grasp the concept of an *associative array*; which is how tables in Lua are implemented. An associative array is a collection of paired elements, where each pair has both a key and a value. A table can be indexed using a specific key, and it will return (or store) the given value.

Creating and Indexing Tables

Create a new table for Alice by running this code:

```
> alice = {}
```

In Lua, the expression {} creates a new table, in this case an empty one. Here, the new table has been assigned to the variable alice. You can index this table using square brackets and a key. Run the following:

```
> alice["name"] = "Alice Applebaum"
> alice["phone"] = "+1-212-555-1434"
> alice["address1"] = "114 Auburn Street"
> alice["address2"] = "Apt 14"
> alice["city"] = "Atlanta"
> alice["state"] = "GA"
```

Each line here tells Lua to look in the table alice using the key within the square brackets, and set that value to whatever is on the right side of the assignment operator. These elements can then be accessed later:

```
> print(alice["name"])
Alice Applebaum
> print(alice["address2"])
Apt 14
```

In each case, a key is matched up with a specific value and stored within the table. Each of these examples uses a string as the key, but Lua actually allows any value (except nil) to be used as a key. Test this by running the following:

```
> alice[1] = "Test value"
> alice[2] = 14
> print(alice[1])
Test value
> print(alice[2])
14
```

Clearing an Element from a Table

When a table is indexed with a key that has not been set, the table will return the special value nil. Run the following:

```
> print(alice["fax"])
nil
```

This means, quite literally, that there is nothing stored in the table for the given key. We can use this information to help us clear entries from a table if they are no longer needed:

```
> alice[1] = nil
> alice[2] = nil
```

Shortcuts for String Keys

Lua provides an easier way to index a table by string keys when those strings are a single identifier. This is extremely useful when working with data tables. Instead of typing this,

```
> alice["address1"] = "114 Auburn Street"
```

you can type the following:

```
> alice.address1 = "114 Auburn Street"
```

This shortcut method only works when the key begins with a letter or underscore character and consists of only letters, digits, and underscore characters. In addition, the key cannot be a reserved Lua keyword (such as end). All of the following identifiers are considered valid:

- `myTable.someKey`
- `myTable.someKey12`
- `myTable.some_Key`
- `myTable._someKey`
- `myTable.start`

But these will throw an error:

- `myTable.12someKey`
- `myTable.some-key`
- `myTable.end`

This method of indexing a table is only provided as a convenience, and won't work for all situations. Each of the preceding invalid keys can still be indexed using full bracket notation.

Creating Populated Tables

In addition to using {} to create new empty tables, it can also be used to create an already populated table. This is accomplished by providing a set of key/value pairs within the constructor itself, using the following syntax:

```
myTable = {
  [key1] = value1,
  [key2] = value2,
  ...
}
```

A record for Alice can thus be created by running the following:

```
alice = {
  ["name"] = "Alice Applebaum",
  ["phone"] = "+1-212-555-1434",
  ["address1"] = "114 Auburn Street",
  ["address2"] = "Apt 14",
  ["city"] = "Atlanta",
  ["state"] = "Georgia",
}
```

You can take advantage of shortcuts for string keys in the constructor too, by typing *someKey* instead of `["someKey"]`. This shortcut follows the same rules as dot notation for table indexing. This shortens the example record to:

```
alice = {
  name = "Alice Applebaum",
  phone = "+1-212-555-1434",
  address1 = "114 Auburn Street",
  address2 = "Apt 14",
  city = "Atlanta",
  state = "Georgia",
}
```

The last line of each of these examples has a trailing comma before the closing brace. Lua's syntax allows these within table constructors so new lines can easily be added to the end of the definition. If Lua didn't allow this and you forgot to add a comma before adding a new line, you would have a compilation error. Having trailing commas makes adding new entries much easier, so it's a common practice to include them when creating tables in this format.

Using Tables as Arrays

Lua tables have another unique property when they are used with consecutive integer keys starting at 1. These tables can be used as simple lists of values that can be added, removed, and sorted. Tables used in this manner are typically referred to as *arrays*, due to the similarities they share with arrays in other programming languages. More specifically, the part of a table that has integer keys starting at 1 is referred to as the *array part* of a table.

Creating an Array

You can create a new array using the table constructor in one of the two following ways (they are equivalent):

```
tbl = {
  value1,
  value2,
```

```
    value3,
    ...
}

tbl = {
  [1] = value1,
  [2] = value2,
  [3] = value3,
  ...
}
```

As you can see, arrays are just a special case of tables. Each of the functions covered in this section is only reliable when dealing with *consecutive* integer keys starting at 1.

Getting the Length of an Array

The same length operator (#) that was introduced in Chapter 2 for use on strings is also used to get the length of the array part of a table. Here are some quick examples:

```
> tbl = {"alpha", "beta", "gamma", "delta"}
> print(#tbl)
4
> tbl = {}
> print(#tbl)
0
> tbl = {
>> "alpha",
>> "beta",
>> ["one"] = "uno",
>> ["two"] = "dos",
>> "gamma",
>> }
> print(#tbl)
3
```

You can see that # only counts the elements in the array part. This operator can be used to print the table's elements without your needing to hardcode the upper limit. For example:

```
> for i=1,#tbl do
>> print(tbl[i])
>> end
alpha
beta
gamma
```

Adding Elements to an Array

Adding an element to an array is as simple as associating the value to the next integer key in sequence. More generally:

```
> tbl[#tbl] = "new element"
```

This can get rather tedious and isn't very efficient or easy to read. Lua provides a standard table.insert() library function to make adding elements easier. The syntax for `table.insert()` is:

```
table.insert(tbl, [pos,] value)
```

The arguments are as follows:

- `tbl` — The table to alter
- `pos` (optional) — The position at which to add the new element
- `value` — The value to insert

The second parameter being enclosed in brackets indicates that it is optional and does not need to be included. If the position isn't included, the new value will be added to the end of the table.

Run the following in your interpreter to create a sample table and a function that will allow you to easily print the contents of the table's array part:

```
tmp = {"alpha", "beta", "gamma"}
function print_tmp()
  for i=1,#tmp do
    print(i, tmp[i])
  end
end
```

To print the current list, use the following command:

```
> print_tmp()
1, alpha
2, beta
3, gamma
```

To add a new element to the end of the list, simply call `table.insert()` with the table you'd like to alter and the value you'd like to add:

```
> table.insert(tmp, "delta")
> table.insert(tmp, "epsilon")
> print_tmp()
1, alpha
2, beta
3, gamma
4, delta
5, epsilon
```

To insert a new value at a given position, call `table.insert()` with the optional second parameter `pos`, a number that indicates at what position you'd like to add the element. When you insert a value in this way, all elements after the given position will be renumbered and moved up.

```
> table.insert(tmp, 3, "zeta")
> print_tmp()
1, alpha
2, beta
3, zeta
4, gamma
5, delta
6, epsilon
```

When using the position argument, it's important to make sure you're supplying a valid number. The position should always be between 1 and the last element of the list (`#tmp`). If you supply a value outside this range, the results are unpredictable.

Removing Elements from an Array

Lua includes a function to remove elements from a table, and the syntax is similar to its companion `table.insert()`:

```
value = table.remove(tbl [, pos])
```

This function takes up to two parameters:

- `tbl` — The table to alter
- `pos` (optional) — The element to remove from the table

The syntax statement also shows that this function returns a single value:

- `value` — The value removed from the table

Again, the brackets around pos show that it is an optional parameter. When a position isn't included, Lua will remove the last element in the table (that is, the element at the `#tbl` position).

To remove the last element of a table, use the following command:

```
> table.remove(tmp)
> print_tmp()
1, alpha
2, beta
3, zeta
4, gamma
5, delta
```

By simply calling `table.remove()` with only a table argument, the last element has been removed and we're left with the rest of the table.

Here's how to remove a specific element in a table:

```
> table.remove(tmp, 3)
> print_tmp()
1, alpha
2, beta
3, gamma
4, delta
```

When an element is removed from the middle of the table (including the first element), all other elements are renumbered and shifted down. This ensures that the elements of the array are always numbered properly so the array part functions all work properly.

Sorting the Elements of an Array

When an array contains basic elements such as strings and numbers that can be easily compared, there is a standard library function to sort the list. The syntax of the `table.sort()` function follows:

```
table.sort(tbl [, comp])
```

The second argument to `table.sort()` will be covered in detail in Chapter 5, but the first argument is the table that you would like to sort. Using this function is as simple as calling it, passing the table to be sorted as the first argument:

```
> print_tmp()
1, alpha
2, beta
3, gamma
4, delta
> table.sort(tmp)
> print_tmp()
1, alpha
2, beta
3, delta
4, gamma
```

Because the values in this table are strings, they are sorted alphabetically, in ascending order (this is the default). If the table contained numbers, they would be sorted in the same way.

A simple sort like this won't be effective for more complex values (such as tables), or when the values in an array are mixed (such as strings and numbers). The second argument to `table.sort` allows you to custom tailor the sort function for these situations.

Using Tables as Namespaces

You've already been introduced to a few functions that are grouped together:

- `table.insert()`
- `table.remove()`
- `table.sort()`

When functions are grouped together in this manner, they are said to be part of a *namespace*, in this case, the `table` namespace. Namespaces provide a logical grouping of functions that are related, implemented simply as Lua tables. Because tables can hold function values, the preceding functions are also accessible using:

- `table["insert"]()`
- `table["remove"]()`
- `table["sort"]()`

Creating a new library is as simple as writing your new functions, creating a new table, and setting key/value pairs for your table.

Creating a util Namespace

You've already written a few utility functions that might be handy to keep around, such as `convert_c2f()`. You can create a new namespace to start storing these functions by defining a new table:

```
> util = {}
```

Adding Functions to util

There are two different ways to add functions to a namespace, by indexing the table and storing the value of an existing function, or by defining the function directly as part of the namespace.

Storing an Existing Function

If you've closed your Lua session, redefine your Celsius to Fahrenheit conversion function:

```
function convert_c2f(celsius)
  return (celsius * 1.8) + 32
end
```

Now that you have a function to which you can refer, you can use the following code to store it in the `util` table:

```
util.celsius2fahrenheit = convert_c2f
```

This function can then be accessed directly from the `util` table:

```
> print(util.celsius2fahrenheit(0))
32
> print(util.celsius2fahrenheir(-40))
-40
```

Defining a New Function

Rather than define a function under a global variable and then set it as part of the namespace, you can define the function directly as part of the namespace. Run the following code:

```
function util.factorial(num)
  local total = 1
  for i=1,num do
    total = total * i
  end
  return total
end
```

You may recall from Chapter 3 that this method of function definition is *syntactic sugar* and is translated by Lua into the following:

```
util.factorial = function(num)
  local total = 1
  for i=1,num do
    total = total * i
  end
  return total
end
```

Using the first form is often the most convenient way to define functions, and it makes the code easier to read compared to the alternative methods. More often than not, when you read a namespace definition, you will see it in this form.

Object Oriented Programming with Tables

Tables can also be used for a different type of programming called *object-oriented programming*. In this type of programming, data is described as objects, which contain *methods*, special functions that act directly on or through that object.

Creating a Non-Object-Oriented Counter

To illustrate some of the benefits this type of programming provides, run the following in your interpreter:

```
-- Create a new scope for privacy
do
  -- Private counter
  counter = 0

  -- Global functions to interact with counter
  function counter_get()
    return counter
  end

  function counter_inc()
    counter = counter + 1
  end
end
```

This block of code makes a simple, one-way counter that can't ever go down, but can be retrieved and incremented via the `counter_get()` and `counter_inc()` functions. Unfortunately, this only really allows a single counter when, in fact, we might need more than one. Because these functions work on a specific variable, they are extremely limited.

Using Tables as Simple Objects

The following is a different implementation for the simple counter, making the counter an object with two methods, `get` and `inc`:

```
counter = {
  count = 0
}

function counter.get(self)
  return self.count
end

function counter.inc(self)
  self.count = self.count + 1
end
```

This program allows us to do the following:

```
> print(counter.get(counter))
0
> counter.inc(counter)
> print(counter.get(counter))
1
```

In this implementation, the actual counter variable is stored in a table (which serves as our object). Each of the functions that interact with this value has an argument named `self` expected to be a counter object. We could make a new counter by running the following:

```
> counter2 = {
  count = 15,
  get = counter.get,
  inc = counter.inc,
}
> print(counter2.get(counter2))
15
```

Because the functions are just Lua values and they work on an argument rather than some magical hidden variable, you can copy them into your new counter. As a matter of fact, the functions will work correctly even if you mix them:

```
> print(counter.get(counter2))
15
> print(counter.get == counter2.get)
true
```

This should be no surprise because you're just moving and copying functions around. While this implementation is definitely more convenient than our first attempt, it can be made even easier. Right now, you have to call the function and pass in the counter object, causing you to type the object's name twice. Lua provides a bit of syntactic sugar that helps us.

Using : to Call Object Methods

When calling an object's method, you can use a colon instead of a period, and the object will be passed as the first argument to the method. This means that instead of calling `counter.get(counter)`, you can call `counter:get()`. This works automatically behind the scenes to prevent you from having to pass the object every time you make a method call.

Defining Functions Using :

When defining functions, we can use the : operator to define them, making this type of programming even more natural. The definition `function tbl:MyMethod() end` is equivalent to `function tbl.MyMethod(self) end`. This is why in our previous example we used the variable name `self`, because it's the same variable name Lua uses when defining functions using this method.

```
counter = {
  count = 0
}
```

```
function counter:get()
  return self.count
end

function counter:inc()
  self.count = self.count + 1
end
```

COMMON ERRORS

If you attempt to call a method that expects the self argument with a period instead of a colon, you might get an error similar to this:

```
stdin:2: attempt to index local 'self' (a nil value)
```

Most of the time, when you get this error, it means you are accidentally calling a method without passing a first argument, or you used a period where you meant to use a colon.

Making a Better Counter

This counter program still has room for improvement because the way we make new counters is relatively clunky. Run the following to define a more robust counter system:

```
-- Create a new scope for privacy
do
  local function get(self)
    return self.count
  end

  local function inc(self)
    self.count = self.count + 1
  end

  function new_counter(value)
    if type(value) ~= "number" then
      value = 0
    end

    local obj = {
      count = value,
      get = get,
      inc = inc,
    }

    return obj
  end
end
```

This example provides a single global function called `new_counter`, which takes a single argument value, the initial value of the counter. It returns a new object containing two methods and the counter value itself. This type of function is typically called a *factory function* because it just returns new objects every time you call it. Run a few tests to ensure the system works properly:

```
> counter = new_counter()
> print(counter:get())
0
> counter2 = new_counter(15)
> print(counter2:get())
15
> counter:inc()
> print(counter:get())
1
> print(counter2:get())
15
```

While the implementation may seem a bit more complex than the previous attempts, creating and manipulating new counters is extremely easy.

Extending Tables with Metatables

Each table in Lua is capable of having a *metatable* attached to it. A metatable is a secondary table that gives Lua extra information about how that table should be treated when it is used. For example, by default, when you try to print a table you are given a string that looks something like `table: 0x30d470`, which isn't extremely readable. Lua provides a way to change this behavior using metatables and metamethods.

Adding a Metatable

A metatable is nothing more than a simple table used to store extra information about the tables to which it is attached. They can be passed around, attached to multiple tables, and altered at any time. To begin redefining the behavior of a table, you must create a metatable and attach it to a table object, using the `setmetatable()` function. This function takes two arguments:

- `tbl` — The table to alter
- `mt` — The table to attach to `tbl`

In addition, the `setmetatable()` function returns a single argument, the table you passed in as the first argument. This can be helpful when creating new tables to pass directly to `setmetatable()`. Run the following code to create some tables for us to play with, and attach the same metatable to each of them.

```
tbl1 = {"alpha", "beta", "gamma"}
tbl2 = {"delta", "epsilon", "zeta"}
tbl3 = {}
```

```
mt = {}
setmetatable(tbl1, mt)
setmetatable(tbl2, mt)
setmetatable(tbl3, mt)
```

You can verify the metatable has been set correctly by using the `getmetatable()` function. This function simply takes a table as the first argument and returns the metatable, or `nil` if no metatable is attached.

```
> print(getmetatable(tbl1) == mt)
true
```

Now that you have an object with a metatable, you can begin redefining the behavior of the table.

Defining Metamethods

A *metamethod* is nothing more than a function stored with a specific key in a metatable. There are several possible metamethods, and they take a varying number of arguments. Each metamethod begins with two underscore characters. A full list can be found in the *Lua Reference Manual*, or *Programming in Lua*, but the most relevant ones when dealing with World of Warcraft are shown in Table 4-1.

Table 4-1 Relevant Metamethods

METAMETHOD	ARGS	DESCRIPTION
`__add`	2	Defines the behavior when used in addition operations.
`__mul`	2	Defines the behavior when used in multiplication operations.
`__div`	2	Defines the behavior when used in division operations.
`__sub`	2	Defines the behavior when used in subtraction operations.
`__unm`	1	Defines the behavior when negated (unary minus).
`__tostring`	1	Defines the behavior when the table is an argument to tostring(). This also affects the print() function, which calls tostring() directly.
`__concat`	2	Defines the behavior when used with the concatenation operator (..).
`__index`	2	Defines the behavior when the table is indexed with a key that doesn't exist in that table.
`__newindex`	3	Defines the behavior when a previously unset key in the table is being set.

Defining Basic Arithmetic using __add, __sub, __mul, and __div

Each of these arithmetic metamethods takes two arguments and can (in theory) return anything you'd like. However, keep the following in mind:

- The result of one operation may be part of a larger arithmetic expression.
- If you return a non-number from your metamethod, you should ensure it can handle the arithmetic operations.
- If you return nil, it will break any arithmetic expression it is a part of, so it's best to avoid this.

The following function defines addition between two tables as a new table with the elements of the first table's array part, followed by the elements of the second's array part. Add the following function to your Lua interpreter:

```
function mt.__add(a,b)
  local result = setmetatable({}, mt)

  -- Copy table a in first
  for i=1,#a do
    table.insert(result, a[i])
  end

  -- Copy table b in second
  for i=1,#b do
    table.insert(result, b[i])
  end

  return result
end
```

To simplify the function, the arguments have been named a and b. The first line creates a new results table and makes sure to set the metatable correctly. The rest of the function is straightforward, copying the elements of each table to the new resulting table. Here is a simple test:

```
> add_test = tbl1 + tbl2
> print(#add_test)
6
> for i=1,#add_test do print(i, add_test[i]) end
1, alpha
2, beta
3, gamma
4, delta
5, epsilon
6, zeta
```

The metamethod correctly handles the addition and creates a new table with the results of the addition. The other basic arithmetic operations could be defined in the same way. Instead of returning a table, these functions could return some meaningful number can be used as part of a larger formula. You're only limited by your imagination.

Defining Negation using __unm

The unary minus (negation) operator expects exactly one argument, and should return the result of the argument being negated. In our examples, this will mean reversing the array part of the given table. Run the following code:

```
function mt.__unm(a)
  local result = setmetatable({}, mt)

  -- Reverse through the elements of the array
  for i=#a,1,-1 do
    table.insert(result, a[i])
  end

  return result
end
```

Test table negation with a few examples:

```
> unm_test = -tbl1
> for i=1,#unm_test do print(i, unm_test[i]) end
1, gamma
2, beta
3, alpha
> unm_test = -tbl1 + tbl2
> for i=1,#unm_test do print(i, unm_test[i]) end
1, gamma
2, beta
3, alpha
4, delta
5, epsilon
6, zeta
```

Creating Meaningful Output with __tostring

In the current example, it would be useful to print the table and have it display the elements rather than the unique string Lua provides. This can easily be accomplished using the __tostring metamethod, which takes a single argument (the table) and should return a string.

Run the following code:

```
function mt.__tostring(tbl)
  local result = "{"

  for i=1,#tbl do
    if i > 1 then
      result = result .. ", "
    end

    result = result .. tostring(tbl[i])
```

```
      end

   result = result .. "}"

   return result
end
```

Because we know the input will be a table, we start the string with the { character. This function then loops through each element of the array. If the loop is beyond the first element, then a comma is added to the string to separate each value. This is done so we don't have an extra comma at the end of the output. Then the value itself is concatenated onto the result string. Finally, when the loop is complete, we close the brace and return the string.

```
> print(tbl1)
{alpha, beta, gamma}
> print(tbl2)
{delta, epsilon, zeta}
> print(tbl3)
{}
```

When working with more complex objects, it can be very useful to provide a meaningful text representation of your data, so the __tostring metamethod can be extremely handy.

Concatenating Tables Using __concat

For these tables, concatenation will end up being the same thing as addition, so you can simply use that function for the __concat metamethod, as well. Both metamethods take in two arguments and return a single result. In addition, both are typically chained together, so you'll need to ensure your resulting object is also able to be concatenated. Run the following tests:

```
> mt.__concat = mt.__add
> print(tbl1 .. tbl2)
{alpha, beta, gamma, delta, epsilon, zeta}
```

Because the __tostring metamethod is still active, the resulting table is converted to string representation, even when printed like this.

Exploring Fallback Tables with __index

Normally, when a key isn't associated with a value in a given table nil is returned. However, in a number of situations other responses might make more sense, and the __index metamethod allows this to happen. This is what occurs when an index isn't found:

1. Table is indexed with an unassociated key.
2. If the table has an __index metatable entry that is another table, return the keyed entry from that table (or nil if it doesn't exist).

3. If the table has an `__index` metatable entry that is a function, return the result of calling that function with the table, and the key as arguments.

This is the only metatable entry that can be either a function or a table itself.

Using Tables

Run the following code:

```
deDE_races = {
  ["Night elf"] = "Nachtelf"
}
mt = {}
setmetatable(deDE_races, mt)

-- Create a default tables
enUS_races = {
  ["Human"] = "Human",
  ["Night elf"] = "Night elf",
}

mt.__index = enUS_races
```

This example creates a table containing the German localization of the English phrase `"Night elf"`. In addition, there is a default table that contains the English phrases `"Human"` and `"Night elf"`. When the table `deDE_races` is indexed, if the answer isn't found, Lua will look in the metatable's `__index` entry and return that result. See this in action yourself:

```
> print(deDE_races["Night elf"])
Nachtelf
> print(deDE_races["Human"])
Human
```

The `__index` metatable entry here allows us to provide partial localization for the German language, displaying the English words by default if a translation isn't found.

Using Functions

Instead of using a table for the `__index` entry, you can specify a function that takes two arguments, namely the table and the key. This function allows you to add logic to the indexing of tables, and when coupled with the `__newindex` metamethod, you can do interesting things, such as make read-only tables. For now, run the following code, which will warn you about invalid indices in your code:

```
function mt.__index(tbl,key)
  print("Attempt to access key '"..key.."' in " .. tostring(tbl))
  return nil
end
```

Now test it:

```
> print(tbl1[4])
Attempt to access key '4' in {alpha, beta, gamma}
nil
> print(tbl.apple)
Attempt to access key 'apple' in {alpha, beta, gamma}
nil
```

Catching New Keys with __newindex

The __newindex metamethod takes three arguments:

- tbl — The table being indexed
- key — The key being used to index the table
- value — The value to assign to table[key]

This function can be used to notify you when a new value is set, and can even be used to prevent the value from ever being set. When this metamethod is set, it is responsible for actually making the assignment happen. The following example allows you to set any index other than "banana":

```
function mt.__newindex(tbl,key,value)
  if key == "banana" then
    error("Cannot set a protected key")
  else
    rawset(tbl, key, value)
  end
end
```

While this entry is set, you won't be able to (through conventional means) set the key ["banana"] in any of the three tables:

```
> tbl1.apple = "red"
> print(tbl1.apple)
red
> tbl1.banana = "yellow"
stdin:3: Cannot set a protected key
stack traceback:
        [C]: in function 'error'
        stdin:3: in function <stdin:1>
        stdin:1: in main chunk
        [C]: ?
> print(tbl1.banana)
nil
```

Because error() stops the function entirely, we never get to set the entry, and we have a pseudo "protected" key within the table.

Bypassing Metatables

When writing functions for the `__index` and `__newindex` metamethods, in particular, it may be necessary to bypass the metatable when fetching a value. This is accomplished using the `rawget()` and `rawset()` functions.

value = rawget(tbl, key)

The `rawget()` function takes the table to query and the key to look up, and returns the value of that key in the table without using the metatable for lookups. When you are writing a function that serves as a metamethod for a table, it is typically best to use `rawget()` when accessing values in the same table.

rawset(tbl, key, value)

To set a value in a table without hitting the metatable, you can use the `rawset()` function. This function takes in the table to be altered, the key to use, and the value to be placed in the table. You will encounter tables with `__newindex` metamethods less frequently than those with `__index` metamethods, but it's good to understand what tools are available, in case you need them.

Summary

In this chapter you learned how to use Lua tables to store records of data that can be easily read and indexed. Arrays were introduced as a special subset of tables with helper functions such as insertion, removal, and sorting. Libraries of functions were introduced along with basic object-oriented programming. Finally, you learned how to extend tables using metatables.

# CHAPTER 5

Advanced Functions and Control Structures

James Whitehead II

The functions and control structures introduced in Chapter 3 were relatively simple but gave you the ability to create nontrivial programs. This chapter introduces you to more advanced versions of functions and loops that allow you to accomplish the following:

- Create functions with a variable number of arguments
- Loop through the key/values pairs in the hash part of a table
- Return multiple values from a function
- Sort an array with table data

Multiple Return Values

In Lua, functions are able to return more than one value in a `return` statement, which makes accomplishing some tasks more natural. For example, colors in World of Warcraft are represented as hexadecimal values (such as `99CCFF`) as well as numeric percentages of red, green, and blue (such as `0.6`, `0.8`, `1.0`). As a result, it is useful to convert from a hexadecimal string to the component values of red, green, and blue.

Converting Hex to RGB

An example of a hexadecimal string is `"FFCC99"`, where the first two characters represent the value of the color red as a number between 0 and 255 in hexadecimal. The second set of characters is the value of green, followed by blue. The `string.sub()`

function can be used to split the string up into it's three component color strings, while the `tonumber()` function can convert the string into a number. If the `tonumber()` function is called with the red part of the string `"FF"`, it won't return a meaningful result:

```
> print(tonumber("FF"))
nil
```

By default, the `tonumber()` function expects the number to be a decimal number (that is, in base-10), so it can't convert this base-16 number. The second argument of `tonumber()` specifies the base of the string that is being converted. In this case:

```
> print(tonumber("FF", 16))
255
```

Because the output needs to be a number between 0.0 and 1.0, the result of the conversion can be divided by 255 to get the percentage value. A definition for `ConvertHexToRGB()` might look something like this:

```
function ConvertHexToRGB(hex)
  local red = string.sub(hex, 1, 2)
  local green = string.sub(hex, 3, 4)
  local blue = string.sub(hex, 5, 6)

  red = tonumber(red, 16) / 255
  green = tonumber(green, 16) / 255
  blue = tonumber(blue, 16) / 255

  return red, green, blue
end
```

Test this function with a few sample values:

```
> print(ConvertHexToRGB("FFCC99"))
1, 0.8, 0.6
> print(ConvertHexToRGB("FFFFFF"))
1, 1, 1
> print(ConvertHexToRGB("000000"))
0, 0, 0
```

Assigning Multiple Values

To get the results of a function with multiple return values, you can use the following syntax:

```
var1, var2, var3, var4 = someFunction()
```

This calls `someFunction()` and assigns the first return to `var1`, the second return to `var2`, and so on. If there are more returns than variables, the extra returns are just discarded.

Missing Return Values?

When you are working with multiple return values, a few odd things can happen. Look at the following example:

```
> print(ConvertHexToRGB("FFFFFF"))
1, 1, 1
> print(ConvertHexToRGB("FFFFFF"), "SomeOtherArgument")
1, SomeOtherArgument
```

Where did the other returns go? They were eaten by the following rule:

When a function call with multiple return values is the last argument to another function, or the last argument in a multiple assignment expression, all of the return values are passed or used. Otherwise, only the first return value is used or assigned.

You can see this behavior with the assignment operator in the following example:

```
> a,b,c,d = ConvertHexToRGB("FFFFFF"), "yet", "another", "argument"
> print(a,b,c,d)
1, yet, another, argument
```

Because the call to ConvertHexToRGB() is followed by additional values, Lua only uses the first return from the function call. There are a few technical reasons for this limitation, but you should not find it affects you very often.

TIP When working with multiple return values, you can always wrap the function call in parenthesis to limit it to a single return value, as follows:

```
> print((ConvertHexToRGB("FFFFFF")))
1
```

Multiple Return Values in World of Warcraft

Several World of Warcraft API functions return multiple values. For example, the function GetRaidRosterInfo() takes a character's raid index (a number) and returns the following information:

- The name of the character
- The character's rank in the raid (leader, assistant, and so on)
- What subgroup the character is in
- The character's level
- The character's class (localized)
- The character's class (capitalized, in English)
- The name of the zone the character is currently in
- Whether or not the character is online
- Whether or not the character is dead

- If the character is a main tank or main assist
- Whether or not the character is master looter

This function provides a ton of information, but, typically, when you need one of the items, you need more than one. In this case, it's more efficient for the game client to return each of these items every time the function is queried, rather than having 11 different API functions.

SELECTING SPECIFIC VALUES

Functions with multiple return values provide a unique set of challenges, such as how to get at values that aren't at the start of the return list. There are two easy ways to do this: using a dummy variable and using the `select()` statement.

Taking the `ConvertHexToRGB()` example, how can you extract just the green value?

Using a Dummy Variable

The function is going to return three results regardless of how we call it, but we can use dummy variables to *throw away* the results that aren't interesting. For example, you may see something that looks like this:

```
local _,g = ConvertHexToRGB("FFFFFF")
```

Because the underscore character is a valid identifier, it can be used to store values, but most sane programs choose more valid variable names. The underscore identifier has become somewhat of a de-facto standard when you need to throw away the result of a function call simply because it's easy to type, and most likely not already in use, but it's considered bad practice.

Instead of using the underscore as a dummy variable, it's better to give each variable a meaningful name, and only use those that are necessary. Some situations can't be handled using this method, but Lua provides a utility function to compensate.

USING THE SELECT() Function

The `select()` function was designed to help solve this problem, by allowing you to choose a specific argument from a given list. This function takes any number of arguments, the first of which tells the function what to do. When `select()` is passed the `"#"` string as the first argument, it will simply return the number of arguments in the second part of the function. If `select()` is passed a number value, it returns that argument from the list, followed by anything after it. After this initial argument, `select()` takes any number of arguments, comma separated.

Confused yet? Look at a few examples:

```
> print(select("#", "alpha", "beta", "gamma"))
3
> print(select(1, "alpha", "beta", "gamma"))
alpha, beta, gamma
> print(select(2, "alpha", "beta", "gamma"))
beta, gamma
> print(select(3, "alpha", "beta", "gamma"))
gamma
```

> If you just need to get a single value from the list, you can assign it directly to the variable, or wrap the `select()` call in parentheses so the extra values are thrown away. You may find this function useful when working with some of the longer World of Warcraft API functions, such as `GetRaidRosterInfo()`. If you only need a single return, you can isolate it using a call to `select()`.

Accepting a Variable Number of Arguments

Many functions are designed to take a specific number of arguments, such as the `tonumber()` function, which takes a string, and optionally, a number base for the conversion. Other functions make more sense when they accept a variable number of arguments. Consider a function that calculates the arithmetic mean of a set of numbers. A simple two argument version of this function might look something like this:

```
function mean(num1, num2)
  return (num1 + num2) / 2
end
```

Unfortunately, if you need to compute the mean of three numbers, you would need to do it manually, or write a new function that takes three arguments instead. As you can imagine, this is highly inefficient, and Lua provides an easier way to write these types of functions so they can accept a variable number of arguments.

Declaring a Vararg Function

Functions with variable number of arguments are called *vararg functions* for short, and they use an ellipsis in their function declaration to indicate they take any number of arguments.

In Lua, the ellipsis can appear as the last argument in a function declaration. Whenever the ellipsis is then used in the body of the function, the arguments that were supplied in the vararg slot are substituted. Take the `print()` function, which already accepts a variable number of arguments, and extend it with the following function definition:

```
function test_print(...)
  print("test string", ...)
end
```

This function takes in any number of arguments and then passes them to the `print()` function, adding it's own text to the start of the list. The output from running this function looks like this:

```
> test_print("alpha", "beta", 13, "gamma")
test string, alpha, beta, 13, gamma
```

When the function is run and Lua encounters the . . . symbol, it replaces it with the list of arguments that were passed to the function. As a result, it can be used in the following ways:

```
-- Pass the arguments to another function
print(...)

-- Assign the arguments to variables
local var1, var2, var3 = ...

-- Construct a new table with the arguments
local tbl = {...}
```

The preceding example could be used to make a new function called `newtable()`, which takes in a set of arguments and makes a new table with those arguments in the array part of the table:

```
function newtable(...)
  return {...}
end
```

Test this function:

```
> tbl = newtable("alpha, "beta, "gamma")
> for i=1,#tbl do
>> print(i, tbl[i]))
>> end
1, alpha
2, beta
3, gamma
```

Using select() with ...

The select function makes working with `vararg` functions very easy, because it can provide the number of arguments passed, as well as allow you to easily iterate through them without needing to assign them to variables. Consider the following function that takes a list of arguments and prints their index, followed by the argument itself:

```
function printargs(...)
  local num_args = select("#", ...)
  for i=1,num_args do
    local arg = select(i, ...)
    print(i, arg)
  end
end
```

Sample output:

```
> printargs("alpha", "beta", 13, "gamma")
1, alpha
2, beta
3, 13
4, gamma
```

This method avoids your needing to create a new table every single time, and allows the value `nil` to be passed as an argument. This is important due to the following discrepancy:

```
function test1(...)
  local tbl = {...}
  for i=1,#tbl do
    print(i, tbl[i])
  end
end

function test2(...)
  for i=1,select("#", ...) do
    print(i, select(i, ...))
  end
end
```

One version of the test function uses tables; the other uses the `select()` function:

```
> test1("alpha", "beta", nil, "gamma")
1, alpha
2, beta
> test2("alpha", "beta", nil, "gamma")
1, alpha
2, beta
3, nil
4, gamma
```

The difference here is twofold: The first function needs to create a new table on each call, which will allocate and use more memory in the long run. In addition, it can't handle a `nil` value passed as an argument because of the way the array part of a table is defined in Lua. The version using `select()` handles this case properly because it doesn't have the same limitations.

Generic for Loops and Iterators

In Chapter 3 you were introduced to the `for` statement, which allowed you to repeat a computation over a series of numbers by supplying a start value, end value, and a value by which to increment the counter after each loop. In Chapter 4 you were introduced to storing data in both the array part and the hash part of Lua tables. Up until this point there has been no way to *loop* through the elements of the hash part of the table, but Lua provides a more generic form of the for statement that, when combined with an iterator function, allows just that.

Wikipedia defines an *iterator* as "an object which allows a programmer to traverse through all elements of a collection, regardless of its specific implementation." In Lua specifically, we use an iterator function along with some extra information to loop through a collection.

Syntax of Generic for

The generic for loop syntax is a bit different than the numeric for loop:

```
for val1,val2,val3,... in <expression> do
  -- body of for loop
end
```

A generic for loop can return many variables on each iteration (as many as defined by the iterator function, actually). Immediately after the for keyword, you supply a list of variable names that are assigned by the iterator function. The loop determines what to traverse by evaluating <expression>, which should return the following three values:

- An iterator function that can be called on each iteration of the loop
- A state, used by the iterator function on each subsequent call
- An initial value for the iterator value

Luckily, unless you plan to write your own iterator functions, you won't have to deal with any of this directly. A number of prewritten functions will create your iterators for you.

Traversing the Array Part of a Table

ipairs() is one such example that allows you to traverse the array part of a table without using the numeric for loop. Some programmers prefer this syntax to that of the numeric for loop because it's a bit cleaner:

```
> tbl = {"alpha", "beta", "gamma"}
> for idx,value in ipairs(tbl) do
>> print(idx, value)
>> end
1, alpha
2, beta
3, gamma
```

The ipairs() function takes a table and returns all the information the for loop requires to traverse the array part of the table, including the iterator function itself. Each call to the iterator function returns the numeric index of the element, and the element itself. These variables can be named whatever you'd like and, as always, are local to the scope of the for loop (meaning they cannot be accessed outside of that scope).

You can explore the `ipairs()` function a bit more by running the following in your interpreter:

```
> print(ipairs(tbl))
function: 0x300980, table: 0x3072c0, 0
> print(tbl)
table: 0x3072c0
```

It appears the `ipairs()` function returns an iterator function, the state (in this case it's just the table you passed in), and the initial value for the iterator (`0`). There's no real magic going on here, just a set of useful functions for your use.

Traversing an Entire Table

Another function, called `pairs()`, allows you to traverse a table in its entirety, including both the array part and the hash table part. The usage is the same as `ipairs()`; just pass it the table and use it as part of a generic `for` loop:

```
> tbl = {"alpha", "beta", ["one"] = "uno", ["two"] = "dos"}
> for key,value in pairs(tbl) do
>> print(key, value)
>> end
1, alpha
2, beta
one, uno
two, dos
```

TRAVERSING USING PAIRS()

In the preceding example, the `pairs()` function seemed to traverse the table in the order the elements were added to the table, but this is just a coincidence. The specific order in which elements will be visited is unspecified by this function, even for numeric keys. If you specifically need to traverse the table's numeric elements in order, you should instead use the `ipairs()` function, which can guarantee this. The lack of order when using `pairs()` is due to the way hash tables are implemented, as a collection of associated key/value pairs with no internal order.

When using the `pairs()` function, you must ensure you don't add any elements to the table. This is because `pairs()` calls the `next()` function, which carries the following warning in the Lua 5.1 Reference Manual:

"The behavior of `next` is *undefined* if, during the traversal, you assign any value to a nonexistent field in the table. You may, however, modify existing fields. In particular, you may clear existing fields."

This means that `next()` may simply not work, it may terminate early, or it may throw an error if you add an element to the table during the traversal. It's important to keep this in mind when working with an iteration using pairs().

Clearing a Table

As stated in the Lua 5.1 Reference Manual for `next()`, you can clear the elements of a table while traversing it using `pairs()`. The following code will clear a table of all set elements:

```
for key,value in pairs(tbl) do
  tbl[key] = nil
end
```

Because `pairs()` works for all keys of a table, this is a quick way to ensure you've cleared all elements (in the event you need to re-use a table, for example).

Using Other Iterators

A number of other functions in Lua can be used to generate iterators that are extremely useful. The `string.gmatch()` function can be used with Lua pattern matching to create iterators over strings, and specific matches within that string. You will learn more about this function and Lua pattern matching in Chapter 6, but here are some examples:

```
> for word in string.gmatch("These are some words", "%S+") do
>> print(word)
>> end
These
are
some
words
> for char in string.gmatch("Hello!", ".") do
>> print(char)
>> end
H
e
l
l
o
!
```

Sorting an Array of Table Data

The built-in `table.sort()` function only allows you to sort number and string data by default. Fortunately, `table.sort()` allows you to pass in a function to do the actual comparisons between elements, with the library function doing the overall sort based on the results of your function. This means you can write your own function to determine which of two tables is *bigger* when it comes to sorting.

Define Example Data

For the examples in this section you will need some sample data to sort. Define the following in your Lua interpreter:

```
guild = {}

table.insert(guild, {
  name = "Cladhaire",
  class = "Rogue",
  level = 70,
})

table.insert(guild, {
  name = "Sagart",
  class = "Priest",
  level = 70,
})

table.insert(guild, {
  name = "Mallaithe",
  class = "Warlock",
  level = 40,
})
```

Default Sort Order

By default, this list is sorted in the order it was inserted, because it's using the array part of the table. Run the following to verify this:

```
> for idx,value in ipairs(guild) do
>> print(idx, value.name)
>> end
1, Cladhaire
2, Sagart
3, Mallaithe
```

Rather than print `value` itself, which would show `table: 0x3003a0` instead of something meaningful, this code indexes it and prints the value associated with the key `"name"`. The code segment could be altered to print the class, or the level if so desired.

Creating a Comparison Function

If you try to sort this data using `table.sort()`, you will get an error because Lua doesn't know how to compare table values (to determine what makes one table less than another).

```
> table.sort(guild)
attempt to compare two table values
```

```
stack traceback:
      [C]: in function 'sort'
      stdin:1: in main chunk
      [C]: ?
```

The `table.sort()` function takes a second argument specifically for this purpose, to allow you to define how values should be compared. The second argument is a comparison function that takes two arguments, returning true if the first argument is less than the second argument, and false if the second argument is less than the first argument. That means you can sort two tables based on their member fields, or some other criteria you specify. Write the following function, which will compare two of the elements based on name:

```
function sortNameFunction(a, b)
  return a.name < b.name
end
```

Although the function is extremely short, that's all that is required to sort the array by name. Pass this function in as the second argument to `table.sort()`:

```
> table.sort(guild, sortNameFunction)
> for idx,value in ipairs(guild) do
>> print(idx, value.name)
>> end
1, Cladhaire
2, Mallaithe
3, Sagart
```

If you would like to reverse the sort order, just reverse the order of the comparison (note that the position of `b.name` and `a.name` in the comparison have changed).

```
function sortNameFunctionDesc(a, b)
  return b.name < a.name
end
```

Sort with this new function:

```
> table.sort(guild, sortNameFunctionDesc)
> for idx,value in ipairs(guild) do print(idx,value.name) end
1, Sagart
2, Mallaithe
3, Cladhaire
```

Creating a More Complex Sort Function

Assume you'd like to sort the preceding data by level and then by character name. You can write a function to sort by level, but there's no way to tell in what order it will put the two level 70 characters. The following comparison function will accomplish this more complex sort:

```
function sortLevelNameAsc(a, b)
  if a.level == b.level then
    return a.name < b.name
  else
    return a.level < b.level
  end
end
```

All that is required is a simple check to see if the two levels are the same, and if they are, to compare the names of the characters. A sort function can be as complex as you need, as long as it returns true when the first argument should be sorted *less* than the second argument:

```
> table.sort(guild, sortLevelNameAsc)
> for idx,value in ipairs(guild) do print(idx, value.name) end
1, Mallaithe
2, Cladhaire
3, Sagart
```

Summary

This chapter introduced the concepts of variable argument functions, generic `for` loops, iterators, and sorting complex data in arrays. These concepts are relatively advanced, but come up often when designing and writing a new addon.

# CHAPTER 6

Lua Standard Libraries

James Whitehead II

Throughout the first part of this book, a number of Lua standard library functions have been introduced and used in code examples. While this book does not cover every single Lua function included in the World of Warcraft implementation of Lua, this chapter introduces you to the most prevalent functions that you need when developing addons.

In addition to covering the Lua standard libraries, this chapter covers some functions specific to WoW that aren't really part of the game API itself. These functions are grouped at the end of the chapter.

> **NOTE** The details in this chapter cover the parts of the Lua API that are most relevant to WoW. A full reference for Lua can be found online at `http://www .lua.org/manual/5.1`. This manual is also available in print: *Lua 5.1 Reference Manual* by R. Ierusalimschy, L. H. de Figueiredo, and W. Celes, Lua.org, August 2006 (ISBN 85-903798-3-3).

In addition, the chief architect of Lua has written a very easy-to-read book about the Lua programming language that covers these (and more) functions in depth. An older version of this book written for an older version of Lua can be found online at `http://www.lua.org/pil/`. Reading the older version may be confusing, so the second edition can be found at many online bookstores: *Programming in Lua* (second edition) by Roberto Ierusalimschy, Lua.org, March 2006 (ISBN 85-903798-2-5).

Each function is this chapter is presented with what is called the function's signature. A full function signature describes what values are returned by the function, as well as what arguments are taken by the function. For example, consider the fictional function `foo()`:

```
someReturn = foo(arg1, arg2)
```

In this example, the function `foo()` takes two arguments (`arg1` and `arg2`) and returns a single value *someReturn*. These signatures can also indicate optional arguments, by enclosing them in square brackets:

```
somereturn = foo(arg1 [, arg2])
```

This notation indicates that the second argument to `foo()` is optional. When you see this, you should consult the description of the function and arguments to determine the behavior of the function because it varies.

This chapter only shows the argument portion of the function signature, but any return values are indicated in the function's description.

Table Library

The table library provides several functions that allow you to easily add elements, remove elements, and sort array tables. In addition, a utility function is provided that works outside of the array part of the table, returning the maximum numeric index used in the table. The former functions all operate exclusively on the array part of the table, while the latter can be used on any type of table.

table.concat (table [, sep [, i [, j]]])

This function concatenates all entries of the array part of a table, with an optional separator string `sep`. Given an array where all elements are strings or numbers, it returns `table[i]..sep..table[i+1] ... sep..table[j]`. The default value for `sep` is the empty string, the default for `i` is `1`, and the default for `j` is the length of the table. If `i` is greater than `j`, it returns the empty string.

```
> tbl = {"alpha", "beta", "gamma"}
> print(table.concat(tbl, ":"))
alpha:beta:gamma
> print(table.concat(tbl, nil, 1, 2))
alphabeta
> print(table.concat(tbl, "\n", 2, 3))
beta
gamma
```

This function is a simple and easy way to print the elements of the array part of a table. As you can see, `sep` can be any string (including the newline character) as it's just concatenated with the entries in the table.

table.insert (table, [pos,] value)

This function inserts a new element into the array, optionally as position pos, shifting up other elements to open space, if necessary. The default value for pos is n+1, where n is the length of the table. Therefore, a call of table.insert(t,x) inserts x at the end of table t.

```
> tbl = {"alpha", "beta", "gamma"}
> table.insert(tbl, "delta")
> table.insert(tbl, "epsilon")
> print(table.concat(tbl, ", "))
alpha, beta, gamma, delta, epsilon
> table.insert(tbl, 3, "zeta")
> print(table.concat(tbl, ", "))
alpha, beta, zeta, gamma, delta, epsilon
```

table.maxn (table)

This function returns the largest positive numerical index of the given table, or zero if the table has no positive numerical indices. (To do its job, this function does a linear traversal of the entire table.) Unlike most table functions, table.maxn() considers numerical keys instead of integer keys, so numerical constants and rational numbers are counted as well.

```
> tbl = {[1] = "a", [2] = "b", [3] = "c", [26] = "z"}
> print(#tbl)
3
> print(table.maxn(tbl))
26
> tbl[91.32] = true
> print(table.maxn(tbl))
91.32
```

table.remove (table [, pos])

This function removes an element from the given table, shifting down other elements to close the space, if necessary. It returns the value of the removed element. The default value for pos is n, where n is the length of the table, so a call table.remove(t) removes the last element of table t.

```
> tbl = {"alpha", "beta", "gamma", "delta"}
> print(table.remove(tbl))
delta
> print(table.concat(tbl, ", "))
alpha, beta, gamma
```

table.sort (table [, comp])

This function sorts the array part of a table by reordering the elements within the same table. If `comp` is given, then it must be a function that receives two table elements and returns `true` when the first is less than the second (so that `not comp(a[i+1],a[i])` will be `true` after the sort). If `comp` is not given, the standard Lua operator `<` is used instead.

This sort algorithm is not stable, which means that elements considered equal by the given comparison function may have their order changed by the sort.

```
> tbl = {"alpha", "beta", "gamma", "delta"}
> table.sort(tbl)
> print(table.concat(tbl, ", "))
alpha, beta, delta, gamma
> sortFunc = function(a,b) return b < a end
> table.sort(tbl, sortFunc)
> print(table.concat(tbl, ", "))
gamma, delta, beta, alpha
```

Math Library

The math library provides an interface to several standard math functions and constants. Table 6-1 describes some of the more common functions in the math library. (It is not a full listing of the library; for that, please consult a proper Lua reference, which includes a full set of trigonometric functions such as `math.cos`, `math.sin`, `math.tan`, and so on.)

Table 6-1: Math Functions

FUNCTION	DESCRIPTION	EXAMPLE(S)

`math.abs(x)`	Returns the absolute value of x.	`> print(math.abs(13))`
		`13`
		`> print(math.abs(-13))`
		`13`

`math.ceil(x)`	Returns the smallest integer larger than or equal to x.	`> print(math.ceil(1.03))`
		`2`
		`> print(math.ceil(13))`
		`13`
		`> print(math.ceil(17.99))`
		`18`

`math.deg(x)`	Returns the angle x (given in radians) in degrees.	`> print(math.deg(math.pi))`
		`180`
		`> print(math.deg(math.pi * 2.5))`
		`450`

Table 6-1 *(continued)*

FUNCTION	DESCRIPTION	EXAMPLE(S)
`math.exp(x)`	Returns the value of the mathematical constant `e` raised to the `x` power.	`> print(math.exp(27))` `532048240601.8`

`math.floor(x)`	Returns the largest integer smaller than or equal to `x`.	`> print(math.floor(1.03))`
		`1`
		`> print(math.floor(13.0))`
		`13`
		`> print(math.floor(17.99))`
		`17`

`math.fmod(x, y)`	Returns the remainder of the division of `x` by `y`. You can also use the expression `x % y` to compute the same value.	`> print(math.fmod(14, 3))`
		`2`
		`> print(math.fmod(14, 2))`
		`0`

`math.log(x)`	Returns the natural logarithm of `x`.	`> print(math.log(532048240601.8))` `27`
`math.log10(x)`	Returns the base-10 logarithm of `x`.	`> print(math.log10(10^2))` `2`
`math.max(x, y, z, …)`	Returns the maximum value among its arguments.	`> print(math.max(-13, 7, 32))` `32`
`math.min(x, y, z, …)`	Returns the minimum value among its arguments.	`> print(math.max(-13, 7, 32, 17))` `-13`

`math.modf(x)`	Returns two numbers, the integral part of `x` and the fractional part of `x`.	`> print(math.modf(10.23))`
		`10, 0.23`
		`> print(math.modf(7/22))`
		`0, 0.31818181818182`

`math.pi`	The value of the mathematical constant pi.	`> print(math.pi)` `3.1415926535898`

`math.pow(x, y)`	Returns `x` raised to the `y` power. (You can also use the expression `x^y` to compute this value.)	`> print(math.pow(2, 10))`
		`1024`
		`> print(math.pow(2, -10))`
		`0.0009765625`

`math.rad(x)`	Returns the angle `x` (given in degrees) in radians.	`> print(math.rad(180))`
		`3.1415926535898`
		`> print(math.rad(180) == math.pi)`
		`true`
		`> print(math.rad(450))`
		`7.8539816339745`

Continued

Table 6-1 *(continued)*

FUNCTION	DESCRIPTION	EXAMPLE(S)

`math.random([m [, n]])`	Generate pseudo-random numbers. The numbers generated may not be sufficient for statistical analysis but provide an easy way to create pseudo-randomness in a program. For example, this function can be used along with the `SendChatMessage()` World of Warcraft API function to allow your character to make random sayings based on certain events.
	When called without arguments, returns a pseudo-random real number between 0 and 1 (not including 1). When called with a number m, returns a pseudo-random integer between and including 1 and m. When called with two numbers m and n, returns a pseudo-random integer between and including m and n
		`> print(math.random())`
		`7.8263692594256e-06`
		`> print(math.random(100))`
		`14`
		`> print(math.random(10, 20))`
		`18`

`math .randomseed(x)`	The pseudo-random number generator used by Lua takes an initial seed and generates a sequence of numbers based on that seed. As a result, the same initial seed will always produce the same sequence.	`> math.randomseed(1000)`
		`> print(math.random(100))`
		`1`
		`> print(math.random(100))`
		`54`
		`> print(math.random(100))`
		`61`
		`> -- reset the seed`
		`> math.randomseed(1000)`
		`> print(math.random(100))`
		`1`
		`> print(math.random(100))`
		`54`
		`> print(math.random(100))`
		`61`

Table 6-1 *(continued)*

FUNCTION	DESCRIPTION	EXAMPLE(S)
math.sqrt(x)	Returns the square root of x. (You can also use the expression x^0.5 to compute this value.)	> print(math.sqrt(169) 13 > print(math.sqrt(2)) 1.4142135623731 > print(2 ^ 0.5) 1.4142135623731

NOTE Lua doesn't include a math.round() function because there are so many possible variations on what it means to "round" a number. http://lua-users.org/wiki/SimpleRound shows how to implement the following function, which rounds a number to a given decimal place:

```
function round(num, idp)
  local mult = 10^(idp or 0)
  return math.floor(num * mult + 0.5) / mult
end
```

String Utility Functions

Lua provides several utility functions for working with and manipulating strings. Each of these functions is available as object-oriented method calls, as well as the library calls themselves. For example, the following two calls accomplish the same thing:

```
> test = "This is a string"
> print(string.len(test))
16
> print(test:len())
16
```

Table 6-2 describes the utility functions.

Table 6-2: String Utility Functions

FUNCTION	DESCRIPTION	EXAMPLE(S)
string.len(s)	Receives a string and returns its length. The empty string "" has length 0. Embedded zeros are counted, so "a\000bc\000" has length 5.	> print(string.len("Monkey")) 5

Continued

Table 6-2 *(continued)*

FUNCTION	DESCRIPTION	EXAMPLE(S)

`string.lower(s)`	Receives a string and returns a copy of this string with all uppercase letters changed to lowercase. All other characters are left unchanged. The definition of what an uppercase letter is depends on the current locale.	```> test = "Hello World!"```
		```> print(string.lower(test))```
		```hello world!```
		```> print(test:lower())```
		```hello world!```

`string.rep(s, n)`	Returns a string that is the concatenation of `n` copies of the string `s`.	```> print(string.rep("Hello", 3)```
		```HelloHelloHello```
		```> test = "foo"```
		```> print(test:rep(3))```
		```foofoofoo```

`string .reverse(s)`	Returns a string that is the string `s` reversed.	```> print(string.reverse("Test"))```
		```tseT```
		```> test = "Hello world!"```
		```> print(test:reverse())```
		```!dlrow olleH```

`string.sub( s, i [, j])`	Returns the substring of `s` that starts at `i` and continues until `j`; `i` and `j` may be negative. If `j` is absent, then it is assumed to be equal to `-1` (which is the same as the string length). In particular, the call `string .sub(s,1,j)` returns a prefix of `s` with length `j`, and `string.sub(s, -i)` returns a suffix of `s` with length `i`.	```> test = "Hello world"```
		```> print(string.sub(test, 1, 3))```
		```Hel```
		```> print(test:sub(1, -1)```
		```Hello world```
		```> print(test:sub(-3, -1)```
		```rld```

`string.upper (s)`	Receives a string and returns a copy of this string with all lowercase letters changed to uppercase. All other characters are left unchanged. The definition of what a lowercase letter is depends on the current locale.	```> test = "Hello World!")```
		```> print(string.upper(test))```
		```HELLO WORLD!```
		```> print(test:upper())```
		```HELLO WORLD!```

Formatting New Strings

Throughout the book, you've used the concatenate operator to make new strings and format longer messages. This code to generate longer strings ends up being extremely difficult to read, and difficult to maintain. Lua provides a utility function called `string.format(formatstring, ...)` that will format a list of arguments, according to a defined format.

The `string.format(formatstring, ...)` function is used to format any number of arguments into an output string based on `formatstring`. A format string can contain literal characters and conversion codes that are formatted and copied directly into the result. Conversion codes are used to format the string based on arguments that are passed to `string.format()`.

Conversion codes begin with a percent sign (%) and contain one of the following specifiers, indicating what type of data the argument should be treated as:

- `%c` — Takes a number argument and formats it as the ASCII character that corresponds to the number.

- `%d`, `%i` — Takes a number argument and formats it as a signed integer.

- `%o` — Takes a number argument and formats it as an octal number.

- `%u` — Takes a number argument and formats it as an unsigned integer.

- `%x` — Takes a number argument and formats it as a hexadecimal number, using lowercase letters.

- `%X` — Takes a number argument and formats it as a hexadecimal number, using capital letters.

- `%e` — Takes a number argument and formats it as scientific notation, with a lowercase `e`.

- `%E` — Takes a number argument and formats it as scientific notation, with an uppercase `E`.

- `%f` — Takes a number argument and formats it as a floating point number.

- `%g` and `%G` — Takes a number and formats it according to either `%e` (or `%E` if `%G` is specified) or `%f`, depending on which is shortest.

- `%q` — Formats a string so it can safely be read back into a Lua interpreter.

- `%s` — Takes a string and formats it according to the supplied options.

Several options can be used in a conversion specification between the percent sign and the type specifier. The following options can be included, in this specific order:

- A sign specification (either a + or a -) that causes a sign to be printed with any number. By default, the sign is only printed with negative numbers.

- A padding character (either a space, or a 0) that will be used when padding the result to the correct string width. By default, any results will be padded with spaces to meet the correct width, if specified.

- An alignment specification that causes the result to be left-justified or right-justified. The default is right-justification, while a - character will make the result left-justified.

- (Optional) A width specification that specifies the minimum width of the resulting string.

- (Optional) A precision specification that dictates how many decimal digits should be displayed when formatting a floating-point number. When specified for strings, the resulting string will be cut off at this number of characters.

- A type specification indicating what type of data the argument should be treated as.

Confused yet? More often than not, you'll only use a very small subset of these options, but it's good to understand the abilities and limitations of the string formatting system. The examples in Table 6-3 should help clarify the basics of string formatting.

Table 6-3: Example Format Strings

COMMAND	RESULT
string.format("%%c: %c", 83)	S
string.format("%+d", 17.0)	+17
string.format("%05d", 17)	00017
string.format("%o", 17)	21
string.format("%u", 3.14)	3
string.format("%x", 13)	d
string.format("%X", 13)	D
string.format("%e", 1000)	1.000000e+03
string.format("%E", 1000)	1.000000E+03
string.format("%6.3f", 13)	13.000
string.format("%q", "One\nTwo")	"One\ Two"
string.format("%s", "monkey")	monkey
string.format("%10s", "monkey")	monkey
string.format("%5.3s", "monkey")	mon

IN WORLD OF WARCRAFT

WoW includes an extra option for `string.format()` that allows you to choose a specific argument from the argument list, rather than having the next one used for a given type identifier. This option is not included in standard Lua 5.1, so you will need to be using the special Lua511WoW distribution that has been created to test this in your interpreter. If you are using WoWLua, it should work correctly.

To select a specific argument, include the number of the argument, followed by the dollar sign (`$`), immediately after the percent sign (`%`). For example:

```
> print(string.format("%2$d, %1$d, %d", 13, 17))
17, 13, 13
```

As you can see, the first type identifier is modified to request the second argument, while the second identifier consumes the second argument to the format string. When selecting parameters in this way, you can't skip any and leave them unused. If you use parameters 1 and 3, you must also use parameter 2. You can mix parameter selection and normal type identifiers in the same format string without any issues.

Uses in localization

WoW specifically includes this functionality to provide support for multiple languages. For example, the following string appears in English:

```
Cladhaire's Shadow Word: Pain is removed.
```

In German, the phrase used in this same situation is:

```
'Shadow Word: Pain' von Cladhaire wurde entfernt.
```

As you can see, the order of the arguments is swapped based on the way the phrase is constructed for German clients. Without parameter selection, WoW would have to handle each of these cases specifically, which would get very messy. Instead, the client uses `string.format()` along with parameter selection to craft these messages.

The English format string is `"%s's %s is removed."`, while the German format string is `"'%2$s' von %1$s wurde entfernt."`. Rather than maintain a long list of special messages, format strings are used to make the client consistent.

Pattern Matching

A common theme you will find when writing addons is the need to match and parse text supplied by the game against a given pattern. Lua provides a number of utility functions to accomplish these tasks. These functions can use *patterns* to describe what to search for when matching against a given string.

Character Classes

Patterns can use any of the character classes described in Table 6-4. Each class is designed to match a subset of all characters in a specific way. For example, the character class %s can be used to match any whitespace character, while %a can be used to represent any letter.

Table 6-4: Character Classes

CLASS	MATCHES
x (where x is not one of the magic characters ^$()%.[]*+-?)	The character x itself
. (a period)	Any character
%a	Any letter
%c	Any control character
%d	Any digit
%l	Any lowercase letter
%p	Any punctuation character
%s	Any space character
%u	Any uppercase letter
%w	Any alphanumeric character
%x	Any hexadecimal digit
%z	The character with representation 0 (for example,\000)
%x (where x is any non-alphanumeric character)	Represents the character x. This is the standard way to escape the magic characters. Any punctuation character (even the non-magic ones) can be preceded by a % when used to represent itself in a pattern.
[set]	Any characters included in set, which can be specified as a range of characters by listing the range with a hyphen (such as A-Z). All classes defined in this table may also be used as a part of set, including the other characters, which just represent themselves. For example, [%w_] matches all alphanumeric characters plus the underscore character, while [0-9%l%-] matches all digits plus the lowercase letters and the - character.
[^set]	The complement of any set (as previously defined). Therefore, [^%s] matches any non-space character.

In addition, with any of the character classes that have a percent sign followed by a letter, the letter can be changed to uppercase to serve as a shortcut for the complement to the character class. In other words, %s will match any character that is *not* a space, and %A will match any character that is *not* a letter.

Take a look at some examples. Given the test string `"abc ABC 123 !@# \n \000 %"`, Table 6-5 shows what will be matched by a given pattern.

Table 6-5: Example Patterns

PATTERN	STRING MATCHED
`"a"`	a
`"."`	a
`"%a"`	a
`"%c"`	\n
`"%d"`	1
`%l"`	a
`%p`	!
`%s`	space
`%u`	A
`%w`	a
`%x`	a
`%z`	\000
`%%`	%

Pattern Items

Each of the character classes previously defined can be used in the pattern items described in Table 6-6.

Table 6-6: Using Pattern Items

PATTERN	MATCHES
A single character class	Any single character in the class.
A single character class followed by an *	Zero or more repetitions of a character in the class. These repetition items always match the longest possible sequence.

Continued

Table 6-6 *(continued)*

PATTERN	MATCHES
A single character class followed by a +	Zero or more repetitions of characters in the class. These repetitions items always match the longest possible sequence.
A single character class followed by a -	Zero or more repetitions of characters in the class. Unlike *, these repetition items always match the shortest possible sequence.
A single character class followed by a ?	Zero or one occurrence of a character in the class.
%n	For n between 1 and 9; such item matches a substring equal to the nth captured string (see the section later in this chapter on captures).
%bxy, where x and y are two distinct characters	Strings that start with x, end with y, and where the x and y are balanced. This means that if you read the string from left to right, counting +1 for an x and -1 or a y, the ending y is the first y where the count reaches 0. For instance, the item %b() matches expressions with balanced parentheses.

These pattern items can be very simple to use when you need to match a specific part of a string in a very general way. Table 6-7 gives a number of example patterns and the corresponding matches when run against the string `"abc ABC 123 !@# \n \000 %"`.

Table 6-7: Example Patterns

PATTERN	STRING MATCHED
%a	a
%a*	abc
%a+	abc
%a	no string matched
%a-%s	Abc
%a?	A
%ba3	abc ABC 123

Pattern Captures

A pattern can contain subpatterns enclosed in parentheses, called captures. When a match succeeds, the part of the pattern enclosed in parentheses is stored (captured) for future use. Captures are numbered according to the order of their left parenthesis, because they can be nested. For instance, in the pattern `"(a*(.)%w(%s*))"`, the part of the string matching `"a*(.)%w(%s*)"` is stored as the first capture (with number 1); the character matching `"."` is captured as number 2, and the part matching `"%s*"` has number 3.

Additionally, the empty capture `()` captures the current string position (a number). For instance, if you apply the pattern `"()aa()"` on the string `"flaaap"`, there will be two captures, the number 3 and the number 5.

Pattern Anchors

A pattern is quite literally a sequence of characters to be matched. Using ^ at the beginning of a pattern can match the beginning of a string, while using $ at the end of a pattern can match the end of a string. When used anywhere else in the pattern, these strings will match their literal equivalent. Anchors can be used to make a pattern more explicit.

Pattern Examples

Table 6-8 illustrates a number of common requirements for pattern matching and shows what that pattern might look like. These are general examples and may only work in specific cases.

Table 6-8: Example Patterns

REQUIREMENT	PATTERN
Match a nonspace token in a string.	`"%S+"`
Match all strings beginning with the text MYADDON:, capturing the rest of the string.	`"^MYADDON:(.+)"`
Match a number, optionally with a fractional part after a decimal point, capturing the entire number.	`"(%d+%.?%d*)"`
Match each assignment in the form xxxx=yyyy, where xxxx is alphanumeric and yyyy contains no spaces, and capture each individually.	`"(%w+)=(%S+)"`
Match all single quoted strings, such as `'foo'` and `'bar'`.	`"%b''"`
Match the last nonspace token in a string.	`"%S+$"`

Pattern Matching Functions

Lua provides four functions that accept pattern strings:

- `string.gmatch(s, pattern)`
- `string.gsub(s, pattern, repl [, n])`

- ```
  string.match(s, pattern [, init])
  ```

- ```
  string.find(s, pattern [, init [, plain]])
  ```

These functions are also available as object-oriented method calls on the string itself, as with the utility functions discussed earlier. Each of them accomplishes a different task for strings, as you'll see.

The `string.gmatch(s, pattern)` function returns an iterator function that, each time it is called, returns the next captures from `pattern` over string `s`. If `pattern` specifies no captures, then the entire match is produced in each call.

For example, the following loop iterates over all the words from string `s`, printing one per line:

```
s = "hello world from Lua"
for w in string.gmatch(s, "%a+") do
  print(w)
end
```

And here's an example that collects all pairs' key=value from the given string into a table:

```
t = {}
s = "from=world, to=Lua"
for k, v in string.gmatch(s, "(%w+)=(%w+)") do
  t[k] = v
end
for k,v in pairs(t) do
  print(k, v)
end
```

When working with `string.gmatch()`, remember that the pattern needs to match each and every occurrence, so the pattern shouldn't be anchored too heavily (in particular using the ^ and $ anchors would make the preceding example work incorrectly).

The `string.gsub(s, pattern, repl [, n])` function returns a copy of `s` in which all (or the first `n`, if given) occurrences of the pattern have been replaced by a replacement string specified by `repl`, which may be a string, a table, or a function. `string.gsub()` also returns as its second value the total number of matches that occurred.

If `repl` is a string, its value is used for replacement. The character % works as an escape character: any sequence in `repl` of the form %n, with n between 1 and 9, stands for the value of the nth captured substring (see the following example). The sequence %0 stands for the whole match. The sequence %% stands for a single %.

If `repl` is a table, the table is queried for every match, using the first capture as the key; if the pattern specifies no captures, then the whole match is used as the key.

If `repl` is a function, this function is called every time a match occurs, with all captured substrings passed as arguments, in order; if the pattern specifies no captures, then the whole match is passed as a sole argument.

If the value returned by the table query or by the function call is a string or a number, it is used as the replacement string; otherwise, if it is `false` or `nil`, there is no replacement (that is, the original match is kept in the string).

Here are some examples:

```
> print(string.gsub("hello world", "(%w+)", "%1 %1"))
hello hello world world 2
> print(string.gsub("hello world", "%w+", "%0 %0", 1))
hello hello world 1
> print(string.gsub("hello Lua", "(%w+)%s*(%w+)", "%2 %1"))
Lua hello 1
> lookupTable = {["hello"] = "hola", ["world"] = "mundo"}
> function lookupFunc(pattern)
>> return lookupTable[pattern]
>> end
> print(string.gsub("hello world", "(%w+)", lookupTable))
hola mundo 2
> print(string.gsub("hello world", "(%w+)", lookupFunc))
hola mundo 2
```

The `string.match(s, pattern [, init])` function looks for the first match of pattern in the string `s`. If it finds one, the match returns the captures from the pattern; otherwise, it returns `nil`. If `pattern` specifies no captures, the whole match is returned. A third, optional numerical argument — `init` — specifies where to start the search; its default value is 1 and may be negative.

The `string.find(s, pattern [, init [, plain]])` function looks for the first match of `pattern` in the string `s`. If it finds a match, `find` returns the indices of `s` where this occurrence starts and ends; otherwise, it returns `nil`. A third, optional numerical argument — `init` — specifies where to start the search; its default value is 1 and may be negative. A value of `true` as a fourth, optional argument, `plain`, turns off the pattern matching facilities, so the function does a plain "find substring" operation, with no characters in `pattern` being considered "magic." Note that if `plain` is given, `init` must also be given.

If the pattern has captures, then in a successful match the captured values are also returned, after the two indices.

World of Warcraft Additions to Lua

Several functions have been added to the Lua implementation in WoW as utility functions for developers:

- `strsplit(sep, str)`
- `strjoin(sep, ...)`
- `strconcat(...)`
- `getglobal(name)`
- `setglobal(name, value)`
- `debugstack([start[, count1[, count2]]])`

These functions are available in the WowLua addon, on the WebLua webpage, and in the two interpreters that are available for download via the book's companion website. They may not be available in Lua distributions obtained elsewhere.

The `strsplit(sep, str)` function takes a given string `str` and splits it into separate strings on each occurrence of the separator string `sep`. This function will return each individual string (with separator characters removed) to the caller.

```
> print(strsplit(":", "foo:bar:blah"))
foo, bar, blah
> print(strsplit(" ", "This is a string"))
This, is, a string
```

The `strjoin(sep, ...)` function takes a list of strings and concatenates them together with the separator character `sep`, returning the result.

```
> print(string.join(" ", "This", "is", "a", "test", "string"))
This is a test string
> print(string.join(", ", "alpha", "beta", "gamma"))
alpha, beta, gamma
```

The `strconcat(...)` function takes a list of strings and concatenates them together into one long string, which is returned.

```
> print(strconcat("This", "is, "a", "test"))
Thisisatest
> print(strconcat("alpha, ", 'beta, ", "gamma"))
alpha, beta, gamma
```

The `getglobal(name)` function takes a variable name as a string and returns the so named global variable, if it exists. This function is used extensively by the WoW user interface when dealing with frame children and parents.

```
> greek1,greek2,greek3 = "alpha","beta","gamma"
> for i=1,3 do
>> print(getglobal("greek"..i))
>> end
alpha
beta
gamma
```

The `setglobal(name, value)` function takes a variable name as a string, along with a corresponding value, and sets the so named global variable to the new value. This function is again used by the default WoW interface.

```
> print(myVariable)
nil
> setglobal("myVariable", 17)
> print(myVariable)
17
```

The debugstack([start[, count1[, count2]]]) function returns the current calling stack according to three inputs, as described in Table 6-9.

Table 6-9: debugstack Inputs

INPUT	TYPE	DESCRIPTION
start	Number	The stack depth at which to start the stack trace (defaults to 1, the function calling debugstack)
count1	Number	The number of functions to output at the top of the stack (default 12)
count2	Number	The number of functions to output at the bottom of the stack (default 10)

This function only operates correctly in WoW. The standalone Lua interpreter has its own method of providing stack traces.

Function Aliases

In World of Warcraft, many of the library functions have been given shorter aliases so they are easier to access and type. Table 6-10 contains a full listing of these aliases.

Table 6-10: Global Aliases

ALIAS	ORIGINAL FUNCTION	ALIAS	ORIGINAL FUNCTION
abs	math.abs	tan	math.ran
acos	math.acos	format	string.format
asin	math.asin	gmatch	string.gmatch
atan	math.atan	gsub	string.gsub
atan2	math.atan2	strbyte	string.byte
ceil	math.ceil	strchar	string.char
cos	math.cos	strfind	string.find
deg	math.deg	strlen	string.len
exp	math.exp	strlower	string.lower
floor	math.floor	strmatch	string.match
frexp	math.frexp	strrep	string.rep
ldexp	math.ldexp	strrev	string.reverse

Continued

Table 6-10 *(continued)*

ALIAS	ORIGINAL FUNCTION	ALIAS	ORIGINAL FUNCTION
log	math.log	strsub	string.sub
max	math.max	strupper	string.upper
min	math.min	foreach	table.foreach
mod	math.fmod	foreachi	table.foreachi
rad	math.rad	getn	table.getn
random	math.random	sort	table.sort
Randomseed	math.randomseef	tinsert	table.insert
Sin	math.sin	tremove	table.remove
Sqrt	math.sqrt		

Summary

Lua has three major libraries that contain utility functions. The table library provides ways to insert, remove, and sort array tables; the string library has a number of useful utilities for tasks such as turning a string into all lowercase, uppercase, or even reversing the string. In addition to these utility functions, you were introduced to the basics of Lua pattern matching and string formatting using `string.format()`, `string.match()`, and `string.find()`.

# CHAPTER 7

Learning XML

James Whitehead II

As mentioned in Chapter 1, you use two languages to build user interfaces for World of Warcraft. You have already been introduced to Lua, the programming language that defines the behavior of the interface, but you haven't yet tackled eXtensible Markup Language (XML), the language used to create the graphical frames that comprise WoW's user interface. That's what this chapter is all about.

XML as a Markup Language

A markup language takes text content and adds extra information to the document, mixing it in with the text itself. The markup typically describes something about the text itself, such as the structure of the document or how the text should be displayed on screen. Following are examples of two notable markup languages. First is HTML:

```
<html>
  <head>
    <title>My Document</title>
  </head>
  <body>
    <h1>Heading One</h1>
      This text is <strong>bold</strong>.
  </body>
</html>
```

And then LaTeX:

```
\documentclass{article}
\title{My Document}
\begin{document}
\maketitle
\section{Heading One}
This text is \textbf{bold}.
\end{document}
```

Each of these examples provides basic information about the structure of the content by creating new headings and sections, and delimiting the actual body of the document. In addition, the `<strong>` and `\textbf{}` tags are intermixed with the text to indicate that a specific word should be displayed in a bold face font.

XML's Relationship to HTML

While HTML is a markup language describing presentation with a minimal amount of structural information, XML is entirely a structural language, describing the relationship between elements but providing no cues about how they should be presented. Consider this example XML document:

```
<addressbook name="Personal">
  <entry>
    <firstname>Alice</firstname>
    <lastname>Applebaum</lastname>
    <phone>+1-212-555-1434</phone>
    <address>
       114 Auburn Street
       Apt 14
       Atlanta, GA
    </address>
  </entry>
</addressbook>
```

Unlike the earlier HTML example, this has no presentation cues, and modern web browsers wouldn't know how to display this information. An XML document typically structures information according to some set of rules (such as a schema definition, which you will explore later this chapter). In short, XML is a cousin of the HTML standard that is generalized for multiple uses, and is stricter in its syntax and structure.

Components of XML

XML is designed to be both human-readable and computer-readable, so it has a strict required structure. As a result, a limited number of constructs can be used to build a document (other than the *content* of the document, which can be free-form text or include further markup).

An XML document includes tags, elements, attributes, and entities, each of which is discussed in the following sections.

XML Tags

An XML tag is an identifier that begins and ends with angle brackets, such as `<tag>`. The tags are case-sensitive, so `<Tag>` is a different tag name than `<tag>`. A closing tag is the same as an opening tag, but has a forward slash immediately after the open bracket, such as `</tag>`. The XML standard doesn't define any specific tags, only the rules defining how and when tags should appear.

XML Elements

Elements are the lowest level of structure and content in an XML document, taking some content and enclosing it in a set of open/close tags. A basic element from the earlier XML example is the `<entry></entry>` section, which defines an XML element of type `entry`. An XML element can contain any type of content, including more XML definitions. Elements are governed by the following rules:

- A nonempty element must begin with an opening tag and end with a closing tag.
- An element with no content can either be delimited with start/end tags or be a self-closing tag. A self-closing tag has a forward slash immediately before the closing angle bracket, such as `<tag />` or `<tag/>`.

Again, the XML standard doesn't really define any element types or tags, but merely describes how the document should be structured so it conforms to the standard.

XML Attributes

In addition to containing generic content, each XML element can have any number of attributes, which are named values belonging to that element. An attribute is declared in the start tag (or the self-closing tag, if used) like this:

```
<tag attribute="value"></tag>
```

Attributes can have any name, but the XML standard requires that all values be quoted using either balanced single quotes or balanced double quotes. This ensures the document can be parsed by any program conforming to the XML standards.

Unlike an element's content, which describes more of a parent/child relationship, attributes describe something specific about the element, such as the name of the element. The `addressbook` element has the name `Personal`, so it can be distinguished easily from any other `addressbook` that has been defined. The distinction isn't made through the XML standard but is extremely useful when parsing and validating an XML document.

XML Entities

The XML specification forbids the ampersand (`&`) and the less than sign (`<`) from appearing within an element. To compensate for this, XML provides a number of escaped entities that can be included in the place of these characters. Table 7-1 shows a list of the most common XML entities:

Table 7-1: XML Entities

CHARACTER	EQUIVALENT ENTITY
&	&amp;
<	&lt;
>	&gt;
"	&quot;
'	&apos;

Creating Well-Formed XML

A well-formed XML document is one that is valid and parsable from a syntactic point of view; that is, it follows all the required rules defined by the standard. Before jumping into the rules for a well-formed document, we need to define root and nonroot elements, which are used in the rules.

- **root element:** A root element is an element that is not nested within another element. The first element in an XML file is a root element, as is any other element on that same level.

- **non-root element:** An element that is nested within another element.

For a document to be well-formed, it must comply with the following:

- Any nonempty elements begin with a start tag and end with an end tag.

- Empty elements may either be delimited with start and end tags or be marked as a self-closing element.

- All attribute values are quoted with balanced single or double quotes.

- Tags may be nested, but must not overlap. In particular, each non-root element must be contained entirely within another element. This disallows something like `<b>Some <i>Text</b></i>`, because the `<i>` element is not contained entirely within another element.

Checking the syntax of an XML document is as simple as opening it in your favorite web browser, although more specialized tools are available. Most modern browsers are XML-capable and can tell you which line of the document failed.

Validating an XML Document

The XML format itself describes the syntax of the language — that is, the rules that make an XML document well-formed — but doesn't delve into the semantics, such as what attributes can belong to a given element, and what relationships can exist between given elements.

One method of describing the semantics of a given XML document is to use a schema definition. These definitions can come in a few forms, such as:

- Document Type Definition (DTD), a format native to XML.
- XML Schema, a W3C standard for declaring a schema.
- RELAX NG, a simple schema language available in XML formats as well as a shorter version.

World of Warcraft defines its schema using the XML Schema standard. The following section of the chapter focuses on this standard, and how to read it and use it for validating your files.

Example Schema Definition

The following is a simple XML Schema definition for an address book:

```
<xs:schema
  xmlns:xs="http://www.w3.org/2001/XMLSchema">
  <xs:element name="addressbook" type="AddressBook"/>
  <xs:complexType name="AddressBook">
    <xs:sequence>
      <xs:element name="name" type="xs:string"/>
      <xs:element name="phone" type="xs:string"/>
      <xs:element name="address" type="xs:string"/>
    </xs:sequence>
  </xs:complexType>
</xs:schema>
```

The initial line is standard for declaring a schema; it simply points to the standard document for the W3C definition of the XML Schema definition. The second tag defines a new element named addressbook, creating a new <addressbook> tag, and associating it with the named type AddressBook. The rest of the sequence defines what it means to be of type AddressBook, namely a sequence of four different named elements that is simply string content.

Example XML Document

The following is a file that declares its schema to exist in the file addressbook.xsd. Assuming both files are in the same directory, this file can be validated against the schema directly:

```
<addressbook
  xmlns:xsi="http://www.w3.org/2001/XMLSchema-instance"
  xsi:noNamespaceSchemaLocation="addressbook.xsd">
  <name>Alice Applebaum</name>
  <phone>+1-212-555-1434</phone>
  <address>
    114 Auburn Street
```

```
        Apt 14.
        Atlanta, GA
    </address>
</addressbook>
```

You can use a number of utilities to validate an XML schema on different platforms:

- XMLNanny (MacOSX), `www.xmlnanny.com`
- Microsoft Visual Studio (Windows), `www.microsoft.com/express/`
- XMLSpy, `www.altova.com/products/xmlspy/xml_editor.html`
- Decision Soft's Online XML Validator, `tools.decisionsoft.com/schemaValidate/`

Figure 7-1 shows this XML document being validated against the given schema.

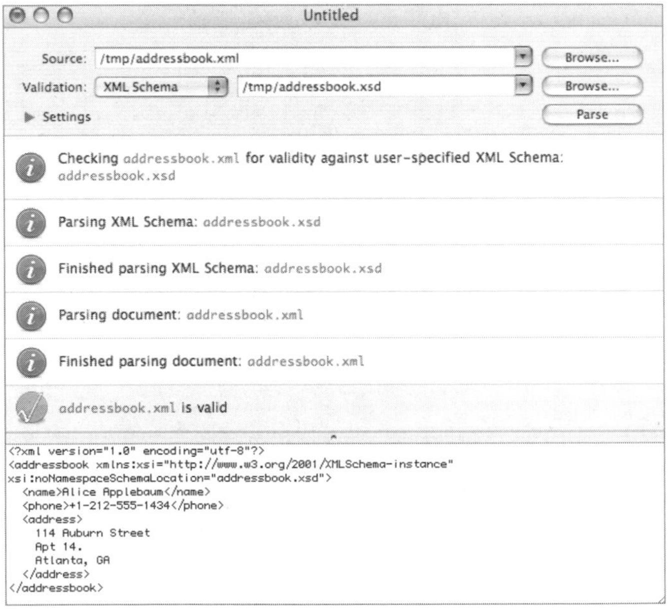

Figure 7-1: Validating with XMLNanny

The document passes the validation step because it's been structured correctly and the schema has been followed exactly. As a matter of fact, the example schema requires the elements of `<addressbook>` to appear in the exact order shown. If you were to swap the order of `<name>` and `<phone>`, the document would no longer validate. To add the elements in any order, as long as you include them all, you can change the `<xs:sequence>` and its matching close tag to read `<xs:all>`.

XML in World of Warcraft

The WoW user interface has an incredibly detailed XML schema that dictates exactly what tags, attributes, and values are valid when defining frames. To better understand how everything is structured, you can unpack the latest XML schema following the directions given in Chapter 8. It will extract to the `Blizzard Interface Data (enUS)/FrameXML/UI.xsd` file under your WoW installation, where enUS is your locale. Here's an excerpt from the file:

```xml
<xs:simpleType name="ORIENTATION">
  <xs:restriction base="xs:NMTOKEN">
    <xs:enumeration value="HORIZONTAL"/>
    <xs:enumeration value="VERTICAL"/>
  </xs:restriction>
</xs:simpleType>

<xs:simpleType name="ColorFloat">
  <xs:restriction base="xs:float">
    <xs:minInclusive value="0.0"/>
    <xs:maxInclusive value="1.0"/>
  </xs:restriction>
</xs:simpleType>

<xs:complexType name="ColorType">
  <xs:attribute name="r" type="ColorFloat" use="required"/>
  <xs:attribute name="g" type="ColorFloat" use="required"/>
  <xs:attribute name="b" type="ColorFloat" use="required"/>
  <xs:attribute name="a" type="ColorFloat" default="1.0"/>
</xs:complexType>

<xs:complexType name="GradientType">
  <xs:sequence>
    <xs:element name="MinColor" type="ColorType"/>
    <xs:element name="MaxColor" type="ColorType"/>
  </xs:sequence>
  <xs:attribute name="orientation" type="ORIENTATION"
default="HORIZONTAL"/>
</xs:complexType>
```

This excerpt from the WoW XML schema defines a series of types that are used later in the schema, along with attributes and valid values. The first block defines a new type called ORIENTATION. This value is an enumeration, which means it must be one of the listed values, specifically HORIZONTAL or VERTICAL.

The second block defines a new type called ColorFloat, which must be a floating point number. In this case, it must be between the values 0.0 and 1.0 inclusive. Next, a complex type called ColorType is defined; it has three required attributes and one optional attribute. Any element of this type must supply values for r, g, and b (which must conform to the rules for ColorFloat), and may optionally provide a value for a. These correspond to the red, green, blue, and alpha values of a given color.

Finally, a complex type GradientType is defined; it takes exactly two items in sequence, a <MinColor> tag and a <MaxColor> tag, both of type ColorType. Additionally, this tag can take an orientation attribute orientation, described earlier.

Using a GradientType

Assuming there is a `<Gradient>` tag with the type `GradientType` defined somewhere, the following would be a valid usage of this schema:

```
<Gradient orientation="VERTICAL">
  <MinColor r="1.0" g="0.0" b="0.3" a="1.0"/>
  <MaxColor r="0.0" g="0.0" b="0.0" a="1.0">
</Gradient>
```

When used as part of a texture in the game, this appears as a gradient from red to black, with the gradient traveling vertically. This is exactly how the `<Gradient>` tag should be used.

Exploring the Schema

The advantage of a strict markup like XML being used for layout is that all the information necessary to write complex layouts is within the schema itself. The schema reveals to you all of the valid options for any given tag or attribute. In addition, there are a number of tools you can use when editing XML files to make your life easier.

For example, XMLSpy, Visual Studio, and other XML editors can provide auto-complete when you're creating a new file, so attribute names are automatically completed, and some editors even give you dropdowns to select the values when they are defined.

Summary

XML is a broad specification that allows virtually endless combinations of schemas and structure, but when dealing with World of Warcraft, you focus on a very particular subset defined by the schema. The default user interface uses XML for all of its frame layout and creation, and you can take advantage of this by using Blizzard's own code to learn more about the system.

Part

II

Programming in
World of Warcraft

Programming Within World of Warcraft

James Whitehead II

Now it's time to begin working within the game and creating your own meaningful addons.

This chapter shows you the differences between a standalone programming environment and the one that runs inside your World of Warcraft client, points you to tutorials and resources provided by Blizzard, and introduces a number of addons you may find useful as you begin creating your own.

Running and Testing Code In-Game

There are a number of differences between running Lua code outside World of Warcraft and trying to run it within the game. In particular, the `print()` function doesn't exist in the game because there isn't a Lua interpreter to output the given text. This can be remedied by using the WowLua addon created for this book, which gives you an interactive interpreter within the game, or by defining a print function of your own.

Setting Up

First things first; you want to change your client preferences to display Lua errors. When you first install World of Warcraft, or log on to a new account with no addons, errors are silenced by default. This works for most users, but as a developer you will want access to your error messages. Enable Lua errors by doing the following:

1. Open your Main menu by pressing Esc, or by clicking the button near your bags.

2. Click the Interface button to open the interface options.

3. In the second grouping of options, toward the center of your screen, check the Display Lua Errors option.

4. Click Okay to save the options, and exit to the main game.

5. Press Enter to bring up the chat frame's edit box.

6. Type `/run message("Hello World")` and press Enter.

A window similar to the one shown in Figure 8-1 should open in the center of your screen. This is a simple pop-up window that can be used for output by calling the `message()` function. If you didn't enable Lua errors (step 3), this window will not appear. That's because the same function is used for both `error()` and `message()` in the game client, so the setting affects both of them.

Figure 8-1: "Hello World" message

Using /script and /run

As the preceding example shows, you can run code directly from the chat edit box using the slash commands `/script` and `/run`. Both commands run the custom code supplied on the command line as if it were entered into a Lua interpreter. Run the following command:

```
/run print("Hello World")
```

You might expect this line to work in a Lua interpreter, but it gives an error, as shown in Figure 8-2. That's because there is no global function `print()` in World of Warcraft unless you run all of your code through the WowLua interpreter.

Figure 8-2: Error message from running /run print("Hello World")

Displaying Output

There are two primary ways to display output in World of Warcraft:

1. Using the `message()` function. The output window is limited, so long strings or messages will be truncated. In addition, this method pops a window up in the middle of your game, which can be inconvenient, so it's typically used only when writing and debugging code.

2. Using the `:AddMessage()` method and friends to send text to the chat frames. These functions add your output to the normal chat windows. This method is the primary way of displaying information to the user.

Seven chat frames are defined by default in World of Warcraft, and each of them has a function that will add a message to the frame. By default, ChatFrame1 will be the primary window for any WoW user, so it is typically used as the main output window. Run the following:

```
/run ChatFrame1:AddMessage("Hello World!")
```

This function addresses the `ChatFrame1` global object and calls the `:AddMessage()` method with a string to output. This should appear in your chat window, as shown in Figure 8-3.

Figure 8-3: Hello World in a ChatFrame

HINT Unlike the `print()` **function in a Lua interpreter, both** `message()` **and** `ChatFrame1:AddMessage()` **expect the argument to be a string value, so you cannot directly print a table value. Instead, you can call** `tostring()` **before calling the output function, such as:**

```
/run message(tostring(ChatFrame1))
```

Editing Code In-Game

Being able to execute code from the edit box is handy but somewhat limited because it allows a maximum of only 255 characters to be input at a time. Even macros (which enable you to use the `/script` and `/run` commands) are limited to 255 characters. Fortunately, several custom addons let you actually edit code in an in-game text editor, and then run it with a single click. Three of them are TinyPad, Omnibus, and WowLua.

TinyPad

TinyPad, created by Gello, is an extremely compact addon for World of Warcraft that serves as both a simple notepad and an easy to way to write and execute Lua code within WoW. TinyPad enables you to add and delete pages of text, search through any pages that already exist, and "undo" a page back to its last saved version. This addon can be downloaded from the following locations:

```
http://wowui.incgamers.com/ui.php?id=1718
```

```
http://wowinterface.com/downloads/fileinfo.php?id=4417
```

In-game, TinyPad can be accessed through the /tinypad slash command. Figure 8-4 shows the TinyPad window, which has just a few buttons at the top and a basic resizable editing frame.

Figure 8-4: TinyPad's editor

At the top of the window there are buttons to create a new page (the parchment), delete the current page (the bomb), run the code on the current page (the sprinting boot), and revert the page to the last saved version (the paw). In addition, there are buttons to navigate from page to page, open the options screen, and close the window.

The code shown in the figure defines a simple print() function, and outputs a message to the main chat frame.

Omnibus

Based on the visual style and feel of TinyPad, Omnibus adds a few nice features to the in-game code editor, such as tagging and naming of scripts, as well as sending scripts from one user to another via the in-game communication channels.

The latest (potentially unstable) version can be downloaded from http://files .wowace.com/Omnibus/Omnibus.zip. Omnibus was created by JJSheets.

WowLua

WowLua, introduced in Chapter 1, serves as both an interactive Lua interpreter and as a code editor within the game. While WowLua offers similar functionality to the other options, it adds a number of features that make it feel more like a real text editor.

All Lua code in WowLua will be syntax highlighted using the For All Indents and Purposes library, written by Krka. This library is included with WowLua and can be disabled through the options screen. In addition, WowLua includes a custom fixed-width font that makes code more readable, and includes line numbers for convenience. When a script is run and an error occurs, the cursor is taken to the offending line, and the line number is highlighted in red to indicate an error.

WowLua, created by Cladhaire, can be obtained from the book's companion website: http://wowprogramming.com/addons/wowlua.

Writing a Custom print() Function

WowLua defines a global print() function that can be used to print any output to the WowLua output window. You may choose not to use WowLua as your scripting editor, and you may find it useful to implement a function of your own. The following code implements the same functionality for ChatFrame1, directing all your output to the main chat window:

```
local argsToString(arg, ...)
  if select("#", ...) > 0 then
    return tostring(arg), argsToString(...)
  else
    return tostring(arg)
  end
end

function print(...)
  local output = strjoin(", ", argsToString(...))
  ChatFrame1:AddMessage("Print: " .. output)
end
```

The first function takes a list of arguments and runs tostring() on each of them. This allows them to be passed to the strjoin() function, which combines them into one big string. Without this first function you wouldn't be able to print tables or functions without manually running tostring() because you would get an error.

NOTE Chapter 12, "Creating Your First Addon: CombatTracker," will show you how to create your first addon (where you can include this function if you'd like). In addition, Appendix E, "Utilizing Addon Libraries," will show you how to create a library of functions where you can define your print function.

Limitations of Addons and Scripting

Addons for World of Warcraft are given large-scale access to the client API, providing tons of information and functions to accomplish various tasks within the game, but there are a number of important restrictions to keep in mind when designing an addon:

- There is no manner of file input or output in theLua implementation in WoW. Addons can store data using saved variables but these are loaded only when the game starts, and saved only when the game closes or the user interface is reloaded.

- An addon cannot intelligently target units for you, so there is no way, for example, to target the party member with the lowest health.

- An addon cannot intelligently choose a spell for you, so there is no way, for example, to cast the correct rank of a spell to kill the player without spending more mana than necessary.

- Addons cannot control character movement in any way.

A general rule for creating addons is to display as much information as necessary to cue the player to make the correct decision, but the player must actually make the decision and click the button himself. This means you can highlight a specific target to cast, along with which rank of the spell on your hotbar you should use, but the player must ultimately make the decision. Providing an arrow that directs the player to his next objective is kosher because the player must ultimately make the movements himself.

Blizzard Addon Writing Resources

Blizzard includes a number of resources for writing new addons within the game files themselves. To access these files you must download a tool from the World of Warcraft website that unpacks them. These resources are explored in the following sections.

User Interface Customization Tool

Download the User Interface Customization tool from www.blizzard.com/support/ wow/?id=aww01671p. This website contains versions for Microsoft Windows as well as for Mac OS X. Once you've downloaded the zip file, extract the program and run it. On loading, you'll see the screen shown in Figure 8-5.

You have two options:

- Install Interface Data — Extracts all of the code that defines the default user interface, the XML schema that defines the markup, as well as two tutorial addons with step-by-step descriptions.

- Install Interface Art — Extracts all the graphics files that are used in the default interface, such as icons, border textures, and so on.

Most users extract both portions using the Interface Customization tool, creating the following subdirectories in the World of Warcraft directory:

- Blizzard Interface Art (enUS)
- Blizzard Interface Data (enUS)
- Blizzard Interface Tutorial

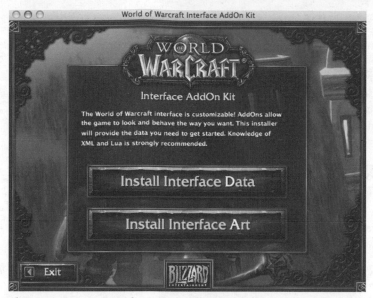

Figure 8-5: User Interface Customization tool

You may find that your directories extract with a different locale in parenthesis. The enUS stands for U.S. English, the language that the interface files use. If you use a German WoW client, you may instead see deDE, for example. You will learn more about localization a little later in the book.

The Blizzard Interface Data directory contains two subdirectories, FrameXML and AddOns. The FrameXML data is loaded every time the client starts, while the AddOns code is loaded optionally if certain conditions are met. For example, the `Blizzard_AuctionUI` addon isn't loaded until you interact with an auctioneer.

BLIZZARD INTERFACE ART

Although Blizzard provides a way to extract the art that is used throughout the game, the graphics files are in a proprietary format called BLP2. Blizzard uses that format for its graphics and, unfortunately, no official tools have been written to support it.

Foxlit, an enterprising member of the user interface community, has written a web page that can convert these files on demand, and we have the opportunity to host a version of it on the book's companion website:

```
http://wowprogramming.com/utils/blp2png
```

Simply select a BLP file that you'd like converted, and the web page will return a PNG image that can be saved and edited. Remember, however, that World of Warcraft only loads BLP and TGA files, so you'll have to convert it after making any changes.

UI and Macros forums

Blizzard provides an on-line forum for the user interface community: `forums .worldofwarcraft.com/board.html?forumId=11114`.

This is often the first place that new information about the user interface is posted, particularly when a new API function is introduced or there's a change to the existing systems. A new post containing a summary of all the upcoming user interface changes is created for each patch, which is then open for discussion and suggestion.

Community Resources

Although the addon community at large is discussed in Appendix F, there are two community resources that deserve a specific mention here because they are more focused as resources and tools, rather than community websites.

WowWiki

Started during the Beta for World of Warcraft, WowWiki (`http://wowwiki.com`) has quickly become a compendium of information about every aspect of the game, including lore, theory crafting, and even interface customization. While the data has grown somewhat out of date, the wiki continues to have an extremely large set of "how-to" documents and reference pages. The interface customization portal can be accessed directly via the following URL: `http://www.wowwiki.com/WoWWiki:Interface_customization`.

WoW Version Tracker

Hosted by WowInterface.com, WoW Version Tracker (`http://wdn.wowinterface.com`) provides in-depth comparisons of the different versions of the interface files released by Blizzard. With a single click anyone can view the difference between any version of any file since the game was released. This can be extremely useful when trying to determine when a bit of functionality was introduced or simply for exploring Blizzard's interface files via the web.

Summary

While a number of differences exist between programming with Lua outside of World of Warcraft and actually writing code for addons, they are rather minor. Experiment with one of the in-game tools or the `/run` and `/script` commands to become familiar with the way interacting with the game client works. You may find it useful to label yourself as `/afk` in-game while you're writing addons — otherwise your guild may think you've gone crazy!

The next chapter introduces you to the basic structure of an addon and shows you how to create frames via XML.

# CHAPTER 9

Anatomy of an Addon

James Whitehead II

At the most basic level, addons for World of Warcraft are just a collection of text and media files that are packaged together with some metadata and loaded by the game client. In practice, however, addons include scripts and media used to extend the core functionality provided by the game client.

Including adding new action buttons, displaying player information, and providing for easier communication, the number of custom addons available for WoW has become immense. This chapter introduces you to the basic components of an addon, explaining in detail what role each of them plays.

Exploring Your Addons Folder

For an addon to be loaded and recognized by the game, it must exist in a specific subdirectory of your World of Warcraft installation. If you've loaded WoW at least once, you will find a subdirectory called Interface that contains a directory named AddOns. That's where every addon directory must reside.

Blizzard Addons

Much of the functionality in the default user interface is implemented via separate addons that are loaded when they are needed by the game client, for example, the Auction House UI. When the player visits an auctioneer, the game loads the Blizzard_AuctionUI addon. This helps speed up load times when opening the game because those functions and frames don't have to be processed. Table 9-1 describes the player's action that triggers the loading of each of the current Blizzard addons.

Table 9-1: Blizzard Load-on-Demand Addons

ADDON NAME	LOADS WHEN THE PLAYER. . .
Blizzard_AuctionUI	Talks to an auctioneer in order to open the auction house interface.
Blizzard_BattlefieldMinimap	Shift+clicks on the Battleground/Arena icon, or presses the keybind to toggle the battlefield minimap.
Blizzard_BindingUI	Opens the Key Binding option in the main menu.
Blizzard_CombatText	Enables the Blizzard Floating Combat Text feature in Advanced Interface Options.
Blizzard_CraftUI	Opens something that uses the CraftUI (such as Enchanting, or Pet Training).
Blizzard_GMSurveyUI	Has had an interaction with a game master and is asked to complete a survey.
Blizzard_InspectUI	Inspects another player.
Blizzard_ItemSocketingUI	Shift+right clicks an item to socket it.
Blizzard_MacroUI	Opens the macro editor from the main menu.
Blizzard_RaidUI	Enters a raid.
Blizzard_TalentUI	Accesses the talent trees from the button or via keybinding.
Blizzard_TradeSkillUI	Opens a tradeskill that uses the TradeSkill interface.
Blizzard_TrainerUI	Interacts with an NPC trainer to learn new skills.

Each of the Blizzard addons has a single file in its directory that has the name of the addon followed by the .pub extension. As far as we can tell, this is some sort of signature used by the game to verify the authenticity of the addon, because the addons written by Blizzard count as secure addons, something that is covered in detail in Chapter 17.

You will learn more about addons that load on demand and how they work later in this chapter, but they provide a nice way to delay loading an addon until it's actually needed by the user.

Custom Addons

Any custom addons should be placed in the same directory as the Blizzard Addons, but unlike the official addons, all components of the addon are included in the single subdirectory named after the addon. There are no restrictions on what these directories can be named, other than the restrictions your operating system places on file creation.

Unlike the Blizzard addons, each addon directory holds all files necessary to load and use that addon, so you will find several different types of files, ways of organizing addons, and different naming conventions.

Addon Components and Files

The files included with each addon will be slightly different, but certain things (such as the table of contents file) will always be the same. This section explains the different types of files that may be included with an addon.

Table of Contents Files (.toc)

The one file that must be included in every addon is the table of contents (TOC) file, which must have the same name as the addon's folder. If an addon's directory is `MyAddon`, then it must contain a file called `MyAddon.toc`. The TOC file provides vital information about the addon (such as title, description, author, and so on) along with directives to load specific addon files. A sample `.toc` file might look like this:

```
## Interface: 20300
## Title: My Addon Name
## Notes: This is my sample addon

MyAddon.xml
MyAddon.lua
```

Each line beginning with `##` contains a directive providing some sort of metadata. The lines after the directives are simply a list of files to be loaded by the addon. In this example, the Title line is the text that is displayed when the addon is listed on the addon selection screen, and Notes contains a longer description that is displayed when you mouse over the addon in that list.

Interface:

The `## Interface` directive (`## Interface: 20300` in the preceding example) provides a basic versioning mechanism that the client uses for the addon selection screen. This number is used by the game client to label the addon with one of two states:

- Out of Date — The game client is newer than this addon's `## Interface` version and may have changed in ways that will cause problems if the addon is loaded. This is only a warning; the addon may work just fine if you check "Load out of date AddOns" at the top of the screen.

- Incompatible — The game client won't load this addon because there have been major changes to the UI system since the version indicated by this addon's `## Interface` directive. A new version of the addon should be downloaded to ensure it operates correctly.

Figure 9-1 shows two addons, one flagged as "Out of date" and the other as "Incompatible." TinyPad could be loaded by checking the "Load out of date AddOns" checkbox, while nothing can force the "Incompatible" addon to load.

Figure 9-1: Addon selection screen

Just because an addon is listed as Out of Date doesn't mean there's anything particularly wrong with it, only that the interface directive in the .toc file hasn't been updated to the latest interface number. When this happens, it's a good reminder to update your addons and make sure you're using the latest versions. This helps you get the latest bug fixes and features. Making sure you're using the latest version of an addon makes it easier for its author to support you.

The interface number is generally built from the version number of the WoW client. For example, the interface number for the 2.3.0 client is 20300, however, this does not necessarily change each time there is a patch. If after a WoW patch you're not sure what interface number to use in building your own addons, you can extract the latest FrameXML files using the User Interface Customization Tool introduced in Chapter 8 and consult the FrameXML.toc file.

ADDON SELECTION SCREEN

The addon selection screen can be accessed by clicking the "Addons" button in the bottom-left corner of the character selection screen. This button will only appear if the user has downloaded and installed an addon in the appropriate place.

From this selection screen, addons can be enabled and disabled on a per-character or global basis. The global settings only work for a single server, so if your characters are on different servers, those settings will need to be configured independently. The addon selection screen can be used to browse the addons that are available on a given system, as well as any dependencies they may have.

When things go wrong with an addon, checking the addon selection screen to ensure the addon isn't flagged as "Out of date" or "Incompatible" is a good place to start to ensure the addon is actually being loaded.

Title: MyAddonName

When addons are listed in the addon selection screen, they are sorted and shown by their ## Title directive, rather than by the name of the addon's TOC file or directory. This can be somewhat confusing as you try to determine which directory corresponds to which addon title in game, but this is relatively infrequent and easy to resolve. The default value for this option is the name of the addon's directory.

This directive can be localized, meaning it can display different text depending on which language the user's client is set to display. To localize the `## Title` directive for the Korean language users, add a hyphen followed by a locale code, such as `## Title-koKR: My Addon Name`. When your addon is loaded on a WoW client with that locale, the custom name will be displayed instead of the generic one supplied in the `## Title` directive. Localization is covered in more depth later in this chapter.

Notes: This is a description for MyAddonName.

The `## Notes` directive gives you the capability to provide a longer description of your addon so users can easily see what it's supposed to do and where to go for more information. This field can also be localized to provide a different description depending on client locale. As with `## Title`, this field may also contain color codes to highlight portions of the text. Figure 9-2 shows the tooltip displayed by the WoWLua addon `.toc` file.

Figure 9-2: WowLua tooltip, generated from ## Title and ## Notes directives

Dependencies or ## RequiredDeps: AddonA, AddonB

Occasionally, an addon requires another addon to function, such as a configuration interface that is only loaded when the user runs a specific slash command. The `## Dependencies` directive takes a list of addon names, and the game client loads the given addon only if all of its dependencies are loaded or can be loaded.

If an addon has a dependency that is disabled in the addons screen (or missing entirely), an error message is displayed, as shown in Figures 9-3 and 9-4. You can move your mouse over the addon name to view a list of dependencies and see which one is missing.

Figure 9-3: Addon with dependency disabled

Figure 9-4: Addon with dependency missing

Dependencies also ensure addons are loaded in the proper order, so if `Beta` relies on `Alpha`, the client will load `Alpha` before it loads `Beta`. This is even true for a long chain of dependencies. `## Dependencies` and `## RequiredDeps` both work the same for this directive.

OptionalDeps: AddonA, AddonB

When an addon can interact with another addon, but doesn't want to require it as a hard dependency, it can be listed as an optional dependency using the `## OptionalDeps` directive. All this directive does is ensure load order between dependent addons, if they are enabled and exist. This directive takes a comma-separated list of addon names. The names listed must match the `.toc` file and the directory names of the given addons.

LoadOnDemand: 1 or 0

As previously mentioned, each of the Blizzard addons is configured to load on demand, meaning that in response to something specific, the game client will load and initialize the addon. This saves memory and load time by not loading the auction house user interface every time the player logs in to the game, but only when the player visits the auction house. Because not all addons may be written in a way that supports load on demand (LoD), there is a directive that flags an addon as LoD capable.

An LoD addon can still use the other directives, and still appears in the addon list, but will not be loaded until explicitly requested by another addon. Many addons use this functionality for their configuration systems, only loading them when the user tries to make a configuration change.

This option takes either a `1` or a `0`, where `1` means the addon is `LoadOnDemand` capable, and `0` means it is not. If this value isn't supplied in the TOC, it defaults to `0`.

LoadsWith: AddonA, AddonB

The `## LoadsWith` directive can be combined with `## LoadOnDemand` to load an addon as soon as another is being loaded. For example, an addon that alters the default Blizzard Raid UI could include `## LoadsWith: Blizzard_RaidUI` to be loaded as soon as the default raid UI is loaded by the client. This directive has rather limited use but expands the usefulness of LoD components quite a bit. If multiple addons are listed, the addon will be loaded as soon as one of those listed is initialized.

DefaultState: enabled or disabled

Not all addons are designed to be enabled or loaded on each and every character, so there is a directive that sets the default state of an addon. This flag tells the client whether or not an addon should be checked (enabled) in the addon selection screen by default. As soon as a user overrides this setting by checking or unchecking the addon, the user preference will be respected. This value defaults to enabled, if not supplied.

LoadManager: AddonA

Adding to the complexity (and versatility) of the LoD system is the `##LoadManager` directive. This directive allows an addon to be flagged as LoD if the LoadManager is present and enabled; otherwise, it will be loaded as a normal addon.

Using this directive is a bit different from simply flagging the addon as LoD. In particular, this method requires a second addon that handles the loading of the first addon; otherwise, it will be loaded unconditionally (as if it wasn't LoD).

A very simple addon called AddonLoader, available at `files.wowace.com` is used by several addons as a LoadManager. The developer can provide conditions in the TOC that AddonLoader then uses to decide when the addon should be loaded. For example, an addon that is specific to Rogues (call it RogueHelper) can be flagged with `## X-LoadOn-Class: Rogue,` and it will be loaded for any rogue characters but not for any others.

This method requires the developer to add these flags to the TOC file and the user to download AddonLoader, but it provides major benefits when used correctly.

SavedVariables: VariableName

The only way an addon can save information between sessions is to define a Lua variable and list its name in the `## SavedVariables` directive in its TOC file. This tells the game to save the contents of that variable out to a file when the game is closed, and read it back in when the game is started up again. The variable can be a string, number, or a table.

SavedVariablesPerCharacter: VariableName

The `## SavedVariablesPerCharacter: VariableName` directive operates in the same way as SavedVariables, except a different file is saved and loaded for each character you log in with. If you log in to character Alice, then her settings will be saved separately from those for Bob. Nothing special needs to happen in the addon; this is all handled automatically by the client.

NONSTANDARD METADATA DIRECTIVES

Beyond the officially supported metadata tags, you may see any number of other tags that are included in the `.toc` file of custom addons. Two customary directives are `##`
`Author: AuthorName` **and** `## Version: 1.0`. **This information isn't displayed by default, but can be accessed by other addons in-game.**

In addition, any field that begins with an X and contains a label with some value is considered addon metadata and can be accessed from within the game. For example, an addon could include a web address using an `## X-Website: http://www.myaddon`
`.com` **directive.**

Each of the `X-Label` directives is localized by the game client, so you can include all of the following and only the correct version will be available through the `GetAddOnMetadata()` **API function:**

```
## X-FAQ-Website: http://www.myaddon.com/faq/
## X-FAQ-Website-esES: http://www.myaddon.com/faq/esES
## X-FAQ-Website-deDE: http://www.myaddon.com/faq/deDE
```

Addon Categories

The Ace addon community has developed a standard set of addon categories that can be included in the metadata for an addon, making it easier to group similar types of addons together when listing or displaying them. Here's the list of categories:

Action Bars	Frame Modification	Priest
Auction	Guild	Quest
Audio	Healer	Raid
Battlegrounds/PvP	Hunter	Rogue
Buffs	Interface Enhancements	Shaman
Caster	Inventory	Tank
Chat/Communication	Library	Tradeskill
Combat	Mage	UnitFrame
Compilations	Mail	Warlock
Data Export	Map	Warrior
Development Tools	Miscellaneous	
Druid	Paladin	

You could use one of these categories or define your own set — that's the beauty of addon metadata. To supply your category, simply use the `## X-Category:`
`CategoryName` **directive.**

Lua Script Files

The TOC file can list any number of Lua files, potentially in subdirectories. Each of these files is loaded and parsed, then executed by the game client in the order listed in the TOC file. This means you can define local variables at the file level and they will be unavailable to other files your addon loads. Keep this in mind when you need to share data between two different files.

Typically, the Lua file is used to define the behavior of an addon rather than the visual style, but it can also be used to create frames dynamically (something you will explore in Chapter 16).

XML Files

A `.toc` file can also load any number of `.xml` files from addons. Markup in these files will be validated against the `UI.xsd` schema file as it's parsed and loaded. This means that an XML file can use the `<Script file="`*SomeFile*`.lua"/>` tag to load a Lua file (this is what the default UI does). Each XML file should begin with the proper declaration of the `<Ui>` element (which must be the root of all XML files loaded):

```
<Ui xmlns="http://www.blizzard.com/wow/ui/" ↵
xmlns:xsi="http://www.w3.org/2001/XMLSchema-instance" ↵
xsi:schemaLocation="http://www.blizzard.com/wow/ui/ ↵
..\FrameXML\UI.xsd">
</Ui>
```

As these files are loaded, any errors will appear in the `Logs\FrameXML.log` file in your base World of Warcraft installation. If your addons aren't behaving properly, it's always a good idea to check this file to ensure there wasn't an error in validating the document.

Media Files

Addons are able to include custom graphics, sounds, and fonts to be displayed (or played) within the game client, providing a different visual style or audio cues. These files are included within the addon directories themselves, and addressed by full pathname from the WoW directory.

Music

Assuming you have a file called `mysound.mp3`, and you have it as part of your addon `MySound`, it will reside in the following location:

```
Interface\Addons\MySound\mysound.mp3
```

This file could then be played by running the following command in-game (remember to escape the backslash character because Lua uses it as the escape character):

```
/run PlaySoundFile("Interface\\Addons\\MySound\\mysound.mp3")
```

The WoW client can natively play MP3 files as well as WAV files. Converting files to these formats can be accomplished through a number of tools freely available on the Internet.

Graphics

WoW accepts two different graphics formats when loading textures for frames. Each graphic must meet the following basic requirements to be loaded, along with being one of the two correct file types:

1. The file's height and width must be greater than or equal to 2, and smaller than 512 pixels.

2. The height and width of the file must be a power of two, although they need not be the same.

For example, a file that is 32 x 64 is acceptable, while a file that is 512 x 400 is not (because the height is not a power of two). In addition, the file can, and should, contain an alpha channel, something that is particular to the specific graphics editing software you are using.

Chapter 20 is dedicated to creating custom graphics, so that isn't covered in detail in this section. Instead, the two primary graphics formats are introduced.

BLP Format

If you have extracted the Blizzard Interface Art using the User Interface Customization Tool (as shown in Chapter 8), you may have noticed that all the files that were created have a `.blp` extension. This file format was created by Blizzard, and has been used in both Warcraft III and World of Warcraft. Even though they provide a way to extract the files, there is still no official tool that can convert these files. The companion website for the book provides a way to convert these graphics (see Chapter 8 for more information). The only time this book will deal with `.blp` files is if we alter any original game art, in which case we will provide the texture in the `.tga` format instead.

TGA Format

Wikipedia defines a `.tga` file as a Truevision Advanced Raster Graphics Adapter file (or TARGA file). This is a simple graphics file format that can be used to store color images, including transparency information. TGA files never use lossless compression, which means the image is not degraded as a result of saving the image, as happens with JPG files. Most modern graphics editors can save to this file format natively, and Chapter 20 provides an extensive tutorial on creating files to be used in the game.

Localizing Your Addons

Localization as it relates to addon development is the process of converting the text and icons used in the application to a format that is meaningful for users from other regions of the world, who may speak different languages. WoW boasts over ten million subscribers, many of them coming from regions in Europe and Asia.

Valid Locales

Blizzard provides a number of game locales with World of Warcraft. Table 9-2 shows a list of the current valid game locale codes. For each of these languages, Blizzard has translated each in-game message and string so they are meaningful to users from that region.

Table 9-2: Valid Client Locales

LOCALE CODE	CORRESPONDING LANGUAGE
deDE	German
enUS	American English
enGB	British English
esES	Spanish
frFR	French
koKR	Korean
zhCN	Simplified Chinese
zhTW	Traditional Chinese

In addition, the Auctioneer set of addons provides localization for the Russian language. Wow doesn't natively support this localization, but the Auctioneer addon suite has most of its messages translated.

Reasons for Providing Localization

When a user plays the game in a specific language, it's often easier for them to make split-second decisions if they aren't trying to read an entirely different language as part of a custom addon. Imagine if you spoke native Spanish but played the game entirely in English. Even if you're a fluent reader, your brain may find difficulty in switching between the two languages quickly.

From a purely practical standpoint, why not? Most users are willing and able to help authors with the addon localization, and if the addon is organized well, it can be a very easy task to keep localizations up to date.

Encouraging Users to Contribute

More often than not, users will approach authors with localization files, but the author can take some steps to ensure the addon is easy to localize. This typically means the following:

1. Rather than including string messages throughout the code, you should provide a set of constants, or a lookup table that can be used for translation.

2. Provide information in the `readme.txt` file for your addon, or the addon's website on how users can contact you to help with localization.

3. Provide comments about what a specific message means so it can easily be translated. Although the word "speed" means only one thing in English, it may translate to different words depending on the language.

Implementing Localization

Implementing localization in your addon can be done in several ways. This section describes one suggested way of structuring your addon so localization files are easy to update and to use. The same techniques can be used in different ways, so experiment and find a method that works best for you.

Add a File for Each Locale

Begin by adding a new localization file for each locale for which you have translations. If you don't have any translations to begin with, simply create a file for the "base" locale in which you've developed the addon. For my addons, this means adding a `Localization.enUS.lua` file to my directory structure. Add the file to the top of the `.toc` file to ensure that it's loaded first.

Create a Global Table Containing the Base Strings

If the addon is called MyAddon, create a new global table called `MyAddonLocalization` in the `Localization.enUS.lua` file. The base translations can be added to this file in two ways: using full strings or using tokens.

Using Full Strings

The following is a set of table definitions that takes the entire string to be translated and uses it as both the key and the value. The reason for this will become apparent later.

```
MyAddonLocalization = {}
MyAddonLocalization["Frames have been locked"] = "Frames have ↵
been locked"
MyAddonLocalization["Frames have been unlocked"] = "Frames have ↵
been unlocked"
```

This tends to work for smaller strings but, as you can see, can be quite verbose for longer string keys.

Using Tokens

Instead of using the entire string as the table key, you can use a smaller string or "token." The same localization file might look like this:

```
MyAddonLocalization = {}
MyAddonLocalization["FRAMES_LOCKED"] = "Frames have been locked"
MyAddonLocalization["FRAMES_UNLOCKED"] = "Frames have been unlocked"
```

Using the Localization Table

Because you've ensured that the localization files have already loaded when the main addon's files are loaded, you can use the table instead of simply writing the strings themselves. For example, you can display the "locked" message using the following:

```
ChatFrame1:AddMesage(MyAddonLocalization["Frames have been locked"])
```

or

```
ChatFrame1:AddMessage(MyAddonLocalization["FRAMES_LOCKED"])
```

If that appears too verbose for you, you could make a shortcut to the global table. This is typically done with the variable L, which is used in other software realms for localization:

```
local L = MyAddonLocalization
ChatFrame1:AddMessage(L["Frames have been locked"])
```

If you've opted for the token method, you can even use syntactic sugar to make it easier to type:

```
ChatFrame1:AddMessage(L.FRAMES_LOCKED)
```

Adding New Locales

New languages can be added by defining new files and using the method described in the previous section. These new files should be loaded after the base locale in the .toc file, but before the main addon. For example, the following could be added as Localization.deDE.lua:

```
if  GetLocale() == "deDE" then
  if not MyAddonLocalization then
    MyAddonLocalization = {}
  end
  MyAddonLocalization["FRAMES_LOCKED"] = "Frames wurden gesperrt"
  MyAddonLocalization["FRAMES_UNLOCKED"] = "Frames wurden entsperrt"
end
```

The first line checks to ensure that the user's locale is deDE; otherwise, the translation file is skipped. The second line creates the global table if it doesn't already exist, and the rest is the same as the base locale file, with the values of the table being the translated strings.

Now, on a German client, if the message is printed to the client, it will be displayed in the native language rather than in English.

Handling Partial Translations

What happens if there are some strings that have been translated into German but not others? Currently, because the main English table is created first, and then the German table is loaded after it, any English strings that haven't been translated to German will be displayed in English. This gives you a mix of the two rather than an error message.

Creating an Addon Skeleton

Chapters 10 and 11 lead you through a number of examples using XML as the basis for creating new frames for your addons. To follow those directions, you need to create a basic addon skeleton that you can alter without having to create a new addon for each example. Work through the following sections to create your first addon skeleton.

Naming your Addon (Creating a Directory)

Your addon must reside in the `Interface\Addons` directory, underneath the World of Warcraft base install location in a subdirectory of its own. For these examples, name your addon `WowXMLExample` by creating a new directory called `WowXMLExample`. The relative path of this directory should be:

```
World of Warcraft\Interface\AddOns\WowXMLExample
```

All new files you create in the next two chapters will reside in this directory.

Creating a .toc File

An addon is useless without a TOC file, so create one now using the following code:

```
## Interface: 20300
## Title: WowXMLExample
## Description: Example addon for World of Warcraft Programming

WowXMLExample.xml
```

The interface number may have changed since this book was published, so consult `FrameXML.toc` to find the latest version.

This minimal file declares the interface number, as well as a title and description for the addon. The only file it loads is the `WowXMLExample.xml` file, which you'll create next.

Generating a Skeleton .xml file

Create `WowXMLExample.xml` in your addon's directory with the following code:

```
<Ui xmlns="http://www.blizzard.com/wow/ui/" ↵
xmlns:xsi="http://www.w3.org/2001/XMLSchema-instance" ↵
```

```
xsi:schemaLocation="http://www.blizzard.com/wow/ui/ ↵
..\FrameXML\UI.xsd">
</Ui>
```

This basic declaration is required for the file to validate properly without errors. Any code you write will be a child of the main <Ui> tag that is defined.

Using External Libraries

Several addon writing libraries and frameworks have been created over the course of time. While these tools can be useful to a developer, the authors of this book recommend you learn how to write basic addons using the World of Warcraft API and XML definitions before trying to learn one specific library's set of helper functions. Appendix E contains a list of the major libraries and frameworks, with detailed information about each.

Summary

This chapter introduced you to the basic components that are included within an addon, including the table of contents file, XML definitions, and Lua scripts. Specific types of media files can be included and used within addons.

# CHAPTER 10

Creating Frames in XML

James Whitehead II

The graphical portions of the World of Warcraft user interface are created using a series of objects more commonly referred to as frames, textures, and font strings. Textures are used to display colors, gradients, or graphics, while font strings are used to display bits of text. Frames are the various buttons, windows, and status bars throughout the user interface, used to group together collections of textures and font strings for display. This chapter introduces you to the basics of the WoW frame system, and teaches you to create basic frames in XML.

Understanding UI Objects

Although the rules for creating user interface objects are relatively straightforward, it's extremely useful to understand how the user interface system works before jumping head-first into XML. Three main user interface objects can be created:

- Texture — A texture is used to display some sort of graphic, color, or color gradient within the game. Textures are created using the <Texture> XML element.

- FontString — A font string can be used to display text in a specific font, size, and color. Font strings can be further customized to display outlines, drop shadows, and other standard effects. Font strings are created using the <FontString> XML element.

- Frame — Frames are the containers that "own" all the textures and font strings throughout the user interface. There are a number of special subtypes of frames, such as buttons, edit boxes, and scroll message frames that you will be introduced later in this chapter. In addition to containing textures and font strings, frames may contain other frames, making them extremely versatile. Frames are created using the `<Frame>` XML element.

When creating any of these objects, there are attributes and elements available that let you indicate the name, size, position, and visibility of the object.

Naming Objects

Each of the basic user interface objects can be given a name using the `name` attribute. These names allow you to refer back to the object later on in the XML file, as well as through Lua once the game has loaded. While names are not mandatory in all cases, it's generally a good rule to name those frames that you may need to interact with later on.

Parenting Objects

In addition to a name, each object can also have a single parent. Parenting helps define a hierarchy for different aspects of the user interface:

1. When a parent is hidden, all child frames are hidden, as well. If this weren't the case, you'd have to manually hide all the other elements that might be attached to a frame.

2. A frame's effective scale is defined by multiplying the frame's scale by its parent's effective scale. Scaling allows a user interface's size to be "shrunk" or "grown" in size.

3. A frame's effective alpha (opacity) value is defined by multiplying the frame's alpha by its parent's effective alpha. This enables you to make not only a button transparent, but all of the individual child elements transparent, as well.

Many of the Blizzard default frames are parented to `UIParent`, which is a special frame used to hide the entire user interface on command, and provide UI scaling. When creating your own frames, it's a good idea to see they end up parented to `UIParent` at some point to ensure they work the same as the other frames to which the user may be accustomed.

There are three different ways to set the parent/child relationship between objects: specifying a parent explicitly using XML attributes, using the hierarchy of XML elements to define the relationship, or calling the `:SetParent()` method on an object directly.

Using Attributes

Use the `parent` attribute to define a parent/child relationship in an XML frame. This attribute should be the name of a frame that is to be set as parent. This method only works for frames. For example:

```
<Frame name="MyFrame" parent="UIParent">
</Frame>
```

Using XML Hierarchy

Each object can be given a parent simply through its nested location within the XML file. The following example shows a frame that contains a single texture and a single font string:

```
<Frame name="MyFrame" parent="UIParent">
  <Layers>
    <Layer level="BACKGROUND">
      <FontString name="MyText"/>
      <Texture name="MyGraphic"/>
    </Layer>
  </Layers>
</Frame>
```

Three new tags are introduced in this example. First, the `<Layers>` tag is used to group layers together. The `<Layer>` tag is then used to declare a specific layer level, and this is where font strings and textures are declared. Layers will be covered in full later in this chapter, but the preceding example creates a frame with a single background layer that contains a font string and a texture. These two graphical elements are both parented to the frame `MyFrame`, because they are declared within that frame.

Using the :SetParent() Method

Once an object has been created, you can call the `:SetParent()` method to change the parent (it takes one argument, the frame, to use as parent). Using the preceding example with `MyFrame`, you could call `MyFrame:SetParent(Minimap)` anytime after the frame has been loaded to parent the frame to the minimap. The argument must be a frame object, not a string.

> **HINT** When naming a frame, you can include the name of the parent simply by adding the string `$parent`. **For example, the following frame will be named** `UIParentMyParent` **because the** `$parent` **string is expanded to the full name of the object's parent:**

```
<Frame name="$parentMyFrame" parent="UIParent"/>
```

The same trick works for textures and font strings, as well.

Giving Objects Sizes

Naturally, before the user interface can know what to do with your objects, it needs to know how large or small they are. The size of an object can be given using the `<Size>` XML element, using either absolute or relative dimensions.

Absolute Dimensions

Absolute dimensions are specific pixel values that define how large an object will be. For example, a frame could be defined as being 100 pixels wide by 50 pixels tall. This definition would look like this in XML:

```
<Frame name="MyFrame">
  <Size x="100" y="50"/>
</Frame>
```

You may also see this done in the following way (particularly in Blizzard's own XML):

```
<Frame name="MyFrame">
  <Size>
    <AbsDimension x="100" y="50"/>
  </Size>
</Frame>
```

Each of these XML definitions creates a frame that is 100 pixels in width and 50 pixels in height.

Relative Dimensions

Instead of using absolute values, a frame can express its height and width as a percentage of its parent. The following XML definition creates two frames:

```
<Frame name="MyFrame1">
  <Size x="100" y="50"/>
</Frame>

<Frame name="MyFrame2" parent="MyFrame1">
  <Size>
    <RelDimension x="0.5" y="0.5"/>
  </Size>
</Frame>
```

The first frame has a size in absolute dimensions, but the second is given using relative dimensions. As a result, MyFrameName2 will be 50 pixels wide by 25 pixels high. You won't see this method of sizing used very often in the default UI (as a matter of fact, it's not currently used at all), but it is still available as an option.

Anchoring Objects

All object placement in World of Warcraft is done through a series of anchors that attach one point on a frame to some other point on another frame. Table 10-1 shows these anchor points, and where they occur on the edge of the frames.

Table 10-1: Available Anchor Points

TOPLEFT	TOP	TOPRIGHT
LEFT	CENTER	RIGHT
BOTTOMLEFT	BOTTOM	BOTTOMRIGHT

Anchors are all defined within the `<Anchors>` element, using the `<Anchor>` tag with the following attributes:

- `point` — The point being anchored.

- `relativeTo` — The frame to which the point is being anchored. This attribute is optional; if omitted, the default is the frame's parent.

- `relativePoint` — The point to attach to on the `relativeTo` frame. This attribute is optional; if omitted, the default is the point being anchored.

In addition to these attributes, the `<Anchor>` element can contain an `<Offset>` element, with which you can specify an offset in absolute or relative dimensions (this tag is used in the same way as the `<Size>` tag). For example, the following code snippet creates a new frame, `MyFrame`, and anchors it to the center of the `UIParent`:

```
<Frame name="MyFrame" parent="UIParent">
  <Size x="100" y="100"/>
  <Anchors>
    <Anchor point="CENTER" relativePoint="CENTER" ↵
relativeTo="UIParent">
      <Offset x="0" y="0"/>
    </Anchor>
  </Anchors>
</Frame>
```

Along the same lines, the following example creates a new frame, `MyFrame2`, which sits to the right of `MyFrame1`, with the top edges aligned by anchoring the opposite top corners to each other:

```
<Frame name="MyFrame2" parent="UIParent">
  <Size x="50" y="50"/>
  <Anchors>
    <Anchor point="TOPLEFT" relativePoint="TOPRIGHT" ↵
relativeTo="MyFrame"/>
  </Anchors>
</Frame>
```

In this example, the top-left corner of `MyFrame2` is attached to the top-right corner of `MyFrame1`, aligning their top edges and placing them side-by-side. When there is no offset, the `<Offset>` tag can be left out entirely, and the `<Anchor>` tag can be made self-closing.

Sticky Anchors

When you are anchoring a frame, it's not a one-time placement used to position the frame, but rather a sticky attachment between two objects. If FrameA is anchored to FrameB and, at some point later, FrameB is moved from one place to another, FrameA will follow it in order to obey the defined anchor points.

Anchor Examples

The easiest way to visualize anchoring is to look at examples and determine how the objects might be anchored together. Table 10-2 contains a number of anchor examples, along with the anchor points that were used. Each of these examples attaches FrameA to FrameB.

Table 10-2: Anchoring Examples

DESCRIPTION	EXAMPLE
FrameB's TOPLEFT anchored to FrameA's TOPRIGHT	
FrameB's TOPLEFT anchored to FrameA's RIGHT	
FrameB's TOPLEFT anchored to FrameA's BOTTOMRIGHT	
FrameB's TOP anchored to FrameA's BOTTOM	
FrameB's RIGHT anchored to FrameA's LEFT	

Layering Frames and Graphical Elements

The WoW user interface system provides a very granular way for graphical elements to be layered on top of another. This allows you to create frames that appear entirely over another frame, or graphical elements that are layered to create a final image. There are three different levels of layering: frame strata, frame level, and texture/fontstring layers.

Frame Strata

The most basic level of frame layering is the frame strata. Simply, all the frames in a given frame strata are rendered later than frames in a lower strata, and before those in a higher strata. Overlapping frames will be displayed layered from lowest to highest. Table 10-3 shows a list of the available frame strata.

Table 10-3: Possible Frame Strata Values from Lowest To Highest

FRAME STRATA	DESCRIPTION
BACKGROUND	Meant for frames that don't interact with the mouse. Any frame in this strata is blocked from receiving mouse events unless the frame level is higher than 1.
LOW	Used by the default user interface for the buff frame, durability frame, party interface, and pet frame.
MEDIUM	The default frame level for UIParent, and all children of UIParent, unless overwritten.
HIGH	Used by the default user interface for the action buttons and tutorial frames, as well as the interface error and warning frames.
DIALOG	Used for any dialog-type frame that pops up and expects user interaction.
FULLSCREEN	Any full-screen frame such as the World Map or the User Interface options should reside in this frame strata.
FULLSCREEN_DIALOG	A dialog strata that exists above the FULLSCREEN strata, for dialogs and dropdown menus.
TOOLTIP	The highest frame strata available, used for mouseover tooltips so they are displayed regardless of the strata.

Setting a frame to be drawn on a specific strata is easy; you simply include the frameStrata attribute in the XML definition. For example:

```
<Frame name="MyFrame" frameStrata="HIGH">
</Frame>
```

This is the technique used by the default user interface to allow pop-up windows such as the confirmation dialog to appear over any other frames that might be displayed on screen.

Frame Levels

Within a strata, each frame has a frame level, which determines the order in which it is rendered (from lowest to highest). Frame levels can be messy to set, but sometimes they are the only way to accomplish a specific type of layering. When `FrameA` contains a child, `FrameB`, the frame level of `FrameB` will automatically be one higher than that of `FrameA`. This allows children to be rendered on top of their parent, if they are overlapping elements. The frame level can be set using the `frameLevel` attribute, which should be a number.

In addition, a frame can use the `toplevel` attribute, which should be a boolean flag. If `toplevel` is set to true, when the frame is clicked it will automatically be promoted to the highest frame level on the given strata, so it is shown on top. This is useful when frames are movable to bring the frame that is being moved to the front. The following is an example frame with `frameStrata`, `frameLevel` and `toplevel` all set:

```
<Frame name="MyFrame" frameStrata="HIGH" frameLevel="5"
toplevel="true">
</Frame>
```

Graphical Layers

As mentioned earlier in this chapter, all `Textures` and `FontStrings` must belong to the `<Layers>` element of a given frame and, in particular, a specific `<Layer>` element. These layers are used to allow textures and font strings to be layered on a more granular basis than frame levels and frame strata allow. Table 10-4 shows the different graphical layers that are available.

Table 10-4: Description of Graphical Layers

LAYER	DESCRIPTION
BACKGROUND	The background of your frame should be placed here.
BORDER	Any graphical borders or artwork that needs to be above the BACKGROUND layer but below the rest of the frame should reside here.
ARTWORK	Your frame's artwork should reside in this layer. This is typically any nonfunctional decorative or separating artwork that needs to be above the background and border but below the functional portions of the frame.
OVERLAY	The functional part of a frame, including buttons, text labels, and other active widgets, should reside here.
HIGHLIGHT	Anything can reside in this frame, but it is only shown when the mouse is over the frame and will be displayed on top of any other layer for the frame. For the HIGHLIGHT layer to be active, the frame must have the `enableMouse` attribute set to true.

Figure 10-1 shows the first four layers using colored textures and different font strings. These images are then placed on top of each other and layered by the user interface.

Figure 10-1: Graphics layers rendered in-game

Figure 10-2 shows the highlight layer being displayed by holding the mouse over the containing frame.

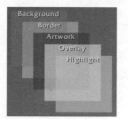

Figure 10-2: Highlight layer being shown on mouseover

Different layers are created using the `<Layer>` element, and the `level` attribute, as in the following example:

```
<Frame name="MyFrame">
  <Layers>
    <Layer level="BACKGROUND">
    </Layer>
    <Layer level="HIGHLIGHT">
    </Layer>
  </Layers>
</Frame>
```

Common Attributes

In addition to the basic naming, sizing, and placement, there are a set of attributes that are common to the three basic user interface objects. Table 10-5 shows a list of these attributes along with a description of each.

Table 10-5: Common Attributes

ATTRIBUTE	DESCRIPTION
Name	The name of the object being created. Objects are not required to be named, but if they are named, they will be accessible via the Lua scripting system, using the name as a global variable. The name string may include the string $parent, which is expanded to the name of the parent at the time of creation.
Inherits	WoW has an inheritance system that allows a developer to create templates that can be used when creating new frames. This attribute accepts a comma-separated list of templates names to inherit from.
Virtual	A boolean value indicating whether or not a frame is a virtual template. In this case, no actual objects are created; a template is established instead.
setAllPoints	A boolean value indicating whether or not a frame should be attached to all points on its parent frame. This gives the frame the same size and position of its parent.
Hidden	A boolean value indicating whether a frame is created hidden or shown by default.

Inheritance and templates will be explored further in Chapter 11.

Creating Textures

Textures are two-dimensional graphics that are rendered by the game client for the user interface. They can be a graphics file that is loaded from disk, a solid color with optional alpha, or a gradient from one color to another. All begin using the `<Texture>` tag.

A texture element can have the following attributes, along with the common attributes previously listed:

- `file` — The path to a texture file to be loaded and used as the graphic.
- `alphaMode` — The blending mode to be used when layering multiple textures. Can be any of the following values: DISABLE, BLEND, ALPHAKEY, ADD, or MOD.

Adding Colors

To use a solid color for the texture, include the `<Color>` element in the texture definition. This element accepts four attributes (r, g, b, a) as the three color components red, green, and blue, and the alpha (opacity) value. Each should be a number between 0.0 and 1.0.

```
<Frame name="MyFrame">
  <Layers>
    <Layer level="BACKGROUND" setAllPoints="true">
      <Color r="1.0" g="0.1" b="0.1" a="1.0"/>
    </Layer>
  </Layers>
</Frame>
```

The preceding example creates a frame that contains a single red texture. This texture uses setAllPoints to indicate that it should be the exact size and placement of its parent, which is the frame itself.

Adding a Gradient

In addition to solid colors, a texture can also be a gradient between two different colors. To do this, you define a gradient with a minimum color and a maximum color, using the <Gradient> tag. Figure 10-3 shows two example gradients.

Figure 10-3: Horizontal gradient (top) and vertical gradient (bottom)

The <Gradient> element takes a single, optional attribute, orientation, which can be either HORIZONTAL or VERTICAL. The default is a horizontal gradient. The tag must contain two elements, <MinColor> and <MaxColor>, each of type ColorType.

A <Gradient> tag alone won't create a gradient; it must be combined with a <Color> tag. At each step in the gradient, the color values from the <Color> tag are multiplied by the current gradient value to determine what color is displayed on screen. The easiest way to handle this is to have the following color value:

```
<Color r="1.0" g="1.0" b="1.0" a="1.0"/>
```

This ensures that your gradient begins at your <MinColor> and ends at your <MaxColor> because each component value is 1.0, which doesn't change the value it's multiplied against. Here's the XML used to create the gradients shown in Figure 10-3:

```
<Ui xmlns="http://www.blizzard.com/wow/ui/" ↵
xmlns:xsi="http://www.w3.org/2001/XMLSchema-instance" ↵
xsi:schemaLocation="http://www.blizzard.com/wow/ui/
..\FrameXML\UI.xsd">
  <Frame name="GradientTest" parent="UIParent">
    <Size x="200" y="200"/>
    <Anchors>
      <Anchor point="CENTER" relativePoint="CENTER"
relativeTo="UIParent"/>
    </Anchors>
    <Layers>
      <Layer level="BACKGROUND">
        <Texture name="$parentHorizontal">
          <Size x="200" y="100"/>
          <Anchors>
            <Anchor point="TOPLEFT" relativePoint="TOPLEFT"/>
          </Anchors>
          <Color r="1.0" g="0.0" b="0.0" a="1.0"/>
          <Gradient orientation="HORIZONTAL">
            <MinColor r="1.0" g="0.0" b="0.0" a="1.0"/>
            <MaxColor r="0.0" g="0.0" b="0.0" a="1.0"/>
          </Gradient>
        </Texture>
        <Texture name="$parentVertical">
          <Size x="200" y="100"/>
          <Anchors>
            <Anchor point="BOTTOMLEFT" relativePoint="BOTTOMLEFT"/>
          </Anchors>
          <Color r="1.0" g="1.0" b="1.0" a="1.0"/>
          <Gradient orientation="VERTICAL">
            <MinColor r="0.0" g="0.0" b="0.0" a="1.0"/>
            <MaxColor r="1.0" g="1.0" b="0.0" a="1.0"/>
          </Gradient>
        </Texture>
      </Layer>
    </Layers>
  </Frame>
</Ui>
```

Adding a Graphic

Adding a graphic to a texture is as simple as supplying the correct filename in the `file` attribute. The following XML definition creates a 100x100 frame in the center of your screen that shows the icon for a priest's Shadow Word: Pain spell:

```
<Ui xmlns="http://www.blizzard.com/wow/ui/" ↵
xmlns:xsi="http://www.w3.org/2001/XMLSchema-instance" ↵
```

```
xsi:schemaLocation="http://www.blizzard.com/wow/ui/
..\FrameXML\UI.xsd">
  <Frame name="GraphicTest" parent="UIParent">
    <Size x="100" y="100"/>
    <Anchors>
      <Anchor point="CENTER" relativePoint="CENTER"
relativeTo="UIParent"/>
    </Anchors>
    <Layers>
      <Layer level="BACKGROUND">
        <Texture name="$parentPainIcon" ↵
file="Interface\Icons\Spell_Shadow_ShadowWordPain" setAllPoints="true">
        </Texture>
      </Layer>
    </Layers>
  </Frame>
</Ui>
```

Figure 10-4 shows how this example is displayed on screen.

Figure 10-4:
GraphicTest frame
displayed in-game

Creating Text using FontStrings

Adding text to your frames is a matter of creating a `FontString` object within your frame and anchoring it to the frame. As mentioned earlier in this chapter, the `<FontString>` element must be inside a `<Layer>` element. In addition to the basic attributes, a `FontString` has several attributes that can be used to change the style of the displayed text, shown in Table 10-6.

Table 10-6: Attributes Available to FontString Elements

ATTRIBUTE	DESCRIPTION/USAGE
font	The path to a font file to be used when displaying the text. This can be a file included with WoW, or a true type font supplied by a custom addon.

Continued

Table 10-6 *(continued)*

ATTRIBUTE	DESCRIPTION/USAGE
bytes	A positive number expressing a limit on the number of characters to be displayed in the FontString.
text	The text to be displayed.
spacing	Sets the spacing, in pixels, between lines if the FontString has multiple lines.
outline	Specifies the outline type of the FontString. Should be one of the following values: NONE, NORMAL, THICK.
monochrome	A boolean value specifying if the font should be monochromatic (grayscale) or not.
nonspacewrap	A boolean value that specifies whether long strings without spaces are wrapped or truncated. When this is true, the string is wrapped.
justifyV	Specifies the vertical justification of the text using one of the following values: TOP, MIDDLE, BOTTOM.
justifyH	Specifies the horizontal justification of the text as one of the following values: LEFT, CENTER, RIGHT.
maxLines	Specifies the maximum number of lines to be displayed in a FontString.

Using Templates

Rather than specifying each of these attributes for every new display of text, most FontStrings take advantage of inheritance to define these values. Although inheritance and templates are explained more in-depth in Chapter 11, using them is simple enough using the inherits attribute. Figure 10-5 shows some of the available templates (which can be found in Fonts.xml in the extracted interface data).

Example Use

The following code creates a single frame that displays a font string in the center of your screen (using the GameFontNormalHuge template):

```
<Ui xmlns="http://www.blizzard.com/wow/ui/"
xmlns:xsi="http://www.w3.org/2001/XMLSchema-instance"
xsi:schemaLocation="http://www.blizzard.com/wow/ui/
..\FrameXML\UI.xsd">
```

```
<Frame name="FontTest" parent="UIParent">
  <Size x="200" y="50"/>
  <Anchors>
    <Anchor point="CENTER" relativePoint="CENTER"/>
  </Anchors>
  <Layers>
    <Layer level="OVERLAY">
      <FontString setAllPoints="true" justifyV="MIDDLE" ↵
justifyH="CENTER" inherits="GameFontNormalHuge" text="Hello Azeroth!"/>
    </Layer>
  </Layers>
</Frame>
</Ui>
```

Figure 10-5: Listing of FontString templates

Further Customization

The following elements can be used to customize a FontString's display:

- <FontHeight> — Can be specified using the val attribute, or using <AbsValue> or <RelValue>. Specifies the height of the font string in pixels or a relative value.

- <Color> — Changes the color of the font string; specified using the r, g, b, and a attributes.

- <Shadow> — Adds a drop shadow to the font. The color and placement of the shadow is specified by the <Color> and <Offset> elements, which are required.

OBJECT VISIBILITY

A somewhat confusing topic when dealing with UI objects is the concept of visibility. For an object to be actually drawn on screen, it must fulfill the following requirements:

1. The object must have some visual component, such as text, graphics, background color, or border. A frame with none of these is not visible, and a texture or font string without any contents is equally invisible.

2. The object must have a positive height and width. While this may seem obvious, it's easy to forget one or the other.

3. The object must be placed somewhere within the bounds of the screen. If it's anchored outside the viewable window, it can't be displayed.

4. The object and each of its parents must be shown.

In this case, the word "shown" means that the object is not hidden. An object can be hidden in two different ways:

■ By setting the `hidden` attribute in the XML definition to true

■ By calling the object's `:Hide()` method

Luckily, there are two API functions that can be used to assist any troubleshooting. The `:IsShown()` method returns 1 if the frame isn't hidden, while the `:IsVisible()` method tests the requirement that the object and each of its parents are shown.

Exploring Frame Types

As previously mentioned, there are frame types other than `<Frame>`. This section examines actual examples of each kind of frame type in the game to demonstrate its use. Each of these frame types can be substituted for the basic `<Frame>` element and used in the same way. Full details about each of these types are available in the XML schema that can be extracted using the Interface Tooltip (see Chapter 8).

When exploring these frame types, it's often useful to look at an existing example to see how they are used, and what other attributes and elements might exist in the XML definition.

Buttons

Buttons are used to allow user input by clicking a meaningful icon or visual button with text. Buttons can react to clicks and, in some cases, even cast spells and target units. Examples of buttons include the Main Menu and the Action buttons (shown in Figure 10-6). Buttons often show different textures when they are moused over, pressed, or disabled. Many buttons display text or icons to convey more meaning.

Figure 10-6: Main Menu
buttons (left) and default
Action buttons (right)

Check Buttons

Check buttons are a special kind of buttons that have only two states: checked and
unchecked. They are used to convey toggleable options, and normally come with text
labels to explain which options the checkbox alters. Checkboxes are used primarily in
custom configuration interfaces and the User Interface Options screen, as shown
in Figure 10-7.

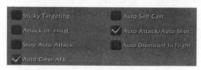

Figure 10-7: Checkboxes in the
interface options screen

ColorSelect

The ColorSelect frame type is used by the chat interface to change output color for
channels, along with the background of the chat windows. It pops up as a dialog box
that enables you to select a color (possibly with alpha) to use for a specific option.
Figure 10-8 shows an example ColorSelect frame.

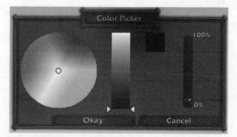

Figure 10-8: ColorSelect example frame
as a dialog box

EditBox

The EditBox type of frame is used to allow for text input, along with basic history and editing capabilities. The simplest example of an EditBox is attached to the chat frame, allowing you to run commands and communicate with other players, as shown in Figure 10-9.

Figure 10-9: Chat frame's EditBox

GameTooltip

A GameTooltip is a simple frame that can display two columns of data that further describe the UI element you currently have your mouse over, including buttons, items, and even players in the 3-D world. An item tooltip is shown in Figure 10-10.

Figure 10-10: Item tooltip

MessageFrame

MessageFrames are used by the game to send a stream of errors, warnings, or messages to the user. This is most often seen with the UIErrorsFrame, which displays any issues with spellcasting, as shown in Figure 10-11.

Figure 10-11:
UIErrorsFrame showing
spellcasting errors

Minimap

The Minimap is used for simple navigation in World of Warcraft, and only exists with the default minimap, as shown in Figure 10-12. The minimap is only the map-specific portion of the image, while the rest of the image is attached graphics, buttons, and fontstrings.

Figure 10-12:
Minimap used for
navigation

Model

Models are used to display three-dimensional models in-game, potentially with the capability to pan and zoom in on the model. Models are used in the default UI within the character window, dressing room at the auction house, and the tabard planner in the major cities. Figure 10-13 shows the tabard vendor window, using models.

Figure 10-13: Tabard vendor, showing
player model

ScrollingMessageFrame

WoW, being a massively multiplayer online role-playing game, has a fair amount of communication between its players, and these are typically displayed in scroll messages frames, namely the ChatFrames (refer to Figure 10-9).

ScrollFrame

When something is too large to be displayed in its native window, a scroll frame can be included to allow the user to scroll either vertically or horizontally. This is used frequently throughout the user interface, particularly within the friends window, the skills window, the auction house, and the quest log (shown in Figure 10-14).

Figure 10-14: Scroll frame used in the Quest Log

SimpleHTML

For presenting data, scrolling messages frames aren't always suitable, such as when reading a book or item in-game. In these situations, a special type of frame is used that allows for basic HTML-like markup. When combined with multiple pages or a scroll frame, data becomes easier to present. Figure 10-15 shows a player reading a plaque in Stormwind, which uses a SimpleHTML frame.

Slider

Sliders are used when there is a range of numbers that can possibly be selected. They're used primarily in the default user interface options screen (shown in Figure 10-16). Sliders enable the developer to set a minimum value, a maximum value, and the default step that the slider will allow, so you can control precision.

StatusBar

StatusBars are used throughout the default user interface to show progress or percentages, such as in the skills window (shown in Figure 10-17). To use a status bar, you must supply a texture to be shown, as well as minimum/maximum values for the bar. Then you can simply set the value of the bar to show the correct value.

Figure 10-15: ItemTextFrame using SimpleHTML to present descriptions

Figure 10-16: Sliders used in the User Interface Options panel

TaxiRouteFrame

The TaxiRouteFrame is a special frame used for the flight path maps when visiting a flight master to draw lines between given points inside it (see Figure 10-18).

Figure 10-17: Skill progress using StatusBars

Figure 10-18: Flight master map using the TaxiRouteFrame

Summary

This chapter introduced the basics of creating frames using XML, including how to define frame sizes, manage complex frame positions, and add graphics and text on your frames. In addition, concepts of frame and graphics layering were explained, and examples were given.

# CHAPTER 11

Adding Behavior to XML Frames

James Whitehead II

Although you've created frames, graphics, and font strings, and sized and placed frames, each of those frames was static and couldn't interact with the user or change in response to any game events. In this chapter, you'll explore XML templates and begin to add dynamic behavior to your XML frames. This chapter is meant as an introduction to adding behavior to XML frames; for a full listing of the available frame scripts and methods, please refer to the Widget Reference in Chapter 31.

Understanding Events and Scripts

The user interface changes along with the state of the game through game events, and allows for interaction with the user via frame scripts.

Frame Scripts

The frames that are used to create the user interface each have specific types of behavior to which they can respond, helping to make the interface truly interactive. For example, buttons can respond to being clicked, and edit boxes need to respond to character input. The `<OnClick>` and `<OnValueChanged>` scripts can be used to respond to these frame behaviors.

Game Events

A game event is a message sent from the client to the user interface. The UNIT_HEALTH event, for example, fires anytime a unit of interest (for example, someone in your party or raid, or your target) has a change in its health. These events are tied directly to the game client, and are typically fired due to combat, communication, or any change in the state of the game.

To respond to game events, a frame must use its :RegisterEvent() method to register with the client to listen for a specific event. This causes the game client to call the <OnEvent> script for that frame each time the event fires.

Each frame can register for as many events as necessary, but can only have one <OnEvent> script. As a result, the game passes the event name to that handler so it can act on different kind of events.

Responding to Frame Events with Scripts

To make frames truly interactive, you can define frame scripts that are called in response to user interaction. You can use XML to create these scripts, by adding a <Scripts> element to your frame definition and a script handler for each type of behavior. This section covers several frame scripts, giving examples of how they can be used.

<OnEnter> and <OnLeave>

Any frame that has the enableMouse attribute set can respond to the <OnEnter> and <OnLeave> behaviors with custom scripts. The following code is the XML definition for a frame that responds to these behaviors; place it between the <Ui> section of WowXMLExample.xml:

```
<Frame name="EnterLeaveTest" parent="UIParent">
  <Size x="100" y="100"/>
  <Anchors>
    <Anchor point="CENTER" relativePoint="CENTER"
relativeTo="UIParent"/>
  </Anchors>
  <Layers>
    <Layer level="BACKGROUND">
      <Texture name="$parentIcon" ↵
file="Interface\Icons\Spell_Shadow_ShadowWordPain" setAllPoints="true"/>
    </Layer>
  </Layers>
  <Scripts>
    <OnEnter>
      ChatFrame1:AddMessage("++ Entered frame: " .. self:GetName())
    </OnEnter>
    <OnLeave>
```

```
      ChatFrame1:AddMessage("-- Leaving frame: " .. self:GetName())
    </OnLeave>
  </Scripts>
</Frame>
```

Handlers are defined using specific elements within the frame's `<Scripts>` element. Each handler inside this element is just Lua code wrapped as a function definition and set to respond to the given behavior. Each handler is passed the `self` variable as the first argument, which is the frame object itself. In addition, some other handlers are passed extra named arguments (detailed later in this chapter).

Each of these scripts prints a message to the chat frame telling you whether you have entered or left the frame, and uses the `self:GetName()` function to retrieve the name of the frame. This is a special Widget API function that can be used on any frame to retrieve its name. If you load the game with this definition included in an addon, a frame with the Shadow Word: Pain icon is shown in the center of the screen; you can move your mouse over it to see the messages printed to the chat frame.

<OnLoad>

Every frame defined in XML is capable of having an `<OnLoad>` script that is executed when the frame is first created. This script is typically used for registering events and other initialization behavior. The script handler is called with the `self` variable set to the frame object itself. As a result, the following XML can be used to register for the `UNIT_HEALTH` event:

```
<Scripts>
  <OnLoad>
    self:RegisterEvent("UNIT_HEALTH")
  </OnLoad>
</Scripts>
```

<OnEvent>

To actually do anything in response to a game event, an `<OnEvent>` script must be created to handle the response. Each `OnEvent` script is passed the frame object that is responding to the event, the event name itself (a string), and a series of arguments that are different depending on the event. In short, whatever is between your `<OnEvent>` and `</OnEvent>` script is put inside the following function definition, and then set as the `OnEvent` script.

```
function OnEvent(self, event, ...)
  if event == "UNIT_HEALTH" then
    -- Run UNIT_HEALTH code here
  elseif event == "UNIT_MANA" then
    -- Run UNIT_MANA code here
  end
end
```

This single handler is responsible for responding to all game events for which the frame is registered. As a result, you should check to see which event has been fired so you can respond properly. For more information about each different type of event, please consult the Event Listing in Chapter 30.

Add the following definition to `WowXMLExample.xml` (within the `<Ui>` section) to test event registration and response:

```
<Frame name="UnitHealthTest">
  <Scripts>
    <OnLoad>
      self:RegisterEvent("UNIT_HEALTH")
    </OnLoad>
    <OnEvent>
      local unit = ...
      ChatFrame1:AddMessage("UNIT_HEALTH - unit=" .. unit)
    </OnEvent>
  </Scripts>
</Frame>
```

The UNIT_HEALTH event receives only one argument, namely the unit whose health was affected. Because the OnEvent handler uses Lua's variable argument notation to pass arguments, we assign . . . to a local variable so we can easily print it out. This frame will print a message to the chat frame every time the game receives a UNIT_HEALTH event, indicating which unit's health was affected (shown in Figure 11-1).

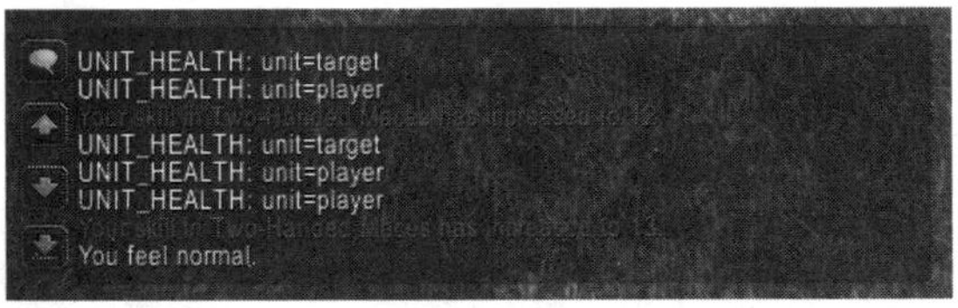

Figure 11-1: UNIT_HEALTH tracker working in-game

<OnClick>

Buttons and CheckButtons are able to respond to button clicks with the `<OnClick>` script. This function is passed three arguments:

- self — The button that was clicked.
- button — The mouse button that was clicked.
- down — The direction of the mouse click.

World of Warcraft can recognize up to five different mouse buttons, named LeftButton, RightButton, MiddleButton, Button4, and Button5. In addition, WoW can differentiate between the down portion of a click, and the up portion of a click. By default, buttons are only registered to accept LeftButtonUp mouse events. This can be changed using the :RegisterForClicks() method.

To register for left-clicks and right-clicks, and receive both up and down events, you would call the following in your <OnLoad> script:

```
self:RegisterForClicks("LeftButtonUp", "LeftButtonDown", ↵
"RightButtonUp", "RightButtonDown")
```

The easiest way to register a button for clicks is to use the "AnyUp" and "AnyDown" virtual buttons in the RegisterForClicks() method. The following code is an example XML definition that illustrates an <OnClick> script (place this in your WowXMLExample.xml file, within the <Ui> section):

```
<Button name="OnClickTest" parent="UIParent">
  <Size x="100" y="100"/>
  <Anchors>
    <Anchor point="CENTER" relativePoint="CENTER"
relativeTo="UIParent"/>
  </Anchors>
  <Layers>
    <Layer level="BACKGROUND">
      <Texture name="$parentIcon" ↵
file="Interface\Icons\Spell_Shadow_ShadowWordPain" setAllPoints="true"/>
    </Layer>
  </Layers>
    <Scripts>
      <OnLoad>
        self:RegisterForClicks("AnyUp", "AnyDown")
      </OnLoad>
      <OnClick>
        ChatFrame1:AddMessage(self:GetName() .. " - Button: " .. ↵
tostring(button) .. " Down: " .. tostring(down))
      </OnClick>
    </Scripts>
  </Button>
```

Figure 11-2 shows the output from a number of sample clicks.

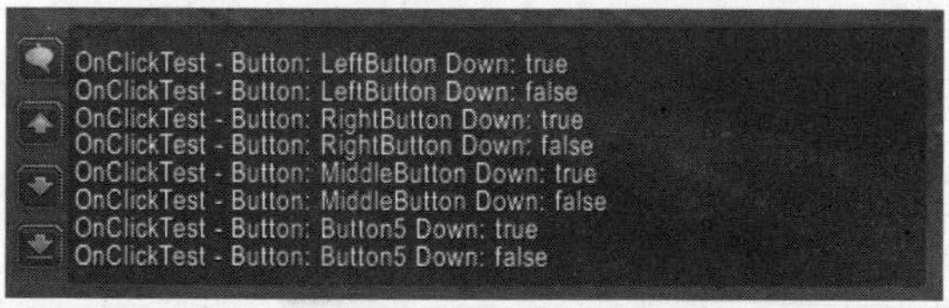

OnClickTest - Button: LeftButton Down: true
OnClickTest - Button: LeftButton Down: false
OnClickTest - Button: RightButton Down: true
OnClickTest - Button: RightButton Down: false
OnClickTest - Button: MiddleButton Down: true
OnClickTest - Button: MiddleButton Down: false
OnClickTest - Button: Button5 Down: true
OnClickTest - Button: Button5 Down: false

Figure 11-2: <OnClick> script test output

<OnUpdate>

<OnUpdate> is a special type of script that is called every time the WoW client redraws the frame. As a result, it only fires when the frame is shown (but not necessarily seen by the player). A frame can have no textures or visual elements and still have an OnUpdate

script to manage periodic tasks. This script will be used in Chapter 18 when creating the MapZoomOut addon, to create a timer of sorts.

Available Frame Scripts

Table 11-1 lists the most commonly used frame scripts and which frames types can register those scripts, along with descriptions of each.

Table 11-1: Frame Scripts

SCRIPT	DESCRIPTION	AVAILABLE TO
OnChar(self, text)	When the frame's `enableMouse` attribute is set to `true`, any keyboard input will be sent to the frame using this script. The second argument is the text that was input from the keyboard.	All frame types
OnClick(self, button, down)	When the mouse is clicked on the button, this script is used to convey the click to the button, along with which mouse button was used. A button will only receive the clicks for which it is registered (using the `:RegisterForClicks()` function). By default, a button is only registered for `LeftButtonUp`.	Button, CheckButton
OnDoubleClick(self, button)	When the mouse is double-clicked on the button, this script allows the button to respond to the click. A button will only receive this click if it is registered for the up portion of a mouse button (for example, LeftButtonUp); LeftButtonDown will not trigger it.	Button, CheckButton
OnDragStart(self, button) OnDragStop(self, button)	A frame can call `self:RegisterForDrag()` to register for drag events. This function takes a list of mouse button names, such as `"LeftButton"`, `"RightButton"`, `"Button4"`, and so on. When a user clicks on the frame and holds the mouse button down while moving the pointer, this script will be called. When the user releases the mouse button afterward, the `OnDragStop` script will be called.	All frame types

Table 11-1 *(continued)*

SCRIPT	DESCRIPTION	AVAILABLE TO
OnEnter(self, motion) OnLeave(self, motion)	When a frame is set to receive mouse events, the OnEnter and OnLeave scripts can be set up to handle these situations. The second argument passed indicates whether or not the enter was a result of mouse movement (instead of the frame being shown while your mouse was over it already).	All frame types
OnHide(self) OnShow(self)	These scripts can be used when a frame is shown or hidden. Because a hidden frame will continue to receive events and this isn't always desirable, you can use the OnHide script to unregister specific events, and then re-register them when the frame is shown. The default user interface uses this to avoid processing unnecessary events.	All frame types
PreClick(self, button, down) PostClick(self, button, down)	Not everything can be handled in an OnClick script, so the WoW client provides pre-click and post-click scripts for more flexibility. They are fired with the same arguments that the OnClick script receives.	Button, CheckButton

Altering Frames with Frame Methods

Each named frame you create in World of Warcraft is accessible through the Lua scripting interface, meaning you can interact with it directly. These frames have a multitude of functions that make querying and setting attributes easy. For example, if your frame is called MyFrame, you can call MyFrame:GetHeight() to return the height, or MyFrame:GetScale() to return the scale attribute.

This chapter has already introduced you to a few methods, such as :RegisterForClicks() to register a button for mouse clicks, and the :RegisterEvent() function to listen for game events. A comprehensive list of all frame types and their methods is available in the Widget Reference (Chapter 31).

Common Methods

When dealing with frames, texture, and font strings in XML, there are several attributes and elements that each can use and take advantage of. The same applies to working with frame methods. Table 11-2 describes some of the methods common to these UI objects.

Table 11-2: Methods Common to Frames, Textures, and Font Strings

METHOD	DESCRIPTION
`Object:GetAlpha()`	Gets the current alpha (opacity) value for the given object.
`Object:GetName()`	Gets the name of the given object or nil.
`Object:GetObjectType()`	Returns a string containing the type of the object.
`Object:IsObjectType("type")`	Returns 1 if the object is of the given object type, or nil.
`Object:SetAlpha(alpha)`	Sets the opacity of the given object. Alpha should be a number between 0.0 and 1.0.
`Object:Show()`	Shows the object. This may not cause it to appear on screen, for example, if it hasn't been placed or its parent is hidden.
`Object:Hide()`	Hides the object.
`Object:IsShown()`	Returns 1 if the object is currently shown or nil if the object is currently hidden. This does not indicate that the object is visible, only that `Object:Hide()` has not been called on the object.
`Object:IsVisible()`	Returns 1 if the object, its parent, its parent's parent, and so on, are all shown.

Type-Specific Functions

Certain methods are only available to frames of a specific type. `RegisterForClicks()`, for instance, is only accessible from `Buttons` and `CheckButtons`. With each frame type, there is a way to accomplish any task using method calls that you can accomplish in XML. There are too many frame methods to cover in this section, so please see the Widget Reference in Chapter 31 for more information.

Creating and Using Templates

XML can be quite verbose when used to describe frames; naturally, there's a shortcut you can use to make your life easier. Many of the frames that appear in the default user interface (buttons, in particular) are actually defined through a series of templates. In reality, hundreds of different templates are provided and used by the default user interface to make development of a consistent user interface easier. This section discusses templates, why they are useful, and how to create your own XML templates.

Why Are Templates Useful?

An XML template enables you to accomplish certain tasks more quickly, such as creating a 32x32 button with a texture in the OVERLAY level and a few predefined frame scripts. Later, when you need to alter the series of buttons, you must only edit the template instead of each instance you've created.

Creating New XML Templates

All that is required to make an XML template is a name for the template in the name attribute and the virtual attribute set to true. Everything else is up to your imagination; you can supply as much or as little detail as necessary.

Create the following XML definition inside the `<Ui>` section of your WowXMLExample .xml file:

```
<Button name="IconTestTemplate" virtual="true">
  <Size x="32" y="32"/>
  <Layers>
    <Layer level="OVERLAY">
      <Texture name="$parentIcon" ↵
file="Interface\Icons\Spell_Shadow_ShadowWordPain" setAllPoints="true"/>
    </Layer>
  </Layers>
  <Scripts>
    <OnLoad>
      self.Icon = getglobal(self:GetName().."Icon")
    </OnLoad>
    <OnEnter>
      self.Icon:SetDesaturated(true)
    </OnEnter>
    <OnLeave>
      self.Icon:SetDesaturated(nil)
    </OnLeave>
    <OnClick>
      ChatFrame1:AddMessage("You clicked on " .. self:GetName())
    </OnClick>
  </Scripts>
</Button>
```

This template creates a button that is 32x32 and contains a single texture in the OVERLAY layer that shows the Shadow Word: Pain spell icon. When the template is inherited, it gets the name supplied in the creating XML definition.

During the OnLoad handler, this script runs some Lua code that gets the name of the current frame, adds the string "Icon" to it, and tries to access that global variable, storing it in the self.Icon table. This takes the texture object and stores it in the frame object (which is just a special Lua table). This is done so you can easily access the icon in the OnEnter and OnLeave scripts.

self.Icon:SetDesaturated(true) is called whenever the mouse enters any of these buttons. This grays out the icon so it appears black and white. When the mouse exits, the effect is reversed. In addition, when the buttons are clicked, the name of the button is printed to ChatFrame1 along with a message.

Using XML Templates

Create a few of these buttons by adding the following XML at some point after the template definition in WowXMLExample.xml (remember, these should only be inside the <Ui> element in that file):

```
<Button name="IconTest1" inherits="IconTestTemplate" parent="UIParent">
  <Anchors>
    <Anchor point="BOTTOMRIGHT" relativePoint="CENTER" ↵
relativeTo="UIParent"/>
  </Anchors>
</Button>
<Button name="IconTest2" inherits="IconTestTemplate" parent="UIParent">
  <Anchors>
    <Anchor point="BOTTOMLEFT" relativePoint="CENTER" ↵
relativeTo="UIParent"/>
  </Anchors>
</Button>
<Button name="IconTest3" inherits="IconTestTemplate" parent="UIParent">
  <Anchors>
    <Anchor point="TOPLEFT" relativePoint="CENTER"
relativeTo="UIParent"/>
  </Anchors>
</Button>
<Button name="IconTest4" inherits="IconTestTemplate" parent="UIParent">
  <Anchors>
    <Anchor point="TOPRIGHT" relativePoint="CENTER"
relativeTo="UIParent"/>
  </Anchors>
</Button>
```

This should create a block of four buttons in the center of your screen, as shown in Figure 11-3.

Figure 11-3:
Buttons created
with IconTestTemplate

Figure 11-4 shows the output when the buttons are clicked.

You clicked on IconTest1
You clicked on IconTest3
You clicked on IconTest2
You clicked on IconTest4

Figure 11-4: Output from clicking on test buttons

If you later need to alter these buttons by making them larger, changing the icon, or varying the script behavior, you can change the master template. When the user interface is next reloaded, the frames will take on their newly inherited attributes.

> **TIP** XML templates enable you to easily inherit default values when creating a new frame, but any of the values can be overwritten in the new frame. If the template you inherit has a default size, you can overwrite it with your own `<Size>` tag in the new frame. Scripts can also be overwritten by creating a new script, even if it's blank.

Using Default UI Widget Templates

WoW provides hundreds of user interface templates that are used throughout the game. This section introduces you to several of the most frequently used templates.

TEMPLATE	
UIPanelButtonTemplate is used for the game buttons within the game.	UIPanelButtonTemplate
UIPanelButtonTemplate2 is a bit more forgiving when being resized, but serves the same purpose as UIPanelButtonTemplate; it's used for the game buttons.	UIPanelButtonTemplate2

Continued

TEMPLATE

UIPanelCloseButton is used to create simple "close" buttons for many of the user interface panels.

InputBoxTemplate is used by the default user interface for the chat frame, and by addons for any text entry that may be required.

UICheckButtonTemplate allows you to create a familiar checkbutton. It includes a font string for the label.

TabButtonTemplate can be used to create tabbed buttons on the top or bottom of a window. It's designed to integrate well with the default UI style.

GameMenuButtonTemplate is a specific size, because it is used for the game menu that appears when you press the escape key.

UIRadioButtonTemplate can be used to make simple radio buttons. It is similar to UICheckButtonTemplate.

OptionsSliderTemplate presents you with a main label, as well as sub-labels, for the minimum and maximum values (set to Low and High by default). Sliders provide an easy way to select a numeric value out of a range.

Summary

This chapter introduced you to the technique of creating more interactive user interfaces by setting frame scripts, and registering for and responding to game events. You learned how to create XML templates and new frames based on templates.

# CHAPTER 12

Creating Your First Addon: CombatTracker

James Whitehead II

At this point, you've been introduced to the Lua programming language and understand how to create your own functions. You've explored creating frames using XML and responding to game events and frame behavior using scripts. You have all the basic building blocks required to create a fully functional addon. This chapter leads you step-by-step through creating an addon called CombatTracker.

Defining Specifications

Before sitting down to code, it's important to understand exactly what an addon will be expected to do and have a general idea of how it should operate from the user perspective. What isn't important at this stage is how you will implement the addon; the design needs to be decided first.

CombatTracker User Experience

The specification for CombatTracker covers the following specific details:

1. A frame will be created on screen that can be dragged and moved by the user.

2. When the player enters combat, the addon will store the current time and change the frame to display "In Combat."

3. Each time the player takes damage from an NPC, the frame's display will be updated to show the amount of time that has been spent in combat, the amount of damage that has been sustained, and the incoming damage per second.

4. When combat has ended, the frame will display final statistics.

5. The frame will be a button and, when clicked, will send the incoming damage per second summary to the player's party, if they are in one; otherwise, it will simply be displayed on the screen.

Finding the Right Game Events

The next step when building an addon is figuring out which game events are needed for it to properly function. This is often a very difficult process and can take some time, because not all of the Blizzard events are named intuitively or fire exactly when you'd expect them to. This section details the three events that CombatTracker needs to function.

PLAYER_REGEN_DISABLED

Upon entering combat, a player no longer regenerates health over the course of time, with the exception of spells, talents, and equipment that provide specific amounts of health regeneration every five seconds. As a result, the PLAYER_REGEN_DISABLED event can be used to indicate when the player has engaged in combat, according to the game client. This event doesn't necessarily mean that the player has sustained any damage; it just indicates to the game client that the player is now considered to be in combat.

From a user interface perspective, this event also allows addon authors to do any last-minute setup for any addons that use secure templates. You will learn more about secure templates in Chapter 17 but, in short, they allow for addons to cast spells and target units through a special system that cannot be altered while in combat. This event gives those addons one last chance to configure themselves.

This event has no arguments included when it fires.

PLAYER_REGEN_ENABLED

The PLAYER_REGEN_ENABLED event fires when the player begins normal health regeneration again. This event means the player's normal health regeneration has started and is fired consistently when the player exits combat. As a result, it can be used by an addon to track the player exiting combat (even though the event isn't named PLAYER_EXIT_COMBAT or something similar). This event has no arguments included when it fires.

UNIT_COMBAT

Several events deal with the player sustaining damage, but you will be using the UNIT_COMBAT event. Anytime a unit the player is interested in (such as party members, raid members and their targets, and so on) has a change in hit points that relates to combat, this event fires. It fires with the following arguments describing the change:

- unit — The identifier for the unit that experienced the change.
- action — The type of combat action that happened. Some example values are the strings HEAL, DODGE, BLOCK, WOUND, MISS, PARRY, RESIST, and so forth.

- `modifier` — If the action was a combat attack, it could possibly be a glancing hit, critical hit, or crushing blow. Example values are the strings GLANCING, CRUSHING and CRITICAL.

- `damage` — The amount of damage sustained, or the amount of health healed.

- `damagetype` — The type of damage that occurred, using one of the following number values:

  - 0 — physical damage

  - 1 — holy damage

  - 2 — fire damage

  - 3 — nature damage

  - 4 — frost damage

  - 5 — shadow damage

  - 6 — arcane damage

FINDING THE RIGHT EVENT

Determining the proper event to respond to in order to react properly in-game can be challenging, but tools have been written that make this job much easier. Iriel, an extremely prominent contributor to the UI community and one of the Blizzard UI & Macros forum MVPs, has written an addon called DevTools, which allows you to easily track events.

DevTools can be downloaded from www.wowinterface.com/downloads/fileinfo.php?id=3999.

Once you have this addon downloaded and installed, log in to the game. You won't see anything different, but you will be able to use the /dtevents slash command, which will help you figure out the order and timing of events. This pops up the DevTools Event Trace window that logs all sorts of event information, as shown here.

In this example, the UNIT_COMBAT event is selected, and you can see the specific time that the event fired, as well as the arguments that were sent with the event. In this case, the "player" unitid took one damage from a WOUND type of physical damage. In addition, you can see other events firing such as UNIT_HEALTH and UNIT_MANA, along with SPELL_UPDATE_USABLE. When you have a sequential view of the game events to look at, figuring out exactly what you need to listen to can be much easier.

DevTools is an extremely powerful development tool and has several slash commands you might find useful as you create and edit your addons.

Creating Your Addon's Skeleton

Although this entire addon (and most addons, actually) could be written in just a single Lua file or a single XML file, this implementation will separate the design and layout of the frames from the code that defines the addon's behavior. Create your addon skeleton:

1. In your AddOns directory, create a new directory called CombatTracker.

2. In this new directory create a file called CombatTracker.toc, with the following content:

```
## Interface: 20300
## Title: CombatTracker
## Description: Tracks incoming DPS, and how long you spend in combat

CombatTracker.lua
CombatTracker.xml
```

3. Create an empty file called CombatTracker.xml, which will be used to create the frames.

4. Create an empty file called CombatTracker.lua, which will be used to define the addon's behavior.

If you exit the game entirely and then open the WoW client back up, you should see CombatTracker listed in the addon listing along with the description, as shown in Figure 12-1.

Figure 12-1: CombatTracker in the Addon Listing

Defining CombatTracker's XML Frame

For the visual style of CombatTracker, you'll use the DialogBox backdrop and edgefile that was used in Chapter 10. Because the frame needs to be clickable, it will need to be a button. Open CombatTracker.xml and add the following:

```
<Ui xmlns="http://www.blizzard.com/wow/ui/" i
xmlns:xsi="http://www.w3.org/2001/XMLSchema-instance" ↵
xsi:schemaLocation="http://www.blizzard.com/wow/ui/
..\FrameXML\UI.xsd">
  <Button name="CombatTrackerFrame" parent="UIParent" enableMouse="true" ↵
```

```
      movable="true" frameStrata="LOW">
        <Size x="175" y="40"/>
        <Anchors>
          <Anchor point="TOP" relativePoint="BOTTOM" relativeTo="Minimap">
            <Offset x="0" y="-10"/>
          </Anchor>
        </Anchors>
        <Backdrop bgFile="Interface\DialogFrame\UI-DialogBox-Background" ↵
      edgeFile="Interface\DialogFrame\UI-DialogBox-Border" tile="true">
          <BackgroundInsets>
            <AbsInset left="11" right="12" top="12" bottom="11"/>
          </BackgroundInsets>
          <TileSize>
            <AbsValue val="32"/>
          </TileSize>
          <EdgeSize>
            <AbsValue val="32"/>
          </EdgeSize>
        </Backdrop>
        <Layers>
          <Layer level="OVERLAY">
            <FontString name="$parentText" inherits="GameFontNormalSmall" ↵
      justifyH="CENTER" setAllPoints="true" text="CombatTracker"/>
          </Layer>
        </Layers>
      </Button>
    </Ui>
```

Most of this should look familiar from your work with XML in previous chapters. A new Button is created named CombatTrackerFrame with mouse events enabled and a frameStrata of LOW. This ensures that frames (such as the bag frames or character panel) will show on top of CombatTracker if there's an overlap. By default, the frame is anchored directly below the Minimap, with a small 10-pixel offset to push it further below the Minimap.

A single FontString is created named CombatTrackerFrameText that is anchored to all points of the frame and aligned CENTER horizontally, so the text will always appear in the middle of the frame.

Testing CombatTrackerFrame

It's always a good idea to log in to the game and make sure your frame looks right before diving too deeply into the code. You should see something similar to Figure 12-2, showing the Minimap and the new CombatTrackerFrame directly below it.

At this point, nothing can be done with the frame because no scripts have been written to define its behavior. To make the addon fully functional, it will need scripts to handle clicking, dragging, and event handlers for our events.

Figure 12-2:
CombatTrackerFrame
anchored below the
Minimap

Adding Script Handlers to CombatTrackerFrame

In this addon, the behavior will be defined in `CombatTracker.lua`, but before you can write those functions you must refer to them in the frame definition in `CombatTracker.xml`. Open this file and add the following section right after the `</Layers>` tag in the `Button` definition:

```
<Scripts>
  <OnLoad>
    CombatTracker_OnLoad(self)
  </OnLoad>
  <OnEvent>
    CombatTracker_OnEvent(self, event, ...)
  </OnEvent>
  <OnClick>
    CombatTracker_ReportDPS()
  </OnClick>
  <OnDragStart>
    self:StartMoving()
  </OnDragStart>
  <OnDragStop>
    self:StopMovingOrSizing()
  </OnDragStop>
</Scripts>
```

<OnLoad>

The basic initialization function for CombatTracker will be called `CombatTracker_OnLoad()`; it's called from the `<OnLoad>` handler on the frame. Remember that each script handler in XML gets a certain set of arguments that need to be passed to the handling function (if it's not written directly in the XML file).

\<OnEvent\>

Because the addon needs to respond to three different events (PLAYER_REGEN_ENABLED, PLAYER_REGEN_DISABLED, and UNIT_COMBAT), the CombatTracker_OnEvent() function will be responsible for each of the events. The handling function will need to know which event it's being passed, so ensure you are passing the frame self, the event name event and the variable set of arguments . . . to the function.

\<OnClick\>

When the player right-clicks on CombatTrackerFrame, it will report the current combat stats to the party, or in the chat frame if the player isn't part of a party. This will be handled by the CombatTracker_ReportDPS() function, which will be defined in the next section.

\<OnDragStart\>

The code for allowing a frame to be dragged and placed is very simple, so the code is written directly in the script handler rather than in a function defined in CombatTracker.lua. Later, if you wanted to add options to the addon, such as allowing the user to lock the frame in place, you could move this code into the Lua file to consolidate everything.

Each frame that has the movable attribute set to true can call the self:StartMoving() method, which causes the frame to follow the mouse. As a result, all that's required to set up frame movement when dragged is to call this function.

\<OnDragStop\>

Stopping the frame from following the mouse is a matter of calling self: StopMovingOrSizing(). This function also flags the frame as *user placed*, meaning the next time the addon loads, the frame will be put in the same place the user dropped it. This is quite a handy side effect.

Adding Functions to CombatTracker.lua

To properly calculate the incoming damage, the time spent in combat, and the average incoming DPS during combat, a few values will need to be stored. These will be created as local variables at the top of CombatTracker.lua. Open that file and add the following lines:

```
-- Set up some local variables to track time and damage
local start_time = 0
local end_time = 0
local total_time = 0
local total_damage = 0
local average_dps = 0
```

Although they aren't necessarily needed by anything, the `total_time` and `average_damage` variables will be used when updating the frame and right-clicking to report DPS, so the average doesn't need to be calculated each and every time.

There are four more functions to create to have a fully functional addon:

- `CombatTracker_OnLoad(frame)`
- `CombatTracker_OnEvent()`
- `CombatTracker_UpdateText()`
- `CombatTracker_ReportDPS()`

These functions are discussed in the following sections.

CombatTracker_OnLoad(frame)

As you might recall from your work in Chapter 4, when a function inside a table is called using colon syntax, the first argument passed is called `self`. In addition, when the World of Warcraft client calls a frame script, the first argument is called `self` and points to the frame itself. This can get confusing, so when defining functions that are called from the XML is a good time to make the variable names more meaningful. In this case, the handler script will pass the `self` variable, but the `CombatTracker_OnLoad()` function will bind that value to the variable `frame`. That way, there's no question about what type of value it contains.

Add the following function definition to the bottom of `CombatTracker.lua`:

```
function CombatTracker_OnLoad(frame)
  frame:RegisterEvent("UNIT_COMBAT")
  frame:RegisterEvent("PLAYER_REGEN_ENABLED")
  frame:RegisterEvent("PLAYER_REGEN_DISABLED")
  frame:RegisterForClicks("RightButtonUp")
  frame:RegisterForDrag("LeftButton")
end
```

There is nothing new or special introduced in this function; it simply registers for the events with which the addon is concerned, and registers for the correct mouse buttons for clicking and dragging.

CombatTracker_OnEvent(frame, event, ...)

The `CombatTracker_OnEvent()` function handles three different types of events, so it will be one large conditional with special code for each event name. Add the following function to the bottom of `CombatTracker.lua`:

```
function CombatTracker_OnEvent(frame, event, ...)
  if event == "PLAYER_REGEN_ENABLED" then
    -- This event is called when the player exits combat
    end_time = GetTime()
    total_time = end_time - start_time
    average_dps = total_damage / total_time
    CombatTracker_UpdateText()
```

```
  elseif event == "PLAYER_REGEN_DISABLED" then
    -- This event is called when we enter combat
    -- Reset the damage total and start the timer
    CombatTrackerFrameText:SetText("In Combat")
    total_damage = 0
    start_time = GetTime()
  elseif event == "UNIT_COMBAT" then
    if not InCombatLockdown() then
      -- We are not in combat, so ignore the event
    else
      local unit,action,modifier,damage,damagetype = ...
      if unit == "player" and action ~= "HEAL" then
        total_damage = total_damage + damage
        end_time = GetTime()
        total_time = end_time - start_time
        average_dps = total_damage / total_time
        CombatTracker_UpdateText()
      end
    end
  end
end
```

PLAYER_REGEN_ENABLED

The PLAYER_REGEN_ENABLED section of the conditional happens when the player exits combat, which means it's time to clean up and display the final results. The GetTime() function is used to set the end_time variable. This function returns the current value of the in-game timer. The actual value doesn't matter, because you're just going to subtract the start time from the end time to give you the difference (in seconds).

Finally, the CombatTracker_UpdateText() function is called to handle the update of the actual text on the frame. Instead of calling a function, you could do that updating right here, but as you'll see later, the same code would need to happen in the UNIT_COMBAT handler. As a result, it's easier and cleaner to make it a called function.

PLAYER_REGEN_DISABLED

The PLAYER_REGEN_DISABLED event fires when the player enters combat, so it needs to set up the accounting variables to ensure the addon gets a clean slate for each combat. It simply calls CombatTrackerFrameText:SetText() to change the frame to say "In Combat." It also sets the total_damage variable back to 0 and initializes the start_time variable with the current time.

UNIT_COMBAT

Most of the magic happens in this section, so it's a bit larger than the other two. First, you need to get the arguments that were passed to you so you can check them before processing. From the Event Documentation you know this function passes five arguments, and you name them `unit`, `action`, `modifier`, `damage`, and `damagetype`. Because the `OnEvent` function uses the vararg (`...`) symbol, you can just assign that directly to the new local variables.

The `UNIT_COMBAT` event also fires for heals, so you want to filter those out (otherwise they would show up as extra incoming damage). In addition, the addon is only interested in those messages where `unit` is equal to `"player"`. The inner conditional statement helps filter those out, only completing the logic if the message is actually showing damage to the player.

Next, the damage is added to the total, the end time is updated, and the total time and average DPS are calculated. Finally, the `CombatTracker_UpdateText()` function is called to update the frame.

CombatTracker_UpdateText()

`CombatTracker_UpdateText()` is just a simple function wrapper that updates the status on the `CombatTrackerFrame` using `string.format()`. Add the following function definition to the bottom of `CombatTracker.lua`:

```
function CombatTracker_UpdateText()
  local status = string.format("%ds / %d dmg / %.2f dps", ↵
total_time, total_damage, average_dps)
  CombatTrackerFrameText:SetText(status)
end
```

When displayed in-game, this format string shows the number of seconds in combat, followed by the amount of damage taken, and then the average incoming DPS for the combat period.

CombatTracker_ReportDPS()

`CombatTracker_ReportDPS()` is a rather simple function once you know which API functions are available to you and what they return. In this case, the `GetNumPartyMembers()` function will be used to determine whether the player is in a party. The function takes no arguments, and returns the number of people that are currently in your party. If this number is greater than `0`, the player is in a party. Add the following function to your `CombatTracker.lua`:

```
function CombatTracker_ReportDPS()
  local msgformat = "%d seconds spent in combat with %d incoming ↵
damage.  Average incoming DPS was %.2f"
  local msg = string.format(msgformat, total_time, total_damage, ↵
average_dps)
  if GetNumPartyMembers() > 0 then
    SendChatMessage(msg, "PARTY")
  else
    ChatFrame1:AddMessage(msg)
  end
end
```

Fairly simple, this function uses a format string to craft the outgoing message, and then uses `GetNumPartyMembers()` to decide where to send it. If the player is in a party, the `SendChatMessage()` function is used to send the message to the party; otherwise, `ChatFrame1:AddMessage()` is used to send it to the chat frame so the player can see it.

Testing CombatTracker

You have completed all the code necessary for a fully functional CombatTracker addon. Load the game and select a character. You should be greeted with the Combat-Tracker frame below your Minimap.

Testing is a very important part of addon writing if you plan to release your addons to the public. When you write a set of features, it's prudent to test them yourself before you ship the addon to the public to ensure that users won't get error messages and be reporting them to you after the fact. That sort of troubleshooting is always more difficult than errors you encounter on your own. Systematically test each portion of the addon.

Frame Dragging

By clicking on the frame, holding down the mouse button, and dragging your mouse to another part of the screen, you should be able to move the CombatTracker frame. Figure 12-3 shows it placed beneath the PlayerFrame.

Figure 12-3:
CombatTracker
anchored beneath
the player frame

Just testing that the frame starts and stops dragging isn't enough. Make sure you can reload your UI and have the frame be restored to the new position by running `/console relodui`. This is a slash command that reloads all of the Blizzard User Interface and all custom addon code. It's quite useful when making changes during development, or for testing purposes.

> **NOTE** Once you've moved the frame from its initial anchored position, you may need to adjust it any time you switch between windowed and full-screen mode, or when you change screen resolution. You can re-anchor the frame to the Minimap with the following slash command:
>
> ```
> /run CombatTrackerFrame:SetPoint("TOP", Minimap, ↵
> "BOTTOM", 0, -10)
> ```

This command just re-establishes the anchor point that is in the XML file.

Right-Click Reporting: Part I

The addon is set to print a status report or send it to your party chat when Combat-Tracker is right-clicked. What happens if the user clicks the frame before CombatTracker has had a chance to track any data? You can't assume your users will wait until they've already gone through combat to click, so test that now.

Luckily, because of the way you initialized the local variables (with 0s), the game can print a meaningful message, like the one shown in Figure 12-4.

Figure 12-4: CombatTracker reporting before entering combat

Testing Combat Tracking

Log in to a character and go find something to fight. Hopefully, it's something you won't have much difficulty killing but whose level is close enough to yours that it can hurt you. Immediately upon entering combat, you should see the frame change, as shown in Figure 12-5.

Figure 12-5: CombatTracker showing "In Combat"

After each hit of incoming damage, the frame should be updated to show the current statistics. If you are fighting something from range, you won't see the frame update until the mob actually tries to hit you. Figure 12-6 shows CombatTracker working in combat.

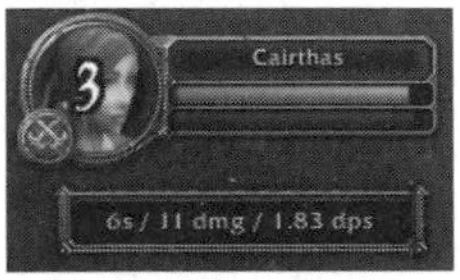

Figure 12-6: CombatTracker showing running statistics

Right-Click Reporting: Part II

When combat has ended, your frame updates with the final statistics and remains there until you enter combat again or reload the user interface. There is one more test that needs to be run on the right-click reporting, and that's making sure it displays correct statistics at the end of combat, and that it properly sends a message to party chat when the player is in a party.

Figure 12-7 shows CombatTracker reporting before joining a party, as well as after joining forces with another player.

Figure 12-7: CombatTracker reporting both in and out of a party

Summary

Creating an addon involves making decisions about the user experience and scope of the addon, investigating what functions and events are required to make the addon functional, and writing the addon itself. The process of deciding how the user will experience your addon and what features make it into the final product is often the most difficult part of writing an addon.

# CHAPTER 13

Using the World of Warcraft API

Matthew Orlando

World of Warcraft is an incredibly in-depth game. At any given moment — even with the default UI — there can be a massive amount of information on the screen: unit frames showing players' and mobs' health, mana, hostility, and PvP status; buffs and their durations; action buttons with various states such as cooldown, number of uses, and range indication; tracked quests; and so on.

Much of this information can be gleaned from event arguments, as seen in previous chapters, but events still leave many gaps. For instance, the UNIT_MANA event identifies the unit to which it applies, but gives no indication of how the unit's mana has changed. Beyond that, events alone give you no way to do anything; they can only react to various happenings outside your control. These gaps are filled by the application programming interface (API).

> **NOTE** API is a generic term in the software field describing a set of functions and data structures that are used by a program to interact with its environment. Another example of an API is Win32, which allows Windows programs to read and create files, display controls such as buttons and checkboxes, communicate over a network, launch other applications, and so on.

Understanding the WoW API

The World of Warcraft API consists of several classes of functions including C functions (functions defined in C and exposed to the Lua environment), Lua-defined functions (found in Blizzard's FrameXML files), and protected functions, which can only be used by Blizzard code because of security and automation concerns.

The functions cover quite a wide range of topics from changing game settings to posting auctions. Some operate like Lua library functions; others provide a specific interface to some aspect of gameplay.

As you progress through this chapter, you may want to flip to Chapter 28, "API Reference," to see the details of the various APIs presented. It will both help you to understand the content of this chapter and give you a glimpse into the kinds of functions available to you. You will also see functions there that may not be discussed at all throughout the instructional chapters.

Normal APIs

Most of the functions you'll encounter on a regular basis are C functions. They interact with the various subsystems of the WoW client to gather information about the state of the game and to take action in several ways. One example is `UnitHealth`, which returns the health of a specified unit (a creature or player referenced by a unit ID). Run the following statement in WowLua, and it will display your current number of hit points:

```
print(UnitHealth("player"))
```

The unit ID in this case is `"player"`, which always refers to you, the player. Use `"target"` instead, and it will print the health of your target, or `nil` if you have no target.

> **NOTE** You may see a number lower than you expected if you use `"target"`. `UnitHealth` **only returns the absolute number of hit points for your target if you are targeting yourself, your pet, or someone in your party/raid. Otherwise, it returns a number from 0 to 100 representing the percentage of hit points left.**

This introduces a recurring theme in the WoW API. Many groups of functions operate on a certain type of data. In the preceding example, the data type is unit ID. While on a fundamental level unit IDs are represented by strings, on a conceptual level they are more like an enumeration in other languages. You'll see the rest of the unit IDs when you examine unit functions in detail a little later in the chapter. Some of the many functions that use unit IDs are `UnitMana`, `UnitExists`, and `UnitLevel`.

Library-like APIs

Lua standard libraries provide a wide range of functions for string manipulation, mathematic operations, and so on. However, many libraries have been deemed inappropriate for inclusion by Blizzard. Addons are not allowed to access files directly, so the I/O library is out. The OS library would be a disaster because anyone would be capable of distributing a malicious executable along with the addon. Even the debug library has some potentially game-breaking ramifications. However, some of the functions provided by these libraries are benign enough that their functionality has been reproduced in new APIs. Table 13-1 shows some of these library–API relationships.

Table 13-1: Library Functions and Their API Equivalents*

STANDARD LIBRARY	EQUIVALENT WOW API
os.date	date
os.time	time
os.difftime	difftime
debug.traceback	debugstack

* Some of the parameters and returns may vary between versions. See Chapter 28, "API Reference," for documentation of each function.

In addition to direct library translations, several functions specific to WoW play a support role in addon development but do not directly relate to anything in-game. These have semantics similar to library functions but are technically part of the WoW API. They are easily identifiable because their names are entirely lowercase — debugprofilestart and hooksecurefunc, for instance.

FrameXML Functions

World of Warcraft's own Lua code defines a number of functions that are useful for addons. While they may not be considered APIs in the strictest sense, their usage is consistent enough with "true" API functions that they deserve documentation here.

The most unique characteristic of Lua-defined functions is that you can examine their inner workings. All of the APIs mentioned so far are hidden behind the Lua-C interface. You can call the functions from Lua and use the values they return, but barring ostensibly illegal activities, there is no way to know exactly how they operate.

A simple FrameXML function is TakeScreenshot, which captures a screenshot and saves it to your World of Warcraft\Screenshots folder. While you could use the Screenshot API function, TakeScreenshot takes the extra step of hiding the "Screen Captured" message that appears when you take a screenshot so it doesn't show in subsequent shots.

Protected Functions

Early in WoW's life, addons had free reign over all functions available in the API. Some of these functions included movement control, combat activities, and other features the designers have since deemed inappropriate for addons. That early leeway made it relatively trivial — especially with a bit of help from external programs — to write "grinding bots" that would completely control your character while you went out shopping. Set it up before work and by the time you got home you could have gained a few levels and received massive amounts of loot to sell.

A similar problem were the "button masher" addons like Emergency Monitor or Decursive. A player could repeatedly press a single key or mouse button and the addon would do all the decision-making: who to target, what spell to cast, etc.

Subsequent patches removed these capabilities by marking the offending functions as protected. Protected functions can be called only by built-in code. WoW can tell when the running code is from an addon or macro versus a built-in file, so it prevents the "illegal" function from operating when necessary. Table 13-2 describes a small sampling of protected functions to give you an idea of their nature.

Table 13-2: Sample of Protected Functions

FUNCTION	DESCRIPTION
Jump	Causes the character to jump
CastSpellByName	Attempts to cast the given spell
ToggleAutoRun	Controls the character's auto-run
TargetUnit	Targets the specified unit
PetAttack	Sends your pet to attack
RegisterUnitWatch	Registers a frame to be shown/hidden based on a unit

These are just examples. All movement, targeting, ability use, and action bar manipulation functions are completely protected.

NOTE You may be wondering how it is possible to write an action bar or unit frame addon at this point, considering that spell-casting and targeting functions are protected. This problem is resolved by using secure templates, which are covered in Chapter 17.

Unit Functions Up Close

The first logical grouping of APIs to examine is unit functions. As previously mentioned, unit functions expose several types of data about players, mobs, and NPCs. Most of them are quite simple: one or two unit IDs in, one or two pieces of information out. Table 13-3 provides a sampling of the unit functions that you'll use throughout this chapter.

Table 13-3: Example Unit Functions

UNIT FUNCTION	DESCRIPTION
exists = UnitExists(unit)	Returns 1 if the unit exists, nil otherwise. For example, UnitExists("target") returns 1 only if you have a target selected. Many of the other unit functions return nil if UnitExists is nil.
name, realm = UnitName(unit)	Returns the name of the specified unit. If the unit is a player in a cross-realm battleground, the second return is the server name.

Table 13-3 *(continued)*

UNIT FUNCTION	DESCRIPTION
level = UnitLevel(unit)	Returns the level of the unit or –1 if you're not supposed to know the level (special bosses, enemy players more than 10 levels above you).
reaction = UnitReaction(unit, other)	Determines the reaction of unit to otherUnit. Returns a number from 1–7, where 1 is extremely hostile, 7 is as friendly as possible, and nil is returned if unknown.
health = UnitHealth(unit)	Returns the health of the unit. For the player, the player's pet, party/raid members and their pets, health is the absolute number of hit points. All other units return a number from 0–100.
mana = UnitMana(unit)	Same as UnitHealth but for mana, rage, energy, and focus (collectively referred to as mana throughout the API).
healthMax = UnitHealthMax(unit)	Returns the maximum health of the unit (actual number of hit points or 100 depending on the same criteria as UnitHealth).
manaMax = UnitManaMax(unit)	Same as UnitHealthMax but for mana.

All of these functions take unit IDs that follow a simple pattern. There are several base unit IDs onto which you can tack "target" an arbitrary number of times. "party1target" would be the first party member's target, for example, and "party1targettarget" would be that unit's target). Table 13-4 shows a list of base units and their meaning. Unit names are not case-sensitive.

NOTE Some functions that accept a unit ID will only operate on certain units or provide differing results. For instance, unless a unit is in your party, UnitHealthMax returns 100 and UnitHealth is a number from 0 to 100.

Table 13-4: Base Unit IDs

UNIT ID	REFERS TO…
"player"	The character controlled by the player.
"pet"	The player's pet.
"target"	The player's target (equivalent to "playertarget").
"focus"	The player's focus target.

Continued

Table 13-4 *(continued)*

UNIT ID	REFERS TO...
"mouseover"	The unit underneath the mouse cursor. Includes characters in the 3-D world and any frame with a set unit attribute.
"partyN"	The party member where N is a number from 1–4. None of the party unit IDs refers to the player.
"partypetN"	The Nth party member's pet.
"raidN"	The raid member where N is a number from 1 to however many members there are in the raid. The highest N always refers to the player, and the lowest N always refers to the raid leader. There is no correlation between the N for raid units and the N for party units.
"raidpetN"	The Nth raid member's pet.
"npc"	The currently selected NPC. UnitExists will only return true for this unit while you are interacting with an NPC (that is, when you are turning in a quest).
"none"	Nothing. It was created to allow activation of the target selection cursor even when you are targeting something vulnerable to the spell you are casting.

Creating a Simple Unit Frame

Unit frames play a vital role in World of Warcraft gameplay. They are our windows into the other players and creatures of Azeroth. Without them there would be no way to tell how injured an opponent is, the levels of mobs in your area, or even whether something is liable to attack you. While the information they provide is highly valuable, many players are still left wanting. This is exactly the situation where addons shine. Unit frames are one of the most customized elements of the UI for several reasons.

Much of the information presented by the built-in unit frames is graphical. Health and mana are represented by status bars; the hostility of the unit is depicted by the color behind the unit's name; PvP status is indicated by a faction icon next to the unit's portrait. Yet, some information that many players find relevant is missing, including class and faction. The addon presented in this chapter, TargetText, provides a simple, text-only unit frame for your target that addresses these concerns. It has fields for the target's name, class, health, mana, reaction, and difficulty. It also uses color to augment the meaning of the data. Figure 13-1 shows an example of the TargetText frame:

Figure 13-1: TargetText in action

It may not be much to look at, but all the vital stats are there as well as some other information the default UI lacks.

Building the Frame

Before we begin, you will need to set up the basic skeleton for TargetText. Create the TargetText folder inside Interface\AddOns and add **TargetText.toc**, **TargetText.lua**, and **TargetText.xml**. (Refer to Chapter 9 for the format of the .toc file.) The Title should be TargetText and it should load TargetText.lua and TargetText.xml in that order.

Next, you need to set up the frame in XML. As you can see, you want a few text fields (FontStrings) and a simple border/background. Borrowing the backdrop from the game's tooltip template, enter the following code into the XML file:

```
<Ui xmlns="http://www.blizzard.com/wow/ui/" ↵
xmlns:xsi="http://www.w3.org/2001/XMLSchema-instance" ↵
xsi:schemaLocation="http://www.blizzard.com/wow/ui/
..\UI.xsd">

  <Frame name="TargetTextFrame" enableMouse="false" parent="UIParent">
    <Size x="200" y="86"/>
    <Anchors>
      <Anchor point="CENTER" relativePoint="CENTER"/>
    </Anchors>
    <Backdrop bgFile="Interface\Tooltips\UI-Tooltip-Background" ↵
edgeFile="Interface\Tooltips\UI-Tooltip-Border" tile="true">
      <EdgeSize val="16"/>
      <TileSize val="16"/>
      <Color r="0.75" g="0.75" b="0.75"/>
      <BackgroundInsets left="5" right="5" top="5" bottom="5"/>

    </Backdrop>

    <!-- We will be adding more elements here  -->

  </Frame>
</Ui>
```

The frame is fairly straightforward. It is a small rectangle anchored in the center of the screen. The Backdrop tag was adapted from the built-in GameTooltipTemplate

(FrameXML\GameTooltipTemplate.xml). The Color tag was added because the background texture is a bit too bright for our purposes.

Because the TargetText frame is not meant to be interactive, enableMouse is set to false. Any mouse clicks will pass through the frame to whatever is underneath.

Adding Data Fields

Now to add all the FontStrings. There will be 10 text fields in total. The first four will be for the name, level, class, and PvP status; they will be normal-sized text. The rest will be slightly smaller because they will need to fit quite a bit of text. These smaller fields will indicate reaction, faction, health, and mana. The health and mana fields will also have corresponding labels. Immediately after </Backdrop>, add the following:

```
<Layers>
  <Layer level="ARTWORK">
    <FontString name="$parentName" inherits="GameFontHighlight" ↵
justifyH="LEFT">
      <Size x="150" y="14"/>
      <Anchors>
        <Anchor point="TOPLEFT">
          <Offset x="10" y="-9"/>
        </Anchor>
      </Anchors>
    </FontString>
    <FontString name="$parentLevel" inherits="GameFontHighlight">
      <Anchors>
        <Anchor point="TOPRIGHT">
          <Offset x="-10" y="-9"/>
        </Anchor>
      </Anchors>
    </FontString>
  </Layer>
</Layers>
```

The first field is for the name of the target and is named $parentName. This FontString is unique to TargetText in that you must specify a size. If you did not, any long names would simply extend off the right side of the frame. By specifying a size, the name that's too long will be truncated with an ellipsis ("Shattrath City Peacek...", for example). This also means you have to specify justifyH="LEFT" because the default justification is CENTER. The rest of the FontStrings do not require this treatment because they all have predictable text lengths. The second FontString is for the level of the target. It is anchored to the frame's upper-right corner.

> **TIP** If you do not specify a size for a FontString, it automatically sizes itself to fit the text. Even though the default justification is CENTER, FontStrings behave as if they were justified to their anchor point. For example, a FontString anchored by its LEFT side will grow rightward as the text inside expands.

The rest of the `FontString`s are straightforward. Add these within the `<Layer>` tag already in the XML:

```
        <FontString name="$parentClass" inherits="GameFontHighlight">
          <Anchors>
            <Anchor point="TOPLEFT" relativeTo="$parentName" ↵
relativePoint="BOTTOMLEFT">
                <Offset x="0" y="-2"/>
            </Anchor>
          </Anchors>
        </FontString>
        <FontString name="$parentPvP" inherits="GameFontHighlight"↵
 text="PvP">
          <Anchors>
            <Anchor point="TOPRIGHT" relativeTo="$parentLevel" ↵
relativePoint="BOTTOMRIGHT">
                <Offset x="0" y="-2"/>
            </Anchor>
          </Anchors>
        </FontString>
        <FontString name="$parentReaction"
inherits="GameFontNormalSmall">
          <Anchors>
            <Anchor point="TOPLEFT" relativeTo="$parentClass" ↵
relativePoint="BOTTOMLEFT">
                <Offset x="0" y="-2"/>
            </Anchor>
          </Anchors>
        </FontString>
        <FontString name="$parentFaction"
inherits="GameFontNormalSmall">
          <Anchors>
            <Anchor point="TOPRIGHT" relativeTo="$parentPvP" ↵
relativePoint="BOTTOMRIGHT">
                <Offset x="0" y="-2"/>
            </Anchor>
          </Anchors>
        </FontString>
        <FontString name="$parentHealthLabel" inherits=↵
"GameFontNormalSmall" text="HEALTH">
          <Anchors>
            <Anchor point="TOPLEFT" relativeTo="$parentReaction" ↵
relativePoint="BOTTOMLEFT">
                <Offset x="0" y="-2"/>
            </Anchor>
          </Anchors>
        </FontString>
        <FontString name="$parentHealth" inherits="GameFontNormalSmall">
          <Anchors>
            <Anchor point="LEFT" relativeTo="$parentHealthLabel" ↵
```

```
relativePoint="RIGHT">
                <Offset x="10" y="0"/>
             </Anchor>
          </Anchors>
       </FontString>
       <FontString name="$parentManaLabel"
inherits="GameFontNormalSmall">
          <Anchors>
            <Anchor point="TOPLEFT" relativeTo="$parentHealthLabel" ↵
relativePoint="BOTTOMLEFT">
               <Offset x="0" y="-2"/>
            </Anchor>
          </Anchors>
       </FontString>
       <FontString name="$parentMana" inherits="GameFontNormalSmall">
          <Anchors>
            <Anchor point="TOPLEFT" relativeTo="$parentHealth" ↵
relativePoint="BOTTOMLEFT">
               <Offset x="0" y="-2"/>
            </Anchor>
          </Anchors>
       </FontString>
```

$parentPvP and $parentHealthLabel have text attributes because they will never change during gameplay. Note that "HEALTH" will become a localized version of the word "Health," as defined in FrameXML\GloablaStrings.lua.

Setting Up Frame Event Handlers

The last step for the XML is to add frame event handlers. You need an OnLoad handler for initialization and an OnEvent handler for the various updates. You'll also use OnShow and OnHide to register and unregister the update events to prevent TargetText from consuming unnecessary CPU time when the frame is hidden. After the </Layers> tag, add the following code:

```
<Scripts>
  <OnLoad>
    TargetText:OnLoad()
  </OnLoad>
  <OnEvent>
    TargetText:OnEvent(event, ...)
  </OnEvent>
  <OnShow>
    TargetText:RegisterUpdates()
  </OnShow>
  <OnHide>
    TargetText:UnregisterUpdates()
  </OnHide>
</Scripts>
```

USING A TABLE AS A NAMESPACE

As you're aware, you need to give your addon's globals unique names so they don't conflict with other code. One method you've seen so far is to prefix your function names with the name of your addon, such as:

```
CombatTracker_OnLoad
```

Another option is to store all of your globally accessible functions in a table. This means you are only creating a single global variable to store all of the behavior. You can do this rather simply by creating an empty CombatTracker table and replacing the underscore in the example with a period. There is another technique with a few advantages.

You may have noticed the method syntax (introduced in Chapter 4) used to call the `TargetText` script handlers. Calling a function in this way implicitly passes the table (`TargetText`) as the `self` parameter. This allows you to call other functions from the addon via `self:function`, saving some typing and allowing easier renaming of the addon, if necessary. Because `self` is a local variable, there is also a slight performance gain from this method (although it's usually negligible).

This technique is widely used in the addon community, especially in conjunction with various frameworks such as Ace and Dongle. We will be using this style for this and a few other chapters.

Now switch over to the Lua file to start implementing some of these functions. First, create a namespace for the TargetText addon and some empty functions to be filled in later:

```lua
TargetText = {}

function TargetText:OnLoad()
end

function TargetText:OnEvent(event, ...)
end

function TargetText:RegisterUpdates()
end

function TargetText:UnregisterUpdates()
end
```

OnLoad

The `OnLoad` function is simple. All it needs to do is register for the two fundamental events that require you to update the state of the frame.

```lua
function TargetText:OnLoad()
  TargetTextFrame:RegisterEvent("PLAYER_ENTERING_WORLD")
  TargetTextFrame:RegisterEvent("PLAYER_TARGET_CHANGED")
end
```

The PLAYER_ENTERING_WORLD event fires whenever you see a loading screen (entering or leaving an instance, logging in, changing continents, and so on), and the PLAYER_TARGET_CHANGED event fires when your target changes. These events will be used to show or hide the frame when necessary.

OnEvent

To keep the event handler as simple as possible, you will create separate functions to update each piece of data and call them when the relevant event is fired. The two events you have registered so far will call an all-in-one function, UpdateAll, that shows or hides the frame, as necessary, and calls all the other update functions to set up the initial state of the frame (when shown). All the other events we will register have the unit as their first argument. They are wrapped in an elseif clause that checks if the unit is "target"; other units will be ignored.

```
function TargetText:OnEvent(event, unit)
  if event == "PLAYER_ENTERING_WORLD" or event == ↵
"PLAYER_TARGET_CHANGED" then
    self:UpdateAll()
  elseif unit == "target" then

    -- Rest of the events will go here

  end
end
```

The first update event to respond to is UNIT_NAME_UPDATE, which fires whenever the name of a unit changes. This is obviously a rare occurrence, but it does happen. One quest in Hellfire Peninsula, for instance, requires you to "zap" an elite mob turning him non-elite and changing his name in the process.

```
if event == "UNIT_NAME_UPDATE" then
  self:UpdateName()
```

Next, you want to call UpdateLevel on the UNIT_LEVEL event in case you are targeting someone who gains a level. To signify that a target is elite, UpdateLevel adds a plus symbol to the level (for example, "72+"). For this reason, we will also respond to the UNIT_CLASSIFICATION_CHANGED event.

```
elseif event == "UNIT_LEVEL" or event == ↵
"UNIT_CLASSIFICATION_CHANGED" then
  self:UpdateLevel()
```

The next event, UNIT_FACTION, will require us to update three different text fields. The most obvious is TargetTextFrameFaction, which shows whether your target is Horde, Alliance, or not affiliated. However, UNIT_FACTION also fires when a unit becomes hostile (at the start of a duel, for example), even if their faction remains the same. Because we want to color the level of the target based on difficulty and the reaction of the target based on hostility, we will need to call three other update functions.

```
elseif event == "UNIT_FACTION" then
  self:UpdateFaction()
  self:UpdateReaction()
  self:UpdateLevel()
```

If our target becomes flagged for PvP combat, we will receive the UNIT_PVP_UPDATE event and call UpdatePvP.

```
elseif event == "UNIT_PVP_UPDATE" then
  self:UpdatePvP()
```

The UNIT_HEALTH and UNIT_MAX_HEALTH events fire when a unit's health and maximum health change, respectively. Both of these will cause our health readout to change, so we need to call the update function for the health field.

```
elseif event == "UNIT_HEALTH" or event == "UNIT_MAXHEALTH" then
  self:UpdateHealth()
```

As previously mentioned, most of the APIs collectively refer to mana, rage, energy, and focus as mana. When a unit changes the type of power used (a Druid changing forms, for instance), the UNIT_DISPLAYPOWER event fires, signifying the new meaning of "mana." You will use this event to change the TargetTextFrameManaLabel to reflect the new power type.

```
elseif event == "UNIT_DISPLAYPOWER" then
  self:UpdatePowerType()
```

While the APIs use a unified nomenclature for the various power types, the event system treats them separately. Each power type has an event for when the value changes and when the maximum changes, just like UNIT_HEALTH and UNIT_MAX_HEALTH. The last set of events will call UpdateMana to change the mana field:

```
elseif event == "UNIT_MANA" or
    event == "UNIT_MAXMANA" or
    event == "UNIT_RAGE" or
    event == "UNIT_MAXRAGE" or
    event == "UNIT_ENERGY" or
    event == "UNIT_MAXENERGY" or
    event == "UNIT_FOCUS" or
    event == "UNIT_MAXFOCUS" then
  self:UpdateMana()
end
```

OnShow and OnHide

When the frame is hidden, you no longer care about any of the UNIT_XXXXX events because there is no data being displayed. This provides you with a chance to use Lua's excellent data-description capabilities. Rather than manually registering and unregistering each and every event, you can create a simple table of events and then iterate through it with a `for` loop. The following table should appear outside of any functions and must be defined earlier in the file than the `RegisterUpdates` and `UnregisterUpdates` functions:

```
local events = {
    "UNIT_NAME_UPDATE", "UNIT_LEVEL", "UNIT_CLASSIFICATION_CHANGED",
    "UNIT_FACTION", "UNIT_PVP_UPDATE", "UNIT_HEALTH", "UNIT_MAXHEALTH",
    "UNIT_DISPLAYPOWER", "UNIT_MANA", "UNIT_MAXMANA", "UNIT_RAGE",
    "UNIT_MAXRAGE", "UNIT_ENERGY", "UNIT_MAXENERGY", "UNIT_FOCUS",
    "UNIT_MAXFOCUS",
}
```

This has been condensed to save space. Normally, you would want each table entry on a separate line for clarity.

TIP The exact arrangement of your source code is a matter of personal preference. Some authors like to consolidate data tables at the beginning of the file; others may prefer to define the data immediately before the function(s) that use it, and you may even see a combination of both, depending on the nature of the data. Whatever you choose, it is always best to remain consistent. Not only will it help other people who may look at your code, but it will also help you when you have been away from the source for a while and need to readjust.

Now that you have this events table, the `RegisterUpdates` and `UnregisterUpdates` functions are trivial to implement:

```
function TargetText:RegisterUpdates()
  for _, event in ipairs(events) do
    TargetTextFrame:RegisterEvent(event)
  end
end
```

```
function TargetText:UnregisterUpdates()
  for _, event in ipairs(events) do
    TargetTextFrame:UnregisterEvent(event)
  end
end
```

Putting the API to Use

How long have you gone on in this chapter without seeing a single, real-world usage of an API function? All mockery aside, this is a fundamental fact of software development. Every nontrivial project requires a good amount of busywork developing the interface layout, planning behaviors, structuring the code, and so forth, before you start seeing results. Because you finally have all the physical pieces of TargetText in place, you can now throw the switch and give them life.

Showing and Hiding the Frame

The most fundamental characteristic of unit frames is that they are only visible when the given unit exists. To implement the UpdateAll function, check whether you have a target. If so, show the frame and call all the update functions. If not, hide the frame.

Here's the UpdateAll code:

```
function TargetText:UpdateAll()
  if UnitExists("target") then
    TargetTextFrame:Show()
    self:UpdateName()
    self:UpdateLevel()
    self:UpdateClass()
    self:UpdateReaction()
    self:UpdateFaction()
    self:UpdatePvP()
    self:UpdateHealth()
    self:UpdatePowerType()
    self:UpdateMana()
  else
    TargetTextFrame:Hide()
  end
end
```

As you can see, the check for your target's existence is simple. Earlier in this chapter you looked at the UnitExists function, which returns 1 if the unit exists or nil otherwise, and now you can see it in action. In fact, you will create empty stubs for all the UpdateXxxx functions and start up WoW:

```
function TargetText:UpdateName()
end

function TargetText:UpdateLevel()
end

function TargetText:UpdateClass()
end

function TargetText:UpdateReaction()
end

function TargetText:UpdateFaction()
end

function TargetText:UpdatePvP()
```

```
end

function TargetText:UpdateHealth()
end

function TargetText:UpdatePowerType()
end

function TargetText:UpdateMana()
end
```

Assuming everything is typed correctly, you should be able to see the new unit frame appear and disappear when you select and deselect targets. Figure 13-2 shows an example of the current state of `TargetText`.

Figure 13-2: TargetText's first breath

Implementing Simple Update Functions

So far, the order in which events and update functions have been presented has corresponded directly to the position of the text fields in the frame. That pattern changes now with the introduction of the rest of the update functions in order of increasing complexity. Feel free to reload your UI after implementing each new function to see how it changes the display.

Setting the Name of Your Target

First up is `UpdateName`, which consists of only two lines of code.

```
function TargetText:UpdateName()
  local name = UnitName("target") or ""
  TargetTextFrameName:SetText(name)
end
```

You use a variable instead of passing `UnitName` directly to `SetText` for a couple of reasons. There is a remote chance that the name of your target will not be available even though `UnitExists` returns `true`. Additionally, `UnitName` can potentially return two values. The second would be the realm name in cross-realm battlegrounds.

Showing PvP Status

`TargetText:UpdatePvP` is also quite simple, because all you need to do is show or hide the `FontString` depending on the target's PvP status.

```
function TargetText:UpdatePvP()
  if UnitIsPVP("target") then
    TargetTextFramePvP:Show()
  else
    TargetTextFramePvP:Hide()
  end
end
```

`UnitIsPvP`, like `UnitExists`, is a simple true/false (or more accurately, `1`/`nil`) check to determine whether the unit is flagged for PvP combat. Based on the return of this function, you show or hide the PvP text field as necessary.

Updating the Target's Power Type

There are two things to do when updating the power type. First, you need to change the `TargetTextFrameManaLabel` to say "Mana," "Rage," "Energy," or "Focus" depending on the power type. You also want to change the color of the mana numbers themselves to reflect the type of power, just like the mana status bars in the default UI.

To be as consistent as possible with the default UI, we looked at FrameXML\Unit-Frame.lua to determine how WoW colors the status bars. It turns out there is a `ManaBar-Color` table with indexes that directly correspond to the returns of `UnitPowerType`, the next API function in our arsenal. This table not only describes the color you want, but also stores localized names of the power types. Fill in the `UpdatePowerType` function as follows:

```
function TargetText:UpdatePowerType()
  local info = ManaBarColor[UnitPowerType("target")]
  TargetTextFrameManaLabel:SetText(info.prefix)
  TargetTextFrameMana:SetTextColor(info.r, info.g, info.b)
end
```

Examining WoW's FrameXML code saved a decent amount of work coding the method to color and name the fields. On top of that, if any of the underlying data changes (more power types are added, colors are adjusted for different locales, and so on), this function will not have to be adjusted in any way — assuming, of course, Blizzard does not decide to change the way *its* mana bars select their color.

Setting the Target's Class

The class of the target should appear in the same color as it would in the raid panel. You approach this similarly to `TargetText:UpdatePowerType` in that you'll use a built-in table to determine the color. `FrameXML\Fonts.xml` defines several types of standard fonts and colors used in the default UI.

You are interested in the RAID_CLASS_COLORS table, which contains red, green, and blue values for each class. The keys to this table are unlocalized (English), all uppercase names of the classes. This matches the second return from the UnitClass function. The first return is the localized version of the class name. Another four lines of code and you have your TargetText:UpdateClass function:

```
function TargetText:UpdateClass()
  local class, key = UnitClass("target")
  local color = RAID_CLASS_COLORS[key]
  TargetTextFrameClass:SetText(class)
  TargetTextFrameClass:SetTextColor(color.r, color.g, color.b)
end
```

One interesting side effect of this addition is the realization that every single unit in the game has a class. Even a level 1 rabbit is considered a Warrior as far as the API is concerned.

The rest of the update functions are a bit more involved. Before you start on them, take a look at the results so far, which are shown in Figure 13-3.

Figure 13-3: TargetText after adding simple update functions

Displaying Health and Mana Values

Health and mana can be represented as proportions and as absolute values. This example will display the absolute values and percentage in the same line so both interpretations are available to the user. For example, if you have 2500 out of 3000 mana, it would look like "2500/3000 (83%)." Creating this string is fairly straightforward thanks to UnitMana and UnitManaMax:

```
function TargetText:UpdateMana()
  local mana, maxMana = UnitMana("target"), UnitManaMax("target")
  local percent = mana/maxMana
  local manaText

  if maxMana == 0 then
    manaText = "N/A"
  else
    manaText = string.format("%d/%d (%.0f%%)", mana, maxMana, ↵
percent * 100)
```

```
     end

     TargetTextFrameMana:SetText(manaText)
  end
```

First, you define a few variables to hold the values you need. Because many NPCs have no mana at all, the function first checks for a return of 0 from `UnitManaMax`. With this, you decide whether to display the mana count or simply "N/A" to indicate its irrelevance. When the target does have mana, `string.format()` creates the mana display as previously specified.

For the health display, start with the `TargetText:UpdateMana` function and replace all of the mana-related values with health-related ones:

```
function TargetText:UpdateHealth()
  local health, maxHealth = UnitHealth("target"), ↵
UnitHealthMax("target")
  local percent = health/maxHealth
  local healthText

  if maxHealth == 0 then
    healthText = "N/A"
  else
    healthText = string.format("%d/%d (%.0f%%)", health, maxHealth, ↵
percent * 100)
  end

  TargetTextFrameHealth:SetText(healthText)
end
```

WARNING Be very careful when copying and pasting code. As much time as you save doing repetitive tasks (or more) can be lost tracking down subtle bugs. While we cannot recommend against copying and pasting entirely, keep it to a minimum. In fact, if you find yourself copying and pasting frequently, chances are there are better ways to accomplish what you are doing, like creating a table and looping through it with a simple function.

At this point, the health display would function adequately. However, you want to make two changes that add a bit of flair. As explained earlier, health values are obfuscated for all units that are not part of your party or raid. Any target with `UnitHealthMax` of 100 should be displayed solely as a percentage. Add the following `elseif` clause before the `else` in the `TargetText:UpdateHealth` function:

```
elseif maxHealth == 100 then
  healthText = string.format("%.0f%%", percent * 100)
```

The color of the health text should also change depending on the percentage. It will start with green at full health, move to yellow at 50 percent, and finally red when your target is nearly dead. To help you accomplish this, define a simple function that returns red, green, and blue values based on a percent argument:

```
function TargetText:GetHealthColor(percent)
  local red, green

  if percent >= 0.5 then
    red = (1 - percent) * 2
    green = 1
  else
    red = 1
    green = percent * 2
  end

  return red, green, 0
end
```

This function is fairly simple because yellow is comprised of both green and red. For health values of 50 percent and up, green stays at 1 and red goes from 1 to 0 as the percent approaches 100. For values less than 50 percent, red stays at 1 and green goes from 1 to 0 as the percent approaches 0. It returns the red and green values as well as 0 for blue because you'll simply pass the return of this function into `TargetText:SetTextColor`, as you can see from the following line, which should be added to the end of `TargetText:UpdateHealth`:

```
TargetTextFrameHealth:SetTextColor(self:GetHealthColor(percent))
```

Figure 13-4 shows the result.

Figure 13-4: TargetText with health and mana (rage) information

Updating Hostility Information

Knowing whether a unit is liable to attack you and/or capable of defeating you is obviously important in games like World of Warcraft. If you are running through a relatively safe area of the woods, on a road perhaps, and suddenly the monsters look a few levels higher, you will probably decide to change directions, or at least watch your step. The final features you'll add to TargetText show just that information.

Two of these functions will use colors that are not defined in a variable in the FrameXML code. Somewhere before the `TargetText:UpdateLevel` and `TargetText: UpdateReaction` functions, add the following table:

```
local colors = {
  white = { r = 1, g = 1, b = 1},
  blue = { r = 0, g = 0, b = 1}
}
```

Setting Your Target's Faction

WoW has been focusing a healthy amount of attention on PvP combat recently. This renewed interest makes it vital that players know when a unit of the opposite faction approaches. TargetText presents this information as Alliance, Horde, or No Faction. To emphasize the meaning, the player's faction will be colored green, no faction will be yellow, and the opposing faction will be red. Fill in the `UpdateFaction` function as follows:

```
function TargetText:UpdateFaction()
  local faction = select(2, UnitFactionGroup("target"))
  local color

  if not faction then
    color = NORMAL_FONT_COLOR
    faction = "No Faction"
  elseif faction == select(2, UnitFactionGroup("player")) then
    color = GREEN_FONT_COLOR
  else
    color = RED_FONT_COLOR
  end

  TargetTextFrameFaction:SetText(faction)
  TargetTextFrameFaction:SetTextColor(color.r, color.g, color.b)
end
```

The `UnitFactionGroup` function, like `UnitClass`, returns both localized and unlocalized versions of the faction, although they're in the opposite order (the default UI rarely displays faction names, so it's usually only concerned with the unlocalized version). You use Lua's `select` to retrieve the second return. The faction is checked for existence and hostility to the player, and the colors are selected accordingly. Finally, you update the text field.

Showing the Target's Level

It may seem a bit trivial to have left it until this point, but you will be doing more in `TargetText:UpdateLevel` than simply setting the text. In a manner consistent with numerous quest log addons, you want to mark elite targets with a plus symbol. You will also take further advantage of color to indicate the potential difficulty of an opponent.

```
function TargetText:UpdateLevel()
  local level = UnitLevel("target")

  local color
  if UnitCanAttack("player", "target") then
    color = GetDifficultyColor(level)
  else
    color = colors.white
  end

  if level == -1 then
    level = "??"
  end

  local classification = UnitClassification("target")
  if classification == "worldboss" or
    classification == "rareelite" or
    classification == "elite" then

    level = level.."+"
  end

  TargetTextFrameLevel:SetText(level)
  TargetTextFrameLevel:SetTextColor(color.r, color.g, color.b)
end
```

UnitLevel returns either the level of the unit or -1 to indicate that you are not supposed to know. First, you use UnitCanAttack to check whether the opponent is attackable (attackability is directional; one unit may be able to attack another but not vise versa). If you can attack it, you use GetDifficultyColor, a function from FrameXML\QuestLogFrame.lua, to set the color based on difficulty. Otherwise, you set the color to the white that you previously defined.

Next, you turn any -1 into "??" to give it more meaning. Finally, you use the Unit-Classification function to add a "+" to the level of elite units.

Displaying the Target's Reaction

The last feature to implement is the TargetTextFrameReaction field. This is essentially a textual representation of the colored background on the default target frame. The basic logic of TargetText:UpdateReaction is borrowed from FrameXML\Target-Frame.lua's TargetFrame_CheckFaction. Here it's compressed a bit for clarity, and a few conditions that seem appropriate to this field are added.

First you need to define a few variables to help you. The first is a table of hostility names. UnitReaction returns a number from 1 to 7, but because the default UI never needs to name them (only to change a color), you have to define them yourself. Again, these should go somewhere in the source code before TargetText:UpdateReaction:

```
local reactionNames = {
  "Extremely Hostile",
  "Very Hostile",
  "Hostile",
  "Neutral",
  "Friendly",
  "Very Friendly",
  "Extremely Friendly"
}
```

Next, you define a few constants because you will be manually picking some of the colors. These are equivalent to the returns from UnitReaction:

```
local HOSTILE = 2
local NEUTRAL = 4
local FRIENDLY = 6
```

As with many of the other functions you've developed, you need to come up with a description and a color for the reaction. First, set up the default values of "No Reaction" and the color blue to help keep the logic simple:

```
function TargetText:UpdateReaction()
  local description, color = "No Reaction", colors.blue
```

If the target is dead, you want to set the text to a gray color. Depending on the type of dead unit, you will label it as "Corpse," "Ghost," or simply "Dead."

```
  if UnitIsDead("target") then
    color = GRAY_FONT_COLOR
    if UnitIsCorpse("target") then
      description = "Corpse"
    elseif UnitIsGhost("target") then
      description = "Ghost"
    else
      description = "Dead"
    end
```

The next few checks apply strictly to player-controlled characters. If a player is disconnected, you set the color to gray and label it so:

```
  elseif UnitPlayerControlled("target") then
    if not UnitIsConnected("target") then
      description = "Disconnected"
      color = GRAY_FONT_COLOR
```

If the player and the target can attack each other, set the reaction as hostile:

```
    elseif UnitCanAttack("target", "player") and ↵
UnitCanAttack("player", "target") then
        description = reactionNames[HOSTILE]
        color = UnitReactionColor[HOSTILE]
```

If the player can attack the target but not vise versa (that is, a PvP flagged opponent but the player is not flagged), set the reaction as `"Attackable"` with a yellow color:

```
    elseif UnitCanAttack("player", "target") then
        description = "Attackable"
        color = UnitReactionColor[NEUTRAL]
```

Any other player-controlled characters are either not PvP-enabled or are friendly:

```
    elseif UnitIsPVP("target") and not UnitIsPVPSanctuary("target") ↵
and not UnitIsPVPSanctuary("player") then
        description = reactionNames[FRIENDLY]
        color = UnitReactionColor[FRIENDLY]
    end
```

Flagged players should be marked as friendly unless the target and/or player is in a PvP sanctuary like Shattrath where players are not allowed to attack each other.

Now that you have players out of the way, only two more color decision sections are left. First, if a unit is tapped by another player (meaning they attacked it first and you are not eligible for experience or loot from it), you will label it as such and color it gray.

```
    elseif UnitIsTapped("target") and not ↵
UnitIsTappedByPlayer("target") then
        description = "Tapped"
        color = GRAY_FONT_COLOR
```

Finally, any other case not handled specifically will be determined by the return of `UnitReaction`. The description will be provided by the `reactionNames` table you defined earlier, and the color will come from a table defined in FrameXML\TargetFrame.lua called `UnitReactionColor`. With this final addition, TargetText should now match Figure 13-1:

```
    else
      local reaction = UnitReaction("target", "player")
      if reaction then
        description = reactionNames[reaction]
        color = UnitReactionColor[reaction]
      end
    end

    TargetTextFrameReaction:SetText(description)
    TargetTextFrameReaction:SetTextColor(color.r, color.g, color.b)
end
```

Summary

Previous chapters introduced you to general programming concepts, creating frames in XML and programming in an event-driven environment. With TargetText under your belt, you now have the foundation necessary to write World of Warcraft addons.

This chapter introduced you to APIs in the general sense, and gave you an in-depth example of one of the categories of APIs included in WoW, the unit functions. Understanding the way these functions interact with the game is essential to creating effective addons that accomplish a variety of goals. At this point, you have enough information in combination with the references provided later in the book, to begin creating your own fully featured addons.

In Part III, you'll see more specific examples of common tasks. While all of this information can be gleaned from FrameXML source code and the various references, it would obviously be a tremendous amount of work to discover all the methods for doing simple things such as creating slash commands, using saved variables effectively, and creating more active addons like action bars or interactive unit frames.

Before you tackle that, though, Chapter 14 shows you how to create addons with AddOn Studio for World of Warcraft. It builds on the techniques you've seen so far with XML and Lua to create a simple "hello world" addon, and introduces you to the visual design features of AddOn Studio.

Building a Basic Addon with AddOn Studio

Dan Fernandez

One of the most exciting things about addon development is the richness of the WoW community where addon developers release tools and frameworks to assist other addon creators in their craft.

AddOn Studio for World of Warcraft is exactly that, a free, open source community-based project built by Warcraft players at Microsoft that aims to provide a Visual Studio-like experience for building addons. AddOn Studio includes features like the ability to visually design frame XML files, schema validation for frames, a great Lua code editing experience including IntelliSense for WoW functions, and even the ability to automatically generate the TOC files for your project.

In this chapter, you'll tour the features in AddOn Studio by building a basic "Hello World" addon.

> **NOTE** AddOn Studio for World of Warcraft is a standalone application that works completely independently of Visual Studio. You do not need to install Visual Studio to use AddOn Studio.

Getting Started with AddOn Studio

You can download the latest version of AddOn Studio from `http://www.codeplex.com/WarcraftAddOnStudio` under the Releases tab. After downloading the zip file for AddOn Studio, simply extract the contents into a folder and click `setup.exe` to start the installer. The installer will check your system requirements and, if you are missing system prerequisites, it will prompt you to automatically install them. Once the program is installed, you will see an entry in your Start ⏵ Programs menu for AddOn Studio for World of Warcraft.

NOTE Depending on whether your machine has the correct system prerequisites installed, the installer may take up to 30 minutes to fully install.

Select File ⏵ New Project to create a new World of Warcraft AddOn project. In the New Project window that appears (see Figure 14-1), choose the Basic Warcraft Addon template, enter the name of the new project (for example, `MyFirstAddOn`), select the location where you want to store all the files associated with this project, and click OK.

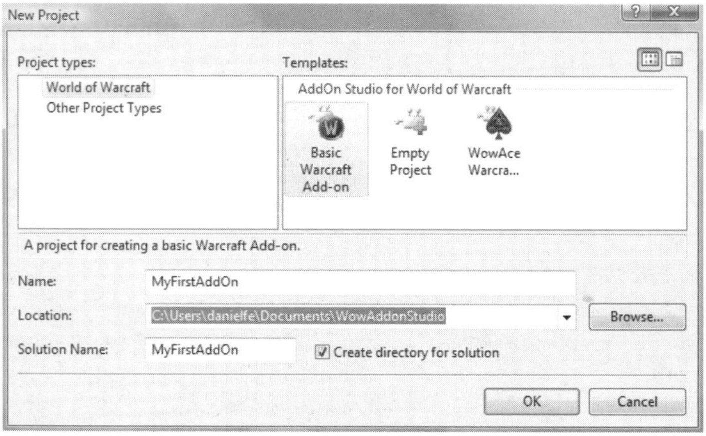

Figure 14-1: New Project dialog

AddOn Studio will now build a project that contains a `frame.xml` file for the interface, a corresponding `frame.lua` file for the code to drive the `frame.xml` file, as well as an autogenerated table of contents (TOC) file for your project, which is discussed at the end of the chapter.

Visually Designing your Interface

By default, your project opens in the `frame.xml` visual designer with the Toolbox visible. The new project shows your addon's user interface, where you can add various controls from the Toolbox by simply dragging and dropping them onto the frame designer. As Figure 14-2 illustrates, when you click on the frame, a few options show up that you can use to manipulate how the frame will appear. These options include a cursor icon in the top-left corner that you can use to click and drag the frame to set its starting position; small, white, resizing squares that you can use to resize the frame; and the Frame Tasks that you can use to automatically generate code to make the frame moveable. For now, simply select the Make Frame Moveable task; you will resize the frame later in the chapter using the Properties window.

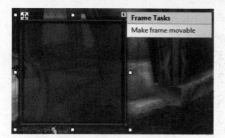

Figure 14-2: Selecting a frame

Using the Toolbox

The Toolbox (see Figure 14-3) contains most of the basic WoW controls you'll need to design your user interface.

Figure 14-3: Toolbox
controls

To use the Toolbox, simply select the control you want to use and drag it onto the form. For the simple example in this chapter, drag a FontString and a Button onto the frame designer. As with the frame, you can move and resize the controls visually. One of the nice features of the visual designer is that it has what are called *snap lines* that, as you can see in Figure 14-4, are guidelines that appear as you reposition controls to easily align them vertically or horizontally.

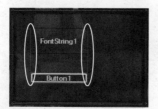

Figure 14-4: Snap lines
help align controls

TIP   Even though AddOn Studio provides a rich graphical interface for designing your UI, at the end of the day it is simply autogenerating FrameXML just like any other addon. You can look at the designer-generated XML by right-clicking on the form and selecting View Code. AddOn Studio includes a powerful XML editor and schema validation tool that you can use to ensure the correctness of your FrameXML design.

Setting Properties

Now that we've designed the basic interface for the addon, you can use the Properties window to change the properties and event handlers for any element in the designer. To select which control's properties to change, you can either click the control on the form designer or choose the control from the dropdown list at the top of the Properties window. Figure 14-5 shows the Properties window with the closeButton control selected.

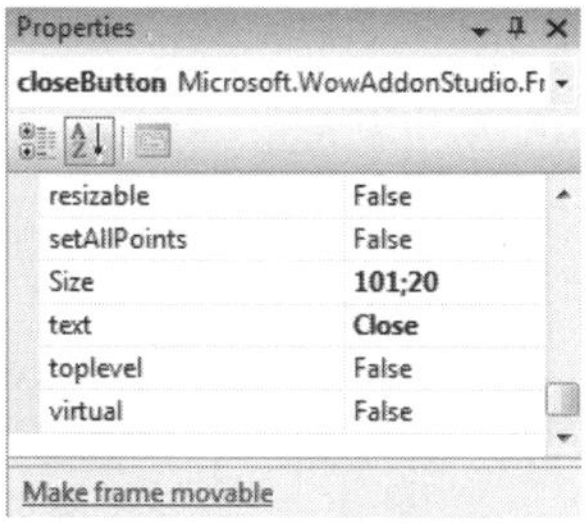

Figure 14-5: Properties and events

To finish designing this addon, make the property changes listed in Tables 14-1, 14-2, and 14-3.

Table 14-1: Frame Properties

PROPERTY	VALUE
Name	helloWorldFrame
Size	Abs 295;180

Table 14-2: FontString Properties

PROPERTY	VALUE
Name	addonMessage
Size	200;26
Text	Hello World!

Table 14-3: Button Properties

PROPERTY	VALUE
name	closeButton
text	Hello World!

Writing the Code

Adding code to your frames is extremely easy in AddOn Studio, using the same familiar Visual Studio interface.

Listening to Events

You will need to register the helloWorldFrame to the PLAYER_TARGET_CHANGED event when the frame loads. To do this in AddOn Studio, simply double-click on the frame. That will automatically generate an OnLoad event handler and switch you to the frame.lua code file:

```
function helloWorldFrame_OnLoad()
    frame:RegisterEvent("PLAYER_TARGET_CHANGED");
end
```

Adding Event Handlers Automatically

The next step is to add the OnEvent event handler for the frame that will be called when your target changes and the PLAYER_TARGET_CHANGED event fires. AddOn Studio can automatically generate the code stubs for events; switch to the designer view and select the control for which you want to generate an event in the Properties window, as shown in Figure 14-6.

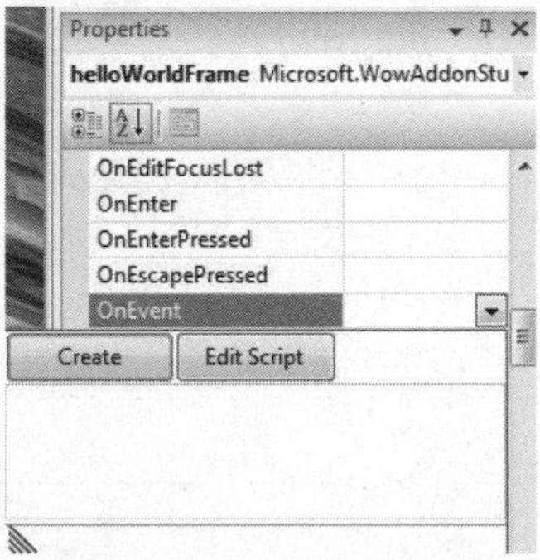

Figure 14-6: Creating events

Doing this adds the following code stub:

```
function helloWorldFrame_OnEvent()
    --put your event handler logic here
end
```

Next, you'll add a couple of snippets of code to check whether the unit exists. If it does, you'll update the `addonMessage` text string property with the name of the unit.

Verifying a Unit Exists

Although the code to verify whether a unit exists is very basic, you'll notice some of the advanced IntelliSense features in AddOn Studio. For example, just typing the `if` keyword and hitting Ctrl+Space automatically generates a code snippet for an `if` statement with the expression highlighted for you to fill in, as shown in Figure 14-7. These are called IntelliSense Code Snippets and are customizable snippets of pre-written Lua scripts for common Lua language constructs such as `for`, `foreach`, printing text, and more.

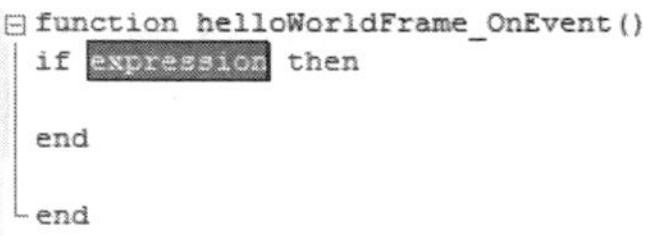

```
function helloWorldFrame_OnEvent()
  if expression then

  end
end
```

Figure 14-7: Code Snippet for if keyword

> **TIP** You can build your own or customize the included code snippets simply by updating the XML files located at `\\Program Files\AddOn Studio for World of Warcraft\Lua\Snippets\1033\`.

Next, you'll add an expression to the `if` statement to verify you are listening to the PLAYER_TARGET_CHANGED event. If you are, you'll make sure that your current target exists using the `UnitExists()` function. To do this, press Ctrl+Space to show the IntelliSense menu and choose `UnitExists()` from the full list of WoW API functions, as shown in Figure 14-8.

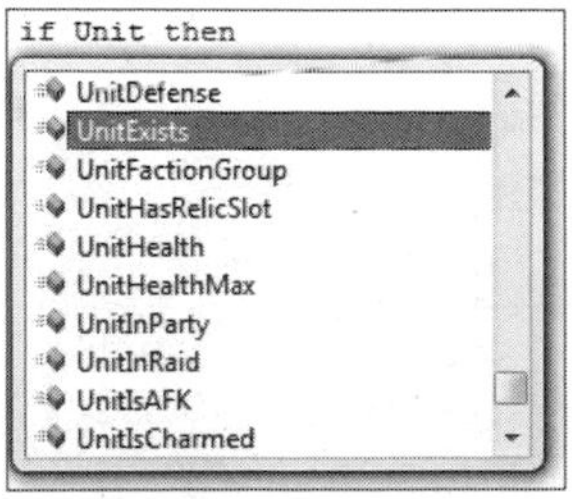

```
if Unit then
  ◈ UnitDefense
  ◈ UnitExists
  ◈ UnitFactionGroup
  ◈ UnitHasRelicSlot
  ◈ UnitHealth
  ◈ UnitHealthMax
  ◈ UnitInParty
  ◈ UnitInRaid
  ◈ UnitIsAFK
  ◈ UnitIsCharmed
```

Figure 14-8: IntelliSense displaying WoW functions

Similarly, when you partially type the name of a control like the addonMessage FontString and hit Ctrl+Space, IntelliSense automatically completes the name of the control. It can also show you a filtered list of the properties, methods, and events for that control, as illustrated in Figure 14-9.

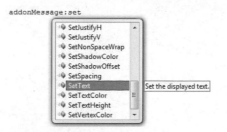

Figure 14-9: IntelliSense for the FontString control

Setting the name of the selected unit as the text for the fontstring control makes the final code look like this:

```
function helloWorldFrame_OnEvent()
  if (event == "PLAYER_TARGET_CHANGED") then
    if UnitExists("target") then
      addonMessage:SetText("Hello " .. UnitName("target") .. "!");
    end
  end
end
```

Add the Close Button Code

The last piece of code to add hides the frame when the user clicks the Close button. Switch back to the designer view and double-click the button to autogenerate the event handler. Just like before, you can use IntelliSense to filter the completion list to select the Hide() function:

```
function closeButton_OnClick()
    helloWorldFrame.Hide();
end
```

Deploying your Addon

Before you deploy the addon, you want to update the TOC file to better describe the addon. While this is normally a manual process that involves editing a text file, AddOn Studio will automatically generate the TOC files for you. It will include any resource files (textures or audio files), Lua scripts, XML frames, and anything else that you've added to the project. To edit settings like the name, e-mail, and title of your addon, select the Project *<project name>* Properties menu option, which will display the Information window shown in Figure 14-10. From here you can manually update settings like the name or description of your addon, saved variables, dependencies, and more.

Figure 14-10: Editing the TOC

To deploy your addon, click the Build option, which will make sure there are no obvious Lua errors with your project (errors would appear in the Error List window), and it will automatically copy your addon to the WoW installation directory using the registry key that WoW sets during installation. Figure 14-11 shows the finished addon.

Figure 14-11: The completed addon

Summary

While the example in this chapter is quite basic, you've hopefully seen how tools like AddOn Studio can help reduce the time it takes to build addons by simplifying the design of your user interface, automatically generating event handlers, using IntelliSense and code snippets to ensure your code doesn't have typos, and, of course, auto-generating your TOC file.

While AddOn Studio is constantly being improved with new features added regularly, it's always critical to understand the fundamentals of building addons, including FrameXML syntax, the basics of Lua code, and how to package and share your addons.

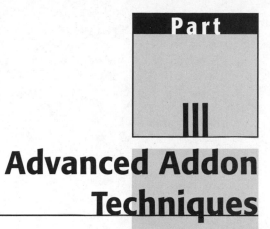

Part

III

Advanced Addon Techniques

Using Templates Programmatically

Matthew Orlando

Templates are a wonderful tool for code re-use in XML frame design. Rather than spelling out every single detail of a number of similar user interface (UI) elements, you can define the basic attributes in one location and inherit them in another. This system does have its limitations, though. If you need to instantiate a large number of templates with only minor variations, more of your time is spent exercising your patience with copy and paste than with creating the ultimate behavior of your addon. The old FlexBar addon (pre-2.0), for example, had 120 identical buttons whose only real differences were their names. All of this repetition is not only time-consuming, but also error-prone.

For everyone's sake, Blizzard introduced the `CreateFrame` function to combat this problem. It allows UI code to create frames on demand, optionally inheriting from a template specified in XML. With this feature comes tremendous flexibility in addon creation. Not only can you create several frames in a loop when your addon is loaded, but you can also delay a frame's instantiation until it is actually needed. Because frame creation is a relatively expensive operation, this can improve loading times.

Beyond the initial creation with `CreateFrame`, frames have several methods to set various attributes that would normally be handled by tags or attributes in XML. For instance, the `SetPoint` method provides the same functionality as an `<Anchor>` tag.

Using CreateFrame

While dynamic frame creation is a highly versatile tool, the root procedure is actually quite simple. The signature of `CreateFrame` says basically everything you need to know (parameters in brackets `[ ]` are optional):

```
frame = CreateFrame(frameType[, name[, parent[, template]]])
```

The `frameType` is the name of the equivalent XML tag (`Frame`, `Button`, `CheckButton`, and so on). If you want to give the frame a global name, pass a string as the second argument. Otherwise, you can make the frame anonymous by leaving out the `name` or passing `nil`. The `parent` parameter accepts a frame reference — the actual frame object, not a string of the name — and sets that frame as the parent of the new frame. Finally, the `template` parameter is a string for the name of the virtual template you want to inherit.

Here's a quick example; run the following command to open up WoWLua in interactive mode and create an action button:

```
/lua CreateFrame("Checkbutton", "MyAction", UIParent, ↵
"ActionBarButtonTemplate")
```

If you are worried that it was a bit anticlimactic, you can rest easy. Although the entire on-demand frame system is built upon `CreateFrame`, the real power lies in the frames' methods. Because `ActionBarButtonTemplate` does not define an anchor, WoW does not have enough information to display the new button yet. You can rectify this by entering the following command in WoWLua:

```
MyAction:SetPoint("CENTER")
```

When passed a single anchor point, `SetPoint` assumes you mean relative to the same point on the frame's parent (in this case, `UIParent`, as specified in the call to `CreateFrame`). This line of Lua code is equivalent to the following XML block:

```
<Anchors>
  <Anchor point="CENTER"/>
</Anchors>
```

With that taken care of, you should see a lone action button right in the middle of your screen — unless you do not have an action in the first slot. (In that case, drag an existing action from one of your bars and the new empty button will appear.)

Take some time to experiment with `CreateFrame` and the various widget methods. When you are done, reload the UI to clean up any unneeded frames.

Adding Buffs to TargetText

In this chapter, you will create a plugin for TargetText called TargetTextBuffs. The plugin (see Figure 15-1) will add buff and debuff icons (sometimes referred to collectively as buffs) to the TargetText frame similar to those on the default UI's target frame.

Like the default UI, the buffs will appear in rows eight icons wide. As the rows fill up, they expand downward to make room. Buffs and debuffs are separated by a small gap, with buffs on top for friendly targets and debuffs on top for hostile ones.

Go ahead and create the basic addon skeleton for TargetTextBuffs, including a Lua and an XML file (see Chapter 10). Be sure to add the following line to the `.toc` file to establish TargetText as a dependency:

```
## Dependencies: TargetText
```

Figure 15-1: TargetTextBuffs in all its glory

Creating the Basic Templates

You need to lay a bit of groundwork before you can begin dynamically creating the buff icons. TargetTextBuffs needs to respond to a couple events, so you will first create a minimal frame. This frame will also serve as the basic anchor point for the buff icons, so you will parent it to TargetText's frame. The specified anchor offset will make a full row of buffs appear centered below the TargetText frame. Here is the beginning of the XML file:

```xml
<Ui xmlns="http://www.blizzard.com/wow/ui/" ↵
xmlns:xsi="http://www.w3.org/2001/XMLSchema-instance" ↵
xsi:schemaLocation="http://www.blizzard.com/wow/ui/
..\UI.xsd">

  <Frame name="TargetTextBuffsFrame" parent="TargetTextFrame">
    <Size x="1" y="1"/>
    <Anchors>
      <Anchor point="TOPLEFT" relativePoint="BOTTOMLEFT">
        <Offset x="8" y="0"/>
      </Anchor>
    </Anchors>
    <Scripts>
      <OnLoad>
        TargetTextBuffs:OnLoad(self)
      </OnLoad>
      <OnEvent>
        TargetTextBuffs:OnEvent(event, ...)
      </OnEvent>
    </Scripts>
  </Frame>
```

Note Although `TargetTextBuffsFrame` does not define any of its own visual elements, you still need to specify a size. WoW does not show a frame if its size is zero in either dimension. Because the buff icons will be children of this frame, you'll use a "dummy" size of 1 x 1 to force WoW to show it.

The buff and debuff icons themselves will be based on predefined templates from FrameXML\TargetFrame.xml. Because those two templates specify different sizes, you will create a new debuff template that matches the built-in buff template's size. Another problem with the debuff template is that it specifies an absolute size for the colored border that indicates the debuff's type. You cannot selectively override a single texture within a Layer tag, so use an OnLoad script to resize the border, like this:

```
<Frame name="TargetTextBuffsDebuffTemplate" ↵
inherits="TargetDebuffButtonTemplate" virtual="true">
   <Size x="21" y="21"/>
   <Scripts>
     <OnLoad>
       local border = _G[self:GetName().."Border"]
       border:SetWidth(23)
       border:SetHeight(23)
     </OnLoad>
   </Scripts>
</Frame>

</Ui>
```

THE GLOBAL ENVIRONMENT

In Lua, all global variables are stored in a table called the *Global Environment*. You can reference this table by the global variable, _G, as seen in the preceding example. This construct operates similarly to the getglobal function: It allows you to retrieve a global variable using a string of its name instead of typing the variable name directly in code. Because _G is a global variable, it contains itself. In other words:

```
_G["_G"]._G == _G.
```

Each Lua function can have its own global environment. You can set the global table for a function using setfenv, as in the following:

```
setfenv(someFunction, someTable)
```

Conversely, the getfenv function allows you to retrieve the environment for a given function or the current code path:

```
local otherEnv = getfenv(someFunction)
local thisEnv = getfenv()
```

A function with a custom environment can also access the "main" global environment by passing 0 to getfenv:

```
local baseEnv = getfenv(0)
```

Both of these functions have other more advanced forms and many usage scenarios. However, describing them is beyond the scope of this book. You can learn more about them from the Lua website at http://www.lua.org.

Defining Fundamental Behaviors

First, create some front matter in the Lua file including a namespace for your functions (see Chapter 13), tables to store the buff and debuff icon frames, and a few constants for controlling the appearance of the buffs:

```
TargetTextBuffs = {}

local buffFrames = {}
local debuffFrames = {}

local BUFFS_PER_ROW = 8
local BUFF_SPACING = 2
local BUFF_TYPE_OFFSET_Y = -7
```

Storing the icons in tables allows you to iterate through them much more efficiently than accessing them by name. You use one table for each type because they will be grouped visually by type. The constants are fairly self-explanatory and will be clarified later when you develop the code that uses them.

Event Handlers

Like the TargetText frame, you want to handle the PLAYER_TARGET_CHANGED event to update the buffs when you get a new target. You will also handle UNIT_AURA, which is triggered whenever a unit's buffs change. Add the following OnLoad function to register the event handlers:

```
function TargetTextBuffs:OnLoad(frame)
  frame:RegisterEvent("PLAYER_TARGET_CHANGED")
  frame:RegisterEvent("UNIT_AURA")
end
```

The OnEvent handler uses a small shortcut. Because UNIT_AURA is only relevant if its first argument is "target" and PLAYER_TARGET_CHANGED does not use the first argument, you can simply check for "target" as the first argument or PLAYER_TARGET_CHANGED as the event:

```
function TargetTextBuffs:OnEvent(event, unit)
  if unit == "target" or event == "PLAYER_TARGET_CHANGED" then
    local anchorBuff = self:UpdateBuffs()
    local anchorDebuff = self:UpdateDebuffs()

    if UnitIsFriend("player", "target") then
      self:UpdateAnchors(buffFrames[1], debuffFrames[1], anchorBuff)
    else
      self:UpdateAnchors(debuffFrames[1], buffFrames[1], anchorDebuff)
    end
  end
end
```

The first job of the event handler is to update the buffs and debuffs. The update functions iterate through the target's buffs and debuffs. As they go along, they create buff frames as needed and set various attributes of the frame (icon, count, number, and so on). They return the first frame of the last row of the given group, which you'll use in the next step.

Arranging the Buffs and Debuffs

UpdateAnchors is the function that places the buffs above the debuffs or vice versa, the choice of which is made by the UnitIsFriend API. The best way to explain this function is to describe its code:

```
function TargetTextBuffs:UpdateAnchors(firstFrame, secondFrame, ↵
anchorTo)
  if firstFrame and firstFrame:IsShown() then
    firstFrame:SetPoint("TOPLEFT", TargetTextBuffsFrame)
    if secondFrame and secondFrame:IsShown() then
      secondFrame:SetPoint("TOPLEFT", anchorTo, "BOTTOMLEFT", 0, ↵
BUFF_TYPE_OFFSET_Y)
    end
  elseif secondFrame and secondFrame:IsShown() then
    secondFrame:SetPoint("TOPLEFT", TargetTextBuffsFrame)
  end
end
```

The firstFrame parameter is the first icon of the set that should appear immediately under the TargetText frame. If this frame exists and is shown, the function calls SetPoint to anchor it appropriately. All of the other frames of the same type are anchored, at least indirectly, to the first one so they will automatically follow.

Once firstFrame is in place, secondFrame is attached to the top group's last row with a gap the size of BUFF_TYPE_OFFSET_Y. In other words, if the debuffs are on top and there are 10 of them, the first buff will be anchored to the ninth debuff (see Figure 15-2). If the firstFrame does not exist, the secondFrame is attached directly to TargetTextBuffsFrame just like the firstFrame would have been.

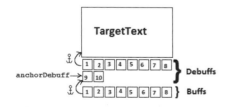

Figure 15-2: Anchoring diagram

Creating the Buff Icons

The work you've done so far has been from the top down, and the high-level logic has been simple and essentially trivial to the goal of this chapter. At this point, there are two layers left: the system that applies the buff characteristics to the frames, and the one that creates the buff frames themselves. You will be doing a bit of abstraction in regard to the differences between buffs and debuffs. For each system, the process is nearly identical between the two types of icons. This lends the rest of the chapter to a bottom-up approach.

Building the "Grid"

As you gain buffs and create frames, you want to arrange the frames into rows. The buffFrames and debuffFrames tables are used as arrays to store these frames, making it trivial to anchor each new frame to the one before it or to the row above it. The CreateBuffBase function handles these tasks.

CreateBuffBase takes the buff index (1 to the number of buffs), the array to store the buff frame, the global name for the new frame, and the template to inherit. First, create the frame with the specified properties; set the parent to TargetTextBuffsFrame to make sure the buffs are hidden when you no longer have a target:

```
function TargetTextBuffs:CreateBuffBase(index, frames, name, template)
  local frame = CreateFrame("Button", name, TargetTextBuffsFrame, template)

  frame.icon = _G[name.."Icon"]
  frame.cooldown = _G[name.."Cooldown"]
  frame.count = _G[name.."Count"]
  frame.border = _G[name.."Border"]
  frame.id = index
```

The subsequent lines give you easy access to various elements of the template, which saves time typing and provides better performance than generating the names each time you need to access them. The frame.id is used by the templates to show the appropriate tooltip when you mouse over a buff.

Setting Anchors

Now that you have the frame, you need to position it. It might be easiest to visualize the logic with some pseudocode:

```
If this is the first buff button then
  Anchor to the bottom left corner of the TargetText frame
Elseif this is the first buff of a row then
  Anchor to the bottom of the first buff of the previous row
Else
  Anchor to the right of the previous buff
```

First, you define a few variables to store the anchor parameters. You can shortcut the first clause of the pseudocode because the buff frame's parent, `TargetTextBuffsFrame`, is already anchored in the desired position. By leaving these variables empty, the `SetPoint` at the end of the next snippet will set the buff's top-left corner to the same as its parent.

```
local relativeTo, relativePoint, offsetX, offsetY
if index == 1 then
  -- Use default (empty) values
elseif index % BUFFS_PER_ROW == 1 then
  relativeTo = frames[index - BUFFS_PER_ROW]
  relativePoint = "BOTTOMLEFT"
  offsetX = 0
  offsetY = - BUFF_SPACING
else
  relativeTo = frames[index - 1]
  relativePoint = "TOPRIGHT"
  offsetX = BUFF_SPACING
  offsetY = 0
end
frame:SetPoint("TOPLEFT", relativeTo, relativePoint, offsetX, offsetY)
```

You first eliminate the initial button of the group with an empty `if` clause, including a comment for clarity. Then you check whether this is the first buff of a row by calculating the remainder from dividing the index by the maximum number of buffs in each row. If the remainder is 1, you set the anchor parameters to appropriate values. Otherwise, you set the anchor to the previous button.

All that is left now is to add the newly created frame to the table passed into the function and return the buff to the calling function:

```
  frames[index] = frame
  return frame
end
```

Creating Specialized Wrappers

You now have a generic function that can create buff or debuff frames depending on the parameters passed to it. To simplify the rest of the code, create two wrapper functions: one for buffs, the other for debuffs. Each one will take the index as its only parameter and generate all the necessary parameters for `CreateBuffBase`, as follows:

```
function TargetTextBuffs:CreateBuff(index)
  return self:CreateBuffBase(
    index,
    buffFrames,
    "TargetTextBuff"..index,
    "TargetBuffButtonTemplate"
  )
end

function TargetTextBuffs:CreateDebuff(index)
```

```
    return self:CreateBuffBase(
      index,
      debuffFrames,
      "TargetTextDebuff"..index,
      "TargetTextBuffsDebuffTemplate"
    )
  end
```

These functions are nothing special. Each is simply a single `return` statement that calls the base function with the appropriate parameters.

TIP Notice how each parameter is placed on its own line. Because the parameters themselves are really the focus of these functions, doing so serves to emphasize their meaning. Feel free to experiment with the layout of your code. Sometimes a nonstandard approach like this actually makes for more readable code.

Updating the Buffs

With the means to create the buff icons out of the way, you can now focus on the "when." Any time you acquire a new target or your target's buffs change, you need to cycle through them, showing, creating, and hiding buff frames, as necessary. Again, you'll start with a more abstract approach and work your way toward the code presented first in this chapter.

`UpdateBuffsBase` accepts three parameters: a function to get buff data from the given index, the table of buff or debuff frames, and a string of the `TargetTextBuffs` method to call for frame creation (these will be explained in more detail as you progress).

Looping Through the Buffs

Iterating through the target's buffs is as easy as starting at 1 and working your way up until there are no more buffs. A `while` loop works nicely. Start by setting up the data for the first pass through the loop:

```
function TargetTextBuffs:UpdateBuffsBase(BuffFunc, frames, method)
  local index = 1
  local icon, count, duration, timeLeft, debuffType = BuffFunc(index)
  local anchorBuff

  while icon do
```

The `BuffFunc` passed in should be a wrapper for either `UnitBuff` or `UnitDebuff` and return the items listed in the third line, as follows:

- `icon` — Texture path of the icon for the buff.
- `count` — Number of applications.

- `duration` — Total length of time the buff lasts.

- `timeLeft` — The amount of time remaining for the buff.

- `debuffType` — For debuffs, this is an index used by the `DebuffTypeColorTable` for setting the border color of the debuff icon. For buffs, this will be `nil`.

The values `duration` and `timeLeft` are only provided for abilities the player is able to cast.

If you pass an index to `BuffFunc` and there is no corresponding buff on the target, all of the returns will be `nil`. That's how the `while` loop decides whether to continue. You use the `icon` because it is the only return from `BuffFunc` that applies to all existing buffs.

Showing or Creating the Buff

The first step inside the loop is to get the current buff frame or, if none exists, to create one. Once you have the frame, you show it (in case it was previously hidden) and set various attributes based on the buff data. As the loop goes along, you also check whether the current buff is the first one in a row. If so, you store it in `anchorBuff` to be returned later. Add the following code:

```
local buff = frames[index] or self[method](self, index)
buff:Show()

if index % BUFFS_PER_ROW == 1 then
  anchorBuff = buff
end
```

Line one of this snippet is where the real power reveals itself. If the frame for the given index already exists, it is assigned to the `buff` variable. Otherwise, you use the `method` parameter to call either `CreateBuff` or `CreateDebuff`. To better understand how this works, recall two pieces of syntactic sugar from Chapter 4:

- `table.element` is equivalent to `table["element"]`.

- `table:function()` is shorthand for `table.function(table)` (when calling, not defining the function).

To create the new buff or debuff, you combine the two in order to call the appropriate method of TargetTextBuffs.

Setting Visual Attributes

Once you have the reference to the relevant buff frame, you need to give it the required appearance. Use the returns of `BuffFunc` to set the icon, count, cooldown, and border color. Because every buff has an icon, displaying it is trivial. Add the following line:

```
buff.icon:SetTexture(icon)
```

`BuffFunc` always returns a number for the count, but you're only interested in numbers above zero:

```
if count > 1 then
  buff.count:SetText(count)
```

```
      buff.count:Show()
   else
      buff.count:Hide()
   end
```

Buffs that show timers (that is, ones that you can cast) use a `Cooldown` element to indicate the time left. `Cooldown`s use the duration and start time of the buff to initiate their animation. However, `UnitBuff` and `UnitDebuff` return duration and time left instead (this is probably because the tooltip displayed time remaining before the timers were implemented). Luckily, it is easy to calculate the start time of the buff using `GetTime`, the duration, and the time left. Here's how:

```
   if duration and duration > 0 then
      local startTime = GetTime() - (duration - timeLeft)
      buff.cooldown:SetCooldown(startTime, duration)
      buff.cooldown:Show()
   else
      buff.cooldown:Hide()
   end
```

The final visual element applies only to debuffs, hence the check for `buff.border`, which would be `nil` for buffs. If the border exists, use the `debuffType` return from `BuffFunc` to pick the color for the border:

```
   if buff.border then
      local color
      if debuffType then
         color = DebuffTypeColor[debuffType]
      else
         color = DebuffTypeColor["none"]
      end
      buff.border:SetVertexColor(color.r, color.g, color.b)
   end
```

The last step in the loop increments the buff index and calls `BuffFunc` for the next round:

```
      index = index + 1
      icon, count, duration, timeLeft, debuffType = BuffFunc(index)
   end
```

When you have no more buffs, you use the current index position as the beginning of a `for` loop to hide any remaining buff frames. Finally, you return `anchorBuff` to be used in `UpdateAnchors`:

```
   for i = index, #frames do
      frames[i]:Hide()
   end

   return anchorBuff
end
```

Wrapping the Update

As you did with `CreateBuffBase`, you must wrap `UpdateBuffsBase` with two functions that pass the appropriate values for buffs and debuffs. The first parameter to the base function is another function that returns the icon, count, duration, time left, and debuff type. Because the `UnitBuff` and `UnitDebuff` APIs return their parameters in a slightly different order, you define a wrapper function for them in the call to `UpdateBuffsBase`:

```
function TargetTextBuffs:UpdateBuffs()
  return self:UpdateBuffsBase(
    function(index)
      local icon, count, duration, timeLeft = select(3, ↵
UnitBuff("target", index))
      return icon, count, duration, timeLeft
    end,
    buffFrames,
    "CreateBuff"
  )
end

function TargetTextBuffs:UpdateDebuffs()
  return self:UpdateBuffsBase(
    function(index)
      local icon, count, debuffType, duration, timeLeft = ↵
select(3, UnitDebuff("target", index))
      return icon, count, duration, timeLeft, debuffType
    end,
    debuffFrames,
    "CreateDebuff"
  )
end
```

In the first function, it would be possible to return the results of `select` directly. However, if new returns are added to `UnitBuff`, they would be passed along as well, which would be misinterpreted by the base function as a debuff type. By specifically assigning and returning four variables, you add a bit of future-proofing to the code, reducing the likelihood that TargetTextBuffs will break in upcoming patches. For the debuff version, the variables are absolutely necessary because the debuff type is returned between the count and the duration.

These functions finally bridge the gap between the high-level logic developed at the beginning of this chapter and the frame-building functions covered more recently. Loading this addon into WoW now provides the results you saw in Figure 15-1.

Summary

In this chapter, you explored the basic concepts of dynamic frame creation using XML templates. You looked at one of the important widget methods, `SetPoint`, which enables you to control the arrangement of frames in the UI. Beyond the strictly procedural concepts, you also examined the common practice of abstracting similar functionality to reduce code duplication.

In Chapter 16, you'll build on these techniques and learn how to create an entire addon without writing a single line of XML.

Writing an Addon Without XML

Bryan McLemore

Originally, addon developers could only build graphical interfaces using XML. To show any frame of significant complexity, you had to write a quite lengthy XML document describing every detail of the content and presentation of the frame. Some developers found this difficult to work with, resulting in addons that either had no graphical components or very poor ones.

To resolve this problem, Blizzard decided to provide an additional API that you could use to create your interfaces completely with Lua. This API also has the benefits of dynamically created frames, potential memory usage savings, and the ability to create addons completely in Lua. It is this API and its applications on which this chapter focuses.

Exploring Basic Frame Creation

Lua-based frames start with a single function. In Chapter 15, you used `CreateFrame` to dynamically generate frames based on XML templates. In this chapter, you'll use `CreateFrame` and related functions to do everything. Generally, you will always start with a `"Frame"` object. Run the following command inside of WowLua:

```
frame = CreateFrame("Frame", nil, UIParent)
```

This gives you a basic empty frame parented to UIParent, but at this point, the frame is fairly meaningless. So let's give it some life by typing the following into WowLua.

```
frame:SetHeight(70)
frame:SetWidth(290)

frame:SetPoint("CENTER", UIParent, "CENTER", 0, 0)

frame:SetBackdrop( {
  bgFile = [[Interface\Tooltips\UI-Tooltip-Background]],
  edgeFile = [[Interface\Tooltips\UI-Tooltip-Border]],
  tile = true, tileSize = 16, edgeSize = 16,
  insets = { left = 5, right = 5, top = 5, bottom = 5 }
})

frame:SetBackdropColor(.75, .75, .75)
frame:SetBackdropBorderColor(1, 1, 1)
```

NOTE Every function used in this code is a replacement for a corresponding XML tag or set of tags. It is pretty much a universal truth that there is a correlation between these Lua functions and XML tags.

Figure 16-1 shows the resulting frame.

Figure 16-1: The frame

Using CreateFontString()

The frame may seem boring right now, but you can use other functions to add more content. These functions differ from CreateFrame in that they do not belong to the global namespace but, instead, must be called directly on a frame. You can use CreateFontString to add more info to your empty frame. Here's that function's signature:

```
fontstring = Frame:CreateFontString([name[, layer[ ,template]]])
```

All the arguments are optional, and all of them should be strings. In this example, however, you won't use any of them. Run the following commands in WowLua to display info on the frame:

```
name = frame:CreateFontString()
name:SetPoint('TOPLEFT', frame, 'TOPLEFT', 10, -10)
```

```
name:SetFontObject(GameFontNormal)
name:SetText(UnitName('player') .. '\nWants to say hi to the World of
Warcraft\n and the expanse of 100% Lua\n driven addons')
```

Figure 16-2 shows the result.

Figure 16-2: The frame with a message just for you

Using CreateTexture()

CreateTexture is similar to CreateFontString; the only major difference is that CreateTexture returns a Texture object instead of a FontString object. Here's the signature for CreateTexture:

```
fontstring = Frame:CreateTexture([name[, layer[ ,template]]])
```

Again, all of its arguments are optional and strings. Textures are used to display just about all forms of graphics on the frames.

Creating a Better PlayerFrame

To further illustrate the use of Lua-based frame API, you'll put together an addon that will display additional information on the PlayerFrame. As always, begin by creating your addon skeleton in your addons directory. However, this time you only need the .toc and .lua files and, in this case, one image file. After creating the .toc and .lua files, copy the image file from this book's code download into the directory. Call this addon **PlayerFramePlus** and use that in your naming scheme on your directory and .toc file. After all is said and done, you should have a folder in your addon's directory with roughly the following structure:

```
PlayerFramePlus
   PlayerFramePlus.toc
   PlayerFramePlus.lua
   PlayerFramePlus.tga
```

An earlier chapter covered what should be in your TOC file. For now, we're concentrating on the .lua file.

Setting Up the Lua

Start by putting in a shell for the LUA file:

```
local PlayerFramePlus = {}

-- This function will do any initial bookkeeping on loading WoW.
function PlayerFramePlus:Initialize()
    Message("PlayerFramePlus Loaded")
end


PlayerFramePlus:Initialize()
```

`Message("PlayerFramePlus Loaded")` is used inside of the `Initialize()` function to verify that your addon is set up properly. Now load up WoW. You should have an annoying popup message; if you don't, try reloading WoW. Once it works, remove that line so that it doesn't happen every time you log in to WoW.

The last line of this code looks innocent enough, but you usually don't want an addon to initialize when the code is parsed. At that particular point, some information that many addons use will not be available. To do this properly, you want the addon to initialize when the `PLAYER_ENTERING_WORLD` event fires. Adjust the stub so that it looks like this:

```
local PlayerFramePlus = {}

-- This function will do any initial bookkeeping on loading WoW.
function PlayerFramePlus:Initialize()

end

local frame = CreateFrame("Frame", nil, PlayerFrame)

frame:RegisterEvent("PLAYER_ENTERING_WORLD")
frame:SetScript("OnEvent", function()
    if event == "PLAYER_ENTERING_WORLD" then
        PlayerFramePlus:Initialize()
    end
end)

PlayerFramePlus.frame = frame
```

Now you have basic event handling in your frame. While the `if` clause inside the `OnEvent` handler is not needed, strictly speaking, it is a good idea to use it anyway. Because the frame is a local reference, the last line saves the reference under the Player-FramePlus table for future use.

Creating the Frames

Now that you have a core stub for this addon, you can create the actual display area for the addon to use. First, use the graphics file that you copied into the folder:

```
function PlayerFramePlus:Initialize()
  local frame = self.frame

  --Create the graphical outline out of the image file
  local border = frame:CreateTexture(nil, "OVERLAY")
  border:SetHeight(128)
  border:SetWidth(256)
  border:SetPoint("TOPLEFT", PlayerFrame, "TOPLEFT", 77, -37)
  border:SetTexture[[Interface\AddOns\PlayerFramePlus\PlayerFramePlus]]
end
```

Then reload the UI by typing **/console reloadui** into WoW. Your PlayerFrame should be similar to that shown in Figure 16-3.

Figure 16-3: Basic wire frame for the PlayerFrame addition

Even with the graphics file, the addon still doesn't look like much, but you're going to add a few more widgets to the frame: a FontString, a StatusBar, and a background texture. You'll examine some of the highlights of the code in a moment but, first, here's the code to insert in the Initialize() function:

```
local xpText = frame:CreateFontString(nil, "OVERLAY",
"GameFontNormalSmall")
  xpText:SetPoint("CENTER", border, "CENTER", 0, 30)
  xpText:SetTextColor(.9, .7, 1)
  xpText:SetText("PlaceHolder")
  frame.xpText = xpText -- Save for future reference

  local xpBar = CreateFrame("StatusBar", nil, frame, "TextStatusBar")
  xpBar:SetWidth(218)
  xpBar:SetHeight(12)
  xpBar:SetPoint("TOPLEFT", border, "TOPLEFT", 12, -28)
  xpBar:SetStatusBarTexture[[Interface\TargetingFrame\UI-StatusBar]]
  xpBar:SetStatusBarColor(.5, 0, .75, 1)
  xpBar:SetFrameLevel("1")

  frame.xpBar = xpBar -- Save for future reference

  local bg = xpBar:CreateTexture(nil, "BACKGROUND")
```

```
bg:SetTexture(0, 0, 0, .5)
bg:SetWidth(218)
bg:SetHeight(12)
bg:SetPoint("BOTTOM", PlayerFrame, "BOTTOM", 84, 22)
```

Now reload again and you should see a full StatusBar (that's a progress meter) in the bottom row of the wire frame with the word PlaceHolder, as shown in Figure 16-4.

Figure 16-4: The almost complete frame

Reading that segment of code, you should see a general cycle: Create the widget and define its properties. Pay special attention to the lines marked with the comment Save for future reference. These lines are used to save the reference to the PlayerFrame-Plus table so you have access to the widget while the addon runs.

Also of interest is xpBar:SetFrameLevel("1"). That line is part of a layering trick that enables you to do things like have the experience bar appear behind the Player-Frame and FontStrings above other widgets.

Making It Work

Now you have a pretty addition to the frame, but it doesn't do anything. An experience bar that doesn't update when you gain experience is fairly useless, so you need the code that will handle the update of the widget:

```
function PlayerFramePlus:ShowExp()
  local currXP, nextXP = UnitXP("player"), UnitXPMax("player")
  local restXP, percentXP = GetXPExhaustion(), floor(currXP / nextXP * ↵ 100)
  local str

  if restXP then
    str = ("%s / %sxp %s%% (+%s)"):format(currXP, nextXP, percentXP, ↵
restXP/2)
  else
    str = ("%s / %sxp %s%%"):format(currXP, nextXP, percentXP )
  end

  self.frame.xpText:SetText(str)

  self.frame.xpBar:SetMinMaxValues(min(0, currXP), nextXP)
  self.frame.xpBar:SetValue(currXP)
end
```

To make this code functional, you need to listen for more events. Do so by adding the following code after the line that reads `frame:RegisterEvent("PLAYER_ENTERING_WORLD")`:

```
frame:RegisterEvent("PLAYER_XP_UPDATE")
frame:RegisterEvent("PLAYER_LEVEL_UP")
frame:RegisterEvent("UPDATE_EXHAUSTION")
```

Now that your frame is listening for the correct events, you must tell it what to do when those events occur. There is also another problem to fix. Right now, when you load the game it's still going to show `PlaceHolder` and a full status bar until you gain some experience, which obviously is not the behavior you want. Let's change the original `OnEvent` handler to look like the following:

```
frame:SetScript("OnEvent", function()
    if event == "PLAYER_ENTERING_WORLD" then
        PlayerFramePlus:Initialize()
        PlayerFramePlus:ShowExp()
    elseif event == "PLAYER_XP_UPDATE"
     or event == "PLAYER_LEVEL_UP"
     or event == "UPDATE_EXHAUSTION" then
    PlayerFramePlus:ShowExp()
  end
end)
```

After reloading the interface one more time, you should see a fully functional experience bar added to your PlayerFrame. It's simple and minimalistic, but it works.

Comparing Lua Frames to XML Frames

So what's the difference between Lua and XML frame declarations? In this section, you compare and contrast Lua and XML frame declarations — seeing the two side by side, as it were. You'll see the analysis of the two in a moment but, first, look at this code from the addon you just created:

```
    local frame = self.frame

    --Create the graphical outline out of the image file
    local border = frame:CreateTexture(nil, "OVERLAY")
    border:SetHeight(128)
    border:SetWidth(256)
    border:SetPoint("TOPLEFT", PlayerFrame, "TOPLEFT", 77, -37)

  border:SetTexture[[Interface\AddOns\PlayerFramePlus\PlayerFramePlus]]

    local xpText = frame:CreateFontString(nil, "OVERLAY", ↵
"GameFontNormalSmall")
    xpText:SetPoint("CENTER", border, "CENTER", 0, 30)
```

```
xpText:SetTextColor(.9, .7, 1)
xpText:SetText("PlaceHolder")

frame.xpText = xpText -- Save for future reference

local xpBar = CreateFrame("StatusBar", nil, frame, "TextStatusBar")
xpBar:SetWidth(218)
xpBar:SetHeight(12)
xpBar:SetPoint("TOPLEFT", border, "TOPLEFT", 12, -28)
xpBar:SetStatusBarTexture[[Interface\TargetingFrame\UI-StatusBar]]
xpBar:SetStatusBarColor(.5, 0, .75, 1)
xpBar:SetFrameLevel("1")

frame.xpBar = xpBar -- Save for future reference

local bg = xpBar:CreateTexture(nil, "BACKGROUND")
bg:SetTexture(0, 0, 0, .5)
bg:SetWidth(218)
bg:SetHeight(12)
bg:SetPoint("BOTTOM", PlayerFrame, "BOTTOM", 84, 22)
```

The following is a listing of the equivalent XML:

```
<Ui xmlns="http://www.blizzard.com/wow/ui/" xmlns:xsi=↵
"http://www.w3.org/2001/XMLSchema-instance" xsi:schemaLocation=↵
"http://www.blizzard.com/wow/ui/FrameXML/UI.xsd">
  <Frame name="PlayerFramePlus" parent="PlayerFrame">
    <Layers>
    <Layer level="OVERLAY">
      <Texture name="PlayerFramePlusBorder"
      file="Interface\AddOns\PlayerFramePlus\PlayerFramePlus">
        <Size>
          <AbsDimension x="256" y="128"/>
        </Size>
        <Anchors>
          <Anchor point="TOPLEFT" relativeTo="PlayerFrame"
          relativePoint="TOPLEFT">
            <Offset>
              <AbsDimension x="77" y="-37"/>
            </Offset>
          </Anchor>
        </Anchors>
      </Texture>
      <FontString name="$parentExpString"
inherits="GameFontNormalSmall">
        <Size>
          <AbsDimension x="204" y="12"/>
        </Size>
        <Anchors>
          <Anchor point="CENTER" relativeTo="PlayerFramePlusBorder"
            relativePoint="CENTER">
```

```
        <Offset>
          <AbsDimension x="0" y="30"/>
          </Offset>
        </Anchor>
      </Anchors>
      <Color r="0.90" g="0.70" b="1.0"/>
    </FontString>
  </Layer>
</Layers>
<Frames>
  <StatusBar name="$parentExpBar" inherits="TextStatusBar">
    <Size>
      <AbsDimension x="218" y="12"/>
    </Size>
    <Anchors>
      <Anchor point="TOPLEFT" relativeTo="PlayerFramePlusBorder"
relativePoint="TOPLEFT">
        <Offset>
          <AbsDimension x="12" y="-28"/>
        </Offset>
      </Anchor>
    </Anchors>
    <Layers>
      <Layer level="BACKGROUND">
        <Texture>
          <Size>
            <AbsDimension x="214" y="12"/>
          </Size>
          <Anchors>
            <Anchor point="BOTTOM" relativeTo="PlayerFrame">
            <Offset>
                <AbsDimension x="84" y="22"/>
            </Offset>
            </Anchor>
          </Anchors>
          <Color r="0" g="0" b="0" a="0.5"/>
        </Texture>
      </Layer>
    </Layers>
    <BarTexture file="Interface\TargetingFrame\UI-StatusBar"/>
    <BarColor r="0.5" g="0.0" b="0.75"/>
    <Scripts>
      <OnLoad>
        this:SetFrameLevel("1")
      </OnLoad>
    </Scripts>
  </StatusBar>
  </Frames>
</Frame>
</Ui>
```

The first and most notable difference is the length. The Lua frame code is less than 30 lines including whitespace and comments; the XML is more than 70 lines long. A subjective but popular statement is that the Lua is more readable and less clunky; however, the opposite has also been said. When it comes down to it, it's pretty much a draw.

Summary

In this chapter you explored the basics of creating completely Lua-based addons and frames. You then wrote a complete addon to display an experience bar below your PlayerFrame. While the complete widget API is extensive, you at least have a basic familiarity that will let you dig in a little bit more.

# CHAPTER 17

Taking Action with Secure Templates

Matthew Orlando

World of Warcraft players can engage in an enormous variety of activities. However, few can argue that the central aspect of gameplay is combat. With this importance comes no shortage of sensitivity. The designers have spent, and continue to spend, countless hours adjusting and fine-tuning every aspect of combat. To protect this balance from abuse, only *secure code* — the UI code that is built into the game — is allowed to directly cast spells, use items, or select targets. This allows Blizzard direct control over how the player engages in combat.

Thankfully, they recognize the value that addons bring to the table and have created specific mechanisms for us to affect combat. This chapter introduces *secure templates*. These are XML templates you can inherit that have pre-defined, but configurable behaviors. By picking the right template and setting its various attributes, you can write addons to replace the action bars or unit frames, to add click casting to the default UI, or to provide more specialized functionality, such as a button to cast buffs requested by party members (outside of combat).

Understanding Taint

WoW uses a system of *taint* to differentiate addon code from secure code. Any Lua code that runs from an addon or macro is considered tainted. If tainted code attempts to use a protected function (one whose use is only allowed to built-in code) it generates an error. Using `CastSpellByName` in WowLua, for instance, produces the error shown in Figure 17-1.

Figure 17-1: Protected function error

Notice that the message references WowLua. When WoW loads a Lua file, every value created by the addon (functions and other globals) is marked as such. In this case, the code in WowLua that executes your commands is known to be tainted. When it tries to access `CastSpellByName`, the WoW game code refuses to comply. Instead, it throws an error with the name of the addon that caused the taint.

NOTE The `CastSpellByName` **function itself is not blocked for tainted code. Rather, it is the actual casting of spells that is blocked. For example, if you try to cast a spell that you do not have,** `CastSpellByName` **will fail silently. Additionally, you can safely use** `CastSpellByName` **to cast trade skills.**

Enabling Taint Logging

It can be quite important, depending on the nature of your addon, to understand how taint propagates through the UI environment. Sometimes, the way it spreads can appear mysterious because of the various and complex interactions of different parts of the UI code (addons, macros, and built-in code). First, run the following command to turn on taint logging:

```
/console taintLog 1
```

The taint log shows you a timeline of when taint occurs and how the taint blocks an action. Level 1 only shows taint events if they lead up to a blocked action. Level 2 records every single occurrence of taint including those that are completely innocuous (and indeed inevitable). To turn off taint logging, pass it a zero (0). The following is an example taint log attempting to run `CastSpellByName`.

```
11/20 09:17:09.218  An action was blocked because of taint from ↵
WowLua - CastSpellByName()
11/20 09:17:09.218      CastSpellByName("Attack"):1
11/20 09:17:09.218      pcall()
11/20 09:17:09.218      Interface\AddOns\WowLua\WowLua.lua:277 ↵
ProcessLine()
11/20 09:17:09.218      Interface\AddOns\WowLua\WowLua.lua:147
```

The first line shows the actual event, the call to `CastSpellByName` that generated the error message shown in Figure 17-1. The other indented lines show a stack trace leading up to the event to help you track down the source of any problems. Upcoming sections take a closer look at some other taint logs.

Taint logs are saved as `taint.log` in the `Logs` folder of your WoW installation. Like chat logs, they are only written to disk when the game exits or the UI is reloaded. To see the taint log for your current session, you must manually reload the UI. Be sure to open up the file quickly, as WoW sometimes likes to empty it during gameplay.

Execution Taint

There are two ways to spread taint. One is temporary and only exists when a particular chain of code is executing. The other is more persistent and the cause of many headaches. The first is what you experienced in the preceding example. The taint travels up the call stack from one function to another. For example, enter the following command in the chat box (not WowLua):

```
/run WowLua:ProcessLine("CastSpellByName('Attack')")
```

WowLua works by reading each line of text you enter and then running it as Lua code. With the preceding command, you are manually calling the function that does this, telling it to attempt to cast the `Attack` spell. The important point to note is that the game blames WowLua for the infraction, not the macro command. Figure 17-2 illustrates the taint path and the state of the blame.

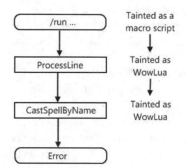

Figure 17-2: Execution taint path

The taint begins when the macro processes the `/run` command (remember that macros fall under the same restrictions as addons). At this point, the taint is attributed to the macro command. If you were to call `CastSpellByName` directly, the error would mention "A macro script." Instead, you call `WowLua:ProcessLine`, which now receives blame for the taint. The function executes the code sent, which in turn tries to call `CastSpellByName`. You can also follow this path through the taint log.

```
11/20 08:40:29.301  An action was blocked because of taint from ↵
WowLua - CastSpellByName()
11/20 08:40:29.301      CastSpellByName('Attack'):1
```

```
11/20 08:40:29.301        pcall()
11/20 08:40:29.301        Interface\AddOns\WowLua\WowLua.lua:277 ↵
ProcessLine()
11/20 08:40:29.301
WowLua:ProcessLine("CastSpellByName('Attack')"):1
11/20 08:40:29.301        RunScript()
11/20 08:40:29.301        Interface\FrameXML\ChatFrame.lua:1768 value()
11/20 08:40:29.301        Interface\FrameXML\ChatFrame.lua:3108 ↵
ChatEdit_ParseText()
11/20 08:40:29.301        Interface\FrameXML\ChatFrame.lua:2800 ↵
ChatEdit_SendText()
11/20 08:40:29.301        Interface\FrameXML\ChatFrame.lua:2821 ↵
ChatEdit_OnEnterPressed()
11/20 08:40:29.301        ChatFrameEditBox:OnEnterPressed()
```

Working from bottom to top, it starts by pressing Enter in the chat box. Next, it works its way up to RunScript(), which applies the first taint in the sequence, blaming it on "A macro script." The macro script then calls WowLua:ProcessLine, which receives blame for the taint.

Execution taint is transient because none of the functions involved are permanently affected in any way. The default UI uses CastSpellByName for certain cases of spell casting. Even after erroneously calling, as shown here, WoW still behaves correctly. The taint itself goes away as soon as the original /run command finishes.

Variable Taint

Less forgiving than execution taint, variable taint can permanently (for the session) affect certain aspects of the built-in code. Variable taint is not really an opposite of execution taint; they both play off of each other, and even overlap in some ways. Any tainted execution path has the potential to cause variable taint.

Recall from Part I the ideas of values and references. World of Warcraft has modified its Lua engine to store a taint flag with every value in the Lua environment that identifies the addon that caused the taint. This is how the preceding example determined the blame. Variable taint is caused when a tainted code path creates a new value or reference. Any time your code makes a new global variable, function, table, and so on, that new value is now tainted. Where you begin to run into trouble is when you start modifying variables used by the default UI. Here's an example in action. Type the following line into WowLua:

```
> NUM_ACTIONBAR_BUTTONS = NUM_ACTIONBAR_BUTTONS
```

Now try to use any ability on your action bar and you will see the same error as shown in Figure 17-1. The function ActionButton_CalculateAction in FrameXML\ActionButton.lua uses this variable to determine which action slot to activate when you press the button. As soon as the code accesses the tainted value, the execution path becomes infected with execution taint. This causes an error when the code attempts to run the UseAction function. The only way to "cure" this condition is to reload the UI.

NOTE The error will probably not appear if you are using a custom bar mod. The default UI's action buttons calculate which action slot to use based on NUM_ACTIONBAR_BUTTONS, **the button's ID (set via the** id **XML attribute) and some other pieces of data. Addons' action buttons usually do not use IDs, so** ActionButton_CalculateAction **never runs into the tainted value.**

NUM_ACTIONBAR_BUTTONS could be set to some number directly, but it is important to realize that the taint is caused simply by the act of assignment itself. The fact that the value came from a secure variable does not exempt you from taint.

Another chart is helpful to picture the interactions. Figure 17-3 shows the series of events that occurs when you press the action button after tainting NUM_ACTIONBAR_BUTTONS. Again, note that it's the simple action of reading the tainted variable that causes the execution path to be tainted.

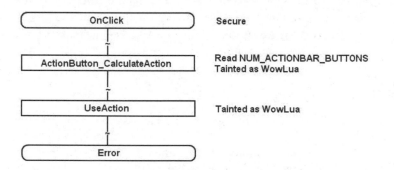

Figure 17-3: Code path tainted by a modified variable

Take a look at the resulting taint log:

```
11/20 08:38:36.801  Global variable NUM_ACTIONBAR_BUTTONS tainted ↵
by WowLua - NUM_ACTIONBAR_BUTTONS = NUM_ACTIONBAR_BUTTONS:1
11/20 08:38:36.801      pcall()
11/20 08:38:36.801          Interface\AddOns\WowLua\WowLua.lua:277 ↵
ProcessLine()
11/20 08:38:36.801          Interface\AddOns\WowLua\WowLua.lua:147
11/20 08:38:36.801  Execution tainted by WowLua while reading ↵
NUM_ACTIONBAR_BUTTONS - Interface\FrameXML\ActionButton.lua:133 ↵
ActionButton_CalculateAction()
11/20 08:38:36.801          Interface\FrameXML\SecureTemplates.lua:261 ↵
SecureActionButton_OnClick()
11/20 08:38:36.801          BonusActionButton6:OnClick()
11/20 08:38:36.801  An action was blocked because of taint from ↵
WowLua - UseAction()
11/20 08:38:36.801          Interface\FrameXML\SecureTemplates.lua:266 ↵
SecureActionButton_OnClick()
11/20 08:38:36.801          BonusActionButton6:OnClick()
```

The first "Global variable tainted" event shows the taint being applied to NUM_ACTIONBAR_BUTTONS. The next "Execution tainted" event, which was originally triggered by the button's OnClick handler, occurs during ActionButton_CalculateAction, as anticipated. Finally, UseAction is blocked from executing because the code path was tainted.

> **NOTE** This particular taint log illustrates a particular distinction between taint log levels 1 and 2. Notice that all three events share the same time stamp. At level 1, WoW waits until taint actually causes a blocked action before reporting it. When the action blocked message is generated, WoW goes back through its taint history and retrieves the first two events, and all three events are then output to the log. If you were to click the action button a second time, all three events would be logged again, even though the first one happened some time ago.

On the other hand, level 2 records each event exactly as it happens. Every global variable set by an addon generates a tainted message. Every time Blizzard code reads an insecure variable, it generates an execution tainted message. This makes level 2 extremely verbose, but it can also be more telling for a given issue.

Creeping Taint

One of the problems you may come across when dealing with taint issues is the gradual spreading of variable taint. Say you have a tainted variable used by the default UI (such as the earlier NUM_ACTIONBAR_BUTTONS example). As explained, as soon as the built-in code accesses this variable, it becomes tainted. Well, what happens when the tainted execution path then modifies some other variable? That variable is now afflicted with the same taint that is affecting the current execution path.

This process can happen repeatedly, often unnoticed, with each new tainted variable potentially causing even more taint. In this way, your addon can taint entire subsystems of the UI without modifying more than a single variable. Not only can it spread far and wide, but the speed of the spreading can be misleading. Some code in the default UI runs based on events that are not exactly frequent. One piece of misplaced taint may not cause any problems until you join a raid group or travel to another continent, for example.

These situations are where the taint logs can really shine. When you receive an action blocked message during development, simply turn on taint logging and you can track down the problems. Level 2 is especially helpful in a case like this, as it allows you to see exactly when each variable becomes tainted.

Understanding Protected Frames

Addons are not supposed to be able to make sensitive combat decisions. The taint mechanism prevents you from programmatically taking any action deemed inappropriate by the designers. Taint alone, however, still cannot protect against all abuse.

Consider the `ActionBarButtonTemplate` mentioned in the exercise for Chapter 14. Imagine creating one button for every capability of yours in the same spot on the screen. During combat, your addon selectively shows one button at a time, making it possible to repeatedly click the stack of buttons and have the addon choose every spell for you based on changing combat conditions.

As you have probably guessed, this is not possible to do, and *protected frames* are the reason why. Like protected functions, protected frames restrict the actions addons are allowed to take by disallowing tainted code to execute certain frame methods. Unlike protected functions, these restrictions only apply during combat. When a frame action is blocked it does not produce an error message like a blocked spell cast. Instead, the action will fail silently save for a meek announcement in your chat window that an "Interface action failed because of an addon." Here is a list of all protected methods:

AllowAttributeChanges	Lower	SetHorizontalScroll
ClearAllPoints	Raise	SetParent
Disable	SetAllPoints	SetPoint
Enable	SetAttribute	SetScale
EnableKeyboard	SetFrameLevel	SetToplevel
EnableMouse	SetFrameStrata	SetVerticalScroll
EnableMouseWheel	SetHeight	SetWidth
Hide	SetHitRectInsets	Show

You should probably be able to identify a pattern in these functions. The protection prevents you from making changes to a frame that could modify its "clickability." This stops our sneaky idea dead in its tracks.

One issue to recognize is that many of these methods can indirectly affect protected frames. For instance, if you have a nonprotected frame with protected children, you will not be able to use protected methods on the parent. In fact, the methods related to `ScrollFrame`s operate entirely indirectly. If any of the frames in the `ScrollChild` are protected, you will not be able to programmatically modify the scroll position.

The protection itself is accomplished by defining an XML template with the `protected` attribute set to `true`. This feature is not exactly useful for our own purposes; the true power comes to us indirectly via secure templates.

Setting Frame Properties without Taint

`SetAttribute` provides you with a taint-free way to set an arbitrary value associated with a frame. As previously indicated, you cannot call `SetAttribute` on a protected frame during combat. Its usage is fairly simple:

```
frame:SetAttribute("name", value)
```

The *value* argument can be any Lua value, but *name* must be a string. You can retrieve the value of an attribute with the `GetAttribute` method, like this:

```
frame:GetAttribute("name")
```

> **WARNING** The choice of the word "attribute" is rather unfortunate.
> Attribute is the term in XML lingo that describes the properties given to an
> element within the element's start tag (for example, `name="$parentButton"`,
> `inherits="UIPanelButtonTemplate"`, and so on). The attributes referred to in
> this chapter, however, are completely unrelated. In a sense, they function like
> member variables of the frames but, as discussed, they are free from taint.

> **NOTE** The name parameter of both `SetAttribute` and `GetAttribute` is *not*
> case sensitive. `B1` and `b1` refer to the same attribute.

Using Secure Templates

With all the time spent telling you how WoW prevents you from doing things, you are
probably craving something a bit more encouraging. You had a small glimpse of secure
templates in action with the `ActionBarButtonTemplate`, but now you get to see exactly
what is going on under the hood.

`FrameXML\SecureTemplates.xml` defines several templates to use for your addons.
The focus in this chapter is `SecureActionButtonTemplate`. The XML for this template is
surprisingly simple. All it defines is an `OnClick` script that calls `SecureActionButton_`
`OnClick`. The trick here is that because the scripts are defined in secure code, as long as
you do not modify them in any way, they have free reign with protected functions. A
secure script remains secure when you inherit it.

Defining Behaviors for Action Buttons

Earlier, you saw that attributes — in the `SetAttribute` sense — are used to control the
secure templates. At first glance, this is accomplished very easily. However, it is decep-
tively powerful.

To test some of these new techniques, create a simple addon that puts a single button on the screen. Use a basic button style to emphasize the fact that secure action
buttons define nothing more than the click behavior. This keeps the XML nice and
simple so you can concentrate on the functional bits:

```
<Button name="SABTest" inherits="SecureActionButtonTemplate, ↵
UIPanelButtonTemplate2">
  <Anchors>
    <Anchor point="CENTER"/>
  </Anchors>
  <Attributes>
    <Attribute name="type" value="spell"/>
  </Attributes>
</Button>
```

The unfamiliar part is the `<Attributes>` element and its `<Attribute>` child. These comprise the XML counterpart to the `SetAttribute` method; the `name` and `value` attributes correspond directly to the `name` and `value` parameters described earlier. In this case, you are defining a single attribute, called `"type"`, with the value of `"spell"`. This tells the `SecureActionButtonTemplate`'s `OnClick` handler to treat this button as a spell-casting button.

> **NOTE** There is a third possible XML attribute for the `<Attribute>` tag called `type` (apologies for any confusion). This tells WoW how to interpret the `value` attribute by specifying a Lua type. The default is `string`, which is perfect for the purposes in this section. Other possible values are `nil`, `boolean`, and `number`. The rest of the Lua types would not make sense inside an XML attribute.

Casting a Spell

Load up WoW with your new addon. You now have a button in the middle of your screen that does absolutely nothing. To make it cast something, you must give it a spell. Open the WowLua window and enter the following command:

```
> SABTest:SetAttribute("spell", "Spell Name")
```

Replace *Spell Name* with a spell you are able to easily test. Be sure to type the name exactly as it appears in the tooltip, including all spaces and punctuation. Once you run this command, clicking the button will cast the spell you chose.

You could have simply added another `<Attribute>` tag to the XML file. However, most addons that use secure action buttons create them dynamically from templates or, at the very least, modify them on demand depending on user settings. As you will soon see, there are many different attributes and ways to use them, so it is a good idea to become comfortable manipulating them in Lua.

If you have a character that can cast beneficial spells (healing, cleansing, or buffing), take a look at one more example before digging around in the meat of the secure action buttons. First, run the preceding command with the name of the beneficial spell. Verify that you are able to cast it on a friendly target (you may want to pick an NPC so you know it won't be going anywhere). Now run the following command:

```
> SABTest:SetAttribute("unit", "player")
```

Now, whenever you click the button it will cast the spell directly on you no matter who you are targeting. This illustrates just one of the many ways multiple attributes on the same frame can interact to bring varied results.

Looking Under the Hood

So what is actually going on when you click the button? Open up `FrameXML\SecureTemplates.lua` and scroll down to `SecureActionButton_OnClick`. Some of the front matter in this function prepares for more advanced features that are covered later in this and other chapters. The most important steps right now are as follows:

1. The `"type"` attribute is checked to determine which type of action to take. In this case, your button is using a `"spell"` type.

2. The `"spell"` attribute is retrieved and `CastSpellByName` is called with the spell name and unit.

This is where the nature of protected frames, protected functions, taint, and attributes finally come together. Only secure code is allowed to call `CastSpellByName`. `SecureActionButton_OnClick` is secure and it gets its instructions from taint-free attributes. The only way to take advantage of `SecureActionButton_OnClick` is by inheriting a secure, protected template, `SecureActionButtonTemplate`. Because the frame is protected, your addon can only call `SetAttribute` outside of combat. In this way, Blizzard can precisely control when and how the player is allowed to activate abilities with addons.

Specifying Units to Affect

Many templates can act on units in various ways. For example, quite a few types of `SecureActionButtons` do their actions on the specified unit. You can control the unit directly via the `"unit"` attribute, as you will see shortly.

Alternatively, if you use a `"unitsuffix"` attribute, its value will be appended to the `"unit"` attribute of the button's parent. The unit suffix can be in either of the following forms (items in brackets [ ] are optional):

```
pet[target][target]...
target[target]...
```

For example, if the parent's `unit` is `"raid5"` and the button's `"unitsuffix"` is `"targettarget"`, the button will use `"raid5targettarget"` as its unit.

You can also make the button respond to your self-cast modifier by setting its `"checkselfcast"` attribute to a true value.

Other Types and Their Uses

If you were following along in the source code during the previous section, you undoubtedly noticed the wide range of `"type"` attributes the `OnClick` handler recognizes. Each type defines its own set of subordinate attributes that control the button's behavior. In the preceding case, the `"spell"` type buttons use a `"spell"` attribute to determine which spell to cast. Similarly, `"action"` type buttons use an `"action"` attribute to use an action slot. Following is a comprehensive list of types and their uses. This list follows the same order as the FrameXML code. Types marked with a U respond to the unit attribute, if present.

> **actionbar** — Used to manipulate your action bar page. Subordinate attribute:
> **action** — Describes how to change the action bar page. A single number means change directly to that page. A string with two numbers separated by a comma (for example, `"1, 2"`) will swap between the two given pages. It

will switch directly to the first number if you are on a page other than the two given. Finally, you can use either `"increment"` or `"decrement"` to go up one page or down one page, respectively. They will both wrap to the other end if you go too far.

action (U) — Activates an action slot. Subordinate attribute:

action (optional) — The action slot number to use. If you omit this attribute, the action will be determined by the button's ID in the same manner as the default UI. In other words, if you have a button with an ID of 1, the actual action used would depend on your stance, action bar page, and so on, just like the first button on the main action bar. See `UseAction` (API) for more information.

pet (U) — Uses one of your pet's abilities. Subordinate attribute:

action — The pet action index of the ability you wish to use. See `CastPetAction` (API) for more information.

spell (U) — Casts the named spell. Subordinate attribute:

spell — The name of the spell to cast. See `CastSpellByName` (API) for more information.

item (U) — Uses the given item. Subordinate attributes (we are intentionally omitting two deprecated attributes you may notice in the FrameXML code):

item — Specifies the item to use. This attribute can take a number of forms depending on how you want to access the item:

- `"Name of Item"` — By name.
- `"item:12345"` — By item ID.
- `"13"` — By inventory slot number for equipped items.
- `"3 12"` — By bag and slot number for items in your bags.

macro — Run a macro. Subordinate attributes:

macro — The macro to run. This can be the numerical index or the name of a macro to run.

macrotext — The text of a macro. Set this to a Lua string containing the macro you want to run. This text is *not* limited to 255 characters. A `"macro"` attribute will override a `"macrotext"` one.

stop — Cancels the target selection cursor (glowing blue hand). No subordinate attributes are used.

target (U) — Target a particular unit.

focus (U) — Focus on the given unit.

assist (U) — Assist the specified unit.

maintank (U) — Set the main tank to the unit.

mainassist (U) — Set the main assist to the unit

click — Securely simulate a click on another button. Subordinate attribute:

clickbutton — The button to click. This must be a direct reference, not the name of the button.

function — If specified, the button will call `self:function(unit, click)`.

If an action targets an item instead of a unit — using a poison, for example — you can use the following attributes to specify what item to target:

- `target-slot` — An inventory slot number by itself, or a bag slot number along with `target-bag`.

- `target-bag` — Specifies a bag number (0-4, right to left on the default bag bar). You must also include a `target-slot` attribute.
- `target-item` — The name of the item.

Take a look at a few simple examples with the SABTest addon before moving on to something a bit more substantial. One of the most common requests on the World of Warcraft UI & Macros forum is for a way to cast a spell or use an item directly on the player without changing targets. Both of the following examples will accomplish this using bandages, but with two different approaches.

Using an "item" Type Button

With the testing addon from earlier loaded, run the following commands in WowLua to set up the new behavior on your button. You will want to log into a character that has a couple bandages to spare for testing to see the full effect. Wherever you see *Heavy Netherweave Bandage* in the following code samples, rename it to whatever bandages you have available.

```
> SABTest:SetAttribute("type", "item")
> SABTest:SetAttribute("item", "Heavy Netherweave Bandage")
> SABTest:SetAttribute("unit", "player")
```

The first line tells the button to use an item when it's clicked. The second specifies the bandages you want to use. Finally, the `"unit"` attribute tells the button to use the item on the player. If your bandages were in the first slot of your backpack, you could use an `"item"` attribute of `"0 1"` instead of the name of the bandage, and it would always use whatever was in that slot.

Because bandages can only be used when you're missing some health, you'll want to head out into the wilderness and pick a fight with some easy mob. There are plenty of other creative ways to reduce your health percentage (like un-equipping and re-equipping a piece of stamina gear). Whenever you feel like bandaging yourself, click the SABTest button and enjoy.

Using an Item With a "macro" Type Button

If you have spent any time in the UI customization community before diving into addon programming, you should be at least marginally familiar with macros. One very simple example is a self-use macro. On an action button this macro will behave exactly like the SABTest example from the preceding section.

```
/use [target=player] Heavy Netherweave Bandage
```

Attaching this macro to the SABTest button is fairly straightforward:

```
> SABTest:SetAttribute("type", "macro")
> SABTest:SetAttribute("macrotext", ↵
"/use [target=player] Heavy Netherweave Bandage")
```

Notice that even if you still have the `"unit"` attribute from the previous self-bandage configuration, it will be completely ignored. `"macro"` type action buttons leave that sort of decision entirely up to the macro itself.

NOTE A thorough treatment of the macro system is beyond the scope of this book. However, you can find further information in several places. Blizzard recently began work on an official macro guide. As of this writing, it is still in its early stages, although it does look promising: `http://worldofwarcraft.com/info/basics/macroguide-one.html`

This chapter's author (Orlando) currently maintains Cogwheel's Complete Macro Guide on the World of Warcraft UI & Macros forum. The guide has detailed descriptions of all the common (and many obscure) slash commands and macro options:

`http://forums.worldofwarcraft.com/thread.html?topicId=3881820910`

Finally, *Hacking World of Warcraft* (Wiley, 2007) has a comprehensive — if slightly outdated — chapter on creating macros, written by James Whitehead, one of this book's authors.

Making Simple Choices

Being able to perform combat actions is great, but what has been shown so far is not very flexible. Sure, you can configure a button any way you want — while you're out of combat. And there's the real trick: to make an addon behave even like the default UI, you have to be able to make certain changes *during combat*. A bar mod needs to be able to change pages when you switch forms. A "totem stomper" needs to flip to the next totem in the sequence. Unit frames that you can actually click to target need a way to show and hide themselves.

While you won't see the full gamut of options right away, you will see the two most fundamental: modifier keys and mouse buttons. The keyboard and mouse are the only ways of controlling your characters' actions, and there are some simple ways to exploit their features. (For the pedants among you, voice commands, joysticks, game controllers, and the like merely emulate keyboard or mouse input to interact with WoW.)

As an added bonus, you'll see how to react to a well-known state: the hostility of your target. This will serve as a bridge piece to the *state headers* discussed in Chapter 25.

Deconstructing a Modified Attribute

Shrinking the space their UI occupies and increasing the view of their game world — known as minimalism — is the primary focus of many addon users. Multipurpose buttons provide a great way of reducing the UI's footprint. One of the simplest ways to control which action to take is by holding down a *modifier key*. Click the button normally, cast one spell. Click it while holding down the SHIFT key, cast a different one. Perhaps CTRL-clicking could cause the button to target your 2v2 team member. Alternatively (or additionally), you may want to choose a different action based on which mouse button you clicked.

Choosing an Action by Modifier Key

Behaviors like these can be created by adding modifiers to the various attributes used by the button. For example, choosing a spell based on the SHIFT key might look like the following.

```
> SABTest:SetAttribute("type", "spell")
> SABTest:SetAttribute("shift-spell*", "Power Word: Fortitude")
> SABTest:SetAttribute("spell", "Shadow Word: Pain")
```

The most important bit is the second attribute, `shift-spell*`. There are three components to modified attributes:

1. The *prefix* determines which modifier keys to check. In this example, you specify the SHIFT key with a prefix of `shift-`.

2. The *root*, or name, is the actual basis of the attribute — the object that the prefix and suffix modify. The root of the preceding attribute is `spell`.

3. Finally, there's the *suffix*, which establishes the mouse button to look for. The preceding example uses an asterisk (*)as a wildcard. This means that as long as you hold SHIFT, it doesn't matter which mouse button you use; it will always cast `Power Word: Fortitude`.

Modifiers can be used on most attributes in the secure template system, including all of the ones shown so far. They are the basis of the more advanced decision-making features you will see in later in the book. The core of the modified attribute system is the aptly named function, `SecureButton_GetModifiedAttribute`. This function looks for several variations of attributes based on your modifier keys, the root attribute, and the mouse button used to click the button. For example, if you right-click the `SABTest` button while holding your Ctrl and Alt keys, it will check for the following `"spell"` attributes in order:

1. `alt-ctrl-spell2`

2. `*spell2`

3. `alt-ctrl-spell*`

4. `*spell*`

5. `spell`

The only match it will find is the `"spell"` attribute, so it returns the spell `"Shadow Word: Pain"`. If, instead, you are holding Shift and no other modifier keys, `SecureButton_GetModifiedAttribute` will find a match with `"shift-spell*"` (the third step of the list).

NOTE The order of the elements in the prefix is always the same, regardless of which are included: `"alt-ctrl-shift-"`. For example, `"alt-shift-"` would be recognized, but `"shift-alt-"` would not.

You can also map modifier keys to arbitrary names by using a `"modifiers"` attribute on the button. This attribute uses the following format, with items in brackets (`[ ]`) being optional:

```
MODIFIER[:name][,MODIFIER[:name]]...
```

`MODIFIER` can be a normal modifier (`ALT`, `CTRL`, or `SHIFT`) or a modifier variable, such as `SELFCAST`. See `IsModifiedClick` (API) for details. If no `name` is specified, the lower-case version of the modifier will be returned. For example:

```
SPLITSTACK:split,ALT
```

This value will give a prefix of `"split-"` if you are holding down the stack-splitting modifier or `"alt-"` if you are holding the Alt key.

Choosing an Action by Mouse Button

You have most likely guessed that to pick a spell based on a mouse button you need to specify a suffix. The most basic suffixes are the numbers 1 to 5, which indicate mouse buttons:

1. Left button
2. Right button
3. Middle button
4. Button 4
5. Button 5

Expanding on the previous example, run the following command to add a right-click behavior to the button:

```
> SABTest:SetAttribute("*spell2", "Power Word: Fortitude")
```

Now when you click it with the right mouse button, regardless of any modifier keys, it will cast Power Word: Fortitude.

> **WARNING** The prefix/suffix system is a bit stricter than you might first assume. The five attribute variations mentioned earlier create some specific situations worth noting. For example, while you can use `"spell"` as a last resort fallback, `"spell2"` will only match if you're not holding any modifier keys. This is why the wildcard was used in the most recent example.

Note, as well, that the prefixes it checks will always include all the modifier keys you're holding down. There is no way to mix a wildcard in a prefix like `"*shift-spell2"` to allow shift in combination with any other modifier. To achieve the desired result, you must use multiple attributes: `"shift-spell2"`, `"alt-shift-spell2"`, `"ctrl-shift-spell2"` and `"alt-ctrl-shift-spell2"`.

Delegating Attribute Responsibility

You will often have a number of secure action buttons that are closely related, perhaps an action bar. To make it easier to apply configurations to multiple buttons, modified attributes provide a `"useparent"` facility to delegate an attribute to the button's parent. If `SecureButton_GetModifiedAttribute` does not find a match with one of the five variations, it will check for a `"useparent-root"` or `"useparent*"` attribute. If it finds one, it will then get the modified attribute from the parent.

For example, the default UI's action buttons have a `"useparent-unit"` attribute. With one simple setting, you can make all of the buttons on the main bar cast normally with a left click, or always on yourself with a right click.

```
> MainMenuBarArtFrame:SetAttribute("*unit2", "player")
```

Choosing an Action by Hostility

The last concept presented before moving on to something more concrete is a way to customize the "mouse button" that is checked against the suffix. That phrase is in quotes because from here on out the physical mouse button plays much less of a role in the suffix of modified attributes.

Two new attributes allow you to change the nature of the button based on the nature of the specified unit: `"helpbutton"`, meaning you can cast beneficial spells on the unit, and `"harmbutton"`, meaning you can attack the unit. The value of these attributes is a string that will be used for the suffix in subsequent modified attribute checks. You can continue the previous example with Shadow Word: Pain and Power Word: Shield by making a single button that automatically picks between the two.

```
> SABTest:SetAttribute("unit", "target")
> SABTest:SetAttribute("harmbutton", "swp")
> SABTest:SetAttribute("helpbutton", "pws")
> SABTest:SetAttribute("*spell-swp", "Shadow Word: Pain")
> SABTest:SetAttribute("*spell-pws", "Power Word: Shield")
```

NOTE Some targets can be neither helped nor harmed (neutral NPCs, for instance). In cases like that, the preceding example will do nothing.

WARNING You must explicitly set a `"unit"` attribute; otherwise, `"helpbutton"` and `"harmbutton"` will be ignored.

The easiest way to understand the interactions is to follow the steps of `SecureActionButton_OnClick`. For the first case, assume you have a hostile target.

1. Fetch the `"unit"` attribute.
2. Because the `"unit"` attribute exists, check to see whether you can attack it.

3. Because you can attack the target, check for a `"harmbutton"` attribute.

4. The `"harmbutton"` exists, so now you set the "clicked" button (the new suffix) to the value of `"harmbutton"`: `"swp"`.

5. Re-evaluate the `"unit"` attribute given the new suffix (nothing happens in this case because you don't have any `"unit"` attributes with a suffix of `"-swp"`).

6. Fetch the `"type"` attribute (defined as `"spell"` in the XML).

7. Because the type is `"spell"`, look for a modified `"spell"` attribute using the `"swp"` suffix.

8. Cast Shadow Word: Pain as specified by `"*spell-swp"`.

With a friendly target, follow these steps:

1. Fetch the `"unit"` attribute.

2. Because the `"unit"` attribute exists, check to see whether you can attack it.

3. Because you can't attack the target, check if you can heal it.

4. Because you can heal the target, check for a `"helpbutton"` attribute.

5. The `"helpbutton"` attribute exists, so now set the new suffix to `"pws"`.

6. Re-evaluate `"unit"` (again, nothing happens).

7. Fetch the `"type"` attribute.

8. Look for the modified `"spell"` using the `"pws"` suffix.

9. Cast Power Word: Shield as specified by `"*spell-pws"`.

It is worth noting that `"helpbutton"` and `"harmbutton"` themselves can also be modified. This way you can create different suffixes depending on which actual mouse button was used to click the button.

Giving Life to Your Unit Frame

At this point, all the fundamentals of the secure template system have been covered. Now that you have a grasp of the various interactions among attributes, suffixes, protected frames, and taint, let's put it into practice by making `TargetText` (from Chapter 13) do more than just sit there and look pretty.

Your first order of business is to enable `TargetTextFrame` to take action. You can accomplish this by adding `inherits="SecureActionButtonTemplate"` to the frame's definition. Then you need to clean up some other areas of the code to accommodate the new features.

TIP You could have used `SecureUnitButtonTemplate` instead, but it does not really offer you anything you intend to use. In fact, it sets up some attributes that you will have to discard.

Removing Forbidden Code

TargetText uses an event handler to manually show or hide the frame when you gain or lose a target. Now that the frame is marked as protected, this event handler will fail during combat, resulting in an "Interface action failed" message and a hefty taint log. All you have to do is remove the Show/Hide commands and the else from TargetText:UpdateAll. The resulting function should look like this:

```
function TargetText:UpdateAll()
  if UnitExists("target") then
    self:UpdateName()
    self:UpdateLevel()
    self:UpdateClass()
    self:UpdateReaction()
    self:UpdateFaction()
    self:UpdatePvP()
    self:UpdateHealth()
    self:UpdatePowerType()
    self:UpdateMana()
  end
end
```

Accepting Clicks

Another problem with the current state of TargetText is that it is incapable of receiving clicks. First, make a few more changes to the frame's definition. The <Frame> needs to be changed into a <Button>, and you must remove enableMouse="false". While you're at it, also add hidden="true" because you will not be using the frame until the player acquires a target. The final definition should look like this:

```
<Button name="TargetTextFrame" hidden="true" parent="UIParent" ↵
inherits="SecureActionButtonTemplate">

  ...
</Button>
```

Now that the button is structurally capable of receiving clicks, you must tell it to what clicks it should respond. Adding the following line to the end of TargetText:OnLoad will allow the button to respond to any mouse click:

```
TargetTextFrame:RegisterForClicks("AnyUp")
```

Showing and Hiding the Frame

Now you have a perfectly useless, invisible frame in the middle of your screen. You cannot show or hide it yourself because that would be blocked in combat. However, a function called RegisterUnitWatch will do exactly what you want. It looks for a "unit" attribute on the given frame and shows or hides it depending on whether the unit exists. First, give it a unit. Because the unit is so fundamental to the behavior of `TargetText`, define it in the XML, as follows:

```
<Attributes>
  <Attribute name="unit" value="target"/>
</Attributes>
```

Now you can activate the unit watch by adding the following line to `TargetText:OnLoad`:

```
RegisterUnitWatch(TargetTextFrame)
```

At this point, `TargetText` should act as it did before this chapter, with one exception: Mouse clicks no longer pass through the frame.

Setting up Actions

`TargetTextFrame` is now a functional, secure action button and can do anything the `SABTest` button could. To help get your gears spinning, set the frame up with the following behaviors:

- **Left click** — Cast Greater Heal on a friendly target or Mind Blast on an enemy.
- **Right click** — Focus on your target.
- **Shift+left click** — Cast Renew on a friendly target or Shadow Word: Pain on an enemy.
- **Shift+right click** — Cast Shackle Undead on your focus.

To make the process a bit smoother, a common practice is to create a `SetManyAttributes` function like the following:

```
function TargetText:SetManyAttributes(frame, ...)
  for i = 1, select("#", ...), 2 do
    frame:SetAttribute(select(i, ...), select(i+1, ...))
  end
end
```

Now you can set up the attributes for these behaviors much more cleanly, like the following addition to `TargetText:OnLoad`:

```
self:SetManyAttributes(TargetTextFrame,
  "type", "spell",

  -- Unmodified left click
  "helpbutton1",  "heal",
  "*spell-heal",  "Greater Heal",
  "harmbutton1",  "blast",
  "*spell-blast", "Mind Blast",

  -- Unmodified right click
```

```
        "type2", "focus",

        -- Shift left click
        "shift-helpbutton1", "renew",
        "*spell-renew",      "Renew",
        "shift-harmbutton1", "pain",
        "*spell-pain",       "Shadow Word: Pain",

        -- Shift right click
        "shift-unit2",  "focus",
        "shift-spell2", "Shackle Undead"
    )
```

Feel free to adjust the attributes to your liking and experiment with different configurations.

Summary

This chapter covered a lot of ground. The secure template system uses a wide assortment of specific features — taint, protected functions and frames, attributes, and so on. — to achieve a much larger goal. It needs to protect the game against too much automation and, at the same time, allow addons to alter the way you interact in combat. There is still a lot to cover in upcoming chapters (25 and 26, in particular), but once you understand the basics laid out here, the rest will flow much more freely.

# CHAPTER 18

Creating Slash Commands

Bryan McLemore

World of Warcraft players interact daily with slash commands. Whether it's /friend MaleNightElfFemale7 or a hasty /gquit following your ninja looting Kael'thas after your (now former) guild's first takedown, you're using slash commands.

As an addon author, it's often easier or just plain useful to have slash commands to either spur your addon to action or to enable configuration. Generally speaking, it's much quicker and simpler to write out a quick slash command system than to have a fully functioning graphical configuration screen. It is because of these features and reasons that knowing how to create slash commands and leverage their power is important.

Examining the Basics of Slash Commands

Blizzard provides a fairly straightforward way to implement slash commands. There are two basic components: a set of global variables and a table entry. Here is a quick example:

```
SLASH_MESSAGE1 = "/message"
SlashCmdList["MESSAGE"] = function(msg)
    message(msg)
end
```

Type that into WoWLua and then type **"/message My first slash command"** in the regular chat frame. You should see a message pop up with "My first slash command" in it. Congratulations, you did it. Now take a look at the machinery that made this possible.

The global variables must always be in the same format — SLASH_<VARIABLE><NUMBER>. This format allows for great flexibility. Type **SLASH_MESSAGE2 = "/msg"** in WoWLua and then try using that slash command with **"/msg I created a slash command alias"**. Again you should see a message pop up with those words.

As you just saw, incrementing the number in the global format allows for multiple slash commands to be aliased to the same handler. It's worth noting that omitting the number in the global declaration or the / in the handler name results in nothing happening.

You must also assign a handler for the new slash command you registered. This is done by creating the entry in the global table SlashCmdList. As in the preceding sample, the key for this entry must be the same as the <VARIABLE> portion of the global decoration.

Recapping, here is a list of steps to take when creating a new slash command:

1. Define at least one global variable to define the actual handler.

   ■ Ensure that a number is present in the global variable.

   ■ The string you assign must begin with a /.

2. Create a handler entry in SlashCmdList.

   ■ The key for the entry must match the variable portion of the global you created in Part One.

Tips, Tricks, and Good Ideas

One thing you must remember about slash commands is that anything the user types in after the slash command is passed in as a string to the handler. That has some immediate implications to the flexibility and power of slash commands. You've already seen basic usage of slash commands, but you have a few more advanced tricks that you can leverage in your addons: tokenization, validation, and fake switches.

Tokenizing Input

These principles may sound more complex than they really are. *Tokenization* is the process in which you take one larger string and cut it up into smaller ones — called tokens — based on a separating character called a delimiter or deliminator. You can use a few basic methods to do this. Most straightforward is using string.match. The following example of tokenization assumes that the first word is an identifier of the function to pass off execution to, and that everything else will be passed in as arguments.

```
function handler(str)
    local switch, msg = str:match("([^ ]+) (.*)")
    if switch == "alert" then
        message(msg)
    elseif switch == "chat" then
        ChatFrame1:AddMessage(msg)
    end
end
```

While this example may not be the most applicable as a slash handler, it still demonstrates the potential of tokenization. Another tokenization method uses `string.gmatch`. It works basically the same as regular match except it returns an iterator that you can use to loop over all the tokens. Here's a simple example of this function:

```
str = "this is a simple string"
for part in str:gmatch("([^ ]+)") do
    print(part)
end
```

The code will produce output something like the following:

```
this
is
a
simple
string
```

You can use a similar trick for more complicated execution paths and other esoteric usages, such as averaging a list of ordinals:

```
function handler(str)
    local sum, count = 0, 0
    for n in str:gmatch("([^ ]+)") do
        sum = sum + tonumber(n)
        count = count + 1
    end

    ChatFrame1:AddMessage(("Average value: %d"):format(return sum /
count))
end
```

Using Validation for Pattern Matching

Validation just means that if you expect a number or a string, for instance, you need to make sure that the value you receive matches the expected type. For simple type checking, you can use built-in functions like `tostring` or `tonumber`. They return `nil` if the type does not match. Note, however, that things like `tonumber("5 bags")` return `nil` not 5.

Things get a little trickier if you want to validate nonstandard types. For instance, say you have a command that accepts either `run` or `stay` as string literals. Here's what a function might look like:

```
local state = "stay"
function handler(val)
    state = val
end
```

Looks great, except for one thing — it falls apart if someone types **/yourcommand bobdole**. This can lead to some oddities in the execution of your code that relies on that variable. So, change it to look like the following:

```
local state = "stay"
local errmsg = 'Valid values are either "stay" or "run", you entered %s"
function handler(val)
    if ("stay run"):match( val) then
        state = val
    else        message(errmsg:format(val))

    end
end
```

The same method can be leveraged for more robust pattern matching, like this:

```
local number, type = 0, "flowers"
function handler(val)
    local n, t = val:match("^([0-9]) ([a-zA-Z]+)$")
    if n and t then
        number, type = n, t
    end
end
```

This code grabs two variables from the pattern and makes sure they are the only values presented on the line (by use of anchors). That one line validated the correct number of arguments and their types, and even the fact that only a single digit is allowed for the number. If either had returned `nil`, you could have given a meaningful usage message.

Faking a Switch

You can do a few other things to make your code cleaner (and therefore easier to read and manage). Look at this example:

```
local function handler(val)
    local switch, args = val:match("([^ ]+) (.+)")
    if switch == "run" then
        return doRun(args)
    elseif switch == "stay" then
        return doStay(args)
    elseif switch == "jump" then
        return doJump(args)
    else
        return printUsage(args)
    end
end
```

As you can see, the code can quickly get pretty clunky. If you ever have a lot that you need to do under a single main command, your code will either explode to monumental proportions, or you'll end up not keeping things logically encapsulated. You can use the following method to keep yourself a little more sane:

```
local slashHandlers = {
    run = doRun,
    stay = doStay,
    jump = doJump
}

local function handler(val)
    local switch, args = val:match("([^ ]+) (.+)")
    if slashHandlers[switch] then
        return slashHandlers[switch](args)
    else
        return printUsage(args)
    end
end
```

By using a table to provide a quick lookup for what function to call the code inside handler already looks much better. The number of slash handlers you can add is limitless. It is subjective but, generally, a single line in a table is a lot easier to read than a complicated if then elseif block.

There's another tweak to the table switch method that can clean up your handler function a little bit more. The main advantage of using this method is the default handler is moved closer to the rest of the handler definitions.

```
local slashHandlers = {
    run = doRun,
    stay = doStay,
    jump = doJump
}

local mt = {__index = function() return printUsage end}
setmetatable(slashHandlers, mt)

local function handler(val)
    local switch, args = val:match("([^ ]+) (.+)")
    return slashHandlers[switch](args)
end
```

Using a table to express the handlers like this enables you to add as many options as you'd like to a given slash handler, and all you have to do is add a row to a table. This trick is really just borrowing a principle from other languages that support a switch control structure. Thus, you're really just faking a switch.

Good Ideas

This chapter's shown you methods for doing things programmatically; now explore some of the thoughts involved in doing that well.

No matter how you look at it, when dealing with slash commands, two conventions immediately come to mind as good ideas. First, always clear feedback from your slash commands. A user has no way of knowing he did something wrong if you don't tell him.

An out-of-game documentation of the options you provide in your slash handlers can be helpful. In fact, we believe that if you provide slash commands you should always document their intended functionality in an online and publicly accessible place. However, remember that out-of-game documentation should never replace a solid in-game help system; not every user will refer to a website or a printout to understand what your slash commands should be doing.

The second good idea is consistency. It is absolutely imperative that you enforce some standards on your slash commands. Here is a small list of things to consider:

- Do your responses to the users make sense?
- Do the responses carry a common "feel" across all the messages?
- Can each action be easily reversed or changed again?
- Do the names of the commands make sense?
- Are you using the easiest method to provide this functionality?

If you answer "no" to any of these questions, it's time to revisit your slash commands and make the answer "yes."

Summary

In this chapter you learned the basics of slash commands and how to get a barebones command up and running. You also examined a set of tips and tricks you can use to make your code more flexible and cleaner. Finally, you read some honest advice that can be applied to your slash commands. Slash commands aren't flashy, and in some circles they get a bad wrap, but they're powerful, flexible and, if implemented correctly, elegant.

# CHAPTER 19

Altering Existing Behavior with Function Hooking

James Whitehead II

Many addons are designed as self-contained additions to the default user interface. In these cases, you may trigger code in the default interface, but don't seek to change its functionality. Sometimes, though, it makes sense to alter some existing behavior of the UI. One of the ways you can do this is known as *function hooking*. This chapter introduces you to the concept of function hooking, including specific rules to follow and pitfalls to avoid.

What Is Function Hooking?

"Hooking a function" is mostly just a fancy way of saying "replacing a function." Like any other Lua variable, you can overwrite a function with a new one of your creation. Then, any time some other piece of code calls the function, it will use yours instead. More specifically, though, function hooking means that the original function still runs, at least when a function hook behaves properly.

Function hooking is used to alter the behavior of an existing function by modifying its arguments or return values, preventing the original from running in certain situations, or simply taking extra action each time the function runs. The following code, for example, adds a timestamp to any message that is sent though the `ChatFrame1:AddMessage()` function:

```
local origAddMessage = ChatFrame1.AddMessage

function ChatFrame1.AddMessage(self, text, ...)
  local timestamp = date("%X")
```

```
    text = string.format("%s %s", timestamp, text)
    return origAddMessage(self, text, ...)
end
```

The first code line takes the function referenced by `ChatFrame1.AddMessage` and stores it in the local variable `origAddMessage`. Then, a new function is created in its place. This new function gets the current time of day and adds it to the text argument. Finally, it calls `origAddMessage`, passing it the new, modified text.

There are a couple important points to note in the example. First, the new function takes a variable number of arguments. The purpose of this is twofold. Selfishly, it allows us to only pay attention to the first couple of parameters. More importantly, though, it prevents the function from breaking expected behavior. If the number or order of parameters ever changes in the default UI's `AddMessage` function, as long as the text remains in the same position, our hook will still operate as expected, and will play nicely with other code that uses it.

The other point to note is that we return the results of `origAddMessage` as the last step. This may seem a bit redundant, because at the time of this writing `AddMessage` does not return anything. However, like the use of vararg, this practice future-proofs our function in case the default UI begins expecting a return value.

Modifying Return Values

There are two basic types of function hooking. The preceding example is what's known as a *pre-hook*, indicating that the hook takes its primary action before triggering the original function. This is directly visible in the code with the call to (and return from) `origAddMessage` as the last step.

A *post-hook*, on the other hand, does its business after the original function returns. This can allow you to change return values from the function, altering the behavior of any code that calls it. You can, of course, combine the two techniques, though the differentiation will prove useful when we start dealing with secure hooks.

Post-hooks can be a bit trickier to get right using the preceding techniques. Because there is no direct way to store a variable number of returns, you must use an extra vararg function to store the results of the original.

The following example works as a simple "piggy bank" for World of Warcraft. It will hook the `GetMoney()` function, changing the result. When you open your backpack, the amount of gold displayed will be different than the actual amount you have on hand. This will be controlled by a global variable, `SAVED_MONEY`, which will be subtracted from the "real" amount that you have.

```
SAVED_MONEY = 10000
local origGetMoney = GetMoney

local function newGetMoney(realMoney, ...)
  return realMoney - SAVED_MONEY, ...
end

function GetMoney(...)
  return newGetMoney(origGetMoney(...))
end
```

Again, you may be tempted to omit the extra layer of function calls because, in its current state, GetMoney only returns one value and doesn't take any arguments. However, it is your responsibility to make sure your hook still works correctly with other code, so it is always a good idea to ensure that it can handle any future changes without modification.

This example won't prevent you from spending the money in your invisible store; in fact, if your character has less than SAVED_MONEY money (1 gold in the preceding example), then your backpack display may show a nonsense value because the money frames aren't designed to show negative values.

Hooking Widget Scripts

Hooks are often used when dealing with frame scripts. For example, your addon may want to react to the click of some button in the default UI while still allowing the button to behave normally. Consider the Abandon Quest button in the Quest Log that enables you to drop a quest from your log. It currently pops up a confirmation dialog but doesn't give any specific warning when a quest is already complete.

The first step in a frame script hook is to use the GetScript method to retrieve the function currently used by the script handler:

```
local origOnClick = QuestLogFrameAbandonButton:GetScript("OnClick")
```

The GetScript() method returns either a reference to the function handler, or nil if no handler is currently set. This is equivalent to the first line of each of the last two examples.

WARNING Always check to see if a script is already set before replacing it, even if the frame you're hooking doesn't normally specify one. Another addon may be interested in the same button you are, and blindly replacing the script would break that other addon. If there is no original function, you can skip that step in your new function — but always check.

Next you need to create the replacement function:

```
local function newOnClick(...)
  local questIndex = GetQuestLogSelection()
  local completed = select(7, GetQuestLogTitle(questIndex))
  if completed then
    ChatFrame1:AddMessage("*** WARNING YOU ARE ABOUT TO ABANDON ↵
AN ALREADY COMPLETED QUEST ***", 1.0, 0.1, 0.1, 1.0)
  end

  return origOnClick(...)
end
```

The code to check and warn in this situation is relatively simple. First, you use the GetQuestLogSelection() function to get the current selected quest index, and then use GetQuestLogTitle() to determine whether you have completed it yet. If so, it prints the warning and then dispatches the call to the original handler function.

Now that you have the replacement function, you need to set it as the new `OnClick` handler for the frame:

```
QuestLogFrameAbandonButton:SetScript("OnClick", newOnClick)
```

Here's the final code for the abandon warning addon:

```
local origOnClick = QuestLogFrameAbandonButton:GetScript("OnClick")

local function newOnClick(...)
  local questIndex = GetQuestLogSelection()
  local completed = select(7, GetQuestLogTitle(questIndex))
  if completed then
    ChatFrame1:AddMessage("*** WARNING YOU ARE ABOUT TO ABANDON ↵
AN ALREADY COMPLETED QUEST ***", 1.0, 0.1, 0.1, 1.0)
  end
  -- Call and return the original, if it exists
  if origOnClick then
    return origOnClick(...)
  end
end

QuestLogFrameAbandonButton:SetScript("OnClick", newOnClick)
```

Hooking a Function Securely

As you learned in Chapter 17, mucking around with variables used by the default UI can cause any number of problems due to taint. You may hook a seemingly benign function but, if it's used in any secure code paths, the taint can have far-reaching side effects. This is, in fact, one of the intended purposes of the taint system. If you hook `UseAction` and try to pass it customized values of your choosing, you will generate an action blocked message, which is as it should be.

Sometimes, though, you may want to react to a function call without changing its behavior. For this purpose, WoW provides a `hooksecurefunc` function that creates a taint-free post-hook. Because the hook runs after the original function, you cannot change the original function's behavior. Furthermore, any returns from your hook are discarded so you cannot change the behavior of code that calls the hook. The signature for `hooksecurefunc` is as follows:

```
hooksecurefunc([table,] functionName, hookFunction)
```

Note that you can only hook functions with names, either global or as members of a table. For example, the following code prints a message every time you press an action button or otherwise trigger `UseAction`:

```
hooksecurefunc("UseAction", function(slot, unit)
  ChatFrame1:AddMessage(format(
    "You used action %d on %s",
```

```
        slot, unit or "<no unit>"
  ))
end)
```

To hook a table method securely, simply add the table as the first argument. For example, say you want to be notified when any code calls the `Show` method on a frame. This hook is different than responding to `OnShow` because it covers explicit attempts to show the frame. These will not trigger `OnShow` if the frame is already shown or the parent is hidden. The following code prints a message any time you try to show `someFrame`:

```
hooksecurefunc(someFrame, "Show", function(self)
  ChatFrame1:AddMessage("Attempting to show someFrame")
end)
```

Notice in both of these examples that you are much freer with regard to parameters and returns. Because the returns are discarded and changing any arguments has no effect on the rest of the code path, you can arrange your function in whatever way makes the most sense.

Hooking Scripts Securely

Reacting to a widget method call without changing its behavior is actually simpler than the "normal" hook method you saw earlier. Analogous to `hooksecurefunc`, every widget has a `HookScript` method that achieves essentially the same result. Your new hook will be called with all the same arguments after the original script, and any returns will be discarded. For example, the following will safely hook an action button's `OnClick` handler and keep track of each click of the button:

```
ActionButton1:HookScript("OnClick", function()
  clickCounter = clickCounter + 1
end)
```

This hook only applies to the specified button. To capture every secure button click, use `hooksecurefunc` on `SecureActionButton_OnClick` instead.

Deciding When to Hook

While function hooks are undoubtedly a useful tool, they do have a few important caveats. These range from performance issues to the potential breakage of elements in the default UI or other addons. In many cases, function hooking is unnecessary, and there are less obtrusive alternatives.

Understanding the Hook Chain

To fully appreciate some of the problems that can arise from sloppy hooking, think for a moment what would happen if two addons hooked the same function. Take the `GetMoney` example from earlier. When any piece of code calls GetMoney, it first activates the hook from your addon, and then your addon calls the original function. If another addon comes along and hooks it again, another layer is added to the *hook chain*. The hook chain is simply a way to visualize the interaction between the two addons and the base function. In this example it looks like the following:

```
Other Addon@@raYour Addon@@raBuilt-in GetMoney
```

Secure hooks (via hooksecurefunc and HookScript) don't really follow the same chain analogy. Instead, they're more like a key ring where each hook is a key. After the function does its business, the secure hook system goes through each hook one by one, executing them independently. This does not make them immune to the following problems, though.

You Can't Rely on Order

Your addon has no way of knowing the order in which the hooks take place. If the other addon is loaded before yours, the hook chain would look like this instead:

```
Your Addon@@raOther Addon@@raBuilt-in GetMoney
```

Never rely on your addon being in a certain place in the chain. The order of addon loading is arbitrary and controlled entirely by the game engine. You can buy a little bit of leeway with dependencies and such, but that requires keeping a list of every addon that interferes. If you find yourself in a situation where the order matters, you could probably stand to re-evaluate the overall design of your addon.

There Is No "Unhook"

Another issue the hook chain brings to the table is that it's dangerous to "unhook" a function. With the earlier hook chain, if you were to remove your hook (à la GetMoney = origGetMoney) you would also be removing the hook from the other addon, because your origGetMoney was stored before the other addon got a chance to hook it. More fundamentally, secure hooks are impossible to remove; the API simply does not have any facility for it.

If you do need to unhook a function, it's best to simply check a flag in your hook and change the flag whenever you need to apply or remove the hook. Of course, this leads to the next potential problem.

Hooking Hits Performance

Each hook on a given function adds a new layer of function calls. In pseudo-code, that looks like this:

```
LastHook(...)
  AnotherHook(...)
    SecondHook(...)
      FirstHook(...)
```

```
        return ...
      return ...
    return ...
  return ...
```

At each new level, Lua has to copy the argument stack to call the next function, and then copy the return as it comes back out. With secure hooks, the calls are not nested like that, but there's still just as much data copying going on. Most of the time, this doesn't cause any noticeable problems. However, if you hook a function that is called many times per frame, you may create a perceptible drop in frame rate.

Finding Alternatives

We don't want to scare you away from hooking completely; it definitely has its time and place. However, you should consider possible alternatives first to avoid these problems. To help you along, Table 19-1 contains some common scenarios in which your first instinct might be to hook, along with possible alternatives. Don't hesitate to ask for help from the UI community either. With a wider experience base, you may end up with new ideas that help your entire addon function more efficiently.

Table 19-1: Hooking Alternatives

POTENTIAL HOOK	ALTERNATIVE
OnShow of a frame from the default UI or another addon	Create a new frame with its own OnShow handler as a child of the target frame. Any time the target frame is shown or hidden, yours will be, too. Removing your hook is as simple as re-parenting your frame.
MerchantFrame_OnShow to respond to opening a vendor window	Register for the MERCHANT_SHOW event and process the merchant data on your own. Unregister the event to unhook. This also prevents any conflicts if the user has a custom merchant frame.
SetAttribute to track attribute changes on a frame	Set or hook OnAttributeChanged instead. The nature of the widget handler fits the purpose of the hook better than the method.

Designing an Addon: MapZoomOut

MapZoomOut is a simple addon that, whenever the player changes the zoom of the minimap, starts a timer that returns the map to full zoom after 20 seconds. This ensures that the player can change the zoom temporarily, but that the map always reverts to the full size (to help with things like tracking and tradeskills).

Specifying the behavior:

- When the minimap zoom is changed (via the `Minimap:SetZoom()` method), a timer will begin.
- When the timer reaches 20 seconds, the zoom will be changed until it is fully zoomed out again.

Implementation details:

- The `Minimap:SetZoom(zoomLevel)` function is used to change the zoom of the minimap.
- The minimum zoom level is 0, which is fully zoomed out.
- The maximum zoom level can be obtained by calling `Minimap:GetZoom-Levels()`.
- The two minimap zoom buttons (the plus and minus) use the `SetZoom()` function to change the zoom level.
- When the minimap zoom buttons are used, they include logic to enable or disable themselves (so the zoom out button is disabled when you are at zoom level 0).
- The current zoom level can be obtained using the `Minimap:GetZoom()` function.
- To start the timer, the `Minimap.SetZoom()` function will need to be hooked.

Creating a Timer

Creating a timer for World of Warcraft is a matter of using the `OnUpdate()` handler for a frame and tracking the amount of time the handler has been running. You may recall that the `OnUpdate()` handler is called on every screen refresh, so it's called quite a bit. The WoW client passes two arguments to each `OnUpdate` handler: the frame for which it's being triggered, and the amount of game time that has passed since the last update. As a result, this can be used directly for your running total.

Following is a small code sample that creates a frame, and then sends "Hello World" to ChatFrame1 after 20 seconds. The code is written so it can be run multiple times through an in-game code editor without creating duplicate frames.

```
-- If we haven't already created TimerFrame, do so
if not TimerFrame then TimerFrame = CreateFrame("Frame") end

local delay - 20
local counter = 0
local function OnUpdate(self, elapsed)
  counter = counter + elapsed
  ChatFrame1:AddMessage("DEBUG: " .. counter)

  if counter >= delay then
    ChatFrame1:AddMessage("Hello World")
    counter = 0
    self:Hide()
```

```
    end
end

TimerFrame:SetScript("OnUpdate", OnUpdate)
TimerFrame:Show()
```

The first code line creates a frame called TimerFrame if one doesn't already exist. It then sets two local variables — one holds the amount the timer should delay, and the other is the running counter for the timer. On each frame refresh, the elapsed time is added to the counter and the current value of the counter is printed as a debug message.

If the counter is larger than the delay time, then the payload code runs, the counter resets itself, and the frame hides (remember that a hidden frame will not have its OnUpdate handler called). Finally, once the function is created, it is set as the OnUpdate handler, and the frame is shown to start the timer. Figure 19-1 shows the timer in action (your numbers will be different).

Figure 19-1: Simple OnUpdate timer running

WARNING Remember that the code in your OnUpdate handler is called on every screen update (if you normally get 60 frames per second, then this function is called 60 times per second). As a result, these functions need to be as quick as possible, and you should be conscious of your memory usage. Don't over-scrutinize your code into some monster, but be aware of the potential impact of a poorly written OnUpdate function because that can affect the frame rate.

In addition, the preceding example uses a counter variable to throttle its timer, to ensure it only runs every 20 seconds. Keep this in mind when writing your own OnUpdate functions; you may not need to update every single frame.

Creating MapZoomOut

MapZoomOut won't require an .xml file, so create the basic addon directory and then add MapZoomOut.toc using the following content:

```
## Interface: 20300
## Title: MapZoomOut
## Notes: Zooms the map out to the full level after a given time

MapZoomOut.lua
```

Creating a Timer Frame

Create a new file called **MapZoomOut.lua**, and add the following line to the top of the file:

```
local timerFrame = CreateFrame("Frame")
```

This creates a frame with no global name and assigns it to a local variable so it can be used later in the file. This frame will be used to trigger the timer with OnUpdate.

Initial Setup

Add these lines to the bottom of the MapZoomOut.lua file, creating a variable to store the delay amount for the timer, a variable for the timer counter, and a reference to the original Minimap:SetZoom() function:

```
local delay = 20
local counter = 0
local origSetZoom = Minimap.SetZoom
```

These local variables will be used later in the file to check the timer, as well as to call the original SetZoom function.

Create the Function Hook

The new function is simple; it just calls timerFrame:Show() and changes the counter to 0 to reset the timer. It then calls the original SetZoom function to change the zoom level. Add this function definition to the bottom of MapZoomOut.lua:

```
function Minimap.SetZoom(...)
    -- Show the timer frame, starting the timer
    timerFrame:Show()
    counter = 0

    -- Call the original SetZoom function
    return origSetZoom(...)
end
```

The function parameters or returns are simply passed to the original function using ..., and the results are returned to the calling function. This ensures that the function will operate well with whatever calls it, because it augments behavior rather than altering the original function.

Writing the Timer Code

The timer is a bit more complex than the earlier example simply for aesthetic reasons. The easy way to write this addon would be to call origSetZoom(0) when the timer expires, but this causes a pretty large change in the minimap and doesn't look all that pleasing. Instead, this function will zoom out step by step, producing a more gradual zoom.

Add the following code to the bottom of MapZoomOut.lua:

```
local function OnUpdate(self, elapsed)
        -- Increment the counter variable
        counter = counter + elapsed

        if counter >= delay then
            -- Check current zoom level
            local z = Minimap:GetZoom()
            if z > 0 then
                origSetZoom(Minimap, z - 1)
            else
                -- Enable/Disable the buttons
                MinimapZoomIn:Enable()
                MinimapZoomOut:Disable()
                self:Hide()
            end
        end
end
```

The beginning of the timer is the same, incrementing the counter and checking it against the delay. Inside the conditional, you store the current zoom level in local variable z so it can be referenced. If the minimap is currently zoomed in (z > 0), the map is zoomed out by one level, but the counter isn't reset. That ensures the timer's payload will run on the next frame update as well. This alone accomplishes the gradual zoom-out rather than the single frame change.

Finally, if the minimap is zoomed all the way out, the MinimapZoomIn button is enabled, and the MinimapZoomOut button is disabled. Then the timer frame hides itself so its OnUpdate won't be called again.

Final Setup

The last step is setting the OnUpdate script for timerFrame, and then deciding what to do when the addon first loads. Because the user may load the game with the minimap already zoomed in, the code will check to see if it should start the timer or hide it to begin with (so it doesn't run).

Add the following code to the bottom of your MapZoomOut.lua file:

```
timerFrame:SetScript("OnUpdate", OnUpdate)
if Minimap:GetZoom() == 0 then
        timerFrame:Hide()
end
```

Testing MapZoomOut

As with any addon you create, you should test the functionality to ensure it works properly with no side effects. In this case, you should test the following:

- Using the zoom-in button, zoom in to each level, and verify that the map is zoomed out after `delay` seconds each time.

- Manually call the `Minimap:SetZoom()` function by running `/script Minimap:SetZoom(3)`. The addon should detect the change, and begin the timer even though the buttons weren't pushed.

Summary

Function hooking can be a useful tool in a programmer's box, but it comes with a hefty instruction booklet and set of warnings. In particular, function hooks should follow these principles:

- Use the same parameters and returns.

- Call the original function and maintain the hook chain.

- Don't alter the order or meaning of arguments or returns, because other functions may rely on them.

- Don't depend on your hook being in a certain part of the chain. This also means you should never unhook a function.

- Look for alternatives first. Hooking may not always be the best solution.

In addition, special care must be taken when hooking Blizzard scripts and functions, because certain actions are restricted to the default user interface.

# CHAPTER 20

Creating Custom Graphics

James Whitehead II

When creating addons for World of Warcraft, you can often build your frames using only the default Blizzard artwork, icons, and buttons. If your addon requires something more specific or custom, it can be created using any major graphics editor. This chapter details the major steps needed to create a custom texture for WoW in the GNU Image Manipulation Program (GIMP), Adobe Photoshop CS, and Corel Paint Shop Pro X.

Common Rules for Creating Graphics

Graphics (or textures) in WoW have a few specific requirements they must meet for them to be loaded and rendered in-game as part of a custom UI:

- The height and width of the texture must be a power of two, although they do not have to be the same power of two. This means 32x256 and 512x512 are both valid, but 50x128 is not. In addition, textures are limited to a maximum of 512 pixels in either dimension. If you have a larger graphic, you can break it into tiles and use multiple Texture objects to display it.

- The graphic must be saved in either BLP or TGA format. BLP is a proprietary format that Blizzard uses internally, and there are no official tools that allow these files to be easily created or edited. TGA files can be read and written in most major graphics editors.

- Textures should be saved with an 8-bit alpha channel along with the 24-bit color data. This allows for both partial and full transparency in textures.

- Graphics files must reside in an addon's directory to be accessible to the game client.

The GIMP

Creating a texture with transparency is relatively simple in the GIMP because of the way it handles the alpha channel. The trick is creating the image with a transparent background, and paying particular attention to creating the various elements of the image.

Create a New Image

To create a new image with the GIMP:

1. Select File ⇨ New in the main GIMP window.

2. In the window that appears (see Figure 20-1), enter the width and height of your image. Keep in mind that you don't need to fill the entire space, but both the height and width must be a power of two.

3. Expand the Advanced Options section of the New dialog.

4. Ensure RGB color is selected for the Colorspace.

5. Set Fill With to Transparency, so the new base image is fully transparent.

6. Click OK.

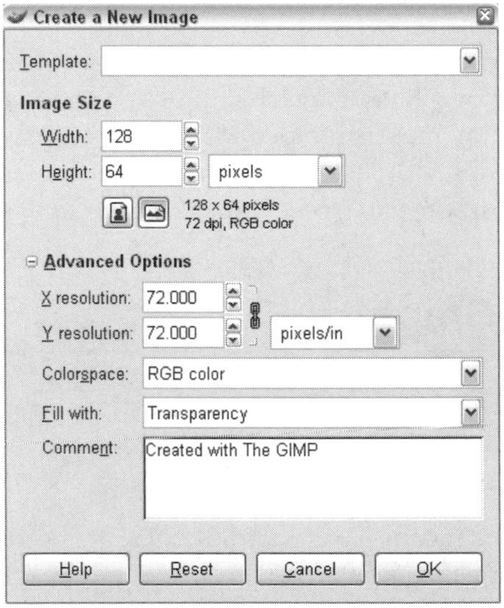

Figure 20-1: GIMP's New Image dialog

Adding Graphical Components

A new window opens showing the base transparent image (see Figure 20-2). You can add any graphical components to this image, including layers. Unfortunately, I'm just a simple programmer and lack any and all graphical manipulation skills, so I can't give you too many pointers. In this example, you create a very simple custom button.

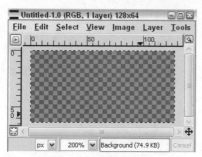

Figure 20-2: Editing window for
new transparent image in the GIMP

Figure 20-3 shows a newly created custom icon, combining a simple border graphic and a picture of my dog Daisy. This image is 64x64 and has transparent edges (specifically for the rounded corners).

Figure 20-3: New custom
icon created in the GIMP

Saving Textures

As long as you've created the graphic properly, you should be golden; saving it is where most people have issues. Save your image taking the following steps:

1. The image will be saved as a nonlayered image, so merge all the layers before attempting to save. This step isn't necessarily required but makes the subsequent steps easier.

2. Select File ⇨ Save.

3. In the Save dialog, name your file with a .TGA extension and click the Save button.

4. An options dialog pops up (shown in Figure 20-4). Check both checkboxes and click OK. This compresses the image in a lossless way (so it loses no quality) but creates a smaller file size.

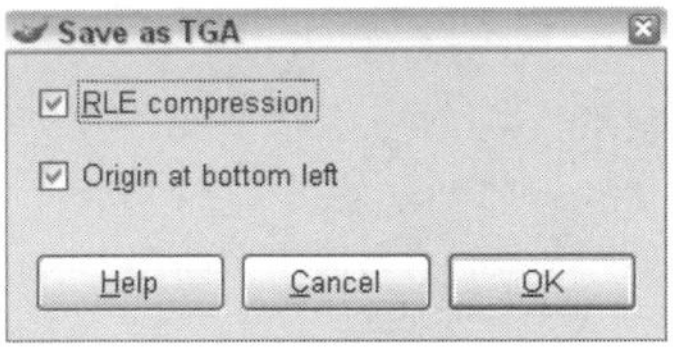

Figure 20-4: Save as TGA
Dialog in the GIMP

As long as the image was created with a transparent background and saved as a TGA file this way, it should load properly in the game.

Adobe Photoshop

Creating a texture in Photoshop is similar to those in the GIMP, but the interface is quite a bit different. The same basic steps apply, the image creation and saving being the most important.

Create a New Image

To create a new image with Photoshop:

1. Open Photoshop and select File ➪ New.

2. The New dialog opens (see Figure 20-5).

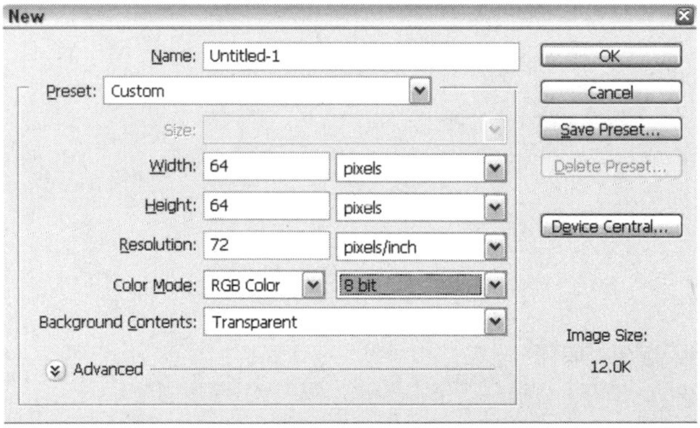

Figure 20-5: Adobe Photoshop file creation dialog

3. Change the height and width to your desired dimensions.

4. Ensure the Background Contents dropdown has Transparent selected.

5. Click OK to create the new image.

Adding Graphical Components

Create the graphic as required (you're the one familiar with Photoshop here), but take care to follow these rules:

■ Make sure there isn't a Background layer in your document when you are ready to save.

■ If you need to merge visible layers, use Merge All, but don't flatten the image. Flattening the image gives it a background, which loses the transparency information.

Transparency in Adobe Photoshop is different than in Gimp. In particular, you won't see an alpha channel created by default in the Channels window. The transparent background means nothing when the image is flattened and saved. To achieve transparency, you must create the alpha channel.

Creating an Alpha Channel

When your image is complete and ready to save, complete the following steps to create an alpha channel:

1. Merge the visible layers so you have a single layer containing the nontransparent portions of your image.

2. Select the layer in the layers palette.

3. Open the Select menu, and select Load Selection.

4. You will be prompted with a dialog box (see Figure 20-6), but the default options should be correct. Click OK. This selects each pixel in the current layer that isn't transparent.

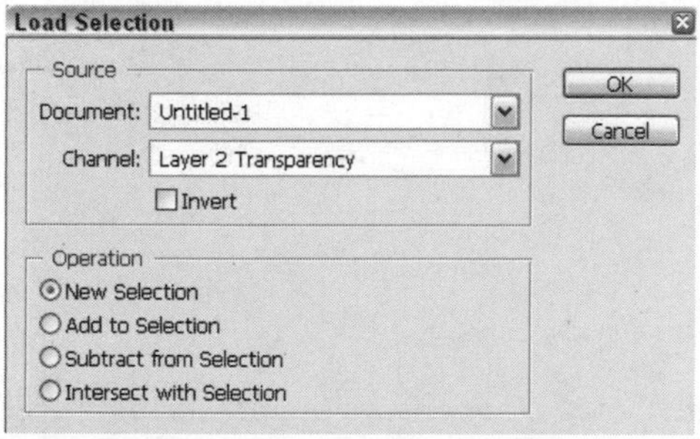

Figure 20-6: Load Selection dialog

5. In the Channels window, there is a small icon that will "Save Selection As Channel" (see Figure 20-7). Click it, creating an alpha channel based on the selection.

Figure 20-7: Save
Selection As Channel
button in the Channels
window

The new 8-bit alpha channel gives you different levels of opacity for an image with more forgiving transparency. At this point you can flatten your image without any issues, but there's no particular reason to do so.

Saving an Image

Once the alpha channel is created, saving the image is a matter of selecting File ⇨ Save As. The Save As dialog provides several options (shown in Figure 20-8).

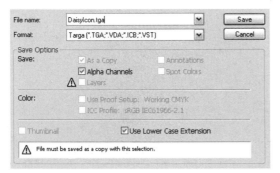

Figure 20-8: Options in Photoshop's
Save As dialog

You can choose any name you'd like for the image, but ensure the file format is set to *Targa (*.tga)* and the filename ends in the .tga extension. If your image has layers, the As A Copy option will be automatically selected, and the Layers option will be des-elected with an error warning next to it. This simply means that TGA doesn't support layers, so the image will be flattened before saving. Ensure that Alpha Channels is selected. Click Save.

A final TGA options dialog (see Figure 20-9) opens to allow you to select the color resolution and add compression to the image. You should select 32 bits/pixel, and check the box for Compress (RLE).

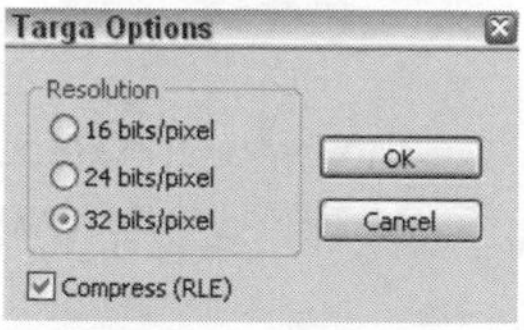

Figure 20-9: Targa
Options dialog

Once the image is saved, it can be copied into your WoW installation and tested.

Paint Shop Pro

Paint Shop Pro is similar to Adobe Photoshop in most respects, particularly in the way it handles transparency. As a result, you'll need to take extra steps to ensure the transparent images you create are saved correctly.

Creating a New Image

To create a new image with Paint Shop Pro:

1. Select File ➪ New.
2. The New Image options dialog (shown in Figure 20-10) opens. Specify the dimensions of your image.
3. Select a Raster Background with a color depth of RGB - 8 bits/channel.
4. Check the Transparent box to give your image a transparent background.
5. Click OK.

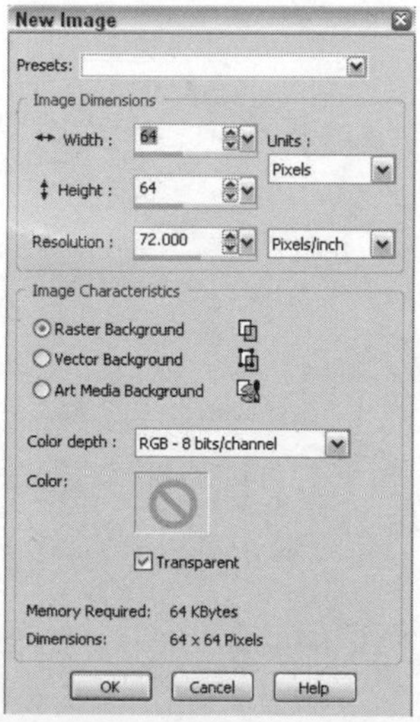

Figure 20-10: Corel Paint
Shop Pro New Image dialog

Adding Graphical Components

Create your image as you usually do in this application, ensuring that you don't use the Flatten Image option. You will need the transparent background to make certain the alpha channel is creating correctly.

Creating an Alpha Channel

Once your image is created, use the following steps to create an alpha channel for transparency:

1. Select Layers ⇨ New Mask Layer ⇨ From Image (see Figure 20-11). This will create a new mask layer consisting only of the pixels in your image.

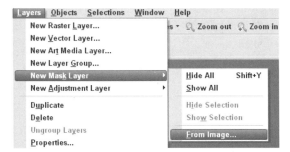

Figure 20-11: New Mask Layer menu option

2. In the Add Mask From Image dialog (see Figure 20-12), select Source Opacity in the Create Mask From section to ensure the new alpha channel is created using the transparency you defined when creating the image.

Figure 20-12: Add Mask From Image dialog box

3. Click OK. This adds a new layer mark to your image.
4. Select Layers ⇨ Load Save Mask ⇨ Save Mask to Alpha Channel.

5. A dialog box displays, allowing you to preview the image transparency and giving you an opportunity to name the new channel. Click OK.

Your image now has a proper alpha channel that can be used to save the image with transparency.

Saving an Image

Follow these steps to save an image in Paint Shop Pro:

1. Select File ➪ Save As.

2. In the dialog that appears, choose TGA Truevision targa (*.*tga*) as the image format, and name your image.

3. Click the Options button.

4. In the Save Options dialog box (see Figure 20-13), select a 24-bit image and compression for your image.

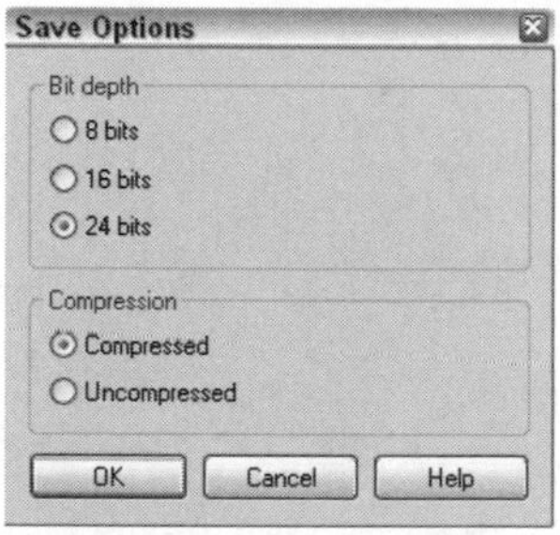

Figure 20-13: Targa options in Paint Shop Pro

5. Click OK to exit the options dialog.

6. Click Save.

7. If you still have layers in your image, you may get a warning dialog (see Figure 20-14) telling you that the image will be merged and then saved. Click Yes.

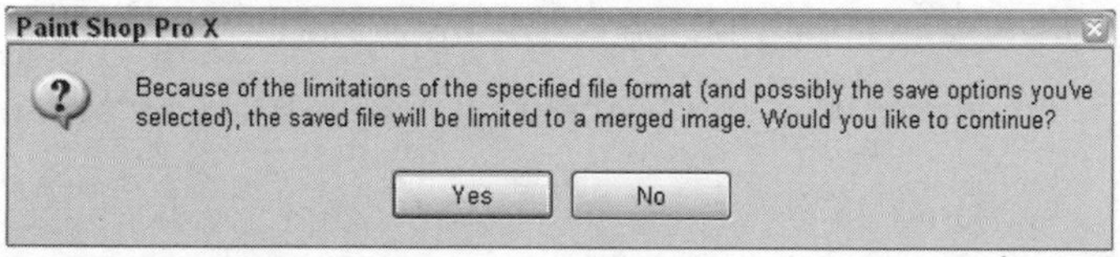

Figure 20-14: File format limitations dialog in Paint Shop Pro

Testing Your Texture

To test the new texture, you need to fully exit World of Warcraft and add a small custom addon to house the image. (You could instead add it to an existing addon, but that exercise is left to the reader, when appropriate.)

1. Create a folder `IconTest` underneath your `AddOns` directory.

2. Add a file `IconTest.toc` with the following contents:

   ```
   ## Interface: 20300
   ## Title: IconTest
   ## Notes: Simple icon test addon

   IconTest.xml
   ```

3. Add a file `IconTest.xml` with the following contents. Change `DaisyIcon` to the name of your icon.

   ```
   <Ui xmlns="http://www.blizzard.com/wow/ui/" ↵
   xmlns:xsi=http://www.w3.org/2001/XMLSchema-instance ↵
   xsi:schemaLocation="http://www.blizzard.com/wow/ui/ ↵
   ..\FrameXML\UI.xsd">
     <Button name="IconTest" parent="UIParent">
       <Size x="64" y="64"/>
       <Anchors>
         <Anchor point="CENTER"/>
       </Anchors>
       <Layers>
         <Layer level="BACKGROUND">
           <Texture name="$parentIcon" ↵
   file="Interface\AddOns\IconTest\DaisyIcon" ↵
   setAllPoints="true"/>
         </Layer>
       </Layers>
     </Button>
   </Ui>
   ```

4. WoW doesn't require you to specify extensions when loading textures; it will try to load both a `.BLP` and a `.TGA` automatically.

5. Copy your icon file to the IconTest directory.

6. Load up World of Warcraft and hope you don't have any errors in your XML.

If you have created the texture correctly, it should appear in the center of your screen (see Figure 20-15).

If you've made any errors, you might experience one of two symptoms: no button appears, or you see only a solid green box.

Figure 20-15:
Custom texture
being viewed
in-game

No Button Appears

If you see no button at all, double-check your XML definition, and ensure you have no errors in your `FrameXML.log` file. You can also use a web browser to check that your XML document is well-formed. Ensure that your test addon appears in the AddOn listing. Did you make sure to exit WoW before you added the new files?

A Green Box Appears

When there is an issue loading a given texture in World of Warcraft, the texture will be colored solid green (see Figure 20-16). Typically, this is a result of a typo on the filename being used for the texture.

Figure 20-16:
Solid green
texture, indicating
an error

Depending on how the texture was created (from an XML definition or through a Lua function call), a number of issues could result in a green texture being displayed.

XML Texture Definition

A texture created in XML may have one of the following issues:

- The filename was specified incorrectly. It should look like `Interface\AddOns\YourAddOnName\Path\To\Texture`.
- XML filename path separators must be backslashes, even on a Mac OS X or UNIX system, because of the way the client loads and parses the filenames.

- The file doesn't exist.
- The graphic was saved incorrectly.

Lua Texture Definition

When troubleshooting texture errors in Lua, the following issues may exist:

- The backslash separator character must be escaped with an extra backslash, making the path `Interface\\AddOns\\YourAddOnName\\Path\\To\\Texture`. Instead of escaping backslashes, you could use a long string, such as `[[Interface\AddOns\YourAddOnName\Path\To\Texture]]`.
- Forward slashes are not valid in texture paths; they must be backslashes.
- The file doesn't exist.
- The graphic was saved incorrectly.

Summary

Each graphical editor has its own set of quirks and settings that are necessary to create an image with partial transparency for use in World of Warcraft. The GIMP enables you to create your image and simply save it as a TGA file, while both Photoshop and Paint Shop Pro require you to create an alpha channel based on a mask or selection.

# CHAPTER 21

Making Frames Move

Bryan McLemore

From a young age we all are fascinated by what catches the eye. We like shiny things; we like things that move. In the same way, your users will be drawn to certain things — they also like it when things can and do move. This chapter tackles making forms movable and shows you how to animate a form.

Drag and Drop

You can never count on users liking things in the same spot that you do. Inevitably, you will want to make a frame draggable. There are several ways to do so and a couple of things that must be true regardless of which method you use. The following should always be true:

- The frame must be set as being movable.
- You must enable the mouse.

Those are pretty much absolutes. You can use the following code to achieve this.

```
frame:SetMovable(1)
frame:EnableMouse()
```

Or, if you're using XML, you can declare this behavior in the `Frame` tag:

```
<Frame movable="true" enablemouse="true">
```

Now let's look at the methods of making your frame movable.

TitleRegion

Perhaps the most straightforward method of making your frame movable is by adding a `TitleRegion`. This can be done in either XML for via the frame API. You simply add a `TitleRegion` and set its size, and then the frame can be dragged easily by clicking on and dragging the `TitleRegion`.

Using OnMouseDown and OnMouseUp

Most of us think of a mouse click as an action, and it *is*. However, when you click a mouse it's really two separate actions: You push down on the mouse and then you lift up your finger. `OnMouseDown` and

`OnMouseUp` are the two frame events that represent those actions. This set of events can easily be used to make a frame draggable. The following code creates your typical drag-and-drop behavior on pretty much any frame:

```
frame:SetScript("OnMouseDown", function()
    this:StartMoving()
end)

frame:SetScript("OnMouseUp", function()
    this:StopMovingOrSizing()
end)
```

Try it on, say, the Auction House frame.

This behavior could be considered feature complete depending on what you're doing. Still, you may want to limit when dragging is functional. One method would be to unhook the scripts when you don't want them to drag. Another, and I'd say preferred method, would be to use an `if` inside the handlers, like this:

```
frame:SetScript("OnMouseDown", function()
    if IsAltKeyDown() then
        this:StartMoving()
    end
end)
```

This code makes it so that a frame would start moving only if the users were holding down the Alt key while they attempt to drag it. Functions also exist to tell if the Control or the Shift keys are down, but any Boolean expression would suffice there.

One small caveat: There's not much of a negative impact if your frame can close, via the Escape key, for example, while you are moving it — your frame doesn't get stuck on the cursor or anything of that sort. However, the frame will not remember where you were and will reappear at its previous location when you open it again, so you may want to include something like the following to stop the moving in the `OnHide` handler.

```
frame:SetScript("OnHide", function()
    this:StopMovingOrSizing()
end)
```

Using OnDragStart/OnDragStop

Blizzard has also created drag events that can be used pretty much as previously outlined, but may not be as responsive. You do, however, need to mark the frame as draggable:

```
frame:SetScript("OnLoad", function()
    this:RegisterForDrag("LeftButton")
end)

frame:SetScript("OnDragStart", function()
    this:StartMoving()
end)

frame:SetScript("OnDragStop", function()
    this:StopMovingOrSizing()
end)
```

Bringing Life to the Frames

Now that you've gotten the various methods of making a frame draggable down pat, let's look at the next level: making your frames move. Take a look at the following example. It assumes that you already have a frame that you're working with and you want it to slide some.

```
local frame = CreateFrame("Frame", nil, UIParent)
frame:SetWidth(300)
frame:SetHeight(250)

frame:SetBackdrop({
            bgFile = "Interface\\ChatFrame\\ChatFrameBackground", ↵
tile = true,tileSize = 16,
            edgeFile = "Interface\\Tooltips\\UI-Tooltip-Border",↵
 edgeSize = 16,
            insets = {left = 5, right = 5, top = 4, bottom = 4},
    })

frame:SetBackdropColor(24/255, 24/255, 24/255)
frame:SetPoint("CENTER", nil, "CENTER")

local pi = math.pi
local cos = math.cos

local function cosineInterpolation(point1, point2, mu)
    return point1+(point2-point1)*(1 - cos(pi*mu))/2
end
```

```
local timeToMove = 5
local start, stop = 0, 400

local totalElapsed = 0

local function onupdate(self, elapsed)
    totalElapsed = totalElapsed + elapsed

    if totalElapsed >= timeToMove then
        totalElapsed = 0
        self:SetScript("OnUpdate", nil)
        self:Hide()
        return
    end
    offset = cosineInterpolation(start, stop, 1/timeToMove*totalElapsed)
    self:SetPoint("LEFT", self:GetParent(), "LEFT", offset, 100)
end

local function startMove(self)
    self:SetPoint("LEFT", self:GetParent(), "LEFT", 0, 100)
    self:SetScript("OnUpdate", onupdate)
end

startMove(frame)
```

There you have it, a basic frame animation that simply makes the frame of your choice slide across the screen. Examining the code, it's fairly straightforward. The beginning creates a frame for the purpose of this example; you'd use this with pretty much any frame. The cosine interpolation, for those no longer familiar with their math courses, is a slow-in, slow-out sinusoidal interpolation between two points. Using this to generate the offset gives you a more stylized movement because it'll speed up at the beginning and then slow to a stop. You can manipulate math a few other ways to make your effects flashy.

In the preceding example, you only use the `cosineInterpolation` to generate the `y` coordinate; you can, however, use it for both `x` and `y` coordinates. Using them together in various ways, you can create interesting curves and diagonal slides. If you don't like this type of slow-in, slow-out movement, you can use a linear interpolation that would look something like this:

```
function linearInterpolation(point1, point2, mu)
    return point1 + mu * (point2 - point1)
end
```

In both the linear and the cosine interpolation, `point1` and `point2` are just points along the graph, representing start and stop points. The variable `mu` is a number between 0 and 1 that represents a point in time along the graph. `0` is the beginning of the timeline and would correlate to `point1`, and `1` is going to render you the value of `point2`. This need for a number between 0 and 1 is the reason you use `1/timeToMove*totalElapsed` in the earlier example that showed the basic frame animation — this is what actually renders the `0` to `1` as a function of time.

Fading

Two Blizzard-supplied functions facilitate fading: `UIFrameFadeIn` and `UIFrameFadeOut`. They are both fairly straightforward. They work based on an `OnUpdate` and can work with the other moving methods, giving you a fade in or out. Here are the function signatures:

```
UIFrameFadeIn(frame, timeToFade, startAlpha, endAlpha)
UIFrameFadeOut(frame, timeToFade, startAlpha, endAlpha)
```

This can allow for some very cool effects, such as text strings that fly off the screen and fade into obscurity, frames fading in as they appear, and other interesting combination effects.

Summary

This chapter showed you how you can make your frames movable and make them dance (and you were reminded of some math that you may have not seen in years, if ever). You also saw some cool Blizzard-provided functions that can facilitate adding visual effects to your addon frames.

# CHAPTER 22

Creating Scroll Frames

James Whitehead II

When creating a custom user interface, you may have a need to display data that is too large for a reasonably sized window. World of Warcraft allows you to create frames that can scroll both horizontally and vertically, giving you more flexibility in the display of your data. This chapter shows you how to create two different types of scroll frames that are used throughout the default user interface.

A ScrollFrame is used to allow horizontal and vertical smooth scrolling of data that is too large for the containing frame. In the default user interface, the Quest Log uses a scroll frame when the quest description is too long for the window (see Figures 22-1 and 22-2). These types of scroll frames allow for pixel-by-pixel, smooth scrolling of the contents.

Figure 22-1: Quest Log scroll frame initially loaded

Figure 22-2: Quest Log scroll frame
showing arbitrary vertical scrolling

A `FauxScrollFrame` is, as the name suggests, a way to provide scrolling without using an actual `ScrollFrame`. It's designed for elements such as lists, where using a `ScrollFrame` would require creating individual frames for each list entry. Instead, a `FauxScrollFrame` lets you create only as many frames as are needed to show one "page" worth of the list, and as the user scrolls it helps you keep track of which list elements those frames should represent. The Auction House UI uses this technique to display lists of auctions (see Figure 22-3). It shows eight auctions at a time using a frame for each row, and as you scroll through the list, it changes the information displayed by each frame. (This is much more memory and CPU efficient than creating frames for each auction — potentially hundreds — and encapsulating them in a `ScrollFrame`.)

Figure 22-3: Auction House using a Faux ScrollFrame

Using Scroll Frames

Creating a scroll frame is relatively easy. It requires a new frame of the `ScrollFrame` type, with a `ScrollChild` element frame that contains the data to be displayed. This creates a scroll frame that can be manipulated, but doesn't create any scroll bars or define any behavior scripts (unless you use one of the Blizzard templates). Creating a scroll frame is simply a matter of defining a new `Slider` frame that alters the display of the `ScrollFrame`.

Create a new addon skeleton called `ScrollFramesTest` that will be used to create a sample scroll frame for this section.

Defining a Scroll Frame

Add the following definition to `ScrollFramesTest.xml` in your addon skeleton:

```
<Ui xmlns="http://www.blizzard.com/wow/ui/" ↵
xmlns:xsi="http://www.w3.org/2001/XMLSchema-instance" ↵
xsi:schemaLocation="http://www.blizzard.com/wow/ui/
..\FrameXML\UI.xsd">
  <ScrollFrame name="ScrollFrameTest">
    <Size x="150" y="150"/>
    <Anchors>
      <Anchor point="CENTER"/>
    </Anchors>
    <Layers>
      <Layer level="BACKGROUND">
        <Texture setAllPoints="true">
          <Color r="0.0" g="0.0" b="0.0"/>
        </Texture>
      </Layer>
    </Layers>
  </ScrollFrame>
</Ui>
```

This definition creates a 150x150 frame in the center of the screen with a black background. A `ScrollFrame` is a very specific type of frame that has different methods and handler scripts available. For example, the following methods can be used on scroll frames:

- `GetHorizontalScroll()` — Returns the current scroll value of the horizontal scroll component.

- `GetVerticalScroll()` — Returns the current scroll value of the vertical scroll component.

- `GetHorizontalScrollRange()` — Returns the maximum scroll range for the horizontal scroll component.

- `GetVerticalScrollRange()` — Returns the maximum scroll range for the vertical scroll component.

- `UpdateScrollChildRect()` — Updates the virtual size of the scroll child. This function should be called when the contents are changed.

Adding a Scroll Child

The contents of your frame are actually defined in the `<ScrollChild>` element when using XML, or with the `:SetScrollChild()` method when using Lua. Add the following section to `ScrollFrameTest.xml` immediately after the `</Layers>` tag:

```
<ScrollChild>
  <Frame>
    <Size x="250" y="250"/>
    <Layers>
      <Layer level="ARTWORK">
        <Texture ↵
file="Interface\Icons\Spell_Shadow_DemonicFortitude">
          <Size x="100" y="100"/>
          <Anchors>
            <Anchor point="CENTER"/>
          </Anchors>
        </Texture>
      </Layer>
    </Layers>
  </Frame>
</ScrollChild>
```

The `<ScrollChild>` element should contain exactly one frame (or frame derivative) that should contain the contents of the scroll frame. This child frame can be any size, but it will be visually capped to the size of the `<ScrollFrame>` element. As a matter of fact, the horizontal and vertical scroll ranges are defined by the size of this child frame.

Load the game and you should see an image in the center of your screen similar to that shown in Figure 22-4.

Figure 22-4:
ScrollFrameTest
as loaded

You can center the image by using the following two scripts in-game:

```
/run ScrollFrameTest:SetHorizontalScroll(-50)
/run ScrollFrameTest:SetVerticalScroll(50)
```

Note that the horizontal scroll ends up being a negative value to scroll the viewport to the right, while vertical scroll is a positive number to scroll the viewport up. This is consistent with the way the UI coordinates work (where 0,0 is in the bottom-left corner). Figure 22-5 shows the frame when adjusted using these commands.

Figure 22-5:
ScrollFrameTest
scrolled 50 pixels
to the left and
50 pixels up

Creating Scroll Bars

Creating a scrolling frame is relatively simple, but it seems quite useless without an easy way to manipulate the frame. Fortunately, adding scroll bars is as simple as creating a `<Slider>` type frame, which adjusts the scroll values `<OnValueChanged>`. Add the following to `ScrollFrameTest.xml`, after the `</ScrollChild>` tag:

```
<Frames>
  <Slider name="ScrollFrameTest_HSlider" orientation="HORIZONTAL"↵
minValue="0" maxValue="100" defaultValue="0" valueStep="1">
    <Anchors>
      <Anchor point="TOP" relativePoint="BOTTOM" ↵
relativeTo="ScrollFrameTest"/>
    </Anchors>
    <Size x="150" y="25"/>
    <ThumbTexture name="$parentThumbTexture" ↵
file="Interface\Buttons\UI-ScrollBar-Knob">
      <Size x="25" y="25"/>
    </ThumbTexture>
    <Scripts>
      <OnValueChanged>
        ScrollFrameTest:SetHorizontalScroll(-1 * self:GetValue())
      </OnValueChanged>
    </Scripts>
```

```
    </Slider>
    <Slider name="ScrollFrameTest_VSlider" orientation="VERTICAL" ↵
minValue="0" maxValue="100" defaultValue="0" valueStep="1">
      <Anchors>
        <Anchor point="LEFT" relativePoint="RIGHT" ↵
relativeTo="ScrollFrameTest"/>
      </Anchors>
      <Size x="25" y="150"/>
      <ThumbTexture name="$parentThumbTexture" ↵
file="Interface\Buttons\UI-ScrollBar-Knob">
        <Size x="25" y="25"/>
      </ThumbTexture>
      <Scripts>
        <OnValueChanged>
          ScrollFrameTest:SetVerticalScroll(self:GetValue())
        </OnValueChanged>
      </Scripts>
    </Slider>
  </Frames>
```

These two XML definitions create two scroll frames with a range between 0 and 100, because the child frame is exactly 100 pixels larger than the scroll frame. When the sliders are moved, the horizontal or vertical scroll is updated on the scroll frame. These simple scroll bars use the `UI-ScrollBar-Knob` graphic for the slider "thumb" graphic, and could be extended to use the border and backgrounds from those scroll bars, as well. Figure 22-6 shows the full product in-game.

Figure 22-6:
ScrollFrameTest scroll
frame, with scroll bars

Creating Faux Scroll Frames

The second type of scroll frame, more of a pseudo scroll frame, is also quite simple to create, but must be carefully tailored to the specific need. This section creates a sequence of onscreen icons that can be scrolled through to display all valid macro icons for selection. The API functions used here are the following:

- `GetNumMacroIcons()` — Returns the number of available macro icons.
- `GetMacroIconInfo(index)` — Returns the texture for the selected macro index.

This addon will display six icons side by side, and will split the total number of macro icons up into pages of five. The slider will then be used to move from page to page. Begin by creating an addon skeleton called `MacroIconTest`. Add the following to `MacroIconTest.xml`:

```xml
<Ui xmlns="http://www.blizzard.com/wow/ui/" ↵
xmlns:xsi="http://www.w3.org/2001/XMLSchema-instance" ↵
xsi:schemaLocation="http://www.blizzard.com/wow/ui/
..\FrameXML\UI.xsd">
  <Button name="MacroIconTest_IconTemplate" virtual="true">
    <Size x="32" y="32"/>
    <NormalTexture name="$parentIcon" setAllPoints="true"/>
    <HighlightTexture alphaMode="ADD" ↵
file="Interface\Buttons\ButtonHilight-Square"/>
  </Button>
</Ui>
```

This simple XML template will be used to create each of the icon slots. It defines a default texture, as well as a highlight texture to give a bit more visual feedback. Insert the following XML before the `</Ui>` tag to create a set of icons:

```xml
<Frame name="MacroIconTest">
  <Size x="160" y="32"/>
  <Anchors>
    <Anchor point="CENTER"/>
  </Anchors>
  <Frames>
    <Button name="$parentIcon1" ↵
inherits="MacroIconTest_IconTemplate">
      <Anchors>
        <Anchor point="TOPLEFT"/>
      </Anchors>
    </Button>
    <Button name="$parentIcon2" ↵
inherits="MacroIconTest_IconTemplate">
      <Anchors>
        <Anchor point="TOPLEFT" relativePoint="TOPRIGHT" ↵
relativeTo="$parentIcon1"/>
      </Anchors>
    </Button>
    <Button name="$parentIcon3" ↵
inherits="MacroIconTest_IconTemplate">
      <Anchors>
        <Anchor point="TOPLEFT" relativePoint="TOPRIGHT" ↵
relativeTo="$parentIcon2"/>
      </Anchors>
    </Button>
    <Button name="$parentIcon4" ↵
inherits="MacroIconTest_IconTemplate">
      <Anchors>
```

```
            <Anchor point="TOPLEFT" relativePoint="TOPRIGHT" ↵
relativeTo="$parentIcon3"/>
        </Anchors>
    </Button>
    <Button name="$parentIcon5" ↵
inherits="MacroIconTest_IconTemplate">
        <Anchors>
            <Anchor point="TOPLEFT" relativePoint="TOPRIGHT" ↵
relativeTo="$parentIcon4"/>
        </Anchors>
    </Button>
    <Button name="$parentIcon6" ↵
inherits="MacroIconTest_IconTemplate">
        <Anchors>
            <Anchor point="TOPLEFT" relativePoint="TOPRIGHT" ↵
relativeTo="$parentIcon5"/>
        </Anchors>
    </Button>
  </Frames>
</Frame>
```

At this point, if you jump into game, you'll have an invisible set of boxes that can be moused over (the highlight texture will still show) but that don't actually display anything. Jump to `MacroIconTest.lua` and add the following function:

```
function MacroIconTest_UpdateIcons(startIcon)
  local name = "MacroIconTestIcon"

  for i=1,5 do
    local texture = GetMacroIconInfo(startIcon + (i - 1))
    local button = getglobal(name .. i)
    button:SetNormalTexture(texture)
  end
end
```

This function accepts a number argument, namely which icon should be displayed first. It then loops through the five different icon buttons and changes their texture accordingly. This loop assumes the first icon is numbered 1, because the `GetMacroIconInfo()` function makes the same assumption.

TIP Not all data is available immediately within the game client. For example, the number of icons and the texture information about each macro icon isn't available until after the client has been partially initialized. Generally, all information is available after the `PLAYER_LOGIN` event, which is fired just before the client begins displaying the 3-D world. Some functions may need to be delayed until after this event to work properly.

Add the following behavior scripts to the `MacroIconTest` frame by putting the following section immediately after the `</Frames>` tag:

```
<Scripts>
  <OnLoad>
    self:RegisterEvent("PLAYER_LOGIN")
  </OnLoad>
  <OnEvent>
    if event == "PLAYER_LOGIN" then
      GetNumMacroIcons()
      MacroIconTest_UpdateIcons(1)
    end
  </OnEvent>
</Scripts>
```

Here you register for the `PLAYER_LOGIN` event, and when it fires, call `GetNumMacroIcons()`, and then `MacroIconTest_UpdateIcons()` function when it fires. When guild banks were introduced, the macro icon system was changed so icon information isn't available until the `GetNumMacroIcons()` function has been called at least once, hence the call here. Load the game client, and you should see something like that shown in Figure 22-7 in the center of your screen.

Figure 22-7: MacroIconTest frame

Test the update function by running some of the following macros:

- `/run MacroIconTest_UpdateIcons(15)`
- `/run MacroIconTest_UpdateIcons(180)`
- `/run MacroIconTest_UpdateIcons(-1)`

Notice that in the last example, rather than error the first two icons are shown blank.

Adding Scroll Bars

As in the previous example, a simple slider can be used to scroll through the list of icons. Add the following to your `MacroIconTest.xml` file after the `</Frame>` tag from the main frame:

```
<Slider name="MacroIconTest_HSlider" orientation="HORIZONTAL">
  <Anchors>
    <Anchor point="TOP" relativePoint="BOTTOM"↵
 relativeTo="MacroIconTest"/>
```

```
    </Anchors>
    <Size x="150" y="25"/>
    <ThumbTexture name="$parentThumbTexture" ↵
file="Interface\Buttons\UI-ScrollBar-Knob">
      <Size x="25" y="25/>
    </ThumbTexture>
    <Scripts>
      <OnLoad>
        local max = math.floor(GetNumMacroIcons())
        self:SetMinMaxValues(1, max)
        self:SetValueStep(1.0)
        self:SetValue(1)
      </OnLoad>
      <OnValueChanged>
        MacroIconTest_UpdateIcons(value)
      </OnValueChanged>
    </Scripts>
  </Slider>
```

This is essentially the same slider used in the preceding example, only it sets the minimum and maximum values based on the number of icons (in case it changes between versions). When the slider changes values, the `MacroIconTest_UpdateIcons()` function is called with the new offset.

Scrolling with the Mouse Wheel

You can add mouse wheel scrolling to this (or any other) scroll frame by ensuring the frame is set to receive mouse events and setting an `OnMouseWheel` script. Add the following to the `<Scripts>` section of the `MacroIconTest` frame:

```
<OnMouseWheel>
  MacroIconTest_OnMouseWheel(self, delta)
</OnMouseWheel>
```

Then add this function to `MacroIconTest.lua`:

```
function MacroIconTest_OnMouseWheel(self, delta)
  local current = MacroIconTest_HSlider:GetValue()

  if (delta < 0) and (current < GetNumMacroIcons()) then
    MacroIconTest_HSlider:SetValue(current + 1)
  elseif (delta > 0) and (current > 1) then
    MacroIconTest_HSlider:SetValue(current - 1)
  end
end
```

This function definition just piggybacks onto the slider bar's min and max values to ensure it doesn't go outside those boundaries. You should now be able to scroll the frame using both the slider (see Figure 22-8) and the mouse wheel.

Figure 22-8: MacroIconTest
addon showing various
macro icons

USING BLIZZARD TEMPLATES

Two Blizzard templates deal with scroll frames: `UIPanelScrollFrameTemplate` **and**
`FauxScrollFrameTemplate`. **Throughout the course of my addon development, I have
found them to be more confusing than anything else, while creating custom scroll frames
is actually relatively simple.**

**A few graphics are available, if necessary, for the scroll bar background and thumb
texture, along with sets of graphics for the up and down arrow buttons (you can find
templates for these in** `UIPanelTemplates.xml`**).**

**Currently, no horizontal scroll bars are used in the default user interface, so there are
no pre-made graphics available to be used.**

Summary

A visual scroll frame is a smooth, pixel-by-pixel scroll frame that can be used to display
contents that are too large for the parent window. Scroll frames of this nature are used in
the default user interface in the Quest Log, and within the edit box in the macro window.

Pseudo scroll frames use a set number of frames to display a list of rows by changing
offsets using the scroll bar. These scroll frames don't change visually when you scroll
through them; rather, they redraw the rows with different information. These faux scroll
frames are used in the Auction House, Friends list, and several other places in the
default user interface.

# CHAPTER 23

Creating Dropdown Menus

James Whitehead II

Popup menus are used throughout the default user interface to provide a list of actions or configuration options based on context, such as the menu that appears when you right-click your target or the chat frame configuration menu.

Some dropdown menus are triggered by a mouse click on a pre-existing frame, such as the menu that appears when you right-click the player frame (shown in Figure 23-1). Other menus have artwork that makes them appear as a more specific dropdown-style menu, such as the dropdown used for column selection in the "Who" tab of the Social pane, shown in Figure 23-2.

Figure 23-1:
Dropdown menu
displayed when
right-clicking on
the player frame

Figure 23-2: Column dropdown
in the "Who List" panel

Creating these menus is relatively easy once you understand how they work. This chapter takes you through using dropdown menus.

Creating a Simple Dropdown

There are four major components to creating a new dropdown menu. Blizzard provides a robust set of templates and functions that make managing dropdowns fairly easy. This section leads you through the following steps:

1. Adding a button that can be clicked to show the dropdown menu. This may be a button that already exists in your addon or something new entirely.

2. Creating a new frame that inherits the `UIDropDownMenuTemplate` template that is provided by Blizzard. Instead of making a new frame, you can re-use an existing dropdown frame, but this method allows you to ensure no one else will be able to modify your frame.

3. Initializing the dropdown menu once it has been created.

4. Writing code that causes a click on the button to toggle the display of the dropdown menu.

For this example, you need to create a new addon called **DropDownTest**. Create the basic addon skeleton including `DropDownTest.lua` and `DropDownTest.xml`.

Adding a Toggle Button

Using the Blizzard template `GameMenuButtonTemplate`, create a button by adding the following code to `DropDownTest.xml`:

```
<Ui xmlns="http://www.blizzard.com/wow/ui/" ↵
xmlns:xsi="http://www.w3.org/2001/XMLSchema-instance" ↵
xsi:schemaLocation="http://www.blizzard.com/wow/ui/
..\FrameXML\UI.xsd">
  <Button name="DropDownTest_Button" ↵
inherits="GameMenuButtonTemplate" parent="UIParent" ↵
text="DropDownTest">
    <Anchors>
      <Anchor point="CENTER"/>
    </Anchors>
    <Scripts>
      <OnClick>
        DropDownTest_ButtonOnClick(self, button, down)
      </OnClick>
    </Scripts>
  </Button>
</Ui>
```

To make a quick and easy button, this code uses the `GameMenuButtonTemplate`. The text is set using the XML attribute, and the new button is anchored to the center of the user interface. When the button is clicked, it will call the `DropDownTest_ButtonOnClick()` function and pass the proper arguments.

Creating a Dropdown Frame

The default Blizzard Interface uses templates for its dropdown menus and, as a result, you can re-use the templates as a basis for your own menus. Add the following frame definition to `DropDownTest.xml`:

```
<Frame name="DropDownTest_DropDown" ↵
inherits="UIDropDownMenuTemplate" ↵
frameStrata="DIALOG_FULLSCREEN">
  <Scripts>
    <OnLoad>
      DropDownTest_DropDownOnLoad(self)
    </OnLoad>
  </Scripts>
</Frame>
```

This frame simply inherits from the given template and sets the `frameStrata` to be `DIALOG_FULLSCREEN` in case the dropdown is used on a frame that is already `FULLSCREEN`. When the frame is first created, `DropDownTest_DropDownOnLoad()` is called to handle the initialization of the dropdown menu.

Initializing the Dropdown

Two things need to happen when you are initializing a dropdown menu. First, you must define a function that will be responsible for describing the actual buttons and adding them to the menu. Second, you must call the global `UIDropDownMenu_Initialize()` to do some setup and accounting on the frame.

Adding Buttons to the Dropdown

The initialization function handles the creation of each menu item through a Lua table definition. This function takes a single argument, `level`, which indicates what level of the dropdown should be displayed (for multilevel menus). This simple example won't use the argument because it will only contain three items on the same level; multilevel menus are covered later in this chapter.

Add the following function to your `DropDownTest.lua` file:

```
function DropDownTest_InitializeDropDown(level)
  -- Create a table to use for button information
  local info = {}

  -- Create a title button
```

```
    info.text = "DropDown Test"
    info.isTitle = 1
    UIDropDownMenu_AddButton(info)

    -- Create a normal button
    info = {}
    info.text = "Sample Item 1"
    UIDropDownMenu_AddButton(info)

    -- Create another normal button
    info = {}
    info.text = "Sample Item 2"
    UIDropDownMenu_AddButton(info)
end
```

Each button is described by a table with several attributes and passed to the `UIDrop-DownMenu_AddButton()` function, which handles the creation and display of the button. This code creates a title element with two basic elements below it.

BEST PRACTICES

In this example, the initialization function creates three new tables each time it is displayed. When the menu is this small that shouldn't be an issue, but larger menus created this way can make quite a bit of tables that are simply thrown away afterward. One technique to counteract this is re-using the same table to add buttons, as in the following example:

```
function DropDownTest_InitializeDropDown(level)
  -- Create a table to use for button information
  local info = {}

  -- Create a title button
  info.text = "DropDown Test"
  info.isTitle = 1
  UIDropDownMenu_AddButton(info)

  -- Create a normal button
  info.text = "Sample Item 1"
  info.isTitle = nil
  UIDropDownMenu_AddButton(info)

  -- Create another normal button
  info.text = "Sample Item 2"
  UIDropDownMenu_AddButton(info)
end
```

BEST PRACTICES *(continued)*

Alternatively, you could define the buttons ahead of time and then simply add them in the initialization function, as demonstrated in the following:

```
local dropdown_title1 = {
  text = "DropDown Test",
  isTitle = 1,
}

local dropdown_item1 = {
  text = "Sample Item 1",
}

local dropdown_item2 = {
  text = "Sample Item 2",
}
function DropDownTest_InitializeDropDown(level)
  UIDropDownMenu_AddButton(dropdown_title1)
  UIDropDownMenu_AddButton(dropdown_item1)
  UIDropDownMenu_AddButton(dropdown_item2)
end
```

There is no solution that is perfect for all applications. You'll need to consider how your dropdowns are being used and what code will be the most readable later on down the line. Later in this chapter you'll see another approach that enables you to create the button definitions ahead of time and have them automatically added to the menu.

Calling UIDropDownMenu_Initialize()

The `UIDropDownMenu_Initialize()` function stores the initialization function so it can be used later on and does other general setup. Call the function by adding the following to `DropDownTest.lua`:

```
function DropDownTest_DropDownOnLoad(self)
  UIDropDownMenu_Initialize(self, DropDownTest_InitializeDropDown);
end
```

When the dropdown is first created, the `OnLoad` script simply calls the Blizzard `UIDropDownMenu_Initialize()` function with the dropdown frame itself as the first argument and the initialization function as the second argument. The initialization function you specify will be called during this function, and then again each time the dropdown is shown (or the menu enters a sublevel).

Toggling the Dropdown Menu

The Blizzard template code defines a toggle function, called `ToggleDropDownMenu()`, that allows you to easily show the dropdown menu as well as specify some basic positioning information. The function takes six arguments:

- `level` (number) — The initial level to display. This number is passed directly to the initialization function.

- `value` — A value used to set `UIDROPDOWNMENU_MENU_VALUE`, which is used primarily in multilevel menus. This is discussed in detail later in this chapter.

- `dropDownFrame` — The actual dropdown frame to display.

- `anchorName` (string) — The name of the frame to which the dropdown should be anchored. This can also be the string `"cursor"`, in which case the dropdown is anchored to the cursor position at the point this function is called.

- `xOffset` (number) — A horizontal offset in pixels for the dropdown menu.

- `yOffset` (number) — A vertical offset in pixels for the dropdown menu.

Add the following function to `DropDownTest.lua` to call `ToggleDropDownMenu()` when the test button is clicked:

```
function DropDownTest_ButtonOnClick(self, button, down)
  ToggleDropDownMenu(1, nil, DropDownTest_DropDown, ↵
self:GetName(), 0, 0)
end
```

Because this example only displays one level of the menu, the function passes `1` as level and doesn't include a menu value. The dropdown will be anchored to the button itself, with no offset from the default location.

Testing the Dropdown

Log in to World of Warcraft with `DropDownTest` enabled; a game button should display in the center of your screen. Click the button and you should see the dropdown menu shown in Figure 23-3.

Figure 23-3:
Dropdown menu
created by
DropDownTest addon

The example menu won't do anything at the moment, but the second section of this chapter shows you how to make the menu elements functional so they can be used for configuration and other purposes. By default, the menu will timeout after a certain period of inactivity, and clicking the test button while the menu is open will close it outright.

Creating Multilevel Dropdowns

Creating a multilevel dropdown menu is relatively straightforward once you understand how a dropdown menu is created and initialized. The dropdown level is a numeric value that indicates what layer in the hierarchy is currently being displayed.

Consider a dropdown with two submenus called Alpha and Beta. Assume each menu has distinct items that will be displayed. Because the root level of the menu is 1, the level for both Alpha and Beta is 2 (because they are children of the main menu). If each of them had another layer, it would be level 3, and so on. To differentiate between Alpha and Beta, you will use a value element in the button table so the initialization function knows which menu to display.

Rewrite the `DropDownTest_InitializeDropDown()` function in your test addon, as follows:

```
function DropDownTest_InitializeDropDown(level)
  if level == 1 then
    local info = {}
    info.text = "DropDown Test"
    info.isTitle = 1
    UIDropDownMenu_AddButton(info, level)

    info = {}
    info.text = "Alpha Submenu"
    info.hasArrow = 1
    info.value = "Alpha"
    UIDropDownMenu_AddButton(info, level)

    info = {}
    info.text = "Beta Submenu"
    info.hasArrow = 1
    info.value = "Beta"
    UIDropDownMenu_AddButton(info, level)
  elseif (level == 2) and (UIDROPDOWNMENU_MENU_VALUE == "Alpha") then
    local info = {}
    info.text = "Alpha Sub-item 1"
    UIDropDownMenu_AddButton(info, level)
  elseif (level == 2) and (UIDROPDOWNMENU_MENU_VALUE == "Beta") then
    local info = {}
    info.text = "Beta Sub-item 1"
    UIDropDownMenu_AddButton(info, level)
  end
end
```

You'll notice quite a few differences between the original function and this one, namely the use of the `hasArrow` and `value` attributes in some of the button tables. `hasArrow` simply tells the template code to treat the button as a menu header and to display the arrow graphic. The `value` attribute is used to distinguish between different submenus.

In the initialization function, if the level is 2, the value of `UIDROPDOWNMENU_MENU_VALUE` is checked. This variable is set to the value attribute of the menu header. These values can be anything — tables, functions, numbers, and strings — as long as you can use them to distinguish between menus.

An optional second argument to the `UIDropDownMenu_AddButton()` function indicates the level at which the new button should be added. Without this, entering a submenu would only add buttons to the root menu instead of popping out an additional level, and that would be confusing.

The resulting menu can be seen in Figures 23-4 and 23-5.

Figure 23-4: Example dropdown menu with Alpha expanded

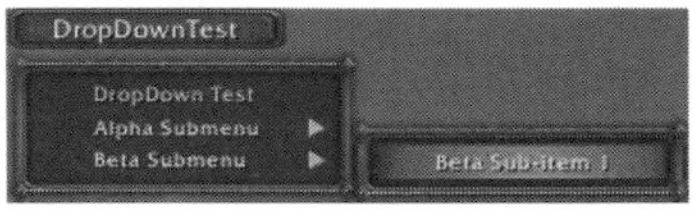

Figure 23-5: Example dropdown menu with Beta expanded

Creating Advanced Dropdowns

Dropdown menus are capable of displaying several different widgets, such as checkboxes and color pickers, in addition to the standard buttons. Each of these widgets is defined using specific sets of attributes in the button table that is passed to `UIDropDownMenu_AddButton()`. The following attributes are always available for a menu item:

- `text` (string) — Text to be displayed on the menu item.
- `textR` (number) — Red color value of the text (0–255).
- `textG` (number) — Green color value of the button text (0–255).
- `textB` (number) — Blue color value of the button text (0–255).
- `isTitle` — A flag (1 or `nil`) indicating if the button should be treated as a title button (not clickable and gold text).

- notClickable — A flag (1 or nil) indicating that the button should not be clickable. This forces the button's color to white, so you cannot color an unclickable item.

- notCheckable — A flag (1 or nil) indicating that the button cannot be checked. This causes the button's width to shrink because the check button graphic is no longer necessary.

- tooltipTitle (string) — Title to be displayed in the tooltip that appears when hovering the mouse over the menu option.

- tooltiptext (string) — Text to be displayed in the tooltip that appears when hovering the mouse over the menu option.

- textHeight (number) — The height of the font used for the button text.

- justifyH — If this attribute is set to CENTER, the text on the button will be centered. No other text justification options are available.

Function Menu Items

A menu item can be set to call a function when it is clicked by using the following list of attributes:

- func — The function to be called when the button is clicked.

- arg1 — The first argument to be passed to the function when it is called.

- arg2 — The second argument to be passed to the function when it is called.

- keepShownOnClick — A value indicating whether the dropdown menu should remain showing instead of disappearing when the button is clicked. A value of 1 keeps the menu visible, while nil causes it to disappear.

A valid definition for a function menu item would look something like this:

```
info = {}
info.text = "Function Button 1"
function info.func(arg1, arg2)
  ChatFrame1:AddMessage("Arg1: " .. tostring(arg1) .. " Arg2: " ↵
.. tostring(arg2))
end
info.arg1 = "MYMENU_NAME"
info.arg2 = "MYITEM_NAME"
UIDropDownMenu_AddButton(info)
```

The function you supply can be as simple as changing a setting in your addon based on the arguments that were supplied, or creating and displaying an elaborate frame.

> **HINT** In reality, most of your buttons will have a func attribute that is used to really do something when the user clicks on a button. If you are using check buttons in your dropdown, they will change their visual state when they are clicked, but you will need to actually toggle the appropriate setting, as well.

CheckButton Menu Items

A dropdown will often be used to toggle configuration items on and off and, as a result, it has a built-in checkbox item for use. These menu items are created by using the `checked` attribute along with some logic in the handler function. For example:

```
info = {}
info.text = "Do Something"
info.checked = SomeSetting
function info.func(arg1, arg2)
  SomeSetting = not SomeSetting
end
UIDropDownMenu_AddButton(info)
```

This code creates a button with the label "Do Something" (see Figure 23-6). When this button is created, the global variable `SomeSetting` is checked and used to set the checked state of the menu item. When the button is clicked, the global setting variable is toggled.

Figure 23-6:
Dropdown Test
showing the
"Do Something"
option

ColorPicker Menu Items

A dropdown menu can contain color swatches that can be opened to show a color picker frame. These allow for easy customization of colors in a hierarchical manner, but using them to the fullest requires a full set of the following attributes:

- `hasColorSwatch` — A flag (`1`, `nil`) that adds a color swatch to the menu item. This swatch can then be clicked to open the color picker frame.

- `swatchFunc` — A function called by the color picker when the color has changed.

- `hasOpacity` — A flag (`1`, `nil`) that adds the opacity slider to the color picker frame.

- `opacity` — The percentage of opacity, as a value between `0.0` and `1.0`, indicating how transparent the color selected is.

- `opacityFunc` — A function called by the color picker when the opacity changes.

- `cancelFunc` — A function called by the color picker when the user clicks the Cancel button. This function is passed the previous values to which the color picker is reverting.

- `r` — The red component of the color swatch (0-255).

- `g` — The green component of the color swatch (0-255).

- `b` — The blue component of the color swatch (0-255).

The following example uses the color picker to change the color of the player's name on the player frame. The code accesses the font string `PlayerName` to get the current color values, as well as to set the new color.

```
info = {}
info.text = "PlayerName Color"
info.hasColorSwatch = 1
local oldr,oldg,oldb,olda = PlayerName:GetTextColor()
info.r = oldr
info.g = oldg
info.b = oldb

function info.swatchFunc()
  local r,g,b = ColorPickerFrame:GetColorRGB()
  PlayerName:SetTextColor(r,g,b)
end

function info.cancelFunc(prev)
  PlayerName:SetTextColor(prev.r, prev.g, prev.g)
end

UIDropDownMenu_AddButton(info)
```

When this code runs, it gets the current color of the text using `PlayerName:GetTextColor()` and stores those values in the `r`, `g`, and `b` attributes of the new menu item. The swatch function fetches the selected color from the color picker frame and handles the selection of the text, while the cancel function takes the values it is passed and restores the previous color.

This definition creates the menu item shown in Figure 23-7. When the user clicks on the color swatch, the color picker frame (see Figure 23-8) opens. The color the user chooses is reflected in the player frame. Figure 23-9 shows the name colored green.

Figure 23-7: Menu item to change the color of the player's name

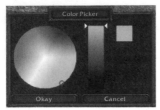

Figure 23-8: The ColorPicker frame that appears when the color swatch is selected

Figure 23-9: Player frame with color changed

Automating Menu Creation

Creating dropdown menus can be a bit tedious, but there are several ways to slightly automate the process. The following example function shows how to define a dropdown using a table to describe the different elements:

```
function DropDownTest_InitializeDropDown(level)
  -- Make sure level is set to 1, if not supplied
  level = level or 1

  -- Get the current level from the info table
  local info = dropdownInfo[level]

  -- If a value has been set, try to find it at the current level
  if level > 1 and UIDROPDOWNMENU_MENU_VALUE then
    if info[UIDROPDOWNMENU_MENU_VALUE] then
      info = info[UIDROPDOWNMENU_MENU_VALUE]
    end
  end

  -- Add the buttons to the menu
  for idx, entry in ipairs(info) do
    UIDropDownMenu_AddButton(entry, level)
  end
end
```

This code uses a table called `dropdownInfo` to define the various levels of a drop-down menu. It allows submenus and also handles the differentiation between different, same-level submenus. A table that makes use of this function might look like this:

```
MyOptionsTable = {
  -- Define level one elements here
  [1] = {
    { -- Title
      text = "Example dropdown",
      isTitle = 1,
    },
    { -- Sample item
      text = "Sample item 1",
    },
    { -- Submenu Alpha item
      text = "Submenu Alpha",
      hasArrow = 1,
      value = "Alpha",
    },
    { -- Submenu Beta item
      text = "Submenu Beta",
      hasArrow = 1,
      value = "Beta",
    },
  },
  [2] = { -- Submenu items, keyed by value
    ["Alpha"] = {
      {
        text = "Alpha subitem 1",
      },
    },
    ["Beta"] = {
      {
        text = "Gamma submenu",
        hasArrow = 1,
      },
    },
  },
  [3] = { -- Third submenu
    {
      text = "Gamma subitem 1",
    },
  },
}
```

While that may seem like a lot of code, it is quite a bit easier to read and update than a set of hardcoded entries. Figures 23-10, 23-11, and 23-12 show the resulting menu.

Figure 23-10:
Example dropdown
menu (Level 1)

Figure 23-11: Example dropdown
menu (Level 2)

Figure 23-12: Example dropdown menu (Level 3)

Summary

Creating a dropdown menu is a matter of learning to use the templates and functions that exist in the default user interface. Dropdowns can be used for anything from a quick configuration interface to displaying hierarchical information to the user.

# CHAPTER 24

Tooltips

Bryan McLemore

Tooltips are by far one of the most visible UI elements in World of Warcraft. Whenever you move your mouse over a player, item, spell, talent, or almost anything else, you see a small tooltip at the bottom right of your screen. It's time to dig into the inner works of the tooltips and how you can bend them to your own whims.

Manipulating Tooltips

The central components of tooltips inside WoW are the `GameTooltip` frame type and the `GameTooltip` object. This is confusing at first because both share the same name. The object `GameTooltip` is the tooltip you normally see when you mouse over items and players in-game. By consistently reusing the same object, Blizzard has a built-in safeguard that only one is showing at a time. However, it is possible, as seen by the item comparison tooltips, to show multiple tooltips by creating more objects of the `GameTooltip` frame type.

Another tooltip object the base UI defines is the `ItemRefTooltip`. It is the tooltip-like frame that shows up when you click on an item link in chat. Unlike other tooltips, the `ItemRefTooltip` remains on the screen until you explicitly close it. This object is what you'll be using to explore basic tooltip functionality.

Using :Set. . . Functions

A multitude of functions are attached to a `GameTooltip` object, showing information about various game elements. Before you look at some of them, you need to display a tooltip object to manipulate.

Clicking on an item link in chat runs the `SetItemRef` function with a reference to the item you want to see. Let's do the same by running `SetItemRef("item:6948")` in WowLua. You should now see the `ItemRefTooltip` for your Hearthstone.

Now that you have the tooltip on display, you can play with it a little. Run the following:

```
ItemRefTooltip:SetTalent(1,1)
```

With a little bit of magic, the function turns the tooltip from your Hearthstone to the tooltip that should match the top-left talent from your first talent tree. By manipulating the arguments, you can display other talents. The first variable passed into SetTalent is which talent tree, and the second is the talent index counting left to right, top to bottom.

As mentioned earlier, you can use a myriad of functions on tooltip objects. One notable function is `:SetHyperlink`, which sets the tooltip to any item that you send in. Internally, `SetItemRef` uses this function. Run the following to return the tooltip to your Hearthstone:

```
ItemRefTooltip:SetHyperlink("item:6948")
```

Now that you've seen how the `:Set...` functions allow you to fill a tooltip with information provided by the WoW client, you can get info on all the other `:Set...` functions in Chapter 31, "Widget Reference."

Tooltips with Custom Content

The various ":Set..." commands are great — they let you show some cool info easily. However, that's only one use for tooltips. Another use is to show custom information such as usage hints or more detailed information. First, though, take a look at the basic ways to add lines to the tooltip. Using the same tooltip you've been playing with in the previous examples, run the following:

```
ItemRefTooltip:ClearLines().
```

Now you should see a very empty tooltip. That's because the tooltip does not redraw when you add or remove content. While the content vanishes when you call `:ClearLines`, it will not change the layout or size of the tooltip.

There are two functions — `:AddLine` and `:AddDoubleLine` — that add arbitrary lines to the tooltip, and they are similar in function. `:AddLine` adds a single text string to a line, whereas `:AddDoubleLine` adds two text strings split into two columns. Run the following commands:

```
ItemRefTooltip:AddLine("The King of the World")
ItemRefTooltip:AddDoubleLine("The King is:", "Me!")
```

Figure 24-1 shows you the results.

Figure 24-1: The messed
up tooltip

A few things you should notice right off: The first line is a header; it has a slightly larger font than the other lines. You can use this as part of your presentation. Second, the tooltip looks horrible. You have a lot of extra space, and some words overlap on the second line. This is a problem.

Remember how the tooltips do not redraw when you add or remove content? They redraw when their :Show function is called. You can trigger this resizing manually by calling ItemRefTooltip:Show(). Go ahead and try it. The tooltip will look much better.

Both :AddLine and :AddDoubleLine have additional optional arguments for specifying the color of the text. The color is split into three arguments, each expecting a number between 0 and 1. Try the following commands:

```
ItemRefTooltip:ClearLines()
-- I like blue for this line
ItemRefTooltip:AddLine("The King of the World", 0, 0, 1)
-- And for this one how about white and then red respectively
ItemRefTooltip:AddDoubleLine("The King is:", "I", 1, 1, 1, 1, 0, 0)
ItemRefTooltip:Show()
```

The numbers represent how much of each color — red, green, and blue, in that order — to put into the mix: 0 for none, and 1 for max.

NOTE A quick way to remember this is the "Roy G Biv" trick. The acronym actually shows the whole color spectrum (Red Orange Yellow Green Blue Indigo Violet), but you're just concerned about his initials: R, G, B.

Creating Custom Tooltips

Everything you've seen so far applies to all objects of the GameTooltip type. However, only two of those are commonly used in the default environment: GameTooltip and ItemRefTooltip. For most of your purposes, these two will serve you well, but there will be times when you want to have another tooltip object to work with.

Keep in mind that in your average use case, you won't need to make more tooltips, but you can reuse the standard GameTooltip. If you need to display a tooltip in addition to the regular tooltip, you'll need to create an additional tooltip object. Look at the following code:

```
CreateFrame("GameTooltip", "MyTip", UIParent, ↵
 "GameTooltipTemplate")

GameTooltip_SetDefaultAnchor(MyTip, UIParent)
tooltip:SetHyperlink("item:6948")
```

There you have it — the bare minimal code you need to create and display a custom tooltip. The first line creates the new tooltip object with the name `MyTip`. Unlike most other frame types, you cannot omit the name argument (`MyTip`, in this example). The internal code that creates the tooltip, sizes it, and adds lines depends on having a named object. Be careful, because forgetting to name a tooltip object can give you hours of headache and frustration. WoW will not complain or gripe about the missing name; instead, all of the methods will leave you with an empty object that won't show anything.

The second line is just a shortcut method for showing the tooltip in the default location. A slightly longer version of this code would reveal the following lines instead:

```
MyTip:SetOwner(UIParent, "ANCHOR_NONE");
MyTip:SetPoint("BOTTOMRIGHT", "UIParent", "BOTTOMRIGHT", ↵
-CONTAINER_OFFSET_X - 13, CONTAINER_OFFSET_Y);
```

These lines are at the heart of all tooltip placements. Like any other frame, a tooltip needs an anchor point to be visible. The concept of an owner condenses the normal frame positioning actions. The first line of the preceding code sets the tooltip's owner to `UIParent` with no anchor. Without the second line, the tooltip would remain invisible because it isn't anchored. The second line anchors its bottom-right corner to the bottom right of the screen, and uses a couple of global variables provided by the default UI to move the tooltip far enough from the bottom-right corner that it doesn't overlap the action bars or other standard UI elements.

Another slightly entertaining variation on these lines would be to replace them with the following line:

```
MyTip:SetOwner(UIParent, "ANCHOR_CURSOR")
```

After running this line you'll notice that the tooltip is stuck to your cursor, and it won't stop. At this point there's no close condition, so the tooltip won't hide. You don't want to reload the UI because that would destroy the tooltip and you're not done with it yet. To stop it from following the cursor, re-anchor it:

```
MyTip:SetOwner(Minimap, "ANCHOR_BOTTOMLEFT")
```

Parsing Tooltip Data

So you've explored how you can create and edit tooltips and make them bend to your will. However, displaying information on the screen is only half of what makes tooltip objects useful. Many of a tooltip's :Set... functions display information that cannot be found anywhere else in the addon API, which gives rise to the need to parse the tooltip data.

Basic Anatomy

The anatomy of a tooltip is simple: It's a series of FontString objects representing the two labels on each line. Luckily, the objects are named according to a logical pattern, which looks something like this:

```
(TooltipName)Text(Left|Right)(lineNumber)
```

That sounds much worse than it really is. For example, the top-left header text on the tooltip we used in the last section would be MyTipTooltipTextLeft1. A mouthful for sure, but it should be easy to see where it goes from there.

In addition to a number of these FontStrings, the tooltip also contains a money frame, which is displayed in cases such as selling equipment or showing repair prices. In general, though, you won't need to scan this frame for information.

There is no explicit limit on how many lines you can have in a tooltip. The tooltip object creates as many FontStrings as needed to display information provided by one of its :Set... methods, and automatically adds more as you call :AddLine or :AddDoubleLine. At any given time, you can use a tooltip's :NumLines method to tell you how many lines a tooltip object has.

Basic Scanning Loop

Now that you know what a tooltip is made of, you can easily examine its contents. If you know exactly on which line and side of a tooltip the information you're looking for is displayed, you can look at only that line. However, if you don't know exactly which line you need to look at, you can simply scan it from top to bottom or bottom to top, if that direction makes more sense. The following code is a basic loop that lets you examine the contents of the tooltip line by line:

```
for i=1, tooltip:NumLines() do
    local left = getglobal(tooltip:GetName().."TextLeft"..i):GetText()
    local right = getglobal(tooltip:GetName().."TextRight"..i):GetText()

    -- Do something with the text here
End
```

You can do a great many things with this text: serialize it to a variable, count the total amount of stats you get from an item, calculate the secondary effects an item has on you based on its primary stats. You can achieve many options with this general method, mostly only limited by your imagination. However, if it's possible to get the information you're looking for without scanning a tooltip, do so. Tooltip processing like this can have performance issues, and race conditions may exist if the tooltip is changing rapidly.

Now you know how to gather information from tooltips. As mentioned earlier, you should only use tooltips to gather information you cannot get elsewhere. When gathering information that can't be gathered elsewhere it is often best to use a custom tooltip object that remains invisible to prevent your users from having their normal tooltip hijacked and changed at random intervals.

Summary

Tooltips: You can make them, fold them, bend them, and break them. Creating your own custom tooltips is within your sphere of power, and scraping them for every drop of information they have is now easily doable.

# CHAPTER 25

Using State Headers

Matthew Orlando

Chapter 17 offered your first glimpse of the decision-making capabilities provided to addons for combat actions such as targeting, spell casting, and so forth. Now we will bring this to a whole new level by adding *state headers* to the mix. A state header is simply a frame inherited (directly or otherwise) from `SecureStateHeaderTemplate`. This template provides an array of features to control decision-making processes (which spell to cast, which macro to use, whether to target or assist, and more), as well as various visual aspects of the header and its children.

Each header you create is in one state at any given moment. With the swath of attributes this chapter introduces, you can configure `SecureActionButtonTemplate` buttons to behave in countless ways based on the state of their header.

A state is simply a label of "the way things are." In and of themselves, states carry no meaning. It is only through the description of behaviors that they come to life. A behavior might be something like, "If you click this button while in state 0, cast Drain Life and then move to state 1."

In WoW, states are stored in the `"state"` attribute of a state header. This can be basically any string, though whole numbers are more readily supported by the template code. When the state changes, the header's children can be shown, hidden, moved, sized, or even have new keys bound to them.

Creating Your First State Header

For experimentation during this chapter, you'll be using `ActionBarButtonTemplate` buttons. This template responds visually to state changes so you will have immediate feedback as you add new behaviors. To that end, please create a test addon with an empty Lua file (no need for an XML file this time).

NOTE Be sure to keep this addon around for the next chapter.

First, you will create the header itself and place it in the center of the screen. The position is only for the purpose of anchoring its children; the header has no visible elements.

```
CreateFrame("Frame", "TestHeader", UIParent, ↵
"SecureStateHeaderTemplate")
TestHeader:SetPoint("CENTER")
```

To make testing as flexible as possible, you will make a function that adds new buttons to the action bar. First, you will create an upvalue for your function, `nextButton`, to help number each button sequentially. The first button created is named `TestButton1`, the second `TestButton2`, and so on.

```
local nextButton = 1
```

Now you can begin defining the function itself. The first step is to create the actual button frame. This is fairly straightforward:

```
function CreateTestButton()
  local button = CreateFrame(
    "CheckButton",
    "TestButton"..nextButton,
    TestHeader,
    "ActionBarButtonTemplate"
  )
```

Next, tell the button to look to its parent for its `"statebutton"` attribute. The `"statebutton"` works just like `"helpbutton"` and `"harmbutton"`, but instead of responding to the hostility of your target, it works with the state of the button's header. You will be using this extensively throughout the chapter.

```
button:SetAttribute("useparent-statebutton", true)
```

NOTE You can use different `"statebutton"` attributes for each button to achieve more intricate behaviors. However, for the purpose of this chapter, delegating it to the parent makes the examples a bit simpler.

TIP If your button is configured to receive clicks on mouse down — see `RegisterForClicks` (Widget API) — the state header will look for a `"statedownbutton"` attribute before it looks for `"statebutton"` when it receives a down click. Because you can register a button for both up and down clicks simultaneously, a single button can take one action on mouse down and another action on mouse up.

Once the button is created, you need to register it with the state header, as shown here:

```
TestHeader:SetAttribute("addchild", button)
```

This makes the button a child of the header and wraps its OnClick method with code that handles state mapping and transitions.

> **TIP** SecureStateHeaderTemplate **uses a neat trick — repeated throughout the secure template code — to accomplish this wrapping securely. When you set the** "addchild" **attribute, it triggers the** OnAttributeChanged **script for the state header. Because both this script and the** "addchild" **attribute (whose value is the button itself) are secure, it can hook the button's** OnClick **handler without worrying about taint. It will also prevent you from adding new children to a state header during combat.**

Now that you have a new button to work with, you need to position it. Any button created after the first will be added to the right side of the bar by anchoring it to the previous button.

```
if nextButton > 1 then
  button:SetPoint("LEFT", _G["TestButton"..(nextButton - 1)], "RIGHT")
end
```

Whenever you add a new button, you should move the first button to the left to keep the bar centered. For each button in the bar (nextButton - 1), you move to the left (the negation at the beginning of the following formula) by half the width of a button (button:GetWidth() / 2), as shown here.

```
local offsetX = - (nextButton - 1) * button:GetWidth() / 2
TestButton1:SetPoint("CENTER", TestHeader, "CENTER", offsetX, 0)
```

Finally, you increment nextButton for the next call to CreateTestButton and return the newly created button.

```
nextButton = nextButton + 1
return button
end
```

Load up WoW with the new testing addon, and in another anticlimactic burst, you will see nothing new. That can be easily remedied by calling CreateTestButton by whatever method you prefer. Create a few buttons to see how the bar expands, as shown in Figure 25-1. At this point, all of the buttons will default to action slot 1 because they have not been instructed otherwise. When you are ready to continue, reload your UI to get rid of any excess buttons.

Figure 25-1: Example layout after calling CreateTestButton three times

NOTE If you do not see a button appear after calling `CreateTestButton`, it means you have no action in slot 1. Simply pick up any spell, macro, or usable item and the button outline will appear, allowing you to place your selection.

Remapping Mouse Clicks

The buttons you just added are children of a state header because you want to be able to change their actions based on predefined states. You use modified attributes with customized suffixes, as you did with `"helpbutton"` and `"harmbutton"` (modified attributes, `"helpbutton"`, and `"harmbutton"` are covered in Chapter 17). A `"statebutton"` attribute defines what virtual mouse button to use in each state to click your action button.

Using State Attributes

A `"statebutton"` follows a particular format known as a *state attribute*. State attributes evaluate to some value based on the current state. The meaning of this value depends on the purpose of the attribute. A state attribute consists of semicolon-separated rules linking states with values. The rules are checked from left to right until a match is found, in which case the attribute will evaluate to the specified value. Rules can appear in one of the following forms.

- *value* — Because no state is specified, this rule will always match.
- *state:value* — Matches if the header is in the specified state. You can substitute `state` with an asterisk (*) to match any state.
- *start-end:value* — Matches if the header is in a numeric state in the range from `start` to `end` (`start` should be less than or equal to `end`).

Consider the following rule set, for example:

```
1:val1;2-4:val2;5:;default
```

When the header is in state 1 it will evaluate to `"val1"`, in states 2 through 4 it will be `"val2"`, and in state 5 it will be `nil`. Any other state will evaluate to `"default"`.

Some state attributes are also modified attributes. With the `"statebutton"` attribute, this means we can assign different rule sets for various combinations of modifier keys and mouse buttons.

Configuring the Buttons

You will be using the same two test buttons over the next few sections, so set up a script in WowLua's script editor to create them. This way, if you need to log out for any reason, you can recreate the buttons with a few clicks rather than configuring it manually each time. If you would like to experiment with more buttons or states than shown here, feel free to change the values for NUM_BUTTONS and NUM_STATES, as shown.

```
local NUM_STATES = 4
local NUM_BUTTONS = 2

local statebutton = ""
for state = 0, NUM_STATES - 1 do
  statebutton = statebutton..format("%d:B%1$d;", state)
end
TestHeader:SetAttribute("statebutton", statebutton)
```

This first snippet sets up a "statebutton" attribute on our header (remember that the "statebutton" is normally associated with each button, but we told our buttons to look to the header instead). For each state you will be using, it adds an item to the list in the form "n:Bn;". As with "helpbutton" and "harmbutton", we can name the values anything we want. In this case, we are using Bn; the B is an abbreviation for "button" and n indicates the state. With four states, the final attribute will be "0:B0;1:B1;2:B2;3:B3;".

Now you have to set up action attributes for each suffix defined by "statebutton". The outer loop creates the buttons themselves, and the inner loop sets the appropriate action attributes.

```
for buttonNum = 0, NUM_BUTTONS - 1 do
  local button = CreateTestButton()
  for state = 0, NUM_STATES - 1 do
    button:SetAttribute("*action-B"..state, (buttonNum*NUM_STATES) ↵
+ state + 1)
  end
end
```

With four states and two buttons, the first button will use actions 1-4, the second will use 5-8, and so on. This loop would be equivalent to the following:

```
TestButton1:SetAttribute("*action-B0", 1)
TestButton1:SetAttribute("*action-B1", 2)
TestButton1:SetAttribute("*action-B2", 3)
TestButton1:SetAttribute("*action-B3", 4)

TestButton2:SetAttribute("*action-B0", 5)
TestButton2:SetAttribute("*action-B1", 6)
TestButton2:SetAttribute("*action-B2", 7)
TestButton2:SetAttribute("*action-B3", 8)
```

Running your new script will now create two buttons fully configured to respond to state changes. You will notice the first button shows whatever action you have in slot 1, and the second will show slot 5. When you first create the state header, its state is `nil`. This is interpreted by the state system as `"0"` for most purposes, hence the mapping to `"*action-B0"`.

Now you can see what happens when the state changes. `SecureStateHeaderTemplate` uses its `OnAttributeChanged` script to handle all the actions associated with a state change. This means that you can trigger a state change manually — out of combat — by setting the `"state"` attribute directly. Enter the following command in WowLua's interactive mode to move to state 1 and the buttons will update to show the actions in the slots specified by their `"*action-B1"` attributes.

```
> TestHeader:SetAttribute("state", "1")
```

USING A DETACHED HEADER

`SecureActionButtonTemplate` **buttons are not required to be children of the state header to have their clicks remapped. Instead of setting the** `"addchild"` **attribute on the header, we can create a** `"stateheader"` **attribute on the button itself. For example, you can replace the** `"addchild"` **line from** `CreateTestButton` **with the following, and the button will behave as expected when clicked.**

```
button:SetAttribute("stateheader", TestHeader)
```

Although this can be useful in certain situations, it has a couple of important drawbacks. Normally, when a header changes state, it sets the `"state-parent"` **attribute on all of its children to the new state. If a button uses a detached header, it will no longer receive this notification. Because** `ActionBarButtonTemplate` **uses its** `OnAttributeChanged` **script to update the icon and other aspects of the button, using a detached header will prevent your buttons from giving you visual feedback about the state changes.**

Read another way, the only characteristic that buttons receive from their detached header is the action to take when clicked. This means that none of the other behaviors triggered by state changes will occur for the buttons, including visual changes and override bindings (covered later in this chapter).

Changing State with a Click

Changing states manually does not really accomplish much in the long run. The first game-managed state transition we will address is triggered by clicking on one of the children of the state header. The changes are controlled by a state attribute on the child called `"newstate"`. `"newstate"` uses *transition rules* to define what new state to enter given the current one. For example, the following command makes TestHeader move up one state each time you click the first button, wrapping back to state 0 when it gets to the end:

```
> TestButton1:SetAttribute("newstate", "0-3")
```

Each transition rule in the list can take one of three forms:

- *state* — Enter the given state. If blank, no state change occurs. If it's an equals sign (=), it will trigger a state change to its current state (useful for triggering visual updates without an actual state change).

- *start-end* — Cycle through the range of numerical states from start to end. After reaching end, it will return to start. If the header is not in any of the states in the range, it will enter start. The order is significant: "1-5" will cycle forward and "5-1" will cycle backward.

- *first, second, ..., last* — Cycle through the individually named states in the list from left to right, entering the first state of the set if not in one already.

For a more complex example, give TestButton2 a "newstate" of "3:1;2-1". Clicking the button while in state 3 will switch directly to state 1. States 1 and 2 will swap with each other. State 0 will transition to state 2 because the range is a catch-all (equivalent to "*:2-1").

Delaying the State Change

Sometimes, you may want some time to pass between the click and the state change. For example, a context menu with protected buttons could hide itself after a few seconds. The "delaystate" attribute allows you to accomplish just that. Like "newstate", "delaystate" uses transition rules to specify state changes.

The "delaystate" attribute also requires another state attribute, "delaytime". If the value retrieved from this attribute for the given state is a number, clicking the button sets up a timer for that many seconds. Once the time is up, the header will transition to the state specified by "delaystate". While the timer is running, any state changes will cancel it. This means that each click of the button restarts the timer. Run the following commands to set up a "delaystate" for TestButton1:

```
> TestButton1:SetAttribute("newstate", nil)
> TestButton1:SetAttribute("delaystate", "0-3")
> TestButton1:SetAttribute("delaytime", "0-1:1;2:2;3:3")
```

Clicking the button in state 0 or 1 will switch to state 1 or 2, respectively, after one second; state 2 will switch to state 3 after 2 seconds, and state 3 will wrap back to state 0 after 3 seconds.

You can also take advantage of "delaystate" and "newstate" at the same time. In this case, "delaystate" uses the original state at the time you click the button to determine the new state. For example, set your newstate to "1-3", your "delaystate" to "2:0", and your "delaytime" to "5". If you repeatedly click the button within five seconds, it will cycle states 1 through 3. If you click the button in state 2, switching immediately to state 3, after five seconds of inactivity it transitions to state 0. In any other state no delayed transition will occur.

In certain situations you may want a frame to remain visible while the mouse is over it. The delay system offers us one last state attribute, "delayhover". If it evaluates to true, the timer will not run until the mouse leaves the state header or any of its children. If the mouse re-enters any of the frames before the time is up, the timer will reset and wait until the mouse leaves again before resuming.

Controlling Visual Properties

Besides changing the action a button performs, you can also use the state to control certain visual aspects of the header and its children. The following sections outline various unmodified state attributes used directly on the header and its children. To make best use of these examples, you should give TestButton1 a "newstate" of "0-3" and clear any lingering "delaystate". You will use the first button to cycle through the states and observe changes occurring on TestButton2.

Showing and Hiding Children

Two attributes control visibility: "showstates" and "hidestates". They both operate in the same manner, but as you might guess, the former specifies which states to show the child (making it hidden by default) and the latter which states to hide (making it shown by default). Which one you choose is entirely up to you. Depending on the intent, one may make more sense than the other. If both are present, only the "showstates" will be respected. For example:

```
> TestButton2:SetAttribute("showstates", "0-1,3")
```

As you cycle through all the states by clicking the first button, you will notice that the second button disappears when you reach state 2. If you clear "showstates" and create a "hidestates" with the same value, you will notice the opposite behavior.

These two attributes consist of a comma-separated list of state rules, which are evaluated from left to right until a match is found. Each rule can be formed as follows.

- *state* — Match the specified state. You can use an asterisk (*) to match any state.

- *start-end* — Match any state in the given range.

A rule may be prefixed with an exclamation mark (!) to match the opposite. For example, "!2-4;1-10" would match all states from 1 to 10 except states 2 to 4.

Repositioning Children

You can position children relative to the parent using the following state attributes:

- "ofsx" — Horizontal offset. Default is 0.

- "ofsy" — Vertical offset. Default is 0.

- "ofspoint" — The point on the child to anchor. Default is "CENTER".

- "ofsrelpoint" — The point on the parent to which the child will be anchored. Default is the same as ofspoint.

NOTE You must provide either "ofsx" or "ofsy" for positioning to occur.

These attributes correspond directly to the parameters for the `SetPoint` widget method. See the Widget API reference for further details. For example, the following command will move the second button above the center of the bar in states 0-1 and below the bar in any other state, as shown in Figure 25-2:

```
> TestButton2:SetAttribute("ofsy", "0-1:40;-40")
```

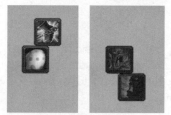

Figure 25-2: Example child repositioning

Resizing Children and the Header

The size of a child can be controlled with the state attributes `"width"`, `"height"`, and `"scale"`. These are equivalent to `SetWidth`, `SetHeight`, and `SetScale`, respectively. The following command multiplies the size of the second button by the given values for each state, as seen in Figure 25-3:

```
> TestButton2:SetAttribute("scale", "0:0.5;1:1;2:2;3:3")
```

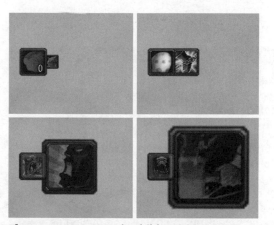

Figure 25-3: Example child resizing

The state header uses `"headwidth"`, `"headheight"`, and `"headscale"` exactly like the children use `"width"`, `"height"`, and `"scale"`.

Repositioning the Header

You can manipulate the position of the header in much the same way as its children. `"headofsx"`, `"headofsy"`, `"headofspoint"`, and `"headofsrelpoint"` operate just like the attributes shown earlier for the children (`"ofsx"`, `"ofsy"`, and so on). The header has a couple of extra features, though, which give it a bit more flexibility.

Anchoring to the Cursor or Screen

The `"headofsrelpoint"` attribute can use two special-purpose strings instead of a standard anchor point: `"screen"` and `"cursor"`. `"screen"` will anchor the header relative to the bottom-left corner of the screen, and `"cursor"` will anchor it relative to the position of the mouse cursor *at the time of the state change*. For example:

```
> TestHeader:SetAttribute("headofsrelpoint", "1-2:cursor;3:screen")
> TestHeader:SetAttribute("headofsx", "1:18;2:100;3:50;*:0")
> TestHeader:SetAttribute("headofsy", "3:300")
> TestButton1:SetAttribute("delaystate", "1-2:1")
> TestButton1:SetAttribute("delaytime", "3")
```

You have quite a few attributes interacting now, so Table 25-1 provides a concise breakdown of what happens when you click the button in a given state.

> **NOTE** Your experiences may differ if your bar does not have exactly two buttons, or if you still have some leftover positioning attributes from previous examples.

Table 25-1: State-by-State Behaviors for Header Anchoring Example

STATE	NEW STATE	ACTION
0	1	Move the bar so that `TestButton1` is directly under the mouse cursor (headofsrelpoint: `"1-2:cursor"`, headofsx: `"1:18"`).
1	2	Move the header 100 units to the right of the cursor (headofsrelpoint: `"1-2:cursor"`, headofsx: `"2:100"`). Set or reset a timer to return to state 1 after 3 seconds (delaystate: `"1-"2:1"`, delaytime: 3). When the time is up, the bar will be moved as if you had clicked in state 0.

Table 25-1 *(continued)*

STATE	NEW STATE	ACTION
2	3	Move the header 50 units to the right and 300 units up from the bottom-left corner of the screen (headofsrelpoint: `"3:screen"`, headofsx: `"3:50"`, headofsy: `"3:300"`).
		Set a timer as in state 1.
3	0	Move the header back to the center of the screen (headofsx: `"*:0"`).

Re-Parenting the Header

In addition to moving the header around relative to its parent, the screen, or the cursor, you can also give it an entirely new parent. You use a single control attribute, `"head-parent"`, to choose a suffix, and then you set the corresponding `"headparent-suffix"` attributes to the desired parent frames.

NOTE The new parent must be explicitly protected, because unprotected frames can be moved programmatically during combat.

For example:

```
TestHeader:SetAttribute("headofsy", "2:100;3:-100;*:0")
TestHeader:SetAttribute("headparent", "0:parent;2:bar;3:player")
TestHeader:SetAttribute("headparent-parent", UIParent)
TestHeader:SetAttribute("headparent-bar", ActionButton12)
TestHeader:SetAttribute("headparent-player", PlayerFrame)
```

Here is what happens when the header enters a given state (Figure 25-4 shows an example):

- State 0
  - Set the header's parent to UIParent (headparent: `"0:parent"`, headparent-parent: UIParent).
  - Re-anchor the header with no offset (headofsy: `"*:0"`).
- State 1
  - Re-anchor the header with no offset (headofsy: `"*:0"`).
  - This will have no noticeable effect on our test button setup because we will be coming from state 0, where this has already occurred. If the transition to state 1 was triggered externally (for example, via a `"delaystate"`), the header would be re-anchored to its parent at the time.

- State 2
    - Set the header's parent to the 12th action button on the main bar (headparent: `"2:bar"`, headparent-bar: `ActionButton12`).
    - Re-anchor the frame 100 units above the action button (headofsy: `"2:100"`).
- State 3
    - Set the header's parent to the player's unit frame (headparent: `"3:player"`, headparent-player: `PlayerFrame`).
    - Re-anchor the frame 100 units below the player frame (headofsy: `"3:-100"`).

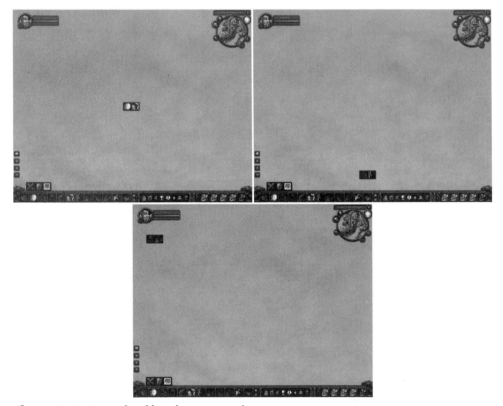

Figure 25-4: Example of header re-parenting

NOTE If there is no action on ActionButton12, it will be hidden. This means the TestHeader will hide as soon as it enters state 2. To bring it back, either place an action on the button or manually set the header's state to anything but 2.

Configuring Other Properties

In addition to the various visual properties, there are a few more subsystems you can use to affect the behavior of the header.

Changing the Header's Unit

A common practice for many addons is to set a `"unit"` attribute on a state header and give each of the children `"useparent-unit"` (as has been done with `ActionBarButtonTemplate`). You already have enough tools at your disposal to provide different units depending on the state. For example, change the button generation script in WowLua to the following and reload the UI:

```
local NUM_STATES = 4
local NUM_BUTTONS = 2

local statebutton = ""
for state = 0, NUM_STATES - 1 do
    statebutton = statebutton..format("%d:B%1$d;", state)
    TestHeader:SetAttribute("*unit-B"..state, "party"..(state + 1))
end
TestHeader:SetAttribute("statebutton", statebutton)

for buttonNum = 1, NUM_BUTTONS do
    local button = CreateTestButton()
    button:SetAttribute("action", buttonNum)
    button:SetAttribute("newstate", "0-3")
end
```

This new script will again create two buttons on a header with four states. Instead of remapping action attributes on the children, though, you are remapping unit attributes on the header. Each state sets the unit to one of your four party members. If you place healing abilities on the buttons, a click will cast on the currently selected party member and then transition to the next one.

While this does get the job done, we have a slightly more concise tool at our disposal. The `"headstateunit"` state attribute allows you to pick unit IDs for each state and will automatically apply them to the `"unit"` or `"unitsuffix"` attributes. Each rule can be in one of the following forms:

- *unitID* — Set the `"unit"` attribute to *unitID* and clear `"unitsuffix"`.
- +*unitID* — Set the `"unitsuffix"` attribute to *unitID* and clear `"unit"`.
- clear — Clear both `"unit"` and `"unitsuffix"`.

Now you can replace the `"statebutton"` block from the preceding script (lines 4-9) with the following:

```
local headstateunit = ""
for state = 0, NUM_STATES - 1 do
```

```
        headstateunit = headstateunit..format("%d:party%d;", state, ↵
state + 1)
end
TestHeader:SetAttribute("headstateunit", headstateunit)
```

If your addon needs to frequently manipulate the unit configuration, number of states, and so on, `"headstateunit"` can make the task much simpler by allowing you to work with a single attribute.

Overriding Key Bindings

Besides mouse button remapping, state headers can change what action you take by binding keys to new frames. Binding overrides use a state attribute on the header called `"statebindings"` to select a set name. Each child then uses its own `"bindings-setName"` attribute to specify which keys are bound to it for the given set. If the child has no bindings for the given set, then previously set override bindings will be removed.

The `"bindings-setName"` attribute is a semicolon-separated list of binding specifications, each using the following syntax. Items in brackets ([ ]) are optional:

```
[*]key[:mouseButton]
```

Each element of the binding specification corresponds to a parameter of `SetOverrideBindingClick`, with the presence of the asterisk representing `isPriority`. `mouseButton` defaults to `"LeftButton"` if unspecified.

You can think of the binding system in layers. At the bottom, you have normal key bindings. These are what you set through the game's key binding interface (and via the `SetBinding` APIs). At the next level up are override bindings. When you remove an override binding for a key, it reverts to the normal binding, if present. At the top are priority overrides. After a priority override is removed, the key will revert to the normal override, if present, or to the normal binding.

One possible use for override bindings might be a two-dimensional action bar where the first key press selects a row and the second uses an action in that row. Let's take a look at an example of just such a setup. You will create a 3x3 grid of `UIPanelButtonTemplate2` buttons that are accessed through number keys. For instance, pressing 1 will choose row 1, and then pressing 3 will click the third button in the row.

First, you will create a state header in the center of the screen and start building a string for the `"statebindings"` attribute. Reload your UI to get rid of buttons from previous examples and open up WowLua's script editor. Enter the following code to set up the basic elements of the 2-D action bar:

```
local NUM_ROWS = 3
local NUM_COLS = 3

local header = CreateFrame("Frame", "TestHeader", UIParent, ↵
"SecureStateHeaderTemplate")
header:SetPoint("CENTER")

local statebindings = "0:selectRow"
```

Each row has an invisible button with a `"bindings-setRow"` attribute. You will also add a new entry to `"statebindings"` in the form `"n:rown"`, which creates a binding set for when the row is selected. The row button then uses a `"newstate"` attribute to move to the state for the selected row:

```
for row = 1, NUM_ROWS do
  statebindings = statebindings..format(";%d:row%1$d", row)

  rowButton = CreateFrame("Button", "TestRow"..row, nil, ↵
"SecureActionButtonTemplate")
  rowButton:SetAttribute("newstate", row)
  rowButton:SetAttribute("bindings-selectRow", row)
  header:SetAttribute("addchild", rowButton)
```

Now you create each of the buttons for the row. Each button uses a `"newstate"` attribute to return to state 0 after use, and `"bindings-rown"` attributes to set the bound key. To easily illustrate the functionality, clicking each button prints a message with the button's name:

```
  for col = 1, NUM_COLS do
    local button = CreateFrame("Button", ↵
format("TestButtonRow%dCol%d", row, col), nil, ↵
"SecureActionButtonTemplate, UIPanelButtonTemplate2")
    button:SetText(row.."-"..col)
    button:SetPoint(
      "TOPLEFT", header, "TOPLEFT",
      (col - 1) * button:GetWidth(),
      -(row - 1) * button:GetHeight()
    )
    button:SetScript("PreClick", function(self)
      DEFAULT_CHAT_FRAME:AddMessage("You clicked: "..self:GetName())
    end)

    button:SetAttribute("newstate", "0")
    button:SetAttribute("bindings-row"..row, col)
    header:SetAttribute("addchild", button)
  end
end
```

Finally, you apply the `"statebindings"` attribute and manually set the state to 0 to make sure all of the bindings are applied as intended:

```
header:SetAttribute("statebindings", statebindings)
header:SetAttribute("state", "0")
```

Now run the script and you will see the buttons appear in the middle of your screen. Press the number keys (from the main row of numbers, not the num pad) to see how the buttons interact.

Storing States in a Stack

The transition rules described earlier (as used in `"newstate"` attributes) are capable of much more complex transitions than shown so far. In addition to specifying a state, range, or comma-separated list, you can use several *state stack* "functions" in transition rules to store and retrieve previous states.

Imagine the state stack as a pile of plates. When you *push* a value onto the stack, it's like setting a new plate on top. When you *pop* a state, you remove the value from the top of the stack. Here are the various stack functions (they're not functions in the strictest sense, but they are syntactically similar):

- `push([newState])` — Push the current state onto the stack and move to `newState`, if specified.

- `pop([defaultState])` — Switch to the state on the top of the stack and pop it from the stack. If there are no states on the stack, switch to `defaultState`, if specified.

- `set([newState])` — Remove all entries from the stack, push the current state, and move to `newState`, if provided.

- `swap([defaultState])` — Swap the current state with the state on top of the stack. If no states are on the stack, this is equivalent to `push(defaultState)`.

You can only use one stack function in each state rule. However, you can combine stack functions with normal transition rules by separating them with a space. If the function does not result in a state change (for example, an empty `push()`), the header uses the normal transition rule for determining the new state. For example, the rule `"1-5:push() 5-1"` pushes the current state and then cycles to the next state down. Other transition rules can then pop the state off the stack.

You can rework the example code from the previous section to use a state stack instead of hard-coded transitions. Replace the line that sets `"newstate"` on `rowButton` with the following:

```
rowButton:SetAttribute("newstate", "push("..row..")")
```

Now replace the line that sets `"newstate"` on each button with:

```
button:SetAttribute("newstate", "pop()")
```

Now when you press a key to select a row, it pushes the current state (0) onto the stack and moves to the new state for the row. Pressing the key a second time returns to state 0 by popping it off the stack. This makes the buttons a bit more generic so they can return to states other than 0, if necessary.

Creating a Macro Sequencer

We suffer no illusions that what you've seen in this chapter is not a huge amount of information. Before we dive into the next major feature of the state header system, let's take a few moments to walk through a simple, useful addon called MacroSequence.

If you have worked with macros for any length of time, you are probably familiar with the /castsequence command. This command takes a list of spells and items and will use them in sequence each time you run the macro (for thorough coverage, see "Cogwheel's Complete Macro Guide" on the WoW UI & Macros forum). While it does its job well, many players feel /castsequence is missing certain features or behaves in undesirable ways, as follows:

- Only spells or items can be used in the sequence. There is no way to sequence chat commands, emotes, equipping gear, and so on.

- All actions in the sequence are taken on a single unit, usually your target, unless the spell/item only operates directly on the player.

- If a spell in the sequence fails to cast, the sequence will remain at that point until it succeeds or the sequence resets. This means you can't spam a sequence with two spells, attempting one after the other until one becomes available.

MacroSequence reproduces most of the functionality of /castsequence while putting the preceding issues to rest. Each item in the sequence is an entire macro in its own right, completely obliterating the first two problems mentioned and adding an enormous amount of flexibility. With some simple "newstate" manipulation, the third point becomes moot, as well.

The last problem in the list is actually useful in certain situations. For instance, a lot of hunters use the following macro for shot rotations:

```
/castsequence Steady Shot, !Auto Shot
```

The first click of this macro casts Steady Shot and then moves to the next spell. The second click attempts to cast Auto Shot but will actually fail because Steady Shot already activated it (the exclamation mark prevents the macro from disengaging Auto Shot). At some point (depending on many specifics), Auto Shot will fire on its own and advance the sequence, resetting it to the beginning. This macro allows hunters to maximize their DPS output for their basic attacks by timing the casts just right. Unfortunately, the mechanics of the state header system prevents us from replicating this behavior, and some may see this as a drawback.

There is one more feature that we will not be able to implement: resetting the sequence when you change targets. This is because there is no way to drive a state change based on a unit *change*, only unit *existence*. All of the other /castsequence reset conditions will work perfectly, though.

TIP As far as we can tell, the unit change limitation is more of an oversight than an intentional restriction. Such a feature has been suggested, so be sure to check the companion site for updates.

As one last benefit to round it all out, the macros in the sequence are not be limited to 255 characters like those in the macro UI. There is also no limit to the number of macros you can create. You can reap these benefits even if you don't create a full-fledged sequence.

ON THE WEB You can find the most recent version of MacroSequence at http://wowinterface.com/downloads/info7911-MacroSequence.html. As of this writing, plans are in the works for a graphical front-end to make editing the sequences much easier.

Please create an addon skeleton for MacroSequence with two Lua files: `MacroSequence.lua` and `Sequences.lua`. In `MacroSequence.toc`, list Sequences first. You will store all sequences in `Sequences.lua` and the addon code in `MacroSequence.lua`.

TIP Keeping user-defined data separate from the implementation like this is always a good idea. It greatly reduces the risk that the user will break the addon and makes maintenance easier.

First thing first: you need to decide how you are going to represent each sequence.

Defining the Sequences

In earlier chapters, we expounded on Lua's superb capabilities as a data description language. This is in no small part due to the incredible flexibility and elegance of its single data structure, the table. We will be taking advantage of the fact that a single table can be interpreted as both an array and dictionary at the same time.

At the most fundamental level, each sequence will simply be a list of strings, each containing the text of a macro. We will also add a subtable called `reset` that will store the various reset conditions. For example, a sequence defined as follows is equivalent to the macro `/castsequence reset=alt/10 Immolate, Corruption, Curse of Agony`:

```
{
  reset = {
    alt = true,
    seconds = 10
  },

  "/cast Immolate",
  "/cast Corruption",
  "/cast Curse of Agony"
}
```

These sequences will be stored by name in a global table called MacroSequenceSequences. Open up `Sequences.lua` and enter the following code:

```
MacroSequenceSequences = {
  TestSequence = {
    [[
/dance
/cheer
    ]],
    [[
```

```
/say Testing
/run ChatFrame1:AddMessage("Second Macro!")
    ]],
    [[
/moan
/scratch
    ]]
  }
}
```

Feel free to modify the sequence with whatever macros you want, or at least go somewhere private so you don't raise too many eyebrows. You'll notice that we have written these out using Lua's long string syntax. This makes multiline macros much easier to edit. You will need to make sure that there are no spaces or tabs at the beginning of each macro line, though, or they will not be interpreted as slash commands.

With the test sequence defined, you can begin working on the implementation.

Setting up the Basic Sequences

We will not be detailing every step of the code, so you may want to print messages at various steps to see what the variables are doing. Open `MacroSequence.lua` and enter the following code:

```
MacroSequence = {}

function MacroSequence:Initialize(sequences)
  if not sequences then
    DEFAULT_CHAT_FRAME:AddMessage("MacroSequencesSequences does ↵
not exist. Please make sure there are no errors in ↵
Interface\\AddOns\\MacroSequence\\Sequences.lua.")
    return
  end

  for name, data in pairs(sequences) do
    self:CreateSequence(name, data)
  end
end

function MacroSequence:CreateSequence(name, data)
end

MacroSequence:Initialize(MacroSequenceSequences)
```

NOTE Any new functions added to MacroSequence must be inserted before the call to `Initialize` (the last line in the preceding code) or they will not exist when `Initialize` runs. Other than that, they can appear in whatever order makes the most sense to you.

`Initialize` is rather straightforward. It includes a helpful error message in case something goes wrong with `Sequences.lua`. Then it iterates through all the sequences in the table, dispatching each one to `CreateSequence`. Now fill in `CreateSequence` with the following code:

```
  if #data == 0 then
    DEFAULT_CHAT_FRAME:AddMessage(format("MacroSequence %s ↵
contains no macros. See ↵
Interface\\AddOns\\MacroSequence\\Sequences.lua.", name))
    return
  end

  local header = CreateFrame("Frame", nil, nil,
"SecureStateHeaderTemplate")
  local button = CreateFrame(
    "Button",
    name,
    header,
    "SecureActionButtonTemplate"
  )
  header:SetAttribute("addchild", button)
  button:SetAttribute("type", "macro")
  button:SetAttribute("newstate", "0-"..(#data - 1))

  self:CreateSequenceEntries(button, data)
  self:ApplyResetConditions(header, button, data)
```

We provide another message to warn about an empty sequence and then proceed to create the state header and button. The `"newstate"` attribute is where the magic happens. Click the button and move to the next state; there's nothing more to it than that. Next, we will add `CreateSequenceEntries` to make `"macrotext"` attributes for each state:

```
function MacroSequence:CreateSequenceEntries(button, data)
  local statebutton = ""
  for state, macro in ipairs(data) do
    state = state - 1
    statebutton = statebutton..format("%d:B%1$d;", state)
    button:SetAttribute("*macrotext-B"..state, macro)
  end
  button:SetAttribute("statebutton", statebutton)
end

function MacroSequence:ApplyResetConditions(header, button, data)
end
```

This function is nothing you haven't seen before. It's essentially the same as the button creation script we worked with at the beginning of the "Changing the Header's Unit" section earlier in this chapter. We have also taken the liberty of creating a stub for

`ApplyResetConditions` because we now have all the code in place to execute a basic sequence. Create a macro with the following command to see it in action:

```
/click TestSequence
```

Now that you have the sequence working, you need to implement the reset conditions.

Resetting the Sequence

The `/castsequence` command resets when you die, and also allows you to specify three other optional reset conditions that you will be implementing:

- `combat` — Reset the sequence when you leave combat.
- *n* — Reset the sequence after *n* seconds of inactivity.
- `alt/shift/ctrl` — Reset the sequence when it's activated while holding down the specified modifier key.

The first step is to make an appropriate sanity check — what's the point of a reset if there's only one entry in a sequence? Add the following code to `ApplyResetConditions`:

```
if #data == 1 then
  return
end
```

Next, you need an event handler to deal with the automatic (as opposed to click-triggered) resets of death and leaving combat. The death event (`PLAYER_DEAD`) occurs before the combat lockdown ends, so if you die in combat you simply set a flag. Otherwise, you reset the sequence immediately. Add the following code:

```
button:SetScript("OnEvent", function(button, event)
  if event == "PLAYER_DEAD" then
    if InCombatLockdown() then
      button.resetDeath = true
    else
      header:SetAttribute("state", "0")
    end
  elseif event == "PLAYER_REGEN_ENABLED" then
    if button.resetCombat or button.resetDeath then
      header:SetAttribute("state", "0")
      button.resetDeath = nil
    end
  end
end)
button:RegisterEvent("PLAYER_DEAD")
button:RegisterEvent("PLAYER_REGEN_ENABLED")
```

The rest of the reset functions only run if you have a `reset` entry in your sequence, so you add another sanity check, like this:

```
if not data.reset then
  return
end
```

Finally, to apply the three optional resets, set the `resetCombat` flag you used earlier and call the two other `Apply` functions that will take care of the timer and modifier keys:

```
button.resetCombat = data.reset.combat
self:ApplyTimerReset(button, data)
self:ApplyModifierResets(button, data)
```

Next, you implement `ApplyTimerReset`, the simpler of the two optional conditions. All you need to do is set the state to 0 after the time specified in `reset.seconds`, as follows:

```
function MacroSequence:ApplyTimerReset(button, data)
  local seconds = data.reset.seconds
  if seconds and seconds > 0 then
    button:SetAttribute("delaystate", "0")
    button:SetAttribute("delaytime", seconds)
  end
end
```

As simple as it may first sound, resetting based on modifier keys is somewhat laborious. For any given modifier key, you must create all possible modified attributes for both `"statebutton"` and `"newstate"`. For example, a reset on shift requires `"shift-root*"`, `"alt-shift-root*"`, `"ctrl-shift-root*"`, and `"alt-ctrl-shift-root*"` attributes because you can't mix wildcards into a prefix. Allowing simplicity to overrule accuracy, create a table with all the prefixes for each modifier key:

```
local modifierPrefixes = {
  alt = {
    "alt",
    "alt-ctrl",
    "alt-shift",
    "alt-ctrl-shift"
  },
  ctrl = {
    "ctrl",
    "alt-ctrl",
    "ctrl-shift",
    "alt-ctrl-shift"
  },
  shift = {
    "shift",
    "alt-shift",
    "ctrl-shift",
    "alt-ctrl-shift"
  }
}
```

Now you can simply iterate over the table and apply each attribute, as needed.

The ultimate goal of ApplyModifierResets is to make the modified click activate the first macro in the sequence and then move to the next one. Once you have all the prefixes, you just need to set the various "statebutton" attributes to state 0's remapped click ("B0") and the "newstate" attributes to state 1. The "statebutton" makes the click run the first entry, and then the "newstate" switches to the second state.

```
function MacroSequence:ApplyModifierResets(button, data)
  for modifier, prefixes in pairs(modifierPrefixes) do
    if data.reset[modifier] then
      for _, prefix in ipairs(prefixes) do
        button:SetAttribute(prefix.."-statebutton*", "B0")
        button:SetAttribute(prefix.."-newstate*", "1")
      end
    end
  end
end
```

With that, MacroSequence is finished — at least in the context of this book.

To test some of the new reset conditions, add the following reset table to MacroSequenceSequences.TestSequence:

```
reset = {
  alt = true,
  seconds = 5,
}
```

Run your sequence a couple times so that it's somewhere in the middle. Hold Alt when you run it and you will see it start from the beginning. Wait 5 seconds, and the next one will start at the beginning. Play with some of the other reset conditions to get a feel for them.

Creating a Pie Button

Before ending this chapter, we will introduce you to one more secure template: SecurePieButtonTemplate. A pie button maps out where you clicked it on a circle and, depending on the location, dispatches the click to some particular child button.

Setting up Pie Buttons

You configure the clickable area of pie buttons with the state attributes described in Table 25-2 (angles are in degrees):

Table 25-2: Pie Button General Configuration Attributes

ATTRIBUTE	DESCRIPTION
`"piecount"`	The number of clickable segments in the pie button, like pizza slices. Required.
`"piemindist"`	The minimum distance from the center of the pie you need to click to trigger an action. This leaves a *dead zone* in the middle like the hole of a doughnut. The size of the frame determines the maximum distance, so there is no counterpart attribute. Default: `1`.
`"piegap"`	An angle that creates a dead zone between each segment. Default: `0`.
`"pieoffset"`	The angle to rotate the pie clockwise. Normally, the first segment is centered at the top of the circle. Default: `0`.

Once it determines which segment you've clicked, it checks the attributes shown in Table 25-3 to see which child to click with which button (items in square brackets [ ] are optional, and those in angle brackets < > are required):

Table 25-3: Pie Button Click Dispatch Attributes

ATTRIBUTE	DESCRIPTION
`"pievariation"`	State attribute that determines which child/button variation to use, if specified.
`"pie[`*variation*`]<`*which*`>child"`	Modified attribute that tells to which child to dispatch the click. Required.
`"pie[`*variation*`]<`*which*`>button"`	Modified attribute that remaps the button sent to the child. Default: the mouse button that clicked the pie.

The *which* element can be a number indicating the segment, an asterisk (*) meaning any segment, or `"none"` meaning the button was clicked in a dead zone. The *variation* element allows you to reconfigure the pie button based on the state of its parent. If either of the selected `"pie...child"` or `"pie...button"` attributes evaluates to `"none"`, no click will be dispatched.

Building the Frame

The addon you create in this section has a pie button cut into sixths. Clicking on segments highlights them. Segment 3 will only respond to right-clicks, and shift-clicking segment 4 will turn off any highlights. See Figure 25-5 for an example.

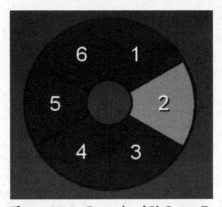

Figure 25-5: Example of PieButtonTest

Begin by creating a skeleton for PieButtonTest. You will need an XML and a Lua file. The pie button template only provides click behaviors, nothing visual, so we have created a set of textures to help illustrate the way pie buttons operate. Navigate to the following URL: http://wowprogramming.com/chapter25/.

Download the pie button texture zip file and extract the contents into your PieButtonTest folder. There should be seven TGA images named PieButtonTest*n*.tga, where *n* is the segment number.

Now open up the XML file and enter the following code to begin the frame:

```
<Ui xmlns="http://www.blizzard.com/wow/ui/" ↵
xmlns:xsi="http://www.w3.org/2001/XMLSchema-instance" ↵
xsi:schemaLocation="http://www.blizzard.com/wow/ui/
..\UI.xsd">

  <Button name="PieButtonTest" parent="UIParent" ↵
inherits="SecurePieButtonTemplate">
    <Size x="256" y="256"/>
    <Anchors>
      <Anchor point="CENTER"/>
    </Anchors>
    <Layers>
      <Layer level="BACKGROUND">
        <Texture name="$parentTexture" setAllPoints="true" ↵
file="Interface\AddOns\PieButtonTest\PieButtonTest"/>
      </Layer>
    </Layers>
    <Attributes>
```

This starts the pie button in the middle of the screen with the nonhighlighted texture. Now you add the various control attributes, beginning with the attribute to set the frame for six segments:

```
        <Attribute name="piecount" value="6"/>
```

The "hole" in the center of our texture has a radius of 34 pixels. Add the following attribute to make it a dead zone:

```
<Attribute name="piemindist" value="34"/>
```

The texture's first segment is not centered at the top of the pie button as the default for the template expects. You will need to turn the clickable area 30° clockwise for it to line up:

```
<Attribute name="pieoffset" value="30"/>
```

This addon will use a single button to handle all the clicks, so you must create the button mappings to give each segment a unique click:

```
<Attribute name="pie1button" value="1"/>
<Attribute name="pie2button" value="2"/>
<Attribute name="pie3button" value="3"/>
<Attribute name="pie4button" value="4"/>
<Attribute name="pie5button" value="5"/>
<Attribute name="pie6button" value="6"/>
```

The final attribute you will define in the XML file implements the special case to clear all the highlights when you shift-click the fourth segment:

```
<Attribute name="shift-pie4button*" value="S4"/>
```

The rest of the XML is fairly straightforward. The scripts are covered in the next section.

```
      </Attributes>
      <Frames>
        <Button name="$parentButton">
          <Scripts>
            <OnLoad>
              PieButtonTest_OnLoad(self)
            </OnLoad>
            <OnClick>
              PieButtonTest_OnClick(self, button)
            </OnClick>
          </Scripts>
        </Button>
      </Frames>
    </Button>

  </Ui>
```

Finishing the Behavior

All you need to do now is define the scripts. Open up the Lua file and add the following line to set up the base image name for the texture:

```
local IMAGE_BASE = "Interface\\AddOns\\PieButtonTest\\PieButtonTest"
```

You will next create the `OnLoad` script. Because the child button does not exist when the `<Attributes>` tag is parsed — not to mention the fact that `<Attribute>` tags can't specify frame references — the first thing you must do is set up the child mappings:

```
function PieButtonTest_OnLoad(self)
    PieButtonTest:SetAttribute("pie3child", "none")
    PieButtonTest:SetAttribute("*pie3child2", self)
    PieButtonTest:SetAttribute("pie*child", self)
```

The first attribute specifies that the third segment should be ignored by default. The second one overrides that default, mapping to the child button when you right-click the third segment. Finally, there is the catchall attribute to map the rest of the segments to the child button.

Now you need to register the button to receive more than just left clicks:

```
    PieButtonTest:RegisterForClicks("AnyUp")
end
```

Finally, the `OnClick` handler sets the image based on the button it receives:

```
function PieButtonTest_OnClick(self, button)
    local image = IMAGE_BASE
    if button ~= "S4" then
        image = image..button
    end
    PieButtonTestTexture:SetTexture(image)
end
```

Summary

This chapter has thrown a lot of new concepts at you: state headers, state attributes, transition rules, and so on. These tools allow you to reconfigure your frames both visually and functionally. The interactions between various attributes and templates is quite complex, but once you understand the fundamentals, everything should become clear.

The next chapter discusses ways to trigger state changes based on external events that are only indirectly controlled by the player.

# CHAPTER 26

Driving State Changes

Matthew Orlando

In the preceding chapter, all of the examples of state transitions we showed you were triggered by clicks of a button or key. Often, though, a state change needs to occur indirectly, such as when you change stance or summon a pet, or by less direct interaction like mousing over a frame. These conditions are still controlled by the player, but it is not the actual click of a button that triggers the state change. The state driver system allows you to register a state header to be notified of various game events. Anchor templates provide you with a few alternative ways to manually trigger state changes, and they also allow you to control some visual aspects of a child header.

Working with State Drivers

Before we begin, load up the state header test addon you created at the beginning of Chapter 25. To keep things simple, you will only be using one button for these examples. However, you still need to set up a few attributes so you can see the state changes. In WowLua's script editor, enter and run the following code, which should be familiar to you:

```
local button = CreateTestButton()

local statebutton = ""
for state = 0, 9 do
    statebutton = statebutton..format("%d:B%1$d;", state)
    button:SetAttribute("*action-B"..state, state + 1)
end
TestHeader:SetAttribute("statebutton", statebutton)
```

There are two fundamental concepts behind state drivers: registering the driver and creating a state map. Registration is accomplished with the `RegisterStateDriver` function defined in `FrameXML\SecureStateDriver.lua`.

`RegisterStateDriver(header, stateName, criteria)`

- `header` (frame) — The state header frame to register for state changes.

- `stateName` (string) — A name for the driver state.

- `criteria` (string) — A set of macro options that specifies driver states based on various criteria (macro options will be covered in depth shortly).

As the driver changes states based on the criteria, it will set an attribute called `"state-stateName"` on your header. State maps are *state attributes* (see Chapter 25) in the form `"statemap-stateName"` that tell the header what state to enter based on these changes to the driver state.

Enter the following lines in WowLua to set up a state driver that responds to the Ctrl key. As you press and release the key, you will see the button swap between action slot 1 and action slot 2.

```
> TestHeader:SetAttribute("statemap-ctrl", "$input")
> RegisterStateDriver(TestHeader, "ctrl", "[modifier:ctrl] 1; 0")
```

The first line sets up a state map for the `"ctrl"` driver state. `"$input"` is a special rule for state maps that maps the driver state directly to the header's state. In other words, when `state-ctrl` changes to 1, `state` will change to 1, as well. The second line registers the state driver to change to 1 when holding down Ctrl, or to 0 otherwise.

State maps can also take the form `"statemap-stateName-newValue"`, which allows you to specify different state maps for specific driver states. The state header will always look for the more specific maps before settling on the generic one. Enter the following commands to remove our `ctrl` driver and register a new driver that uses states 1-6 depending on your action bar page.

```
> UnregisterStateDriver(TestHeader, "ctrl")
> TestHeader:SetAttribute("statemap-bar", "$input")
> TestHeader:SetAttribute("statemap-bar-4", "6")
> TestHeader:SetAttribute("statemap-bar-6", "4")
> RegisterStateDriver(TestHeader, "bar", "[actionbar:1] 1; ↵
[actionbar:2] 2; [actionbar:3] 3; [actionbar:4] 4; [actionbar:5] ↵
5; [actionbar:6] 6")
```

TIP If you omit the second parameter from `UnregisterStateDriver`, **it will unregister all the drivers for the header.**

When you change to action bar 1 through 3, the header will use `"statemap-bar"` and set its state to the action bar page. For action bar pages 4 and 6, however, it will use one of the specific state maps, transitioning to state 6 on bar 4 and vice versa.

NOTE If you have any of the "extra action bars" enabled in the default UI, you will not be able to see all of the page transitions outlined here. For testing purposes, you may want to temporarily disable them.

Delaying Driven State Changes

Driver state changes can also set up delayed transitions on the header. This works much like the `"delaystate"` attribute you saw in the last chapter. Again, there are three classes of state attributes for specifying the delays:

- `delaystatemap-stateName[-newValue]` — Specifies the state map for the delayed transition.

- `delaytimemap-stateName[-newValue]` — Sets the time for the delay.

- `delayhovermap-stateName[-newValue]` — Determines whether to prevent the transition while the mouse is over the header or any of its children.

For example, we can return our state header to state 0 five seconds after changing to action bar page 1, and three seconds after changing to any other page, as follows:

```
> TestHeader:SetAttribute("delaystatemap-bar", 0)
> TestHeader:SetAttribute("delaytimemap-bar-1", 5)
> TestHeader:SetAttribute("delaytimemap-bar", 3)
```

As with `delaystate`, any state changes while the timer is running will cancel a pending delayed change.

For `delaystatemap` to have any effect, there must be a normal state map present on the header. However, this does not mean that the state map must trigger a transition. You can simply set the state map to an empty string signifying that no immediate state change should occur, as in the following example.

```
> TestHeader:SetAttribute("statemap-bar", "")
> TestHeader:SetAttribute("statemap-bar-4", nil)
> TestHeader:SetAttribute("statemap-bar-6", nil)
> TestHeader:SetAttribute("delaystatemap-bar", "$input")
```

Now the header will change to the state for the current action bar page after a delay.

Understanding Macro Options

With the mechanics of state drivers under your belt, you can now tell the driver when to change states.

Macro options provide a concise way to make choices based on specific conditions that share a few common characteristics. They are state-like in the sense that some particular event causes the condition to change. The events themselves are controlled directly by the player for the most part. This means, for example, that you will never see a conditional to detect whether your target has a particular buff.

> **TIP** Macro options were originally developed for patch 2.0 as a way to control which spell to cast, item to use, gear to equip, and so on, in macro commands (hence the name). Recognizing their flexibility and widespread use, Blizzard redesigned the state drivers in 2.1 to use macro option syntax for driving state changes. Prior to this time, the `SecureStateDriverTemplate` was the only way to drive similar state changes.

The mechanics of macro options are similar to state attributes. To dive right into an example, the following macro option set chooses state 0 if you can attack your target, state 1 if you can heal your target, or state 2 if you can neither help nor harm your target.

```
[harm] 0; [help] 1; 2
```

Building Macro Option Sets

At the highest level, you have a set of criteria/parameter groups separated by semicolons. The criteria consist of zero or more sets of conditions. Each condition set is enclosed with square brackets. Here is an illustration of this basic syntax.

```
[conditions] [more conditions] state; [conditions] state …
```

As you saw in the preceding basic example, the set is evaluated from left to right. As soon as it finds a set of conditions that are true, it evaluates to the corresponding state. If there are no conditions in a clause, it will always be true. When the set does not have any conditions that are true, it will evaluate to `nil`.

Creating Conditions

Each condition set is a simple comma-separated list of conditions. Think of the comma as an "and." A condition set like `[help, nodead]` means "My target is friendly *and* not dead."

> **WARNING** Conditions are case-sensitive. If you use `[Help]` instead of `[help]`, the set will generate an error.

Conditions have a few building blocks. First off, as you just saw with `[nodead]`, you can put `no` in front of a condition to mean the opposite. Notice that `[nohelp]` does not mean the same thing as `[harm]`. `[harm]` and `[help]` both return `true` only if there is a target to begin with. Furthermore, there are some targets that can neither be helped nor harmed (non-PvP players of the other faction, noncombat pets, and so forth).

Some conditions also take their own sets of parameters. For example, `[stance]` by itself means "I'm in any stance" (useful for every class with stances except Warriors because they are always in a stance). However, you can also specify one or more particular stances to check. The set of parameters begins with a colon (`:`), and each parameter is separated with a slash (`/`) that means "or." The following is a generic illustration of the syntax for a single condition where everything inside brackets (`[ ]`) is optional.

```
[no]condition[:parameter[/parameter[/...]]]
```

Here is a simple example for a Warrior that chooses state 0 if you're in either Battle or Defensive Stance, and state 1 if you're in Berserker Stance.

```
[stance:1/2] 0; 1
```

> **NOTE** "no" applies to the whole condition and all of its parameters. This means that [nostance:1/2] would mean "anything but stances 1 or 2."

Choosing a Different Unit to Test

In addition to condition checking, the macro option system provides you with a way to set the target of various checks. For example, the following clause will choose state 1 if you have a focus target or state 0 otherwise (see Chapter 13 for a full list of unit IDs):

```
[target=focus, exists] 1; 0
```

The target=*unit* portion can appear in any position within the condition set. It will always be evaluated first before any conditions. This allows you to arrange the conditions in whatever order makes the most sense. For example, the following option set will behave identically to the previous one:

```
[exists, target=focus] 1; 0
```

Exploring Conditionals

The following is the entire list of conditionals that are available to the macro option system. One of the goals in the 2.0 patch was to eliminate a lot of old "smart buttons" that allowed people to essentially play the entire game spamming one key repeatedly. However, many tasks people used macros to simplify were deemed OK and given Blizzard's blessing via the macro options.

If you don't see a condition listed here, then there is no way to check for it and take a combat-related action. These are essentially non-negotiable, although they may be augmented in the future. Abbreviated versions appear in parentheses.

help & harm

As previously covered, these determine whether the unit can be helped or harmed.

exists

This determines whether the given unit exists. In other words, if you don't have a target, [exists] will return false. If you have a focus, [target=focus, exists] would be true. Note that in some cases [exists] is unnecessary. [help], [harm], [dead], [party], and [raid] all imply [exists] if they're true.

dead

If you have a target and it is dead, this will be true.

stance (form)

Stance is the generic term used for Warriors', Druids', Rogues' (Stealth), Priests' (Shadowform) and Shamans' (Ghost Wolf) forms. Stances are only applicable to situations where certain abilities are only usable in specific forms. Because of this, Paladin auras (despite being on the shapeshift bar) and Hunter aspects are *not* considered stances.

[stance] by itself means that you are in any stance whatsoever. It also accepts a numbered parameter indicating the stance of interest (see Table 26-1). [stance:0] is equivalent to [nostance], so you can use a conditional such as [stance:0/3] to evaluate as true if you are either in stance 3 or not in any stance.

The stances are ordered the same way as they appear on your shapeshift bar. So a Druid with Bear, Aquatic, Cat, and Travel forms would have stances 1 through 4.

Table 26-1: Stance Numbers and Their Meanings

STANCE	WARRIOR	DRUID*	PRIEST	ROGUE	SHAMAN
1	Battle	Bear	Shadowform	Stealth	Ghost Wolf
2	Defensive	Aquatic			
3	Berserker	Cat			
4		Travel			
5		Moonkin, Tree of Lifes			
6		Flight			

* If a Druid is missing a form, all the higher-number ones will shift upward on the chart.

stealth

While the Rogues among you may find this redundant because [stance] behaves the same way, [stealth] also applies to Night Elves' Shadowmeld, Mages' Invisibility, and so on.

modifier (mod)

This condition will evaluate to true if you are holding a modifier key. By itself, [modifier] means you are holding any modifier key. You can also specify ctrl, shift, or alt as parameters:

```
[mod:shift] 0; [mod:ctrl, mod:alt] 1; 2
```

In addition, you can use modifier variables as seen in Chapter 17. For example:

```
[modifier:SELFCAST] 1; 0
```

button (btn)

Present only for completeness, this conditional makes no sense in the context of state drivers. In a macro it allows you to determine which mouse button was used to run the macro. However, there is no analogy for triggering a state change because the state drivers do not respond directly to clicks. See "Using an Item With a `macro` Type Button" in Chapter 17 for a list of macro resources where you can learn more.

equipped (worn)

`[equipped]` allows you to determine if a particular type of gear is equipped. The item type can be an inventory slot name, an item type, or an item subtype. See `GetItemInfo` (API) for lists of these types. Example:

```
[equipped:Shields] 0; [equipped:Two-Handed Axes] 1; 2
```

channeling

This option allows you to choose a state depending on whether you are channeling a spell. `[channeling]` alone matches any spell, and you can also list a number of spell names to check. Example:

```
[channeling:Drain Soul]
```

actionbar (bar)

The default UI provides a number of action bar pages. These pages only affect the lower-left action bar that is visible by default. `[actionbar]` allows you to change states based on your current action bar page number. Note that `[actionbar]` only makes sense when used with parameters because everyone is always on some page. Example:

```
[actionbar:1] 1; [actionbar:2] 2; 3
```

bonusbar

Any class whose action bar changes based on certain conditions (stance, stealth, possession, and so on) uses a bonus bar. This determines the range of action slots that replaces page 1 of the main action bar. For instance, a Priest's bonus bar number is 5 when he/she is controlling the mind of some other unit. `[bonusbar]` by itself means you have an active bonus bar. Example:

```
[bonusbar:5] 1; 0
```

See `GetBonusBarOffset` (API) for details on classes and their bonus bar offsets.

pet

Every class with a pet should find this one useful. It allows you to choose a state based on which pet you have out. You can specify your pet's name or your pet's type (Voidwalker, Boar, Imp, Wolf, and so on). `[pet]` by itself matches any pet.

combat

True if you are in combat. In other words, your health is no longer regenerating.

mounted, swimming, flying, indoors, and outdoors

These are all fairly self-explanatory. They all apply to you, the player.

flyable

[flyable] determines whether you are in a location where you can use a flying mount.

party and raid

These return true if the target is in your party or raid, respectively.

group:party/raid

This lets you determine whether you are in the given group type. [group] is equivalent to [group:party]. [group:raid] implies [group:party].

Combining State Types

You may have noticed that RegisterStateDriver allows you to set up multiple state types for a single state header. Most of the time, you can simply create a more complex macro option set that incorporates all the same conditions. However, in certain cases, using multiple state types can be useful or even necessary.

As an example, you will create an action button that enters a different state for each combination of Ctrl and Shift. Reload your UI, run the CreateTestButton script from earlier, and open up a new script.

You need to create state maps for every possible transition. To keep this understandable, you will use named states instead of numbers. The final states for the header are in the form "ctrl0-shift0" to indicate the status of each modifier. When you release the Ctrl key, for instance, the header needs to change to some state that starts with "ctrl0" but leaves the shift part unchanged. Because state maps are state attributes, you can use the current state to specify the new state for each particular driver state transition.

```
TestHeader:SetAttribute("statemap-ctrl-0", ↵
"ctrl1-shift0:ctrl0-shift0;ctrl1-shift1:ctrl0-shift1")
```

This translates to plain English as follows: When the ctrl driver state changes to 0, if the current state is ctrl1-shift0, change to ctrl0-shift0. Otherwise, if the state is ctrl1-shift1, change to ctrl0-shift1. Notice that you do not need to specify transitions for when the current state is already ctrl0-*, because the ctrl driver state can never transition from 0 to 0.

Now you can define the rest with a couple of very careful copy/pastes:

```
TestHeader:SetAttribute("statemap-ctrl-1", ↵
"ctrl0-shift0:ctrl1-shift0;ctrl0-shift1:ctrl1-shift1")
TestHeader:SetAttribute("statemap-shift-0", ↵
```

```
"ctrl0-shift1:ctrl0-shift0;ctrl1-shift1:ctrl1-shift0")
TestHeader:SetAttribute("statemap-shift-1", ↵
"ctrl0-shift0:ctrl0-shift1;ctrl1-shift0:ctrl1-shift1")
```

With the state maps out of the way, you need to give the button a new `statebutton` attribute to map our now-named states to button clicks.

```
TestHeader:SetAttribute("statebutton", ↵
"ctrl0-shift0:B0;ctrl0-shift1:B1;ctrl1-shift0:B2;ctrl1-shift1:B3")
```

Because the header starts out in state 0 and none of our state maps use 0 or * as a selection criteria, the header will have no way of knowing what state to enter initially. Before you register the state drivers, you need to put the header into a state that will be recognized for transitions. The exact state you pick does not matter, because registering the state driver will trigger a transition to the correct state.

```
TestHeader:SetAttribute("state", "ctrl0-shift0")
```

Finally, you can go ahead and register state drivers for `ctrl` and `shift`.

```
RegisterStateDriver(TestHeader, "ctrl", "[mod:ctrl] 1; 0")
RegisterStateDriver(TestHeader, "shift", "[mod:shift] 1; 0")
```

After running the script, the button now maps to four different actions depending on the status of your Ctrl and Shift keys.

Sharing States Among Headers

State headers can be used as state drivers for other headers. As mentioned in the "Using a Detached Header" sidebar in Chapter 25, whenever a state header changes state, it sets the `"state-parent"` attributes on all its children to the new state. This means you can use various `"statemap-parent"` attributes on a child header to control its state based on that of the parent.

You can also send state transitions to the parent by setting an `"exportstate-stateName"` attribute to `true`. Whenever the header changes states, it will set the `"state-stateName"` attribute on its parent to the new state.

Using Anchor Templates

Anchor templates allow you to share a single header among several different frames. When an anchor is triggered, it manipulates the frame specified in its `"anchorchild"` modified attribute based on some other familiar-looking attributes (also modified), as follows:

▪ `childofsx` — Horizontal offset for re-anchoring.

▪ `childofsy` — Vertical offset for re-anchoring.

- `childpoint` — Point on the child to anchor.

- `childrelpoint` — Point on the anchor frame to which the anchor child will be anchored.

As with state headers, either `childofsx` or `childofsy` must be specified for any re-anchoring to occur. You can also use a few other attributes to control the anchor child, as follows:

- `childreparent` — If set to a true value, the anchor child will have its parent set to the anchor frame.

- `childraise` — If set to a true value, the child will be raised to the top of the frame stack. See `Raise` (Widget API).

- `childstate` — If present, the anchor child's `"state-anchor"` attribute will be set to the value of `childstate`. You can prefix the state with a carat (^) to force the state transition even if the child is already in the given state (for example, `"^1"`).

- `childverify` — If set to a true value, the anchor child must be the actual child of the anchor frame in order to receive a new `"state-anchor"`.

Triggering Anchor Changes

Each type of anchor trigger has its own template. See Table 26-2 for a complete list.

Table 26-2: Anchor Template Specifications

TEMPLATE	TRIGGER	BUTTON	REMAP BUTTON
SecureAnchorButtonTemplate	Click	Mouse*	onclickbutton
SecureAnchorEnterTemplate	Mouse Enter	OnEnter	onenterbutton
	Mouse Leave	OnLeave	onleavebutton
SecureAnchorUpDownTemplate	Down Click	Mouse*	onmousedownbutton
	Up Click	Mouse*	onmouseupbutton

* "Mouse" uses the mouse button or state button that was used to click the anchor.

With multiple inheritance, you can create a single anchor that can be triggered by different types of interaction. Because all of the attributes are modified, you can create suffixed attributes to respond differently for a particular interaction. For example, the following will create an anchor that sets its child state to 1, 2, or 0 when you mouse over, click, or mouse leave, respectively:

```
local anchor = CreateFrame(
  "Button",
  "TestAnchor",
  UIParent,
  "SecureAnchorButtonTemplate, SecureAnchorEnterTemplate"
)
```

```
anchor:SetAttribute("anchorchild", SomeHeader)
anchor:SetAttribute("*childstate-OnEnter", 1)
anchor:SetAttribute("childstate", 2)
anchor:SetAttribute("*childstate-OnLeave", 0)
```

TIP Both SecureAnchorButtonTemplate **and** SecureAnchorUpDownTemplate **can also be triggered by keyboard clicks. You can use** SetBindingClick **(API) to set a binding directly, or you can make the anchor frame a child of a state header and use binding attributes.**

Remapping Anchor Transitions

As you saw in the preceding example, you can use modified attributes to give the anchor different effects depending on how it was triggered. However, you may notice, for instance, that the UpDown template uses the same button for each action. This is where the Remap Buttons from Table 26-2 come in handy. They work just like the "helpbutton" and "harmbutton" attributes from Chapter 17, allowing you to change the suffix used for the rest of the modified attributes on the anchor. For example, say you want to change the child state as follows:

ACTION	NEW CHILD STATE
Left button down	1
Right button down	2
Either button up	0

The code for this might look something like the following (using the SetManyAttributes function you saw in Chapter 17 for clarity):

```
local anchor = CreateFrame(
  "Button",
  "TestAnchor",
  UIParent,
  "SecureAnchorUpDownTemplate"
)
SetManyAttributes(anchor,
  "anchorchild",          SomeHeader,

  "*onmousedownbutton1",  "down1",
  "*onmousedownbutton2",  "down2",
  "onmouseupbutton",      "up",

  "*childstate-down1",    1,
  "*childstate-down2",    2,
  "*childstate-up",       0
)
```

Creating an Action Popup

The `UnitActionPopup` addon will modify the default UI's unit frames so that clicking on them will bring up a circle of six action buttons that will do their action on the given unit (see Figure 26-1). When you move the mouse away from the group of buttons, it will hide itself after a few seconds. You can still use the frames to target their respective units by holding down any modifier key when you click.

Figure 26-1: Example
UnitActionPopup display

Building the Frame

Create a skeleton for `UnitActionPopup` including both a Lua and an XML file. Open the XML file and enter the following code to set up the basic frame:

```
<Ui xmlns="http://www.blizzard.com/wow/ui/" ↵
xmlns:xsi="http://www.w3.org/2001/XMLSchema-instance" ↵
xsi:schemaLocation="http://www.blizzard.com/wow/ui/
..\UI.xsd">
  <CheckButton name="UnitActionPopupButtonTemplate" virtual="true" ↵
inherits="ActionBarButtonTemplate">
    <Scripts>
      <OnLoad>
        UnitActionPopup:ButtonOnLoad(self)
      </OnLoad>
    </Scripts>
  </CheckButton>

  <Frame name="UnitActionPopupHeader"
inherits="SecureStateHeaderTemplate" ↵
enableMouse="true" clampedToScreen="true">
    <Size x="36" y="36"/>
    <Frames>

      <!-- You will be inserting code for each button here -->

    </Frames>
    <Scripts>
```

```
      <OnLoad>
        UnitActionPopup:OnLoad(self)
      </OnLoad>
      <OnEvent>
        UnitActionPopup:OnEvent(self, event, ...)
      </OnEvent>
    </Scripts>
  </Frame>
</Ui>
```

The template at the top is used for each of the six buttons. Its `OnLoad` script is used to configure the buttons' attributes and register them with the state header.

`UnitActionPopupHeader` is the frame you will use as the anchor child for the various unit frames. The area in the middle of the popup will not have a button, so you need to enable mouse input on the header and give it a size that fills up the blank space (in this case, the size of a button: 36 x 36). This prevents the header from hiding after the delay while the mouse is in the center of the group.

Adding the Buttons

As shown in Figure 26-1, the buttons are arranged in a hexagon around the header frame. Figure 26-2 shows a more detailed diagram of the arrangement with important features marked.

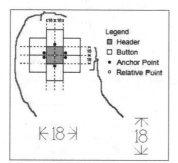

Figure 26-2:
UnitActionPopupHeader
button anchoring diagram

In the code, each button will take the following form:

```
<CheckButton name="$parentButtonName" ↵
inherits="UnitActionPopupButtonTemplate" id="ID">
    <Anchors>
        <Anchor point="point" relativePoint="CENTER">
            <Offset axis="offset"/>
        </Anchor>
    </Anchors>
</CheckButton>
```

The five variables in the snippet are used as follows:

VARIABLE	DESCRIPTION
Name	An arbitrary name for the frame, because `ActionBarButtonTemplate` buttons must have a name in order to behave correctly. You will be using names that describe the position of the button in the popup.
ID	This will be used to determine the action slot for the button, adding it to the offset you will define later in the Lua file.
point	The point on the button to anchor to the header.
axis	Specifies the axis along which to offset the button (either x or y).
offset	The distance to offset the button.

Inside the `<Frames>` tag of the XML file, add buttons following the preceding template according to Table 26-3.

Table 26-3: UnitActionPopup Button Specifications

NAME	ID	POINT	AXIS	OFFSET
Top	1	BOTTOM	y	18
TopRight	2	BOTTOMLEFT	x	18
BottomRight	3	TOPLEFT	x	18
Bottom	4	TOP	y	-18
BottomLeft	5	TOPRIGHT	x	-18
TopLeft	6	BOTTOMRIGHT	x	-18

Here is what the first button will look like in code:

```
<CheckButton name="$parentButtonTop" ↵
inherits="UnitActionPopupButtonTemplate" id="1">
    <Anchors>
      <Anchor point="BOTTOM" relativePoint="CENTER">
        <Offset y="18"/>
      </Anchor>
    </Anchors>
</CheckButton>
```

Defining the Basic Behavior

Once you have created the final button, close the XML file and open up the Lua. Unless otherwise instructed, you should add each snippet presented in the following sections to the end of the Lua file.

First, set up a few constants for readability and ease of maintenance. ACTION_OFFSET sets the starting action slot (less one) for the six buttons. Use slot 108, because it isn't used by the default UI.

```
local ACTION_OFFSET = 108
```

The next constants specify the states used by the header for hiding, showing, and configuring the buttons:

```
local HIDE_STATE   = 0
local SHOW_STATE   = 1
local CONFIG_STATE = 2
```

Whenever the buttons should be hidden, the state header will be put into state 0. When the anchor frames are clicked, they will put the header in state 1, which shows the buttons and sets up a delay to return it to state 0. When the user enters the /unitactionpopup config command (shown next), it will place the state header into state 2, which shows the buttons in the center of the screen indefinitely.

The final constant specifies how long to wait before hiding the popup after moving the mouse away:

```
local HIDE_DELAY   = 2
```

Creating the Slash Commands

This addon has two slash command options: config, described in the last section, and hide, to hide the popup. The base slash command is /unitactionpopup or /uap for short:

```
SLASH_UNITACTIONPOPUP1 = "/unitactionpopup"
SLASH_UNITACTIONPOPUP2 = "/uap"
```

Both config and hide are protected actions, so the addon displays a message and stops processing the command if you are in combat:

```
SlashCmdList["UNITACTIONPOPUP"] = function(text)
  if InCombatLockdown() then
    DEFAULT_CHAT_FRAME:AddMessage("You cannot configure ↵
UnitActionPopup in combat.")
    return
  end
```

Now you add the command options. If the command is config, set the state on the header to the configuration state.

```
  if text == "config" then
    UnitActionPopupHeader:SetAttribute("state", CONFIG_STATE)
```

WARNING At the time of this writing, there is a bug in the UI rendering code. Under certain circumstances, changing the state as shown here will not successfully show the popup. Until this is fixed you will need to manually show the frame, which is OK to do because you are guaranteed to be out of combat by this point in the code. Add the following line if necessary:

```
UnitActionPopupHeader:Show()
```

Next, you repeat the process for the `hide` command using the appropriate state:

```
elseif text == "hide" then
    UnitActionPopupHeader:SetAttribute("state", HIDE_STATE)
```

Finally, if the user enters some other command or none at all, the addon will display a usage message. Notice we are using two `AddMessage` calls to make scrolling through the chat messages a bit cleaner:

```
else
    -- Using two AddMessages to make for better scrolling
    DEFAULT_CHAT_FRAME:AddMessage([[
Usage:
  /unitactionpopup |cff33ff33command|r
  /uap |cff33ff33command|r]]
    )
    DEFAULT_CHAT_FRAME:AddMessage([[
Commands:
  |cff33ff33config|r - Show the buttons for configuration
  |cff33ff33hide|r - Hide the buttons]]
    )
  end
end
```

Configuring the Buttons

Now you need to give each button an appropriate action attribute and define a few other behaviors. You will set a lot of attributes in the following sections so, first, you should add a `SetManyAttributes` function to make it go a bit more smoothly.

```
local function SetManyAttributes(frame, ...)
  for i = 1, select("#", ...), 2 do
    frame:SetAttribute(select(i, ...))
  end
end
```

Next, create a namespace table to store the functions that you called from the XML.

```
UnitActionPopup = {}
```

The first step of the buttons' `OnLoad` function will be to retrieve and clear their ID. This might seem wasteful save for two important points: Identifying the buttons by ID is much easier than parsing their names, and it is more automatic than creating a table to iterate. You need to clear the ID from the button or the template will ignore the presence of the action attributes:

```
function UnitActionPopup:ButtonOnLoad(button)
  local id = button:GetID()
  button:SetID(0)
```

The buttons only need three attribute changes because a lot of their functionality is already provided by the template (for example, `"useparent-statebutton"`, which we will explore later): one to set the action slot, one to hide the button when necessary, and one to ignore the self-cast modifier key.

```
SetManyAttributes(button,
  "action",        id + ACTION_OFFSET,
  "hidestates",    HIDE_STATE,
  "checkselfcast", nil
)
```

All that remains for the buttons is to add them to register them with the state header and call `ActionBarButtonTemplate`'s `OnLoad` function, as we overwrote it in our button template:

```
  button:GetParent():SetAttribute("addchild", button)
  ActionButton_OnLoad()
end
```

Configuring the Header

All of the unit frames in the default UI are near the edge of the screen. This is why you set `clampedToScreen` on the header in the XML file. However, the clamping code uses the header's size of 36 x 36, so there's still a chance that at least parts of some buttons will appear off-screen. You can use `SetClampRectInsets` (Widget API) with negative values to expand the area that is used to clamp. Unfortunately, this function has a bug that reverses the meaning of the right and top insets. To make the code clearer, create a function to fix the parameters:

```
local function FixedSetClampRectInsets(frame, left, right, top, bottom)
  frame:SetClampRectInsets(left, -right, -top, bottom)
end
```

Now you can begin the header's `OnLoad`, setting its insets to `-36`, which will expand the clamping rectangle by the width of a button in every direction:

```
function UnitActionPopup:OnLoad(frame)
  FixedSetClampRectInsets(frame, -36, -36, -36, -36)
```

> **TIP** There is every possibility that the `SetClampRectInsets` **bug will be fixed by the time this book reaches your hands. You may want to test this by replacing the call to** `FixedSetClampRectInsets` **with the following:**

```
frame:SetClampRectInsets(-36, -36, -36, -36)
```

If the user enters combat while in configuration mode, there will be no easy way to hide the buttons. Because he probably won't want the popup in the middle of the screen as he fights, the addon will go ahead and hide it immediately before the combat lockdown. To that end, add the following line to register for entering combat:

```
frame:RegisterEvent("PLAYER_REGEN_DISABLED")
```

As mentioned earlier, the buttons will do their action on the unit specified by the frame you click to trigger the popup. You can accomplish this with a chain of `useparent-unit` attributes. The buttons already have this attribute set, so now you set it on the header:

```
SetManyAttributes(frame,
    "useparent-unit",        true,
```

After all is said and done, the chain of unit delegation looks like this:

Button → Header → Anchor → Unit Frame

You want the header to take a few positioning activities. When you click on the anchor, thereby showing the header, the popup will appear directly under the cursor. That gives you the least distance to travel to click any particular action button. When you enter config mode, the header changes its parent to `UIParent` and then centers itself on the screen.

When entering state 0 to hide the popup, the header itself does not actually hide; only the buttons will. Because the header accepts mouse input, this leaves a 36 x 36 invisible "dead area" on the screen. This can be resolved in a few ways. Because the `headofsx`, `headofsrelpoint`, and `headparent` attributes will already exist for the other anchoring tasks, you can use them to move the button off one side of the screen:

```
    "headofsx",               "%d:-18;0",
    "headofsrelpoint",        format("%d:cursor;%d:LEFT", ↵
SHOW_STATE, HIDE_STATE),
    "headparent",             format("%d,%d:uiparent", ↵
CONFIG_STATE, HIDE_STATE),
    "headparent-uiparent", UIParent
  )
end
```

Before moving on to the anchors, add the "entering combat" event handler as follows, and take a moment to see what you've got so far.

```
function UnitActionPopup:OnEvent(frame, event, ...)
  if event == "PLAYER_REGEN_DISABLED" then
    if frame:GetAttribute("state") == CONFIG_STATE then
```

```
        frame:SetAttribute("state", HIDE_STATE)
      end
    end
  end
```

The two slash commands should be working as promised. You can also see a pre-view of the cursor anchoring if you manually set UnitActionPopupHeader's state to 1. If you put the cursor near the edge of the screen, you will notice how the buttons remain fully visible.

Applying the Anchors

The anchor-header interaction for this addon is actually fairly simple. Enter state 1 when the anchor is clicked; enter state 0 a few seconds after mousing out. Add the fol-lowing lines to the preceding SetManyAttributes call. Don't forget to add a comma to the end of the headparent-uiparent line.

```
"statemap-anchor",      SHOW_STATE,
"delaystatemap-anchor", HIDE_STATE,
"delaytimemap-anchor",  HIDE_DELAY,
"delayhovermap-anchor", "true"
```

To the end of UnitActionPopup:OnLoad, add the following line to call the anchor creation function:

```
self:AddAnchors(frame)
```

Selecting the Unit Frames

Besides the raid frames, which are arguably too compact for this addon to be practical, there are 12 unit frames in the default UI for the player, the player's pet, the target, the target's target, and the four party members and their pets. Below the combat event handler, create a list of these frames and add the AddAnchors function to iterate through them, as follows:

```
local unitFrames = {
  PlayerFrame,
  PetFrame,
  TargetFrame,
  TargetofTargetFrame,
  PartyMemberFrame1,
  PartyMemberFrame2,
  PartyMemberFrame3,
  PartyMemberFrame4,
  PartyMemberFrame1PetFrame,
  PartyMemberFrame2PetFrame,
  PartyMemberFrame3PetFrame,
  PartyMemberFrame4PetFrame,
```

```
  }
function UnitActionPopup:AddAnchors(header)
  for _, unitFrame in pairs(unitFrames) do
    self:AddAnchor(unitFrame, header)
  end
end
```

Creating the Anchors

All you have left to add is the `AddAnchor` function. The first step is to create the anchor frame as a child of the given unit frame:

```
function UnitActionPopup:AddAnchor(parent, header)
  local anchor = CreateFrame(
    "Button",
    parent:GetName().."UAPAnchor",
    parent,
    "SecureAnchorButtonTemplate"
  )
```

To make sure the buttons appear above the unit frames, add the following line:

```
anchor:SetFrameStrata("DIALOG")
```

The user will not be clicking the anchor directly, so you need to give the unit frame a new left-click behavior that passes the click on to the anchor. Note the lack of an asterisk (*) in the type attribute. This allows the unit frame to behave like normal if you hold any modifier key. For example, shift-clicking the frame for your first party member will target them.

```
SetManyAttributes(parent,
  "type1",        "click",
  "clickbutton",  anchor
)
```

Next, you will complete the unit attribute chain we mentioned earlier:

```
SetManyAttributes(anchor,
  "useparent-unit", true,
```

Finally, you must configure the anchor's interactions with the header. Note the use of the carat (^) to force the header to refresh its state even if it's already shown.

```
    "anchorchild",    UnitActionPopupHeader,
    "childreparent",  "true",
    "childstate",     "^"..SHOW_STATE
  )
end
```

`UnitActionPopup` is now finished.

Summary

Over the last two chapters you have witnessed the enormous power — and complexity — of the state header system. From action bars to popup menus, to remapping key bindings and sequencing macros, with just a handful of attributes you can create an impressive array of features.

Since before 2.0 was released, state headers have had an air of mystery about them. The documentation has been sparse for such a broad subject. The endless possible combinations of attributes and templates are quite literally a frontier where new discoveries are made all the time. We hope that these chapters will help you stake your claim.

The next chapter presents one final class of secure templates: group headers. These provide a range of features specific to unit frame addons used in groups and raids.

# CHAPTER 27

Creating Unit Frames with Group Templates

James Whitehead II

Earlier in this book you learned how to create a very simple unit frame, and then later extended it by making it clickable using secure templates. With some work, you could extend this simple addon to show your party or raid, but because they are secure templates, they are unable to be created or configured when the player is in combat. Because a raid frequently has new members joining, this means you would be unable to see those players until you've exited combat.

Blizzard provides several templates that allow developers to create raid, party, and pet frames that will update and configure themselves even while the player is in combat. The templates allow you to pre-program the type and configuration of the frames, as well as where the frames should be placed or sorted.

This chapter introduces two templates: `SecureGroupHeaderTemplate` and `SecureGroupPetHeaderTemplate`. The first is used to display player characters, and the second is used to display their pets. There is currently no template that can display players and pets intermixed, so they will most often be displayed in two distinct groups.

How Do the Templates Work?

Each of the secure group headers allows you to specify a named XML template to be used when creating the individual unit frames. As players join your party or raid, the secure template handles the creation of new frames for each of them. If the player is in combat, these frames would normally be locked down, unable to be modified. The templates give your addon a chance to do last-minute configuration before the frame is ever locked down. The process for using `SecureGroupHeaderTemplate` is as follows:

1. Create a new header frame that inherits from `SecureGroupHeaderTemplate`. This may be a custom XML template that inherits from the Blizzard template and adds things such as artwork and labels, or just the raw template itself.

2. Set attributes on the new header for some of the following:

   ▪ What characters, classes, groups should be displayed in the header?

   ▪ Should the header be displayed when the player is in a party, raid, solo, or all of the above?

   ▪ When new frames are created, to what point on the previous frame should they be anchored?

   ▪ How should the frames be sorted?

   ▪ Should the frames be grouped, or displayed in some sort of grid?

3. Supply an XML template (optionally) that the header will use to create new unit frames. This could be a custom template with artwork and elements, or simply `SecureUnitButton`.

4. Provide a configuration function (optionally) that will be called when a new unit frame is created, allowing for last-minute customization by addons.

Of course, creating a fully functional raid addon is a bit more complicated than this, but once you've mastered the basics of using the template, other features can be added to your addon, as necessary.

Configuring a SecureGroupHeader

A `SecureGroupHeader` has plenty of options that can be set using attributes. These options can be grouped into three major classes: filtering, grouping and sorting, and display. Tables 27-1, 27-2, and 27-3 describe these attributes.

Table 27-1: Filtering Attributes

ATTRIBUTE	TYPE	DESCRIPTION
showRaid	boolean	When `true`, the group header is shown when the player is in a raid.
showParty	boolean	When `true`, the group header is shown when the player is in a party. This attribute doesn't imply `showRaid` but can work alongside it.
showPlayer	boolean	When `true`, the header includes the player when not in a raid (normally, the player would not be visible in a party listing).

Table 27-1 *(continued)*

ATTRIBUTE	TYPE	DESCRIPTION
showSolo	boolean	When `true`, the header is shown when the player is not in any group. This option implies `showPlayer`.
nameList	string	A comma-separated list of player names to be included in the listing. This option is not used if `groupFilter` is specified.
groupFilter	string	A group number, or any combination of the following strings: A comma-separated list of raid group numbers A comma-separated list of uppercase class names in English (`WARRIOR`, `PRIEST`, and so on) A comma-separated list of uppercase group roles (`MAINTANK`, `MAINASSIST`)
strictFiltering	Boolean	When `true`, a character must match both a group and a class from the `groupFilter` list. This allows you to specify `"1,WARRIOR"`, which will show all warriors in group 1.

Table 27-2: Grouping and Sorting Attributes

ATTRIBUTE	TYPE	DESCRIPTION
groupBy	string	Specifies a grouping to apply before the list of players is sorted. Can be one of the following values: `"GROUP"`, `"CLASS"`, or `"ROLE"`. The sorting within these groups can be specified with the `groupingOrder` attribute.
groupingOrder	string	Specifies what order should be applied to the groups before they are sorted individually. This should be a comma-separated string of group numbers, uppercase class names, or uppercase role names (depending on what type of grouping was specified).
sortMethod	string	Specifies what sorting method should be used for ordering raid frames. Can be either `"NAME"` or `"INDEX"`, where index will sort the raid by the internal raid id. This value defaults to `"INDEX"`.
sortDir	string	Specifies the sort order using `"ASC"` for ascending, and `"DESC"` for descending. This value defaults to `"ASC"`.

When specifying a `groupBy` attribute, you must also supply a `groupingOrder` or the template will err because `groupingOrder` doesn't have any default values.

Table 27-3: Display Attributes

ATTRIBUTE	TYPE	DESCRIPTION
template	string	The name of an XML template to use when creating new frames. This can be a custom template, or the simple `SecureUnitButtonTemplate`.
templateType	string	The frame type of the XML template being used (`Button`, `StatusBar`, etc.).
point	string	A valid XML anchor point. This point will be used to anchor a new frame to an existing frame. The code will intelligently use the opposing anchor points, so if you specify `"TOP"`, it will anchor the `"TOP"` point of the new frame to the `"BOTTOM"` point of the previous frame.
xOffset	number	An `x` offset (in pixels) to be used when anchoring new frames.
yOffset	number	A `y` offset (in pixels) to be used when anchoring new frames.
maxColumns	number	The maximum number of columns that the header will create. The default for this attribute is a single column.
unitsPerColumn	number	The maximum number of units that will be displayed in a single column. When this value is `nil`, there is no limit.
startingIndex	number	The index in the final sorted list at which to start displaying units. This value defaults to `1`.
columnSpacing	number	The amount of space (in pixels) between the columns. This value defaults to `0`.
columnAnchorPoint	string	The anchor point for each new column. A value of `"LEFT"` will cause the columns to grow to the right.
initial-anchor	string	The initial anchor point for new unit frames. This can be used to place the frame in a different starting location (such as growing from the bottom up instead of top down). This value should be a comma-separated list containing anchor point, relative anchor point, x offset and y offset.
initial-width	number	The initial width of the unit frames in pixels.
initial-height	number	The initial height of the unit frame in pixels.
initial-scale	number	The initial scale of the unit frame.

A column in this context is simply the initial level of grouping for the raid frames. Because you can specify a custom anchor point for the frames (using the `point` attribute), your columns could actually be horizontal, and your rows could be vertical. In addition, when using a multicolumn display, you must specify a `columnAnchorPoint` or the template will generate an error.

SecureGroupPetHeaderTemplate Attributes

Two attributes can be used with the `SecureGroupPetHeader` template to customize the display of party/raid pets:

- `useOwnerUnit` (boolean) — When `true`, the `unit` attribute on the created frames corresponds to the owner's unit instead of the pet's unit.

- `filterOnPet` (boolean) — When `true`, the pet's names are used when sorting and filtering.

In addition to these specific attributes, the pet header accepts the same attributes as the normal secure group header.

Creating a New SecureGroupHeader

Begin by creating an addon skeleton called **BasicUnitFrames** that will be used throughout this chapter to create a very simple unit frame addon. You will use both `BasicUnitFrames.xml` and `BasicUnitFrames.lua` to separate the frame creation from the behavior logic.

Add the following to `BasicUnitFrames.xml`:

```
<Ui xmlns="http://www.blizzard.com/wow/ui/" ↵
xmlns:xsi="http://www.w3.org/2001/XMLSchema-instance" ↵
xsi:schemaLocation="http://www.blizzard.com/wow/ui/
..\FrameXML\UI.xsd">
  <Frame name="BasicUnitFrames_Header" parent="UIParent" ↵
inherits="SecureGroupHeaderTemplate" movable="true" hidden="false">
    <Anchors>
      <Anchor point="CENTER"/>
    </Anchors>
  </Frame>
</Ui>
```

> **HINT** When creating your header frame, you must avoid creating handlers for OnLoad, OnEvent, OnShow, or OnAttributeChanged. Each of these handlers is defined by the template, and any new ones will stop the old ones from being called. This will effectively break your header.

This XML snippet creates a new group header by inheriting from Blizzard's `SecureGroupHeaderTemplate`. Group headers must be created and configured prior to entering combat. Once the header has been created it must be configured using a set of attributes. Define these directly in the XML file by adding the following section to your frame definition:

```
<Attributes>
  <Attribute name="showParty" type="boolean" value="true"/>
  <Attribute name="showRaid" type="boolean" value="true"/>
  <Attribute name="showPlayer" type="boolean" value="true"/>
  <Attribute name="showSolo" type="boolean" value="true"/>
  <Attribute name="maxColumns" type="number" value="8"/>
  <Attribute name="unitsPerColumn" type="number" value="5"/>
  <Attribute name="columnAnchorPoint" type="string" value="LEFT"/>
  <Attribute name="point" type="string" value="TOP"/>
  <Attribute name="template" type="string" ↵
value="BasicUnitFrames_ButtonTemplate"/>
  <Attribute name="templateType" type="string" value="Button"/>
</Attributes>
```

This set of attributes defines a header that will be shown when the player is playing solo, grouped in a party, or part of a raid. It will show eight columns of five players, with frames growing down and columns growing to the right. New frames will be created using the `BasicUnitFrames_ButtonTemplate` that will be defined in the next section.

SETTING ATTRIBUTES USING XML

In Chapter 17, you learned how to use attributes to configure secure frames, using the `Frame:SetAttribute()` method call. Blizzard provides an alternative method of setting attributes using XML.

Any frame can contain an `<Attributes>` element, which should contain a list of `<Attribute>` tags. Each of these tags should have three set attributes:

- `name` — **The name of the attribute**
- `type` — **The Lua type of the value**
- `value` — **The value to be set**

The name is required to identify the attribute (and corresponds directly with the first argument to the `:SetAttribute()` method). Because XML only allows string values, you must specify the type of the value being set so it can be converted. If the type wasn't specified, the value `"true"` in the previous example would be set as the string `"true"` instead of the boolean value true, which could mean something entirely different.

Both methods of setting attributes have their own set of advantages and can be used interchangeably and even mixed together. Defining a default set of attributes in an XML template could give your `<OnLoad>` script a bit less to do over the course of the program.

Defining an XML Template

The header defined in the preceding section expects to find an XML template called `BasicUnitFrames_ButtonTemplate` that will be used when creating new frames. This template must exist when the header is first created, so add the following definition above the header, in the `BasicUnitFrames.xml` file:

```
<Button name="BasicUnitFrames_ButtonTemplate" virtual="true">
  <Size x="35" y="35"/>
  <Layers>
    <Layer level="ARTWORK">
      <FontString name="$parent_Name" setAllPoints="true" ↵
text="Unknown Entity" inherits="GameFontHighlight"/>
    </Layer>
  </Layers>
  <Frames>
    <StatusBar name="$parent_HealthBar" minValue="0" maxValue="100" ↵
defaultValue="100" setAllPoints="true">
      <BarTexture file="Interface\TargetingFrame\UI-StatusBar"/>
      <BarColor r="1.0" g="1.0" b="1.0"/>
      <Scripts>
        <OnLoad>
          -- This is done to ensure the status bar doesn't block
          -- the name text
          self:SetFrameLevel(self:GetFrameLevel() - 1)
        </OnLoad>
      </Scripts>
    </StatusBar>
  </Frames>
</Button>
```

This is a simple square button with a font string for the player's name that inherits from `GameFontHighlight` (this is the basic white font you see in most places). It also contains a status bar element that is initialized with a minimum value of `0` and a maximum value of `100`, with the default being `100`. The status bar is the full size of the button and has a default color of white.

When the status bar is first created, it will be shown above the name font string because its frame level is higher than the button's (by default, a child is created with a frame level of one greater than its parent). To get everything to layer properly, the `OnLoad` script lowers the frame level of the status bar.

Adding Behavior Scripts

Behavior scripts can be added to the button template by including the following after the `</Frames>` tag:

```
<Scripts>
    <OnLoad>
```

```
      BasicUnitFrames_Button_OnLoad(self)
    </OnLoad>
    <OnShow>
      BasicUnitFrames_Button_OnShow(self)
    </OnShow>
    <OnEvent>
      BasicUnitFrames_Button_OnEvent(self, event, ...)
    </OnEvent>
    <OnDragStart>
      BasicUnitFrames_Button_OnDragStart(self, button)
    </OnDragStart>
    <OnDragStop>
      BasicUnitFrames_Button_OnDragStop(self, button)
    </OnDragStop>
    <OnHide>
      BasicUnitFrames_Button_OnDragStop(self, button)
    </OnHide>
  </Scripts>
```

Each button created with this template will have the following scripts set:

- OnLoad — Handles event registration and creating shortcuts for the status bar and name text.

- OnShow — Called each time the unit associated with the frame is changed, and should handle things like changing the name and color of the status bar.

- OnEvent — Handles the UNIT_HEALTH and UNIT_MAXHEALTH events that will be registered for each button.

- OnDragStart/OnDragStop — Allows the entire header to be dragged by click-dragging on any of the unit buttons.

- OnHide — Because the buttons are hidden and shown when the unit changes, they could be hidden while you are in the middle of dragging the header around. If that happens, it will stay attached to the mouse. By running the OnDragStop code OnHide, you ensure this won't happen.

Initializing Frames

Open BasicUnitFrames.lua and add the following:

```
function BasicUnitFrames_Button_OnLoad(self)
  self:RegisterForDrag("LeftButton")
  self:RegisterEvent("UNIT_HEALTH")
  self:RegisterEvent("UNIT_MAXHEALTH")
  self.healthbar = getglobal(self:GetName().."_HealthBar")
  self.name = getglobal(self:GetName().."_Name")
end
```

This function sets the frame up for dragging support with the left button and registers the events necessary to monitor unit health. In addition, it creates two shortcuts, one to the health bar and one to the name text, so they can be easily updated in other functions.

When writing your OnLoad function, make sure to take no actions that are protected during combat (such as :Show(), :Hide(), or :SetAttribute()). Because the frame may be created during combat, those functions won't have any effect and, instead, should be put in the configuration function (shown later in this section).

Updating Unit Information

The OnShow handler for your frames can be used to update the unit-specific information because the frame is hidden and then shown again each time the unit attribute changes. Add the following code to update the color of the status bar and the name text:

```
function BasicUnitFrames_Button_OnShow(self)
  local unit = self:GetAttribute("unit")
  if unit then
    self.name:SetText(UnitName(unit))
    local class = select(2, UnitClass(unit)) or "WARRIOR"
    local color = RAID_CLASS_COLORS[class]
    self.healthbar:SetStatusBarColor(color.r, color.g, color.b)
  end
end
```

RAID FRAME LAG

In the current version of World of Warcraft, BasicUnitFrames_Button_OnShow(self) may be called many times if you join any raid that is constantly having members added and removed from it (in particular Battlegrounds). Here's an alternate version of the function that takes this into account with a unit cache:

```
function BasicUnitFrames_Button_OnShow(self)
  local unit = self:GetAttribute("unit")
  if unit then
    local name, server = UnitName(unit)
    if server then
      name = name .. server
    end
    if name ~= self.currentName then
      self.name:SetText(name)
      local class = select(2, UnitClass(unit)) or "WARRIOR"
      local color = RAID_CLASS_COLORS[class]
      self.healthbar:SetStatusBarColor(color.r, color.g,↵
color.b)
      self.currentName = name
    end
  end
end
```

Continued

RAID FRAME LAG *(continued)*

You can't use `unitIds` to track changes directly because those can change as someone joins the raid; instead, you use the player's name. A player's name should be unique on a single server, but once you get into the cross-realm battlegrounds there could be a potential conflict. As a result, if the unit's name includes a server name, this is appended to the name that is stored. If the name of the new unit is the same as the old unit's name, then you can skip the update.

Updating Maximum Health

Add the following definition to `BasicUnitFrames.lua`:

```
function BasicUnitFrames_Button_OnEvent(self, event, ...)
  local unit = ...
  if self:GetAttribute("unit") == unit then
    if event == "UNIT_MAXHEALTH" then
      self.healthbar:SetMinMaxValues(0, UnitHealthMax(unit))
      self.healthbar:SetValue(UnitHealth(unit))
    elseif event == "UNIT_HEALTH" then
      self.healthbar:SetValue(UnitHealth(unit))
    end
  end
end
```

Simply enough, this handles the maximum health of a unit changing, as well as the current health value, by changing the status bar limits and setting the value directly.

Adding Dragging Support

The behavior code for BasicUnitFrames is finished off with the following function definitions, which enable dragging to move the group header:

```
function BasicUnitFrames_Button_OnDragStart(self, button)
  BasicUnitFrames_Header:StartMoving()
  BasicUnitFrames_Header.isMoving = true
end

function BasicUnitFrames_Button_OnDragStop(self, button)
  if BasicUnitFrames_Header.isMoving then
    BasicUnitFrames_Header:StopMovingOrSizing()
  end
end
```

Testing BasicUnitFrames

Log in to World of Warcraft and ensure BasicUnitFrames is listed and enabled in your addon selection screen. You should see a small box in the center of your screen (see Figure 27-1). You can click and drag this frame around, and it should update as your health changes (see Figure 27-2).

Figure 27-1:
BasicUnitFrames
showing a Paladin

Figure 27-2:
BasicUnitFrames
responding to
health events

As new members join your party, you should see the frame expand to add a new square for each member of the party or raid (see Figure 27-3).

Figure 27-3: BasicUnitFrames
displaying a raid

Of course, you can continue adding new features to your addon, customizing it specifically to your needs by changing the template, registering new events, and changing the behavior logic.

> **NOTE** If you happen to do some digging, you may find that all
> of the frames are named in an easy-to-guess format, specifically
> `<HeaderName>UnitButton<childIndex>`. In the preceding addon, this means
> `BasicUnitFrames_HeaderUnitButton1`, and so on. You can obtain these names by
> running the following macro while hovering the mouse over one of the frames:
>
> ```
> /run ChatFrame1:AddMessage(GetMouseFocus():GetName() or "")
> ```

This consistent naming makes it easy for other addons to interact with your frames by simply knowing the name of your header.

Summary

The secure template system for raid frames is extremely flexible and allows you to create robust unit frames with minimal amounts of code.

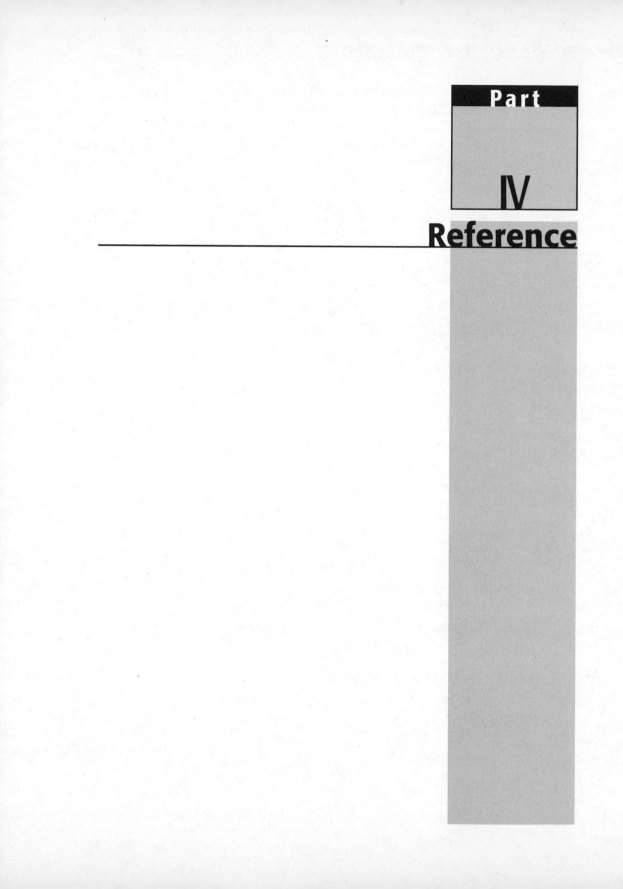

Part

IV

Reference

API Reference

The World of Warcraft API contains more than a thousand functions that can be used to obtain information from the game client. This chapter provides an alphabetic listing of these functions, along with detailed descriptions of what each function does, what arguments it takes, and what it returns to the caller.

Although all efforts were made to provide the most up-to-date listing of functions, the API does change from patch to patch. For the most current listings, please visit the book's companion website at `http://wowprogramming.com/api`. Information about upcoming changes can be found on the World of Warcraft UI & Macros Forums: `http://forums.worldofwarcraft.com/board.html?forumId=11114`.

API Reference Conventions

This chapter contains function names listed alphabetically. Following each function is a description of what the function does. Then comes the function signature (if necessary), followed by any arguments or returns.

Function Signatures

A function signature is a short way to express the name of a function, the arguments that the function expects to be called with, and any values that the function may return. Consider the following signature for the `CalculateAuctionDeposit()` function:

```
deposit = CalculateAuctionDeposit(runTime)
```

This notation indicates that the function accepts a single argument called `runTime`, and returns a single value called `deposit`. These aren't requirements for names: they are simply names given to each of the arguments and returns, to make the signature easier to read.

If a function signature is omitted, then the function takes no arguments, and returns no values. This is equivalent to the function signature `FunctionName()`, so these signatures are not listed.

Optional Arguments

When a signature contains an optional argument, it is wrapped in square brackets to indicate this. The following is the function signature for `BuyMerchantItem()`:

```
BuyMerchantItem(index [,quantity])
```

This signature shows that the function returns no arguments and takes an argument `index`, along with an optional argument `quantity`. The specific details of what the optional argument does are listed in the description for that argument, which is displayed below the signature.

A function may have multiple nested optional arguments, such as `SendChatMessage()`:

```
SendChatMessage("text" [,"chatType" [,"language" [,"channel"]]])
```

This function requires the first argument `text`, but can also take up to three more arguments. The optional arguments are nested in this way because to include the argument `language`, you must also include something for `chatType` (even if it's the value `nil`). Likewise, to supply a `channel` argument, you must also supply values for `chatType` and `language`.

Argument Choices

Certain functions, such as `IsAddOnLoaded()`, have alternative choices in their arguments:
loaded = IsAddOnLoaded(index or "name")This function can take either the index of an addon in the addon listing, or the name of an addon. It then returns whether or not the addon is currently loaded by the game client. When a function has multiple choices for a single argument, each is simply added to the list of options in the signature and description.

Argument and Return Listings

Following a function signature is a detailed listing of the arguments and returns for the given function. The arguments and returns are all given in a similar format. Here is the listing for the `GetSocketTypes()` function:

Argument:

index — The index of the socket to query. (number)

Return:

gemColor — The color of the given gem socket. (string)

- ▪ Blue
- ▪ Yellow
- ▪ Red
- ▪ Meta

Under each section is a list of named arguments, followed by a description of the argument. After the description is an indicator that tells you what Lua type to pass (or what to expect from the function). In this case, the function accepts a numeric argument called index, and returns a string that is the color of the socket.

If an argument is optional, it will be specified in the argument listing as well as in the function signature. When there is an argument choice, that also is reflected in these listings.

API Pseudo-Types

For the purposes of this chapter, we have created a number of pseudo-types to help describe what sort of values are accepted in an argument, or are returned from an API function. These are not actual Lua types, but a classification of accepted values in various API functions. Table 28-1 describes these types.

Table 28-1: API Pseudo-Types

TYPE	DESCRIPTION
1nil	This variable type indicates that a function returns a boolean result, by returning 1 for true, and nil for false. While in most cases these operate the same as boolean values, they aren't the actual values true and false.
unitID	unitIDs are used throughout the API to provide an alias to certain units of interest. Valid base values are player, pet, target, partyX, raidX, partypetX, raidpetX, focus, mouseover, and npc (where X is a number from 1 to the number of party or raid members). These correspond to the player, the player's pet, the player's target, a member of the player's party, a member of the player's raid, the player's focus, the unit that the mouse is currently hovering over, and the NPC with which the player is currently interacting. In addition, any unitID can have target added to the end of it to reference that unit's target, such as partypet2target, which resolves to the second party member's pet's target. Longer values such as targettargettarget are also legal.

Continued

Table 28-1 *(continued)*

TYPE	DESCRIPTION
	Functions that accept a `unitID` will also accept the name of a player in your party or raid instead of a `unitID`. For example `UnitHealth` (`"Cladhaire"`) will return the same value as `UnitHealth("party1")` if the unit `party1` is the player named `Cladhaire`. To access the target of a player in this format, simply add a hyphen between the name and target, for example `UnitHealth("Cladhaire-target")`.
`Team`	Arena teams are specified by the index in which they appear in the PvP tab of the character window. These teams are listed in increasing size order, so if the player is a member of a 3v3 and a 5v5 team, the index `1` will refer to 3v3, and `2` will refer to 5v5.
`inventoryID`	The API functions that query the inventory take a number that identifies one of the queriable inventory slots. These numbers may be obtained using the `GetInventorySlotInfo()` function.
`bagID`	Functions that operate on containers take a numeric index that represents a specific bag. The player's backpack has index `0`, and the normal bags have indices `1-4`. The player's keyring is index `-2`. The bank itself has index `-1`, and the bank bags are indices `5-11`.
`itemID`	An item's ID is the internal number used by the client to identify specific items. For the item Mantle of the Avatar, the ID is `30154`.
`itemString`	The `itemString` for a given item is the information portion of the `itemLink` without the color information or the item's name. Partial strings are accepted so you can provide as much or as little information as you have. For the item Mantle of the Avatar, an example `itemString` could be `"item:30154:2993:2741:2741"`. The extra numbers indicate the specific enchantments of gems that are included with this item.
`itemLink`	The full hyperlink, including the color information, item name and the full `itemString` for the given item. For Mantle of the Avatar this might be `"|cffa335ee|Hitem:30154:2993:2741:2741:0:0:0:0|h[Mantle of the Avatar]|h|r"`.

Alphabetic API Listing

AbandonQuest

Confirms abandoning a quest. This function is used by the default user interface to confirm the abandoning of a quest in your log. `SetAbandonQuest()` is used to select which quest should be abandoned. See also: `SetAbandonQuest()`

AbandonSkill

Confirms abandoning a skill. This function is called by the default user interface when confirming the abandoning of a tradeskill or profession.

```
AbandonSkill(index)
```

Argument:

`index` — The index of the skill to abandon. `(number)`

AcceptAreaSpiritHeal

Notifies the server that you are ready to accept the periodic area resurrection from a battleground spirit healer. (This is called automatically by the default UI when your ghost is within range of the spirit healer. The incoming resurrection can still be canceled by calling `CancelAreaSpiritHeal()`.)

AcceptArenaTeam

Accepts an invitation to join an arena team.

AcceptBattlefieldPort

Accepts the offered teleport to a battleground, or leaves the queue for a given battleground.

```
AcceptBattlefieldPort(index, accept)
```

Arguments:

`index` — The index of a battleground for which the player is currently queued. `(number)`

`accept` — `1` to accept the offered port, `nil` to leave the queue for the given battleground. `(1nil)`

AcceptDuel

Accepts a proposed duel.

AcceptGroup

Accepts an invitation to a party.

AcceptGuild

Accepts an invitation to join a guild.

AcceptQuest

Accepts the quest that is currently displayed.

AcceptResurrect

Accepts a pending resurrection spell. This function cannot be used to accept a self-resurrect. *See also:* `UseSoulstone()`

AcceptSockets

Accepts the current socketed gems without confirmation.

AcceptTrade

Accepts a proposed trade.

AcceptXPLoss

Confirms the loss of 25 percent durability when being resurrected at the spirit healer, without confirmation. (This function was not renamed when the spirit healing penalty was changed from a loss of experience to loss of inventory durability.)

ActionHasRange

Returns whether an action has a range restriction.

```
hasRange = ActionHasRange(slot)
```

Argument:

`slot` — The action bar slot. (number)

Return:

`hasRange` — 1 if the action has a range restriction, otherwise `nil`. (1nil)

AddChatWindowChannel

Maps a channel in a specific chat frame to a numeric index.

```
zoneChannel = AddChatWindowChannel(index, "channel")
```

Arguments:

`index` — The index of a chat frame (1–7). (number)

`channel` — The name of a chat channel. (number)

Return:

`zoneChannel` — 0 for nonzone channels; otherwise, a numeric index specific to that channel. (number)

AddChatWindowMessages

Sets a chat frame to receive and show messages of the given message group.

```
AddChatWindowMessages(index, "messageGroup")
```

Arguments:

`index` — ChatFrame index (1–7). (number)

`messageGroup` — Message group to add to the chat frame. (string)

AddFriend

Adds a player or unit to the friends list.

```
AddFriend("unit")
```

Arguments:

`unit`

`unit` — The unit ID of the player to add to the friends list. (unitid)

AddIgnore

Adds a player or unit to the ignore list.

```
AddIgnore("unit")
```

Arguments:

```
unit
```

unit — The unit ID of the player to add to the ignore list. (unitid)

AddMute

Mutes a player in voice chat.

```
AddMute("fullname")
```

Argument:

fullname — The name of the player to be muted. (string)

AddOrDelIgnore

Adds or removes a player from the ignore list.

```
AddOrDelIgnore("fullname")
```

Argument:

fullname — The player to add or remove from the ignore list. (string)

AddOrDelMute

Adds or removes a player/unit from the voice mute list.

```
AddOrDelMute("unit")
```

Arguments:

```
unit
```

unit — The unit to mute. (unitid)

AddQuestWatch

Adds a quest to the quest tracker.

```
AddQuestWatch(questIndex)
```

Argument:

questIndex — The index of a quest in the quest log. (number)

AddTradeMoney

Adds the money currently on the cursor to the trade window.

ArenaTeamDisband

Disbands an arena team.

```
ArenaTeamDisband(team)
```

Argument:

team — The index of the arena team to disband. These indices begin at 1, with 1 always being the smallest team of which the player is a part. For example, if the player is only a member of a 3v3 and 5v5 team, then the index 1 will be the 3v3 team, and the index 2 will be the 5v5 team. (number)

Note: This function requires the player to be the team leader

ArenaTeamInviteByName

Invites a player to one of the player's arena teams.

```
ArenaTeamInviteByName(team, "name")
```

Arguments:

team — The index of the arena team. (number)

name — The name of the player to invite. (string)

ArenaTeamLeave

Leaves an arena team.

```
ArenaTeamLeave(team)
```

Argument:

team — The index of the team to leave. (number)

ArenaTeamRoster

Queries the server for roster information about an arena team. This function sends a query to the server requesting roster information about one of the player's arena teams. The function doesn't return any information directly because it has to communicate with the server. Once the information has been requested, an addon can respond to the ARENA_TEAM_ROSTER_UPDATE event, and then use the GetNumArenaTeamMembers() and GetArenaTeamRosterInfo() functions to get more details about specific members.

This function will only update arena team information once every 10 seconds for each index. If you call ArenaTeamRoster(1), the ARENA_TEAM_ROSTER_UPDATE event will fire, but if you call it again within 10 seconds, no event will be fired. Each team index has its own throttling timer, so you can call ArenaTeamRoster(1) and ArenaTeamRoster(2), and both will raise their own events.

```
ArenaTeamRoster(team)
```

Argument:

team — The index of the team to be queried. (number)

ArenaTeamSetLeaderByName

Promotes an arena team member to team leader.

```
ArenaTeamSetLeaderByName(team, "name")
```

Arguments:

team — The index of the arena team. (number)

name — The name of the player to promote to team leader. (string)

ArenaTeamUninviteByName

Uninvites a player from an arena team.

```
ArenaTeamUninviteByName(team, "name")
```

Arguments:

team — The index of the arena team. (number)

name — The name of the player to uninvite from the given arena team. (string)

AscendStop

Called when the player releases the binding for Jump. The Jump binding is also used for ascending while in flight.

Note: This function is protected and cannot be called via addons.

AssistUnit

Assists a player, targeting their current target. This is used to allow players to easily follow another player's target.

```
AssistUnit("unit")
```

Arguments:

unit

unit — The unit ID of the player to add to the friends list. (unitid)

Note: This function is protected and cannot be called via addons.

AttackTarget

Enables melee auto-attacking against the currently selected target.

Note: This function is protected and cannot be called via addons.

AutoEquipCursorItem

Tries to equip the item currently held on the cursor.

AutoStoreGuildBankItem

Withdraws an item from the guild bank, automatically storing it in your inventory.

```
AutoStoreGuildBankItem(tab, slot)
```

Arguments:

tab — The index of a guild bank tab. (number)

slot — A slot in the guild bank tab. (number)

BankButtonIDToInvSlotID

Returns an inventory slot ID mapped from a bank location. This allows the items in the bank to be used as if they were in your local inventory.

```
inventoryId = BankButtonIDToInvSlotID(buttonId [, isBag])
```

Arguments:

`buttonID` — A button ID from the bank interface. `(number)`

`isBag` (optional) — Indicates if the given slot is a bag. `(1nil)`

Returns:

`inventoryId` — An inventory slot ID that can be used in the inventory functions. `(number)`

Example:

```
-- While mousing over a button in the bank
local button = GetMouseFocus()
ChatFrame1:AddMessage("Inventory Slot: " .. ↵
BankButtonIDToInvSlotID(button:GetID(), button.isBag))
```

BindEnchant

Confirms enchanting an item when it would cause the item to become soul-bound. Certain enchantments cause the item being enchanted to become soulbound. When this happens, the game asks for confirmation before applying the enchantment, and this function is used to confirm that it should proceed.

BuyGuildBankTab

Purchases the next available guild bank tab, without confirmation.

BuyGuildCharter

Purchases a guild charter with a given name.

```
BuyGuildCharter("guildName")
```

Argument:

`guildName` — The name of the guild. `(string)`

Note: This function only works when speaking with a guild master.

BuyMerchantItem

Purchases an item available from a merchant, without confirmation.

```
BuyMerchantItem(index [,quantity])
```

Arguments:

`index` — The index of an item available from the merchant. `(number)`

`quantity` — The number of items to purchase. `(number)`

BuyPetition

Purchases a petition (used for arena charters).

```
BuyPetition(index, "name")
```

Arguments:

index — The index of the petition to purchase. For purchasing arena charters, these are 1 for 2v2, 2 for 3v3 and 3 for 5v5. (number)

name — The name to use for the petition. (string)

BuyStableSlot

Purchases the next available stable slot, without confirmation.

Note: This function works only when speaking with a stable master.

BuyTrainerService

Purchases a service available at a trainer.

```
BuyTrainerService(index)
```

Argument:

index — The index of a service available at a trainer. (number)

BuybackItem

Purchases an item from the buyback tab.

```
BuybackItem(slot)
```

Argument:

slot — The slot on the buyback tab. (number)

CalculateAuctionDeposit

Returns the cost of an auction house deposit for a given runtime.

```
deposit = CalculateAuctionDeposit(runTime)
```

Argument:

runTime — The runtime of the proposed auction. (number)

- 720 — 12 hours
- 1440 — 24 hours
- 2880 — 48 hours

Return:

deposit — The cost of the deposit, in copper. (number)

Note: This function operates based on the item placed in the auction house create auction item slot.

CameraOrSelectOrMoveStart

Called when left-clicking in the 3-D world.

Note: This function is protected and cannot be called via addons.

CameraOrSelectOrMoveStop

Ends a left-click in the 3-D world.

```
CameraOrSelectOrMoveStop(isSticky)
```

Argument:

isSticky — If 1, the camera will remain static until canceled. Otherwise, the camera will pan back to be directly behind the character. (1nil)

Note: This function is protected and cannot be called via addons.

CameraZoomIn

Zooms the camera in a specified distance. The maximum distance of the camera is set in the Interface Options screen and the maximum distance allowed is enforced by this setting, and the game client. Depending on the setting, this is between 15.0 and 24.0 in the current version of the client.

```
CameraZoomIn(distance)
```

Argument:

distance — The distance to zoom in. (number)

CameraZoomOut

This function is used to zoom the camera out. The maximum distance of the camera is set in the Interface Options screen, and the maximum distance allowed is enforced by this setting and the game client. Depending on the setting, this is between 15.0 and 24.0 in the current version of the client.

```
CameraZoomOut(distance)
```

Argument:

distance — The distance to zoom out. (number)

CanComplainChat

Returns whether a given chat line can be reported.

```
canComplain = CanComplainChat(lineID)
```

Argument:

lineID — The unique identifier of a given chat line. (number)

Returns:

canComplain — 1 if the player can complain about the given chat line, otherwise nil. (1nil)

CanComplainInboxItem

Queries an inbox mail item for complain status. This determines if you can report this mail as spam. Returns 1 if you can, nil otherwise. This function only works at the mailbox, and it will return nil for anyone on your friends list.

```
complain = CanComplainInboxItem(mailID)
```

Argument:

mailID — The index of the message in the mailbox. (number)

Returns:

complain — 1 if the inbox item can be complained about, otherwise nil. (1nil)

CanEditGuildInfo

Returns whether the player can edit the guild information.

```
canEdit = CanEditGuildInfo()
```

Returns:

canEdit — 1 if the player can edit the guild information, otherwise nil. (1nil)

CanEditMOTD

Returns whether the player can edit the guild MOTD.

```
canEdit = CanEditMOTD()
```

Returns:

canEdit — 1 if the player can edit the guild MOTD, otherwise nil. (1nil)

CanEditOfficerNote

Returns whether the player can edit officer notes.

```
canEdit = CanEditOfficerNote()
```

Returns:

canEdit — 1 if the player can edit officer notes, otherwise nil. (1nil)

CanEditPublicNote

Returns whether the player can edit public notes.

```
canEdit = CanEditPublicNote()
```

Returns:

canEdit — 1 if the player can edit public notes, otherwise nil. (1nil)

CanGuildDemote

Returns whether the player can demote lower-ranked guild members.

```
canDemote = CanGuildDemote()
```

Returns:

canDemote — 1 if the player can demote lower-ranked guild members. This is determined by the player's guild rank permissions. (1nil)

CanGuildInvite

Returns whether the player can invite members to his or her guild.

```
canInvite = CanGuildInvite()
```

Returns:

canInvite — 1 if the player can invite members to their guild, otherwise nil. (1nil)

CanGuildPromote

Returns whether the player has the ability to promote other players within the guild.

```
canPromote = CanGuildPromote()
```

Returns:

canPromote — 1 if the player has the ability to promote within the guild, otherwise nil. (1nil)

CanGuildRemove

Returns whether the player can remove a member from his or her guild.

```
canRemove = CanGuildRemove()
```

Returns:

canRemove — 1 if the player can remove a member from his or her guild, otherwise nil. (1nil)

CanInspect

This function returns whether the given unit can be inspected. This function will return nil if the unit is out of inspection range, if the unit is an NPC, or if the unit is a member of the opposing faction.

```
canInspect = CanInspect(unitId [, showError])
```

Arguments:

unitId — The unit ID that you want to check to see if you can inspect it. This function only accepts unit IDs, not player names. (string)

showError — Returns true to display an error in the UIErrorsFrame, otherwise false. (boolean)

Returns:

canInspect — 1 if you can inspect the unit, otherwise nil. (1nil)

CanJoinBattlefieldAsGroup

Returns whether the currently displayed battlefield supports joining as a group.

```
canGroupJoin = CanJoinBattlefieldAsGroup()
```

Returns:

canGroupJoin — 1 if the currently displayed battlefield supports joining as a group. (1nil)

CanMerchantRepair

Returns whether the open merchant can repair equipment.

```
canRepair = CanMerchantRepair()
```

Returns:

`canRepair` — 1 if the merchant can repair equipment, otherwise `nil`. (1nil)

CanSendAuctionQuery

Returns whether the player can perform a given auction house query. Mass auction queries were added in Patch 2.3 to allow auction house addons to query the entire auction house at once, instead of page by page. This mass query system is throttled to only allow one query entry every 15 minutes.

```
canQuery, canMassQuery = CanSendAuctionQuery("list")
```

Argument:

`list` — The type of auction listing. (string)

- `bidder` — Auctions on which the player has bid
- `list` — Available auctions listing
- `owner` — Auctions the player placed

Returns:

`canQuery` — 1 if the player can submit an auction query, otherwise `nil`. (1nil)

`canMassQuery` — 1 if the player can submit a mass auction query, otherwise `nil`. (1nil)

CanSendLFGQuery

Returns whether the player can submit an LFG/LFM request for the given type and index.

```
canSend = CanSendLFGQuery(type, index)
```

Arguments:

`type` — The type of LFG query. The valid values can be obtained from `GetLFGTypes()`. (number)

`index` — The specific LFG dungeon/quest index. The valid values can be obtained from `GetLFGTypeEntries()`. (number)

Returns:

`canSend` — Returns `true` if the player can submit an LFG query for the given type/index, otherwise `false`. (boolean)

CanShowResetInstances

Returns whether the player can reset instances. This function is used to determine if the "Reset Instance" option should be displayed on the unit popup menu.

```
canResetInstances = CanShowResetInstances()
```

Returns:

`canResetInstances` — 1 if the player can currently reset instances, otherwise `nil`. (1nil)

CanSignPetition

Returns whether the player can sign the currently offered petition.

```
canSign = CanSignPetition()
```

Returns:

`canSign` — 1 if the player can sign the currently offered petition, otherwise `nil`. (1nil)

Note: Petitions can only be signed once per account, rather than once per character.

CanViewOfficerNote

Returns whether the player can view officer notes.

```
canView = CanViewOfficerNote()
```

Returns:

`canView` — 1 if the player can view officer notes, otherwise `nil`. (1nil)

CanWithdrawGuildBankMoney

Returns whether the player can withdraw money from the guild bank.

```
canWithdraw = CanWithdrawGuildBankMoney()
```

Returns:

`canWithdraw` — 1 if the player can withdraw money from the guild bank, otherwise `nil`. (1nil)

CancelAreaSpiritHeal

Cancels resurrection if one is pending from a battleground spirit healer. Area spirit heals repeat periodically; this function only cancels the currently pending resurrection.

CancelAuction

Cancels an auction that has been placed by the player. This causes the player to lose the deposit and, as a result, is called from a popup confirmation dialog.

```
CancelAuction(index)
```

Argument:

`index` — The index of the auction in the `owner` listing. (number)

CancelDuel

Cancels a proposed duel, or declines a duel that has been offered.

CancelItemTempEnchantment

Cancels a temporary item enchantment.

```
CancelItemTempEnchantment(slot)
```

Argument:

slot — 1 to cancel the main-hand item enchant, 2 to cancel the off-hand item enchant. (number)

CancelLogout

Cancels a pending logout. This function only has an effect while the logout countdown timer is displayed.

CancelPendingEquip

Cancels a pending equip action. When the player tries to equip a bind-on-equip item, a confirmation dialog is displayed asking the user if he or she wants to bind the item by equipping it. This function is used by the confirmation dialog when the player cancels the pending equip.

```
CancelPendingEquip(index)
```

CancelPendingLFG

Removes the player from all open LookingForGroup queues.

CancelPlayerBuff

Cancels one of the player's buffs by name or index.

```
CancelPlayerBuff("name" or index)
```

Arguments:

name or index

name — The name of the buff to cancel. (string)

index — The index of the player buff to cancel. This number can be obtained with GetPlayerBuff(). (number)

CancelShapeshiftForm

Cancels the current shapeshift form. The game considers the following shapeshift forms: druid shapeshifts, shadowform, stealth, and ghost wolf form.

CancelTrade

Cancels an active trade.

CancelTradeAccept

Cancels a trade that is currently pending acceptance by the other party.

CastPetAction

Casts a pet action on a specific target.

`CastPetAction(index, "target")`

Arguments:

`index` — The index of a pet action in the pet's action bar. (`number`)

`target` — The unit to use as the target of the given action. (`unitid`)

Note: This function is protected and cannot be called via addons.

CastShapeshiftForm

Casts a shapeshift form by index.

`CastShapeshiftForm(index)`

Note: This function is protected and cannot be called via addons.

CastSpell

Casts a spell by the ID of the spell in the spellbook.

`CastSpell(spellID, "bookType")`

Arguments:

`spellID` — The index of a spell in the spellbook. (`number`)

`bookType` — The type of spellbook to use. (`string`)

- ▪ `pet` — The pet's spellbook
- ▪ `spell` — The player's spellbook

Note: This function is protected and cannot be called via addons.

CastSpellByName

`CastSpellByName("name" [, "target"])`

Arguments:

`name` — The name of a spell to cast. (`string`)

`target` — The unit to use as the target of the given action. (`unitid`)

Note: Although this function is protected in most cases, it can be used by addons to call up the tradeskill and craft windows; for example, `CastSpellByName("First Aid")`. It cannot be used to cast other types of spells.

ChangeActionBarPage

Changes the current action bar page.

`ChangeActionBarPage(page)`

Argument:

`page` — The action bar page to which to change. (`number`)

Note: This function cannot be called while in combat.

ChangeChatColor

Changes the color of a message type in the chat windows. This change takes effect immediately.

```
ChangeChatColor("messageType", red, green, blue)
```

Arguments:

messageType — The message type, as listed in chat-cache.txt. Examples of values are "SAY" and "CHANNEL1". (string)

red — The value of the red component color (0.0–1.0). (number)

green — The value of the green component color (0.0–1.0). (number)

blue — The value of the blue component color (0.0–1.0). (number)

ChannelBan

Bans a player from a given chat channel. This function requires the player to be a moderator of the given channel.

```
ChannelBan("channel", "fullname")
```

Arguments:

channel — The name of the channel. (string)

fullname — The name of the player to be banned. (string)

ChannelInvite

Invites a player to a given channel.

```
ChannelInvite("channel", "name")
```

Arguments:

channel — The channel name. (string)

name — The player's name. (string)

ChannelKick

Kicks a player from the given channel. This function requires the player to be a moderator of the given channel.

```
ChannelKick("channel", "name")
```

Arguments:

channel — The name of the channel. (string)

name — The name of the player to kick. (string)

ChannelModerator

Grants a player moderator status on the given channel. This function requires the player to be owner of the given channel.

```
ChannelModerator("channel", "fullname")
```

Arguments:

channel — The name of the channel name. (string)

fullname — The name of the player to give moderator status. (string)

ChannelMute

Turns off the specified player's ability to speak in the channel. This function requires the player to be a moderator of the given channel.

```
ChannelMute("channel", "player")
```

Arguments:

channel — The channel on which to mute the selected player. (string)

player — The name of the player to mute on the selected channel. (string)

ChannelSilenceAll

Removes both voice and chat permissions for the given player in the specified channel. The player must be a moderator of the given channel to perform this action.

```
ChannelSilenceAll("channel" or channelIndex, "name")
```

Arguments:

channel or channelIndex

channel — The name of the given channel. (string)

channelIndex — The index of the given channel. (number)

name — The exact name of the player to silence. (string)

ChannelSilenceVoice

Silences the given character for voice chat on the channel. Can only be done as a raid/party/bg leader or assistant.

```
ChannelSilenceVoice("channel", "name")
```

Arguments:

channel — Channel on which to silence the character. (string)

name — Name of the character to silence. (string)

ChannelToggleAnnouncements

Toggles channel announcements for a given channel.

```
ChannelToggleAnnouncements("channel")
```

Argument:

channel — The channel for which to enable or disable channel announcements. (string)

ChannelUnSilenceAll

Unsilences a player for chat and voice on a given channel.

```
ChannelUnSilenceAll("channelName" or channelIndex, "name")
```

Arguments:

channelName or channelIndex

channelName — The name of the channel. (string)

channelIndex — The index of the channel. (number)

name — The name of a player to unsilence. (string)

ChannelUnSilenceVoice

Unsilences a player on a given channel.

ChannelUnSilenceVoice("channelName" or channelId, "unit" or "name")

Arguments:

channelName or channelId

channelName — The name of a channel. (string)

channelId — The numeric index of a channel. (number)

unit or name

unit — The unit ID to unsilence. (unitid)

name — The name of the player to unsilence. (string)

ChannelUnban

Unbans a player from a given channel.

ChannelUnban("channel", "player")

Arguments:

channel — The name of the channel. (string)

player — The name of the player. (string)

ChannelUnmoderator

Revokes moderator status from a given player on a specific channel

ChannelUnmoderator("channel", "player")

Arguments:

channel — The name of the channel. (string)

player — The player from whom to revoke moderator status. (string)

ChannelUnmute

Unmutes the specified player on that channel.

ChannelUnmute("channel", "player")

Arguments:

channel — The channel in which to unmute the player. (string)

player — The player to unmute. (string)

ChannelVoiceOff

Disables voice chat in the given channel.

```
ChannelVoiceOff("channel" or channelIndex)
```

Arguments:

channel or channelIndex

channel — The name of the given channel. (string)

channelIndex — The index of the given channel. (number)

ChannelVoiceOn

Enables voice chat in the given channel.

```
ChannelVoiceOn("channel" or channelIndex)
```

Arguments:

channel or channelIndex

channel — The name of the given channel. (string)

channelIndex — The index of the given channel. (number)

CheckBinderDist

Returns whether the player is in range of an NPC that can bind his hearthstone. This function is used to hide the Hearthstone confirmation dialog.

```
inRange = CheckBinderDist()
```

Returns:

inRange — 1 if the player is in range of a hearthstone binder, otherwise nil. (1nil)

CheckInbox

Requests the player's mailbox information from the server. When the client has received the inbox information the MAIL_INBOX_UPDATE event is fired. When this happens, the mail information is cached and can be accessed anywhere in the world. This function requires that the mailbox window be open.

CheckInteractDistance

Returns whether the player is close enough to interact with a unit.

```
canInteract = CheckInteractDistance("unit", distIndex)
```

Arguments:

unit — The unit to query. (unitid)

distIndex — The distance to check. (number)

- 1 — Inspect
- 2 — Trade
- 3 — Duel
- 4 — Follow

Returns:

canInteract — 1 if the player can perform the given interaction with the given unit, otherwise nil. (1nil)

CheckPetUntrainerDist

Returns whether the player is in range of a pet trainer. This function is used by the default user interface to hide the confirmation dialog that pops up when you attempt to untrain your pet.

```
inRange = CheckPetUntrainerDist()
```

Returns:

inRange — 1 if the player is in range of a Pet Trainer, otherwise nil. (1nil)

CheckSpiritHealerDist

Returns whether the player is in range of a spirit healer.

```
inRange = CheckSpiritHealerDist()
```

Returns:

inRange — 1 if the player is in range of a spirit healer, otherwise nil. (1nil)

CheckTalentMasterDist

Returns whether the player is in range of a talent trainer. This function will not return 1 for any NPC until after the player has requested a talent wipe and the CONFIRM_TALENT_WIPE event has fired. In addition, this function only returns a valid value for the NPC from which the player requested a talent wipe, even if other talent trainers are in range.

```
inRange = CheckTalentMasterDist()
```

Returns:

inRange — 1 if the player is in range of a talent trainer, otherwise nil. (1nil)

ClearCursor

Removes whatever is currently attached to the cursor.

ClearFocus

Clears the player's focus unit.

Note: This function is protected and cannot be called via addons.

ClearInspectPlayer

Clears the data for the currently inspected player. This function is called when the inspect frame is hidden, but does not actually clear the item textures from the slots.

ClearLFGAutojoin

Clears the automatic joining functionality in the LFG tool.

ClearLFMAutofill

Stops the LFM interface from auto-adding members to your group.

ClearLookingForGroup

Clears the player from any LFG/LFM listings or requests.

ClearLookingForMore

Clears all active LFM requests, removing the player from the LFG queue.

ClearOverrideBindings

Clears all override bindings for a given owner. An override binding is a temporary key or click binding that can be used to override the default bindings. The bound key will revert to its normal setting once the override has been removed.

```
ClearOverrideBindings(owner)
```

Argument:

owner — The owner of a set of override bindings. (table)

ClearPartyAssignment

Clears a specified assignment (main tank, main assist) for the specified unit, or all raid members if not specified.

```
ClearPartyAssignment("assignment" [,"raidMember"] [,exactMatch]))
```

Arguments:

assignment — The token for the party assigment that you want to clear. (string)

- MAINASSIST — One of the party or raid's main assists

- MAINTANK — One of the party or raid's main tanks

raidMember — The unitID or name of the party or raid member whose assignment you want to clear. If nil it will clear the assignment from every member of the raid. (string)

exactMatch — Set to true if you want an exact match for the player name, otherwise false. (boolean)

ClearSendMail

Clears the send mail window, removing all items, money, and text.

ClearTarget

Clears the player's current target.

Note: This function is protected and cannot be called via addons.

ClearTutorials

Clears any already displayed tutorials so that they are displayed again.

ClickAuctionSellItemButton

Causes the item currently being held by the cursor to be placed in the auction house "Create Auction" item slot. This function simulates the click as if the item had been dropped on the slot when creating a new auction. This function can be used in conjunction with the other auction house API functions to automate the placing of auctions. This function has no effect if the auction house is not open. If there is already an item in the slot, this function will place it on the cursor. If an item is in the slot and an item is already on the cursor, this function will exchange the two.

Example:

```
-- Places the first item in your backpack in the auction house item
slot
PickupContainerItem(0, 1)
ClickAuctionSellItemButton()
```

ClickSendMailItemButton

Causes the item currently being held by the cursor to be placed in the mailbox "Send Item" slot. This function can be used in conjunction with the mail API functions to automate the sending of items in mail. This function has no effect if the mailbox is not open. If an item is already in the slot, this function will pick it up with the cursor. If an item is in the slot and another item is on the cursor, this function will exchange them.

```
ClickSendMailItemButton([index [, autoReturn]])
```

Arguments:

index — The index of an item slot in the "Send Mail" panel (1–12). This value defaults to the first available slot. If an invalid index is specified or the item slots are full, an error message will be printed to the UIErrorsFrame. (number)

autoReturn — If true, items picked up from item slots will automatically be returned to the player's bags; otherwise, they will be placed on the cursor. (boolean)

Example:

```
-- Places the first item in your backpack in a send mail item slot
PickupContainerItem(0, 1)
ClickSendMailItemButton()
```

ClickSocketButton

Picks up or places a gem in the Item Socketing UI. If the Item Socketing UI is open and the cursor is holding a socketable gem, this function places the gem into the socket identified by index. If the cursor does not hold an item and the socket identified by index is not locked, this function picks up the gem in that socket.

```
ClickSocketButton(index)
```

Argument:

index — The index of a socket in the Item Socketing UI. (number)

Example:

```
-- Put the item in the top left slot of the backpack into
-- the first gem socket
PickupContainerItem(0,1)
ClickSocketButton(1)
```

ClickSpellByName

Casts a spell, either on your current target or the given target.

```
ClickSpellByName("name" [, "target"])
```

Arguments:

name — The name of the spell to cast. (string)

target (optional) — The target on which to cast the spell. (string)

Note: This function emulates a real click, so it will toggle auto-repeat actions such as Auto Shot. This function is protected and cannot be called via addons.

ClickStablePet

Simulates a click on the given stable pet index. When the cursor doesn't contain a pet, this function will select the given pet slot and display that pet's model and stats. If the cursor contains the currently active pet and the index is a stable slot, this function will place the pet into the stable (but not necessarily into the given slot). If the cursor contains a stabled pet and the index passed is the active pet slot, this function makes the stabled pet the currently active pet (placing the current pet in the stable).

```
selected = ClickStablePet(index)
```

Argument:

index — The index of the stable slot. (number)

- 0 — The active pet's slot
- 1 — The first stable slot
- 2 — The second stable slot

Returns:

selected — 1 if the function selected a stabled pet rather than moved a pet. (1nil)

ClickTargetTradeButton

Simulates clicking on a specific slot in the target trade window. If the cursor contains an item and the slot is empty, the item will be placed in the given slot. If the cursor does not contain an item and the slot contains an item, the item will be placed on the cursor. If the cursor contains an item and the slot contains an item, the items will be exchanged.

```
ClickTargetTradeButton(index)
```

Argument:

index — The index of a trade slot on the target's side of the trade window. (number)

ClickTradeButton

Clicks a specific trade window button. This function can be used to place items in the trade window from the cursor, or to pick up an item from the trade window. If the cursor is currently holding an item, you can run `ClickTradeButton(1)` to place the item in the trade window, slot 1. If there is an item in the trade window slot 1, you can run `ClickTradeButton(1)` to pickup that item and hold it on the cursor.

`ClickTradeButton(index)`

Argument:

`index` — The index of the trade button window to click. `(number)`

CloseArenaTeamRoster

Closes the arena team roster frame.

CloseAuctionHouse

Closes the auction house UI and stops all data retrieval.

CloseBankFrame

Closes the bank frame.

CloseBattlefield

Closes the battlefield selection UI.

CloseCraft

Closes the craft frame.

CloseGossip

Closes the gossip window.

CloseGuildBankFrame

Closes the guild bank frame.

CloseGuildRegistrar

Closes the guild registrar frame.

CloseGuildRoster

Closes the guild roster frame.

CloseItemText

Closes the item text display frame. This is the frame displayed when reading a book or a plaque.

CloseLoot

Closes the loot window.

CloseMail

Closes the mail window.

CloseMerchant

Closes the open merchant window.

ClosePetStables

Closes the pet stable window.

ClosePetition

Close the petition window.

ClosePetitionVendor

Closes the petition vendor window.

CloseQuest

Closes the open quest frame.

CloseSocketInfo

Closes the socket frame.

CloseTabardCreation

Closes the tabard creation window.

CloseTaxiMap

Closes the taxi (flight master) map.

CloseTrade

Closes the trade window.

CloseTradeSkill

Closes the tradeskill window.

CloseTrainer

Closes the trainer window.

CollapseChannelHeader

Collapses a channel header in the chat channel listing.

```
CollapseChannelHeader(index)
```

Argument:

index — The index of the header in the chat channel window. These indices include the actual channel listings, so the second channel may be at a higher index, depending on how many channels are listed in the first header. (number)

CollapseCraftSkillLine

Collapses a skill line in the craft frame.

```
CollapseCraftSkillLine(index)
```

Argument:

index — The skill line in the craft UI to collapse. Unlike the tradeskill UI, the craft UI will error if an invalid skill line is passed. (number)

CollapseFactionHeader

Collapses a given faction header. Collapses the faction header with the given index. A faction header is the header for several factions, as seen in the reputation tab. Examples include Outland, Shattrath City, and so on.

```
CollapseFactionHeader(index)
```

Argument:

index — The index of the faction header to collapse. (number)

CollapseQuestHeader

Collapses a header in the quest log.

```
CollapseQuestHeader(index)
```

Argument:

index — The index of the quest header. This index is separate from the quest indices, so regardless of how many quests you have showing in the quest log, index 2 will always be the second header. (number)

CollapseSkillHeader

Collapses a skill header in the skills window.

```
CollapseSkillHeader(index)
```

Argument:

index — The index of the skill header to collapse. If this value is a skill instead of a skill header, the enclosing header will be collapsed. (number)

CollapseTradeSkillSubClass

This function collapses the specified index in the TradeSkill UI. Note that this function will error out if the index does not correspond to a header, so check the return values of GetTradeSkillInfo() before calling this function. Also note that if this function succeeds in collapsing a header, any indices after the one that was collapsed will not correspond to the same items or headers as before this function was called.

```
CollapseTradeSkillSubClass(index)
```

Argument:

index — The index of the subclass you want to collapse. (number)

CollapseTrainerSkillLine

Collapses the given skill line in the class trainer frame. This function errs if the given skill line is not a header. This should be verified using GetTrainerServiceInfo().

```
CollapseTrainerSkillLine(index)
```

Argument:

index — The index of the skill line to collapse. (number)

ComplainChat

Files a complaint about a given chat message. This function can either be used by right-clicking the name of the player in the chat window and clicking "Report Spam" or by specifying a specific player name and message.

```
ComplainChat(lineID or "name" [, "text"])
```

Arguments:

lineID or name

lineID — The unique numeric identifier of a message in a chat frame. (number)

name — The name of a player to complain about. (string)

text (optional) — The specific text to complain about. (string)

ComplainInboxItem

Reports an inbox item as spam.

```
ComplainInboxItem(index)
```

Argument:

index — Inbox item to report as spam. (number)

CompleteQuest

Completes the current quest in a quest giver dialog. This function is used to move from the progress portion of a quest to the completion dialog.

ConfirmAcceptQuest

Confirms accepting a quest that someone in your group is starting. When someone in your group begins certain types of quests (such as escort quests) a popup dialog appears asking if you'd like to join the quest. This function is called to confirm the accepting of that quest.

ConfirmBindOnUse

Confirms the "Bind on Use" dialog when using a new item.

ConfirmBinder

Confirms a new hearthstone location. This function is used by the default user interface to confirm setting a new hearthstone location.

ConfirmLootRoll

Confirms a loot roll for a given item that will be bound to your character if you win the roll.

```
ConfirmLootRoll(lootIndex, rollType)
```

Arguments:

lootIndex — The index of the loot on which to roll. (number)

rollType — The roll action to confirm. (number)

- ▪ 0 — Pass on the given loot (not used for this function)
- ▪ 1 — Confirm a "need" roll
- ▪ 2 — Confirm a "greed" roll

ConfirmLootSlot

Confirms the looting of a bind-on-pickup item.

```
ConfirmLootSlot(slot)
```

Argument:

slot — The index of the loot slot. (number)

ConfirmPetUnlearn

Confirms unlearning a pet's skills.

ConfirmReadyCheck

Sends your ready status to the raid leader when asked for a ready check.

```
ConfirmReadyCheck(ready)
```

Argument:

ready — 1 if the player is ready, otherwise nil. (1nil)

ConfirmSummon

Accepts a summon spell. This function has no effect if called when there is no pending summons for the player. The default user interface uses this function to accept a summons from the popup dialog box.

ConfirmTalentWipe

Confirms the player's unlearning all talents.

ConsoleExec

Runs a console command. This function is used by the default UI to handle any /console slash commands.

```
ConsoleExec("console_command")
```

Argument:

console_command — The console command to run. (string)

ContainerIDToInventoryID

Returns the inventory ID that corresponds to a given container ID.

```
inventoryId = ContainerIDToInventoryID(containerID)
```

Argument:

containerId — The container ID. (number)

- 1 — The first bag slot
- 2 — The second bag slot
- 3 — The third bag slot
- 4 — The fourth bag slot
- 5 — The first bank bag slot
- 6 — The second bank bag slot
- 7 — The third bank bag slot
- 8 — The fourth bank bag slot
- 9 — The fifth bank bag slot
- 10 — The sixth bank bag slot
- 11 — The seventh bank bag slot

Returns:

inventoryId — The inventory ID corresponding to the given container. (number)

ConvertToRaid

Converts a party to a raid. Does nothing if the player is not in a party, or the player isn't party leader.

CraftIsEnchanting

Returns whether the current craft window is the enchanting window.

```
enchanting = CraftIsEnchanting()
```

Returns:

enchanting — 1 if the open craft window is the enchanting window, otherwise nil. (1nil)

CraftIsPetTraining

Returns whether the open craft window is the pet training window.

```
isPetTraining = CraftIsPetTraining()
```

Returns:

training — 1 if the open craft window is the pet training window, otherwise nil. (1nil)

CraftOnlyShowMakeable

Enables or disables the "Have Materials" filter in the craft UI.

```
CraftOnlyShowMakeable(enableFilter)
```

Argument:

enableFilter — Any `true` value (other than `0`) or `nil` will enable the filter, while `0` and `false` will disable the filter. (`boolean`)

CreateFont

Creates a new font object.

```
fontObject = CreateFont("name")
```

Argument:

name — The name of the font object to create. (`string`)

Returns:

fontObject — The newly created font object. (`table`)

CreateFrame

Creates a new frame object dynamically.

```
frame = CreateFrame(frameType [, name] [, parent] [, template])
```

Arguments:

frameType — The type of the frame to create. (`string`)

- `Button` — A clickable button widget.
- `CheckButton` — A toggleable button widget.
- `ColorSelect` — A color selection widget used by the color picker frame.
- `Cooldown` — A pie-style cooldown animation widget.
- `DressUpModel` — A 3-D player mesh with functions to dress up in different items.
- `EditBox` — An editbox widget.
- `Frame` — A simple frame widget.
- `GameTooltip` — A tooltip widget.
- `MessageFrame` — A message frame that allows text-fading; used by the `UIErrorsFrame`.
- `Minimap` — A minimap widget.
- `Model` — A widget to display a real 3-D mesh as part of the UI.
- `PlayerModel` — A widget to display a 3-D player mesh.
- `ScrollFrame` — A scrolling frame widget.
- `ScrollingMessageFrame` — A widget to show scrolling messages.
- `SimpleHTML` — A widget to show simple HTML content.
- `Slider` — A simple slider widget.
- `StatusBar` — A statusbar widget.
- `TabardModel` — A 3-D mesh used by the tabard frame for designing a new tabard.

name (optional) — The name of the new frame. If given, will also create an entry in the global namespace for the created frame under the specified name. (string)

parent (optional) — A reference to the parent of the new frame. (table)

template (optional) — The name of the template to be used for creating the new frame, or a comma-separated list of templates to be used (string)

Returns:

frame — A reference to the newly created frame. (table)

CreateMacro

Creates a new macro.

```
index = CreateMacro("name", iconIndex, "body", local, perCharacter)
```

Arguments:

name — The name of the new macro. Names do not need to be unique, but calls to other API functions can be confusing if two macros with the same name exist. (string)

iconIndex — The index of the chosen macro icon. (number)

body — The body of the macro. (string)

local — Determines if the macro should be stored locally or on the server. This argument is currently unused. (1nil)

perCharacter — 1 if the macro should be stored as a character-specific macro, otherwise nil. (1nil)

Returns:

index — The index of the newly created macro. (number)

Example:

```
-- Create a character specific macro
local index = CreateMacro("DanceMonkey", 13, "/emote dances ↵
like a monkey!!!", nil, 1)

-- Create a general macro
local index = CreateMacro("Heal", 73, "/cast Flash Heal\n/say ↵
Let the light of Elune cleanse you!", nil, nil)
```

CursorCanGoInSlot

Returns whether the item on the cursor can be placed in the given slot.

```
canBePlaced = CursorCanGoInSlot(slot)
```

Argument:

slot — The slot number on the PaperDollFrame. (number)

Returns:

canBePlaced — 1 if the item on the cursor can be placed in the given inventory slot, otherwise nil. (1nil)

CursorHasItem

Indicates if the cursor is currently holding an item.

```
hasItem = CursorHasItem()
```

Returns:

hasItem — 1 if the cursor is currently holding an item, otherwise nil. (1nil)

CursorHasMacro

Returns whether the cursor currently holds a macro.

```
hasMacro = CursorHasMacro
```

Returns:

hasMacro — 1 if the cursor currently holds a macro, otherwise nil. (1nil)

CursorHasMoney

Returns whether the cursor is currently holding money.

```
hasMoney = CursorHasMoney()
```

Returns:

hasMoney — 1 if the cursor is currently holding money, otherwise nil. (1nil)

CursorHasSpell

Returns whether the cursor currently holds a spell. This function is used by the default user interface to determine if a spell is being dragged to an action button.

```
hasSpell = CursorHasSpell()
```

Returns:

hasSpell — Indicates if there is currently a spell attached to the cursor. (1nil)

debugprofilestart

Starts and resets the high-resolution debug timer. Subsequent calls to debugprofilestop() will return the running value of the timer.

debugprofilestop

Returns the value of the running debug profile timer.

```
time = debugprofilestop()
```

Returns:

time — The current value of the debug profile timer in milliseconds (with sub-millisecond precision). (number)

debugstack

Returns information about the current function call stack.

```
debugstring = debugstack([start [, countTop [, countBot]]])
```

Arguments:

start (optional) — The stack level at which to start the trace. 0 is the debugstack() function itself, while 1 is the function that called debugstack(). (number)

countTop (optional) — The maximum number of functions to output at the top of the stack trace. (number)

countBot (optional) — The maximum number of functions to output at the bottom of the stack trace. (number)

Returns:

debugstring — The stack traceback as a multiline string. (string)

DeclineArenaTeam

Declines an arena team invitation.

DeclineGroup

Declines a group invitation.

DeclineGuild

Declines a guild invitation.

DeclineQuest

Declines a quest. This function is used internally by the default user interface when the player clicks the decline button on the popup dialog.

DeclineResurrect

Declines a resurrection spell.

DelIgnore

Removes a player from your ignore list.

```
DelIgnore("name")
```

Argument:

name — The name of the player you wish to remove from your ignore list. (string)

DelMute

Removes a voice mute for a given player.

```
DelMute("unit" or "fullname")
```

Arguments:

unit or fullname

unit — The unit ID to be unmuted. (unitId)

fullname — The full name of a player to be muted. (string)

Example:

```
-- Unmute your current target
DelMute("target")

-- Unmute player "Cladhaire"
DelMute("Cladhaire")
```

DeleteCursorItem

Confirms deletion of the item currently held on the cursor. This function is used internally to verify that an item should be deleted after the player types a confirmation word into the popup dialog. As a result, it should not be altered or called by addons.

DeleteGMTicket

Abandons the currently pending GM ticket.

DeleteInboxItem

Deletes the given mail from your inbox.

```
DeleteInboxItem(index)
```

Argument:

index — Inbox item to delete. (number)

DeleteMacro

Deletes a macro by ID.

```
DeleteMacro(id)
```

Argument:

id — The macro ID. The ID of the currently selected macro can be obtained using MacroFrame.selectedMacro. (number)

DemoteAssistant

Demotes the given player from raid assistant status.

```
DemoteAssistant("name")
```

Argument:

name — The name of the player. (string)

DepositGuildBankMoney

Deposits money into the guild bank.

```
DepositGuildBankMoney(money)
```

Argument:

money — The amount of copper to deposit. (number)

DescendStop

Called when the player releases the Sit/Descend binding (while swimming or flying).

Note: This function is protected and cannot be called via addons.

DisableAddOn

Disables an addon by name or index.

```
DisableAddOn("name" or index)
```

Arguments:

name — The name of the addon to disable. (string)

index — The index of the addon in the addon listing. (number)

DisableAllAddOns

Flags all addons as disabled for the current character. This change will not take effect until the user interface is reloaded.

DisableSpellAutocast

Disables autocast for a given pet spell.

```
DisableSpellAutocast("spell")
```

Argument:

spell — The name of a pet spell. (string)

Dismount

Dismounts the player. This will not work on Taxi mounts.

DisplayChannelOwner

Fires a CHANNEL_OWNER event for the given channel.

```
DisplayChannelOwner("channel" or channelIndex)
```

Arguments:

channel or channelIndex

channel — The name of the channel to query. (string)

channelIndex — The index of the channel to query. (number)

Note: This function does not return anything. If no owner exists for the given channel, no event is fired.

DisplayChannelVoiceOff

Disables voice chat in a given channel.

```
DisplayChannelVoiceOff(displayIndex)
```

Argument:

displayIndex — The index of a channel in the chat display window. These indices include the headers that are displayed in this window. (number)

Note: This function requires the player be the moderator of the given channel.

DisplayChannelVoiceOn

Enables voice chat in a given channel.

```
DisplayChannelVoiceOn(displayIndex)
```

Argument:

displayIndex — The index of a channel in the chat display window. These indices include the headers that are displayed in this window. (number)

Note: This function requires the player be the moderator of the given channel.

DoCraft

Performs the selected craft skill.

```
DoCraft(index)
```

Argument:

index — The index of the craft skill in the craft UI. (number)

DoEmote

Executes a preset emote, with optional target.

```
DoEmote("emote"[, "target"])
```

Arguments:

emote — The emote to perform (does not include the /). (string)

■ ARG — A list of emotes can be found in ChatFrame.lua. These tokens are the EMOTE#_TOKEN constants.

target (optional) — Name of a player or NPC at which to direct the emote. (string)

Example:

```
DoEmote("wave")
-- Player waves

DoEmote("doom", "Thrall")
-- Player threatens Thrall with the wrath of doom
```

DoReadyCheck

Perform a ready check. This function displays a message to each member of the raid, asking if they are ready. The results are then reported to the requester. This function can only be run by a party or raid leader.

DoTradeSkill

Casts a tradeskill, optionally multiple times.

```
DoTradeSkill(index [, repeat])
```

Arguments:

index — The index of the skill. (number)

repeat (optional) — The number of times to repeat the craft. (number)

DropCursorMoney

Drops the money currently held to the cursor, returning it to where it was taken from.

DropItemOnUnit

Drops the currently held item on a specific unit. If the cursor holds an item, this function attempts to give it to the specified unit, the effect of which varies depending on the unit. If the unit is a friendly player, this will add the item to the trade window (opening it if necessary). If the unit is pet (or the name of the player's pet) and the player is of the Hunter class, this will attempt to feed the item to the pet (and likely generate a blocked action error, as casting Feed Pet or any other spell from nonsecure Lua isn't allowed). For all other units, nothing happens and the item remains on the cursor.

```
DropItemOnUnit("unit")
```

Arguments:

unit

unit — The unit ID of the player on which to drop the item. (unitId)

EditMacro

Edit Macro command/button. Cannot be used in combat.

```
macroID = EditMacro(index, "name", icon, "body", local, perCharacter)
```

Arguments:

index — Macro index number. (number)

name — Name of the macro to be shown in the UI. Current limit is 16 characters. (string)

icon — An numeric icon index from 1 to GetNumMacroIcons(). (number)

body — The macro command to be executed. Current limit used is 255 characters. (string)

local — Indicates if the macro is stored locally or on the server. This return value is currently unused. (number)

perCharacter — 0 for a per-account macro, 1 for a per-character one. (number)

Returns:

macroID — The index of the macro. (number)

EnableAddOn

Enables an addon for the current character. This function can take either an addon name, or an index in the sorted addon list displayed on the addon selection screen.

```
EnableAddOn(index or "name")
```

Arguments:

index or name

index — The index of the addon to be enabled. (number)

name — The name of the addon to be enabled. (string)

EnableAllAddOns

Enables all addons for the current character (takes effect at the next UI load).

EnableSpellAutocast

Enables autocast for a given pet spell.

```
EnableSpellAutocast("spell")
```

Argument:

spell — The name of a pet spell. (string)

EnumerateFrames

Returns the next frame following the frame passed, or nil if no more frames exist.

```
nextFrame = EnumerateFrames([currentFrame])
```

Argument:

currentFrame (optional) — The current frame to get the next frame, or nil to get the first frame. (table)

Returns:

nextFrame — The frame following current frame; nil if no more frames exist, or the first frame if nil was passed. (table)

Example:

```
-- Print all visible frames under the mouse cursor
local frame = EnumerateFrames(); -- Get the first frame
while frame do
  if ( frame:IsVisible() and MouseIsOver(frame) ) then
    ChatFrame1:AddMessage(frame:GetName() or string.format↵
("<Unnamed Frame: %s>", tostring(frame)));
  end
  frame = EnumerateFrames(frame); -- Get the next frame
end
```

EnumerateServerChannels

Returns the available server channel names.

```
... = EnumerateServerChannels()
```

Returns:

... — A list of the available server channel names. For example: General, Trade, WorldDefense, GuildRecruitment, LookingForGroup. (string)

EquipCursorItem

Attempts to equip the item held on the cursor into a specific inventory slot.

```
EquipCursorItem(slot)
```

Argument:

slot — An inventory slot ID. (number)

EquipItemByName

Equips an item by name, item link, or item ID.

```
EquipItemByName("itemName" or "itemLink" or itemId)
```

Arguments:

itemName or itemLink or itemId

itemName — The name of an item to be equipped (can be a partial match). (string)

itemLink — The item link of an item to be equipped. (string)

itemId — The item ID of an item to be equipped. (number)

EquipPendingItem

Confirms the equipping of a pending bind-on-equip item. This function is used internally by the default UI to confirm the equipping of a bind-on-equip item. Using this function will equip the item, and it will become soulbound.

```
EquipPendingItem(slotId)
```

Argument:

slotId — The inventory slot ID. (number)

ExpandChannelHeader

Expands a channel header in the chat channel listing.

```
ExpandChannelHeader(id)
```

Argument:

id — The index of the header in the chat channel window. These indices include the actually channel listings, so the second channel may be at a higher index, depending on how many channels are listed in the first header. (number)

ExpandCraftSkillLine

Expands a craft skill line header. There are currently no headers in either Enchanting or Beast Training.

```
ExpandCraftSkillLine(index)
```

Argument:

index — The index of the skill line. (number)

ExpandFactionHeader

Expands a given faction header. Expands the faction header with the given index. A faction header is the header for several factions, as seen in the reputation tab. Examples include Alliance, Steamwheedle Cartel, Shattrath City, and so on.

```
ExpandFactionHeader(index)
```

Argument:

index — The index of the faction header to collapse. (number)

ExpandQuestHeader

Expands a quest header in the quest log.

```
ExpandQuestHeader(index)
```

Argument:

index — The index of the quest log entry to expand. If the index supplied is invalid or not a quest header, this function will instead expand all quest headers. This index is separate from the quest indices so that, regardless of how many quests you have showing in the quest log, index 2 will always be the second header. (number)

ExpandSkillHeader

Expands a skill header in the skills window.

```
ExpandSkillHeader(index)
```

Argument:

index — The index of the skill header to expand. (number)

ExpandTradeSkillSubClass

Expands a tradeskill subclass in the tradeskill window.

```
ExpandTradeSkillSubClass(index)
```

Argument:

index — The index of the tradeskill subclass in the tradeskill window. If the index specified is a tradeskill item rather than a subclass heading, this function will produce an error. (number)

ExpandTrainerSkillLine

Expands a skill line in the trainer window. This function will produce an error if called on a skill line that isn't a header to be expanded.

```
ExpandTrainerSkillLine(index)
```

Argument:

index — The index of the line to expand. (number)

FactionToggleAtWar

Toggles the "at war" status towards a specific faction. This can only be done with factions for which the eighth return of `GetFactionInfo` (labeled `canToggleAtWar` in this book) is true. The `UPDATE_FACTION` event will be fired after the change.

```
FactionToggleAtWar(index)
```

Argument:

`index` — The row index of the faction with which to toggle "at war" status. (`number`)

FlagTutorial

Flags a tutorial step as already viewed, so it doesn't appear again.

```
FlagTutorial("tutorial")
```

Argument:

`tutorial` — The identifier for the tutorial step. (`string`)

FlipCameraYaw

Rotates the camera around the player.

```
FlipCameraYaw(degrees)
```

Argument:

`degrees` — The number of degrees to rotate; positive for counterclockwise, negative for clockwise. (`number`)

Example:

```
-- Dramatically Rotate the camera 360 degrees around the player
if not YawFrame then CreateFrame("Frame", "YawFrame") end
local degree = 0
local function OnUpdate(self, elapsed)
  degree = degree + 1
  FlipCameraYaw(1)
  if degree >= 360 then
    self:Hide()
  end
end
YawFrame:SetScript("OnUpdate", OnUpdate)
YawFrame:Show()
```

FocusUnit

Sets the given unit as your focus target. Passing `nil` will clear your focus.

```
FocusUnit("unit" or "name")
```

Arguments:

`unit` or `name`

`unit` — The unit ID to set as focus. (`unitid`)

`name` — The name of the player to set as focus. (`string`)

Note: This function is protected and cannot be called via addons.

FollowUnit

Follows a specified player.

```
FollowUnit("unit" or "name" [, strict])
```

Arguments:

unit or name

unit — The unit ID of the player to follow. (unitid)

name — The name of a player to follow. (string)

strict — Indicates that the name match should be exact. (1nil)

- ■ 1 — Match the supplied name exactly

- ■ nil — Partial matches for name are allowed

ForceQuit

Immediately exits World of Warcraft. This is the same as the Exit Now button that appears when logging out.

FrameXML_Debug

Enables or disables verbose XML logging. This will produce an extremely large log in Logs/FrameXML.log that gives you information about every frame and template created during the load process.

```
FrameXML_Debug(enable)
```

Argument:

enable — 1 if verbose XML logging should be enabled, otherwise nil. (1nil)

GetAbandonQuestItems

Returns any items that would be destroyed by confirming the abandoning of the current quest.

```
items = GetAbandonQuestItems()
```

Returns:

items — A string of items that would be destroyed by abandoning the given quest. (string)

GetAbandonQuestName

Returns the name of the quest being abandoned. This function can be called between clicking the Abandon Quest button, and clicking the confirmation button to retrieve the name of the quest being abandoned.

```
name = GetAbandonQuestName()
```

Returns:

name — The name of the quest being abandoned. (string)

GetAccountExpansionLevel

Returns the expansion level of the player's account.

```
expansionLevel = GetAccountExpansionLevel()
```

Returns:

expansionLevel — The expansion level of the player's account. (number)

- ▪ 0 — World of Warcraft
- ▪ 1 — World of Warcraft: The Burning Crusade

GetActionBarPage

Returns the current action bar page.

```
page = GetActionBarPage()
```

Returns:

page — The current action bar page. (number)

GetActionBarToggles

Returns the current visibility settings for the four secondary action bars.

```
showBar1, showBar2, showBar3, showBar4 = GetActionBarToggles()
```

Returns:

showBar1 — 1 if the interface option is set to show the Bottom Left ActionBar, otherwise nil. (1nil)

showBar2 — 1 if the interface option is set to show the Bottom Right ActionBar, otherwise nil. (1nil)

showBar3 — 1 if the interface option is set to show the Right ActionBar, otherwise nil. (1nil)

showBar4 — 1 if the interface option is set to show the Right ActionBar 2, otherwise nil. (1nil)

GetActionCooldown

Returns cooldown information about a given action slot.

```
start, duration, enable = GetActionCooldown(slot)
```

Argument:

slot — The action slot to query for cooldown information. (number)

Returns:

start — The value of GetTime() at the moment the cooldown began, or 0. (number)

duration — The length of the cooldown, or 0. (number)

enable — 1 if the cooldown is enabled, otherwise 0. (number)

Example:

```
-- Show all actions currently on cooldown
for i=1,120 do
  local start,duration,enable = GetActionCooldown(i)
  if start > 0 and enable == 1 then
    local actiontype,id,subtype = GetActionInfo(i)
    local name

    if actiontype == "spell" then
      name = GetSpellName(id, "spell")
    elseif actiontype == "item" then
      name = GetItemInfo(id)
    end

    local timeLeft = math.floor((start + duration)--GetTime())
    local output = string.format("Cooldown on %s %s (%s seconds ↵
left)", actiontype, name, timeLeft)
    ChatFrame1:AddMessage(output)

  end
end
```

GetActionCount

Returns the number of uses remaining for the given action slot. This function returns the remaining available uses for spells that require reagents, items that stack, or items with charges. This is used to display the count on action buttons. It will return 0 for any action that does not have a count.

```
count = GetActionCount(slot)
```

Argument:

slot — The action slot to check (1–120). (number)

Returns:

count — The number of uses left. (number)

GetActionInfo

Returns information about a given action bar slot.

```
type, id, subtype = GetActionInfo(slot)
```

Argument:

slot — An action slot. (number)

Returns:

type — The type of action bound to the slot. (string)

- ▪ item

- ▪ spell

- ▪ macro

id — The identifier for the spell/macro/item. (number)

subType — The subtype of the action, otherwise nil. (string)

Example:

```
-- Prints all unique action "types" to chat
-- Get all possible types and subtypes we can find
local types = {}
for i=1,120 do
  local type,id,subtype = GetActionInfo(i)
  if type and not types[type] then
    types[type] = subtype or true
  end
end

for k,v in pairs(types) do
  ChatFrame1:AddMessage("Type: " .. tostring(k) .. " (" ..
tostring(v) .. ")")
end
```

GetActionText

Returns the label for a given action slot. Macros that are placed on the action bars have their name as the label. Most actions that are placed on the action bars do not have labels.

```
text = GetActionText(slot)
```

Argument:

slot — The action slot to query. (number)

Returns:

text — The label for the action slot, or nil. (string)

GetActionTexture

Returns the texture for the given action slot. This texture may be an item, spell, or macro icon.

```
texture = GetActionTexture(slot)
```

Argument:

slot — Action ID to query. (number)

Returns:

texture — Texture of the slot. (string)

GetActiveTitle

Returns the name of an active quest in the `QuestFrame`.

```
title = GetActiveTitle(index)
```

Argument:

`index` — The index of an active quest in the `QuestFrame`. (number)

Returns:

`title` — Title of the active quest. (string)

GetActiveVoiceChannel

Returns the currently active voice channel.

```
id = GetActiveVoiceChannel()
```

Returns:

`id` — The numeric identifier of the currently active voice channel. (number)

GetAddOnCPUUsage

Returns the amount of CPU time used by the given addon, in milliseconds.

```
usage = GetAddOnCPUUsage(index or "name")
```

Arguments:

`index` or `name`

`index` — The index of the addon; must be in the range of 1 to `GetNumAddOns()`. (number)

`name` — The name of the addon as it appears in its folder name. (string)

Returns:

`usage` — The amount of CPU time the given addon has used, in milliseconds. (number)

Note: Returns 0 unless CPU profiling is enabled by setting the CVar `scriptProfile` to 1. Furthermore, addon-specific CPU usage statistics are only updated when `UpdateAddOnCPUUsage()` is called.

GetAddOnDependencies

Gets a list of the dependencies of a given addon. Returns `nil` if no dependencies are listed.

```
... = GetAddOnDependencies(index or "name")
```

Arguments:

`index` or `name`

`index` — The index of the addon; must be in the range of 1 to `GetNumAddOns()`. (number)

`name` — The name of the addon as it appears in its folder name. (string)

Returns:

`...` — A list of strings, indicating the dependencies for the given addon. (list)

GetAddOnInfo

Returns information about an addon in the client's addon list.

```
name, title, notes, enabled, loadable, reason, security = ↵
GetAddOnInfo(index or "name")
```

Arguments:

index or name

index — The index of the addon, must be in the range of 1 to GetNumAddOns().
(number)

name — The name of the addon as it appears in its folder name. (string)

Returns:

name — The name of the addon. (string)

title — The title of the addon. (string)

notes — The value of the Notes field from the table of contents. (string)

enabled — 1 if the addon is enabled for the current character, otherwise
nil. (1nil)

loadable — If the addon is capable of being loaded. (1nil)

reason — If the addon isn't loadable, gives the reason. (string)

security — SECURE if the addon is secure, otherwise INSECURE. A secure addon
is one that is released by Blizzard and is digitally signed. (string)

GetAddOnMemoryUsage

Returns the amount of memory used by a given addon.

```
mem = GetAddOnMemoryUsage(index or "name")
```

Arguments:

index or name

index — The index of the addon; must be in the range of 1 to
GetNumAddOns(). (number)

name — The name of the addon as it appears in its folder name. (string)

Returns:

mem — The memory usage of the addon, in kilobytes. (number)

GetAddOnMetadata

Returns the value of certain fields in an addon's TOC file.

```
data = GetAddOnMetadata(index or "name", "variable")
```

Arguments:

index or name

index — The index of the addon; must be in the range of 1 to GetNumAddOns(). (number)

name — The name of the addon as it appears in its folder name. (string)

variable — The variable name that you want to query; only a limited number of values are accepted. (string)

- Author — The author of the addon as outlined in the TOC file.

- Notes — Any notes the author of the addon placed into the TOC file.

- Title — The title of the addon; this defaults to the name of the addon as it appears in its folder name.

- Version — The version string that appears in the TOC file.

- X-*<something>* — These are the only custom tags that can be queried; *<something>* can be anything you want.

Returns:

data — The data available in the TOC for the variable queried, or nil if the variable is not queryable or not defined. (string)

GetAreaSpiritHealerTime

Returns the amount of time until a nearby battleground spirit healer resurrects all players in its area.

```
timeleft = GetAreaSpiritHealerTime()
```

Returns:

timeleft — Seconds left before the area spirit heal is cast. (number)

GetArenaCurrency

Returns the number of available arena currency points.

```
points = GetArenaCurrency()
```

Returns:

points — The number of available arena currency points. (number)

GetArenaTeam

Returns information about one of the player's arena teams. This function is used by the default user interface to render the PvP information tab, including the statistics about a given team, and the border/emblem and colors used to represent the team.

```
teamName, teamSize, teamRating, teamPlayed, teamWins,
seasonTeamPlayed, seasonTeamWins, playerPlayed, seasonPlayerPlayed,
teamRank, playerRating, bg_red, bg_green, bg_blue, emblem,
emblem_red, emblem_green, emblem_blue, border, border_red,
border_green, border_blue = GetArenaTeam(index)
```

Argument:

index — The index of the arena team. These are indexed from smallest to largest, with the first team (normally 2v2) being 1. (number)

Returns:

teamName — The name of the arena team. (string)

teamSize — The size of the team (2 for 2v2, 3 for 2v2, and so on). (number)

teamRating — The team's rating. (number)

teamPlayed — The number of games played in the current arena period. (number)

teamWins — The number of games won in the current arena period. (number)

seasonTeamPlayer — The number of games played in the current arena season. (number)

seasonTeamWins — The number of games won in the current arena season. (number)

playerPlayed — The number of games the player has played in the current arena period. (number)

seasonPlayerPlayed — The number of games the player has played in the current arena season. (number)

teamRank — The current team ranking. (number)

playerRating — The player's personal rating. (number)

bg_red — The red component color value for the background (0.0-1.0). (number)

bg_green — The green component color value for the background (0.0-1.0). (number)

bg_blue — The blue component color value for the background (0.0-1.0). (number)

emblem — The index of the team's emblem graphic. (number)

emblem_red — The red component color value for the emblem (0.0-1.0). (number)

emblem_green — The green component color value for the emblem (0.0-1.0). (number)

emblem_blue — The blue component color value for the emblem (0.0-1.0). (number)

border — The index of the team's border graphic. (number)

border_red — The red component color value for the border (0.0-1.0). (number)

border_green — The green component color value for the border (0.0-1.0). (number)

border_blue — The blue component color value for the border (0.0-1.0). (number)

GetArenaTeamRosterInfo

Returns information about an arena team member.

```
name, rank, level, class, online, played, win, seasonPlayed,
seasonWin, rating = GetArenaTeamRosterInfo(team, index)
```

Arguments:

team — The index of the team to query. Teams are indexed in increasing size from 1 to 3, depending on which teams the player is a member of. (number)

index — The team roster index to query. (number)

Returns:

name — The name of the player. (string)

rank — The rank of the player. (number)

- ■ 0 — Team captain
- ■ 1 — Member

level — The level of the player. (number)

class — The localized name of the player's class. (string)

online — 1 if the player is online, otherwise nil. (1nil)

played — The number of games the player has played this week. (number)

win — The number of games the player has won this week. (number)

seasonPlayed — The number of games the player has played this season. (number)

seasonWin — The number of games the player has won this season. (number)

rating — The player's personal rating with this team. (number)

GetArenaTeamRosterSelection

Returns the currently selected arena team member for a given team.

```
index = GetArenaTeamRosterSelection(team)
```

Argument:

team — The index of an arena team. (number)

Returns:

index — The currently selected arena team member. (number)

GetArenaTeamRosterShowOffline

Returns whether the Show Offline Members filter for arena teams is enabled.

```
showOffline = GetArenaTeamRosterShowOffline()
```

Returns:

showOffline — 1 if the Show Offline filter for arena teams is enabled, otherwise nil. (1nil)

GetAttackPowerForStat

Calculates the amount of attack power that your current character would gain from having the given value for the specified stat.

```
attackPower = GetAttackPowerForStat(statIndex,effectiveStat)
```

Arguments:

`statIndex` — The index of the stat to query. (number)

- 1 — Strength
- 2 — Agility
- 3 — Stamina
- 4 — Intellect
- 5 — Spirit

`effectiveStat` — The value of the stat to use in the attack power calculation. (number)

Returns:

`attackPower` — The amount of attack power your character would gain from having the given amount of the selected stat. (number)

GetAuctionHouseDepositRate

Returns the current auction house deposit rate.

```
rate = GetAuctionHouseDepositRate()
```

Returns:

`rate` — The current auction house deposit rate. (number)

GetAuctionInvTypes

Returns a list of the inventory subtypes for a given auction house item subclass. You do not need to be at an auction house to use this function.

```
token, display, ... = GetAuctionInvTypes(classIndex, subClassIndex)
```

Arguments:

`classIndex` — The class index to query. The only section of the auction house that currently has a third level of drill-down when selecting is Armor, which is `classIndex` 2. (number)

- 2 — Armor

`subClassIndex` — The subclass to query. This corresponds to the indices in the auction house listing, as subclasses for `Armor`. The special subclasses `Shields`, `Librams`, `Idols`, and `Totems` do not have any subinventory types. (number)

- 1 — Miscellaneous
- 2 — Cloth
- 3 — Leather
- 4 — Mail
- 5 — Plate

Returns:

token — An inventory type token such as INVTYPE_FINGER. (string)

display — 1 if the inventory type should be displayed in the auction house listing for this subcategory. This is used in the auction house UI to hide inventory types that shouldn't appear under the given subclass (for example, INVTYPE_TRINKET only shows up under Miscellaneous). (1nil)

... — A list token and display pairs for all possible values. (list)

GetAuctionItemClasses

Returns a list of top-level item classes used to categorize auction items (for example, Weapons, Armor, Container, Consumable, Trade Goods, and so on). You do not need to be at an auction house to use this function.

... = GetAuctionItemClasses()

Returns:

... — List of possible auction item classes. (string)

GetAuctionItemInfo

Returns information about an item up for auction.

name, texture, count, quality, canUse, level, minBid, minIncrement, buyoutPrice, bidAmount, highBidder, owner = GetAuctionItemInfo("type", index)

Arguments:

type — The auction listing type to query. (string)

- bidder — The auctions on which the player has bid.
- list — The default auction house browse listing.
- owner — The auctions the player has placed.

index — The index of the item in the listing. (number)

Returns:

name — The name of the item. (string)

texture — The path to the item's icon texture. (string)

count — The number of items in the stack. (number)

quality — The quality level of the item. (number)

- 0 — Poor
- 1 — Common
- 2 — Uncommon
- 3 — Rare
- 4 — Epic
- 5 — Legendary
- 6 — Artifact

canUse — 1 if the item can be used by the player, otherwise `nil`. (1nil)

`level` — The level of the item. (number)

`minBid` — The minimum bid required, in copper. (number)

`minIncrement` — The minimum required incremental bid, in copper. (number)

`buyoutPrice` — The buyout price, in copper. (number)

`bidAmount` — The current highest bid, or 0 if no one has bid. (number)

`highestBidder` — 1 if the player is currently the highest bidder, otherwise `nil`. (1nil)

`owner` — The owner of the auction. (string)

GetAuctionItemLink

Returns an item link for a given auction item.

```
link = GetAuctionItemLink("type", index)
```

Arguments:

`type` — The type of auction house listing to query. (string)

▪ `bidder` — Auctions on which the player has bid.

▪ `list` — The available auctions.

▪ `owner` — Auctions the player has placed.

`index` — The index of the item in the listing. (number)

Returns:

`link` — An item link for the given item. (string)

GetAuctionItemSubClasses

Returns a list of subclasses that are valid for a specific auction item class (for example, One-Handed Axes, Two-Handed Axes, Bows, Guns, and others under Weapons; Miscellaneous, Cloth, Leather, and others under Armor; Arrow and Bullet under Projectile; and so on). You do not need to be at an auction house to use this function.

```
... = GetAuctionItemSubClasses(index)
```

Argument:

`index` — The index of the auction item class you want to query for subclasses. The number is from 1 to `#{GetAuctionItemClasses()}`. (number)

Returns:

`...` — A list of the subclasses attached to the queried auction class, or `nil` for classes that have no subclasses. (string)

GetAuctionItemTimeLeft

Returns the time left for a given auction listing.

```
duration = GetAuctionItemTimeLeft("type", index)
```

Arguments:

`type` — The type of auction listing (`string`)

- ▪ `bidder` — Auctions on which the player has bid.
- ▪ `list` — Auctions available for purchase.
- ▪ `owner` — Auctions the player has placed.

`index` — The index of the auction. (`number`)

Returns:

`duration` — The amount of time left on the current auction. (`number`)

- ▪ 1 — Short time (less than 30 minutes)
- ▪ 2 — Medium time (30 minutes to 2 hours)
- ▪ 3 — Long time (2 hours to 12 hours)
- ▪ 4 — Very long time (more than 12 hours)

GetAuctionSellItemInfo

Returns information about the item being placed on auction. This function can be called when an item has been placed in the auction house sell slot to get information about the item.

```
name, texture, count, quality, canUse, price =
GetAuctionSellItemInfo()
```

Returns:

`name` — The name of the item. (`string`)

`texture` — The path to the icon texture for the item. (`string`)

`count` — The number of items in the stack. (`number`)

`quality` — The quality level of the item. (`number`)

- ▪ 0 — Poor
- ▪ 1 — Common
- ▪ 2 — Uncommon
- ▪ 3 — Rare
- ▪ 4 — Epic
- ▪ 5 — Legendary
- ▪ 6 — Artifact

`canUse` — 1 if the item can be used by the player, otherwise `nil`. (`1nil`)

`price` — How much the item would sell for to a vendor. (`number`)

GetAuctionSort

Returns the information about a given auction house sort entry.

```
existingSortColumn, existingSortReverse = GetAuctionSort("type", ↵
"index")
```

Arguments:

`type` — The type of auction listing. (string)

- `bidder` — Auctions on which the player has bid.

- `list` — Auctions available for bidding/purchase.

- `owner` — Auctions the player has placed.

`index` — The index of an auction sort entry. (number)

Returns:

`existingSortColumn` — The column by which to sort. (string)

`existingSortReverse` — 1 if the sort on the existing column is reversed, otherwise `nil`. (1nil)

GetAutoLootDefault

Returns whether auto-loot is enabled.

```
value = GetAutoLootDefault()
```

Returns:

`value` — 1 if the client is set to auto-loot, otherwise `nil`. (1nil)

GetAvailableTitle

Queries the title of the selected available quest at a quest NPC.

```
title = GetAvailableTitle(index)
```

Argument:

`index` — The index of the quest to query. (number)

Returns:

`title` — The title of the quest. (string)

GetBagName

Returns the name of a bag.

```
name = GetBagName(index)
```

Argument:

`index` — A bag index. (number)

Returns:

`name` — The name of the bag, or `nil`. (string)

Example:

```
-- Print the name of our bags to chat
for i=0,4 do
  local name = GetBagName(i)
  if name then
    ChatFrame1:AddMessage("Bag " .. i .. ": " .. name)
  end
end
```

GetBankSlotCost

Returns the cost of a bank slot.

```
cost = GetBankSlotCost(index)
```

Argument:

`index` — The index of the bank slot. (number)

Returns:

`cost` — The cost of the bank slot, in copper. (number)

GetBaseMip

Returns the level of texture resolution rendered by the client.

```
baseMip = GetBaseMip()
```

Returns:

`baseMip` — The level of texture resolution rendered by the client. (number)

- ▪ `0` — Low texture resolution
- ▪ `1` — High texture resolution

GetBattlefieldEstimatedWaitTime

Returns the estimated wait time on a battleground or arena queue.

```
waitTime = GetBattlefieldEstimatedWaitTime(index)
```

Argument:

`index` — The index of the battleground or arena as listed in the tooltip for the minimap battle status icon. (number)

Returns:

`waitTime` — The estimated wait time in millseconds. (number)

GetBattlefieldFlagPosition

Returns positioning information on the given flag. The `flagToken` can be used as a texture by prepending it with `Interface\WorldStateFrame\`.

```
flagX, flagY, flagToken = GetBattlefieldFlagPosition(index)
```

Argument:

`index` — Index of the flag between `1` and `GetNumBattlefieldFlagPositions()`. (number)

Returns:

flagX — X location of the flag between 0 and 1. (number)

flagY — Y location of the flag between 0 and 1. (number)

flagToken — Type of flag. (string)

GetBattlefieldInfo

Returns information about a battleground when speaking to a battlemaster NPC or attempting to enter a battleground instance portal.

```
mapName, mapDescription, minLevel, maxLevel, mapID, mapX, mapY, ↵
minBracket, maxBracket = GetBattlefieldInfo()
```

Returns:

mapName — The name of the map. (string)

mapDescription — The description of the map. (string)

minLevel — The minimum level required to enter the battleground. (number)

maxLevel — The maximum level allowed in the battleground. (number)

mapID — Currently unused; always returns -1. (number)

mapX — Currently unused; returns 0 for most battlegrounds. (number)

mapY — Currently unused; returns 0 for most battlegrounds. (number)

minBracket — The minimum level allowed in this battlefield's bracket. (number)

maxBracket — The maximum level allowed in this battlefield's bracket. (number)

GetBattlefieldInstanceExpiration

When a battleground match is over, this returns the amount of time remaining before the instance is closed and all players are returned to the locations from which they entered it.

```
timeLeft = GetBattlefieldInstanceExpiration()
```

Returns:

timeLeft — If in a battleground after a finished match, the amount of time remaining (in milliseconds) before the instance shuts down, otherwise 0. (number)

GetBattlefieldInstanceInfo

Returns a numeric ID for a battleground instance listed in the battleground instance selection window. This number is the number seen in the instance names in said listings and elsewhere in the battlegrounds UI (for example, "You are eligible to enter Warsong Gulch 13.").

```
instanceID = GetBattlefieldInstanceInfo(index)
```

Argument:

index — The index in the battleground instance listing (with 1 corresponding to the first actual instance shown in the list after "First Available"). (number)

Returns:

instanceID — The instance ID that corresponds to the given index. (number)

GetBattlefieldInstanceRunTime

Returns how long the current battleground instance has been running, in milliseconds.

```
time = GetBattlefieldInstanceRunTime()
```

Returns:

`time` — The number of milliseconds since the current battleground instance started. This number can be converted to seconds by dividing by `1000`, or converted to a text string by using `SecondsToTime(GetBattlefield↵`
InstanceRunTime()/1000). (`number`)

Example:

```
-- Print the currently battleground time as a string
ChatFrame1:AddMessage(SecondsToTime(GetBattlefieldInstanceRunTime()/100
0))
```

GetBattlefieldMapIconScale

Returns the scale of the battleground map icons. This function is used to determine the size of the point of interest icons (towers, graveyards, and so on) on the zone map (aka battle minimap). The default size of the icons is set by `DEFAULT_POI_ICON_SIZE` and the scale is used to grow or shrink them depending on the size of the map.

```
scale = GetBattlefieldMapIconScale()
```

Returns:

`scale` — The scale of the map icons from `0` to `1`. (`number`)

Example:

```
-- Set the size of an icon scaled by this value
local size = DEFAULT_POI_ICON_SIZE * GetBattlefieldMapIconScale()
icon:SetWidth(size)
icon:SetHeight(size)
```

GetBattlefieldPortExpiration

Returns the time left on a battleground or arena invitation. If the status returned by `GetBattlefieldStatus(index)` is "confirm," this function will return the number of milliseconds left until your invitation expires. If the status is anything else, it will return `0`.

```
expiration = GetBattlefieldPortExpiration(index)
```

Argument:

`index` — The index of the battleground or arena as listed in the tooltip for the minimap battle status icon. (`number`)

Returns:

`expiration` — Time until your invitation expires (in milliseconds). (`number`)

Example:

```
-- Print the time left for all your active battleground queues
local index = 1
while true do
  local status, name = GetBattlefieldStatus(index)

  if not status then
    break   -- No more valid indexes
  elseif status == "confirm" then
    DEFAULT_CHAT_FRAME:AddMessage(format(
      "Your invitation to %s will expire in %d seconds.",
      name, GetBattlefieldPortExpiration(index) / 1000
    ))
  end

  index = index + 1
end
```

GetBattlefieldPosition

Returns information on the queried player's position in a battleground.

```
x, y, name = GetBattlefieldPosition(index)
```

Argument:

index — Player index between 1 and GetNumBattlefieldPositions(). (number)

Returns:

x — Position on the map between 0 and 1. (number)

y — Position on the map between 0 and 1. (number)

name — Name of the player on the map. (string)

Note: The BattlefieldPosition APIs no longer return useful information now that WoW automatically puts all battleground members into a raid group; use raid APIs instead.

GetBattlefieldScore

Returns information about a specific line in the battleground or arena score list

```
name, killingBlows, honorableKills, deaths, honorGained, faction,
rank, race, class, classToken, damageDone, healingDone =
GetBattlefieldScore(index)
```

Argument:

index — The index of the row in the battlefield score data. (number)

Returns:

name — The name of the player. (string)

killingBlows — The number of killing blows gained in the battlefield. (number)

honorableKills — The number of honorable kills gained in the battlefield. (number)

deaths — The number of deaths the player had during the battlefield. (number)

honorGained — The amount of honor gained during the battlefield. (number)

faction — The faction of the player (number)

- 0 — Horde (Battleground)/Green Team (Arena)
- 1 — Alliance (Battleground)/Gold Team (Arena)

rank — Deprecated; always 0. (number)

race — The player's class. (string)

classToken — The path to the classes icon's texture. (string)

damageDone — The amount of damage done in the battlefield. (number)

healingDone — The amount of healing done in the battlefield. (number)

GetBattlefieldStatData

Returns battleground-specific statistics for a given player. This function is used to determine a player's standing in a battleground. Players in the battleground are represented by a number from 1 to GetNumBattlefieldScores(), which is passed as the playerIndex parameter. Each unique piece of data for a battleground (for example, flag captures in Warsong Gulch or assaulted towers in Alterac Valley) is accessed by a specific statIndex. You can determine the number and meaning of statIndexes with the GetNumBattlefieldStats() and GetBattlefieldStatInfo() functions. This data is cached in the client. If you want to operate on the freshest data, you need to use RequestBattlefieldScoreData() and wait for the UPDATE_BATTLEFIELD_SCORE event.

columnData = GetBattlefieldStatData(playerIndex, statIndex)

Argument:

playerIndex — The index of the player whose statistics you want to retrieve. (number)

statIndex — The column index of the statistic you want to retrieve. (number)

Returns:

columnData — The requested data; nil if either the playerIndex or statIndex is invalid. (number)

Example:

```
-- Print out your personal battleground statistics
local playerName = UnitName("player")
for playerIndex = 1, GetNumBattlefieldStats() do
  local name = GetBattlefieldScore(playerIndex)
  if name == playerName then
    local output = "Battleground stats for "..name..":\n"
    for statIndex = 1, GetNumBattlefieldStats() do
output = output .. "    " .. GetBattlefieldStatInfo(statIndex) .. ↵
": " ..GetBattlefieldStatData(statIndex) .. "\n"
    end
    DEFAULT_CHAT_FRAME:AddMessage(output)
    break
  end
end
```

GetBattlefieldStatInfo

Used to retrieve a list of custom scoreboard columns inside a battleground. For example, in Warsong Gulch the stats are "Flags Captured" and "Flags Returned," while Arathi Basin has "Bases Assaulted" and "Bases Defended."

```
text, icon, tooltip = GetBattlefieldStatInfo(index)
```

Returns:

`text` — The name of the column. (`string`)

`icon` — The path to the stat's icon texture. (`string`)

`tooltip` — The text to be displayed in the tooltip on mouseover. (`string`)

GetBattlefieldStatus

Returns information about an active or queued battleground instance.

```
status, mapName, instanceID, levelRangeMin, levelRangeMax, teamSize,
registeredMatch = GetBattlefieldStatus(index)
```

Argument:

`index` — The index of the battleground or arena as listed in the tooltip for the minimap battle status icon. (`number`)

Returns:

`status` — The status of the battlefield. (`string`)

- ▪ `active` — The player is currently playing in this battlefield.
- ▪ `confirm` — The player currently has a slot for this battlefield and may choose to join it.
- ▪ `queued` — The player is queuing for this battlefield.

`mapName` — The name of the battlefield (such as Alterac Valley, or All Arenas for arena battlefields). (`string`)

`instanceID` — The battlefield instance assigned to you or the instance you are queuing for, or `0` if you are queuing for all instances. (`number`) levelRangeMin — The minimum level to queue for this battlefield instance. (number)

levelRangeMax — The maximum level to queue for this battlefield instance. (number)

teamSize — The number of players on each team for arenas, and 0 for non-arenas. (number)

- 0 — Not an arena
- 2 — 2v2 Arena
- 3 — 3v3 Arena
- 5 — 5v5 Arena

registeredMatch — 1 if the battlefield is rated (that is, rated arena matches), 0 otherwise. (number)

GetBattlefieldTeamInfo

Returns info about teams and their ratings in a rated arena match. This function only produces correct rating results after UPDATE_BATTLEFIELD_SCORE has fired.

teamName, teamRating, newTeamRating = GetBattlefieldTeamInfo(index)

Argument:

index — Team index. (number)

- 0 — Green Team
- 1 — Gold Team

Returns:

teamName — Team name. (string)

teamRating — Rating the team started this match with. (number)

newTeamRating — Rating for the team after this match. (number)

GetBattlefieldTimeWaited

Returns the amount of time the player has queued for the given battleground, in milliseconds.

timeInQueue = GetBattlefieldTimeWaited(index)

Argument:

index — The index of a battleground or arena as listed in the tooltip for the minimap battle status icon. (number)

Returns:

timeInQueue — The amount of time the player has been in a queue for the given battlefield, in milliseconds. (number)

GetBattlefieldWinner

Returns the winner of the current battleground or arena.

```
matchwinner = GetBattlefieldWinner()
```

Returns:

`winner` — The index of the winning team, or nil if not in a match or the match is not yet over. (`number`)

- 0 — Horde (Battleground)/Green Team (Arena)
- 1 — Alliance (Battleground)/Gold Team (Arena)

GetBidderAuctionItems

Retrieves bidding data for items on which you are bidding.

```
GetBidderAuctionItems([page])
```

Argument:

`page` — The page number to retrieve bidding data for, or all pages if nil. (`number`)

GetBillingTimeRested

Returns the number of minutes offline required for full xp.

```
time = GetBillingTimeRested()
```

Returns:

`time` — Minutes of rest required for full experience. (`number`)

Note: This function is used in the Chinese client for World of Warcraft where playtime is limited by law. Always returns 0 in other locales.

GetBindLocation

Returns the value of the Hearthstone bind location.

```
location = GetBindLocation()
```

Returns:

`location` — The current value of the Hearthstone bind location. (`string`)

GetBinding

Returns information about a key binding. This function is used internally to set up the key bindings window, and it can be used by custom addons to build their own key binding interfaces.

```
commandName, binding1, binding2 = GetBinding(index)
```

Argument:

`index` — The index in the key bindings window (headings are included). (`number`)

Returns:

commandName — The name of the command used in the key binding functions. (string)

binding1 — The primary key binding for the command, or nil. (string)

binding2 — The secondary key binding for the command, or nil. (string)

GetBindingAction

Returns the action associated with the given key.

```
action = GetBindingAction("key" [, checkOverride])
```

Arguments:

key — The key or key combination to query (for example, Ctrl-2). (string)

checkOverride (optional) — Set to 1 or true if override bindings should be checked as well (defaults to false). (boolean)

Returns:

action — The action associated with the given key, or an empty string if no action was found. (string)

GetBindingByKey

Returns the actions bound to a specific key combination.

```
action = GetBindingByKey("key")
```

Argument:

key — The key or key combination to query (for example Ctrl-2). (string)

Returns:

action — The action currently bound to the key combination. (string)

GetBindingKey

Returns the key combinations for a given binding command.

```
key1, ... = GetBindingKey("COMMAND")
```

Argument:

COMMAND — The name of a binding command to query. (string)

Returns:

key1 — The primary key combination bound to this command. (string)

... — A list of the other key combinations bound to this command. Although the default user interface only allows two combinations to be bound to a command, more than two can be set via the API. This function returns all known combinations for the given command. (string)

GetBlockChance

Returns your block percentage. This amount is not to be confused with Block Rating or the amount of damage stopped by a block. It's shown in the default UI in the Defenses section of the Character panel.

```
chance = GetBlockChance()
```

Returns:

chance — Percentage chance to block. (number)

GetBonusBarOffset

Returns the bar offset for the bonus bar. This value corresponds to what stance the player is currently in and, more specifically, what action bar should be shown in that stance.

```
offset = GetBonusBarOffset()
```

Returns:

offset — Returns the current offset for the bonus bar. (number)

GetBuildInfo

Returns the version information about the client.

```
version, internalVersion, date = GetBuildInfo()
```

Returns:

version — The version number of the client (such as 2.3.0). (string)

internalVersion — The internal version number of the client (such as 7561). (string)

date — The release date of the client (such as Nov 8 2007). (string)

GetBuybackItemInfo

Returns information about an item in the merchant buyback window.

```
name, texture, price, quantity, numAvailable, isUsable =
GetBuybackItemInfo(slot)
```

Argument:

slot — The slot in the merchant buyback window. (number)

Returns:

name — The name of the item. (string)

texture — The path to the item's icon texture. (string)

price — The price of the item, in copper. (number)

quantity — The number of items per stack. (number)

numAvailable — The number of items available for purchase. (number)

isUsable — 1 if the item is usable, otherwise nil. (1nil)

GetBuybackItemLink

Returns the item link for an item in the buyback window.

```
link = GetBuybackItemLink(slot)
```

Argument:

slot — The index of a slot in the vendor buyback window. (number)

Returns:

link — The item link for the item in the given buyback slot. (string)

Example:

```
-- Print item links for every item in the buyback tab
for i=1,12 do
  local link = GetBuybackItemLink(i)
  if link then
    ChatFrame1:AddMessage(link .. " is available for buyback")
  end
end
```

GetCVar

Returns the value of a stored configuration variable.

```
value = GetCVar("cvar")
```

Argument:

cvar — The name of a configuration variable. If an invalid CVar is passed to this function, it will cause a Lua error. (string)

Returns:

value — The stored value, as a string. (string)

GetCVarDefault

Queries the default value for a given CVar. Will produce an error if CVar does not exist.

```
value = GetCVarDefault("CVar")
```

Argument:

cvar — CVar to query. (string)

Returns:

value — Default value of the CVar. (string)

GetChannelDisplayInfo

Returns information about a given chat channel.

```
name, header, collapsed, channelNumber, count, active, category,
voiceEnabled, voiceActive = GetChannelDisplayInfo(index)
```

Argument:

index — The index of the channel in the channel window. (number)

Returns:

name — The name of the channel. (string)

header — 1 if the entry is a channel header, otherwise nil. (1nil)

collapsed — 1 if the entry is a channel header and the header is collapsed, otherwise nil. (1nil)

channelNumber — The number of the channel. This corresponds to the slash commands used to talk in a channel. If the channel doesn't have a number, this returns nil. (number)

count — The number of members of the channel. (number)

active — 1 if the channel is active, otherwise nil. This is primarily used for the special Trade and LookingForGroup channels, because they are inactive when the player is not in a major city. (1nil)

category — The category to which the chat channel belongs. (string)

- ▪ CHANNEL_CATEGORY_CUSTOM — Custom channels created by players

- ▪ CHANNEL_CATEGORY_GROUP — Group channels (party, raid, battleground)

- ▪ CHANNEL_CATEGORY_WORLD — World channels (General, Trade, and so on)

voiceEnabled — 1 if voice chat is enabled for the given channel, otherwise nil. (1nil)

voiceActive — 1 if voice chat is active for the given channel, otherwise nil. (1nil)

GetChannelList

Returns the list of channels to which the player currently belongs.

```
channel, index, ... = GetChannelList()
```

Returns:

channel — The name of the channel. (string)

index — The index of the channel. (number)

... — A list of channel and index pairs for each result. (list)

GetChannelName

Returns information about a given chat channel.

```
channel, channelName, instanceID = GetChannelName(channelIndex or ↵
"channelName")
```

Arguments:

channelIndex or channelName

channelIndex — A channel ID. (number)

channelName — A channel name. (string)

Returns:

channel — The ID of the channel. (number)

channelName — The name of the channel. (string)

instanceID — The channel's instance ID, or 0 if there are not separate instances of the channel. (number)

GetChannelRosterInfo

Returns information about a user in a given channel.

```
name, owner, moderator, muted, active, enabled = ↵
GetChannelRosterInfo(id, rosterIndex)
```

Arguments:

id — The index of the channel to query. (number)

rosterIndex — The index of the player in the given channel. (number)

Returns:

name — The name of the player. (string)

owner — 1 if the player is the channel owner, otherwise nil. (1nil)

moderator — 1 if the player is the channel moderator, otherwise nil. (1nil)

muted — 1 if the player is muted, otherwise nil. (1nil)

active — 1 if the player is currently speaking in the channel, otherwise nil. (1nil)

enabled — 1 if the player has voice chat enabled in the channel, otherwise nil. (1nil)

Example:

```
-- Counts the number of players in the given channel who do not have
-- voice chat enabled, and prints it to chat.

-- This script should be run with the "Chat" window open and a
channel selected
local index = GetSelectedDisplayChannel()
local count = select(5, GetChannelDisplayInfo(index))
local activeCount = 0
for i=1,count do
  local active = select(6, GetChannelRosterInfo(index, i))
  if active then
    activeCount = activeCount + 1
  end
end

ChatFrame1:AddMessage(activeCount .. " of " .. count .. " users have
voice chat ↵
enabled in this channel.")
```

GetChatTypeIndex

Converts a chat type string to a numeric chat type index. These numeric indices are used for grouping messages of similar types together, for when chat type colors change.

```
index = GetChatTypeIndex("type")
```

Argument:

type — A string indicating the chat type to be converted. This is the key in the table ChatTypeInfo. (string)

Returns:

index — The type index of the given chat type. (number)

GetChatWindowChannels

Returns a list of all channels in which a given chat window is interested.

```
channeName, channelId, ... = GetChatWindowChannels(index)
```

Argument:

index — The index of the chat frame to query. (number)

Returns:

channelName — The name of the channel. (string)

channelId — A numeric ID for the given channel. (number)

... — A repeating list of channelName and channelId for each channel belonging to a given chat window. (list)

GetChatWindowInfo

Retrieves information about a specific chat window.

```
name, fontSize, r, g, b, a, shown, locked, docked = ↵
GetChatWindowInfo(index)
```

Argument:

index — Index of the window on which you wish you get information (starts at 1). (number)

Returns:

name — Name of the chat window. (string)

fontSize — Font size of the text in the chat window. (number)

r — The red component of the window's background color (0.0, 1.0). (number)

g — The green component of the window's background color (0.0, 1.0). (number)

b — The blue component of the window's background color (0.0, 1.0). (number)

alpha — The alpha level (opacity) of the window's background (0.0, 1.0). (number)

shown — Returns 1 if the window is shown, 0 if it is hidden. (number) `locked` — Returns 1 if the window is locked, 0 if it is movable. (`number`)

`docked` — Returns 1 if the window is docked, 0 if free. (`number`)

GetChatWindowMessages

Returns a list of message events (leaving the `CHAT_MSG_` part out) for which a given chat frame is registered. An example return value is `SAY`; this means the chat frame is registered for the `CHAT_MSG_SAY` event.

`... = GetChatWindowMessages(index)`

Argument:

`index` — Chat frame index. (`number`)

Returns:

`...` — List of message types. (`list`)

GetCoinIcon

Returns a texture path for an icon, depending on the amount passed.

`icon = GetCoinIcon(amount)`

Argument:

`amount` — Amount of money in copper. (`number`)

Returns:

`icon` — Texture path for the icon corresponding to the largest coin for the given amount. (`string`)

- `Interface\Icons\INV_Misc_Coin_04` — Copper
- `Interface\Icons\INV_Misc_Coin_02` — Gold
- `Interface\Icons\INV_Misc_Coin_06` — Silver

GetCombatRating

Returns the amount of rating a player has for a given rating statistic.

`rating = GetCombatRating(ratingIndex)`

Argument:

`ratingIndex` — The index of the rating to be queried. (`number`)

- `CR_BLOCK` — Block skill
- `CR_CRIT_MELEE` — Melee critical strike chance
- `CR_CRIT_RANGED` — Ranged critical strike chance
- `CR_CRIT_SPELL` — Spell critical strike chance
- `CR_CRIT_TAKEN_MELEE` — Unknown
- `CR_CRIT_TAKEN_RANGED` — Unknown
- `CR_CRIT_TAKEN_SPELL` — Unknown
- `CR_DEFENSE_SKILL` — Defense skill
- `CR_DODGE` — Dodge skill

- CR_HASTE_MELEE — Melee haste
- CR_HASTE_RANGED — Ranged haste
- CR_HASTE_SPELL — Spell haste
- CR_HIT_MELEE — Melee chance to hit
- CR_HIT_RANGED — Ranged chance to hit
- CR_HIT_SPELL — Spell chance to hit
- CR_HIT_TAKEN_MELEE — Unknown
- CR_HIT_TAKEN_RANGED — Unknown
- CR_HIT_TAKEN_SPELL — Unknown
- CR_PARRY — Parry skill
- CR_WEAPON_SKILL — Weapon skill
- CR_WEAPON_SKILL_MAINHAND — Main-hand weapon skill
- CR_WEAPON_SKILL_OFFHAND — Off-hand weapon skill
- CR_WEAPON_SKILL_RANGED — Ranged weapon skill

Returns:

rating — The amount of rating bonus the player has. (number)

GetCombatRatingBonus

Returns the percentage bonus for a given combat rating. This is used in the PaperDollFrame to show percent increases for each of the possible combat statistics (in tooltips).

```
local ratingBonus = GetCombatRatingBonus(ratingIndex)
```

Argument:

ratingIndex — The index of the rating to be queried. (number)

- CR_BLOCK — Block skill
- CR_CRIT_MELEE — Melee critical strike chance
- CR_CRIT_RANGED — Ranged critical strike chance
- CR_CRIT_SPELL — Spell critical strike chance
- CR_CRIT_TAKEN_MELEE — Unknown
- CR_CRIT_TAKEN_RANGED — Unknown
- CR_CRIT_TAKEN_SPELL — Unknown
- CR_DEFENSE_SKILL — Defense skill
- CR_DODGE — Dodge skill
- CR_HASTE_MELEE — Melee haste
- CR_HASTE_RANGED — Ranged haste
- CR_HASTE_SPELL — Spell haste
- CR_HIT_MELEE — Melee chance to hit

- CR_HIT_RANGED — Ranged chance to hit

- CR_HIT_SPELL — Spell chance to hit

- CR_HIT_TAKEN_MELEE — Unknown

- CR_HIT_TAKEN_RANGED — Unknown

- CR_HIT_TAKEN_SPELL — Unknown

- CR_PARRY — Parry skill

- CR_WEAPON_SKILL — Weapon skill

- CR_WEAPON_SKILL_MAINHAND — Main-hand weapon skill

- CR_WEAPON_SKILL_OFFHAND — Off-hand weapon skill

- CR_WEAPON_SKILL_RANGED — Ranged weapon skill

Returns:

ratingBonus — The percentage increase the rating confers. (number)

GetComboPoints

Returns the number of combo points the player has. This function returns a number from 0 to MAX_COMBO_POINTS, indicating how many combo points are active. This is only applicable to Rogues and Druids in Cat Form; it will always return 0 for other classes.

```
comboPoints = GetComboPoints()
```

Returns:

comboPoints — The number of combo points. (number)

Example:

```
-- Show or hide combo point indicators
local comboPoints = GetComboPoints()
for i = 1, MAX_COMBO_POINTS do
  if i <= comboPoints then
    indicators[i]:Show()
  else
    indicators[i]:Hide()
  end
end
```

GetContainerItemCooldown

Returns information about the cooldown for an item in one of your bags.

```
start, duration, enable = GetContainerItemCooldown(index, slot)
```

Arguments:

index — The index of the container. (number)

- ∎ -1 — Standard Bank
- ∎ -2 — Keyring
- ∎ 0 — Backpack
- ∎ 1 — Bag 1
- ∎ 2 — Bag 2
- ∎ 3 — Bag 3
- ∎ 4 — Bag 4
- ∎ 5 — Bank Bag 1
- ∎ 6 — Bank Bag 2
- ∎ 7 — Bank Bag 3
- ∎ 8 — Bank Bag 4
- ∎ 9 — Bank Bag 5
- ∎ 10 — Bank Bag 6
- ∎ 11 — Bank Bag 7

slot — The slot within the given container. (number)

Returns:

start — The time the cooldown started with millisecond precision. This is the value of GetTime() at the moment the cooldown began. (number)

duration — The duration of the cooldown in seconds. (number)

enable — 1 if the item has a possible cooldown, otherwise 0. (1nil)

GetContainerItemDurability

Returns durability information for an item in one of your bags.

```
curDurability, maxDurability = GetContainerItemDurability(index,
slot)
```

Arguments:

index — The index of the container. (number)

- ∎ -1 — Standard Bank
- ∎ -2 — Keyring
- ∎ 0 — Backpack
- ∎ 1 — Bag 1
- ∎ 2 — Bag 2
- ∎ 3 — Bag 3
- ∎ 4 — Bag 4
- ∎ 5 — Bank Bag 1

- 6 — Bank Bag 2
- 7 — Bank Bag 3
- 8 — Bank Bag 4
- 9 — Bank Bag 5
- 10 — Bank Bag 6
- 11 — Bank Bag 7

`slot` — The slot within the given container (numbered left to right, top to bottom). (`number`)

Returns:

`curDurability` — The current durability of the given item. (`number`)

`maxDurability` — The maximum durability of the given item. (`number`)

GetContainerItemInfo

Returns information about an item in a container.

```
texture, itemCount, locked, quality, readable =
GetContainerItemInfo(index, slot)
```

Arguments:

`index` — Container index to query. (`number`)

- -1 — Standard Bank
- -2 — Keyring
- 0 — Backpack
- 1 — Bag 1
- 2 — Bag 2
- 3 — Bag 3
- 4 — Bag 4
- 5 — Bank Bag 1
- 6 — Bank Bag 2
- 7 — Bank Bag 3
- 8 — Bank Bag 4
- 9 — Bank Bag 5
- 10 — Bank Bag 6
- 11 — Bank Bag 7

`slot` — Slot within container to query. (`number`)

Returns:

texture — Texture path of the item. (string)

itemCount — Number of items in the slot. (number)

locked — 1 if the item is locked, nil otherwise. An item can become locked when splitting stacks or if the item is in the trade/mail/auction windows. (1nil)

quality — Item quality indicator. (number)

- 0 — Poor
- 1 — Common
- 2 — Uncommon
- 3 — Rare
- 4 — Epic
- 5 — Legendary
- 6 — Artifact

readable — 1 if the item is readable, nil otherwise. An item is readable when it is a book or scroll that can be read by right-clicking. (1nil)

GetContainerItemLink

Returns the item link of the item at a specific position in the player's bags or bank.

```
item = GetContainerItemLink(index, slot)
```

Arguments:

index — The index of the container to check. (number)

- -1 — Standard Bank
- -2 — Keyring
- 0 — Backpack
- 1 — Bag 1
- 2 — Bag 2
- 3 — Bag 3
- 4 — Bag 4
- 5 — Bank Bag 1
- 6 — Bank Bag 2
- 7 — Bank Bag 3
- 8 — Bank Bag 4
- 9 — Bank Bag 5
- 10 — Bank Bag 6
- 11 — Bank Bag 7

slot — The slot of the container to check. (number)

Returns:

`item` — The item link of the item at the specified position. `(string)`

GetContainerNumSlots

Returns the number of slots for a given container.

```
numSlots = GetContainerNumSlots(index)
```

Argument:

`index` — The index of a container `(number)`

- `-1` — Standard Bank
- `-2` — Keyring
- `0` — Backpack
- `1` — Bag 1
- `2` — Bag 2
- `3` — Bag 3
- `4` — Bag 4
- `5` — Bank Bag 1
- `6` — Bank Bag 2
- `7` — Bank Bag 3
- `8` — Bank Bag 4
- `9` — Bank Bag 5
- `10` — Bank Bag 6
- `11` — Bank Bag 7

Returns:

`numSlots` — The number of slots for the given container. `(number)`

GetCorpseMapPosition

Returns the position of the player's corpse on the world map.

```
corpseX, corpseY = GetCorpseMapPosition()
```

Returns:

`corpseX` — The X coordinate for the player's corpse on the world map. This number is given as a proportion of the total width of the `WorldMapDetailFrame`. `(number)`

`corpseY` — The Y coordinate for the player's corpse on the world map. This number is given as a proportion of the total height of the `WorldMapDetailFrame`. `(number)`

Note: If this returns (`0, 0`), the coordinates could not be determined for the currently displayed map.

GetCorpseRecoveryDelay

Returns the amount of time left until the player can recover their corpse.

```
timeLeft = GetCorpseRecoveryDelay()
```

Returns:

`timeLeft` — The amount of time left until the player can recover their corpse, in seconds. This returns 0 if the player can recover it immediately. (`number`)

GetCraftButtonToken

Returns the global string token for the craft button in the craft UI.

```
token = GetCraftButtonToken()
```

Returns:

`token` — The global string token that should be used when setting the text on the craft button. (`string`)

- ▪ `ENSCRIBE` — Enchant in the current locale
- ▪ `TRAIN` — Train in the current locale

GetCraftCooldown

Returns the amount of time left on a craft skill cooldown.

```
cooldownTime = GetCraftCooldown(index)
```

Argument:

`index` — The index of the craft skill. (`number`)

Returns:

`cooldownTime` — The amount of time left on the craft cooldown, in seconds. (`number`)

GetCraftDescription

Returns a short description of what a specified craft does.

```
craftDescription = GetCraftDescription(index)
```

Argument:

`index` — The index of a craft recipe, from 1 to `GetNumCrafts()`. (`number`)

Returns:

`craftDescription` — A description of what the indexed craft does. (`string`)

GetCraftDisplaySkillLine

Returns information about the currently open craft (Enchanting or Beast Training).

```
name, rank, maxRank = GetCraftDisplaySkillLine()
```

Returns:

name — The name of the currently open craft, or nil. (string)

rank — The player's current rank in the given craft. (number)

maxRank — The current maximum of the given craft for the player. (number)

GetCraftFilter

Returns whether a given craft filter is enabled.

```
enabled = GetCraftFilter(index)
```

Argument:

index — The index of a craft skill filter. In the Enchanting Craft UI, index 0 is the All Slots filter. (number)

Returns:

enabled — 1 if the filter is enabled, otherwise nil. (1nil)

GetCraftIcon

Returns the texture of a selected craft to be shown in the craft UI.

```
texture = GetCraftIcon(id)
```

Argument:

id — The index of the crafting recipe to query. (number)

Returns:

texture — The texture of the recipe icon. (string)

GetCraftInfo

Returns information about a given craft recipe or skill (Enchanting or Pet Training).

```
craftName, craftSubSpellName, craftType, numAvailable, isExpanded,
trainingPointCost, requiredLevel = GetCraftInfo(index)
```

Returns:

craftName — The name of the craft spell or pet skill. (string)

craftSubSpellName — Any secondary text for the spell name, such as the rank for pet skills. (string)

craftType — The current difficulty level of the craft. (string)

- ▪ easy — The craft is easy to complete and only has a minimal chance of gaining the player a skill point when completed.

- ▪ medium — The craft has a medium chance of gaining the player a skill point when completed.

- ▪ optimal — The craft has an optimal chance of gaining the player a skill point when completed.

- ▪ trivial — The craft is trivial to complete and will not gain the player a skill point.

- ▪ none — The craft is a pet skill.

- ▪ used — The craft is a pet skill that the current pet already knows.

numAvailable — The number of crafts the player can complete with the current number of reagents. (number)

isExpanded — Currently unused, because Enchanting and Pet Training have no headers. Always returns nil. (1nil)

trainingPointCost — The number of training points required for the given pet skill, or 0 if the current pet cannot learn the skill. (number)

requiredLevel — The required level to train the pet skill (pet level, not player level). (number)

GetCraftItemLink

Returns an item link for a craft skill item. For Enchanting, this will return a recipe link (the tooltip for which shows reagents and description) unless the skill produces an actual item. (Always returns nil for Beast Training.)

```
link = GetCraftItemLink(index)
```

Argument:

index — The index of a craft skill item. (number)

Returns:

link — A link for the given item. (string)

GetCraftItemNameFilter

Returns the value of the craft UI item name filter.

```
filter = GetCraftItemNameFilter()
```

Returns:

filter — The value of the current craft UI item name filter. (string)

GetCraftName

Returns the name of the current craft that the player has open. Will return the first profession found in the spellbook (even professions that use the TradeSkill APIs instead of the Craft APIs) if no craft is open.

```
craftName = GetCraftName()
```

Returns:

craftName — Current selected craft. Defaults to the first craft found in the spellbook. (string)

GetCraftNumMade

Returns the number of items crafted for a given recipe. This is used in the Enchanting user interface for recipes that create multiple items (such as Small Prismatic Shard). The count is displayed on the item's icon in the crafting UI.

```
minMade,maxMade = GetCraftNumMade(id)
```

Returns:

minMade — The minimum number of items crafted. (number)

maxMade — The maximum number of items crafted. (number)

Example:

```
-- Print any craft recipes that create multiple items to ChatFrame1
for i=1,GetNumCrafts() do
  local minMade,maxMade = GetCraftNumMade(i)
  if minMade > 1 then
    ChatFrame1:AddMessage("The recipe for " .. ↵
GetCraftItemLink(i) .. " creates " .. minMade .. " items")
  end
end
```

GetCraftNumReagents

Returns the number of reagents required for the given recipe. This count does not include the number of each reagent required, merely the number of different types of reagents that are required.

```
numReagents = GetCraftNumReagents(index)
```

Argument:

index — The index of the recipe. (number)

Returns:

numReagents — The number of different reagents required for the craft. (number)

Example:

```
-- The following code takes the selected item in the Craft UI
(Enchanting)
-- and prints a status message about any missing reagents
local index = GetCraftSelectionIndex()
local name = GetCraftInfo(index)
local numReagents = GetCraftNumReagents(index)

ChatFrame1:AddMessage("Inventory for " .. name)

local missing = false
for i=1,numReagents do
  local name, texture, numRequired, numHave = ↵
GetCraftReagentInfo(index, i)
  if numHave < numRequired then
    ChatFrame1:AddMessage("--missing " .. ↵
```

```
    GetCraftReagentItemLink(index, i) .. " x " .. (numRequired--numHave))
      missing = true
    end
  end
end

if not missing then
  ChatFrame1:AddMessage("You have all the required reagents")
end
```

GetCraftReagentInfo

Returns information about a craft skill reagent.

```
reagentName, reagentTexture, reagentCount, playerReagentCount ↵
= GetCraftReagentInfo(index, reagentIndex)
```

Arguments:

index — The index of a craft skill in the craft UI. (number)

reagentIndex — The reagent index for the given craft skill. (number)

Returns:

reagentName — The name of the reagent. (string)

reagentTexture — The path to the item's icon texture. (string)

reagentCount — The number of reagents required. (number)

playerReagentCount — The number of reagents the player currently has. (number)

GetCraftReagentItemLink

Returns an item link for a specific craft skill reagent.

```
link = GetCraftReagentItemLink(index, reagentIndex)
```

Arguments:

index — The index in the craft window. (number)

reagentIndex — The index of the reagent for the given craft skill. (number)

Returns:

link — An item link for the given craft skill reagent. (string)

Example:

```
-- Print all reagents to the chat window
local index = GetCraftSelectionIndex()
local numReagents = GetCraftNumReagents(index)
for reagentIndex=1,numReagents do
  ChatFrame1:AddMessage(GetCraftReagentItemLink(index, reagentIndex))
end
```

GetCraftRecipeLink

Retrieves the recipe link (the tooltip that shows required reagents and description) for a given craft skill.

```
link = GetCraftRecipeLink(index)
```

Argument:

index — The craft index to query. (number)

Returns:

link — A hyperlink for the given craft recipe. (string)

GetCraftSelectionIndex

Returns the index of the currently selected craft item.

```
index = GetCraftSelectionIndex()
```

Returns:

index — The index of the currently selected craft item. (number)

GetCraftSkillLine

Returns the name of the currently (or last) open craft skill window.

```
skill = GetCraftSkillLine(index)
```

Argument:

index — If this argument is 0, GetCraftSkillLine() will always return nil. If it is any number greater than 0, this function will return the name of the open craft skill. (number)

Returns:

skill — The name of the last open craft skill (Beast Training or Enchanting in the current locale), or nil. (string)

GetCraftSlots

Returns a list of item slot types for which crafted items can be made. Returns a list of strings, which are names of globals with the localized names, such as BACKSLOT or WRISTSLOT.

```
... = GetCraftSlots()
```

Returns:

... — A list of item slot types for which crafted items can be made, as strings. (string)

Note: The CRAFT_UPDATE event must have been fired for this function to return anything.

Example:

```
-- Prints the craftable item slot types as global name/localized ↵
name pairs
function printCrafts(...)
  local globalName;
  for i = 1, select('#', ...) do
    globalName = select(i, ...);
    ChatFrame1:AddMessage(string.format('"%s" => "%s"', ↵
globalName, getglobal(globalName)));
  end
end

printCrafts(GetCraftSlots());
```

GetCraftSpellFocus

Returns a list of required items for a craft skill (for example, Enchanting rods).

```
name, has, ... = GetCraftSpellFocus(index)
```

Argument:

index — The index of the craft spell. (number)

Returns:

name — The name of the required item. (string)

has — 1 if the player has the required item, otherwise nil. (1nil)

Example:

```
-- Print the required list to ChatFrame1
local required =
BuildColoredListString(GetCraftSpellFocus(GetCraftSelectionIndex()))
if required then
  ChatFrame1:AddMessage(required)
end
```

GetCritChance

Returns the player's percent melee critical strike chance.

```
critChance = GetCritChance()
```

Returns:

critChance — The player's percent chance to crit for melee attacks. (number)

GetCritChanceFromAgility

Returns the amount of critical strike chance given by the agility stat.

```
critChance = GetCritChanceFromAgility("unit")
```

Argument:

unit — The unit to query. (unitid)

Returns:

critChance — The percentage crit chance granted by the agility stat. (number)

GetCurrentArenaSeason

Returns the current arena season. The arena season is something that changes every few months, resetting team rankings and introducing new and changed items.

```
season = GetCurrentArenaSeason()
```

Returns:

`season` — The current arena season. (`number`)

GetCurrentBindingSet

Returns the type of key bindings in use.

```
bindingSet = GetCurrentBindingSet()
```

Returns:

`bindingSet` — The binding set currently in use. (`number`)

- ▪ 1 — The key bindings in use are for all characters.
- ▪ 2 — The key bindings in use are character specific.

GetCurrentDungeonDifficulty

Returns the current dungeon difficulty level.

```
dungeonDifficulty = GetCurrentDungeonDifficulty()
```

Returns:

`dungeonDifficulty` — The current dungeon difficulty setting. (`number`)

- ▪ 1 — Normal
- ▪ 2 — Heroic
- ▪ 3 — Epic (currently unused)

GetCurrentGuildBankTab

Returns the currently selected guild bank tab.

```
currentTab = GetCurrentGuildBankTab()
```

Argument:

`currentTab` — The currently selected guild bank tab. (`number`)

GetCurrentKeyBoardFocus

Returns the frame that currently has the keyboard focus.

```
frame = GetCurrentKeyBoardFocus()
```

Returns:

`frame` — The frame that currently has the keyboard focus or nil. This is typically an `EditBox` frame, but could be any frame. (`table`)

Example:

```
-- Putting this in a macro will reveal the name of whatever has ↵
the current keyboard focus
local frame = GetCurrentKeyBoardfocus()
local name = frame:GetName() or "Unknown Frame"
ChatFrame1:AddMessage(name or "nil")
```

GetCurrentMapContinent

Returns the current map continent.

```
continent = GetCurrentMapContinent()
```

Returns:

continent — The continent the player is currently viewing on the world map or the continent on which the player currently resides. (number)

- -1 — Universe Map (showing both Outlands and Azeroth)
- 0 — Azeroth World Map
- 1 — Kalimdor
- 2 — Eastern Kingdoms
- 3 — Outlands

GetCurrentMapZone

Returns the number of the zone currently shown on the world map.

```
zone = GetCurrentMapZone()
```

Returns:

zone — The number of the zone currently shown on the world map. (number)

GetCurrentMultisampleFormat

Returns the index of the currently selected multisample format.

```
index = GetCurrentMultisampleFormat()
```

Returns:

index — The index of the currently selected multisample format. (number)

GetCurrentResolution

Returns the index of the current resolution. To determine the dimensions of the current resolution, use GetScreenResolutions().

```
index = GetCurrentResolution()
```

Returns:

index — The index of the current resolution. (number)

Example:

```
-- Print the current resolution to chat
local index = GetCurrentResolution();
local resolution = select(index, GetScreenResolutions());
ChatFrame1:AddMessage(string.format("The current resolution is %s",
resolution));
```

GetCurrentTitle

Returns the currently selected player title.

```
currentTitle = GetCurrentTitle()
```

Returns:

`currentTitle` — The currently selected title. If the player has no available titles, this will return 0. If the player has available titles and has none selected, this will return -1. (number)

GetCursorInfo

Returns information about the object currently held by the cursor.

```
type, id, subType = GetCursorInfo()
```

Returns:

`type` — The type of object currently held by the cursor. (string)

- ▪ money
- ▪ spell
- ▪ item
- ▪ macro
- ▪ merchant

`id` — The value depends on the return for type but corresponds to the amount of money in copper, the spell ID, the item ID, the macro index, or the index of the merchant item being held. (number)

`subType` — The subtype of the object being held, depending on the return of type. The `spellbookType` for the spell or the `itemLink` for the item being held. (string)

GetCursorMoney

Returns the amount of money currently held by the cursor, in copper.

```
cursorMoney = GetCursorMoney()
```

Returns:

`cursorMoney` — The amount of money currently held by the cursor, in copper. (number)

GetCursorPosition

Returns the coordinate position of the cursor on screen.

```
cursorX, cursorY = GetCursorPosition()
```

Returns:

cursorX — The current scale-independent X coordinate of the cursor. (number)

cursorY — The current scale-independent Y coordinate of the cursor. (number)

GetDailyQuestsCompleted

Returns the number of daily quests the player already completed today.

```
dailyQuestsComplete = GetDailyQuestsCompleted()
```

Returns:

dailyQuestsComplete — The number of daily quests the player completed. (number)

GetDamageBonusStat

This function will return the index of the stat that provides the most (not necessarily the only) bonus melee damage when increased for the player's class. Currently this is either 1 (Strength) or 2 (Agility).

```
bonusStat = GetDamageBonusStat()
```

Returns:

bonusStat — The index of the main stat that grants a damage bonus when increased. (number)

- 1 — Strength (Druids, Mages, Paladins, Priests, Shamans, Warlocks, and Warriors)
- 2 — Agility (Hunters and Rogues)

GetDeathReleasePosition

Returns the location of the graveyard where your spirit will appear when it is released from your body.

```
x, y = GetDeathReleasePosition()
```

Returns:

x — x position on the map between 0 and 1. (number)

y — y position on the map between 0 and 1. (number)

Note: Only works when dead or a ghost.

GetDefaultDungeonDifficulty

Returns the default dungeon difficulty level for the player. This returns the player's setting for dungeon difficulty, which may differ from that of the party leader.

```
difficulty = GetDefaultDungeonDifficulty()
```

Returns:

`difficulty` — The dungeon difficulty (`number`)

- ▪ 1 — Normal
- ▪ 2 — Heroic
- ▪ 3 — Epic (currently unused)

GetDefaultLanguage

Returns the default language that the character speaks.

```
language = GetDefaultLanguage()
```

Returns:

`language` — The default language the player's character speaks. (`string`)

GetDodgeChance

Returns the amount of dodge change the player has, as a percentage.

```
chance = GetDodgeChance()
```

Returns:

`chance` — The amount of dodge change the player currently has, as a percentage. (`number`)

geterrorhandler

Returns a reference to the current error handler.

```
handler = geterrorhandler()
```

Returns:

`handler` — The current error handler. (`function`)

Example:

```
-- displays a message using the current error handler
local currentHandler = geterrorhandler()
currentHandler("Something has gone horribly wrong!")
```

GetEventCPUUsage

Returns information about the CPU usage of events.

```
timeSpent, numEvents, GetEventCPUUsage()
```

Returns:

`timeSpent` — The total amount of time spent while processing events, in seconds. If CPU profiling is disabled, this value will be `0`. (`number`)

`numEvents` — The number of events that have been fired this session. (`number`)

Note: Returns `0` unless CPU profiling is enabled by setting the CVar `scriptProfile` to `1`.

GetExistingLocales

Returns the locale packs currently available to the client.

```
... = GetExistingLocales()
```

Returns:

`...` — A list of the locale packs currently available to the client. (`string`)

GetExistingSocketInfo

Returns information about the jewel in a given socket for the item in the item socketing interface.

```
name, texture, isMatch = GetExistingSocketInfo(index)
```

Argument:

`index` — The index of the socket. (`number`)

Returns:

`name` — The name of the jewel currently in the given socket (`nil` if no jewel is socketed in this socket). (`string`)

`texture` — The texture of the icon of the jewel currently in the given socket (`nil` if no jewel is socketed in this socket). (`string`)

`name` — `1` if the jewel currently in the socket matches the socket's color (`nil` if no jewel is socketed in this socket). (`1nil`)

GetExistingSocketLink

Returns an item link for a socketed gem. If the given socket in the Item Socketing UI contains a permanently socketed gem, returns an item link for that gem (even if a new gem has been dropped in the socket to overwrite the existing gem but has not yet been confirmed). If the socket is empty, returns `nil`.

```
link = GetExistingSocketLink(index)
```

Argument:

`index` — The index of the item socket to query. (`number`)

Returns:

`link` — The item link of the gem already in the given socket. (`string`)

See also: `GetNewSocketLink()`

GetExpertise

Returns the amount of expertise the player currently has.

```
expertise = GetExpertise()
```

Returns:

`expertise` — The amount of expertise rating the player currently has. `(number)`

GetExpertisePercent

Returns the reduced chance to be dodged or parried as a result of the expertise rating.

```
expertisePerc = GetExpertisePercent()
```

Returns:

`expertisePerc` — The reduced chance to be dodged or parried granted by the current level of expertise rating. `(number)`

GetFactionInfo

Returns information about a specified faction index.

```
name, description, standingID, barMin, barMax, barValue, atWarWith,
canToggleAtWar, isHeader, isCollapsed, isWatched =
GetFactionInfo(index)
```

Argument:

`index` — The index of the faction in the reputation window. `(number)`

Returns:

`name` — The name of the faction. `(string)`

`description` — The description of the faction, displayed in the faction detail window. `(string)`

`standingID` — The current standing with the given faction. `(number)`

- 1 — Hated
- 2 — Hostile
- 3 — Unfriendly
- 4 — Neutral
- 5 — Friendly
- 6 — Honored
- 7 — Revered
- 8 — Exalted

`barMin` — The minimum value of the reputation bar at the given standing. `(number)`

`barMax` — The maximum value of the reputation bar at the given standing. `(number)`

barValue — The player's current reputation with the faction. (number)

atWarWith — 1 if the player is at war with the given faction, otherwise nil. (1nil)

canToggleAtWar — 1 if the player can declare war with a given faction, otherwise nil. (1nil)

isHeader — 1 if the given faction index is a faction header. (1nil)

isCollapsed — 1 if the faction index is a faction header, and collapsed. (1nil)

isWatched — 1 if the faction is currently being watched (that is, displayed above the experience bar). (1nil)

GetFarclip

Returns the value of the Terrain Distance video option.

```
distance = GetFarclip()
```

Returns:

distance — The distance that corresponds to Terrain Distance option in Video Options. (number)

GetFirstTradeSkill

Returns the index of the first tradeskill recipe, as opposed to tradeskill headers.

```
index = GetFirstTradeSkill()
```

Returns:

index — The index of the first tradeskill recipe, as opposed to tradeskill headers. (number)

GetFrameCPUUsage

Gets CPU time used and number of function calls for the frame and its children depending on the includeChildren setting, which defaults to true.

```
time, calls = GetFrameCPUUsage(frame [, includeChildren])
```

Arguments:

frame — Frame to query. (table)

includeChildren — Include the children of this frame in the query. (boolean)

Returns:

time — CPU time in milliseconds used. (number)

calls — Number of function calls. (number)

Note: Returns 0 unless CPU profiling is enabled by setting the CVar scriptProfile to 1.

GetFramerate

Returns the current graphical frame rate.

```
framerate = GetFramerate()
```

Returns:

framerate — The current graphical frame rate. (number)

GetFramesRegisteredForEvent

Returns all frames registered for a given event.

```
... = GetFramesRegisteredForEvent("event")
```

Argument:

event — An event name. (string)

Returns:

... — A list of all frames registered for the given event. (table)

Example:

```
-- Print the names of any named frames registered for an event
local function printFrameNames(...)
  for i=1,select("#", ...) do
    local frame = select(i, ...)
    local name = frame:GetName()
    if name then
      ChatFrame1:AddMessage(name)
    end
  end
end

printFrameNames(GetFramesRegisteredForEvent("UNIT_HEALTH"))
```

GetFriendInfo

Returns information about someone on the player's friends list.

```
name, level, class, area, connected, status = GetFriendInfo(index)
```

Argument:

index — The index of a friend in the friends list. (number)

Returns:

name — The name of the friend. (string)

level — The friend's level if he or she is online, otherwise 0. (number)

class — The friend's class if he or she is online, otherwise Unknown. (string)

area — The current location of the friend if he or she is online, otherwise Unknown. (string)

connected — 1 if the friend is online, otherwise nil. (1nil)

status — The status string for the player, <AFK> or <DND>. Otherwise, the empty string. (string)

GetFunctionCPUUsage

Returns CPU usage information about a function.

```
timeUsed, numCalled = GetFunctionCPUUsage(function [,
includeSubroutines])
```

Arguments:

`function` — The function to query. (function)

`includeSubroutines` — 1 to include any subroutines called by the original function, otherwise `nil`. (1nil)

Returns:

`timeUsed` — The amount of CPU time spent inside the function. (number)

`numCalled` — The number of times the function has been called. (number)

Note: Returns 0 unless CPU profiling is enabled by setting the CVar `scriptProfile` to 1.

getglobal

Returns a global variable with a given name. This function is used extensively throughout the default UI to fetch global variables with similar names; for example, `getglobal(self:GetName() .. "Icon")` is typical usage.

```
var = getglobal(str)
```

Argument:

`str` — The name of a global variable to get. (string)

Returns:

`var` — The global variable with the given name. (value)

GetGMTicket

Requests a GM ticket update from the server. This function is a server query that requests an update for your GM ticket. When the data is ready, the game will fire the UPDATE_TICKET event.

GetGMTicketCategories

Returns a list of available GM ticket categories.

Returns:

`...` — A variable number of categories. (string)

GetGameTime

Returns the current in-game time.

```
hour, minute = GetGameTime()
```

Returns:

`hour` — The hour portion of the current in-game time. (number)

`minute` — The minute portion of the current in-game time. (number)

GetGamma

Returns the gamma value for the game client.

```
gamma = GetGamma()
```

Returns:

gamma — The gamma setting of the game client. (number)

GetGossipActiveQuests

Returns a list of the available quests during a gossip interaction.

```
name, level, ... = GetGossipActiveQuests()
```

Returns:

name — The name of the quest. (string)

level — The level of the quest. (number)

... — A repeating list of name and level pairs. (list)

GetGossipAvailableQuests

Gets a list of all available quests of the active gossip frame.

```
name, level, isTrivial, ... = GetGossipAvailableQuests()
```

Returns:

name — The name of the quest. (string)

level — The level of the quest. (number)

isTrivial — 1 if the quest is trivial (low level), nil otherwise. (1nil)

... — A repeating list of all quests on the current gossip frame containing title, level, and isTrivial. (list)

Note: This information is only available after the GOSSIP_SHOW event fired.

GetGossipOptions

Returns the available gossip options for a given NPC.

```
text, gossipType, ... = GetGossipOptions()
```

Returns:

text — The text of the gossip option. (string)

gossipType — A string indicating the type of gossip option. (string)

- banker — Open the bank
- battlemaster — Join a battleground
- binder — Sets hearthstone location
- gossip — Talk to the NPC
- taxi — Open the flight map

■ `trainer` — Open the training dialog

■ `vendor` — Sell items to the vendor

`...` — A repeating list of `text` and `gossipType` values for all available options. (`list`)

GetGossipText

Returns the text that is displayed when initially conversing with an NPC.

```
text = GetGossipText()
```

Returns:

`text` — The NPC gossip text displayed in the initial conversation dialog. (`string`)

GetGreetingText

Returns the greeting text displayed for quest NPCs with multiple quests.

```
greetingText = GetGreetingText()
```

Returns:

`greetingText` — The greeting text displayed for quest NPCs. (`string`)

Note: Several quest NPCs use the `GossipFrame` instead, which uses `GetGossipText()`.

GetGuildBankItemInfo

Returns information about the guild bank item in a given slot.

```
texture, count, locked = GetGuildBankItemInfo(tab, slot)
```

Arguments:

`tab` — The index of the guild bank tab. (`number`)

`slot` — The slot to query. (`number`)

Returns:

`texture` — The item's icon texture. (`string`)

`count` — The amount of items in the stack. (`number`)

`locked` — `true` if the item is currently locked, otherwise `nil`. An item is locked when it is picked up by someone in your guild. (`boolean`)

GetGuildBankItemLink

Returns the item link of the item at a specific position in the guild bank.

```
item = GetGuildBankItemLink(tab, slot)
```

Arguments:

`tab` — The tab index to check. (`number`)

`slot` — The slot within the tab to check. (`number`)

Returns:

`item` — The item link of the item at the specified position. (`string`)

GetGuildBankMoney

Returns the amount of money available in the guild bank, in copper. The return value is cached and returns the last value seen when not in range of a guild bank. This cache works across characters. The cache is updated when the GUILDBANK_UPDATE_MONEY or GUILDBANKFRAME_OPENED events are raised. If neither of those events have been fired since the game client was launched, GetGuildBankMoney() will return 0.

```
guildBankMoney = GetGuildBankMoney()
```

Returns:

guildBankMoney — The amount of money available in the guild bank, in copper. (number)

GetGuildBankMoneyTransaction

Returns information from the guild bank money log.

```
type, name, amount, year, month, day, hour =
GetGuildBankMoneyTransaction(index)
```

Argument:

index — Index in the money log. (number)

Returns:

type — Type of the log event. (string)

- ▪ deposit — Deposit into the guild bank
- ▪ repair — Repair costs from the guild bank
- ▪ withdraw — Withdrawal from the guild bank

name — Player who did the withdrawal/deposit/repair; nil for unknown entries. (string)

year — Amount of years ago this event occurred. (number)

month — Amount of months ago this event occurred. (number)

day — Amount of days ago this event occurred. (number)

hour — Amount of hours ago this event occurred. (number)

Note: Information from the log is cached and can be inaccurate if the guild bank has not been opened recently.

GetGuildBankTabCost

Returns the cost of the next available guild bank tab.

```
tabCost = GetGuildBankTabCost()
```

Returns:

tabCost — The cost of the next guild bank tab, in copper. (number)

GetGuildBankTabInfo

Returns information about a given guild bank tab.

```
name, icon, isViewable, canDeposit, numWithdrawals, ↵
remainingWithdrawals = GetGuildBankTabInfo(tab)
```

Argument:

tab — The index of a guild bank tab. (number)

Returns:

name — The name of the guild tab. (string)

icon — The path to the tab's icon texture. (string)

isViewable — 1 if the guild tab is viewable, otherwise nil. (1nil)

canDeposit — 1 if the player can deposit into the guild bank tab. (1nil)

numWithdrawals — The maximum number of withdrawals the player can do in the tab. (number)

remainingWithdrawals — The number of withdrawals the player can make in the tab. (number)

Note: name and icon will only be set to their correct values if the player has visited the guild bank this session.

GetGuildBankTabPermissions

Returns the permissions the currently selected guild rank has for a given guild bank tab.

```
viewTab, canDeposit, numWithdrawals = GetGuildBankTabPermissions(tab)
```

Argument:

tab — The guild bank tab to query. (number)

Returns:

viewTab — 1 if the currently selected guild rank has permission to view the tab. (1nil)

canDeposit — 1 if the currently selected guild rank has permission to deposit items, otherwise nil. (1nil)

numWithdrawals — The number of withdrawals the currently selected guild rank is allowed for the given tab. (number)

GetGuildBankTransaction

Returns information about a specific guild bank item transaction.

```
type, name, itemLink, count, tab1, tab2, year, month, day, hour ↵
= GetGuildBankTransaction(tab, index)
```

Arguments:

tab — The index of the guild bank tab. (number)

index — The index of the log entry. (number)

Returns:

type — The type of transaction. (string)

- deposit
- withdraw
- repair
- move

name — The name of the player who completed the transaction. (string)

itemLink — The item link for the item involved. (string)

count — The number of items in the stack. (number)

tab1 — The source tab if the item was moved from one tab to another. (number)

tab2 — The destination tab if the item was moved from one tab to another. (number)

year — The number of years ago the transaction occurred. (number)

month — The number of months ago the transaction occurred. (number)

day — The number of days ago the transaction occurred. (number)

hour — The number of hours ago that the transaction occurred. (number)

Note: If this function is called prior to the logs being queried from the server, it will return an unknown type transaction that occurred at midnight on January 1, 1970 (UTC). Once the logs have been queried using QueryGuildBankLog(), the results will continue to be available via this function. This is of particular importance because the results continue to be available on other characters in other guilds as long as the client hasn't been closed.

GetGuildBankWithdrawLimit

Returns the guild bank gold withdrawal limit for the current rank being viewed in the guild control pane.

```
goldWithdrawLimit = GetGuildBankWithdrawLimit()
```

Returns:

goldWithdrawLimit — Gold withdrawal limit, with -1 being unlimited. (number)

Note: Only works for a guild master with the guild control pane open.

GetGuildBankWithdrawMoney

Returns the amount of gold the player can withdraw from the bank daily.

```
withdrawLimit = GetGuildBankWithdrawMoney()
```

Returns:

withdrawLimit — The amount of gold the player is allowed to withdraw from the bank daily, or -1 if no limit. (number)

GetGuildCharterCost

Returns the cost of a guild charter.

```
cost = GetGuildCharterCost()
```

Returns:

cost — The cost of a guild charter, in copper. (number)

Note: This function only works when talking to a guild master.

GetGuildEventInfo

Returns information on the guild log.

```
type, player1, player2, rank, year, month, day, hour =
GetGuildEventInfo(index)
```

Argument:

index — Guild event log index between 1 and GetNumGuildEvens().(number)

Returns:

type — Event Type. (string)

- ▪ demote — player1 demotes player2 to rank.
- ▪ invite — player1 invites player2 to the guild.
- ▪ join — player1 joins the guild.
- ▪ promote — player1 promotes player2 to rank.
- ▪ quit — player1 has quit the guild.
- ▪ remove — player1 removes player2 from the guild.

player1 — First actor in the log. (string)

player2 — Second actor in the log (string)

rank — Rank if applicable to the type of the event. (string)

year — Amount of years ago this event occurred. (number)

month — Amount of months ago this event occurred. (number)

day — Amount of days ago this event occurred. (number)

hour — Amount of hours ago this event occurred. (number)

GetGuildInfo

Retrieves information about a player's guild.

```
guildName, guildRankName, guildRankIndex = GetGuildInfo("unit" or
"name")
```

Arguments:

unit or name

unit — The unit ID to query. (unitid)

name — The name of the player to query. (string)

Returns:

guildName — The name of the guild. (string)

guildRankName — The player's guild rank. (string)

guildRankIndex — The index of the player's guild rank. (number)

GetGuildInfoText

Returns the information text for the player's guild. This is the longer information text that is shown via the Guild Information button on the Guild tab of the social interface. It is designed for longer static information, as opposed to the Guild MOTD.

```
guildInfoText = GetGuildInfoText()
```

Returns:

guildInfoText — A string containing the guild information text (including newline characters). (string)

Example:

```
-- Print the Guild Info Text to chat one line at a time, so it wraps
properly
local guildInfoText = GetGuildInfoText()
if guildInfoText then
  for line in guildInfoText:gmatch("[^\n]+\n") do
    ChatFrame1:AddMessage(line)
  end
end
```

Note: Only returns valid data after calling GuildRoster() and the GUILD_ROSTER_UPDATE event has fired.

GetGuildRecruitmentMode

Returns the current guild recruitment mode.

```
enabled = GetGuildRecruitmentMode()
```

Returns:

enabled — The mode of the guild recruitment channel. (number)

■ 0 — Don't join the guild recruitment channel.

■ 1 — Auto-join the guild recruitment channel if the player isn't in a guild.

GetGuildRosterInfo

Returns information about the selected player in your guild roster.

```
name, rank, rankIndex, level, class, zone, note, officernote, online,
status, classFileName = GetGuildRosterInfo(index)
```

Argument:

index — The player index in the guild roster. (number)

Returns:

name — The name of the player. (string)

rank — The rank of the player. (string)

rankIndex — The rank index of the player. (number)

level — The level of the player (number)

class — The (localized) class of the player. (string)

note — The public note of the player. (string)

officernote — The officer note of the player, if the player has permission to view it. (string)

online — 1 if the player is online, nil otherwise. (1nil)

status — The status of the player. (string)

- <AFK> — The player is currently away from keyboard.

- <DND> — The player does not want to be disturbed.

classFileName — The class filename of the player, unlocalized. (string)

Note: Only returns valid data after calling GuildRoster() and the GUILD_ROS-TER_UPDATE event has fired.

GetGuildRosterLastOnline

Returns the amount of time since a guild members has been seen online.

```
years, months, days, hours = GetGuildRosterLastOnline(index)
```

Argument:

index — The index of a member in the guild roster listing. (number)

Returns:

years — The number of years since the player was last online. (number)

months — The number of months since the player was last online. (number)

days — The number of days since the player was last online. (number)

hours — The number of hours since the player was last online. (number)

Note: Only returns valid data after calling GuildRoster() and the GUILD_ROS-TER_UPDATE event has fired.

GetGuildRosterMOTD

Returns the Message of the Day for your guild.

```
guildMOTD = GetGuildRosterMOTD()
```

Returns:

guildMOTD — The Guild Message of the Day. (string)

GetGuildRosterSelection

Returns the raid roster index of your currently selected guild member. The index for any given member depends on your current sorting and filtering settings in the raid window.

```
index = GetGuildRosterSelection()
```

Returns:

`index` — The index of your currently selected guild member, or `0` if none is selected. (number)

GetGuildRosterShowOffline

Returns whether the Show Offline setting is enabled in the Guild tab.

```
showOffline = GetGuildRosterShowOffline()
```

Returns:

`showOffline` — `1` if the Show Offline setting is enabled in the Guild tab, otherwise `nil`. (1nil)

GetGuildTabardFileNames

Returns the filenames of the textures that comprise the player's guild tabard.

```
tabardBackgroundUpper, tabardBackgroundLower, tabardEmblemUpper,
tabardEmblemLower, tabardBorderUpper, tabardBorderLower =
GetGuildTabardFileNames()
```

Returns:

`tabardBackgroundUpper` — The path to the texture for the upper background of the guild tabard. (string)

`tabardBackgroundLower` — The path to the texture for the lower background of the guild tabard. (string)

`tabardEmblemUpper` — The path to the texture for the upper emblem of the guild tabard. (string)

`tabardEmblemLower` — The path to the texture for the lower emblem of the guild tabard. (string)

`tabardBorderUpper` — The path to the texture for the upper border of the guild tabard. (string)

`tabardBorderLower` — The path to the texture for the lower border of the guild tabard. (string)

Note: If the player is not in a guild, this function will return nil.

GetHonorCurrency

Returns the number of honor points available to purchase rewards.

```
honorPoints = GetHonorCurrency()
```

Returns:

`honorPoints` — The number of honor points available to purchase rewards. (number)

GetIgnoreName

Returns the name of the specified ignored person.

```
name = GetIgnoreName(index)
```

Argument:

index — The index of the ignore. (string)

Returns:

name — The name of the ignored person. (string)

GetInboxHeaderInfo

Returns information on an inbox item.

```
packageIcon, stationeryIcon, sender, subject, money, CODAmount,
daysLeft, itemCount, wasRead, wasReturned, textCreated, canReply,
isGM, itemQuantity = GetInboxHeaderInfo(index)
```

Argument:

index — The index of the mail message to be queried. (number)

Returns:

packageIcon — The icon of the item or package being sent. If the mail contains just gold or a message, this will be nil. (string)

stationeryIcon — The icon for the message stationery. (string)

sender — The name of the sender. (string)

subject — The subject of the message. (string)

money — The amount of money in the message, in copper. (number)

CODAmount — The cost of the COD message, in copper. (number)

daysLeft — The amount of time left on the message, in days. (number)

itemCount — The number of items attached to the message. (number)

wasRead — 1 if the message has been read, otherwise nil. (1nil)

wasReturned — 1 if the message has been returned to the player, otherwise nil. (1nil)

textCreated — 1 if a copy of the message text has been made, otherwise nil. (1nil)

canReply — 1 if the player can reply to the message, otherwise nil. (1nil)

isGM — 1 if the message is from a game master, otherwise nil. (1nil)

itemQuantity — The number of items in the stack. This is only returned when the mail has a single item attachment. (number)

GetInboxInvoiceInfo

Returns information about an auction house invoice.

```
invoiceType, itemName, playerName, bid, buyout, deposit, consignment,
moneyDelay, etaHour, etaMin = GetInboxInvoiceInfo(index)
```

Argument:

`index` — The index of the invoice in the inbox. `(number)`

Returns:

`invoiceType` — The type of invoice. `(string)`

- `buyer` — An invoice for an item the player won.

- `seller` — An invoice for an item the player sold.

- `seller_temp_invoice` — A temporary invoice for an item the player sold. These are sent because there is an hour delay in receiving the funds from the auction house.

`itemName` — The name of the item. `(string)`

`playerName` — The name of the player the item was purchased from, or that purchased the item. `(string)`

`bid` — The winning bid amount, if a bid won the auction. `(number)`

`buyout` — The buyout amount, if a buyout won the auction. `(number)`

`deposit` — The amount of money paid in deposit. `(number)`

`consignment` — The auction house charge for selling your item. `(number)`

`moneyDelay` — The delay of pending payment, in minutes. Every auction house temporary invoice will have a delay of 60 minutes. `(number)`

`etaHour` — The hour portion of the estimated time of arrival for the payment. If the ETA is 9:37 server time, this value will be the number 9. `(number)`

`etaMin` — The minute portion of the estimated time of arrival for the payment. If the ETA is 9:37 server time, this value will be the number 37. `(number)`

GetInboxItem

Returns information about an item attached to received mail.

```
name, itemTexture, count, quality, canUse =
GetInboxItem(messageIndex, attachIndex)
```

Arguments:

`messageIndex` — The index of the message to query. `(number)`

`attachIndex` — The attachment index of the message to query (1-16). `(number)`

Returns:

name — The name of the item. (string)

itemTexture — The path to the item's icon. texture. (string)

count — The number of items in the stack. (number)

quality — The item quality. (number)

- 0 — Poor
- 1 — Common
- 2 — Uncommon
- 3 — Rare
- 4 — Epic
- 5 — Legendary
- 6 — Artifact

canUse — 1 if the item can be used by the player, otherwise nil. (1nil)

GetInboxItemLink

Returns the item link to the specified attachment.

```
itemlink = GetInboxItemLink(messageIndex, attachIndex)
```

Arguments:

messageIndex — The index of the message in your mailbox. (number)

attachIndex — The index of the attachment. (number)

Returns:

itemlink — The item link to the attachment in question. (string)

GetInboxNumItems

Returns the number of mail items currently in your inbox.

```
numItems = GetInboxNumItems()
```

Returns:

numItems — The number of items in the inbox. (number)

GetInboxText

Returns information about the text of an inbox message.

```
bodyText, texture, isTakeable, isInvoice = GetInboxText(index)
```

Argument:

index — The index of a mail item in the inbox. (number)

Returns:

bodyText — The text of the mail message. (string)

texture — The stationery texture to be displayed. (string)

isTakeable — 1 if the text of the message can be taken from the message, otherwise nil. (1nil)

isInvoice — 1 if the inbox message is an auction house invoice, otherwise nil. (1nil)

GetInspectArenaTeamData

Returns information about an inspect target's arena team.

```
teamName, teamSize, teamRating, teamPlayed, teamWins, playerPlayed,
playerRating, bg_red, bg_green, bg_blue, emblem, emblem_red,
emblem_green, emblem_blue, border, border_red, border_green,
border_blue = GetInspectArenaTeamData(index)
```

Argument:

index — The index of the arena team. These are indexed from smallest to largest, with the first team (normally 2v2) being 1. (number)

Returns:

teamName — The name of the arena team. (string)

teamSize — The size of the team (2 for 2v2, 3 for 2v2, and so on) (number)

teamRating — The team's rating. (number)

teamPlayed — The number of games played in the current arena period. (number)

teamWins — The number of games won in the current arena period. (number)

playerPlayed — The number of games the player has played in the current arena period. (number)

playerRating — The player's personal rating. (number)

bg_red — The red component color value for the background (0.0–1.0). (number)

bg_green — The green component color value for the background (0.0–1.0). (number)

bg_blue — The blue component color value for the background (0.0–1.0). (number)

emblem — The index of the team's emblem graphic. (number)

emblem_red — The red component color value for the emblem (0.0–1.0). (number)

emblem_green — The green componen color value for the emblem (0.0–1.0). (number)

emblem_blue — The blue component color value for the emblem (0.0–1.0). (number)

border — The index of the team's border graphic. (number)

border_red — The red component color value for the border (0.0–1.0). (number)

border_green — The green component color value for the border (0.0–1.0). (number)

border_blue — The blue component color value for the border (0.0–1.0). (number)

GetInspectHonorData

Returns honor information about an inspect target.

```
todayHK, todayHonor, yesterdayHK, yesterdayHonor, lifetimeHK, ↵
lifetimeRank = GetInspectHonorData()
```

Returns:

todayHK — The number of honor kills for today. (number)

todayHonor — The amount of honor earned today. (number)

yesterdayHK — The amount of honor kills for yesterday. (number)

yesterdayHonor — The amount of honor earned yesterday. (number)

lifetimeHK — The amount of honor kills over the player's lifetime. (number)

lifetimeRank — The highest earned rank in the old honor system. Valid returns can be determined with GetPVPRankInfo(). (number)

GetInstanceBootTimeRemaining

Returns the amount of time left until the player is removed from the current instance (for example, if the player has left a party and is still in that party's dungeon instance).

```
timeleft = GetInstanceBootTimeRemaining()
```

Returns:

timeleft — The number of seconds until the player is booted from the current instance. (number)

GetInstanceDifficulty

Returns your group's dungeon difficulty setting. This function returns a number from 1 to 3, indicating the current dungeon difficulty. 1 for normal, 2 for heroic, and 3 for epic (epic dungeons have not been implemented yet).

```
difficulty = GetInstanceDifficulty()
```

Returns:

difficulty — The group's dungeon difficulty setting (1–3). (number)

Example:

```
-- Print your current difficulty setting
local difficulty =
getglobal("DUNGEON_DIFFICULTY"..GetInstanceDifficulty())
DEFAULT_CHAT_FRAME:AddMessage("Your dungeon difficulty is set to " ..
difficulty)
```

GetInventoryAlertStatus

Returns the durability level of a given inventory slot. This function returns a durability indicator 0, 1, or 2, which can be used as a key to INVENTORY_ALERT_COLORS to get the corresponding color. This return is used to color the armored man when items go below a certain durability level.

```
status = GetInventoryAlertStatus(index)
```

Argument:

index — Inventory index to query. (number)

- 1 — Head
- 2 — Shoulders
- 3 — Chest
- 4 — Waist
- 5 — Legs
- 6 — Feet
- 7 — Wrists
- 8 — Hands
- 9 — Weapon
- 10 — Shield
- 11 — Ranged

Returns:

status — Number 0,1, or 2 indicating alert status. (number)

GetInventoryItemBroken

Returns whether the given inventory item is broken.

```
isBroken = GetInventoryItemBroken("unit", inventoryID)
```

Arguments:

unit — The unit ID to query. (unitid)

inventoryID — The inventory ID to query. (number)

Returns:

isBroken — 1 if the item is broken, otherwise nil. (1nil)

GetInventoryItemCooldown

Returns cooldown information about a current inventory item.

```
start, duration, enable = GetInventoryItemCooldown(unit, slotId)
```

Arguments:

unit — The unit ID to query. This unit can be the player, or the currently inspected unit. (unitid)

slotId — An inventory slot ID to query. This ID can be obtained by calling GetInventorySlotInfo() with a slot token. (string)

Returns:

start — The value of GetTime() at the moment the cooldown began, or 0. (number)

duration — The length of the cooldown, or 0. (number)

enable — 1 if the cooldown is enabled, otherwise 0. (number)

GetInventoryItemCount

Returns the number of items stacked in an inventory slot. This function currently only returns meaningful information for the ammo slot.

```
count = GetInventoryItemCount("unit", slotid)
```

Arguments:

unit — The unit to query. This is typically player, but this function also works for units that are being inspected. (unitid)

slotid — The inventory slot ID. (number)

Returns:

count — The amount of items stacked in the current inventory slot. (number)

GetInventoryItemDurability

Returns the durability stats for a given item.

```
durability, max = GetInventoryItemDurability(slot)
```

Argument:

slot — The inventory slot ID to query. This slot ID should be generated using the GetInventorySlotInfo function. (number)

Returns:

durability — The current durability. (number)

max — The maximum durability. (number)

Example:

```
-- Query HeadSlot durability
local slot = GetInventorySlotInfo("HeadSlot")
local durability,max = GetInventoryItemDurability(slot)
local msg = string.format("Head armor is currently at %s of %s
durability.", ↵
durability, max)
ChatFrame1:AddMessage(msg)
```

GetInventoryItemLink

Returns an item link for an inventory item.

```
link = GetInventoryItemLink("unit", inventoryID)
```

Argument:

unit — The unit ID to query. (unitid)

inventoryID — The inventory ID to query. (number)

Returns:

link — An item link for the given item. (string)

GetInventoryItemQuality

Returns the quality level of a given inventory item.

```
quality = GetInventoryItemQuality("unit", slotId)
```

Arguments:

unit — The unit ID to query. This unit can be the player or the currently inspected unit. (unitid)

slotId — An inventory slot ID to query. This ID can be obtained by calling GetInventorySlotInfo() with a slot token. (string)

Returns:

quality — The quality level of the item. (number)

- 0 — Poor
- 1 — Common
- 2 — Uncommon
- 3 — Rare
- 4 — Epic
- 5 — Legendary
- 6 — Artifact

GetInventoryItemTexture

Returns the item texture for a specific inventory item.

```
texture = GetInventoryItemTexture("unit", slot)
```

Arguments:

unit — The unit ID to query. This is normally player, but can also work on the unit you are currently inspecting. (unitid)

slot — The inventory slot to query. (number)

Returns:

texture — The path to the inventory item's icon texture. (string)

GetInventorySlotInfo

Returns information about an inventory slot.

`id, textureName, checkRelic = GetInventorySlotInfo("slotName")`

Arguments:

`slotName` — The name of an inventory slot to query. (`string`)

- `AmmoSlot` — Ranged ammo slot
- `BackSlot` — Back/cape slot
- `Bag0Slot` — First bag slot
- `Bag1Slot` — Second bag slot
- `Bag2Slot` — Third bag slot
- `Bag3Slot` — Fourth bag slot
- `ChestSlot` — Chest slot
- `FeetSlot` — Feet/boots slot
- `Finger0Slot` — First finger/ring slot
- `Finger1Slot` — Second finger/ring slot
- `HandsSlot` — Hand/gloves slot
- `HeadSlot` — Head/helmet slot
- `LegsSlot` — Legs/pants slot
- `MainHandSlot` — Main hand slot
- `NeckSlot` — Necklace slot
- `RangedSlot` — Ranged slot
- `SecondaryHandSlot` — Secondary hand/offhand slot
- `ShirtSlot` — Shirt slot
- `ShoulderSlot` — Shoulder slot
- `TabardSlot` — Tabard slot
- `Trinket0Slot` — First trinket slot
- `Trinket1Slot` — Second trinket slot
- `WaistSlot` — Waist/belt slot
- `WristSlot` — Wrist/bracer slot

Returns:

`id` — The numeric slot ID that should be used in other `GetInventory` functions. (`number`)

`texture` — The path to the texture to be displayed when this slot is empty. (`string`)

`checkRelic` — 1 if the slot is a relic slot on the given character, otherwise `nil`. The ranged slot token is reused for the relic slot, and this return distinguishes between the two. (`1nil`)

GetItemCooldown

Returns cooldown information about a given item.

```
start, duration, enable = GetItemCooldown("item" or itemId)
```

Arguments:

`item` or `itemId`

`item` — The name of the item to query. (`string`)

`itemId` — The item ID of the item to query. (`number`)

Returns:

`start` — The value of `GetTime()` at the moment the cooldown began, or `0`. (`number`)

`duration` — The length of the cooldown, or `0`. (`number`)

`enable` — `1` if the cooldown is enabled, otherwise `0`. (`number`)

GetItemCount

Returns the number of a given item the player has in possession (possibly including bank).

```
itemCount = GetItemCount(itemId or "itemName" or "itemLink" [,
includeBank])
```

Arguments:

`itemId` or `itemName` or `itemLink`

`itemId` — An item ID. (`number`)

`itemName` — An item name. (`string`)

`itemLink` — An item link. (`string`)

`includeBank` — `true` to include items in the bank in the returned count, otherwise `false`. (`boolean`)

Returns:

`itemCount` — The number of the given item the player has in his or her possession (possibly including items in the bank). (`number`)

GetItemGem

Returns the name and link for a gem in a specific item socket.

```
name, link = GetItemGem("name" or "itemlink", index)
```

Arguments:

`name` or `itemLink`

`name` — The name of an item. (`string`)

`itemLink` — A valid item link. (`string`)

`index` — The index of the socket to query. (`number`)

Returns:

name — The name of the gem in the socket, or nil. (string)

link — The item link for the gem in the socket. (string)

GetItemInfo

Returns information about an item by name, link, or ID. This function is client-side, so it will only return information if the item being queried is in your local item cache at the time the call is made. If you have not seen the item's tooltip since the last time the cache was cleared, the function will return nil. The item cache is usually cleared on patches and server restarts, but this can also happen when the cache folder is deleted. All of this function's string returns are in the client's locale with the exception of equipSlot, which is a token that points to the localized string.

```
name, link, quality, iLevel, reqLevel, type, subType, maxStack,
equipSlot, texture = GetItemInfo(itemID or "itemName" or "itemLink")
```

Arguments:

itemID or itemName or itemLink

itemID — An item's ID. (number)

itemName — An item's name. (string)

itemLink — An item's link. (string)

Returns:

name — The name of the item. (string)

link — A link for the item. (string)

quality — The item's quality. (number)

- ▪ 0 — Poor
- ▪ 1 — Common
- ▪ 2 — Uncommon
- ▪ 3 — Rare
- ▪ 4 — Epic
- ▪ 5 — Legendary
- ▪ 6 — Artifact

iLevel — The internal item level. (number)

reqLevel — The minimum required level to use the item. (number)

type — The item type. This may be the class of item (such as Armor or Weapon) or another item class such as quest. (string)

subType — The item's subtype. (string)

maxStack — The maximum stack size for the item. (number)

equipSlot — A token indicating where the item can be equipped, or the empty string. (string)

- ■ INVTYPE_2HWEAPON — Two-hand
- ■ INVTYPE_AMMO — Ammo
- ■ INVTYPE_BAG — Bag
- ■ INVTYPE_BODY — Shirt
- ■ INVTYPE_CHEST — Chest
- ■ INVTYPE_CLOAK — Back
- ■ INVTYPE_FEET — Feet
- ■ INVTYPE_FINGER — Finger
- ■ INVTYPE_HAND — Hands
- ■ INVTYPE_HEAD — Head
- ■ INVTYPE_HOLDABLE — Held in Off-hand
- ■ INVTYPE_LEGS — Legs
- ■ INVTYPE_NECK — Neck
- ■ INVTYPE_QUIVER — Quiver
- ■ INVTYPE_RANGED — Ranged
- ■ INVTYPE_RANGEDRIGHT — Ranged
- ■ INVTYPE_RELIC — Relic
- ■ INVTYPE_ROBE — Chest
- ■ INVTYPE_SHIELD — Off-hand
- ■ INVTYPE_SHOULDER — Shoulder
- ■ INVTYPE_TABARD — Tabard
- ■ INVTYPE_THROWN — Thrown
- ■ INVTYPE_TRINKET — Trinket
- ■ INVTYPE_WAIST — Waist
- ■ INVTYPE_WEAPON — One-hand
- ■ INVTYPE_WEAPONMAINHAND — Main-hand
- ■ INVTYPE_WEAPONOFFHAND — Off Hand
- ■ INVTYPE_WRIST — Wrist

texture — The path to the item's icon texture. (string)

GetItemQualityColor

Returns the red, green, and blue components of the color for the given item quality index. Also returns a hex representation of the same color.

```
redComponent, greedComponent, blueComponent, hexColor =
GetItemQualityColor(index)
```

Argument:

index — The item quality index. Any indexes outside of the following values will be interpreted as a request for quality index 1. (number)

- ▪ 0 — Poor
- ▪ 1 — Common
- ▪ 2 — Uncommon
- ▪ 3 — Rare
- ▪ 4 — Epic
- ▪ 5 — Legendary
- ▪ 6 — Artifact

Returns:

redComponent — The red component of the item quality's color. It is a floating point number from 0.0 to 1.0. (number)

greenComponent — The green component of the item quality's color. It is a floating point number from 0.0 to 1.0. (number)

blueComponent — The blue component of the item quality's color. It is a floating point number from 0.0 to 1.0. (number)

hexColor — The hex color code for the given item quality, including the |c at the beginning. (string)

GetItemSpell

Returns information about the spell cast when using a given item.

```
name, rank = GetItemSpell("itemName" or itemId)
```

Arguments:

itemName or itemId

itemName — The name of the item to query. (string)

itemId — An itemId to query. (number)

Returns:

name — The name of the spell that is cast when using the given item. These are internal spell names that can't be cast directly. (string)

rank — The rank of the spell cast. (string)

GetLFGPartyResults

Returns information about a member of a party in the LFG results.

```
name, level, class = GetLFGPartyResults(type, lfgNdx, index,
partyIndex)
```

Arguments:

type — The type of LFG query. Valid values can be obtained using GetLFG-Types(). (number)

lfgNdx — The dungeon/quest index of the query. Valid values can be obtained using GetLFGTypeEntries(). (number)

index — The index of the result in the LFG window. (number)

partyIndex — The index of the member of the party. This does not include the party leader. (number)

Returns:

name — The name of the player. (string)

level — The level of the player, as a string. (string)

class — The localized class of the player. (string)

GetLFGResults

Returns information about a specific line of an LFM/LFG query.

```
name, level, zone, class, criteria1, criteria2, criteria3,
comment, numPartyMembers, isLFM, classFileName = GetLFGResults(type,
lfgNdx, index)
```

Arguments:

type — The type of LFG query. Valid values can be obtained using GetLFG-Types(). (number)

lfgNdx — The dungeon/quest index of the query. Valid values can be obtained using GetLFGTypeEntries(). (number)

Returns:

name — The name of the player. (string)

level — The player's level. (number)

zone — The player's current location. (string)

class — The player's class. (string)

criteria1 — The player's first selected LFG/LFM option. (string)

criteria2 — The player's second selected LFG/LFM option. (string)

criteria3 — The player's third selected LFG/LFM option. (string)

comment — The player's comment, if any. (string)

numPartyMembers — The number of current party members. (number)

isLFM — true if the player is looking for more members, otherwise nil. (boolean)

classFileName — The uppercase English name of the player's class. (string)

GetLFGStatusText

Returns information on your current Looking for Group status.

```
isLFG, numCriteria, ... = GetLFGStatusText()
```

Returns:

`isLFG` — `true` if the character is looking for group, `false` if looking for more. `(boolean)`

`numCriteria` — Number of extra criteria after this parameter. `(number)`

`...` — Repeating list of `isLFG`, `numCriteria` pairs. `(list)`

Note: The criteria are the strings you can select from the dropdown box in the LFG UI (Quest names/Dungeon names/Zone names).

GetLFGTypeEntries

Returns the valid entries of a specific type in the LFG system.

```
entry, token, ... = GetLFGTypeEntries(type)
```

Argument:

`type` — The type of LFG request. `(number)`

- 1 — Dungeon
- 2 — Raid
- 3 — Quest (Group)
- 4 — Zone
- 5 — Heroic dungeon

Returns:

`entry` — The name of the entry. `(string)`

`token` — A token subtype for the entry. For example, the token for each entry of the Zones type returns the name of the continent the zone is on, while the tokens for dungeons return a token representing the dungeon. `(string)`

`...` — A repeating list of entries and tokens. `(list)`

GetLFGTypes

Returns the type of possible LFG queries.

```
... = GetLFGTypes()
```

Returns:

`...` — The type of looking for group queries, as a list of strings. `(string)`

GetLanguageByIndex

Returns the localized name of the language identified by the index being queried.

```
language = GetLanguageByIndex(index)
```

Argument:

`index` — The index of the language being queried. Runs from `1` to `GetNumLanguages()`. (number)

Returns:

`language` — The name of the language, such as Common or Gnomish. (string)

GetLatestThreeSenders

Returns the names of the last three senders of unchecked mail.

```
sender1, sender2, sender3 = GetLatestThreeSenders()
```

Returns:

`sender1` — The name of the sender of an unchecked mail. (string)

`sender2` — The name of the sender of an unchecked mail. (string)

`sender3` — The name of the sender of an unchecked mail. (string)

GetLocale

Returns the four-character locale code indicating what language the client uses.

```
locale = GetLocale()
```

Returns:

`locale` — A four-character locale code indicating what language the client uses. (string)

- `deDE` — German
- `enGB` — British English
- `enUS` — American English
- `esES` — Spanish
- `frFR` — French
- `koKR` — Korean
- `zhCN` — Chinese (simplified)
- `zhTW` — Chinese (traditional)

GetLookingForGroup

Retrieves information about the player's LFG status.

```
type1, name1, type2, name2, type3, name3, lfmType, lfmName, comment,
queued, lfgStatus, lfmStatus, autoaddStatus = GetLookingForGroup()
```

Returns:

type1 — The index of the first selected group type. (number)

name1 — The index of the first selected objective. (number)

type2 — The index of the second selected group type. (number)

name2 — The index of the second selected objective. (number)

type3 — The index of the third selected group type. (number)

name3 — The index of the third selected objective. (number)

lfmType — The index of the selected group type on the LFM tab. (number)

lfmName — The index of the selected objective on the LFM tab. (number)

comment — The comment entered on the LFG tab. (string)

queued — true if the player is queued to join a group (Auto-Join is checked), false otherwise. (boolean)

lfgStatus — true if the player is looking for a group, false otherwise. (boolean)

lfmStatus — true if the player is looking for more players for his group, false otherwise. (boolean)

autoaddStatus — true if the player chooses to automatically add members to his group that fit the criteria, false otherwise. (boolean)

GetLootMethod

Retrieves information about the group's loot setting.

```
lootMethod, partyMaster, raidMaster = GetLootMethod()
```

Returns:

lootMethod — The currently active loot method. (string)

- freeforall — Free for All
- group — Group Loot
- master — Master Looter
- needbeforegreed — Need before Greed
- roundrobin — Round Robin

partyMaster — The party unit ID of the player who is currently the loot master. (number)

raidMaster — The raid unit ID of the player who is currently the loot master. (number)

GetLootRollItemInfo

Returns information about the specified item to roll on.

```
texture, name, count, quality, bindOnPickUp = GetLootRollItemInfo(id)
```

Argument:

id — The index of the loot roll. Each new item that is rolled on increments this number by one, so two items won't have the same roll index. (number)

Returns:

texture — The icon texture of the item. (string)

name — The name of the item. (string)

count — The stack size of the item. (number)

quality — The quality of the item. (number)

- 0 — Poor
- 1 — Common
- 2 — Uncommon
- 3 — Rare
- 4 — Epic
- 5 — Legendary
- 6 — Artifact

bindOnPickUp — 1 if the item is bound on pickup, nil otherwise. (1nil)

GetLootRollItemLink

Returns an item link for the specified item.

```
link = GetLootRollItemLink(id)
```

Argument:

id — The index of the loot roll. Each new item that is rolled on increments this number by one, so two items won't have the same roll index. (number)

Returns:

link — An item link for the given loot roll item. (string)

GetLootRollTimeLeft

Returns the amount of time left on the given loot roll, in milliseconds.

```
timeLeft = GetLootRollTimeLeft(id)
```

Argument:

id — The index of the loot roll. Each new item that is rolled on increments this number by one, so two items won't have the same roll index. (number)

Returns:

timeLeft — The amount of time left on given the loot roll, in milliseconds. (number)

GetLootSlotInfo

Returns the information for a loot slot item.

```
texture, item, quantity, quality, locked = GetLootSlotInfo(slot)
```

Argument:

slot — The index of the loot item. (number)

Returns:

texture — The path of the graphical icon for the item. (string)

item — The name of the item. (string)

quantity — The quantity of the item in the stack. Quantity for coins is always 0. (number)

quality — The quality of the item. (number)

- 0 — Poor
- 1 — Common
- 2 — Uncommon
- 3 — Rare
- 4 — Epic
- 5 — Legendary
- 6 — Artifact

locked — Whether the item is locked by having an action currently run on it. (boolean)

GetLootSlotLink

Returns an item link for a given loot window slot.

```
link = GetLootSlotLink(slot)
```

Argument:

slot — A slot index in the loot window. (number)

Returns:

link — An item link for the given item. (string)

GetLootThreshold

Returns the current loot threshold setting.

```
threshold = GetLootThreshold()
```

Returns:

threshold — Loot threshold. (number)

- ■ 0 — Poor
- ■ 1 — Common
- ■ 2 — Uncommon
- ■ 3 — Rare
- ■ 4 — Epic
- ■ 5 — Legendary
- ■ 6 — Artifact

GetMacroBody

Returns the body of a given macro index.

body = GetMacroBody(index)

Argument:

index — The macro index to query. The global macro IDs are 1–18, while the player-specific macros are stored in 19–36. (number)

Returns:

body — The body of the macro, as a text string. (string)

GetMacroIconInfo

Returns the texture for a given macro icon index.

texture = GetMacroIconInfo(index)

Argument:

index — The index of a macro icon. (number)

Returns:

texture — The path to the macro's icon texture. (string)

GetMacroIndexByName

Converts a macro name to macro index.

index = GetMacroIndexByName("name")

Argument:

name — The name of a macro. (string)

Returns:

index — The index of the given named macro, or 0. (number)

GetMacroInfo

Returns name, texture, and body of a given macro.

```
name, texture, body, isLocal = GetMacroInfo(macroIndex)
```

Argument:

`macroIndex` — The macro index to query. Macros `1–18` are the general macros, while `19–36` are character-specific. `(number)`

Returns:

`name` — The name of the macro. `(string)`

`texture` — The path to the macro's icon texture. `(string)`

`body` — The body of the macro. `(string)`

`isLocal` — Whether the macro is stored locally or on the server (currently unused; all macros are stored locally). `(1nil)`

GetMacroItem

Returns information about an item used in a macro, if its next action would be to use an item. (If the macro doesn't use an item, or if the next action in a macro using conditionals or cast sequences is not to use an item, returns `nil`.)

```
name, link = GetMacroItem(macroIndex or "macroName")
```

Arguments:

`macroIndex` or `macroName`

`macroIndex` — The index of a macro to query. `(number)`

`macroName` — The name of a macro to query. `(string)`

Returns:

`name` — The name of the item that will be used by the given macro. `(string)`

`link` — An item link for the given item. `(string)`

GetMacroItemIconInfo

Returns the texture for macro item icons. This is used by the default UI to display possible icons for the guild bank, consisting of all item icons.

```
texture = GetMacroItemIconInfo(index)
```

Argument:

`index` — The index of the icon to query. `(number)`

Returns:

`texture` — The path to the item's icon texture. `(string)`

GetMacroSpell

Returns the spell a given macro is set to cast. This function can be used by action bar addons to display dynamic macro icons and tooltips. In a macro that uses conditionals or cast sequences, this function can be queried to get the next spell that will be cast.

```
name, rank = GetMacroSpell(slot)
```

Argument:

slot — The macro slot to query. (number)

Returns:

name — The name of the spell the macro is set to cast. (string)

rank — The rank of the spell, if applicable. (string)

GetManaRegen

Returns the mana regeneration statistics for the player. Return values are in mana per second.

```
base, casting = GetManaRegen()
```

Returns:

base — The amount of mana the player regenerates each tick while not casting. (number)

casting — The amount of mana the player regenerates each tick while casting. (number)

GetMapContinents

Returns a list of the map continents.

```
... = GetMapContinents()
```

Returns:

... — The names of all valid continent names, as a list of strings. (string)

GetMapInfo

Returns the map information about the current world map texture.

```
mapFileName, textureHeight, textureWidth = GetMapInfo()
```

Returns:

mapFileName — The name of the file containing the textures for the current world map. (string)

textureHeight — The height of the specified texture. (number)

textureWidth — The width of the specified texture. (string)

GetMapLandmarkInfo

Returns information about a map landmark, such as a PvP objective.

`name, description, textureIndex, x, y = GetMapLandmarkInfo(index)`

Argument:

index — The index of a map landmark, from 1 to `GetNumMapLandmarks()` (number)

Returns:

name — The name of the landmark. (string)

description — The description of the landmark. This may contain dynamic information such as the status of a battleground objective. (string)

textureIndex — The index of the texture to be used for the landmark. These indices map to the `Interface/Minimap/POIIcons.blp` graphic, starting with 1 in the upper-left corner of the image. (number)

x — The X coordinate for the image's location as a proportion of the map's current width (number)

y — The Y coordinate for the image's location as a proportion of the map's current height (number)

GetMapOverlayInfo

Returns information about a world map overlay (the map pieces that appear as you explore the world).

`textureName, textureWidth, textureHeight, offsetX, offsetY, mapPointX, mapPointY = GetMapOverlayInfo(index)`

Argument:

index — The index of a world map overlay. (number)

Returns:

textureName — The path to the overlay texture file. (string)

textureWidth — The width of the texture, in pixels. (number)

textureHeight — The height of the texture, in pixels. (number)

offsetX — The X offset for anchoring the overlay with relation to the world map. (number)

offsetY — The Y offset for anchoring the overlay with relation to the world map. (number)

mapPointX — Unknown, always seems to return 0. (number)

mapPointY — Unknown, always seems to return 0. (number)

GetMapZones

Returns the map zones for a given continent.

```
... = GetMapZones(continentIndex)
```

Argument:

`continentIndex` — The index of a world continent. `(number)`

- ▪ `1` — Kalimdor
- ▪ `2` — Eastern Kingdoms
- ▪ `3` — Outland

Returns:

`...` — A list of strings containing all of the map zones in the given continent. `(string)`

Example:

```
local continent = GetCurrentMapContinent()
local zones = {GetMapZones(continent)}
for idx,zone in ipairs(zones) do
  ChatFrame1:AddMessage("Zone #"..idx .. ": " .. zone)
end
```

GetMasterLootCandidate

Returns information about a given loot candidate. This function is used to build the master looter dropdown and only works when the player is the master looter and the loot frame is open.

```
candidate = GetMasterLootCandidate(index)
```

Argument:

`index` — Party or raid index: `1-4` for party, `1-40` for raid. `(number)`

Returns:

`candidate` — Name of the candidate. `(string)`

GetMaxDailyQuests

Returns the maximum number of daily quests that can be completed each day.

```
max = GetMaxDailyQuests()
```

Returns:

`max` — The maximum number of daily quests that can be completed each day. `(number)`

GetMerchantItemCostInfo

Returns the cost of a merchant item in honor points, arena points, and marks.

```
honorPoints, arenaPoints, itemCount = GetMerchantItemCostInfo(index)
```

Argument:

index — The index of the item to query. (number)

Returns:

honorPoints — The cost of the item in honor points. (number)

arenaPoints — The cost of the item in arena points. (number)

itemCount — The number of different types of items (such as epic set tokens, battleground marks of honor, or Ogri'la crystals) that make up the alternate currency for purchasing this item. (number)

GetMerchantItemCostItem

Returns information about an item used as currency to purchase another item (such as battleground rewards).

```
itemTexture, itemValue = GetMerchantItemCostItem(index, itemIndex)
```

Arguments:

index — The index of an item in the merchant window. (number)

itemIndex — The index of the item cost associated with the item for sale, from 1 to itemCount (where itemCount is the third return from GetMerchantItemCostInfo). (number)

Returns:

itemTexture — The texture for the item that is acting as currency. (string)

itemValue — The number of that item required for the given purchase. (number)

GetMerchantItemInfo

Returns information about an item available at a merchant.

```
name, texture, price, quantity, numAvailable, isUsable, ↵
extendedCost = GetMerchantItemInfo(index)
```

Returns:

name — The name of the item. (string)

texture — The path to the item's icon texture. (string)

price — The price of the item in copper. (number)

quantity — The number of items per stack. (number)

numAvailable — The number of items available for purchase. (number)

isUsable — 1 if the item is usable, otherwise nil. (1nil)

extendedCost — 1 if the item has an extended cost (alternate currency) such as arena points, honor points, or items to be turned in (such as epic loot tokens or battleground marks). Details for such currency can be found by calling GetMerchantItemCostInfo and GetMerchantItemCostItem. (1nil)

GetMerchantItemLink

Returns the full link of the item in question or `nil` if the index is out of range.

```
itemLink = GetMerchantItemLink(index)
```

Argument:

`index` — The index of the item whose link you want returned should be within the range 1 to `GetMerchantNumItems()`. (number)

Returns:

`itemLink` — The link of the item being queried or `nil` if the index is not valid. (string)

GetMerchantItemMaxStack

Returns how many of a merchant item you can purchase in one transaction. This function determines the largest value you can use for the quantity argument of `BuyMerchantItem`. For most merchant items, this will be the same as the maximum stack size of the item. Items that are purchased in preset stacks (most food and drink, spices, ammunition, and so on) will have a `maxStack` of 1 because you can only buy one preset stack at a time.

```
maxStack = GetMerchantItemMaxStack(index)
```

Argument:

`index` — The merchant index of the desired merchant item. (number)

Returns:

`maxStack` — The largest quantity of the item you can purchase at once. (number)

Example:

```
-- Buy the most of a merchant item that you can at once
BuyMerchantItem(index, GetMerchantItemMaxStack())
```

See also: `GetMerchantItemInfo()`, `BuyMerchantItem()`

GetMerchantNumItems

Returns the total number of items that a merchant has to sell.

```
numMerchantItems = GetMerchantNumItems()
```

Returns:

`numMerchantItems` — The number of items that a merchant has to sell. (number)

GetMinimapZoneText

Returns the zone text for use on the minimap.

```
zoneText = GetMinimapZoneText()
```

Returns:

`zoneText` — The name of the area the player is currently in. (string)

GetMirrorTimerInfo

Returns information about a mirror timer (breath, exhaustion, and so on).

```
timer, value, maxvalue, scale, paused, label =
GetMirrorTimerInfo(index)
```

Argument:

index — The index of the timer to query. (number)

Returns:

timer — The name of the timer. (string)

value — The current value of the timer. (number)

maxvalue — The maximum value of the timer. (number)

scale — The scale by which to multiply the timer. (number)

paused — If the timer is paused. (number)

label — The label to be displayed on the timer. (string)

GetMirrorTimerProgress

Returns the progress of a mirror timer (breath, exhaustion, and so on). This function is used to check the status of a mirror timer. Possible timers are BREATH, EXHAUSTION, DEATH, and FEIGNDEATH (keys of the MirrorTimerColors table in FrameXMLMirrorTimer.lua). The progress is the number of milliseconds left on the timer.

```
progress = GetMirrorTimerProgress("timer")
```

Argument:

timer — The type of timer to check. (string)

Returns:

progress — The progress of the timer in milliseconds. (number)

GetModifiedClick

Returns the modifiers set (for example, Ctrl-Shift) for the given modified click.

```
modifiers = GetModifiedClick("name")
```

Argument:

name — The name of the modified click to query. (string)

Returns:

modifiers — The modifiers set for the given modified click (nil if the modified click could not be found). (string)

GetModifiedClickAction

Returns the token/name for a modified click action.

```
action = GetModifiedClickAction(index)
```

Argument:

index — The index of a modified click action. Valid indices seem to be between 1 and GetNumModifiedClickActions(), with not every single index returning an action. (number)

Returns:

action — The name/token for the given action. (string)

GetMoney

Returns the amount of money the player currently possesses.

```
money = GetMoney()
```

Returns:

money — Amount of money the player possesses, in copper. (number)

Example:

```
local money = GetMoney()
local gold = floor(abs(money / 1000))
local silver = floor(abs(mod( cost / 100, 100)))
local copper = floor(abs(mod(cost,100)))

DEFAULT_CHAT_FRAME:AddMessage( string.format("I have %d gold %d ↵
silver %d copper.", gold, silver, copper ) )
```

GetMouseButtonClicked

Returns which mouse button triggered the current click. If called in a line of execution that started with a click handler (OnMouseDown, OnMouseUp, OnClick, OnDoubleClick, PreClick, or PostClick), returns a string identifying which mouse button triggered the handler. Otherwise, it returns nil.

```
button = GetMouseButtonClicked()
```

Returns:

button — The name of the mouse button that triggered the given click. (string)

GetMouseButtonName

Converts a mouse button number to a mouse button name.

```
buttonName = GetMouseButtonName(buttonNumber)
```

Argument:

buttonNumber — A mouse button number (1–5). (number)

Returns:

buttonName — The name of the given mouse button. (string)

- ■ LeftButton

- ■ RightButton

- ■ MiddleButton

- ■ Button4

- ■ Button5

GetMouseFocus

Returns the frame that is currently under the mouse and has mouse input enabled.

```
frame = GetMouseFocus()
```

Returns:

frame — The frame that currently has the mouse focus. (table)

Example:

```
-- Returns the name of the frame under the mouse, if it's named
local frame = GetMouseFocus()
if not frame then
  ChatFrame1:AddMessage("There is no mouse enabled frame under ↵
the cursor")
else
  local name = frame:GetName() or tostring(frame)
  ChatFrame1:AddMessage(name .. " has the mouse focus")
end
```

GetMultisampleFormats

Returns the available multi-sample formats. This function is used to build the multisampling strings in the client, such as "24-bit color 24-bit depth 6x multisample."

```
color, depth, multisample, ... = GetMultisampleFormats()
```

Returns:

color — The color depth as a number. Possible values would include 16 for 16-bit color depth, 24 for 24-bit, and so on (number)

depth — The video depth in bits. (number)

multisample — The multisampling setting. (number)

. . . — A list of color, depth, and multisample values listing the multisample formats available to the client. (list)

GetMuteName

Gets name of a character on the player's mute list.

```
name = GetMuteName(index)
```

Argument:

`index` — The index of an entry in the mute listing. (number)

Returns:

`name` — The name of the player being voice muted. (string)

GetMuteStatus

Returns whether the given player or unit ID is muted. If the optional argument `mode` is specified, the squelch list for that channel will be checked. If the player has explicitly muted another player, this will always return 1 for that player. If a party or raid member has been squelched by the party leader and the `mode` argument is specified, the function will return 1.

```
muteStatus = GetMuteStatus("unitId", "mode")
```

Arguments:

`unitId` or `fullname`

`unitId` — The unit ID to query. (unitId)

`fullname` — The name of the player to query. (string)

`mode` — Either party, raid, or nil. (string)

Returns:

`muteStatus` — 1 if the player is muted, otherwise `nil`. (1nil)

GetNetStats

Returns the game's network statistics.

```
bandwidthIn, bandwidthOut, latency = GetNetStats()
```

Returns:

`bandwidthIn` — The current incoming bandwidth (download) usage, measured in KB/s. (number)

`bandwidthOut` — The current outgoing bandwidth (upload) usage, measured in KB/s. (number)

`latency` — The current latency to the server, measured in milliseconds (number)

Note: The values of the `bandwidthIn` and `bandwidthOut` returns are updated constantly, but the value of the latency return updates once every 30 seconds.

GetNewSocketInfo

Returns information about a gem to be socketed. If the given socket in the Item Socketing UI contains a new gem (one that has been placed in the UI but not yet confirmed for permanent socketing in the item), returns info for that gem. If the socket is empty or has a permanently socketed gem but no new gem, returns nil.

```
name, icon, gemMatchesSocket = GetNewSocketInfo(index)
```

Argument:

index — The socket index. (number)

Returns:

name — The name of the gem that would be socketed. (string)

icon — The path to the new gem's icon texture. (string)

gemMatchesSocket — 1 if the gem being socketed matches the socket color, otherwise nil. (1nil)

GetNewSocketLink

Returns an item link for a gem to be socketed. If the given socket in the Item Socketing UI contains a new gem (one that has been placed in the UI but not confirmed for permanently socketing in the item yet), returns an item link for that gem. If the socket is empty or has a permanently socketed gem but no new gem, returns nil.

```
link = GetNewSocketLink(index)
```

Argument:

index — The index of the item socket to query. (number)

Returns:

link — The item link of the gem to be set in the given socket. (string)

See also: GetExistingSocketLink()

GetNextStableSlotCost

Returns the cost of the next available stable slot.

```
money = GetNextStableSlotCost()
```

Returns:

money — The cost of the next available stable slot, in copper. (number)

GetNumActiveQuests

Returns the number of currently active quests by this player for this NPC.

```
numActiveQuests = GetNumActiveQuests()
```

Returns:

numActiveQuests — Number of currently active quests from this NPC. (number)

GetNumAddOns

Returns the number of addons in the addon listing.

```
numEntrys = GetNumAddOns()
```

Returns:

numEntrys — The number of addons in the addon listing. (number)

GetNumArenaTeamMembers

Returns the number of members in a given arena team.

```
numMembers = GetNumArenaTeamMembers(teamindex [,showOffline])
```

Arguments:

teamindex — The index of the arena team, based on the order in which they are displayed in the PvP tab. (number)

showOffline — 1 to show offline members, otherwise nil. This argument is not working as of Patch 2.3. (1nil)

GetNumAuctionItems

Returns the number of auction items for a given type of listing.

```
numBatchAuctions, totalAuctions = GetNumAuctionItems("type")
```

Argument:

type — The type of auction listing to query. (string)

- ▪ bidder — Auctions on which the player has bid
- ▪ list — Auctions available for purchase
- ▪ owner — Items that the player has placed up for auction

Returns:

numBatchAuctions — The number of auctions in the current page of the listing. (number)

totalAuctions — The number of total auctions available for the given listing. (number)

GetNumAvailableQuests

Returns the number of available quests at the current NPC.

```
numAvailableQuests = GetNumAvailableQuests()
```

Returns:

numAvailableQuests — The number of available quests. If the player is not interacting with a quest-giving NPC, returns 0. (number)

GetNumBankSlots

Returns information about purchased bank bag slots.

`numSlots, isFull = GetNumBankSlots()`

Returns:

`numSlots` — The number of bank slots you have purchased. `(number)`

`isFull` — A flag indicating that you cannot purchase any more slots. `(1nil)`

GetNumBattlefieldFlagPositions

Returns the number of battleground flags in the current zone.

`numFlags = GetNumBattlefieldFlagPositions()`

Returns:

`numFlags` — The number of battleground flags to display. `(number)`

GetNumBattlefieldPositions

Returns the number of battleground team members for which position information can be queried via `GetBattlefieldPosition`.

`numTeamMembers = GetNumBattlefieldPositions()`

Returns:

`numTeamMembers` — Number of players for whom position information is available. `(number)`

Note: The `BattlefieldPosition` APIs no longer return useful information now that WoW automatically puts all battleground members into a raid group; use raid APIs instead.

GetNumBattlefieldScores

Returns the number of scores available in the current battleground.

`numScores = GetNumBattlefieldScores()`

Returns:

`numScores` — Number of scores in the current battleground or `0` if not currently in a battleground. `(number)`

GetNumBattlefieldStats

Returns the number of battleground-specific columns to be displayed in the score frame.

`numStats = GetNumBattlefieldStats()`

Returns:

`numStats` — The number of battlefield-specific columns to be displayed in the score frame. `(number)`

GetNumBattlefields

Returns the number of available battleground instances.

```
numBattlefields = GetNumBattlefields()
```

Returns:

`numBattlefields` — The number of available instances. If the player is not currently conversing with a battlemaster, this function may return `0` or an older cached value. `(number)`

GetNumBindings

Returns the number of key binding actions listed in the Key Bindings window.

```
numBindings = GetNumBindings()
```

Returns:

`numBindings` — The number of key binding actions available to be bound to key combinations. `(number)`

GetNumBuybackItems

Returns the number of items available on the buyback tab.

```
numBuybackItems = GetNumBuybackItems()
```

Returns:

`numBuybackItems` — The number of items available to be repurchased. `(number)`

GetNumChannelMembers

Returns the number of members in a specific chat channel.

```
numMembers = GetNumChannelMembers(id)
```

Argument:

`id` — Chat channel ID. `(number)`

Returns:

`numMembers` — Number of players in the queried chat channel. `(number)`

GetNumCrafts

Returns the number of items in the crafting window.

```
numCrafts = GetNumCrafts()
```

Returns:

`numCrafts` — The number of items present in the crafting window. `(number)`

Note: The crafting window is currently only used for the Enchanting and Pet Training professions.

GetNumDisplayChannels

Returns the number of channels in the channel display.

```
channelCount = GetNumDisplayChannels()
```

Returns:

`channelCount` — The number of channels (including headers) displayed in the chat tab channel display. (`number`)

GetNumFactions

Returns the number of factions the player has encountered.

```
numFactions = GetNumFactions()
```

Returns:

`numFactions` — The number of factions the player has encountered. (`number`)

GetNumFrames

Returns the number of created frame objects (and derivatives).

```
numFrames = GetNumFrames()
```

Returns:

`numFrames` — The number of frame objects (and derivatives) created. This value does not include textures and fontstrings. (`number`)

GetNumFriends

Returns the number of friends on the player's friend list.

```
numFriends = GetNumFriends()
```

Returns:

`numFriends` — The number of friends on the player's friend list. (`number`)

GetNumGossipActiveQuests

Returns the number of currently active quests in the gossip window.

```
num = GetNumGossipActiveQuests()
```

Returns:

`num` — The number of currently active quests in the gossip window. (`number`)

GetNumGossipAvailableQuests

Returns the number of available quests in the gossip window.

```
num = GetNumGossipAvailableQuests()
```

Returns:

`num` — The number of available quests in the gossip window. (`number`)

GetNumGossipOptions

Returns the number of options in the current gossip frame. This function is used by the default user interface to bypass non-quest and non-story pages in the gossip window.

```
numOptions = GetNumGossipOptions()
```

Returns:

numOptions — Number of gossip options available in the current instance. (number)

GetNumGuildBankMoneyTransactions

Returns the number of guild bank money transactions available for the money log.

```
numTransactions = GetNumGuildBankMoneyTransactions()
```

Returns:

numTransactions — The number of guild bank money transactions available for the money log. (number)

GetNumGuildBankTabs

Gives the number of purchased tabs for the guild bank. This function works without being at the actual guild bank.

```
numTabs = GetNumGuildBankTabs()
```

Returns:

numTabs — Number of purchased guild bank tabs. This value returns 0 if the player is unguilded. (number)

GetNumGuildBankTransactions

Returns the number of transactions for the specified guild bank tab.

```
numTransactions = GetNumGuildBankTransactions(tab)
```

Argument:

tab — The index of the guild bank tab to query. (number)

Returns:

numTransactions — The number of transactions that happened on the selected guild bank tab. (number)

Note: The guild bank log is limited to 25 transactions. Also, this function will always return 0 until QueryGuildBankLog(tab) has been called.

GetNumGuildEvents

Returns the number of available guild events for the guild log.

```
numEvents = GetNumGuildEvents()
```

Returns:

`numEvents` — Returns the number of guild log events available. These entries are only made available via event callback from the function `QueryGuildEventLog()`. (number)

GetNumGuildMembers

Returns the number of members in the player's guild.

```
numGuildMembers = GetNumGuildMembers()
```

Returns:

`numGuildMembers` — The number of members in the player's guild. (number)

GetNumIgnores

Returns the number of people currently on the player's ignore list.

```
numIgnores = GetNumIgnores()
```

Returns:

`numIgnores` — The number of people currently on the ignore list. (number)

GetNumLFGResults

Returns the number of results from an LFG query.

```
numResults, totalCount = GetNumLFGResults(type, index)
```

Arguments:

`type` — The type of LFGQuery, obtained from `GetLFGTypes()`. (number)

`index` — The index of an LFG entry, obtained from `GetLFGTypeEntries()`. (number)

Returns:

`numResults` — The number of results available. (number)

`totalCount` — The total number of results. (number)

GetNumLanguages

Returns the number of languages the player is capable of speaking.

```
numLanguages = GetNumLaguages()
```

Returns:

`numLanguages` — The number of languages the player is capable of speaking. (number)

GetNumLootItems

Returns the number of items available to be looted.

```
numItems = GetNumLootItems()
```

Returns:

`numItems` — The number of the items available to be looted. (number)

GetNumMacroIcons

Returns the number of available macro icons.

```
numMacroIcons = GetNumMacroIcons()
```

Returns:

`numMacroIcons` — The number of available macro icons. (number)

GetNumMacroItemIcons

Returns the number of available macro item icons. This is a different set of icons from the normal available macro icons, as it includes the icons for every item in game. This is used by the guild bank interface to allow the user to select an icon for a specific tab.

```
numIcons = GetNumMacroItemIcons()
```

Returns:

`numIcons` — The number of available macro item icons. (number)

GetNumMacros

Returns the number of macros the player has stored.

```
numAccountMacros, numCharacterMacros = GetNumMacros()
```

Returns:

`numAccountMacros` — The number of account-wide macros stored. (number)

`numCharacterMacros` — The number of character-specific macros stored. (number)

GetNumMapLandmarks

Returns the number of points of interest on the world map.

```
numPOIs = GetNumMapLandmarks()
```

Returns:

`numPOIs` — The number of points of interest on the world map. (number)

See also: `GetMapLandmarkInfo()`

GetNumMapOverlays

Returns the number of overlays for the current world map. An overlay is an area that can be discovered, revealing that part of the map.

```
numOverlays = GetNumMapOverlays()
```

Returns:

`numOverlays` — The number of overlays for the given world map. (`number`)

GetNumModifiedClickActions

Returns the number of registered modified click actions.

```
num = GetNumModifiedClickActions()
```

Returns:

`num` — The number of modified click actions. This function may return a nonsense value when there are no modified click actions loaded. (`number`)

GetNumMutes

Returns the number of characters on the player's mute list.

```
numMuted = GetNumMutes()
```

Returns:

`numMuted` — The number of characters on the player's mute list. (`number`)

GetNumPackages

Returns the number of packages. This appears to be a holdover from the stationery system that was never fully implemented.

```
numPackages = GetNumPackages()
```

Returns:

`numPackages` — Number of packages. (`number`)

GetNumPartyMembers

Returns the number of members in your party. This does not include the player. Results can be 0–4.

```
numPartyMembers = GetNumPartyMembers()
```

Returns:

`numPartyMembers` — Number of members in your party. (`number`)

GetNumPetitionNames

Returns the number of people who have signed the open petition.

```
numNames = GetNumPetitionNames()
```

Returns:

`numNames` — The number of names that have currently signed the open petition. (`number`)

GetNumQuestChoices

Returns the number of available options from which the player can choose his or her quest reward in an NPC quest completion dialog.

```
numQuestChoices = GetNumQuestChoices()
```

Returns:

numQuestChoices — The number of quest reward options. (number)

GetNumQuestItems

Returns the number of items necessary to complete the active quest.

```
numRequiredItems = GetNumQuestItems()
```

Returns:

numRequiredItems — The number of required items to complete the quest. (number)

GetNumQuestLeaderBoards

Returns the number of quest objectives for a given quest.

```
numObjectives = GetNumQuestLeaderBoards([index])
```

Argument:

index (optional) — The index of a quest in the quest log. This will default to GetQuestLogSelection() if index isn't supplied. (number)

Returns:

numObjectives — The number of trackable quest objectives. (number)

GetNumQuestLogChoices

Returns the number of reward choices for the currently selected quest in the quest log.

```
numChoices = GetNumQuestLogChoices()
```

Returns:

numChoices — The number of reward choices for the currently selected quest in the quest log. (number)

GetNumQuestLogEntries

Returns the number of quest log entries.

```
numEntries = GetNumQuestLogEntries()
```

Returns:

numEntries — The number of quest log entries. (number)

GetNumQuestLogRewards

Returns the count of the rewards for a particular quest.

```
numRewards = GetNumQuestLogRewards()
```

Returns:

`numRewards` — The number of rewards for this quest. (number)

GetNumQuestRewards

Returns the number of quest rewards for completing a quest. This function does not work in the quest log and only returns the number of guaranteed rewards. If there is a choice of rewards, they will not be included in this count.

```
numQuestRewards = GetNumQuestRewards()
```

Returns:

`numQuestRewards` — The number of quest rewards you are guaranteed to get upon completion of the currently displayed quest. (number)

GetNumQuestWatches

Returns the number of quests currently marked for objective watching.

Returns:

`numWatches` — The number of quests from the quest log currently marked for watching. (number)

GetNumRaidMembers

Returns the number of members of the player's raid.

```
numRaidMembers = GetNumRaidMembers()
```

Returns:

`numRaidMembers` — The number of members in the current raid, or 0. This value will include the player as a member of the raid. (number)

GetNumRoutes

Returns the number of routes available from a given taxi node.

```
numRoutes = GetNumRoutes(index)
```

Argument:

`index` — Taxi node index. (number)

Returns:

`numRoutes` — Number of routes from this node. (number)

GetNumSavedInstances

Returns the number of instances to which the player is saved. (Currently, this is only used for raid instances.)

```
savedInstances = GetNumSavedInstances()
```

Returns:

`savedInstances` — The number of instances to which the player is currently saved. `(number)`

GetNumShapeshiftForms

Returns the number of available shapeshift forms for the player.

```
numForms = GetNumShapeshiftForms()
```

Returns:

`numForms` — The number of available shapeshift forms for the player. `(number)`

GetNumSkillLines

Returns the number of skills to be listed in the Skills window. These are the skills that are listed in the Skills tab on the Character frame, such as professions, languages, and weapon skills.

```
numSkills = GetNumSkillLines()
```

Returns:

`numSkills` — The number of skills the player currently knows. `(number)`

GetNumSockets

Returns the number of sockets in the open item. This function only functions when the item is open in the `ItemSocketingFrame`.

```
numSockets - GetNumSockets()
```

Returns:

`numSockets` — The number of available sockets for the open item. `(number)`

GetNumSpellTabs

Returns the number of spell tabs the player has available.

```
numSkillLineTabs = GetNumSpellTabs()
```

Returns:

`numTabs` — The number of spell tabs. `(number)`

Example:

```
-- Prints the names of all spell tabs to chat
for i = 1, GetNumSpellTabs() do
  local name = GetSpellTabInfo(i);
  ChatFrame1:AddMessage(name);
end
```

GetNumStablePets

Returns the number of stabled pets.

```
numPets = GetNumStablePets()
```

Returns:

numPets — The number of stabled pets. This value does not include your current pet.

GetNumStableSlots

Returns the number of stable slots the player has purchased.

```
numSlots = GetNumStableSlots()
```

Returns:

numSlots — The number of stable slots the player currently owns. (number)

GetNumStationeries

Returns the number of available stationeries.

```
numStationeries = GetNumStationeries()
```

Returns:

numStationeries — The number of available stationeries. (number)

GetNumTalentTabs

Returns the number of talent tabs for the player or the currently inspected unit.

```
numTabs = GetNumTalentTabs(inspect)
```

Argument:

inspect — true to query the currently inspected unit, false to query talent info for the player. (boolean)

Returns:

numTabs — The number of talent tabs. (number)

GetNumTalents

Returns the number of talent spell options in a given tab. This function is used internally by the default interface to draw the talent trees.

```
numTalents = GetNumTalents(tabIndex)
```

Argument:

tabIndex — The index of the talent tab to query. (number)

Returns:

numTalents — The number of talent spells in the given tab. (number)

GetNumTitles

Returns the number of available player titles.

```
numTitles = GetNumTitles()
```

Returns:

numTitles — The number of available player titles. (number)

Example:

```
-- Print all available titles to ChatFrame1
for i=1,GetNumTitles() do
  ChatFrame1:AddMessage(GetTitleName(i))
end
```

GetNumTrackingTypes

Returns the number of available tracking types.

```
count = GetNumTrackingTypes()
```

Returns:

count — The number of available tracking types. (number)

GetNumTradeSkills

Returns the number of available tradeskill items and headers. If you do not have a tradeskill open, this will always return 0. This function is used to control the list view in a tradeskill window.

```
numSkills = GetNumTradeSkills()
```

Returns:

numSkills — The number of tradeskills, including headers. (number)

Note: Enchanting is not considered a tradeskill. Please see the Craft functions for more information.

GetNumTrainerServices

Returns the number of available trainer services.

```
numServices = GetNumTrainerServices()
```

Returns:

numServices — The number of available trainer service. (number)

GetNumVoiceSessionMembersBySessionID

Returns the number of members in a voice channel.

```
numMembers = GetNumVoiceSessionMembersBySessionID(sessionId)
```

Argument:

sessionId — A unique session ID returned from ChannelPulloutRoster_
GetSessionIDByName(). (number)

Returns:

numMembers — The number of members in a given voice channel. (number)

GetNumVoiceSessions

Returns the number of voice sessions the player is in. The number of voice sessions means the number of channels for which the user can choose to activate voice chat. This function returns 0 if voice chat is deactivated.

```
count = GetNumVoiceSessions()
```

Returns:

count — The number of voice sessions. (number)

GetNumWhoResults

Returns the number of results from a who request.

```
numResults, totalCount = GetNumWhoResults()
```

Returns:

numResults — The number of results returned. (number)

totalCount — The number of actual results. (number)

GetNumWorldStateUI

Returns the number of world state lines (Arathi Basin points, Black Morass portals, and so on).

```
numUI = GetNumWorldStateUI()
```

Returns:

numUI — Returns the number of current world state lines. (number)

GetObjectiveText

Returns the objective text for the currently displayed quest.

```
questObjective = GetObjectiveText()
```

Returns:

questObjective — The objective text for the currently displayed quest. (string)

GetOwnerAuctionItems

Queries the server for a page of self-posted auctions. Tells the WoW client to retrieve data from the server for the auctions you've posted. If there are more than 50 such auctions, the index identifies which page to retrieve. This data can then be inspected with the other GetAuction API functions.

```
GetOwnerAuctionItems(page)
```

Argument:

page — Which page of self-posted auctions to query. (number)

GetPVPDesired

Returns whether the player has manually toggled the PvP flag on.

```
isPVPDesired = GetPVPDesired()
```

Returns:

isPVPDesired — 1 if the PvP flag was toggled on by the player manually, 0 otherwise. (number)

GetPVPLifetimeStats

Returns lifetime honorable kills and the highest PvP rank the player has attained.

```
hk, highestRank = GetPVPLifetimeStats()
```

Returns:

hk — The number of honorable kills the player has achieved. (number)

highestRank — The highest PvP rank the player has achieved. (number)

GetPVPRankInfo

Returns information about a given PvP rank index.

```
rankName, rankNumber = GetPVPRankInfo(index [, "unit"])
```

Arguments:

index — The PvP index to query. This index begins at 1, which maps to a negative (and unused) PvP rank called "Pariah." The initial PvP rank is found at index 5. (number)

unit — A unit to use as the base faction for the PvP info. The faction of the rank name (such as Legionnaire versus Knight-Captain for rank 8) is determined by the faction of this unit. (unitid)

Returns:

rankName — The name of the PvP rank for the given faction. (string)

rankNumber — The numeric rank. This will be different from the rank that was passed in as an argument. (number)

Note: These PvP ranks are no longer obtainable.

Example:

```
-- Print all the PvP ranks for your faction to ChatFrame1
for i=1,18 do
  local name,rank = GetPVPRankInfo(i)
  if name then
    ChatFrame1:AddMessage("RankId: " .. i .. " Name: " .. name .. "
Rank: " .. rank)
  end
end
```

GetPVPSessionStats

Returns the PvP stats for the current session.

```
honorKills, honorPoints = GetPVPSessionStats()
```

Returns:

honorKills — The estimated number of honor kills for the given session. (number)

honorPoints — The estimated number of honor points for the given session. (number)

GetPVPTimer

Returns the amount of time until the player's PvP flag expires.

```
timer = GetPVPTimer()
```

Returns:

timer — If PvP is enabled, this value is 300000 (five minutes). If PvP is disabled, this value is -1. If the player has requested to disable PvP, it is the number of milliseconds until the PvP flag turns off. (number)

GetPVPYesterdayStats

Returns the player's PvP stats from yesterday.

```
kills, honor = GetPVPYesterdayStats()
```

Returns:

kills — The number of honor kills the player earned yesterday. (number)

honor — The number of honor points earned yesterday. (number)

GetPackageInfo

Returns information on the given package. Currently unused; index 1 always returns a Test Package.

```
name, texture, somenumber = GetPackageInfo(index)
```

Argument:

index — Package Index. Between 1 and GetNumPackages().(number)

Returns:

name — Package name. (string)

texture — Icon for this package. (string)

somenumber — Use currently unknown. (number)

GetParryChance

Returns the player's percentage parry chance.

```
chance = GetParryChance()
```

Returns:

chance — Player's parry chance as a percentage. (number)

GetPartyAssignment

Returns whether a player is assigned a specific role (main tank, main assist).

```
isAssigned = GetPartyAssignment("assignment" [,"unit"] [,exactMatch])
```

Arguments:

assignment — The assignment to query. (string)

- ▪ MAINASSIST — The player is assigned as a main assist.
- ▪ MAINTANK — The player is assigned as a main tank.

unit or name

unit — The unit ID to query. (unitid)

exactMatch — Used when the name argument is supplied; 1 to match the name exactly; otherwise, match the closest name. (1nil)

Returns:

isAssigned — 1 if the player is assigned the specified role, otherwise nil. (1nil)

GetPartyLeaderIndex

Returns the index of the current party leader.

```
index = GetPartyLeaderIndex()
```

Returns:

index — The index of the party leader, or 0. (number)

- ▪ 0 — The player is not in a party, or the player is the party leader.
- ▪ 1 — party1 is the party leader.
- ▪ 2 — party2 is the party leader.
- ▪ 3 — party3 is the party leader.
- ▪ 4 — party4 is the party leader.

GetPartyMember

Returns whether a given party index exists in the player's party.

```
hasMember = GetPartyMember(index)
```

Argument:

index — The index of the party member to query (1–4). (number)

Returns:

hasMember — 1 if there is a party member at the given index of the player's party, otherwise nil. (1nil)

GetPetActionCooldown

Returns cooldown information about a given pet action slot.

```
start, duration, enable = GetPetActionCooldown(index)
```

Argument:

slot — The pet action slot to query for cooldown information. (number)

Returns:

start — The value of GetTime() at the moment the cooldown began, or 0. (number)

duration — The length of the cooldown, or 0. (number)

enable — 1 if the cooldown is enabled, otherwise 0. (number)

GetPetActionInfo

Returns information about a pet action.

```
name, subtext, texture, isToken, isActive, autoCastAllowed,
autoCastEnabled = GetPetActionInfo(index)
```

Argument:

index — The index of the pet action on the pet's action bar. (number)

Returns:

name — The name of the action. (string)

subtext — The secondary text for the action (for example, Passive, Rank 1, and so on). (string)

texture — The path to the action's icon texture. (string)

isToken — 1 if the name/texture were token strings such as PET_ACTION_ATTACK and PET_ATTACK_TEXTURE rather than raw name/texture. (1nil)

isActive — 1 if the action is currently active, otherwise nil. (1nil)

autoCastAllowed — 1 if autocast is allowed for the given action. (1nil)

autoCastEnabled — 1 if autocast is enabled for the given action. (1nil)

GetPetActionsUsable

Returns whether the pet's actions are usable. This is used in the default user interface to gray out the actions at times when pet actions are not allowed (such as when the player is stunned).

```
petActionsUsable = GetPetActionsUsable()
```

Returns:

petActionsUsable — 1 if the pet's actions are usable, otherwise nil. (1nil)

GetPetExperience

Returns the pet's current experience and the amount required to level.

```
currXP, nextXP = GetPetExperience()
```

Returns:

currXP — The current experience value for the pet. (number)

nextXP — The experience required to reach the next level. (number)

GetPetFoodTypes

Returns a list of strings enumerating the food types your current pet can eat.

```
... = GetPetFoodTypes()
```

Returns:

... — A list of available food types for the current pet or nil if no food types available. (string)

- ■ Bread — Baked goods
- ■ Cheese — Cheese products
- ■ Fish — Fish products
- ■ Fruit — Fruit products
- ■ Fungus — Mushrooms and the like
- ■ Meat — Meat products

GetPetHappiness

Returns information about the player's pet's happiness.

```
happiness, damagePercentage, loyaltyRate = GetPetHappiness()
```

Returns:

happiness — The happiness level of the pet. (number)

- ■ 1 — Unhappy
- ■ 2 — Content
- ■ 3 — Happy

damagePercentage — The percentage multiplier for the pet's damage. This is affected by the pet's happiness. (number)

loyaltyRate — The current rate of loyalty gain or loss. Positive values indicate that the pet is gaining loyalty, while negative values indicate the pet is losing loyalty. (number)

GetPetIcon

Returns the icon the player's pet would have if stabled.

```
icon = GetPetIcon()
```

Returns:

icon — The path to the pet's icon texture or nil. (string)

GetPetLoyalty

Returns the loyalty level for the player's pet.

```
loyaltyText = GetPetLoyalty()
```

Returns:

`loyaltyText` — The localized loyalty text for the player's pet. (`string`)

GetPetTimeRemaining

Returns the time till the despawning of a temporary pet, such as a priest's shadowfriend or a mage's water elemental.

```
petTimeRemaining = GetPetTimeRemaining()
```

Returns:

`petTimeRemaining` — Time till the despawning in milliseconds; `nil` without a temporary pet. (`number`)

GetPetTrainingPoints

Returns training point information for your pet. This function determines how many training points your pet has and how many you have spent so far. If you don't have a pet summoned or your pet doesn't use training points, both values will be `0`.

```
totalPoints, spent = GetPetTrainingPoints()
```

Returns:

`totalPoints` — The total number of training points. (`number`)

`spent` — The number of training points you've already spent. (`number`)

Example:

```
- Print the number of training points your pet has left to spend
local total, spent = GetPetTrainingPoints()
DEFAULT_CHAT_FRAME:AddMessage("Your pet has " .. total-spent ↵
.. " training points remaining.")
```

GetPetitionInfo

Returns information about the currently open petition.

```
petitionType, title, bodyText, maxSignatures, originatorName,
isOriginator, minSignatures = GetPetitionInfo()
```

Returns:

`petitionType` — The type of the petition. (`string`)

- ■ `arena` — An arena team charter
- ■ `guild` — A guild charter

`title` — The title of the petition. (`string`)

`bodyText` — The text (body) of the petition. (`string`)

`maxSignatures` — The maximum number of signatures allowed. (`number`) originatorName — The person who initially purchased the charter. (string)

isOriginator — 1 if the current player is the charter's originator. (1nil)

minSignatures — The minimum number of signatures required for this charter. (number)

GetPetitionItemInfo

Returns information about a given petition to create an arena team.

```
name, texture, price = GetPetitionItemInfo(index)
```

Argument:

index — The index of the petition item. (number)

Returns:

name — The name of the petition. (string)

texture — The path to the petition's icon texture. (string)

price — The cost of the petition, in copper. (number)

GetPetitionNameInfo

Returns the name of the player that has signed a given petition slot.

```
name = GetPetitionNameInfo(index)
```

Argument:

index — The signature slot in the open petition. (number)

Returns:

name — The name of the player who has signed the given slot. (string)

GetPlayerBuff

Returns information about the player's buffs.

```
buffIndex, untilCancelled = GetPlayerBuff(index [, "filter"])
```

Arguments:

index — The index of the buff to query. (number)

filter — A filter to use when querying the buffs. (string)

- CANCELABLE — Show buffs that are cancelable
- HARMFUL — Show harmful buffs
- HELPFUL — Show helpful buffs
- NOT_CANCELABLE — Show buffs that can't be canceled

Returns:

buffIndex — A buff index that can be used in the other PlayerBuff functions. (number)

untilCancelled — 1 if the buff will persist until canceled, otherwise nil. (1nil)

GetPlayerBuffApplications

Returns the number of applications (stacks) for a given buff on the player.

```
count = GetPlayerBuffApplications(buffIndex)
```

Argument:

`buffIndex` — The index of the player's buff. (`number`)

Returns:

`count` — The number of applications (stacks) of the given buff. If the buff is not stackable, this will return `0`. (`number`)

GetPlayerBuffDispelType

Returns the dispel type of a given buff.

```
dispelType = GetPlayerBuffDispelType(buffIndex)
```

Argument:

`buffIndex` — The index of the player buff. (`number`)

Returns:

`dispelType` — The dispel type of the buff as a string or `nil` if not dispellable. (`string`)

- ▪ `Poison`
- ▪ `Magic`
- ▪ `Disease`
- ▪ `Curse`

GetPlayerBuffName

Returns information about a buff on the player.

```
name, rank = GetPlayerBuffName(index or "name" [,"rank"])
```

Arguments:

`index` — Index of the buff to query. Starts at `1` (top-right buff in the default UI) and goes through `16`. (`integer`)

`name` — Name of the buff to query. Same value is returned, so this can be used to see if a buff is present or to query the rank of the buff. (`string`)

`rank` — Rank of the buff to query. Does not include the parentheses. Same value is returned back, so this can be used to see if a specific rank is present. (`string`)

Returns:

`name` — Name of the buff queried, if present, `nil` otherwise. (`string`)

`rank` — Rank of the buff queried, if present; the empty string if buff has no rank; `nil` if not present. (`string`)

Example:

```
local name, rank = GetPlayerBuffName("Inner Fire")
— "Inner Fire", "Rank 4"
local name, rank = GetPlayerBuffName(1)
— "Shadowform", ""
local name, rank = GetPlayerBuffName("Made Up Buff of Pure Win")
— nil
```

GetPlayerBuffTexture

Returns the texture for a given buff on the player.

```
texture = GetPlayerBuffTexture(buffIndex)
```

Argument:

buffIndex — The index of the buff to query. (number)

Returns:

texture — The path to the buff's icon texture. (string)

GetPlayerBuffTimeLeft

Returns the time left on the selected buff on the player.

```
timeLeft = GetPlayerBuffTimeLeft(buffIndex)
```

Argument:

buffIndex — The index of the buff to check. (number)

Returns:

timeLeft — The time left on the selected buff, in seconds. (number)

GetPlayerMapPosition

Returns a unit's position on the current map zoom. Map positions can only be retrieved for player units that are currently in the player's party/raid. If the unit is not anywhere on the map of the current map zoom, both return values will be 0.

```
playerX, playerY = GetPlayerMapPosition("player")
```

Argument:

player — A unit ID that refers to the current player or any player character in their party/raid. (unitid)

Returns:

playerX — A number between 0 and 1 that is the specified unit's X map position on the current map zoom, from the left side of the map. (number)

playerY — A number between 0 and 1 that is the specified unit's Y map position on the current map zoom, from the top of the map. (number)

GetPlayerTradeMoney

Returns the amount of money the player deposited in an open trade window.

```
copper = GetPlayerTradeMoney()
```

Returns:

`copper` — The amount of the player's money (in copper) currently in the trade window. (number)

GetPossessInfo

Returns information about the spells in the possess bar. The possess bar is used by the default user interface to switch the main action bar to the spells of your possession target for Mind Control and similar effects.

```
texture, name = GetPossessInfo(index)
```

Argument:

`index` — The index of the possess bar entry to query. (number)

Returns:

`texture` — Full path to the icon texture of the spell in the queried possess bar slot. (string)

`name` — The name of the spell in the queried possess bar slot. (string)

GetProgressText

Returns the quest progress text given by an NPC.

```
text = GetProgressText()
```

Returns:

`text` — The progress text for a given quest. This is the text displayed when turning a quest in to an NPC. The progress text will be displayed, and the Continue option will be available to turn in the quest, as long as the objectives are complete. (string)

GetQuestBackgroundMaterial

Returns the background material for a given quest.

```
material = GetQuestBackgroundMaterial()
```

Returns:

`material` — The background material for the currently displayed quest. Currently, this returns `nil` and defaults to `parchment` in the `QuestFrame` code. (string)

GetQuestGreenRange

Returns the maximum difference between a quest's level and the player's level at which the quest is still classified as "easy" and labeled with in green by the default UI (as opposed to a "trivial" quest, which is colored gray and will not generate XP when turned in). For example, this returns 8 for a level 70 player, indicating that quests of level 62 and above will generate XP when turned in, but a level 61 quest will not; for a level 10 player this returns 5, indicating that only quests level 5 and above will provide XP.

```
range = GetQuestGreenRange()
```

Returns:

range — The maximum level difference for a quest to show in green. (number)

GetQuestIndexForTimer

Returns the index in the quest log for the given timer in the QuestTimer frame.

```
questIndex = GetQuestIndexForTimer(index)
```

Argument:

index — Timer index to query. (number)

Returns:

questIndex — Index in the quest log. (number)

GetQuestIndexForWatch

Returns the index in the quest log of a currently watched quest.

```
questIndex = GetQuestIndexForWatch(index)
```

Argument:

index — The index of a quest in the "watched" quest list. (number)

Returns:

questIndex — The index of the watched quest in the quest log. (number)

GetQuestItemInfo

Returns basic information about the quest items for the quest currently shown in the gossip window.

```
name, texture, numItems, quality, isUsable =
GetQuestItemInfo(itemType, itemNum)
```

Arguments:

itemType — Type of quest item to filter on. (string)

- ▪ choice — Possible reward for the quest
- ▪ required — Required for the quest
- ▪ reward — Reward for the quest

itemNum — The item number for which to get info. (number)

Returns:

name — The name of the quest item. (string)

texture — The path to the quest item's texture. (string)

numItems — How many of the quest item. (number)

quality — The quality of the quest item. (number)

(number) — If the quest item is usable by the current player. (boolean)

GetQuestItemLink

Returns an item link for a quest item (reward or requirement).

```
link = GetQuestItemLink("type", index)
```

Argument:

type — The type of quest item. (string)

- ▪ required — A quest item required to complete the quest
- ▪ reward — A quest reward

Returns:

link — The item link for the quest item. (string)

GetQuestLogChoiceInfo

Returns information about an item available as a quest reward choice for a quest in the quest log.

```
name, texture, numItems, quality, isUsable =
GetQuestLogChoiceInfo(index)
```

Argument:

index — The index of a quest reward choice. (number)

Returns:

name — The name of the item. (string)

texture — The texture of the item. (string)

numItems — The number of items in the stack. (number)

quality — The quality of the item. (number)

- ▪ 0 — Poor
- ▪ 1 — Common
- ▪ 2 — Uncommon
- ▪ 3 — Rare
- ▪ 4 — Epic
- ▪ 5 — Legendary
- ▪ 6 — Artifact

isUsable — 1 if the item is usable, otherwise nil. (1nil)

GetQuestLogGroupNum

Returns the suggested group size to complete the currently selected quest.

```
suggestedGroup = GetQuestLogGroupNum()
```

Returns:

suggestedGroup — The suggested group size to complete the quest selected in the quest log, or 0. (number)

GetQuestLogItemLink

Returns the item link of a specific item in the quest log reward or progress frame.

```
itemLink = GetQuestLogItemLink(type, index)
```

Argument:

type — The type of item on the questlog frame. (string)

- choice — The reward items the player can choose from upon finishing the quest.

- required — The items required to finish the quest.

- reward — The reward items the player always gets.

Note: The required type is only available when visiting a quest NPC with the gossip frame open and viewing an active quest.

GetQuestLogLeaderBoard

Returns information about objectives for a quest in the quest log.

```
text, type, finished = GetQuestLogLeaderBoard(objective [, questIndex])
```

Arguments:

objective — The index of the objective to query. (number)

questIndex (optional) — The index of the quest in the quest log. If this isn't supplied, it defaults to the currently selected quest log entry. (number)

Returns:

text — The text of the objective. (string)

type — The type of objective. (string)

- item
- object
- monster
- reputation
- event

finished — 1 if the objective is complete, otherwise nil. (1nil)

GetQuestLogPushable

Determines if the currently selected quest can be shared with your party members.

```
pushable = GetQuestLogPushable()
```

Returns:

pushable — 1 if the quest is shareable, nil otherwise. (1nil)

GetQuestLogQuestText

Retrieves the text fields for the quest log details panel of the currently active quest.

```
questDescription, questObjectives = GetQuestLogQuestText()
```

Returns:

questDescription — The description of the quest. (string)

questObjectives — The objectives of the quest. (string)

GetQuestLogRequiredMoney

Returns the amount of money required for the selected quest.

```
money = GetQuestLogRequiredMoney()
```

Returns:

money — The amount of required money for the selected quest. (number)

GetQuestLogRewardHonor

Returns the amount of honor rewarded for completing the currently selected quest in the quest log.

```
honor = GetQuestLogRewardHonor()
```

Returns:

honor — The amount of honor rewarded for completing the quest. (number)

GetQuestLogRewardInfo

Returns information about a quest reward.

```
name, texture, numItems, quality, isUsable =
GetQuestLogRewardInfo(index)
```

Argument:

index — The index of the entry in the quest log. (number)

Returns:

`name` — The name of the item. (`string`)

`texture` — The path to the item's icon texture. (`string`)

`numItems` — The number of items in the stack. (`number`)

`quality` — The quality of the item. (`number`)

- ■ 0 — Poor
- ■ 1 — Common
- ■ 2 — Uncommon
- ■ 3 — Rare
- ■ 4 — Epic
- ■ 5 — Legendary
- ■ 6 — Artifact

`isUsable` — 1 if the item is usable by the player, otherwise `nil`. (`1nil`)

GetQuestLogRewardMoney

Returns the amount of money rewarded on quest completion.

```
money = GetQuestLogRewardMoney()
```

Returns:

`money` — The amount of money rewarded on quest completion, in copper. (`number`)

GetQuestLogRewardSpell

Returns information about a quest reward spell. This is used internally by the default UI to change the text displayed above the reward spell. For example, tradeskill recipes show "You will learn how to create:" whereas normal spells are shown as "You will learn:".

```
texture, name, isTradeskillSpell, isSpellLearned =
GetQuestLogRewardSpell()
```

Returns:

`texture` — The path to the spell icon's texture. (`string`)

`name` — The name of the spell. (`string`)

`isTradeskillSpell` — 1 if the spell is a tradeskill recipe, otherwise `nil`. (`1nil`)

`idSpellLearned` — 1 if the reward spell will be learned, otherwise `nil`. (`1nil`)

GetQuestLogSelection

Returns the index of the currently selected quest in the quest log.

```
questID = GetQuestLogSelection()
```

Returns:

`questID` — The index of the quest that is currently selected. (number)

Example:

```
- Returns information about the currently selected quest
local index = GetQuestLogSelection()
local name = GetQuestLogTitle(index)
if name then
  ChatFrame1:AddMessage("Currently viewing " .. name)
end
```

GetQuestLogTimeLeft

Returns the amount of time left on the current timed quest.

```
questTimer = GetQuestLogTimeLeft()
```

Returns:

`questTimer` — The amount of time left on the current timed quest. (number)

GetQuestLogTitle

Returns information about a quest in your quest log. If `questTag` is not nil, and `isDaily` is true, `questTag` will be formatted with DAILY_QUEST_TAG_TEMPLATE when displayed in the `QuestLogFrame`.

```
questLogTitleText, level, questTag, suggestedGroup, isHeader,
isCollapsed, isComplete, isDaily = GetQuestLogTitle(index)
```

Argument:

`questID` — The index of the quest about which you wish to get information. (number)

Returns:

`questLogTitleText` — The title of the quest or nil if the index is out of range. (string)

`level` — The level of the quest. (number)

`questTag` — The type of quest. (string)

- `Dungeon` — Dungeon or instance quest
- `Elite` — Elite quest
- `Group` — Group quest
- `Heroic` — Heroic quest
- `PVP` — PvP-specific quest
- `Raid` — Raid quest
- `nil` — Standard quest

suggestedGroup — If the `questTag` is `Group`, the positive number of players suggested for the quest or `nil`. (number)

isHeader — Whether the entry is a header. (1nil)

- ▪ 1 — The entry is a header.
- ▪ nil — The entry is not a header.

isCollapsed — Whether the entry is a collapsed header. (1nil)

- ▪ 1 — The entry is a collapsed header.
- ▪ nil — The entry is not a header or not a header that is collapsed.

isComplete — Whether the quest is complete. (number)

- ▪ -1 — The quest was failed.
- ▪ 1 — The quest was completed.
- ▪ nil — The quest has yet to reach a conclusion.

isDaily — Whether the quest is a daily. (1nil)

- ▪ 1 — The quest is a daily.
- ▪ nil — The quest is not a daily.

GetQuestMoneyToGet

Returns the amount of money required for the currently displayed quest.

```
money = GetQuestMoneyToGet()
```

Returns:

money — The amount of money required for the currently displayed quest. (number)

GetQuestResetTime

Returns the amount of time until daily quests reset.

```
time = GetQuestResetTime()
```

Returns:

time — The amount of time until daily quests reset, in seconds. (number)

Example:

```
- Print the amount of time until dailies reset
ChatFrame1:AddMessage("Daily quests reset in " .. ↵
SecondsToTime(GetQuestResetTime()))
```

GetQuestReward

Selects an offered quest reward without confirmation.

```
GetQuestReward(choice)
```

Argument:

choice — The quest reward choice. (number)

GetQuestText

Returns the text for the currently displayed quest.

```
text = GetQuestText()
```

Returns:

`text` — The text for the currently displayed quest. `(string)`

GetQuestTimers

Returns a list of the remaining time of all active quest timers.

```
... = GetQuestTimers()
```

Returns:

`...` — A list of all active quest timers. `(number)`

GetRaidRosterInfo

Returns information about a member of the player's raid.

```
name, rank, subgroup, level, class, fileName, zone, online, isDead,
role, isML = GetRaidRosterInfo(index)
```

Argument:

`index` — The index of the raid member. `(number)`

Returns:

`name` — The name of the player. `(string)`

`rank` — The player's rank in the raid. `(number)`

- `0` — Raid Member
- `1` — Raid Assistant
- `2` — Raid Leader

`subgroup` — The raid subgroup to which the player belongs. `(number)`

`level` — The player's level. `(number)`

`class` — The localized name of the player's class. `(string)`

`fileName` — A nonlocalized token representing the player's class. `(string)`

- `WARRIOR`
- `PRIEST`
- `ROGUE`
- `MAGE`
- `DRUID`
- `HUNTER`
- `WARLOCK`
- `PALADIN`
- `SHAMAN`

zone — The name of the zone the player is currently in. (string)

online — 1 if the player is currently online, otherwise nil. (1nil)

isDead — 1 if the player is currently dead, otherwise nil. (1nil)

role — The player's role or nil. (string)

- ▪ MAINTANK
- ▪ MAINASSIST

isML — 1 if the player is the master looter, otherwise nil. (1nil)

GetRaidRosterSelection

Returns the index of the raid member currently selected by the mouse.

```
raidIndex = GetRaidRosterSelection()
```

Returns:

raidIndex — The index of the raid member currently being dragged by the mouse. If a member is currently selected and moved, this function will continue to return that value until a new raid member has been selected. (number)

GetRaidTargetIndex

Returns a number identifying the raid target icon attached to the given unit.

```
raidTargetIndex = GetRaidTargetIndex(unit)
```

Argument:

unit — The unit to query. (unitid)

Returns:

raidTargetIndex — The index of the current raid target. (number)

- ▪ 1 — Star
- ▪ 2 — Circle
- ▪ 3 — Diamond
- ▪ 4 — Triangle
- ▪ 5 — Moon
- ▪ 6 — Square
- ▪ 7 — Cross
- ▪ 8 — Skull

GetRangedCritChance

Returns the player's ranged critical strike chance.

```
critChance = GetRangedCritChance()
```

Returns:

critChance — The player's critical strike chance with the currently equipped ranged weapon, as a floating point number. (number)

GetRealNumPartyMembers

Returns the number of members in the player's "real" nonbattleground party. When the player is in a raid or party and then joins a battleground or arena, they will be a part of two different parties/raids simultaneously. This function is used to get the count of the actual nontemporary raid group and is used by the LFG/LFM interface to determine if the player's party or raid is full.

```
numMembers = GetRealNumPartyMembers()
```

Returns:

`numMembers` — The number of members in the player's actual party. (`number`)

GetRealNumRaidMembers

Returns the number of members in the player's "real" nonbattleground raid group. When the player is in a raid or party and then joins a battleground or arena, the player will be a part of two different parties/raids simultaneously. This function is used to get the count of the actual nontemporary raid group and is used by the LFG/LFM interface to determine if the player's party or raid is full.

```
numMembers = GetRealNumRaidMembers()
```

Returns:

`numMembers` — The number of members in the player's actual raid group. (`number`)

GetRealZoneText

Returns a canonical name for the zone the player is currently in (as opposed to the name shown in the minimap, which might indicate a subzone otherwise different from the "real" name). For example, returns The Stockade as opposed to Stormwind Stockade, or Orgrimmar instead of Valley of Honor.

```
zoneName = GetRealZoneText()
```

Returns:

`zoneName` — The real name of the instance or zone. (`string`)

GetRealmName

Returns the name of the player's realm (server name).

```
realm = GetRealmName()
```

Returns:

`realm` — The name of the player's realm (server). (`string`)

GetRefreshRates

Returns a list of all available refresh rates for the current system.

```
... = GetRefreshRates()
```

Returns:

`...` — A list of all available refresh rates. (`number`)

GetReleaseTimeRemaining

Returns the amount of time left until the player is automatically released from his or her body.

```
timeleft = GetReleaseTimeRemaining()
```

Returns:

`timeleft` — The amount of time left until the player is autoreleased from their body. (number)

GetRepairAllCost

Returns the cost to repair all damaged items.

```
repairAllCost, canRepair = GetRepairAllCost()
```

Returns:

`repairAllCost` — The cost to repair all items, in copper. If the player doesn't need to repair any items, this returns 0. (number)

`canRepair` — 1 if the player needs to and can repair. This return is used to enable/disable the repair all button in the merchant frame. (1nil)

GetResSicknessDuration

Returns the duration of resurrection sickness at the player's current level.

```
resSicknessTime = GetResSicknessDuration()
```

Returns:

`resSicknessTime` — The duration of resurrection sickness at the player's current level. This function returns nil for players under level 10 because they cannot get resurrection sickness. (string)

GetRestState

Returns the player's current rest state.

```
state, name, multiplier = GetRestState()
```

Returns:

`state` — The player's current rest state. (number)

`name` — The name of the player's current rest state. (string)

- ■ `normal` — Normal Experience
- ■ `rested` — Rested Experience
- ■ `tired` — Tired
- ■ `unhealthy` — Unhealthy

`multiplier` — The experience multiplier currently active for the player. (number)

- ■ 1 — Normal experience
- ■ 2 — 200 percent experience

Note: The `tired` and `unhealthy` states are currently only used in the Chinese locale, where play time is limited by law.

GetRewardHonor

Returns the amount of reward honor for the displayed quest.

```
honor = GetRewardHonor()
```

Returns:

honor — The amount of reward honor for the displayed quest. (number)

GetRewardMoney

Returns the amount of money rewarded for the quest that is currently being viewed.

```
money = GetRewardMoney()
```

Returns:

money — The amount of money rewarded for the quest, in copper. (number)

GetRewardSpell

Returns information about a spell quest reward. This function does not work for quests in the quest log, only for quests that are viewed at the NPC.

```
texture, name, isTradeskillSpell, isSpellLearned = GetRewardSpell()
```

Returns:

texture — The path to the spell's icon texture. (string)

name — The name of the spell. (string)

isTradeskillSpell — 1 if the spell is a tradeskill spell, otherwise nil. (1nil)

isSpellLearned — 1 if the reward teaches the player a new spell. (1nil)

GetRewardText

Returns the reward text of the quest at the quest completion frame.

```
text = GetRewardText()
```

Returns:

text — The reward text of the quest that is waiting to be completed or the empty string. (string)

GetRunningMacro

Returns the index of the currently running macro.

```
macroIdx = GetRunningMacro
```

Returns:

macroIdx — The index of the currently running macro or nil. (number)

GetRunningMacroButton

Returns the mouse button that was used to activate the running macro.

```
button = GetRunningMacroButton()
```

Returns:

`button` — The mouse button that was used to activate the macro. If the macro was triggered by a keybinding, the mouse button will be `LeftButton`. (`string`)

- `LeftButton`
- `RightButton`
- `MiddleButton`
- `Button4`
- `Button5`

GetSavedInstanceInfo

Returns information on a specific instance to which the character is saved. (Currently, this is only used for raid instances.)

```
instanceName, instanceID, instanceReset = GetSavedInstanceInfo(index)
```

Argument:

`index` — Saved instance ID to query between 1 and `GetNumSavedInstances()`. (`number`)

Returns:

`instanceName` — Name of the instance. (`string`)

`instanceID` — ID of the instance. (`number`)

`instanceReset` — Timestamp indicating time till reset. (`number`)

GetScreenHeight

Returns the current screen height. This value is affected by scale. To get the true screen height in pixels, divide by `GetScreenHeightScale()`.

```
height = GetScreenHeight()
```

Returns:

`height` — Current screen height in pixels. (`number`)

GetScreenResolutions

Returns the available screen resolutions.

```
... = GetScreenResolutions()
```

Returns:

`...` — A list of available screen resolutions, as strings. For example, 800x600 and 1024x768. (`string`)

Example:

```
- Print all available screen resolutions:
ChatFrame1:AddMessage("Available resolutions: " .. string.join(", ↵
", GetScreenResolutions())))
```

GetScreenWidth

Queries the width of the screen.

```
screenWidth = GetScreenWidth()
```

Returns:

`screenWidth` — The width of the client's screen, in pixels. Note that this may not be the width you expect from the video settings. For example, 1680x1050 reports back a screen width of 1595.844. (`number`)

GetScriptCPUUsage

Returns the total time used by the scripting subsystem.

```
time = GetScriptCPUUsage()
```

Note: Returns `0` unless CPU profiling is enabled by setting the CVar `scriptProfile` to `1`.

GetSelectedAuctionItem

Returns the index of the currently selected auction house item.

```
index = GetSelectedAuctionItem("type")
```

Argument:

`type` — The type of auction house listing. (`string`)

- ▪ `bidder` — Auctions on which the player has bid

- ▪ `list` — Auctions available for bidding/purchasing

- ▪ `owner` — Auctions the player has placed

Returns:

`index` — The index of the currently selected auction item. (`number`)

GetSelectedBattlefield

Returns the index of the currently selected battleground instance in battlemaster NPC/battleground portal dialog.

```
index = GetSelectedBattlefield()
```

Returns:

`index` — Index of the currently selected battleground instance, starting with `1`, or `0` if First Available is selected. (`number`)

GetSelectedDisplayChannel

Returns the channel ID of the selected channel in the Chat interface.

```
channelID = GetSelectedDisplayChannel()
```

Returns:

`channelID` — The channel ID of the channel selected in the Chat tab of the Social panel. (number)

GetSelectedFaction

Returns the currently selected faction index.

```
factionIndex = GetSelectedFaction()
```

Returns:

`factionIndex` — The currently selected faction index. (number)

GetSelectedFriend

Returns the friend index of the friend you currently have selected.

```
index = GetSelectedFriend()
```

Returns:

`index` — The index of your selected friend or 0 if no friend is selected. (number)

GetSelectedIgnore

Returns the currently selected index in the ignore listing.

```
index = GetSelectedIgnore()
```

Returns:

`index` — The currently selected ignore index. (number)

GetSelectedMute

Returns the index of the selected muted player in the muted list.

```
selectedMute = GetSelectedMute()
```

Returns:

`selectedMute` — The index of the selected muted player in the list of muted players. (number)

Note: Returns 0 when no player is muted or selected.

GetSelectedSkill

Returns the currently selected skill index, as listed in the Skills window.

```
skillIndex = GetSelectedSkill()
```

Returns:

`skillIndex` — The currently selected skill index, as listed in the Skills window. The skill lines are numbered including the headers. (number)

GetSelectedStablePet

Returns the index of the currently selected stable pet.

```
selectedPet = GetSelectedStablePet()
```

Returns:

`selectedPet` — The index of the currently selected stable pet. (number)

- `-1` — The player does not currently control a pet.
- `0` — The currently controlled pet is selected.
- `1` — The first stable slot is selected.
- `2` — The second stable slot is selected.

GetSelectedStationeryTexture

Returns the currently selected stationery texture.

```
texture = GetSelectedStationeryTexture()
```

Returns:

`texture` — The currently selected stationery texture. (string)

GetSendMailItem

Returns information on an item slot in the send mail frame.

```
itemName, itemTexture, stackCount, quality = GetSendMailItem(index)
```

Argument:

`index` — Index of the item in the send mail frame. Between `1` and `ATTACHMENTS_MAX_SEND`. (number)

Returns:

`itemName` — Name of the attachment item. (string)

`itemTexture` — Texture of the attachment item. (string)

`stackCount` — Current stack size of the attachment item. (string)

`quality` — Item quality. (number)

- `0` — Poor
- `1` — Common
- `2` — Uncommon
- `3` — Rare
- `4` — Epic
- `5` — Legendary
- `6` — Artifact

GetSendMailItemLink

Returns an item link for an item in the send mail window.

```
link = GetSendMailItemLink(slot)
```

Argument:

slot — The item slot in the send mail window. If not specified, this value defaults to 1. (number)

Returns:

link — The item link for the given send mail item. (string)

Example:

```
- Scan all the send mail item slots, printing a link for each item
for slot=1,ATTACHMENTS_MAX_SEND do
  local link = GetSendMailItemLink(slot)
  if link then
    ChatFrame1:AddMessage("Item " .. link .. " is in slot " .. slot)
  end
end
```

GetSendMailMoney

Returns the amount of money that will be sent with your next mail message. This function will return 0 until you set an amount with SetSendMailMoney. Opening or closing the mail window will reset it to 0.

```
money = GetSendMailMoney()
```

Returns:

money — The amount of money (in copper) to be sent. (number)

See also: SetSendMailMoney(), SendMail()

GetSendMailPrice

Returns the cost associated with sending an in-game mail message.

```
price = GetSendMailPrice()
```

Returns:

price — The cost of sending a mail message in copper. (number)

Note: Normally returns 30, which is the cost for sending a mail message with zero or one attachment. The return value increases by 30 for every additional item to be sent.

GetShapeshiftForm

Returns the current shapeshift form index.

```
index = GetShapeshiftForm()
```

Returns:

index — The current shapeshift form. (number)

GetShapeshiftFormCooldown

Returns cooldown information about a given shapeshift slot.

`start, duration, enable = GetShapeshiftFormCooldown(slot)`

Argument:

`slot` — The shapeshift slot to query for cooldown information. (`number`)

Returns:

`start` — The value of `GetTime()` at the moment the cooldown began, or `0`. (`number`)

`duration` — The length of the cooldown, or `0`. (`number`)

`enable` — `1` if the cooldown is enabled, otherwise `0`. (`number`)

GetShapeshiftFormInfo

Returns information about a shapeshift form.

`texture, name, isActive, isCastable = GetShapeshiftFormInfo(index)`

Argument:

`index` — The index of a shapeshift form. (`number`)

Returns:

`texture` — The path to the shapeshift form's icon texture. (`string`)

`name` — The name of the shapeshift form. (`string`)

`isActive` — `1` if the shapeshift form is currently active, otherwise `nil`. (`1nil`)

`isCastable` — `1` if the shapeshift form is currently castable, otherwise `nil`. (`1nil`)

GetShieldBlock

Returns the amount of damage stopped by a successful block. This amount is not to be confused with Block Rating or Block Chance; it's shown in the default UI only in the tooltip for Block in the Defenses section of the Character panel.

`damage = GetShieldBlock()`

Returns:

`damage` — The amount of damage stopped by a sucessful block. (`number`)

See also: `GetCombatRatingBonus()`, `GetBlockChance()`

GetSkillLineInfo

Returns information about a given skill line.

`skillName, header, isExpanded, skillRank, numTempPoints,`
`skillModifier, skillMaxRank, isAbandonable, stepCost, rankCost,`
`minLevel, skillCostType, skillDescription = GetSkillLineInfo(index)`

Argument:

`index` — The index of the skill line. (`number`)

Returns:

skillName — The name of the skill. (string)

header — 1 if the skill line is a header instead of a skill. (1nil)

isExpanded — 1 if the skill line is a header and is expanded, otherwise nil. (1nil)

skillRank — The rank of the skill. (number)

numTempPoints — The temporary profession rank increase (for example, 15 for engineering for Gnomes due to the racial trait). (number)

skillModifier — The temporary rank modifier due to buffs, equipment, and so on (for example, +Defense gear and the Defense skill). (number)

skillMaxRank — The max rank available. (number)

isAbandonable — 1 if the skill can be unlearned, otherwise nil. (1nil)

stepCost — Unused return value. (number)

rankCost — Unused return value. (number)

minLevel — The minimum level required to learn the skill. (number)

skillCostType — Unused return value. (number)

skillDescription — The description of the skill. (string)

GetSocketItemInfo

Returns information about the item currently open in the socket UI.

```
name, icon, quality = GetSocketItemInfo()
```

Returns:

name — The name of the item. (string)

icon — The icon of the item. (string)

quality — The item's quality. (number)

- ■ 0 — Poor
- ■ 1 — Common
- ■ 2 — Uncommon
- ■ 3 — Rare
- ■ 4 — Epic
- ■ 5 — Legendary
- ■ 6 — Artifact

GetSocketTypes

Returns the color of a given gem socket in the socketing UI.

```
gemColor = GetSocketTypes(index)
```

Argument:

index — The index of the socket to query. (number)

Returns:

gemColor — The color of the given gem socket. (string)

- ■ Blue
- ■ Yellow
- ■ Red
- ■ Meta

GetSpellAutocast

Returns whether a spell can be autocast and currently has autocast enabled (currently only used for pet spells).

```
autoCastAllowed, autoCastEnabled = GetSpellAutocast(spellid,
"bookType")
```

Arguments:

spellid — The spell ID to query. (number)

bookType — The type of spellbook. (string)

- ■ pet — The pet's spellbook
- ■ spell — The player's spellbook

Returns:

autoCastAllowed — Whether this spell can be autocast. (1nil)

autoCastEnabled — Whether this spell currently has autocast enabled. (1nil)

GetSpellBonusDamage

Returns the spell damage bonus for a given school.

```
minModifier = GetSpellBonusDamage(school)
```

Argument:

school — The spell school to query. (number)

- ■ 1 — Physical
- ■ 2 — Holy
- ■ 3 — Fire
- ■ 4 — Nature
- ■ 5 — Frost
- ■ 6 — Shadow
- ■ 7 — Arcane

Returns:

minModifier — The spell damage bonus for a given school. (number)

GetSpellBonusHealing

Query player's bonus healing from equipment. This value is shown in the Character frame spell stats as Bonus Healing.

```
bonusHealing = GetSpellBonusHealing()
```

Returns:

bonusHealing — Sum of healing bonus on player's equipped items. (integer)

GetSpellCooldown

Returns cooldown information about a given spell.

```
start, duration, enable = GetSpellCooldown(id, "bookType")
```

Arguments:

spellName or spellIndex

spellName — The name of the spell to query. (string)

spellIndex — The spellbook index of the spell to query. (number)

bookType (optional) — The type of spellbook in which to look up spellIndex (required when using spellIndex). (string)

- ■ pet — The pet's spellbook
- ■ spell — The player's spellbook

Returns:

start — The value of GetTime() at the moment the cooldown began, or 0. (number)

duration — The length of the cooldown or 0. (number)

enable — 1 if the cooldown is enabled, otherwise 0. (number)

GetSpellCount

Returns the number of times a spell with a reagent can be cast.

```
numCasts = GetSpellCount("name" or spellId, "bookType")
```

Arguments:

name or spellId

name — The name of a spell to query. (string)

spellId — A spell ID to query. (number)

bookType — The type of spellbook to query. (string)

- ■ pet — The pet's spellbook
- ■ spell — The player's spellbook

Returns:

numCasts — The number of spellcasts that can be made with the current number of reagents. (number)

Example:

```
— Iterate through the spellbook, checking which spells can be cast
— with reagents, printing them to chat
local numTabs = GetNumSpellTabs()
for tabid=1,numTabs do
  local name,texture,offset,numSpells = GetSpellTabInfo(tabid)
  for spellid=1,numSpells do
    local name,rank = GetSpellName(spellid + offset, "book")
    local count = GetSpellCount(spellid + offset, "book")
    if count > 0 then
      ChatFrame1:AddMessage(name .. " ( ".. count .. " casts)")
    end
  end
end
```

GetSpellCritChance

Returns the amount of crit chance for a given spell school.

```
minCrit = GetSpellCritChance(school)
```

Argument:

school — The spell school to query. (number)

- ▪ 1 — Physical
- ▪ 2 — Holy
- ▪ 3 — Fire
- ▪ 4 — Nature
- ▪ 5 — Frost
- ▪ 6 — Shadow
- ▪ 7 — Arcane

Returns:

minCrit — The amount of crit chance for a given spell school. (number)

GetSpellCritChanceFromIntellect

Returns the percent chance to crit granted by Intellect.

```
critChance = GetSpellCritChanceFromIntellect("unit")
```

Argument:

unit — The unit to query. This function appears to only work for player units. (unitid)

Returns:

critChance — The percent chance to crit granted by the player's Intellect stat. (number)

GetSpellName

Returns the name and secondary text of a given spell ID.

```
spellName, subSpellName = GetSpellName(spellid, "bookType")
```

Arguments:

spellid — The spell ID to query. (number)

bookType — The type of spellbook. (string)

- ■ pet — The pet's spellbook
- ■ spell — The player's spellbook

Returns:

spellName — The name of the spell. (string)

subSpellName — The text displayed on the second line of the spellbook, such as Rank 5, Racial Passive, or Artisan. (string)

Example:

```
- Print all spells to chatframe1
for i=1,GetNumSpellTabs() do
  local name,texture,offset,numSpells = GetSpellTabInfo(i)
  for j=1,numSpells do
    local spellId = j + offset
    local name,subSpellName = GetSpellName(spellId, "spell")
    ChatFrame1:AddMessage("Spell: " .. name .. " Sub: " ..
subSpellName)
  end
end
```

GetSpellPenetration

Returns the amount of spell penetration the player currently has.

```
penetration = GetSpellPenetration()
```

Returns:

penetration — The spell penetration rating the player currently has. (number)

GetSpellTabInfo

Returns information about a tab in the spellbook.

```
name, texture, offset, numSpells = GetSpellTabInfo(index)
```

Argument:

index — The index of the spell tab. Valid values are 1 through GetNumSpellTabs() .(number)

Returns:

name — The name of the spell tab. (string)

texture — The path to the spell tab's icon texture. (string)

offset — The offset for spell IDs within this tab. (number)

numSpells — The number of spells in the tab. (number)

Example:

```
- Print the valid spellIds for each tab
local numTabs = GetNumSpellTabs()
for i=1,numTabs do
  local name,texture,offset,numSpells = GetSpellTabInfo(i)
  ChatFrame1:AddMessage("Spell tab \"" .. name .. "\" contains ↵
spells from id " .. offset + 1 .. " through " .. offset + numSpells)
end
```

GetSpellTexture

Returns the texture path for a given spell.

```
texture = GetSpellTexture(id, "bookType")
```

Arguments:

id — The spell ID. (number)

bookType — The type of spell book. (string)

- ▪ pet — The pet's spell book.

- ▪ spell — The default spell book.

Returns:

texture — The path to the spell icon's texture. (string)

GetStablePetFoodTypes

Returns the types of food that a stabled pet will eat.

```
... = GetStablePetFoodTypes(index)
```

Argument:

index — The index of a stabled pet, or 0 for the active pet. (number)

Returns:

... — A list of strings, each containing a food that the stabled pet will eat. (string)

GetStablePetInfo

Returns information about a currently stabled pet.

```
icon, name, level, family, loyalty = GetStablePetInfo(index)
```

Argument:

index — The index of the stabled pet. (number)

Returns:

icon — The path to the pet's icon texture. (string)

name — The name of the pet. (string)

level — The level of the pet. (number)

family — The family of the pet in the current locale. (string)

loyalty — The loyalty level of the pet, as a localized string. (string)

GetStationeryInfo

Returns information about a given stationery.

```
name, texture, cost = GetStationeryInfo(index)
```

Argument:

index — A stationery index. (number)

Returns:

name — The name of the stationery. (string)

texture — The path to the stationery texture. (string)

cost — The cost of the stationery, in copper. (number)

GetSubZoneText

Returns the subzone name of the player's current zone. This corresponds to areas within a larger zone such as Nesingwary's Expedition in Stranglethorn Vale.

```
subzoneText = GetSubZoneText()
```

Returns:

subzoneText — The subzone text for the given zone, or the empty string. (string)

GetSuggestedGroupNum

Returns the size of the suggested group for the currently displayed quest.

```
suggestedGroup = GetSuggestedGroupNum()
```

Returns:

suggestedGroup — The size of a suggested group for the currently displayed quest or 0. (number)

GetSummonConfirmAreaName

Returns the destination area of the pending summon spell.

```
area = GetSummonConfirmAreaName()
```

Returns:

area — The destination area of the pending summon spell. (string)

GetSummonConfirmSummoner

Returns the name of the summoner so that it can be displayed in the confirmation dialog.

```
text = GetSummonConfirmSummoner()
```

Returns:

text — The name of the summoner. (string)

GetSummonConfirmTimeLeft

Returns time left in seconds until summon cancel. Will return 0 with no summon dialog up.

```
timeleft = GetSummonConfirmTimeLeft()
```

Returns:

`timeleft` — Time left in seconds until summon cancel. (number)

GetTabardCreationCost

Returns the cost to create a guild tabard.

```
cost = GetTabardCreationCost()
```

Returns:

`cost` — The cost of creating a guild tabard, in copper. (number)

GetTalentInfo

Returns information about the talents of the player or the currently inspected player.

```
name, iconTexture, tier, column, rank, maxRank, isExceptional,
meetsPrereq = GetTalentInfo(tabIndex, talentIndex [,isInspect])
```

Arguments:

`tabIndex` — The index of the talent tree. (number)

`talentIndex` — The index of the talent. (number)

`isInspect` — 1 if retrieving information from an inspected person, nil otherwise. (1nil)

Returns:

`name` — The name of the talent. (string)

`iconTexture` — The icon texture of the talent. (string)

`tier` — The tier (row) of the talent. (number)

`column` — The column of the talent. (number)

`rank` — The current rank of the talent. (number)

`maxRank` — The maximum rank of the talent. (number)

`isExceptional` — 1 if the selected talent is an ability you gain, nil otherwise. (1nil)

`meetsPrereq` — 1 if you meet the prerequisite to learn the talent, nil otherwise. (1nil)

GetTalentPrereqs

Returns the prerequisites for a given talent. Multiple requirements may be returned; in this case, three values are returned for each requirement.

```
tier, column, isLearnable, ... = GetTalentPrereqs(tabIndex,
talentIndex)
```

Arguments:

`tabIndex` — The index of the chosen tab. (`number`)

`talentIndex` — The index of the talent to query. (`number`)

Returns:

`tier` — The tier of the required talent. (`number`)

`column` — The column of the required talent. (`number`)

`isLearnable` — 1 if the talent is currently learnable, otherwise `nil`. (`1nil`)

`...` — A repeating list of `tier`, `column`, and `isLearnable` for each talent prerequisite. (`list`)

GetTalentTabInfo

Returns information about the specified talent tree from either the player or the unit that is being inspected.

```
name, texture, points, fileName = GetTalentTabInfo(index [,isInspect])
```

Arguments:

`index` — The index of the talent tab. (`number`)

`isInspect` — 1 if inspecting someone, `nil` otherwise. (`1nil`)

Returns:

`name` — The name of the talent tree. (`string`)

`texture` — The texture of the talent tree. (`string`)

`points` — The number of talent points spent in the talent tree. (`number`)

`fileName` — The filename to the background texture for the talent tree. (`string`)

GetTargetTradeMoney

Returns the amount of money the target has placed in the trade window.

```
money = GetTargetTradeMoney()
```

Returns:

`money` — The amount of money the target has placed in the trade window, in copper. (`number`)

GetTaxiBenchmarkMode

Returns whether taxi benchmark mode is enabled.

```
isBenchmark = GetTaxiBenchmarkMode
```

Returns:

`isBenchmark` — 1 if taxi benchmark mode is enabled, otherwise `nil`. (`1nil`)

See also: `SetTexiBenchmarkMode()`

GetTerrainMip

Returns the value of the Terrain Detail Level slider in the video options.

```
terrainDetailLevel = GetTerrainMip()
```

Returns:

`terrainDetailLevel` — The value of the Terrain Detail Level slider in the video options. This is either 0 or 1. (`number`)

GetText

Returns a formatted string from `GlobalStrings`.

```
text = GetText("token" [,suffix] [,ordinal])
```

Arguments:

`token` — The name of the global string to format. (`string`)

`suffix` — A suffix to add to the token before fetching the format string. (`string`)

`ordinal` — Will replace `%d` in the string with this number. (`number`)

Returns:

`text` — Formatted global string. (`string`)

Example:

```
- This will return the string "1 Hour"
GetText("FORMATTED_HOUR", nil, 1)
```

GetTime

Returns a number representing the current time with millisecond precision. The number itself doesn't correspond to any useful value, but it can be compared against itself to give a high prevision time measurement.

```
time = GetTime()
```

Returns:

`time` — A number that represents the current time with millisecond precision. (`number`)

GetTitleName

Retrieve a title string from a title ID.

```
titleName = GetTitleName(titleMaskID)
```

Arguments:

`titleMaskID` — Index of the title name to query. `(integer)`

Returns:

`titleName` — The name of the title requested. `(string)`

Example:

```
local id = GetCurrentTitle()
local titleName = GetTitleName(id)
```

GetTitleText

Returns the title text for the currently displayed quest.

```
text = GetTitleText()
```

Returns:

`text` — The title text for the currently displayed quest. `(string)`

GetTrackingInfo

Returns information about a given tracking option.

```
name, texture, active, category = GetTrackingInfo(id)
```

Argument:

`id` — The tracking index to query. `(number)`

Returns:

`name` — The name of the tracking option. `(string)`

`texture` — The path to the tracking option's icon texture. `(string)`

`active` — 1 if the tracking option is active, otherwise `nil`. `(1nil)`

`category` — The tracking option's category. `(string)`

 ■ `npc` — The tracking option is static.

 ■ `spell` — The tracking option is a spell in the player's spellbook.

Note: Returns nil if the given tracking option could not be found.

GetTrackingTexture

Returns the texture of the active tracking buff if one is active.

```
texture = GetTrackingTexture()
```

Returns:

`texture` — The path of the active tracking buff icon texture, if there is one. `(string)`

GetTradePlayerItemInfo

Returns information about an item the player has placed in the trade window.

```
name, texture, numItems, isUsable, enchantment = ↵
GetTradePlayerItemInfo(index)
```

Argument:

index — The index in the trade window. (number)

Returns:

name — The name of the item. (string)

texture — The path to the item's icon texture. (string)

numItems — The number of items in the stack. (number)

quality — The quality level of the item. (number)

- 0 — Poor
- 1 — Common
- 2 — Uncommon
- 3 — Rare
- 4 — Epic
- 5 — Legendary
- 6 — Artifact

isUsable — 1 if the item is usable by the player, otherwise nil. (1nil)

enchantment — The name of the enchantment being applied to the item, if applicable. (string)

GetTradePlayerItemLink

Returns a link for an item offered by the player in the trade window.

```
link = GetTradePlayerItemLink(index)
```

Argument:

index — The index of the player's trade slot. (number)

Returns:

link — The link for the given trade item. (string)

GetTradeSkillCooldown

Returns the cooldown for a given tradeskill.

```
cooldown = GetTradeSkillCooldown(index)
```

Argument:

index — The index of a tradeskill. (number)

Returns:

cooldown — The remaining cooldown of the tradeskill, in seconds. (number)

Example:

```
- Print any skill with a cooldown to chatframe
for i=1,GetNumTradeSkills() do
    local cooldown = GetTradeSkillCooldown(i)
    if cooldown then
        local name = GetTradeSkillInfo(i)
        ChatFrame1:AddMessage("Cooldown for " .. name .. " is " .. ↵
(cooldown / 60) .. " minutes")
    end
end
```

GetTradeSkillIcon

This function will return the icon for the tradeskill item at the index being queried.

```
texturePath = GetTradeSkillIcon(index)
```

Argument:

index — The index of the line for which you want to query the icon. (number)

Returns:

texturePath — The full path to the icon's texture. (string)

GetTradeSkillInfo

Returns information about the recipes of the currently selected tradeskill.

```
skillName, skillType, numAvailable, isExpanded =
GetTradeSkillInfo(index)
```

Argument:

index — The index of the tradeskill to query. (number)

Returns:

skillName — The name of the tradeskill. (string)

skillType — The skill type of the tradeskill. (string)

- header — This entry is a header and not an actual tradeskill.

- trivial — Trivial skill (gray); you will not gain skill points from this recipe.

- easy — Easy skill (green); there is a slim chance that you will gain skill points from this recipe.

- medium — Medium skill (yellow); there is a high chance that you will gain skill points from this recipe.

- optimal — Optimal skill (orange); you will gain skill points from this recipe.

numAvailable — The number of times you can cast this tradeskill. (number)

isExpanded — 1 if this is a header and is expanded, nil otherwise. (1nil)

GetTradeSkillInvSlotFilter

Returns whether a given tradeskill inventory slot filter is enabled.

```
enabled = GetTradeSkillInvSlotFilter(index)
```

Argument:

index — The index of an inventory slot tradeskill filter or 0 for the All Slots filter. (number)

Returns:

enabled — 1 if the filter is enabled, otherwise nil. (1nil)

GetTradeSkillInvSlots

Returns a list of inventory slots for which the current tradeskill can craft. These values are used to populate the slot filter menu in the tradeskill window.

```
... = GetTradeSkillInvSlots()
```

Returns:

... — A list of inventory slots for which the tradeskill is capable of creating items. (string)

GetTradeSkillItemLevelFilter

Returns the current values for the tradeskill item level filter. This filter limits the list of available recipes returned by other TradeSkill functions based on the required level (not item level) of items produced.

```
minLevel, maxLevel = GetTradeSkillItemLevelFilter()
```

Returns:

minLevel — Lowest required level of items to show in filtered tradeskill list. (number)

maxLevel — Highest required level of items to show in filtered tradeskill list. (number)

GetTradeSkillItemLink

Returns an item link for the given tradeskill item.

```
link = GetTradeSkillItemLink(index)
```

Argument:

index — The index of a tradeskill item. (number)

Returns:

link — The item link for the given item. (string)

GetTradeSkillItemNameFilter

Returns the text of the tradeskill item name filter.

```
text = GetTradeSkillItemNameFilter()
```

Returns:

text — The text of the tradeskill item name filter. (string)

GetTradeSkillItemStats

Returns information about a given tradeskill item.

```
... = GetTradeSkillItemStats(index)
```

Argument:

`index` — The index of the tradeskill recipe in the tradeskill window. `(number)`

Returns:

`...` — Multiple strings that give stats about the given tradeskill item. `(string)`

Example:

```
— Netherweave Net returns the following information:
"Other", "Effect: Netherweave Net", "|cffff2020Requires Tailoring
(300)|r"

— Netherweave Bag returns the following information:
"Uncommon", "Binds when equipped", "16 Slot Bag"
```

GetTradeSkillLine

Returns level information about the active tradeskill profession.

```
tradeskillName, currentLevel, maxLevel = GetTradeSkillLine()
```

Returns:

`tradeskillName` — Name of the current tradeskill. `(string)`

`currentLevel` — Current level in tradeskill. `(number)`

`maxLevel` — Current maximum level for tradeskill. `(number)`

GetTradeSkillNumMade

Returns the number of items possibly created when crafting a tradeskill recipe.

```
minMade,maxMade = GetTradeSkillNumMade(index)
```

Argument:

`index` — The index of a tradeskill recipe in the tradeskill window. `(number)`

Returns:

`minMade` — The minimum number of items created when crafting. `(number)`

`maxMade` — The maximum number of items created when crafting. `(number)`

Example:

```
— Print any multi-create items to chat
local numSkills = GetNumTradeSkills()
for i=1,numSkills do
  local numMade = GetTradeSkillNumMade(i)
  if numMade > 1 then
    local link = GetTradeSkillItemLink(i)
    ChatFrame1:AddMessage(link .. " creates " .. numMade .. " each
craft")
  end
end
```

GetTradeSkillNumReagents

Returns the number of reagents required for a tradeskill recipe.

```
numReagents = GetTradeSkillNumReagents(index)
```

Argument:

index — The index of a tradeskill recipe. (number)

Returns:

numReagents — The number of reagents required for a given recipe. (number)

GetTradeSkillReagentInfo

Returns information about tradeskill recipe's reagent.

```
reagentName, reagentTexture, reagentCount, playerReagentCount = ↵
GetTradeSkillReagentInfo(index, reagentIndex)
```

Arguments:

reagentName — The name of the reagent. (string)

reagentTexture — The path to the reagent's icon texture. (string)

reagentCount — The number of required reagents. (number)

playerReagentCount — The number of reagents the player currently
possesses. (number)

Returns:

index — The index of the tradeskill recipe. (number)

reagentIndex — The index of the reagent to the tradeskill recipe. (number)

Example:

```
— Prints the reagent(s) required for the first trade skill item found

— Iterate over all trade skill items we can make
for i = 1, GetNumTradeSkills() do
  local name, type = GetTradeSkillInfo(i);
  — Make sure we're not accessing a header
  if ( name and type ~= "header" ) then
    ChatFrame1:AddMessage(string.format("%s takes the following
reagent(s):", name));
    — Iterate over all reagents
    for j = 1, GetTradeSkillNumReagents(i) do
local reagentName, _, reagentCount = GetTradeSkillReagentInfo(i, j);
ChatFrame1:AddMessage(string.format("    %dx %s", reagentCount,
reagentName));
    end
    return;
  end
end
ChatFrame1:AddMessage("No valid item found.");
. (1nil)
```

Returns:

name — The name of the talent. (string)

iconTexture — The icon texture of the talent. (string)

tier — The tier (row) of the talent. (number)

column — The column of the talent. (number)

rank — The current rank of the talent. (number)

maxRank — The maximum rank of the talent. (number)

isExceptional — 1 if the selected talent is an ability you gain, nil otherwise. (1nil)

meetsPrereq — 1 if you meet the prerequisite to learn the talent, nil otherwise. (1nil)

GetTalentPrereqs

Returns the prerequisites for a given talent. Multiple requirements may be returned; in this case, three values are returned for each requirement.

```
tier, column, isLearnable, ... = GetTalentPrereqs(tabIndex,
talentIndex)
```

Arguments:

tabIndex — The index of the chosen tab. (number)

talentIndex — The index of the talent to query. (number)

Returns:

tier — The tier of the required talent. (number)

column — The column of the required talent. (number)

isLearnable — 1 if the talent is currently learnable, otherwise nil. (1nil)

... — A repeating list of tier, column, and isLearnable for each talent prerequisite. (list)

GetTalentTabInfo

Returns information about the specified talent tree from either the player or the unit that is being inspected.

```
name, texture, points, fileName = GetTalentTabInfo(index
[,isInspect])
```

Arguments:

index — The index of the talent tab. (number)

isInspect — 1 if inspecting someone, nil otherwise. (1nil)

Returns:

name — The name of the talent tree. (string)

texture — The texture of the talent tree. (string)

points — The number of talent points spent in the talent tree. (number)

fileName — The filename to the background texture for the talent tree. (string)

GetTargetTradeMoney

Returns the amount of money the target has placed in the trade window.

```
money = GetTargetTradeMoney()
```

Returns:

money — The amount of money the target has placed in the trade window, in copper. (number)

GetTaxiBenchmarkMode

Returns whether taxi benchmark mode is enabled.

```
isBenchmark = GetTaxiBenchmarkMode
```

Returns:

isBenchmark — 1 if taxi benchmark mode is enabled, otherwise nil. (1nil)

See also: SetTexiBenchmarkMode()

GetTerrainMip

Returns the value of the Terrain Detail Level slider in the video options.

```
terrainDetailLevel = GetTerrainMip()
```

Returns:

terrainDetailLevel — The value of the Terrain Detail Level slider in the video options. This is either 0 or 1. (number)

GetText

Returns a formatted string from GlobalStrings.

```
text = GetText("token" [,suffix] [,ordinal])
```

Arguments:

token — The name of the global string to format. (string)

suffix — A suffix to add to the token before fetching the format string. (string)

ordinal — Will replace %d in the string with this number. (number)

Returns:

text — Formatted global string. (string)

Example:

```
- This will return the string "1 Hour"
GetText("FORMATTED_HOUR", nil, 1)
```

GetTime

Returns a number representing the current time with millisecond precision. The number itself doesn't correspond to any useful value, but it can be compared against itself to give a high prevision time measurement.

```
time = GetTime()
```

Returns:

`time` — A number that represents the current time with millisecond precision. `(number)`

GetTitleName

Retrieve a title string from a title ID.

```
titleName = GetTitleName(titleMaskID)
```

Arguments:

`titleMaskID` — Index of the title name to query. `(integer)`

Returns:

`titleName` — The name of the title requested. `(string)`

Example:
```
local id = GetCurrentTitle()
local titleName = GetTitleName(id)
```

GetTitleText

Returns the title text for the currently displayed quest.

```
text = GetTitleText()
```

Returns:

`text` — The title text for the currently displayed quest. `(string)`

GetTrackingInfo

Returns information about a given tracking option.

```
name, texture, active, category = GetTrackingInfo(id)
```

Argument:

`id` — The tracking index to query. `(number)`

Returns:

`name` — The name of the tracking option. `(string)`

`texture` — The path to the tracking option's icon texture. `(string)`

`active` — 1 if the tracking option is active, otherwise `nil`. `(1nil)`

`category` — The tracking option's category. `(string)`

- ▪ `npc` — The tracking option is static.
- ▪ `spell` — The tracking option is a spell in the player's spellbook.

Note: Returns nil if the given tracking option could not be found.

GetTrackingTexture

Returns the texture of the active tracking buff if one is active.

```
texture = GetTrackingTexture()
```

Returns:

texture — The path of the active tracking buff icon texture, if there is one. (string)

GetTradePlayerItemInfo

Returns information about an item the player has placed in the trade window.

```
name, texture, numItems, isUsable, enchantment = i
GetTradePlayerItemInfo(index)
```

Argument:

index — The index in the trade window. (number)

Returns:

name — The name of the item. (string)

texture — The path to the item's icon texture. (string)

numItems — The number of items in the stack. (number)

quality — The quality level of the item. (number)

- ▪ 0 — Poor
- ▪ 1 — Common
- ▪ 2 — Uncommon
- ▪ 3 — Rare
- ▪ 4 — Epic
- ▪ 5 — Legendary
- ▪ 6 — Artifact

isUsable — 1 if the item is usable by the player, otherwise nil. (1nil)

enchantment — The name of the enchantment being applied to the item, if applicable. (string)

GetTradePlayerItemLink

Returns a link for an item offered by the player in the trade window.

```
link = GetTradePlayerItemLink(index)
```

Argument:

index — The index of the player's trade slot. (number)

Returns:

link — The link for the given trade item. (string)

GetTradeSkillCooldown

Returns the cooldown for a given tradeskill.

```
cooldown = GetTradeSkillCooldown(index)
```

Argument:

index — The index of a tradeskill. (number)

Returns:

cooldown — The remaining cooldown of the tradeskill, in seconds. (number)

Example:

```
- Print any skill with a cooldown to chatframe
for i=1,GetNumTradeSkills() do
    local cooldown = GetTradeSkillCooldown(i)
    if cooldown then
        local name = GetTradeSkillInfo(i)
        ChatFrame1:AddMessage("Cooldown for " .. name .. " is " .. i
(cooldown / 60) .. " minutes")
    end
end
```

GetTradeSkillIcon

This function will return the icon for the tradeskill item at the index being queried.

```
texturePath = GetTradeSkillIcon(index)
```

Argument:

index — The index of the line for which you want to query the icon. (number)

Returns:

texturePath — The full path to the icon's texture. (string)

GetTradeSkillInfo

Returns information about the recipes of the currently selected tradeskill.

```
skillName, skillType, numAvailable, isExpanded =
GetTradeSkillInfo(index)
```

Argument:

index — The index of the tradeskill to query. (number)

Returns:

skillName — The name of the tradeskill. (string)

skillType — The skill type of the tradeskill. (string)

- header — This entry is a header and not an actual tradeskill.
- trivial — Trivial skill (gray); you will not gain skill points from this recipe.
- easy — Easy skill (green); there is a slim chance that you will gain skill points from this recipe.

- ▪ medium — Medium skill (yellow); there is a high chance that you will gain skill points from this recipe.

- ▪ optimal — Optimal skill (orange); you will gain skill points from this recipe.

numAvailable — The number of times you can cast this tradeskill. (number)

isExpanded — 1 if this is a header and is expanded, nil otherwise. (1nil)

GetTradeSkillInvSlotFilter

Returns whether a given tradeskill inventory slot filter is enabled.

```
enabled = GetTradeSkillInvSlotFilter(index)
```

Argument:

index — The index of an inventory slot tradeskill filter or 0 for the All Slots filter. (number)

Returns:

enabled — 1 if the filter is enabled, otherwise nil. (1nil)

GetTradeSkillInvSlots

Returns a list of inventory slots for which the current tradeskill can craft. These values are used to populate the slot filter menu in the tradeskill window.

```
... = GetTradeSkillInvSlots()
```

Returns:

... — A list of inventory slots for which the tradeskill is capable of creating items. (string)

GetTradeSkillItemLevelFilter

Returns the current values for the tradeskill item level filter. This filter limits the list of available recipes returned by other TradeSkill functions based on the required level (not item level) of items produced.

```
minLevel, maxLevel = GetTradeSkillItemLevelFilter()
```

Returns:

minLevel — Lowest required level of items to show in filtered tradeskill list. (number)

maxLevel — Highest required level of items to show in filtered tradeskill list. (number)

GetTradeSkillItemLink

Returns an item link for the given tradeskill item.

```
link = GetTradeSkillItemLink(index)
```

Argument:

index — The index of a tradeskill item. (number)

Returns:

link — The item link for the given item. (string)

GetTradeSkillItemNameFilter

Returns the text of the tradeskill item name filter.

```
text = GetTradeSkillItemNameFilter()
```

Returns:

`text` — The text of the tradeskill item name filter. (`string`)

GetTradeSkillItemStats

Returns information about a given tradeskill item.

```
... = GetTradeSkillItemStats(index)
```

Argument:

`index` — The index of the tradeskill recipe in the tradeskill window. (`number`)

Returns:

`...` — Multiple strings that give stats about the given tradeskill item. (`string`)

Example:

```
— Netherweave Net returns the following information:
"Other", "Effect: Netherweave Net", "|cffff2020Requires Tailoring
(300)|r"

— Netherweave Bag returns the following information:
"Uncommon", "Binds when equipped", "16 Slot Bag"
```

GetTradeSkillLine

Returns level information about the active tradeskill profession.

```
tradeskillName, currentLevel, maxLevel = GetTradeSkillLine()
```

Returns:

`tradeskillName` — Name of the current tradeskill. (`string`)

`currentLevel` — Current level in tradeskill. (`number`)

`maxLevel` — Current maximum level for tradeskill. (`number`)

GetTradeSkillNumMade

Returns the number of items possibly created when crafting a tradeskill recipe.

```
minMade,maxMade = GetTradeSkillNumMade(index)
```

Argument:

`index` — The index of a tradeskill recipe in the tradeskill window. (`number`)

Returns:

`minMade` — The minimum number of items created when crafting. (`number`)

`maxMade` — The maximum number of items created when crafting. (`number`)

Example:

```
— Print any multi-create items to chat
local numSkills = GetNumTradeSkills()
for i=1,numSkills do
  local numMade = GetTradeSkillNumMade(i)
  if numMade > 1 then
    local link = GetTradeSkillItemLink(i)
    ChatFrame1:AddMessage(link .. " creates " .. numMade .. " each
craft")
  end
end
```

GetTradeSkillNumReagents

Returns the number of reagents required for a tradeskill recipe.

```
numReagents = GetTradeSkillNumReagents(index)
```

Argument:

index — The index of a tradeskill recipe. (number)

Returns:

numReagents — The number of reagents required for a given recipe. (number)

GetTradeSkillReagentInfo

Returns information about tradeskill recipe's reagent.

```
reagentName, reagentTexture, reagentCount, playerReagentCount = i
GetTradeSkillReagentInfo(index, reagentIndex)
```

Arguments:

reagentName — The name of the reagent. (string)

reagentTexture — The path to the reagent's icon texture. (string)

reagentCount — The number of required reagents. (number)

playerReagentCount — The number of reagents the player currently possesses. (number)

Returns:

index — The index of the tradeskill recipe. (number)

reagentIndex — The index of the reagent to the tradeskill recipe. (number)

Example:

```
— Prints the reagent(s) required for the first trade skill item found

— Iterate over all trade skill items we can make
for i = 1, GetNumTradeSkills() do
  local name, type = GetTradeSkillInfo(i);
  — Make sure we're not accessing a header
  if ( name and type ~= "header" ) then
    ChatFrame1:AddMessage(string.format("%s takes the following
```

```
reagent(s):", name));
    - Iterate over all reagents
    for j = 1, GetTradeSkillNumReagents(i) do
local reagentName, _, reagentCount = GetTradeSkillReagentInfo(i, j);
ChatFrame1:AddMessage(string.format("    %dx %s", reagentCount,
reagentName));
    end
    return;
  end
end
ChatFrame1:AddMessage("No valid item found.");
```

GetTradeSkillReagentItemLink

Returns the item link for a tradeskill's reagent.

```
link = GetTradeSkillReagentItemLink(skillIdx, reagentIdx)
```

Arguments:

skillIdx — The index of the skill to be queried. (number)

reagentIdx — The index of the reagent. (number)

Returns:

link — The item link of the given reagent for a tradeskill. (string)

Example:

```
-- Print the required components to chat
local index = GetTradeSkillSelectionIndex()
local num = GetTradeSkillNumReagents(index)
for i=1,num do
    ChatFrame1:AddMessage("Requires: " .. ↵
GetTradeSkillReagentItemLink(index, i))
end
```

GetTradeSkillRecipeLink

Returns a recipe link for a tradeskill recipe. (Unlike an item link for the item produced by the recipe, the recipe link shows the names of the profession and the recipe, and its tooltip shows the reagents required for the recipe as well as a description of the item produced.)

```
link = GetTradeSkillRecipeLink(index)
```

Argument:

index — The index of the tradeskill recipe. (number)

Returns:

link — A link for the given item recipe. (string)

GetTradeSkillSelectionIndex

Returns the index of the currently selected line in the Tradeskill window.

```
index = GetTradeSkillSelectionIndex()
```

Returns:

index — The index of the currently selected line in the Tradeskill window. (number)

GetTradeSkillSubClassFilter

Returns whether the tradeskill list should be filtered to include items of the given subclass.

```
enabled = GetTradeSkillSubClassFilter(index)
```

Argument:

index — The index of a return from GetTradeSkillSubClasses(), or 0 for the All filter. (number)

Returns:

enabled — 1 if the filter is enabled, otherwise nil. (1nil)

GetTradeSkillSubClasses

Returns a list of item subclasses (such as Cloth, Leather, Consumable) that can be created by the current tradeskill; these values can be used for filtering the tradeskill list.

```
... = GetTradeSkillSubClasses()
```

Returns:

... — A string for every tradeskill subclass for the given tradeskill. (string)

Example:

```
-- Print the tradeskill subclasses for the currently opened
tradeskill
local subclasses = string.join(", ",    ↵
GetTradeSkillSubClasses())
ChatFrame1:AddMessage("Subclasses: " .. subclasses)

-- Store the tradeskill subclasses in a table for use later
local subclasses = {GetTradeSkillSubClasses()}
ChatFrame1:AddMessage("Subclasses: " .. table.concat(subclasses, ",
"))
```

GetTradeSkillTools

Returns the required tools for a given tradeskill recipe.

```
toolName, hasTool, ... = GetTradeSkillTools(index)
```

Argument:

`index` — The index of a tradeskill recipe in the tradeskill UI. (number)

Returns:

`toolName` — The name of the tool required for the given tradeskill. (string)

`hasTool` — 1 if the player currently has the required tool, otherwise `nil`. This value is accurate for tools that are items carried by the player (for example, Blacksmith Hammer) but is not always accurate for tools that are external world objects (for example, Anvil, Mana Loom). (1nil)

`...` — Multiple returns are used when there are multiple required tools. (repeat)

GetTradeTargetItemInfo

Returns information about an item in the Trade window. Each item slot in the trade window (1–6 being the actual trade slots and 7 being the no-trade slot) can be queried individually for item information. This information is used by the default user interface to build the information in the Trade window.

```
local name, texture, numItems, quality, isUsable, enchantment  =
GetTradeTargetItemInfo(index)
```

Argument:

`index` — The index in the Trade window. (number)

Returns:

`name` — The name of the item. (string)

`texture` — The path to the item's icon texture. (string)

`numItems` — The number of items in the stack. (number)

`quality` — The quality level of the item. (number)

- 0 — Poor
- 1 — Common
- 2 — Uncommon
- 3 — Rare
- 4 — Epic
- 5 — Legendary
- 6 — Artifact

`isUsable` — 1 if the item is usable by the player, otherwise `nil`. (1nil)

`enchantment` — The name of the enchantment being applied to the item, if applicable. (string)

GetTradeTargetItemLink

Returns an item link for an item being offered by the target in a trade.

```
link = GetTradeTargetItemLink(index)
```

Argument:

index — The index of the target's trade item. (number)

Returns:

link — The link for the given item. (string)

GetTradeskillRepeatCount

Returns the number of times the current tradeskill recipe will repeat.

```
repeatCount = GetTradeskillRepeatCount()
```

Returns:

repeatCount — The number of times the current recipe will be repeated until finished. The start value of this is set when DoTradeSkill() is called and is decremented each time a new item is finished. (number)

GetTrainerGreetingText

Returns the greeting text for the currently (or last) open trainer.

```
text = GetTrainerGreetingText()
```

Returns:

text — The greeting text for the currently (or last) open trainer. This is the text displayed at the top of the Trainer window. (string)

GetTrainerSelectionIndex

Returns the currently selected index in the Trainer window.

```
selectionIndex = GetTrainerSelectionIndex()
```

Returns:

selectionIndex — The currently selected index in the Trainer window. (number)

GetTrainerServiceAbilityReq

Retrieves information about abilities that are required to train a specific skill.

```
ability, hasReq = GetTrainerServiceAbilityReq(index)
```

Argument:

index — The index of the trainer service to query. These indices are affected by the trainer filter. *See* GetTrainerServiceTypeFilter() *and* SetTrainerServiceTypeFilter(). (number)

Returns:

ability — The name of the ability that is required. (string)

hasReq — 1 if the player meets the requirement, otherwise nil. (1nil)

GetTrainerServiceCost

Returns the cost of a given trainer service.

```
moneyCost, talentCost, skillCost  = GetTrainerServiceCost(index)
```

Argument:

`index` — The index of a trainer service. (number)

Returns:

`moneyCost` — The cost of the service, in copper. (number)

`talentCost` — The cost of the service, in talent points. (number)

`skillCost` — The cost of the service of the available profession limit. (number)

GetTrainerServiceDescription

Returns the description of a given trainer service (teaching the player a new spell, tradeskill recipe, and so on).

```
text = GetTrainerServiceDescription(index)
```

Argument:

`index` — The index of a trainer service to query. (number)

Returns:

`text` — The description of the service. (string)

GetTrainerServiceIcon

Returns the icon for a given trainer service (spell or skill to be taught to the player).

```
icon = GetTrainerServiceIcon(index)
```

Argument:

`index` — The index of a service in the Trainer window. (number)

Returns:

`icon` — The path to the service's icon texture. (string)

GetTrainerServiceInfo

Returns information about a service in the Trainer window.

```
serviceName, serviceSubText, serviceType, isExpanded  = ↵
GetTrainerServiceInfo(index)
```

Argument:

`index` — The index of a line in the Trainer window. (number)

Returns:

serviceName — The name of the service. (string)

serviceSubText — The secondary text (for example, Rank 2, Passive) of the service. (string)

serviceType — The type of the service. (string)

■ available — Able to be learned

■ unavailable — Not able to be learned

■ used — Already learned

GetTrainerServiceItemLink

Returns an item link for a given trainer service item.

link = GetTrainerServiceItemLink(index)

Argument:

index — The index of a service in the Trainer window. (number)

Returns:

link — The item link for the given trainer service, or nil. (string)

GetTrainerServiceLevelReq

Returns the level requirement for a trainer service.

reqLevel = GetTrainerServiceLevelReq(index)

Argument:

index — The index of the trainer service. (number)

Returns:

reqLevel — The required level to learn a given service, otherwise nil. (number)

GetTrainerServiceNumAbilityReq

Returns the number of ability requirements to learn a given spell. An *ability requirement* is a prerequisite spell that must be known to learn a future rank, such as Arcane Explosion(Rank 2), which requires Arcane Explosion(Rank 1).

numRequirements = GetTrainerServiceNumAbilityReq(index)

Argument:

id — The index in the Trainer window. (number)

Returns:

numRequirements — The number of ability requirements that must be fulfilled to learn the given skill. The details about each specific requirement can be queried using GetTrainerServiceAbilityReq. (number)

Example:

```
local index = GetTrainerSelectionIndex()
local name, rank, category = GetTrainerServiceInfo(index)
if category ~= "header" then
  ChatFrame1:AddMessage("Requirements to learn " .. name .. " ↵
(" .. category .. ")")
  local numRequirements = GetTrainerServiceNumAbilityReq(index)
  if numRequirements > 0 then
    for i=1,numRequirements do
      local ability, hasReq = ↵
GetTrainerServiceAbilityReq(index, i)
      if hasReq then
        ChatFrame1:AddMessage(" + " .. ability)
      else
        ChatFrame1:AddMessage("--" .. ability, 1, 0.3, 0.3)
      end
    end
  else
    ChatFrame1:AddMessage("None")
  end
end
```

GetTrainerServiceSkillLine

Returns the name of the given skill line.

```
skillLine = GetTrainerServiceSkillLine(index)
```

Argument:

index — The index of the skill line to query. (number)

Returns:

skillLine — The name of the given skill line (for example, Herbalism). (string)

GetTrainerServiceSkillReq

Returns the skill requirement for a given trainer service.

```
skill, rank, hasReq = GetTrainerServiceSkillReq(index)
```

Argument:

index — The index of a trainer service. (number)

Returns:

skill — The name of the required skill. (string)

rank — The rank required. (number)

hasReq — 1 if the player fulfills the requirement, otherwise nil. (1nil)

GetTrainerServiceTypeFilter

Queries the enabled state of a filter in the Trainer window.

```
isEnabled  = GetTrainerServiceTypeFilter("type")
```

Arguments:

type — The filter type to query. (string)

- available — Shows skills that you are able to learn.
- unavailable — Shows skills that you are unable to learn.
- used — Shows skills that you have already learned.

Returns:

isEnabled — 1 if the filter is currently enabled, otherwise nil. (1nil)

Example:

```
-- Table to hold possible filters
local filters = {"available", "unavailable", "used"}
for idx,filter in ipairs(filters) do
  local isEnabled = GetTrainerServiceTypeFilter(filter)
  if isEnabled then
    ChatFrame1:AddMessage(filter .. " filter" .. " is ↵
Enabled")
  else
    ChatFrame1:AddMessage(filter .. " filter" .. " is↵
Disabled")
  end
end
```

GetTrainerSkillLineFilter

Returns whether a trainer skill line filter is enabled.

```
isEnabled = GetTrainerSkillLineFilter(index)
```

Argument:

index — The index of a skill line filter. These are any of the major headings at a trainer, such as Frost, Fire, and Arcane, or Development Skills and Recipes. (number)

Returns:

isEnabled — 1 if the given filter is enabled, otherwise nil. (1nil)

GetTrainerSkillLines

Returns the spell schools available at a given trainer.

```
... = GetTrainerSkillLines()
```

Returns:

... — A list of strings containing the names of the available trainer skill lines. These are the schools that correspond to spellbook tabs, such as Fire, Arcane, and Frost. (string)

GetUnitHealthModifier

Returns the health modifier for a pet. Used to modify the amount of health a pet gains from +stamina.

```
modifier = GetUnitHealthModifier("unit" or "name")
```

Arguments:

unit or name

unit — The unit ID to query. (unitid)

name — The name of the player to query. (string)

Returns:

modifier — The health modifier. (number)

Note

This function only works on player and pet. It will always return 1 for the player.

GetUnitHealthRegenRateFromSpirit

Returns the amount of health gained per second while not in combat, as a result of spirit.

```
regen = GetUnitHealthRegenRateFromSpirit("unit")
```

Arguments:

unit or name

unit — The unit to query. (unitid)

name — The name of the character to query. (string)

Returns:

regen — The amount of health gained per second while not in combat. (number)

GetUnitManaRegenRateFromSpirit

Returns the mana regeneration rate per second the unit has from the spirit stat.

```
regen = GetUnitManaRegenRateFromSpirit("unit")
```

Argument:

unit — The unit to query. (unitid)

Returns:

regen — The amount of mana regeneration the unit gains each second from spirit, while not casting. (number)

GetUnitPowerModifier

Returns the power modifier for a pet. Used to modify the amount of mana a pet gains from +intellect.

```
modifier = GetUnitPowerModifier("unit")
```

Arguments:

unit or name

unit — The unit ID to query. (unitid)

name — The name of the player to query. (string)

Returns:

modifier — Power modifier. (number)

Note: This function only works on player and pet. It will return 1 for the player always.

GetVideoCaps

Returns information about the video subsystem.

```
hasAnisotropic, hasPixelShaders, hasVertexShaders, hasTrilinear,
hasTripleBuffering, maxAnisotropy, hasHardwareCursor  = GetVideoCaps()
```

Returns:

hasAnisotropic — (number)

hasPixelShaders — Indicates if the video subsystem has pixel shaders. (number)

hasVertexShaders — Indicates if the video subsystem has vertex shaders. (number)

hasTrilinear — (number)

hasTripleBufering — Indicates if the video subsystem supports triple buffering. (number)

maxAnisotropy — (number)

hasHardwareCursor — Indicates if the video subsystem supports a hardware cursor. (number)

GetVoiceCurrentSessionID

Returns an identifier for your current voice session. This function returns the voice session ID of your currently selected voice channel. Other channels have other session IDs. If you are not in any voice channel, it will return nil. This can be used as a quick check to see if you are in a voice channel.

```
id = GetVoiceCurrentSessionID()
```

Returns:

id — The voice session ID. (number)

GetVoiceSessionInfo

Returns information about a given voice session.

```
name, active = GetVoiceSessionInfo(session)
```

Argument:

session — The session ID. (number)

Returns:

name — The name of the voice session (channel). (string)

active — 1 if the voice session is active, otherwise nil. (1nil)

GetVoiceSessionMemberInfoBySessionID

Returns information about a member of a given voice session.

```
name, voiceActive, sessionActive, muted, squelched = ↵
GetVoiceSessionMemberInfoBySessionID(session, index)
```

Arguments:

session — ID of the voice session. (number)

index — Index of the voice session member. (number)

Returns:

name — Name of the player. (string)

voiceActive — 1 if the player has voice active, otherwise nil. (1nil)

sessionActive — 1 if the player's voice is set to this session, otherwise nil. (1nil)

muted — 1 if you muted that player, otherwise nil. (1nil)

squelched — 1 if the player was silenced by the channel moderator, otherwise nil. (1nil)

Note: You need voice enabled yourself for this function to work, and it will return *Unknown* as the name for an invalid session or member IDs.

GetVoiceStatus

Returns the voice enabled status of the queried player.

```
status = GetVoiceStatus("name" or "unit", "channel")
```

Arguments:

unit or name

unit — The unit ID to query. (unitid)

name — The name of the player to query. (string)

channel — Channel to query for voice status. (string)

Returns:

status — 1 if voice is enabled, nil if disabled. (1nil)

GetWatchedFactionInfo

Returns information about the faction currently being watched.

```
name, reaction, min, max, value = GetWatchedFactionInfo()
```

Returns:

`name` — The name of the faction being watched. (string)

`reaction` — The current faction standing, as a number. (number)

- 1 — Hated
- 2 — Hostile
- 3 — Unfriendly
- 4 — Neutral
- 5 — Friendly
- 6 — Honored
- 7 — Revered
- 8 — Exalted

`min` — The minimum value for the faction status bar. (number)

`max` — The maximum value for the faction status bar. (number)

`value` — The current value for the faction status bar. (number)

GetWeaponEnchantInfo

Returns information about temporary item enchants on the player's weapons. This function does not work for permanent enchantment, but, rather, weapon buffs such as Mana Oil and Poisons.

```
hasMainHandEnchant, mainHandExpiration, mainHandCharges, ↵
hasOffHandEnchant, offHandExpiration, offHandCharges = ↵
GetWeaponEnchantInfo()
```

Returns:

`hasMainHandEnchant` — 1 if the main hand weapon has a temporary enchant. (1nil)

`mainHandExpiration` — The time until the enchant expires, in milliseconds. (number)

`mainHandCharges` — The number of charges left on the enchantment. (number)

`hasOffHandEnchant` — 1 if the offhand weapon has a temporary enchant. (1nil)

`offHandExpiration` — The time until the enchant expires, in milliseconds. (number)

`offHandCharges` — The number of charges left on the enchantment. (number)

GetWhoInfo

Returns information about a specific index of a who request's results.

```
name, guild, level, race, class, zone, classFileName = ↵
GetWhoInfo(index)
```

Argument:

index — The index of an entry in the who list. (number)

Returns:

name — The name of the player. (string)

guild — The player's guild name. (string)

level — The player's level. (number)

race — The localized name of the player's race. (string)

class — The localized name of the player's class. (string)

zone — The player's current zone. (string)

filename — A nonlocalized token representing the player's class. (string)

GetWorldDetail

Returns the level of rendered world detail in the client.

```
worldDetail = GetWorldDetail()
```

Returns:

worldDetail — The level of world detail. (number)

- ▪ 0 — Low world detail
- ▪ 1 — Medium world detail
- ▪ 2 — High world detail

GetWorldStateUIInfo

Returns information about a WorldState UI element. The WorldState frames are used for PvP objectives as well as certain in-game events such as the Black Morass event in Caverns of Time.

```
uiType, state, text, icon, dynamicIcon, tooltip, ↵
dynamicTooltip, extendedUI, extendedUIState1, ↵
extendedUIState2, extendedUIState3 = ↵
GetWorldStateUIInfo(index)
```

Argument:

index — An index between 1 and GetNumStateWorldUI(). (number)

Returns:

uiType — A value of 1 indicates a conditional UI element, whereas any other value will always be displayed. (number)

state — 1 if the objective is displayed, otherwise nil. (1nil)

text — The text of the objective. (string)

icon — The path to the objective's icon texture. (string)

dynamicIcon — The path to the objective's dynamic icon texture. (string)

extendedUI — CAPTUREPOINT to display a progress bar for a capture point, otherwise the empty string. (string)

extendedUIState1 — The index of the capture bar index. (number)

extendedUIState2 — The current progress bar position; 0 is the right edge, 100 is the left edge. (number)

extendedUIState3 — The width of the neutral zone as a percentage (0–100). If the neutral zone is 50, then 25 percent of the bar is Horde, 25 percent of the bar is Alliance, and 50 percent of the bar is in the middle as neutral. (number)

GetXPExhaustion

Returns the amount of rested experience the player has earned.

```
exhaustionXP = GetXPExhaustion()
```

Returns:

exhaustionXP — The amount of rested experience the player currently has earned. Each time the player gains experience from killing monsters, this value will decrease by the total amount of experience gained, not just the amount of rested experience bonus awarded. (number)

GetZonePVPInfo

Returns PvP information about the current zone.

```
pvpType, isSubZonePvP, factionName = GetZonePVPInfo()
```

Returns:

pvpType — The type of PvP zone. (string)

- arena — If the current zone is a PvP arena.
- contested — If the current zone is PvP contested.
- friendly — If the current zone is controlled by the player's faction.
- hostile — If the current zone is controlled by the opposing faction.
- nil — The equivalent of a contested zone on a Normal server.
- sanctuary — The zone is a sanctuary, and PvP is not allowed.

isSubZonePVP — 1 if the current zone allows free-for-all PvP. (1nil)

factionName — The name of the faction that controls the zone, if the pvpType was friendly or hostile. (string)

GetZoneText

Returns the name of the current zone.

```
zone = GetZoneText()
```

Returns:

zone — The name of the current zone. (string)

GiveMasterLoot

Awards the given loot to the specified candidate.

```
GiveMasterLoot(slot, index)
```

Arguments:

slot — The loot slot item to award. (number)

index — The index of the loot candidate as returned by
GetMasterLootCandidate(). (number)

Note: This function requires the player be master looter

GMSurveyAnswerSubmit

Submits an answer to a GM survey question.

```
GMSurveyAnswerSubmit(question, rank, "comment")
```

Arguments:

question — The index of the question being answered. (number)

rank — The rank selected. (number)

comment — A comment for the given question. (string)

GMSurveyCommentSubmit

Submits a comment to the current GM survey.

```
GMSurveyCommentSubmit("comment")
```

Arguments:

comment — The comment made on the GM survey. (string)

GMSurveyQuestion

Returns the text of a specific question from a GM survey.

```
surveyQuestion  = GMSurveyQuestion(index)
```

Argument:

index — The index of a GM survey question. (number)

Returns:

surveyQuestion — The question being asked. (string)

GMSurveySubmit

Submits the current GM survey.

GuildControlAddRank

Adds a new rank to the player's guild. This rank is added at the bottom.

```
GuildControlAddRank("name")
```

Argument:

name — The name of the new rank. (string)

GuildControlDelRank

Deletes a guild rank.

```
GuildControlDelRank("name")
```

Argument:

name — The name of the rank to delete. (string)

GuildControlGetNumRanks

Returns the number of guild ranks in the guild including the guild master.

```
numRanks = GuildControlGetNumRanks()
```

Returns:

numRanks — Number of guild ranks. (number)

GuildControlGetRankFlags

Returns a list of permission flags for a guild rank. This function retrieves a list of permissions for the currently selected rank. There are currently 14 flags as denoted in GlobalStrings.lua by the various GUILDCONTROL_OPTIONxx strings. If you are not the guild leader or have not selected a rank with GuildControlSetRank(), all of the results will be nil. There are also some situations in which it may return no results, such as immediately after logging in.

```
... = GuildControlGetRankFlags()
```

Returns:

... — The list of permission flags. (1nil)

Example:

```
-- Print rank flags for the first rank in the guild
function PrintFlags(...)
  local output = ""
  for i = 1, select("#", ...) do
    output = output .. getglobal("GUILDCONTROL_OPTION"..i) ..↵
": " .. select(i, ...) .. "; "
  end
  DEFAULT_CHAT_FRAME:AddMessage(output)
end
GuildControlSetRank(1)
PrintFlags(GuildControlGetRankFlags())
```

GuildControlGetRankName

Returns the name of the given guild rank.

```
rankName = GuildControlGetRankName(rankIndex)
```

Argument:

rankIndex — The rank index to query. (number)

Returns:

rankName — The name of the given guild rank. (string)

GuildControlSaveRank

Saves the settings for a guild rank.

```
GuildControlSaveRank(name)
```

Argument:

name — The name of the guild rank. (string)

GuildControlSetRank

Sets the current rank in the Guild Control window.

```
GuildControlSetRank(rank)
```

Argument:

rank — The numeric guild rank to edit. The Guild Master rank is always 1.
(number)

GuildControlSetRankFlag

Sets the current rank permission to enabled or disabled. Calling this functions
allows you to change the value of a rank flag. Changes are not saved until a call
is made to GuildControlSaveRank().

```
GuildControlSetRankFlag(index, enabled)
```

Arguments:

index — The index for the flag you wish to change. (number)

- 1 — Guild chat listen
- 2 — Guild chat speak
- 3 — Officer chat listen
- 4 — Officer chat speak
- 5 — Promote
- 6 — Demote
- 7 — Invite member
- 8 — Remove member
- 9 — Set MOTD
- 10 — Edit Public Notes

- 11 — View Officer Note
- 12 — Edit Officer Note
- 13 — Modify guild info

enabled — Enables or disables the flag. (boolean)

GuildDemote

Demotes a guild member by one guild rank.

```
GuildDemote("name")
```

Argument:

name — A guild member's name. (string)

GuildDisband

Disbands your guild without confirmation. Can only be done by the guild leader.

GuildInfo

Queries the server for the player's guild information. This function sends two messages to the default chat frame, one showing the name of the guild, followed by the date the guild was created and how many players/accounts belong to the guild.

GuildInvite

Invites a player to your guild.

```
GuildInvite("name")
```

Argument:

name — The name of the player to invite to your guild. (string)

GuildLeave

Causes the player to leave his or her current guild without confirmation.

GuildPromote

Promotes a given player to the next highest guild rank.

```
GuildPromote("name")
```

Argument:

name — The name of the player to promote. (string)

GuildRoster

Initiates a guild roster update. This function sends a request to the server for updated guild roster information. When the results are ready, the game will fire the GUILD_ROSTER_UPDATE event. The server will only respond to this request every 10 seconds or so, to reduce server load.

GuildRosterSetOfficerNote

Sets an Officer Note for a guild member.

```
GuildRosterSetOfficerNote(index, "note")
```

Arguments:

index — The index of a guild member in the guild UI. (number)

note — The note to set for the given guild member. (string)

GuildRosterSetPublicNote

Sets the Public Note of a guild member. The index is attainable by counting down from the top to the member, or by using GetGuildRosterSelection() while the guild member is selected.

```
GuildRosterSetPublicNote(index, "note")
```

Arguments:

index — The position where the member is on the guild roster. (number)

note — Text to be set as the Public Note of the index. (string)

GuildSetLeader

Promotes the specified player to be the new guild leader.

```
GuildSetLeader("name")
```

Argument:

name — The name of the guild member to promote to leader. (string)

Note: The specified player has to be in the guild and must be online, and you have to be the guild leader for the command to have any effect.

GuildSetMOTD

Sets the guild message of the day. This function allows for longer messages and embedded newlines when used instead of the /gmotd command or the Edit box on the guild interface. Remember that the Guild MOTD can't be turned off in the Interface options — keep your messages concise.

```
GuildSetMOTD("message")
```

Argument:

message — The message to set as the guild MOTD. (string)

Example:

```
-- Set a message of the day
GuildSetMOTD("This is a message of the day")
-- Set a two-line message of the day
GuildSetMOTD("Please vote for the following applicants on our
forums:\nCladhaire\nCairthas")
```

GuildUninvite

Removes a player from the guild.

```
GuildUninvite("name")
```

Argument:

name — The name of the player to remove. (string)

HasAction

Returns a flag if an action slot is occupied.

```
HasAction(slot)
```

Argument:

slot — Action slot number. (number)

Returns:

hasAction — Returns 1 if the slot contains an action, or else nil. (boolean)

HasFilledPetition

Returns whether the player has a completed petition. This function is used by the default user interface to show and hide the buttons that allow you to turn in an arena charter.

```
hasPetition = HasFilledPetition()
```

Returns:

hasPetition — 1 if the player has a filled-in petition, otherwise nil. (1nil)

HasFullControl

Returns whether the player has full control over his or her character.

```
hasControl = HasFullControl()
```

Returns:

hasControl — 1 if the player has full control over his or her character (for example, isn't feared, charmed, and so on), otherwise nil. (1nil)

HasInspectHonorData

Returns whether the client has honor data for the currently inspected player.

```
hasHonorData = HasInspectHonorData()
```

Returns:

hasHonorData — 1 if the client has honor data for the currently inspected player, otherwise nil. (1nil)

HasKey

Returns whether the player currently has a key. This is used by the default UI to show and hide the keychain.

```
hasKey = HasKey()
```

Returns:

hasKey — Returns 1 if the player has a key, otherwise nil. (1nil)

HasNewMail

Returns whether the player has new mail.

```
newMail = HasNewMail()
```

Returns:

hasMail — 1 if the player has new mail, otherwise nil. (1nil)

HasPetSpells

Returns whether the player's current active pet has spells or not.

```
hasPetSpells, petType = HasPetSpells()
```

Returns:

hasPetSpells — 1 if the player has an active pet with spells/abilities currently, otherwise nil. (1nil)

petType — Type of pet used. (string)

HasPetUI

Returns whether the client should show the pet UI.

```
hasPetUI, isHunterPet = HasPetUI()
```

Returns:

hasPetUI — 1 if the client should show the pet UI. (1nil)

isHunterPet — 1 if the player's pet is a hunter pet. (1nil)

HasSoulstone

Returns whether the player has a soulstone resurrection available. Only works when the player is dead and has not yet released his spirit.

```
text = HasSoulstone()
```

Returns:

text — The text to be displayed on the dialog box if the player has a soulstone resurrection available, otherwise nil. (string)

HasWandEquipped

Returns whether the player has a wand equipped.

```
isEquipped = HasWandEquipped()
```

Returns:

isEquipped — 1 if a wand is equipped, otherwise nil. (1nil)

HideFriendNameplates

Hides friendly nameplates.

HideNameplates

Hides nameplates for hostile units.

HideRepairCursor

Stops displaying the item repair cursor.

hooksecurefunc

Adds a function to be called after the original secure function. This function allows you to post-hook a secure function without tainting the original. The original function will still be called, but the function you supply will be called after the original, with the same arguments. The return values from your function will not be used anywhere.

Please note that there is no API to unhook a function.

```
hooksecurefunc([table,] "function", hookfunc)
```

Arguments:

table (optional) — A table object that contains the function to be hooked. (table)

function — The name of the function to be hooked. (string)

hookfunc — The function to be called each time the original function is called. (function)

Example:

```
-- Keep a counter of how many times your character has
-- jumped, and display the count in the chat window
local counter = 0
local function hook_JumpOrAscendStart(...)
  counter = counter + 1
  ChatFrame1:AddMessage("Boing! Boing!--" .. counter .. ↵
" jumps.")
end
hooksecurefunc("JumpOrAscendStart", hook_JumpOrAscendStart)

-- Hook GameTooltip:SetAction() to display how many spell
-- casts you can make without running out of mana
-- It does this by scanning the second line of the tooltip,
-- and matching it against the pattern "(%d+) " .. MANA,
-- where MANA is the global string for "Mana"
local function hook_SetAction(self, ...)
local line = getglobal(self:GetName() .. "TextLeft2")
  local text = line:GetText() or ""
  local manaCost = text:match("(%d+) " .. MANA)
  if manaCost then
    -- Convert the mana cost to a number
    manaCost = tostring(manaCost)
```

```
    -- Get the player's current mana, and calculate
    local mana = UnitMana("player")
    local numCasts = math.floor(mana / manaCost)
    -- Add the line to the tooltip, colored blue
    self:AddLine("You can cast this spell " .. numCasts .. " ↵
times", 0.4, 0.4, 1.0)
    -- Call this to ensure the tooltip is properly resized
    self:Show()
  end
end
hooksecurefunc(GameTooltip, "SetAction", hook_SetAction)
```

InCinematic

Returns whether the character is viewing a cinematic (refers to the in-engine cinematic displayed when first logging in to a new character, not the pre-rendered movies).

```
inCinematic = InCinematic()
```

Returns:

inCinematic — Tells whether the character is viewing a cinematic or not. (1nil)

InCombatLockdown

Queries the game client to see if the user interface is currently in protected lock-down mode.

```
inLockdown = InCombatLockdown()
```

Returns:

inLockdown — 1 if the user interface is in protected lockdown mode as a result of combat, otherwise nil. (1nil)

InRepairMode

Returns whether the player is currently in item repair mode. This function is used by the default user interface to repair items when they are clicked in repair mode and to display repair prices in item tooltips.

```
inRepair = InRepairMode()
```

Returns:

inRepair — 1 if the player is currently in repair mode, otherwise nil. (1nil)

InboxItemCanDelete

Returns whether an inbox item can be deleted.

```
canDelete = InboxItemCanDelete(index)
```

Argument:

index — The index of the message in the inbox. (number)

Returns:

canDelete — 1 if the mail message can be deleted, otherwise nil. (1nil)

InitiateTrade

Initiates a trade with a given unit.

```
InitiateTrade("unit")
```

Argument:

unit — The unit with which to initiate a trade. (unitid)

InviteUnit

Invites a player or unit to the player's party.

```
InviteUnit("unit" or "name")
```

Arguments:

unit or name

  unit — The unit to invite. (unitid)

  name — The name of a unit to invite. (string)

IsActionInRange

Returns whether the action is in range of the current target.

```
inRange = IsActionInRange(action)
```

Argument:

action — The action ID. (number)

Returns:

inRange — 1 if the action is in range of the current target, 0 if out of range, and nil if the target is invalid for this spell. (number)

IsActiveBattlefieldArena

Returns whether the current battlefield is an arena match.

```
isArena, isRegistered = IsActiveBattlefieldArena()
```

Returns:

isArena — 1 if the current battlefield is an arena match. (1nil)

isRegistered — 1 if the current arena match is a ranked match. (1nil)

IsActiveQuestTrivial

Returns whether an active quest in the QuestFrame is considered trivial. This function is used to display (low level) following the quest name.

```
isTrivial = IsActiveQuestTrivial(index)
```

Argument:

index — The index of an active quest in the QuestFrame. (number)

Returns:

isTrivial — 1 if the quest is considered trivial. (1nil)

IsAddOnLoadOnDemand

Returns whether a given addon can be loaded on demand. This function returns the value of the `##` `LoadOnDemand` field in the table of contents file if it's set to `1`, otherwise `nil`.

```
isLod = IsAddOnLoadOnDemand(index or "name")
```

Arguments:

`index` — The index of the addon to query. (`number`)

`name` — The name of the addon to query. (`string`)

Returns:

`isLod` — 1 if the addon is capable of load on demand, otherwise `nil`. (`1nil`)

IsAddOnLoaded

Query if an addon is loaded (running).

```
loaded = IsAddOnLoaded(index or "name")
```

Arguments:

`index` — The addon index to query. Between `1` and `GetNumAddOns()`. Blizzard addons cannot be queried by index. The addon index is OS-specific; in some versions of Windows, it is alphabetically sorted on the folder name. (`integer`)

`name` — Name of the addon to query; not case-sensitive; uses the addon folder name, not the title from the TOC. (`string`)

Returns:

`loaded` — 1 if the addon is loaded, otherwise `nil`. (`1nil`)

IsAltKeyDown

Returns whether an `Alt` key on the keyboard is held down.

Returns:

`isDown` — 1 if an `Alt` key on the keyboard is currently held down. (`1nil`)

IsArenaTeamCaptain

Returns whether the player is the team captain for a given arena team.

```
isCaptain = IsArenaTeamCaptain(index)
```

Argument:

`index` — The index of an arena team. (`number`)

Returns:

`isCaptain` — 1 if the player is the captain of the given arena team or an invalid index is supplied, otherwise `nil`. (`1nil`)

IsAttackAction

Returns whether the given action flashes when engaged in melee auto-attacking.

```
isAttack = IsAttackAction(slot)
```

Argument:

slot — The action slot to query. (number)

Returns:

isAttack — 1 if the action is a type of auto-attack, otherwise nil. (1nil)

Note: Does not work for Shoot or Auto Shot abilities

IsAttackSpell

Returns whether a given spell is an attack spell. This is used by the default user interface to indicate if the spell should flash while auto-attacking.

```
isAttack = IsAttackSpell(spellId or "name" [, "bookType"])
```

Arguments:

spellId or name

- ■ spellId — The index of a spell in the spellbook. (number)
- ■ name — The name of a spell. (string)

bookType — The type of spellbook. (number)

- ■ pet — The pet's spellbook
- ■ spell — The player's spellbook

Returns:

isAttack — 1 if the spell is an attack spell, otherwise nil. (1nil)

IsAuctionSortReversed

Returns whether a column in the auction house interface is reverse-sorted or not.

```
isReversed, isSorted = IsAuctionSortReversed("type", "sort")
```

Arguments:

type — Type of the auction listing. (string)

- ■ bidder — Auctions on which the player has bid
- ■ list — Auctions available for bidding/purchase
- ■ owner — Auctions the player has placed

sort — Column that can be sorted on. (string)

Returns:

isReversed — 1 if the queried sort is reversed, otherwise nil. (1nil)

isSorted — 1 if the queried sort has been sorted on, otherwise nil. (1nil)

IsAutoRepeatAction

Checks if an action is an autorepeat action (for example, Auto Shot).

```
repeat = IsAutoRepeatAction(action)
```

Argument:

action — The action ID to check. (number)

Returns:

repeat — 1 if the action is an autorepeat action, otherwise nil. (1nil)

IsAutoRepeatSpell

Returns whether the given spell is an autorepeat spell.

```
isAutoRepeat = IsAutoRepeatSpell("spellName")
```

Argument:

spellName — The name of the spell to query. (string)

Returns:

isAutoRepeat — If the spell is an autorepeating spell. (1nil)

Note: This doesn't appear to return 1 for any spells, including Auto Shot and Shoot (wand).

IsAvailableQuestTrivial

Returns the trivial state for the quests available at a quest NPC.

```
trivial = IsAvailableQuestTrivial(index)
```

Argument:

index — The index of the quest to check. (number)

Returns:

trivial — 1 if the available quest is trivial, otherwise nil. (1nil)

Note: A quest is trivial if it is way below the player's level.

IsBattlefieldArena

Returns whether the NPC the player is interacting with can queue for arenas.

```
isArena = IsBattlefieldArena()
```

Returns:

isArena — 1 if the interacting NPC can queue the player for arenas, otherwise nil. (1nil)

IsConsumableAction

Returns 1 if the action ID contains a consumable, otherwise `nil`.

```
isConsumableAction = IsConsumableAction(slot)
```

Argument:

`slot` — The action ID of the slot to be queried. (number)

Returns:

`isConsumableAction` — 1 if the action is a consumable, otherwise `nil`. (1nil)

IsConsumableItem

Whether a given item is consumable.

```
consumable = IsConsumableItem(itemID or "itemName" or "itemLink")
```

Arguments:

`itemID` or `itemName` or `itemLink`

`itemID` — An item's ID. (number)

`itemName` — An item's name. (string)

`itemLink` — An item's link. (string)

Returns:

`consumable` — 1 if the item is a consumable, `nil` for invalid or nonconsumable items. (1nil)

IsConsumableSpell

Returns whether a spell requires a consumable reagent.

```
isConsumable = IsConsumableSpell("spell" or spellId [, "bookType"])
```

Arguments:

`spell` or `spellId`

- `spell` — The name of the spell to query (string)

- `spellId` — The spellbook slot index of the spell to query (string)

`bookType` (optional) — The spellbook type in which to look up the slot index (required when slot index is used). (string)

- `pet` — Looks up the slot index in the pet's spellbook of the player

- `spell` — Looks up the slot index in the normal spellbook

Returns:

`isConsumable` — 1 if the spell requires a consumable reagent, otherwise il. (1nil)

IsControlKeyDown

Returns whether a control key on the keyboard is held down.

Returns:

`isDown` — 1 if a Control key on the keyboard is currently held down. (1nil)

IsCurrentAction

Returns whether a specific action is currently being cast, or awaiting targeting.

```
isCurrent = IsCurrentAction(slot)
```

Argument:

slot — An action bar slot. (number)

Returns:

isCurrent — 1 if the given action is currently being cast or the action is currently awaiting targeting, otherwise nil. (1nil)

IsCurrentItem

Returns true if the item is being used and nothing if it is not. This function is used for conditionals when you need to know if the current item is being used or not.

```
IsCurrentItem(itemID or "itemName" or "itemLink")
```

Arguments:

itemID or itemName or itemLink

  itemID — An item's ID. (number)

  itemName — An item's name. (string)

  itemLink — An item's link. (string)

Returns:

isItem — 1 if the item is being used or awaiting input (such as a targeted effect). (1nil)

IsCurrentQuestFailed

Queries the failed state for the currently selected quest.

```
isFailed = IsCurrentQuestFailed()
```

Returns:

isFailed — 1 if the current quest is failed, otherwise nil. (1nil)

IsCurrentSpell

Returns whether a given spell is currently being cast or awaiting targeting.

```
isCurrent = IsCurrentSpell("spellName" or spellId [, "bookType"])
```

Arguments:

spellName or spellId

  ▪ spellName — The name of a spell. (string)

  ▪ spellId — The spell ID of a spell. (number)

bookType (optional) — The type of spellbook for which the spell ID is supplied. (string)

  ▪ pet — The pet's spellbook.

  ▪ spell — The player's spellbook.

Returns:

isCurrent — 1 if the given spell is currently being cast, or awaiting targeting. (1nil)

IsDisplayChannelModerator

Returns whether the player is a moderator of the currently selected display channel in the Chat tab.

isModerator = IsDisplayChannelModerator()

Returns:

isModerator — 1 if the player is a moderator of the currently selected display channel, otherwise nil. (1nil)

IsDisplayChannelOwner

Returns whether the player is the owner of the currently displayed channel.

isOwner = IsDisplayChannelOwner()

Returns:

isOwner — 1 if the player is the owner of the currently displayed channel. (1nil)

IsEquippableItem

Returns whether a given item is equipable.

isEquippable = IsEquippableItem(name)

Returns:

isEquippable — 1 if the item is equipable, otherwise nil. (1nil)

IsEquippedAction

Returns whether an action slot contains an equipped item. If the action slot contains an item that is currently equipped, this function returns 1. If the slot is empty, contains an item that is not equipped, or contains a spell, this function returns nil. If the slot contains a macro, this function's behavior depends on the contents of the macro. If executing the macro under current conditions will /use an item, or if the macro is set to #show an item, it will return 1 if the item is equipped.

IsEquippedAction(slot)

Argument:

slot — The action bar slot. (number)

Returns:

isEquipped — 1 if the slot has an equipped item, otherwise nil. (1nil)

IsEquippedItem

Returns whether the supplied item is currently equipped by the player.

```
isEquipped = IsEquippedItem("name" or itemId)
```

Arguments:

name or itemId

- name — A name of an item. (string)

- itemId — An item's item ID. (itemId)

Returns:

isEquipped — 1 if the item is equipped, otherwise nil. (1nil)

Example:

```
-- Check to see if your Alliance PvP trinket is equipped
if IsEquippedItem("Medallion of the Alliance") then
  ChatFrame1:AddMessage("Your PvP trinket is already equipped.")
else
  ChatFrame1:AddMessage("*** Make sure to equip your PvP trinket ***")
end


-- Check to see if Staff of Infinite Mysteries (itemId 28633) ↵
is equipped
if IsEquippedItem(28633) then
  ChatFrame1:AddMessage("Your staff is equipped")
else
  ChatFrame1:AddMessage("Your staff is not equipped")
end
```

IsEquippedItemType

Returns whether an item of a given type is currently equipped.

```
isEquipped = IsEquippedItemType("type")
```

Argument:

type — The item type to query. (string)

Returns:

isEquipped — 1 if the given item type is currently equipped, otherwise nil. (1nil)

Example:

```
-- Print if the player currently has a shield equipped
local hasShield = IsEquippedItemType("Shields")
if hasShield then
  ChatFrame1:AddMessage("You currently have a shield equipped")
else
  ChatFrame1:AddMessage("You do not have a shield equipped")
end
```

IsFactionInactive

Returns whether a faction is flagged as inactive.

`isInactive = IsFactionInactive(index)`

Argument:

`index` — The index of a faction to query. (number)

Returns:

`isInactive` — 1 if the faction is currently flagged as inactive, otherwise `nil`. (1nil)

IsFalling

Returns whether the player is falling.

`falling = IsFalling()`

Returns:

`falling` — 1 if the player is falling, otherwise `nil`. (1nil)

IsFishingLoot

Returns whether the currently displayed loot is fishing loot. This function is used by the default user interface to play the "reel in" sound and change the circle texture on the Loot window to a fish.

`isFishing = IsFishingLoot()`

Returns:

`isFishing` — 1 if the currently displayed loot is fishing loot, otherwise `nil`. (1nil)

IsFlyableArea

Returns whether the player's current location is an area in which flying mounts and other flight abilities are usable.

`isFlyable = IsFlyableArea()`

Returns:

`isFlyable` — 1 if the current area is a flyable area, otherwise `nil`. (1nil)

IsFlying

Returns whether the player is currently flying.

`isFlying = IsFlying()`

Returns:

`isFlying` — 1 if the player is currently flying, otherwise `nil`. (1nil)

IsGuildLeader

Returns whether the current player is guild leader.

```
isLeader = IsGuildLeader()
```

Returns:

isLeader — 1 if the player is a guild leader, otherwise nil. (1nil)

IsHarmfulItem

Returns whether an item is harmful (has a "use" action that can be cast only against hostile targets).

```
isHarmful = IsHarmfulItem("itemName")
```

Argument:

itemName — The name of the item to query. (string)

Returns:

isHarmful — 1 if the item is harmful, otherwise nil. (1nil)

IsHarmfulSpell

Returns whether a given spell is harmful (can be cast only against hostile targets).

```
isHarmful = IsHarmfulSpell("name")
```

Argument:

spell — The name of the spell to query. (string)

Returns:

isHarmful — 1 if the spell is harmful, otherwise nil. (1nil)

Example:

```
-- Go through the spellbook
local numTabs = GetNumSpellTabs()
for i=1,numTabs do
  local name,texture,offset,numSpells = GetSpellTabInfo(i)
  for spellId=1,numSpells do
    local harmful = IsHarmfulSpell(i, "spell")
    if harmful then
      local name,rank = GetSpellName(i, "spell")
      ChatFrame1:AddMessage(name .. " is a harmful spell")
    end
  end
end
```

IsHelpfulItem

Returns whether the item is helpful (has a "use" action that can only be cast on friendly targets). Helpful items include health potions, food, and drink.

```
helpful = IsHelpfulItem(itemID or "itemName" or "itemLink")
```

Arguments:

itemID or itemName or itemLink

itemID — An item's ID. (number)

itemName — An item's name. (string)

itemLink — An item's link. (string)

Returns:

helpful — 1 if the item is helpful, nil for invalid or non-helpful items. (1nil)

IsHelpfulSpell

Returns whether a given spell is helpful (can be cast only on friendly targets).

```
isHelpful = IsHelpfulSpell(name)
```

Argument:

spell — The name of the spell to query. (string)

Returns:

isHelpful — 1 if the spell is helpful, otherwise nil. (1nil)

IsIgnored

Returns whether you are ignoring a specific unit.

```
isIgnored = IsIgnored("unit" or "name")
```

Arguments:

unit or name

unit — The unit ID to query. (unitid)

name — The name of the player to query. (string)

Returns:

isIgnored — 1 if the given player is being ignored, otherwise nil. (1nil)

IsIgnoredOrMuted

Returns if the queried unit is currently ignored or muted by the player.

```
isIgnoredorMuted = IsIgnoredOrMuted("unit")
```

Argument:

unit — Unit to query. (unitid)

Returns:

isIgnoredorMuted — 1 if a unit is ignored or muted, otherwise nil. (1nil)

IsInGuild

Returns whether the player is in a guild.

```
inGuild = IsInGuild()
```

Returns:

inGuild — 1 if the player is in a guild, otherwise nil. (1nil)

IsInInstance

Returns whether the player is currently in an instance, and if so, what type.

```
inInstance, instanceType = IsInInstance()
```

Returns:

isInstance — 1 if the player is in an instance, otherwise nil. (1nil)

instanceType — The type of instance the player is in. (string)

- ▪ pvp — Battleground instance
- ▪ arena — PvP arena instance
- ▪ party — Five-man instance
- ▪ raid — Raid instance
- ▪ none — Not in an instance

IsInLFGQueue

Returns whether the player is currently queued to automatically join a group (or add members to her group) via the LFG system.

```
inQueue = IsInLFGQueue()
```

Returns:

inQueue — 1 if the player is currently in the LFG queue, otherwise nil. (1nil)

IsIndoors

Returns whether the player is currently indoors.

```
inside = IsIndoors()
```

Returns:

inside — 1 if the player is currently indoors, otherwise nil. (1nil)

IsInventoryItemLocked

Returns whether the given inventory slot is locked (has been picked up, is in the player's side of the Trade window, is in an attachment slot of the Send Mail window, and so on).

```
isLocked = IsInventoryItemLocked(slot)
```

Argument:

slot — An inventory slot ID. (number)

Returns:

isLocked — 1 if the item in the inventory slot is locked, otherwise nil. (1nil)

IsItemInRange

Returns whether a usable item is in range of a given unit.

```
inRange = IsItemInRange(itemid or "itemname" or "itemlink", "unit")
```

Arguments:

`itemid` or `itemname` or `itemlink`

   `itemid` — The item's ID. (number)

   `itemname` — The name of an item. (string)

   `itemlink` — A valid item link. (string)

`unit` — The name of the unit to query. (unitid)

Returns:

`inRange` — 1 if the item is in range of the given unit, otherwise `nil`. (1nil)

IsLeftAltKeyDown

Returns whether the left Alt key is currently held down. Returns 1 if the Alt key on the left side of the keyboard is currently held down, otherwise `nil`.

Note: The Mac WoW client does not distinguish between left and right modifier keys, thus both Alt keys are reported as "Left Alt."

```
isDown = IsLeftAltKeyDown()
```

Returns:

`isDown` — 1 if the left Alt key on the keyboard is currently held down. (1nil)

IsLeftControlKeyDown

Returns whether the left Control key is held down. Returns 1 if the Control (ctrl) key on the left side of the keyboard is currently held down, otherwise nil.

Note: The Mac WoW client does not distinguish between left and right modifier keys, thus both Control keys are reported as "Left Control."

```
isDown = IsLeftControlKeyDown()
```

Returns:

`isDown` — 1 if the left Control key is held down. (1nil)

IsLeftShiftKeyDown

Returns whether the left Shift key on the keyboard is held down. Returns 1 if the Shift key on the left side of the keyboard is currently held down, otherwise `nil`.

Note: The Mac WoW client does not distinguish between left and right modifier keys, thus both Shift keys are reported as "Left Shift."

Returns:

`isDown` — 1 if the left Shift key on the keyboard is currently held down. (1nil)

IsLinuxClient

Returns whether the game client is running on Linux. (Currently, Blizzard does not offer an official Linux client; this function is provided for possible forward compatibility.)

```
isLinux = IsLinuxClient()
```

Returns:

IsLinux — 1 if the client is a Linux client, otherwise nil. (1nil)

IsLoggedIn

Returns whether the PLAYER_LOGIN event has already fired.

```
loggedIn = IsLoggedIn()
```

Returns:

loggedIn — 1 if the PLAYER_LOGIN even has already happened, otherwise nil. (1nil)

IsMacClient

Returns whether the running client is the Mac version of WoW.

```
isMac = IsMacClient()
```

Returns:

isMac — 1 if the client is a Mac client, otherwise nil. (1nil)

IsModifiedClick

Determines if the modifiers specified in the click type had been held down while the button click occurred.

```
modifiedClick = IsModifiedClick(type)
```

Argument:

type — The name of the click type. (string)

Returns:

modifiedClick — 1 if the click was modified, otherwise nil. (1nil)

IsModifierKeyDown

Returns whether a modifier key is held down. Modifier keys include Shift, Control, or Alt on either side of the keyboard.

```
isDown = IsModifierKeyDown()
```

Returns:

isDown — 1 if any modifier key is held down, otherwise nil. (1nil)

IsMounted

Returns whether or not your character is mounted.

```
mounted = IsMounted()
```

Returns:

mounted — 1 if the player is mounted, otherwise nil. (1nil)

IsMouseButtonDown

Returns whether the given mouse button is held down.

```
isDown = IsMouseButtonDown(button)
```

Arguments:

button — The mouse button to query. (string)

- ▪ LeftButton
- ▪ RightButton
- ▪ MiddleButton
- ▪ Button4
- ▪ Button5

Returns:

isDown — 1 if the mouse button is held down, otherwise nil. (1nil)

IsMouselooking

Returns whether the mouselook mode is active.

```
isLooking = IsMouselooking()
```

Returns:

isLooking — Returns true if the mouselook mode is active, otherwise false. (boolean)

IsMuted

Returns the mute status for a given player.

```
muted  = IsMuted(unit)
```

Argument:

unit — The name of the unit to query. (string)

Returns:

muted — 1 if the unit is muted, otherwise nil. (1nil)

IsOutOfBounds

Returns whether the player is currently outside the bounds of the world.

`outOfBounds = IsOutOfBounds()`

Returns:

`outOfBounds` — 1 if the player is currently outside the bounds of the world, otherwise `nil`. (1nil)

Note: This function is used with `IsFalling()` to allow the user to release his body if he has fallen through the world.

IsOutdoors

This function returns whether the player is currently outdoors. Note that this function's return value corresponds to the ability to use a mount in that specific location, not whether there is a roof on top of your head. For example, it will return 1 inside of Ironforge and `nil` inside most instances, including those that are otherwise open, such as Stratholme and Shadowfang Keep. Even if this function returns 1, you might not be able to mount at that location if you are standing on specific models that are flagged internally as "do not mount."

`isOutdoors = IsOutdoors()`

Returns:

`isOutdoors` — 1 if the player is currently outdoors, otherwise `nil`. (1nil)

IsPartyLeader

Returns whether a unit is the current party leader.

`isLeader = IsPartyLeader("unit")`

Argument:

`unit` — The unit to query. (unitid)

Returns:

`isLeader` — 1 if the unit is the party leader, otherwise `nil`. (1nil)

IsPassiveSpell

Returns whether a given spell is passive (that is, cannot be actively cast).

`isPassive  = IsPassiveSpell(id, bookType)`

Arguments:

`id` — The index of the spell being queried. (number)

`bookType` — A string indicating which spellbook type should be queried. This is either the value BOOKTYPE_SPELL or BOOKTYPE_PET, which correspond to the strings `spell` and `pet`. (string)

- BOOKTYPE_PET — The pet spellbook
- BOOKTYPE_SPELL — The standard player spellbook

Returns:

isPassive — 1 if the spell is passive, otherwise nil. (1nil)

Example:

```
ChatFrame1:AddMessage("Scanning your spellbook for passive
spells...")
local numTabs = GetNumSpellTabs()
for tabID=1,numTabs do
  local name,texture,offset,numSpells = GetSpellTabInfo(tabID)

  for spellID = offset + 1, offset + numSpells do
    if IsPassiveSpell(spellID, BOOKTYPE_SPELL) then
      local spell,rank = GetSpellName(spellID, BOOKTYPE_SPELL)
      ChatFrame1:AddMessage("--" .. spell)
    end
  end
end
```

IsPetAttackActive

Returns whether the pet's attack action is currently active.

```
isActive = IsPetAttackActive(index)
```

Argument:

index — The index of the pet's attack action. (number)

Returns:

isActive — 1 if the pet's attack action is currently active, otherwise nil. (1nil)

Note: Applies only to pets that have an auto-attack action (as opposed to an attack/follow/stay behavior control like Hunter and Warlock pets), such as Mind Control targets. In such cases, the index of the auto-attack pet action is usually 1.

IsPossessBarVisible

Returns whether the possession bar should be visible. This function is used by Blizzard in response to the UPDATE_BONUS_ACTIONBAR event to toggle between the ShapeshiftBar and the PossessBar (if applicable).

```
isVisible = IsPossessBarVisible()
```

Returns:

isVisible — 1 if the possession bar should be visible, otherwise nil. (1nil)

IsQuestCompletable

Returns whether the currently viewed quest can be completed.

```
isCompletable = IsQuestCompletable()
```

Returns:

isCompletable — 1 if the currently viewed quest is completable, otherwise nil. (1nil)

IsQuestWatched

Returns whether a given quest is currently being watched. This is used by the default UI to handle the quest objective tracking.

isWatched = IsQuestWatched(index)

Argument:

index — The index of a quest in the quest log. (number)

Returns:

isWatched — 1 if the quest is being watched, otherwise nil. (1nil)

IsRaidLeader

Returns whether the player is the leader of their current raid.

isLeader = IsRaidLeader()

Returns:

isLeader — 1 if the player is the leader of her current raid, otherwise nil. (1nil)

IsRaidOfficer

Returns whether the player is a Raid Officer or not.

isRaidOfficer = IsRaidOfficer()

Returns:

isRaidOfficer — Whether the player is a Raid Officer. (boolean)

IsRealPartyLeader

Returns whether the player is the leader of his "real" party. When the player is in a raid or party and then joins a battleground or arena, he will be a part of two different parties/raids simultaneously. This function is used to determine if the player is the leader of the non-battleground party.

isLeader = IsRealPartyLeader()

Returns:

isLeader — 1 if the player is the party leader of the "real" party, otherwise nil. (1nil)

IsRealRaidLeader

Returns whether the player is the leader of his non-battleground raid party. When the player is in a raid or party and then joins a battleground or arena, he will be a part of two different parties/raids simultaneously. This function is used to determine if the player is the leader of the non-battleground raid group.

isLeader = IsRealRaidLeader()

Returns:

isLeader — 1 if the player is the leader of the "real" raid. (1nil)

IsResting

Returns the player's resting status. You are resting if you are in an Inn or Major City. While resting, you will gain XP bonus.

```
resting = IsResting()
```

Returns:

`resting` — Whether the player is resting. `(boolean)`

IsRightAltKeyDown

Returns whether the right Alt key is currently held down. Returns `1` if the Alt key on the right side of the keyboard is currently held down, otherwise `nil`.

Note: The Mac WoW client does not distinguish between left and right modifier keys, thus both Alt keys are reported as "Left Alt."

```
isDown = IsRightAltKeyDown()
```

Returns:

`isDown` — 1 if the right Alt key on the keyboard is currently held down. `(1nil)`

IsRightControlKeyDown

Returns whether the right Control key on the keyboard is held down. Returns `1` if the Control (Ctrl) key on the right side of the keyboard is currently held down, otherwise `nil`.

Note: The Mac WoW client does not distinguish between left and right modifier keys, thus both Control keys are reported as "Left Control."

```
isDown = IsRightControlKeyDown()
```

Returns:

`isDown` — 1 if the right Control key on the keyboard is held down. `(1nil)`

IsRightShiftKeyDown

Returns whether the right Shift key on the keyboard is held down. Returns `1` if the Shift key on the right side of the keyboard is currently held down, otherwise `nil`.

Note: The Mac WoW client does not distinguish between left and right modifier keys, thus both Shift keys are reported as "Left Shift."

```
isDown = IsRightShiftKeyDown()
```

Returns:

`isDown` — 1 if the right Shift key on the keyboard is currently held down. `(1nil)`

issecure

Returns whether the current execution path is secure.

```
secure = issecure()
```

Returns:

`secure` — 1 if the current execution path is secure, otherwise `nil`. `(1nil)`

issecurevariable

Returns whether a variable is secure and, if not, which addon tainted the variable.

```
issecure, taint = issecurevariable([table,] "variable")
```

Arguments:

table (optional) — A table to be used when checking table elements. (table)

variable — The name of a variable to check. To check the status of a table element, you should specify the table and then the key of the element. (string)

Returns:

issecure — 1 if the variable is secure, otherwise nil. (1nil)

taint — The name of the addon that tainted the variable. (string)

IsSelectedSpell

Returns whether a specific spell is currently selected in the spellbook.

```
isSelected = IsSelectedSpell(id, bookType)
```

Arguments:

id — The index of a spell in the spellbook. (number)

bookType — The spellbook type. (string)

- pet — The pet's spellbook
- spell — The player's spellbook

Returns:

isSelected — 1 if the given spell is currently selected, otherwise nil. (1nil)

IsShiftKeyDown

Returns whether a Shift key on the keyboard is held down. Returns 1 if either Shift key on the keyboard is currently held down, otherwise nil.

Returns:

isDown — 1 if a Shift key on the keyboard is currently held down. (1nil)

IsSilenced

Returns whether the given unit is silenced for voice chat on a channel.

```
isSilenced = IsSilenced("name", "channel")
```

Arguments:

name — The name of the player to query. (string)

channel — The channel to query. (string)

Returns:

isSilenced — 1 if the player is silenced on the given channel, or nil. (1nil)

IsSpellInRange

Returns whether a spell is in range of a given unit.

```
inRange = IsSpellInRange("spell", "unit")
```

Arguments:

spell — The name of a spell to query. (string)

unit — The unit ID to query. (unitid)

Returns:

inRange — 1 if the spell is in range of the given unit, otherwise nil. (1nil)

IsStackableAction

Returns whether a given action slot contains a stackable action. A stackable action is typically an item dragged to an action slot that is capable of stacking. These are the slots that are displayed with a counter on the action button. Spells that require reagents are not considered stackable actions; their counts are updated elsewhere.

```
isStackable = IsStackableAction(slot)
```

Argument:

slot — The number of an action slot. (number)

Returns:

isStackable — 1 if the action is a stackable action, otherwise nil. (1nil)

Example:

```
-- Print all "stackable actions" to your chat window
for i=1,120 do
  if IsStackableAction(i) then
    local count = GetActionCount(i)
    local t,id = GetActionInfo(i)
    local name = GetItemInfo(id)

    ChatFrame1:AddMessage("Action: " .. i .. " Item: " .. name .. ↵
" (" .. count ..")")
  end
end
```

IsStealthed

Returns whether the player is currently stealthed.

```
stealthed = IsStealthed()
```

Returns:

stealthed — 1 if the player is stealthed, otherwise nil. (1nil)

Note: This function considers a druid's "Prowl" to be stealthed.

IsSubZonePVPPOI

Returns whether the current subzone is a PvP point of interest.

```
isPVPPOI = IsSubZonePVPPOI()
```

Returns:

isPVPPOI — 1 if the current subzone is a PvP point of interest. This is used when the "Display World PvP Objectives" setting is set to Dynamic. In this case, the PvP objectives are only shown when the player is in a PvP point of interest. (1nil)

IsSwimming

This function returns whether the player is currently swimming. Note that this function's return value depends on whether you can use water-only abilities such as the Druid's Seaform or cannot use land-only abilities such as a ground mount. Simply being in shallow water will not make this function return 1.

```
isSwimming = IsSwimming()
```

Returns:

isSwimming — 1 if the player is currently swimming, otherwise nil. (1nil)

IsTitleKnown

Returns whether a given title is known (available) to the player.

```
isKnown = IsTitleKnown(titleId)
```

Argument:

titleId — A title index from 1 to GetNumTitles(). (number)

Returns:

isKnown — 1 if the title is known (available) to the player, otherwise nil. (1nil)

IsTradeskillTrainer

Returns whether the currently open training window is a tradeskill trainer.

```
isTradeskill = IsTradeskillTrainer()
```

Returns:

isTradeskill — 1 if the currently open training window is a tradeskill trainer. (1nil)

IsTrainerServiceLearnSpell

Returns whether the given trainer service teaches a spell.

```
isLearnSpell, isPetLearnSpell = IsTrainerServiceLearnSpell(index)
```

Argument:

index — The index of the line in the Trainer window. (number)

Returns:

isLearnSpell — 1 if the trainer service teaches the player a spell, otherwise nil. (1nil)

isPetLearnSpell — 1 if the trainer service teaches the player a pet spell, otherwise nil. (1nil)

IsTrainerServiceSkillStep

Returns whether the given trainer service is a skill step, rather than a recipe.

```
isSkillStep = IsTrainerServiceSkillStep(index)
```

Argument:

index — The index of a skill in the Trainer window. This index is affected by filtering, thus the first shown skill is index 1. (number)

Returns:

isSkillStep — 1 if the service offered by the trainer will affect the player's skill (such as Journeyman Leatherworking or Apprentice First Aid). (1nil)

IsTrainerServiceTradeSkill

Returns whether the given trainer service is a tradeskill recipe.

```
isTradeSkill = IsTrainerServiceTradeSkill(index)
```

Argument:

index — The index of a trainer service. (number)

Returns:

isTradeSkills — 1 if the given trainer service is a tradeskill recipe, otherwise nil. (1nil)

Note: Enchanting is not a tradeskill by API standards; it uses the Craft APIs.

IsUnitOnQuest

Checks if a specified unit is on a quest from the player's quest log.

```
state = IsUnitOnQuest(index, "unit")
```

Arguments:

index — The quest index to query. (number)

unit — The name of the unit to query. (string)

Returns:

state — 1 if the unit is on that quest, otherwise nil. (1nil)

IsUsableAction

Returns whether the action is usable.

```
isUsable, notEnoughMana = IsUsableAction(slot)
```

Argument:

slot — The slot ID of the action to query. (number)

Returns:

isUsable — 1 if the skill is usable, otherwise nil. (1nil)

notEnoughMana — 1 if the player is lacking the mana to take the action, otherwise nil. (1nil)

IsUsableItem

Determines the usability of an item.

```
isUsable, outOfMana = IsUsableItem(itemID or "itemName" or "itemLink")
```

Arguments:

itemID or itemName or itemLink

  itemID — An item's ID. (number)

  itemName — An item's name. (string)

  itemLink — An item's link. (string)

Returns:

isUsable — 1 if the item is currently usable, otherwise nil. (1nil)

outOfMana — 1 if the item cannot be used because of lack of mana, otherwise nil. (1nil)

Note: Will return nil for missing reagents, or not high enough level, but will return 1 for items of your level for which you do not have the armor proficiency.

IsUsableSpell

Returns whether a given spell is usable or cannot be used because of lack of mana.

```
isUsable, outOfMana = IsUsableSpell("spellName" or spellIndex [,
"bookType"])
```

Arguments:

spellName or spellIndex

  spellName — The name of the spell to query. (string)

  spellIndex — The spellbook index of the spell to query. (number)

bookType (optional) — The type of spellbook in which to look up spellIndex (required when using spellIndex). (string)

Returns:

isUsable — 1 if the spell is usable, otherwise nil. (1nil)

outOfMana — 1 if the spell cannot be used because of lack of mana, otherwise nil. (1nil)

IsVoiceChatAllowed

Returns whether the current client/account is allowed to use the voice chat feature.

```
isAllowed = IsVoiceChatAllowed()
```

Returns:

isAllowed — 1 if voice chat is allowed, otherwise nil. (1nil)

IsVoiceChatEnabled

Returns whether the voice chat system is enabled.

```
isEnabled = IsVoiceChatEnabled()
```

Returns:

isEnabled — 1 if the voice chat system is enabled, otherwise nil. (1nil)

IsWindowsClient

Returns whether the currently running version of the client is the Windows version.

```
isWindows = IsWindowsClient()
```

Returns:

isWindows — true if the user runs Windows, false if Mac or Linux. (boolean)

ItemHasRange

Returns whether the item has a range for use.

```
hasRange = ItemHasRange(itemid or "itemname" or "itemlink")
```

Arguments:

itemid or itemname or itemlink

   itemid — The item's ID. (number)

   itemname — The name of an item. (string)

   itemlink — A valid item link. (string)

Returns:

hasRange — 1 if the item has a range, otherwise nil. (1nil)

ItemTextGetCreator

Gets the creator of the text currently being viewed. Used for books, parchments, and the like.

```
creator = ItemTextGetCreator()
```

Returns:

creator — Creator of the text, or nil if the creator is not available.. (string)

ItemTextGetItem

Returns the name of the currently viewed ItemText item.

```
text = ItemTextGetItem()
```

Returns:

`text` — The name of the currently viewed item. (`string`)

ItemTextGetMaterial

Returns a token used in generating the visual style for the current book/parchment being displayed in the ItemTextFrame; this token can be used to get the texture paths needed for displaying the appropriate background (for example, `"Interface\ItemTextFrame\ItemText-"` .. `material` .. `"-TopLeft"`), as well as to look up appropriate header and body colors in `MATERIAL_TITLETEXT_COLOR_TABLE` and `MATERIAL_TEXT_COLOR_TABLE`. A return value of `nil` means that parchment is being used.

```
material = ItemTextGetMaterial()
```

Returns:

`material` — Texture for the current book/parchment being displayed. (`string`)

Note: This value is only valid following the `ITEM_TEXT_READY` event.

ItemTextGetPage

Returns the page number of the current item text.

```
page = ItemTextGetPage()
```

Returns:

`page` — The page number of the currently viewed page of the item text. (`number`)

ItemTextGetText

Returns the text associated with the open item. This is used when right-clicking an item such as a book, to display its text.

```
text = ItemTextGetText()
```

Returns:

`text` — The text associated with the open item. (`string`)

ItemTextHasNextPage

Determines if the currently open book has another page following the current one.

```
next = ItemTextHasNextPage()
```

Returns:

`next` — 1 if the currently open book has a page following the current one, otherwise `nil`. (`1nil`)

ItemTextNextPage

Asks the game to move the currently open book or other readable object to the next page of text. The ITEM_TEXT_READY event will be generated when the next page is ready to be displayed. Does nothing if you are already viewing the last page of text.

ItemTextPrevPage

Asks the game to move the currently open book or other readable object to the previous page of text. The ITEM_TEXT_READY event will be generated when the previous page is ready to be displayed. Does nothing if you are already viewing the first page of text.

JoinBattlefield

Adds the player to the queue for the specified battleground instance, optionally adding the player's entire party or raid group.

```
JoinBattlefield(index, asGroup)
```

Arguments:

index — The index of the specific battleground instance to join. A value of 0 will join the first instance (of whichever battleground is currently represented in the join UI) in which a spot for the player or group becomes available. (number)

asGroup — 1 will queue your entire group for the chosen battlefield; otherwise only the player will be queued. (1nil)

JoinPermanentChannel

Joins a channel, saving any relevant settings in chat-cache.txt.

```
zoneChannel, channelName = JoinPermanentChannel("name" [, ↵
"password" [, "chatFrameIndex" [, enableVoice]]])
```

Arguments:

name — The name of the channel to join. (string)

password (optional) — The password to use when joining. (string)

chatFrameIndex (optional) — The index of a chat frame. (number)

enableVoice (optional) — 1 to enable voice in the channel, otherwise nil. (1nil)

Returns:

zoneChannel — The index of the zone channel, or 0. (number)

channelName — The display name of the channel, if the channel was a zone channel. (string)

Example:

```
-- Join a custom channel "Monkeys" with voice enabled
JoinPermanentChannel("Monkeys", nil, 1, 1)
```

JoinTemporaryChannel

Joins a channel. Although the name of this function indicates that the channel join will be temporary, this is not the case. The channel will persist between sessions, but not all of the window/color settings are guaranteed to be saved out for the new channel.

```
JoinTemporaryChannel("channel")
```

Argument:

`channel` — The name of a channel to join. `(string)`

JumpOrAscendStart

Called when the player presses the Jump key (the space bar by default), which is also used to ascend when on a flying mount. (Releasing the key calls `AscendStop`.)

Note: This function is protected and cannot be called via addons.

KBArticle_BeginLoading

Requests a specific knowledge base article from the server.

```
KBArticle_BeginLoading(articleId, searchType)
```

Arguments:

`articleId` — The unique article ID to request. `(number)`

`searchType` — The search type of the request. `(number)`

- 1 — No search text was entered.
- 2 — Search text was entered.

KBArticle_GetData

Returns information about the last requested knowledge base article.

```
id, subject, subjectAlt, text, keywords, languageId, isHot = ↵
KBArticle_GetData()
```

Returns:

`id` — The unique article ID for the article. `(number)`

`subject` — The subject of the article. `(string)`

`subjectAlt` — Alternate text for the article subject. `(string)`

`text` — The body of the article. `(string)`

`keywords` — A comma-separated list of keywords for the article. `(string)`

`languageId` — The language ID for the given article. See the returns from `API_KBSetup_GetLanguageData()` for these values. `(number)`

`isHot` — `true` if the article is a Hot Item, otherwise `false`. `(boolean)`

KBArticle_IsLoaded

Returns whether the requested knowledge base article has been loaded.

```
isLoaded = KBArticle_IsLoaded()
```

Returns:

isLoaded — true after the KNOWLEDGE_BASE_ARTICLE_LOAD_SUCCESS event has fired by fetching a specific article. This value will be retained through reloading the UI, selecting a new character. It will be reset if the client is closed entirely. (boolean)

KBQuery_BeginLoading

Queries the knowledge base server for articles.

```
KBQuery_BeginLoading(searchText, categoryIndex, ↵
subcategoryIndex, numArticles, page)
```

Arguments:

searchText — The search string to use. The empty string will search for all articles in the given category. (string)

categoryIndex — The category index. (number)

subcategoryIndex — The subcategory index. (number)

numArticles — The number of articles to be returned for each page. (number)

page — The page of the total results that should be displayed. (number)

KBQuery_GetArticleHeaderCount

Returns the number of articles on the current knowledge base search result page.

```
articleHeaderCount  = KBQuery_GetArticleHeaderCount()
```

Returns:

articleHeaderCount — The number of articles on the current knowledge base search result base page. (number)

KBQuery_GetArticleHeaderData

Returns information about an article returned in a knowledge base query.

```
articleId, title, isHotIssue, isRecentlyUpdated = ↵
artiKBQuery_GetArticleHeaderData(index)
```

Argument:

index — The index of the article to query. (number)

Returns:

articleId — A unique article ID for the article. (number)

title — The title of the article. (string)

isHotIssue — true if the article is a Hot Issue, otherwise false. (boolean)

isRecentlyUpdated — true if the article has been recently updated, otherwise false. (boolean)

KBQuery_GetTotalArticleCount

Returns the total number of articles returned for the given query.

```
totalArticleHeaderCount  = KBQuery_GetTotalArticleCount()
```

Returns:

`totalArticleHeaderCount` — The total number of articles returned for the given query. (`number`)

KBQuery_IsLoaded

Returns whether a knowledge base query was loaded successfully.

```
isLoaded = KBQuery_IsLoaded()
```

Returns:

`isLoaded` — `true` if the previous knowledge base query was successful, otherwise `false`. (`boolean`)

KBSetup_BeginLoading

Loads a maximum number of Top Issues from a given page.

```
KBSetup_BeginLoading(numArticles, page)
```

Arguments:

`numArticles` — The number of articles displayed per page. This is typically the constant `KBASE_NUM_ARTICLES_PER_PAGE`. (`number`)

`currentPage` — The page to display. (`number`)

KBSetup_GetArticleHeaderCount

Returns the number of Top Issue articles on the current page.

```
articleHeaderCount = KBSetup_GetArticleHeaderCount()
```

Returns:

`articleHeaderCount` — The number of Top Issue articles on the current page. (`number`)

KBSetup_GetArticleHeaderData

Returns header information about a Top Issue article.

```
articleId, title, isHotIssue, isRecentlyUpdated = ↵
KBSetup_GetArticleHeaderData(index)
```

Argument:

`index` — The index of the article to query. (`number`)

Returns:

`articleId` — A unique article ID for the article. (`number`)

`title` — The title of the article. (`string`)

`isHotIssue` — `true` if the article is a Hot Issue, otherwise `false`. (`boolean`)

`isRecentlyUpdated` — `true` if the article has been recently updated, otherwise `false`. (`boolean`)

KBSetup_GetCategoryCount

Returns the number of available knowledge base categories.

`numCategories = KBSetup_GetCategoryCount()`

Returns:

`numCategories` — The number of available knowledge base categories. `(number)`

KBSetup_GetCategoryData

Returns information about a knowledge base category.

`categoryId, name = KBSetup_GetCategoryData(index)`

Argument:

`index` — The index of the category. `(number)`

Returns:

`categoryId` — The unique identifier for the given category. `(number)`

`name` — The name of the category. `(string)`

KBSetup_GetLanguageCount

Returns the number of available knowledge base languages.

`numLanguages = KBSetup_GetLanguageCount()`

Returns:

`numLanguages` — The number of available knowledge base languages. `(number)`

KBSetup_GetLanguageData

Returns information about a given knowledge base language.

`languageId, name = KBSetup_GetLanguageData(index)`

Argument:

`index` — The index of the language to query. `(number)`

Returns:

`languageId` — A numeric identifier for the language. `(number)`

`name` — The name of the language. `(string)`

KBSetup_GetSubCategoryCount

Returns the number of available subcategories for a given category.

`numSubCategories = KBSetup_GetSubCategoryCount(index)`

Argument:

`index` — The index of the category. `(number)`

Returns:

`numSubCategories` — The number of available subcategories. `(number)`

KBSetup_GetSubCategoryData

Returns information on a knowledge base subcategory.

```
categoryId, name = KBSetup_GetSubCategoryData(index, subindex)
```

Arguments:

index — The index of the category. (number)

subindex — The index of the subcategory. (number)

Returns:

categoryId — The unique category ID for the given subcategory. (number)

name — The name of the subcategory. (string)

KBSetup_GetTotalArticleCount

Returns the number of Top Issue articles.

```
numArticles = KBSetup_GetTotalArticleCount()
```

Returns:

numArticles — The total number of Top Issue articles. (number)

KBSetup_IsLoaded

Returns whether the knowledge base setup has loaded successfully.

```
isLoaded = KBSetup_IsLoaded()
```

Returns:

isLoaded — This function returns true if the knowledge base setup has loaded successfully; otherwise it returns false. This function has the following behavior:

- On first login after opening the client, this function will return false until the knowledge base has been opened and the KNOWLEDGE_BASE_SETUP_LOAD_SUCCESS event has fired.

- When reloading the UI or changing characters, the value will initially be true. If the knowledge base UI is opened, the value will be set to false on the UPDATE_GM_STATUS event and set to true again after KNOWLEDGE_BASE_SETUP_LOAD_SUCCESS. (boolean)

KBSystem_GetMOTD

Returns the current knowledge base MOTD.

```
text = KBSystem_GetMOTD()
```

Returns:

text — The message of the day for the knowledge base system. (string)

KBSystem_GetServerNotice

Returns the text of the knowledge base server system notice.

```
text = KBSystem_GetServerNotice()
```

Returns:

text — The text of the knowledge base system server notice. (string)

KBSystem_GetServerStatus

Returns the knowledge base server system status message.

```
statusMessage = KBSystem_GetServerStatus()
```

Returns:

statusMessage — The knowledge base server status message, or nil. (string)

KeyRingButtonIDToInvSlotID

Converts a key ring slot ID to an inventory slot ID.

```
inventoryID = KeyRingButtonIDToInvSlotID(buttonID)
```

Argument:

buttonID — The index of the key in the key ring. The top-left slot is 1, and proceeds from left to right, top to bottom. (number)

Returns:

inventoryID — The inventory ID that corresponds to the given key ring slot. (number)

LFGQuery

Sends a looking for group request, optionally filtered by class.

```
LFGQuery(typeID, lfgNdx [, class])
```

Arguments:

typeID — The type of LFG Query. This value can be obtained using GetLFGTypes(). (number)

lfgNdx — The index of a specific quest/dungeon. Acceptable values can be obtained using GetLFGTypeEntries() with the previously listed type argument. (number)

class — A class filter to apply to the results. (number)

- 1 — All classes
- 2 — Warrior
- 3 — Paladin
- 4 — Hunter
- 5 — Rogue
- 6 — Priest
- 8 — Shaman
- 9 — Mage
- 10 — Warlock
- 12 — Druid

LearnTalent

Learns the selected talent in the selected talent tree.

```
LearnTalent(tabIndex, talentIndex)
```

Arguments:

tabIndex — The index of the talent tree. (number)

talentIndex — The index of the talent. (number)

LeaveBattlefield

Exits the current battleground. Removes you from a battleground match immediately, returning you to the battleground entrance or battlemaster NPC where
you queued to enter it and applying the Deserter debuff.

LeaveChannelByName

Leaves a channel by name.

```
LeaveChannelByName("name")
```

Argument:

name — The channel to leave. (string)

LeaveParty

Call this function to leave the current party or raid. This function sends a
request to the server to leave the current party or raid. If there are only two
characters in the party or raid, calling this function will cause the party or raid
to be disbanded.

ListChannelByName

Prints the members of a channel to ChatFrame1.

```
ListChannelByName("channelName")
```

Argument:

channelName — The exact name of a channel to list. (string)

ListChannels

Prints a list of the channels to which the player currently belongs to
DEFAULT_CHAT_FRAME.

LoadAddOn

Loads an addon manually if it is Load on Demand. Will also load the dependencies of an addon.

```
loaded, reason = LoadAddOn(index or "name")
```

Arguments:

index or name

index — Addon index between 1 and GetNumAddOns(). Blizzard addons cannot be loaded by index. (number)

name — Name of the addon to load. Not case-sensitive. Uses the addon folder name, not the title from the TOC. (string)

Returns:

loaded — 1 if the addon is loaded, otherwise nil. (number)

reason — Will contain the reason when an addon fails to load. (string)

- BANNED — Banned
- CORRUPT — Corrupt
- DEP_BANNED — Dependency banned
- DEP_CORRUPT — Dependency corrupt
- DEP_DISABLED — Dependency disabled
- DEP_INCOMPATIBLE — Dependency incompatible
- DEP_INSECURE — Dependency insecure
- DEP_INTERFACE_VERSION — Dependency out of date
- DEP_MISSING — Dependency missing
- DEP_NOT_DEMAND_LOADED — Dependency not loadable on demand
- DISABLED — Disabled
- INCOMPATIBLE — Incompatible
- INSECURE — Insecure
- INTERFACE_VERSION — Out of Date
- MISSING — Missing
- NOT_DEMAND_LOADED — Not loadable on demand

Note: Reason values are in GlobalStrings and can be retrieved by prefixing them with ADDON_. Example: ADDON_DEP_MISSING = "Dependency missing". LoadAddOn will not enable disabled addons.

LoadBindings

Loads a set of key bindings from disc, or loads the default set of key bindings. The UPDATE_BINDINGS event is fired when the settings have been loaded.

LoadBindings(set)

Arguments:

set — Which set of key bindings should be loaded. (number)

- 0 — Default key bindings
- 1 — Account key bindings
- 2 — Character key bindings

LoggingChat

Toggle logging of chat to `Logs/WowChatLog.txt`. Toggle = `true` to turn on logging, Toggle = `false` to turn off logging, and `nil` to query logging status.

`isLogging = LoggingChat([toggle])`

Argument:

`toggle` — Toggles on or off, defaults to `nil`. (boolean)

Returns:

`isLogging` — Chat logging flag. (1nil)

Note: Will return `isLogging` regardless of passed toggle.

LoggingCombat

Toggle combat logging to `Logs/WoWCombatLog.txt`. Toggle = `true` to turn on logging, Toggle = `false` to turn off logging, and `nil` to query logging status.
isLogging = LoggingCombat([toggle])

Argument:

`toggle` — Toggles on or off, defaults to `nil`. (boolean)

Returns:

`isLogging` — Chat logging flag. (1nil)

Note: Will return `isLogging` regardless of passed toggle.

Logout

Logs out of the current character, taking you back to the character selection screen.

LootSlot

Attempts to loot the item in the specified slot.

`LootSlot(slot)`

Argument:

`slot` — The slot to loot. (number)

Note: You have to confirm your loot with `ConfirmLootSlot()` for bind-on-pickup items.

LootSlotIsCoin

Returns whether a given loot slot contains coins.

`isCoin = LootSlotIsCoin(slot)`

Argument:

`slot` — The loot slot index to query. (number)

Returns:

`isCoin` — 1 if the loot slot contains coins, otherwise `nil`. (1nil)

LootSlotIsItem

Returns whether a given loot slot contains an item.

```
isItem = LootSlotIsItem(slot)
```

Argument:

slot — A slot index in the current loot window. (number)

Returns:

isItem — 1 if the loot slot contains an item, otherwise nil. (1nil)

MouselookStart

Enables mouselook mode, where cursor movement rotates the camera.

MouselookStop

Disables mouselook mode, where cursor movement rotates the camera.

MoveAndSteerStart

This function is called when the player begins moving and steering at the same time (via the "Move and Steer" key binding).

Note: This function is protected and cannot be called via addons.

MoveAndSteerStop

This function is called when the player exits move and steer mode.

Note: This function is protected and cannot be called via addons.

MoveBackwardStart

This function is called when the player begins moving backward via the "Move Backward" key binding.

Note: This function is protected and cannot be called via addons.

MoveBackwardStop

This function is called when the player stops moving backward.

Note: This function is protected and cannot be called via addons.

MoveForwardStart

This function is called when the player begins moving forward via the "Move Forward" key binding.

Note: This function is protected and cannot be called via addons.

MoveForwardStop

This function is called when the player stops moving forward.

Note: This function is protected and cannot be called via addons.

MoveViewRightStart

Starts your camera orbiting around you to the right (counterclockwise).

MovieRecording_Cancel

Cancels a currently recording video.

Note: Currently, movie recording APIs are only functional on the Mac OS X client.

MovieRecording_DataRate

Returns the data rate required per second for recording video. This value is calculated from the width of the final video, the frame rate of the recording, and if sound is being recorded as well. This data rate is for the raw video being recorded, not any compressed versions.

```
dataRate = MovieRecording_DataRate()
```

Example:

```
-- Calculate the data rate required for the following:
-- 1024x768 video at 29.97 frames per second with sound
local dataRate = MovieRecording_DataRate(1024, 29.97, 1)
ChatFrame1:AddMessage(dataRate .. " is required for this recording.")
```

Note: Currently, movie recording APIs are only functional on the Mac OS X client.

MovieRecording_DeleteMovie

Deletes a movie currently pending compression.

```
MovieRecording_DeleteMovie("filename")
```

Argument:

`filename` — The full path to a movie's filename. (string)

Note: Currently, movie recording APIs are only functional on the Mac OS X client.

MovieRecording_GetAspectRatio

Returns the aspect ratio used in any movie recordings.

```
ratio = MovieRecording_GetAspectRatio()
```

Returns:

`ratio` — The aspect ratio of any resulting movie recordings. This is calculated by dividing the height of the resulting video by the width. (number)

Note: Currently, movie recording APIs are only functional on the Mac OS X client.

MovieRecording_GetMovieFullPath

Returns the full path of the movie currently being recorded or compressed.

```
path = MovieRecording_GetMovieFullPath()
```

Returns:

`path` — Returns the path to the movie currently being recorded or compressed. If the client isn't compressing or recording, it will return either the last file to have been recorded or compressed, or the empty string. (string)

Note: Currently, movie recording APIs are only functional on the Mac OS X client.

MovieRecording_GetProgress

Returns information about the movie that is currently being compressed.

```
recovering, progress  = MovieRecording_GetProgress()
```

Returns:

`recovering` — If a previous compression was interrupted (such as WoW being forcefully closed or crashing), this value will be `true`, indicating that recovery is being attempted on the file. `(boolean)`

`progress` — The progress of the compression process, as a number between `0` and `1`. This number can be converted to a percentage using `math.floor(progress * 100)`. `(number)`

Note: Currently, movie recording APIs are only functional on the Mac OS X client.

MovieRecording_GetTime

Returns the amount of time since the last videorecording operation was started.

```
time = MovieRecording_GetTime()
```

Returns:

`time` — The amount of time since the last videorecording operation was started, as a string `HH:MM:SS`. `(string)`

Note: Currently, movie recording APIs are only functional on the Mac OS X client.

MovieRecording_GetViewportWidth

Queries the current width of the game's viewport. This function is used by the default user interface when recording video on Mac OS X. In the Movie Recording options screen, there is a menu that allows you to select the resolution of the final video. That menu uses this function to determine what the current viewport width is so that the current window size can be selected.

```
width  = MovieRecording_GetViewportWidth()
```

Returns:

`width` — The current width of the World of Warcraft viewport. `(number)`

MovieRecording_IsCodecSupported

Returns whether a given videorecording codec is supported by the client.

```
isSupported = MovieRecording_IsCodecSupported("codecName")
```

Arguments:

`codecName` — The name of a video compression codec. `(string)`

- `Motion JPEG` — This codec is faster to compress than H.264, but it will generate a bigger file.
- `H.264` — This codec is supported natively by Apple devices like the iPod, iPhone, and AppleTV. This codec has the best ratio quality/size, but it is also the slowest to compress.

- ■ Apple Intermediate — Exclusive to Mac OS X. This codec is the fastest to compress.

- ■ MPEG-4 — MPEG-4 is supported by many digital cameras and iMovie.

Returns:

isSupported — true if the codec is supported by the client, otherwise false. (boolean)

Note: Currently, movie recording APIs are only functional on the Mac OS X client.

MovieRecording_IsCompressing

Returns whether the client is currently compressing a recording.

```
isCompressing = MovieRecording_IsCompressing()
```

Returns:

isCompressing — true if the client is currently compressing a recording, otherwise false. (boolean)

Note: Currently, movie recording APIs are only functional on the Mac OS X client.

MovieRecording_IsRecording

Returns whether the client is currently recording a movie.

```
isRecording = MovieRecording_IsRecording()
```

Returns:

isRecording — 1 if the client is currently recording, otherwise nil. (1nil)

Note: Currently, movie recording APIs are only functional on the Mac OS X client.

MovieRecording_IsSupported

Returns whether movie recording is supported by the client.

```
isSupported = MovieRecording_IsSupported()
```

Returns:

isSupported — true if the client supports videorecording, otherwise nil. (boolean)

Note: Currently, movie recording APIs are only functional on the Mac OS X client.

MovieRecording_MaxLength

Returns the maximum length of a recorded video.

```
time = MovieRecording_MaxLength(width, framerate, capturesound)
```

Arguments:

width — The width in pixels of the video resolution. (number)

framerate — The frame rate of the resulting video. (number)

capturesound — 1 to capture sound, otherwise nil. (1nil)

Returns:

`time` — The maximum length of a recorded video as a string `HH:MM:SS`. (`string`)

Note: Currently, movie recording APIs are only functional on the Mac OS X client.

MovieRecording_QueueMovieToCompress

Adds a movie to the compression queue. If there are no items currently in the queue, the movie will begin compressing immediately. There appears to be no limit to the number of queued movies.

```
MovieRecording_QueueMovieToCompress("filename")
```

Argument:

`filename` — The filename of a movie to add to the compression queue. (`string`)

Example:

```
-- This function is called in the following manner when the player
-- clicks the "Compress" button on the compression popup
MovieRecording_QueueMovieToCompress(MacOptionsCompressFrameFileName
:GetText())
```

Note: Currently, movie recording APIs are only functional on the Mac OS X client.

MovieRecording_SearchUncompressedMovie

Enables or disables a search for uncompressed movies.

```
MovieRecording_SearchUncompressedMovie(enable)
```

Argument:

`enable` — `true` to enable searching for uncompressed movies, `false` to end the running search. (`boolean`)

Note: Currently, movie recording APIs are only functional on the Mac OS X client.

MovieRecording_Toggle

Begins recording a new video, or stops the currently recording video.

Note: Currently, movie recording APIs are only functional on the Mac OS X client.

MovieRecording_ToggleGUI

Toggles recording of the user interface when recording a video.

Note: Currently, movie recording APIs are only functional on the Mac OS X client.

MusicPlayer_BackTrack

Goes back a track in iTunes. WoW has a set of key bindings that can control iTunes on Mac OS X. This function can be used to go back a track in this situation.

Note: This function is protected and cannot be called via addons.

MusicPlayer_NextTrack

Goes to the next track in iTunes. WoW has a set of key bindings that can control iTunes on Mac OS X. This function can be used to move to the next track in the playlist.

Note: This function is protected and cannot be called via addons.

MusicPlayer_PlayPause

Plays or pauses playback in iTunes. WoW has a set of key bindings that can control iTunes on Mac OS X. This function can be used to trigger the Pause/Play button.

Note: This function is protected and cannot be called via addons.

MusicPlayer_VolumeDown

Turns the volume down in iTunes.

Note: This function is protected and cannot be called via addons.

MusicPlayer_VolumeUp

Turns the volume up in iTunes.

Note: This function is protected and cannot be called via addons.

NewGMTicket

Opens a new GM support ticket.

```
NewGMTicket(type, "text")
```

Arguments:

type — The type of ticket that should be opened. (number)

- 1 — Game Play
- 2 — Harassment
- 3 — Stuck
- 4 — Bug

text — The text to be sent in the ticket. (string)

Note: This function is protected and cannot be called via addons.

NextView

Changes the camera view to the next pre-defined camera angle. There are five slots for camera angles indexed 1–5. These views can be set and accessed directly using the SaveView() and SetView() functions and cycled through using the NextView() and PrevView() functions.

NoPlayTime

Returns whether the player is out of play time. This function is only used in locales where play time is limited by law, such as mainland China.

```
hasNoTime = NoPlayTime()
```

Returns:

hasNoTime — 1 if the player is out of play time, otherwise nil. (1nil)

NotWhileDeadError

Fires a UI_ERROR_MESSAGE event, with the argument ERR_PLAYER_DEAD.

NotifyInspect

Queries the server for an inspected unit's talent information. The event INSPECT_TALENT_READY fires when the talent information for the inspected unit is available.

```
NotifyInspect(unit)
```

Argument:

unit — The unit to inspect. (unitid)

NumTaxiNodes

Returns the current number of taxi nodes defined.

```
num_nodes = NumTaxiNodes()
```

Returns:

num_nodes — Number of nodes. (number)

OfferPetition

Requests a signature from the targeted player.

OffhandHasWeapon

Determines whether the player has a weapon in the offhand slot.

```
hasWeapon = OffhandHasWeapon()
```

Returns:

hasWeapon — 1 if the player has a weapon equipped in the offhand, otherwise nil. (1nil)

OpenTrainer

Closes the Trainer window if it is open, otherwise appears to do nothing.

OpeningCinematic

Displays the player's race's opening cinematic. This function only works if the player has never gained any experience.

PartialPlayTime

Returns whether the character gains partial experience points.

```
partialPlayTime = PartialPlayTime()
```

Returns:

`partialPlayTime` — 1 if the character gains only partial xp, `nil` if not. (1nil)

Note: This function is used only in the Chinese client for World of Warcraft, where play time is limited by law.

PetAbandon

Releases the player's current pet. For Hunter pets, this function sends the pet away, never to return (in the default UI, it's called when you confirm the "Are you sure you want to permanently abandon your pet?" dialog). For other pets, this function is equivalent to `PetDismiss`.

PetAggressiveMode

Sets your pet to aggressive mode.

Note: This function is protected and cannot be called via addons.

PetAttack

Instructs your pet to attack your current target.

Note: This function is protected and cannot be called via addons.

PetCanBeAbandoned

Returns whether the player's pet can be abandoned.

```
canAbandon = PetCanBeAbandoned()
```

Returns:

`canAbandon` — 1 if the player's pet can be abandoned, otherwise `nil`. (1nil)

PetCanBeRenamed

Returns whether the currently controlled pet can be renamed.

```
canRename = PetCanBeRenamed()
```

Returns:

`canRename` — 1 if the player can rename the currently controlled pet, otherwise `nil`. (1nil)

Note: Currently, only Hunter pets can be renamed, and each can only be renamed once.

PetDefensiveMode

Sets the pet into defensive mode, only attacking when the player or itself is attacked.

Note: This function is protected and cannot be called via addons.

PetDismiss

Dismisses the currently controlled pet. Does nothing for Hunter pets; those can only be dismissed using the Dismiss Pet spell. This function is used for dismissing Warlock pets, Mind Control targets, and so on.

PetFollow

Sets the pet into Follow mode.

Note: This function is protected and cannot be called via addons.

PetHasActionBar

Returns whether the player's current pet has an action bar.

```
hasActionBar = PetHasActionBar()
```

Returns:

hasActionBar — Returns 1 if the player's current pet has an action bar, otherwise nil. (1nil)

PetPassiveMode

Sets the pet into passive mode.

Note: This function is protected and cannot be called via addons.

PetRename

Renames the currently controlled pet.

```
PetRename("name")
```

Argument:

name — The name to give the pet. (string)

Note: Only Hunter pets can be renamed, and each can only be renamed once. Calling this function multiple times will not cause the pet to be renamed.

PetStopAttack

Stops your pet auto-attacking.

PetWait

Orders the player's pet into Stay mode.

Note: This function is protected and cannot be called via addons.

PickupAction

Picks up an action bar slot and holds it on the cursor.

```
PickupAction(slot)
```

Argument:

slot — An action bar slot. (number)

Note: This function cannot be called while in combat.

PickupBagFromSlot

Picks up a bag from an inventory slot or bank bag slot and holds it on the cursor.

```
PickupBagFromSlot(inventoryID)
```

Argument:

inventoryID — The inventory ID of a bag slot. (number)

PickupContainerItem

Picks up an item from a container and holds it on the cursor.

```
PickupContainerItem(index, slot)
```

Arguments:

index — The index of the container that holds the item to be picked up. (number)

slot — The slot that contains the item to be picked up. (number)

Example:

```
-- Pickup the first item in your backpack
PickupContainerItem(0, 1)
```

PickupGuildBankItem

Picks up an item from the guild bank and holds it on the cursor.

```
PickupGuildBankItem(tab, slot)
```

Arguments:

tab — The guild bank tab. (number)

slot — The slot in the given guild bank tab. (number)

PickupGuildBankMoney

Withdraws money from the guild bank, placing it on the cursor.

```
PickupGuildBankMoney(amount)
```

Argument:

amount — The amount of money to pick up, in copper. (number)

PickupInventoryItem

Picks an inventory item up and holds it on the cursor.

```
PickupInventoryItem(id)
```

Argument:

id — The ID of an inventory slot. (number)

PickupItem

Picks up an item by name or ID and holds it on the cursor.

```
PickupItem("name" or itemId)
```

Arguments:

name or itemId

  name — The name of an item. (string)

  itemId — The item ID of an item. (number)

PickupMacro

Simulates picking up a macro from the Macro window and placing it on the cursor. This function can be used to pick up a macro from the Macro window and place it on the cursor. Each macro has a unique ID that is passed as an argument to `PickupMacro()`. Currently, this is 1–18 for the general macros and 19–36 for character-specific macros.

```
PickupMacro(macroId or "name")
```

Arguments:

macroId or name

  macroId — The macro ID of the macro to pick up. (number)

  name — The name of a macro. (string)

Example:

```
-- Pickup the macro currently under the cursor
local macroIndex = MacroFrame.macroBase + GetMouseFocus():GetID()
PickupMacro(macroIndex)
```

PickupMerchantItem

Picks up an item from the Merchant window, holding it on the cursor.

```
PickupMerchantItem(slot)
```

Argument:

slot — The merchant item slot. (number)

PickupPetAction

Picks up the pet action in the given slot and places it under the cursor.

```
PickupPetAction(slot)
```

Argument:

slot — The index of the pet action on the pet's action bar. (number)

PickupPlayerMoney

Picks up money from the player's inventory and holds it on the cursor.

```
PickupPlayerMoney(amount)
```

Argument:

amount — The amount of money to pick up, in copper. (number)

PickupSpell

Picks up a spell from the spellbook, placing it on the cursor.

```
PickupSpell(id, "bookType")
```

Arguments:

id — The numeric ID of a spell in the spellbook. (number)

bookType — The type of spellbook, either spell or pet. (string)

■ pet — The pet's spellbook

■ spell — The player's spellbook

PickupStablePet

Picks up a stabled pet and holds it on the cursor.

```
PickupStablePet(index)
```

Argument:

index — The index of the pet. (number)

■ 0 — The current pet

■ 1 — The first stabled pet

■ 2 — The second stabled pet

PitchDownStart

Begins pitching the camera downward.

Note: This function is protected and cannot be called via addons.

PitchDownStop

Stops pitching the camera after PitchDownStart() is called.

Note: This function is protected and cannot be called via addons.

PitchUpStart

Begins pitching the camera upward.

Note: This function is protected and cannot be called via addons.

PitchUpStop

Stops pitching the camera after PitchUpStart() has been called.

Note: This function is protected and cannot be called via addons.

PlaceAction

Places the action held on the cursor in a specified action bar slot.

```
PlaceAction(slot)
```

Argument:

slot — Places the action held on the cursor in a specific action bar slot. (number)

PlaceAuctionBid

Places a bid on an auction item.

```
PlaceAuctionBid("type", index, bid)
```

Arguments:

`type` — The auction listing type. (`string`)

- ▪ `bidder` — Auctions on which the player has already bid.

- ▪ `list` — Auctions in the main auction house listing.

`index` — The index of the auction in the listing. (`number`)

`bid` — The bid amount, in copper. (`number`)

PlayMusic

Plays a music file. Any other background music that is currently playing will be faded out as the new file begins. Supported codecs include MP3 and Ogg Vorbis (and exclude WMA, RM, and MP4/AAC).

```
PlayMusic("musicfile")
```

Argument:

`musicfile` — The path to a music file. This can be a path in the MPQ files or a file located within an addon directory. (`string`)

Note: Only files that have been in an addons directory since the time the client was started are capable of being played. If new files are added, the client will need to be restarted to play them.

PlaySound

Plays one of the built-in interface sounds (found in `Sound\interface` within the WoW MPQ files).

```
PlaySound("sound")
```

Argument:

`sound` — The name of a built-in sound to play, minus the `.wav` (or other) extension. (`string`)

Example:

```
-- Play the ready check sound
PlaySound("ReadyCheck")
```

PlaySoundFile

Plays a specified sound file. This can be a sound that is packaged with the WoW client, such as `Sound\Creature\MobileAlertBot\MobileAlertBotIntruderAlert01.wav` or a custom addon's sound.

```
PlaySoundFile("soundfile")
```

Argument:

`soundFile` — A path to the sound file to be played. (`string`)

Example:

```
-- Play the "Intruder Alert" sounds from Gnomeregan
PlaySoundFile("Sound\\Creature\\MobileAlertBot\\↵
MobileAlertBotIntruderAlert01.wav")
```

PlayerHasSpells

Returns whether the player has any spells. Effectively always returns 1 for all characters.

```
hasSpells = PlayerHasSpells()
```

Returns:

hasSpells — Returns 1 if the player has any spells, otherwise nil. (1nil)

PrevView

Changes the camera view to the previous pre-defined camera angle. There are five slots for camera angles indexed 1–5. These views can be set and accessed directly using the SaveView() and SetView() functions and cycled through using the NextView() and PrevView() functions.

ProcessMapClick

Possibly changes the World Map based on a mouse click. This function is used internally by the World Map frame to change the map zone or zoom based on where the mouse was clicked in the given map. The coordinates specified should be a value between 0.0 and 1.0, relative to the WorldMapDetailFrame.

```
ProcessMapClick(x, y)
```

Arguments:

x — The *x* coordinate of the click, as a number between 0 and 1. (number)

y — The *y* coordinate of the click, as a number between 0 and 1. (number)

PromoteToAssistant

Promotes a player or unit to raid assistant.

```
PromoteToAssistant("unit" or "name" [, exact])
```

Arguments:

unit or name

- ▪ unit — The unit to promote. (unitid)
- ▪ name — The name of the player to promote. (string)

exact — When using the name argument, a value of 1 will force an exact match. (1nil)

PromoteToLeader

Promotes a player to party/raid leader.

```
PromoteToLeader("name")
```

Argument:

name — The name of the player to promote. (string)

PurchaseSlot

Purchases a bank slot without confirmation.

Note: This function only works when the Banker window is open.

PutItemInBackpack

Puts the currently held item into the first open slot in the player's backpack. Puts the item currently held by the cursor into the first open slot in the player's backpack. If the backpack is full, the function will not place the item into another bag; it will fail.

PutItemInBag

Attempts to place an item under the cursor inside the specified bag.

```
hadItem = PutItemInBag(bagId)
```

Argument:

`bagId` — The ID of the target bag. `(number)`

Returns:

`hadItem` — 1 if the cursor had an item, otherwise `nil`. `(1nil)`

Note: Returns 1 if the cursor actually held an item, otherwise `nil`. Also, you cannot place items in the backpack using this function; use `PutItemInBackpack()` instead.

QueryAuctionItems

Queries the auction house's listings for the attributes specified.

```
QueryAuctionItems([name[, minLevel[, maxLevel[, invTypeIndex[,
classIndex[, subclassIndex[, page[, isUsable[, qualityIndex[,
getAll]]]]]]]]]])
```

Arguments:

`name` (optional) — The name for which you want to search. This is a substring match, not an exact one. `(string)`

`minLevel` (optional) — The minimum item use level you want returned. `(number)`

`maxLevel` (optional) — The maximum item use level you want returned. `(number)`

`invTypeIndex` (optional) — The inventory type for which you want to search; this must be specified as an index according to the following table. The `INVTYPE_*` tokens are taken from the return values of `GetItemInfo()`. `(number)`

- 1 — INVTYPE_HEAD
- 2 — INVTYPE_NECK
- 3 — INVTYPE_SHOULDER
- 4 — INVTYPE_BODY
- 5 — INVTYPE_CHEST
- 6 — INVTYPE_WAIST
- 7 — INVTYPE_LEGS

- 8 — INVTYPE_FEET
- 9 — INVTYPE_WRIST
- 10 — INVTYPE_HAND
- 11 — INVTYPE_FINGER
- 12 — INVTYPE_TRINKET
- 13 — INVTYPE_WEAPON
- 14 — INVTYPE_SHIELD
- 15 — INVTYPE_RANGEDRIGHT
- 16 — INVTYPE_CLOAK
- 17 — INVTYPE_2HWEAPON
- 18 — INVTYPE_BAG
- 19 — INVTYPE_TABARD
- 20 — INVTYPE_ROBE
- 21 — INVTYPE_WEAPONMAINHAND
- 22 — INVTYPE_WEAPONOFFHAND
- 23 — INVTYPE_HOLDABLE
- 24 — INVTYPE_AMMO
- 25 — INVTYPE_THROWN
- 26 — INVTYPE_RANGED

classIndex (optional) — The auction item class index as returned by the
GetAuctionItemClasses() function. (number)

subclassIndex (optional) — The auction item class index as returned by the
GetAuctionItemSubClasses() function. (number)

page (optional) — The page of possibilities that you want returned. For example,
if the query would return 1,000 items, and you want items 300 to 350, you would
ask for page number 7. (number)

isUsable (optional) — true if you only want items that you can use returned,
otherwise false. *Use* is defined as at or below your current character's level
for items, and at or below your current character's skill for recipes and
schematics. (boolean)

qualityIndex (optional) — The quality of the items you want returned. (number)

- 0 — Poor
- 1 — Common
- 2 — Uncommon
- 3 — Rare
- 4 — Epic
- 5 — Legendary
- 6 — Artifact

`getAll` (optional) — `true` if you want all of the pages returned at one, otherwise `false`. This option can only be used once every 15 minutes. (boolean)

Note: This function can currently be called every 0.5 to 2.0 seconds, depending on server load if used normally, or every 15 minutes if used with the `getAll` parameter. This function runs asynchronously; you need to wait until the `AUCTION_ITEM_LIST_UPDATE` event before requesting any info on those returned items.

QueryGuildBankLog

Queries the server for a guild bank log for a specific tab. This function causes the `GUILDBANKLOG_UPDATE` function to fire when the log has been successfully queried.

`QueryGuildBankLog(tab)`

Argument:

`tab` — The index of a guild tab. (number)

QueryGuildBankTab

Queries the server for the contents of the specified guild bank tab. This causes the `GUILDBANKBAGSLOTS_CHANGED` event to fire.

`QueryGuildBankTab(tab)`

Argument:

`tab` — Guild bank tab to query. Between 1 and `GetNumGuildBankTabs()`. (num)

QueryGuildEventLog

Queries the server for the guild event log. This log isn't populated immediately but, rather, will fire the `GUILD_EVENT_LOG_UPDATE` event.

QuestChooseRewardError

Triggers the client's error when the player hasn't chosen a quest reward from the available choices.

QuestLogPushQuest

Shares the currently selected quest with the other party members.

Note: You have to call `SelectQuestLogEntry(id)` on a quest before using this function.

Quit

Quits the game normally. This function asks the game to quit normally. If the player is currently in combat, it will result in an error saying that you cannot quit right now.

If the player is currently resting, the game will quit immediately; otherwise, the game generates an event that prompts the default UI to show the "20 seconds until quit" popup dialog.

RandomRoll

Rolls a random number between min and max.

```
RandomRoll(min, max)
```

Arguments:

min — The minimum amount to roll. (number,string)

max — The maximum amount to roll. (number,string)

RegisterCVar

Registers a configuration variable to be saved.

```
RegisterCVar("cvar" [, default])
```

Arguments:

cvar — The name of a CVar to register. (string)

default — The default value of the CVar. (string)

RegisterForSave

Registers a variable to be saved between sessions. This function is only available to Blizzard's code; addons should use the ##SavedVariables TOC declaration instead.

```
RegisterForSave("variable")
```

Note: This function is an internal/debug function.

RegisterForSavePerCharacter

Registers a variable to be saved between sessions. This function is only available to Blizzard's code; addons should use the ##SavedVariablesPerCharacter TOC declaration instead.

```
RegisterForSavePerCharacter("variable")
```

Note: This function is an internal/debug function.

ReloadUI

Reloads the user interface. This function saves out any saved variables and reloads the user interface completely.

RemoveChatWindowChannel

Removes a chat channel from the given chat window.

```
RemoveChatWindowChannel(index, "channel")
```

Arguments:

index — The index of the chat frame. (number)

channel — The name of the channel to remove. (string)

RemoveChatWindowMessages

Hides a group of messages from a chat frame. This function is used when selecting different types of chat messages to display. When a class of chat messages is unchecked, this function will be called to hide those messages.

```
RemoveChatWindowMessages(index, "messageGroup")
```

Arguments:

index — The index of the chat frame (1–7). (number)

messageGroup — The identifying string for the given message group. (string)

RemoveFriend

Removes a friend from your Friends list.

```
RemoveFriend(["name"] or [index])
```

Arguments:

name or index

name — The name of a friend to remove. (string)

index — The index of an entry in the Friends list. (number)

RemoveQuestWatch

Stops tracking objectives for a quest in the quest log.

```
RemoveQuestWatch(questIndex)
```

Argument:

questIndex — The index of a quest in the quest log. (number)

RenamePetition

Renames the open petition.

```
RenamePetition("name")
```

Argument:

name — The new name for the petition. (string)

RepairAllItems

Attempts to repair all items. Requires the player to be at a merchant that repairs. Passing 1 to the function will attempt to make use of guild bank money for repairs.

```
RepairAllItems(useGuildMoney)
```

Argument:

useGuildMoney — 1 to try and use guild bank money to repair, nil to use your own money. (1nil)

ReplaceEnchant

Confirms replacing an existing enchant.

ReplaceTradeEnchant

Confirms the replacement of an existing enchant being applied in the Trade window.

RepopMe

Will release your spirit and send you to the graveyard when dead.

Note: This function only works after your character has died.

ReportPlayerIsPVPAFK

Reports a player or unit as AFK in a PvP battleground.

```
ReportPlayerIsPVPAFK("name" or "unit")
```

Arguments:

name or unit

name — The name of the player to report. (string)

unit — The unit to report. (unitid)

RequestBattlefieldPositions

Requests new battleground position information from the server (called automatically every frame by UIParent's OnUpdate handler).

Note: The BattlefieldPosition APIs no longer return useful information now that WoW automatically puts all battleground members into a raid group; use raid APIs instead.

RequestBattlefieldScoreData

Requests the latest battlefield score from the server. The UPDATE_BATTLEFIELD_SCORE event fires when the data is received.

RequestInspectHonorData

Requests honor data for the currently inspected target. The INSPECT_HONOR_UPDATE event fires when the data is received.

RequestRaidInfo

Requests information about saved raid instances from the server. This UPDATE_INSTANCE_INFO event fires when the data is received.

RequestTimePlayed

Queries the server for the amount of time played on the given character.

Note: This function fires the TIME_PLAYED_MSG event.

ResetCPUUsage

Reset the current CPU usage statistics.

Note: CPU profiling must be enabled by setting the CVar scriptProfile to 1 for related functions to return meaningful results.

ResetChatColors

Resets the colors of the chat channels back to default. This change does not take effect until after the UI has been reloaded.

ResetChatWindows

Resets the Chat windows to hard-coded defaults.

ResetCursor

Resets the mouse cursor to the default glove pointer.

ResetDisabledAddOns

Resets the enabled status of addons before the change is committed via a reload. For addons that have been disabled via `DisableAddOn()` but have not yet been unloaded via a UI reload or by logging out and back in, this function resets their status to enabled.

ResetInstances

Resets all unsaved instances.

ResetTutorials

Resets tutorials from the beginning. This function tells the game to show all tutorials you may have already seen. The first tutorial will pop up whether you have tutorials enabled or not.

ResetView

Resets the given view mode and switches to that view mode.

```
ResetView(viewModeIndex)
```

Argument:

`viewModeIndex` — view mode index to reset to default (2–5). (number)

RestartGx

Restarts the client's graphic subsystem.

RestoreVideoDefaults

Restores all video settings to default values and reloads the user interface.

ResurrectHasSickness

Determines if using a spirit healer to resurrect will give you resurrection sickness.

```
hasSickness = ResurrectHasSickness()
```

Returns:

`hasSickness` — 1 if resurrecting at the spirit healer will give you resurrection sickness, otherwise `nil`. (1nil)

Note: On a very low level, using the spirit healer has no side effects.

ResurrectHasTimer

Returns whether the player must wait to accept the pending resurrection spell.

```
hasTimer = ResurrectHasTimer()
```

Returns:

`hasTimer` — 1 if the player must wait to accept the pending resurrection spell, otherwise `nil`. (1nil)

RetrieveCorpse

Confirms resurrection by returning to the player's corpse.

ReturnInboxItem

Returns the given inbox item to its sender.

```
ReturnInboxItem(index)
```

Argument:

index — Inbox item to return to sender. (number)

RollOnLoot

Performs a type of roll (pass/need/greed) on a given loot.

```
RollOnLoot(lootIndex, rollType)
```

Arguments:

lootIndex — The index of the loot to roll on. (number)

rollType — The roll action to perform. (number)

- ■ 0 — Pass on the given loot.
- ■ 1 — Roll a need roll.
- ■ 2 — Roll a greed roll.

RunBinding

Runs a key binding action by name.

```
RunBinding("COMMAND")
```

Arguments:

COMMAND — The key binding command or action to run. (string)

Example:

```
-- Take a screenshot
RunBinding("SCREENSHOT")
```

RunMacro

Runs a macro by name or index, as if it had been clicked with a specified button.

```
RunMacro(macro [, "button"])
```

Note: This function is protected and cannot be called via addons.

RunMacroText

Runs a macro string, as if it had been clicked with a specified button.

```
RunMacroText("text" [, "button"])
```

Note: This function is protected and cannot be called via addons.

RunScript

Runs a string as a Lua script.

```
RunScript("script")
```

Argument:

`script` — A Lua script to be run. (string)

Example:

```
-- Print to chat frame
local script = "ChatFrame1:AddMessage(\"Hello World\")"
RunScript(script)
```

SaveBindings

Saves the current key bindings set to disk. These settings can be saved as account-wide key bindings or character-specific key bindings based on the arguments.

```
SaveBindings(set)
```

Arguments:

`set` — Which key bindings set the current settings should be saved to. (number)

- 1 — Account key bindings
- 2 — Character key bindings

SaveGuildRoster

Saves the guild roster `GuildRoster.txt` in the Logs folder. `GuildRoster.txt` is tab separated with the following fields: Name, Level, Class, Location, Rank, Note, and Timestamp.

Note: This function is used by the `/saveguildroster` command.

SaveView

Saves the current camera view to one of the stored camera positions.

```
SaveView(index)
```

Argument:

`index` — A camera index between 1 and 6. (number)

Screenshot

Takes a screenshot, displaying a message when done.

securecall

This function is used by the default user interface to call a tainted function without tainting the current execution path.

Note: This function is protected and cannot be called via addons.

SecureCmdOptionParse

Parses a secure command (macro, slash command) into an action and possible target. This function is used by the secure templates to handle complex conditionals and other macro options.

```
action, target = SecureCmdOptionParse("cmd")
```

Arguments:

cmd — A command to be parsed (typically the body of a macro, macrotext attribute, or slash command). (string)

Returns:

action — The action to take. (string)

target — The target to use for the given action, or nil. (string)

SelectActiveQuest

Selects an active quest in the quest log.

```
SelectActiveQuest(index)
```

Argument:

index — The index of a quest in the quest log. (number)

SelectAvailableQuest

Selects an available quest from the given NPC.

```
SelectAvailableQuest(index)
```

Argument:

index — The index of the available quest in the QuestFrame. (number)

Note: This function only works for interactions that use the QuestFrame and is only available after a QUEST_GREETING event.

SelectCraft

Selects a given item for the active craft (used by Enchanting and Pet Training).

```
SelectCraft(index)
```

Argument:

index — The active craft's item index to select. (number)

SelectGossipActiveQuest

Selects an active quest in the gossip dialog.

```
SelectGossipActiveQuest(index)
```

Argument:

index — The index of an active quest in the gossip dialog. (number)

SelectGossipAvailableQuest

Selects the specified quest on the gossip frame for further processing.

```
SelectGossipAvailableQuest(index)
```

Argument:

index — The index of the quest on the gossip frame. (number)

SelectGossipOption

Selects an option in the NPC dialog (gossip) window. If the GOSSIP_CONFIRM event fires, a dialog box will be created that will ask the user to confirm the gossip option they have selected. This is used for special event turn-ins, such as the Murloc Suit given out at BlizzCon 2007. The NPC will prompt the user for an access code and confirmation. The second and third arguments are used in this situation.

```
SelectGossipOption(index [, text, confirm])
```

Arguments:

index — The option in the NPC gossip window to select, from 1 to GetNumGossipOptions(). (number)

text (optional) — The text of the string to send on confirmation. (string)

confirm (optional) — true to confirm, false or nil to not confirm. (boolean)

SelectPackage

Not yet implemented.

```
SelectPackage(index)
```

SelectQuestLogEntry

Selects a quest from the quest log as the currently active quest to be shown in the details panel. This is required by other functions that do not take a quest index as argument (for example, GetQuestLogQuestText()).

```
SelectQuestLogEntry(index)
```

Argument:

index — The index of the quest to select. (number)

SelectStationery

Selects a given stationery for usage when sending mail.

```
SelectStationery(index)
```

Argument:

index — The index of the stationery to select for usage. (number)

Note: The stationery system is currently not implemented.

SelectTradeSkill

Sets the currently selected tradeskill item.

```
SelectTradeSkill(index)
```

Argument:

index — The index of a tradeskill in the Tradeskill window. (number)

SelectTrainerService

Selects the given trainer service in the class trainer frame.

```
SelectTrainerService(index)
```

Arguments:

index — The trainer service index to select. (number)

SendAddonMessage

Sends a chat-like message to players that will not show up in their Chat windows by default. SendAddonMessage is at the core of client-to-client addon communication. Unlike SendChatMessage, messages sent with this function will not appear in anyone's chat log by default. This means you don't have to take special care to accommodate players who do not have your mod installed; they simply won't process your addon's messages. Because addon messages are hidden, there is no special throttling to relieve spam, although they do still contribute to the client's overall traffic. Another benefit of addon messages is that they are immune to the effects of inebriation like "... hic!"

This function uses an arbitrary prefix for identification purposes. Generally, this will be the name of your addon or some abbreviation thereof, although some libraries will use a standardized prefix for all related communications. You can use the prefix in any way you see fit. The prefix appears as the first argument of the CHAT_MSG_ADDON event on the receiving end, so your addon can easily discard any uninteresting messages. Note that the combined length of the prefix and message must be 254 characters or less, and the prefix cannot contain the tab (\t) character. (A tab is used to separate the prefix from the message in the underlying server transmission.)

Addon messages are limited to a subset of types compared to chat messages to ease server load: PARTY, RAID, GUILD, BATTLEGROUND, or WHISPER. If you use any of the first four, everyone who is in the normal channel will also receive all addon messages sent to the channel. RAID messages will be sent to PARTY if you are not in a raid. WHISPER messages use the target parameter to specify the name of the recipient (Name or Name-Realm). If no type is specified, it will use PARTY by default.

```
SendAddonMessage("prefix", "message", [, "type" [, "target"]])
```

Arguments:

prefix — An arbitrary label for the message. (string)

message — The message to send. (string)

type (optional) — The type of message to send (Guild, Party, Whisper, and so on). (string)

target (optional) — The target of a whisper addon message. (string)

Example:

```
-- Hypothetical communication using addon messages
local MSG_PREFIX = "MY_MOD"
SendAddonMessage(MSG_PREFIX, "Resync", "GUILD")
SendAddonMessage(MSG_PREFIX, "VersionCheck", "WHISPER", player)
```

SendChatMessage

Sends a chat message.

```
SendChatMessage("text" [,"chatType" [,"language" ] [,"channel"]])
```

Arguments:

text — The message to be sent, maximum of 255 characters. (string)

type (optional) — The type of chat message to be sent. Defaults to SAY. (string)

- AFK — Not a real channel. Will set your AFK message. Set an empty message to clear status.

- BATTLEGROUND — Messages to a battleground raid group (/bg).

- CHANNEL — Message to a specific chat channel (/1, /2, ...). Channel number provided as channel.

- DND — Not a real channel. Will set your DND message. Set an empty message to clear status.

- EMOTE — Text emotes to nearby players (/em).

- GUILD — Messages to guild members (/g).

- OFFICER — Messages to guild officers (/o).

- PARTY — Messages to party members (/p).

- RAID — Messages to raid members (/raid).

- RAID_WARNING — Warning to raid members (/rw).

- SAY — Speech to nearby players (/say).

- WHISPER — Message to a specific player (/whisper). Player name provided as channel.

- YELL — Yell to not so nearby players (/yell).

`language` (optional) — The language in which to send the message. Defaults to the common language for the faction (Common, for Alliance, Orcish for Horde). The following list includes all languages known to the UI; however, using a language other than the one or two known to your character (Common/Orcish and possibly a racial language) will cause an error to be printed in the Chat window. (`string`)

- `COMMON` — Alliance and Human language
- `DARNASSIAN` — Night Elf Language
- `DEMONIC` — Demon language
- `DRACONIC` — Dragon language
- `DRAENEI` — Draenei Language
- `DWARVEN` — Dwarf Language
- `GNOMISH` — Gnome language
- `GUTTERSPEAK` — Undead language
- `KALIMAG` — Elemental language
- `ORCISH` — Horde and Orc Language
- `TAURAHE` — Tauren Language
- `TITAN` — Giant language
- `TROLL` — Troll language

`channel` (optional) — The channel or player receiving the message for CHANNEL/WHISPER-type communications. If sending to a channel, you must use the number. This field is required for CHANNEL/WHISPER-type chats and ignored for others. (`string`)

SendMail

Sends mail to a player.

```
SendMail("dest", "subject", "body")
```

Arguments:

`target` — The destination of the mail. (`string`)

`subject` — The subject of the mail. (`string`)

`body` — The body of the mail. (`string`)

SendWho

Sends a who request to the server. Whether results are returned in the Chat window or in a `WHO_LIST_UPDATE` event is determined by the `SetWhoToUI` function and the number of results.

```
SendWho("query")
```

Arguments:

query — A who query. A blank query (the empty string) can be submitted, but the argument must be supplied. Text in the query will match against any of the six searchable fields unless one of the specifiers that follow is used; multiple specifiers can be used in one query. (string)

- c-"class" — Search for players whose class name contains "class."
- g-"guild" — Search for players in guilds whose name contains "guild."
- x — Search for players of level X.
- x-y — Search for players between levels X and Y (inclusive).
- n-"name" — Search for players whose name contains "name."
- r-"race" — Search for players whose race name contains "race."
- z-"zone" — Search for players in zones whose name contains "zone."

Example:

```
-- Searches for Night Elf Rogues in Teldrassil, of levels 10-15, ↵
with the string "bob" in their names.
SendWho('bob z-"Teldrassil" r-"Night Elf" c-"Rogue" 10-15');
```

SetAbandonQuest

Marks the currently selected quest to be abandoned.

Note: You need to call this function before using any other *AbandonQuest*() functions.

SetActionBarToggles

Configures the display of the additional action bars.

```
SetActionBarToggles(SHOW_MULTI_ACTIONBAR_1, SHOW_MULTI_ACTIONBAR_2,
SHOW_MULTI_ACTIONBAR_3, SHOW_MULTI_ACTIONBAR_4, ALWAYS_SHOW_MULTIBARS)
```

Arguments:

SHOW_MULTI_ACTIONBAR_1 — 1 to show the bottom left action bar, otherwise nil. (1nil)

SHOW_MULTI_ACTIONBAR_2 — 1 to show the bottom right action bar, otherwise nil. (1nil)

SHOW_MULTI_ACTIONBAR_3 — 1 to show the right action bar, otherwise nil. (1nil)

SHOW_MULTI_ACTIONBAR_4 — 1 to show the second right action bar, otherwise nil. (1nil)

ALWAYS_SHOW_MULTIBARS — 1 to always show the action bar buttons even when empty, otherwise nil. (1nil)

SetActiveVoiceChannel

Sets the currently active voice channel.

```
SetActiveVoiceChannel(index)
```

Argument:

index — The index of the channel in the channel display window. These indices are offset by any headers that are displayed in this window. (number)

SetActiveVoiceChannelBySessionID

Sets the currently active voice chat channel.

```
SetActiveVoiceChannelBySessionID(session)
```

Argument:

session — The session ID of the voice chat channel. This can be obtained by enumerating GetVoiceSessionInfo(). (number)

SetArenaTeamRosterSelection

Selects a specific member from an arena team roster. This function is used to set the selection that is then used to query information about a specific arena team member.

```
SetArenaTeamRosterSelection(team, index)
```

Arguments:

team — The index of the arena team. (number)

index — The index of the player to select. (number)

SetAutoLootDefault

Enables or disables auto-looting.

```
SetAutoLootDefault(enabled)
```

Argument:

enabled — 1 to enable auto-loot, nil to disable. (1nil)

SetBagPortraitTexture

Sets a texture to a circular rendering of the specified bag's icon. This function is used to create the circular bag icon you see in the upper-left of the bag windows of the default UI. The UI graphics engine does not support alpha masks, thus the game has to generate rounded textures like this on the fly.

Bag slots are numbered from 0 to 4, with 0 being the backpack and 4 being the left-most bag in the default UI. The bank slots are also usable, with numbers 5–12 when the player has the bank open.

```
SetBagPortraitTexture(texture, slot)
```

Arguments:

texture — The texture object to change. (table)

slot — The bag slot used for the generated texture. (number)

Example:

```
-- Set a texture to the rounded icon of your first bag (not ↵
the backpack)
SetBagPortraitTexture(MyBagTexture, 1)
```

SetBaseMip

Sets the level of texture resolution rendered by the client.

```
SetBaseMip(value)
```

Arguments:

value — The desired level of texture resolution rendered by the client. (number)

- ▪ 0 — Low-texture resolution
- ▪ 1 — High-texture resolution

SetBattlefieldScoreFaction

Sets the faction of the battlefield scoreboard.

```
SetBattlefieldScoreFaction(faction)
```

Argument:

faction — The faction to select. (number)

SetBinding

Sets a key combination to a given binding. This is used for certain actions in the default user interface (such as FOLLOWTARGET) as well as an addon's custom bindings. There are more specific functions to bind spells, actions, and macros directly to key/mouse combinations.

```
success = SetBinding("key"[, "command"])
```

Arguments:

key — The name of the key or button to be bound, such as CTRL-P, ALT-SHIFT-#, or ALT-CTRL-SHIFT-1. Note that for multiple modifiers, the order in which they are accepted is a strict one; it will only work if ALT is before CTRL and CTRL is before SHIFT; any other order will result in the function returning success, but the binding being broken. (string)

command (optional) — The command to be bound to the given key. If not specified, the key binding will be unbound. (string)

Returns:

success — 1 if the key binding (or unbinding) was successful, otherwise nil. (1nil)

Example:

```
-- Bind FOLLOWTARGET to Control-Y
SetBinding("CTRL-Y", "FOLLOWTARGET")

-- Unbind MouseButton4
SetBinding("BUTTON4")
```

SetBindingClick

Set a key binding directly to a Button object. The click sends a mouse down when the key is pressed and a mouse up when released.

```
SetBindingClick("KEY", "buttonName"[, "mouseButton"])
```

Arguments:

KEY — The name of the key or button to be bound, such as CTRL-P, ALT-SHIFT-#, or ALT-CTRL-SHIFT-1. Note that for multiple modifiers, the order in which they are accepted is a strict one; it will only work if ALT is before CTRL and CTRL is before SHIFT; any other order will result in the function returning success, but the binding being broken. (string)

buttonName — The Button object to which to bind the key combination. (string)

mouseButton (optional) — The mouse button to use as a trigger. (string)

SetBindingItem

This function will bind a specific key to a specific item. Hitting that key after calling this function will cause the item to be used or activated.

```
success = SetBindingItem("keyCombination", "itemName" or "itemLink"
or "partialItemName")
```

Arguments:

keyCombination

- ■ keyCombination — The name of the key or button to be bound, such as CTRL-P, ALT-SHIFT-#, or ALT-CTRL-SHIFT-1. Note that for multiple modifiers, the order in which they are accepted is a strict one; it will only work if ALT is before CTRL and CTRL is before SHIFT; any other order will result in the function returning success, but the binding being broken. (string)

itemName or itemLink or partialItemName

- ■ itemName — The name of the item you want to bind to a key. (string)

- ■ itemLink — The full link of the item you want to bind to a key. (string)

- ■ partialItemName — A partial name of the item you want to bind to a key. Note that *Hearth* will work if you want to invoke your Hearthstone, but *stone* will not work for the same item. Also note that if the partial name you specify matches several items in your inventory, the first one that appears in your bags will be the one that gets activated. (string)

Returns:

success — 1 if the binding was successful, otherwise nil. (1nil)

SetBindingMacro

Assigns a key binding to a specific macro.

```
SetBindingMacro("KEY", "macroname"|macroid)
```

Arguments:

KEY — The name of the key or button to be bound, such as CTRL-P, ALT-SHIFT-#, or ALT-CTRL-SHIFT-1. Note that for multiple modifiers, the order in which they are accepted is a strict one; it will only work if ALT is before CTRL and CTRL is before SHIFT; any other order will result in the function returning success, but the binding being broken. (string)

macroName or macroID

- macroName — The name of the macro. If Macros are named the same, it will return the first. (string)

- macroID — The Macro ID of the macro required. 1–18 are the account-wide ones, and 19–32 are character-specific. (number)

SetBindingSpell

Binds a spell directly to a key combination.

```
SetBindingSpell("KEY", "spellname")
```

Arguments:

KEY — The name of the key or button to be bound, such as CTRL-P, ALT-SHIFT-#, or ALT-CTRL-SHIFT-1. Note that for multiple modifiers, the order in which they are accepted is a strict one; it will only work if ALT is before CTRL and CTRL is before SHIFT; any other order will result in the function returning success, but the binding being broken. (string)

spellname — The name of a spell to bind. (string)

Example:

```
-- Bind Flash Heal to ALT-Y
SetBindingSpell("ALT-Y", "Flash Heal")
```

SetCVar

Sets the value of a configuration variable.

```
SetCVar("cvar", "value" [, raiseEvent])
```

Arguments:

cvar — The name of the CVar to set. (string)

value — The value for the CVar. (any)

raiseEvent (optional) — If set, this causes the CVAR_UPDATE event to be fired with this as its first argument (note that numbers work, too). (string)

SetChannelOwner

Gives channel ownership to another player.

```
SetChannelOwner("channel", "newowner")
```

Arguments:

channel — The name of the channel. (string)

newowner — The name of the player to give ownership. (string)

Example:

```
-- Give "Cladhaire" ownership in the channel "monkeys"
SetChannelOwner("monkeys", "Cladhaire")
```

SetChannelPassword

Sets a password on a custom chat channel.

```
SetChannelPassword("name", "password")
```

Arguments:

name — The name of the channel to change. (string)

password — The password to set on the channel. (string)

SetChatWindowAlpha

Sets the value of the Chat window alpha in chat-cache.txt. To set and save a Chat window alpha value, the color must be set on the textures in-game, and this function must be called to ensure that the new values are saved between sessions.

```
SetChatWindowAlpha(index, alpha)
```

Arguments:

index — The index of the Chat window to modify. (number)

alpha — The alpha value for the window (0.0–1.0). (number)

SetChatWindowColor

Sets the value of the Chat window color in chat-cache.txt. To set and save a Chat window alpha value, the color must be set on the textures in-game, and this function must be called to ensure that the new values are saved between sessions.

```
SetChatWindowColor(index, r, g, b)
```

Arguments:

index — The index of the chat frame. (number)

r — The red value of the color (0.0–1.0). (number)

g — The green value of the color (0.0–1.0). (number)

b — The blue value of the color (0.0–1.0). (number)

SetChatWindowDocked

Sets the value of the docked setting for the given Chat window in `chat-cache`
`.txt`. This function simply stores the value in `chat-cache.txt` and will only take
effect after a reload of the UI.

```
SetChatWindowDocked(index, docked)
```

Arguments:

`index` — The index of the Chat window to modify. `(number)`

`docked` — 1 if the chat frame is docked with the main frame, otherwise
`nil`. `(1nil)`

SetChatWindowLocked

Locks a Chat window, so it can't be dragged or resized. This function doesn't
actually handle the locking during a WoW session, but rather sets the variables
that cause the locked state to be stored between sessions in `chat-cache.txt`. To
lock the ChatFrame immediately, you should set the `isLocked` variable on the
frame to 1. You can unlock by setting it to `nil`.

```
SetChatWindowLocked(index, locked)
```

Arguments:

`index` — The index of the Chat window. `(number)`

`locked` — 1 to lock the window, `nil` to unlock. `(1nil)`

Example:

```
-- Lock ChatFrame1
SetChatWindowLocked(1, 1)
ChatFrame1.isLocked = true
```

SetChatWindowName

Sets the name for a Chat window in `chat-cache.txt`. This does not set the
name of the window immediately, but instead sets the value to be saved in
`chat-cache.txt` so that it persists between sessions.

```
SetChatWindowName(index, "name")
```

Arguments:

`index` — The index of a Chat window. `(number)`

`name` — The name to give the Chat window. `(string)`

SetChatWindowShown

Sets if a Chat window is shown in `chat-cache.txt`. This allows the setting to
persist between sessions.

```
SetChatWindowShown(index, shown)
```

Arguments:

`index` — The index of the Chat window. `(number)`

`shown` — 1 to show the window, `nil` to hide. `(1nil)`

SetChatWindowSize

Sets the value of the Chat window's font size in `chat-cache.txt`. To set and save a Chat window font size, the font object must be set within the game, and this function must be called to ensure that the new values are saved between sessions.

```
SetChatWindowSize(index, size)
```

Arguments:

`index` — The index of the Chat window to modify. (number)

`size` — The font size for the Chat window. (number)

SetCraftFilter

Sets a specific craft filter as active.

```
SetCraftFilter(index)
```

Argument:

`index` — The craft filter to use. The available filters can be found using the example code that follows. (number)

Example:

```
-- Print the available craft filters to chat
-- This code only works for the Enchanting Craft, if the Craft UI ↵
is open
local slots = {GetCraftSlots()}
for idx,slot in ipairs(slots) do
  local name = getglobal(slot)
  ChatFrame1:AddMessage("Filter #" .. idx .. " is " .. name)
end
```

SetCraftItemNameFilter

Sets the Craft UI to only show items whose names contain a search string.

```
SetCraftItemNameFilter("text")
```

Argument:

`text` — The search string. (string)

SetCurrentGuildBankTab

Sets the currently selected guild bank tab.

```
SetCurrentGuildBankTab(tab)
```

Argument:

`tab` — The guild bank tab index. (number)

SetCurrentTitle

Sets the player's title.

```
SetCurrentTitle(titleMaskID)
```

Arguments:

`titleMaskID` — Sets your player's title to the given ID; should be between 1 and `GetNumTitles()`, or –1 to clear. (number)

Example:

```
-- set your title to a random one:
SetCurrentTitle( math.random(1, GetNumTitles()) )

-- set your title to none:
SetCurrentTitle(-1)
```

SetCursor

Sets the cursor image.

```
SetCursor("cursor")
```

Arguments:

`cursor` — One of the cursor tokens listed below, the path to a 32 ´ 32 blp cursor image, or `nil`. If `nil` is specified, any set cursor will be cleared. (string)

- ATTACK_CURSOR
- ATTACK_ERROR_CURSOR
- BUY_CURSOR
- BUY_ERROR_CURSOR
- CAST_CURSOR
- CAST_ERROR_CURSOR
- GATHER_CURSOR
- GATHER_ERROR_CURSOR
- INNKEEPER_CURSOR
- INNKEEPER_ERROR_CURSOR
- INSPECT_CURSOR
- INSPECT_ERROR_CURSOR
- INTERACT_CURSOR
- INTERACT_ERROR_CURSOR
- ITEM_CURSOR
- ITEM_ERROR_CURSOR
- LOCK_CURSOR
- LOCK_ERROR_CURSOR

- LOOT_ALL_CURSOR

- LOOT_ALL_ERROR_CURSOR

- MAIL_CURSOR

- MAIL_ERROR_CURSOR

- MINE_CURSOR

- MINE_ERROR_CURSOR

- PICKUP_CURSOR

- PICKUP_ERROR_CURSOR

- POINT_CURSOR

- POINT_ERROR_CURSOR

- QUEST_CURSOR

- QUEST_ERROR_CURSOR

- REPAIRNPC_CURSOR

- REPAIRNPC_ERROR_CURSOR

- REPAIR_CURSOR

- REPAIR_ERROR_CURSOR

- SKIN_ALLIANCE_CURSOR

- SKIN_ALLIANCE_ERROR_CURSOR

- SKIN_CURSOR

- SKIN_ERROR_CURSOR

- SKIN_HORDE_CURSOR

- SKIN_HORDE_ERROR_CURSOR

- SPEAK_CURSOR

- SPEAK_ERROR_CURSOR

- TAXI_CURSOR

- TAXI_ERROR_CURSOR

- TRAINER_CURSOR

- TRAINER_ERROR_CURSOR

Note: This is a temporary change of cursor, and if called alone will likely be immediately overwritten by the default cursor. To change the cursor while mousing over a frame, call this from the OnEnter handler for the frame.

Example:

```
-- The following code sample will give you a button in the center of your
screen
-- That can be moused over to view all available default cursors
local cursors = {
    "ATTACK_CURSOR", "ATTACK_ERROR_CURSOR", "BUY_CURSOR",
"BUY_ERROR_CURSOR", ↵
    "CAST_CURSOR", "CAST_ERROR_CURSOR", "GATHER_CURSOR",
"GATHER_ERROR_CURSOR", ↵
    "INNKEEPER_CURSOR", "INNKEEPER_ERROR_CURSOR", "INSPECT_CURSOR", ↵
    "INSPECT_ERROR_CURSOR", "INTERACT_CURSOR", ↵
"INTERACT_ERROR_CURSOR", "ITEM_CURSOR", "ITEM_ERROR_CURSOR",
"LOCK_CURSOR", "LOCK_ERROR_CURSOR", ↵
    "LOOT_ALL_CURSOR", "LOOT_ALL_ERROR_CURSOR", "MAIL_CURSOR", ↵
    "MAIL_ERROR_CURSOR", "MINE_CURSOR", "MINE_ERROR_CURSOR",
"PICKUP_CURSOR", ↵
    "PICKUP_ERROR_CURSOR", "POINT_CURSOR", "POINT_ERROR_CURSOR",
"QUEST_CURSOR", ↵
    "QUEST_ERROR_CURSOR", "REPAIRNPC_CURSOR", ↵
"REPAIRNPC_ERROR_CURSOR", "REPAIR_CURSOR", "REPAIR_ERROR_CURSOR", ↵
"SKIN_ALLIANCE_CURSOR", ↵
    "SKIN_ALLIANCE_ERROR_CURSOR", "SKIN_CURSOR", "SKIN_ERROR_CURSOR", ↵
    "SKIN_HORDE_CURSOR", "SKIN_HORDE_ERROR_CURSOR", "SPEAK_CURSOR", ↵
    "SPEAK_ERROR_CURSOR", "TAXI_CURSOR", "TAXI_ERROR_CURSOR", ↵
    "TRAINER_CURSOR", "TRAINER_ERROR_CURSOR",
}

local current = 1

CreateFrame("Button", "CursorTestFrame", UIParent,
"GameMenuButtonTemplate")
CursorTestFrame:SetPoint("CENTER", 0, 0)
CursorTestFrame:SetText(cursors[current])
local function OnEnter(self)
  SetCursor(cursors[current])
  current = current + 1
  if current > #cursors then
    current = 1
  end
  self:SetText(cursors[current])
end

CursorTestFrame:SetScript("OnEnter", OnEnter)
```

SetDungeonDifficulty

Sets the dungeon difficulty mode.

```
SetDungeonDifficulty(difficulty)
```

Arguments:

`difficulty` — The level of difficulty. (number)

- ▪ 1 — Normal
- ▪ 2 — Heroic
- ▪ 3 — Epic (currently unused)

seterrorhandler

Sets the default error handler to a specific function.

```
seterrorhandler(errHandler)
```

Argument:

`errHandler` — The function to use as the error handler. (function)

Example:

```
-- changes the error handler to print to the default chat frame ↵
in red text
local function printError(error)
    DEFAULT_CHAT_FRAME:AddMessage(error, 1, 0, 0)
end
seterrorhandler(printError)
```

SetEuropeanNumbers

Enables using comma as the decimal separator.

```
SetEuropeanNumbers(enable)
```

Argument:

`enable` — `true` to enable European numbers, otherwise `nil`. (boolean)

SetFactionActive

Sets a faction as the active faction. This faction will be displayed on a bar above the experience bar.

```
SetFactionActive(index)
```

Argument:

`index` — The index of the faction to set as active. (number)

SetFactionInactive

Flags a faction as inactive.

```
SetFactionInactive(index)
```

Argument:

`index` — The index of the faction in the faction list (including headers). (number)

SetFarclip

Sets the value of the "Terrain Distance" slider in the Video Options.

`SetFarclip(value)`

Argument:

`value` — The value of the "Terrain Distance" slider in the Video Options. `(number)`

setglobal

Sets a global variable to a specified value.

`setglobal(name, value)`

Arguments:

`name` — The name of a global variable. `(string)`

`value` — The value to set in the given variable. `(value)`

SetGuildBankTabInfo

Sets the name and icon for a guild bank tab.

`SetGuildBankTabInfo(tab, "name", iconIndex)`

Arguments:

`tab` — The index of a guild bank tab. `(number)`

`name` — The name for the tab. `(string)`

`iconIndex` — The index of the icon to display. This should be a number between 1 and `GetNumMacroItemIcons()`. `(number)`

SetGuildBankTabPermissions

Enables or disables a specific guild bank tab permission.

`SetGuildBankTabPermissions(tab, permission, enabled)`

Argument:

`tab` — The index of a guild bank tab. `(number)`

`permission` — The index of the permission to enable/disable. `(number)`

- 1 — View tab.
- 2 — Deposit items.

`enabled` — 1 to enable the permission, otherwise `nil`. `(1nil)`

SetGuildBankTabWithdraw

Sets the number of withdrawals allowed for the currently selected guild rank, on the given guild bank tab.

```
SetGuildBankTabWithdraw(tab, amount)
```

Arguments:

`tab` — The index of a guild tab. (`number`)

`amount` — The number of stacks of items allowed for withdrawal per day. (`number`)

SetGuildBankWithdrawLimit

Sets the number of money withdrawals allowed for the selected guild rank.

```
SetGuildBankWithdrawLimit(amount)
```

Argument:

`amount` — The amount of copper that can be withdrawn per day. (`number`)

SetGuildInfoText

Sets the guild information text. This text can be multi-line, and is displayed on-demand through the Guild tab on the Social window.

```
SetGuildInfoText("text")
```

Argument:

`text` — The guild information text to be set. (`string`)

SetGuildRecruitmentMode

Enables or disables auto-joining of the guild recruitment channel.

```
SetGuildRecruitmentMode(mode)
```

Arguments:

`mode` — The auto-join mode for the guild recruitment channel. (`number`)

- ▪ `0` — Do not join the guild recruitment channel.
- ▪ `1` — Auto-join the guild recruitment channel if not already in a guild.

SetGuildRosterSelection

Sets the selection in the guild roster.

```
SetGuildRosterSelection(index)
```

Argument:

`index` — The index in the guild roster. (`number`)

SetGuildRosterShowOffline

Sets the value for the Show Offline guild setting.

```
SetGuildRosterShowOffline(showOffline)
```

Argument:

`showOffline` — The value to set for the Show Offline guild setting. (`1nil`)

SetInventoryPortraitTexture

Sets a portrait texture using an inventory item.

```
SetInventoryPortraitTexture(texture, unit, slot)
```

Arguments:

texture — The texture to be changed. (table)

unit — The unit whose inventory should be queried. (unitid)

slot — The inventory slot ID to query. (number)

SetLFGAutojoin

Enables auto-join in the LFG system.

SetLFGComment

Adds a comment to your listing in the LFG system. Sets a comment that can be viewed by others when mousing over your name in the Looking For More window.

Note: SetLFGComment(nil) will not remove an existing comment; use SetLFGComment("") instead.

```
SetLFGComment("comment")
```

Argument:

comment — A comment to be shown with your listing in the LFG system. (string)

Example:

```
-- Sets your LFG comment to a quick summary of your talent spec
-- (Requires you to already be participating in the LFG UI)
local _, _, tab1Points = GetTalentTabInfo(1);
local _, _, tab2Points = GetTalentTabInfo(2);
local _, _, tab3Points = GetTalentTabInfo(3);
SetLFGComment(tab1Points.."/"..tab2points.."/"..tab3points)
```

SetLFGType

Sets a filter for the LFG system in a specific slot.

```
SetLFGType(slot, type)
```

Arguments:

slot — The slot to select (1–3). (number)

type — The type of LFG query to select. Valid options can be obtained by indexing the results of GetLFGTypes(). (number)

SetLFMAutofill

Turns on the autofill option in the Looking For More interface.

SetLFMType

Sets the type of the current LFM request.

```
SetLFMType(id)
```

Arguments:

id — The type of LFM request to query. (number)

- ▪ 1 — Dungeon
- ▪ 2 — Raid
- ▪ 3 — Quest (Group)
- ▪ 4 — Zone
- ▪ 5 — Heroic Dungeon

SetLookingForGroup

Sets one of the three Looking For Group slots.

```
SetLookingForGroup(slot, type, index)
```

Arguments:

slot — The index of a slot in the LFG tab of the Looking For Group system. There are three slots available, thus this value should be a number 1–3. (number)

type — The index of a type as listed from GetLFGTypes(). (number)

index — The index of a dungeon/quest entry as listed from GetLFGTypeEntries(). (number)

SetLookingForMore

Starts looking for more members for the given activity type and index.

```
SetLookingForMore(activityType, activityIndex)
```

Arguments:

activityType — The type of activity. See the return values of GetLFGTypes() for valid indices. (number)

activityIndex — The specific activity index for which to look for more members. See the return values of GetLFGTypeEntries() for valid indices. (number)

SetLootMethod

Sets the loot method when in a group or party. Requires leader.

```
SetLootMethod("method" [,master])
```

Arguments:

method — Method to use for loot distribution. (string)

- ■ freeforall — Free for All
- ■ group — Group Loot
- ■ master — Master Looter
- ■ needbeforegreed — Need before Greed
- ■ roundrobin — Round Robin

master — Name of the master looter. (string)

SetLootPortrait

Sets a texture to the current loot portrait. It seems the loot portrait is typically just the image of the object/monster that is being looted.

```
SetLootPortrait(texture)
```

Argument:

texture — The portrait texture to set. (table)

Example:

```
-- Use when the loot window is open, sets the PlayerFrame portrait
SetLootPortrait(PlayerPortrait)
```

SetLootThreshold

Sets the loot threshold to a specific item quality.

```
SetLootThreshold(quality)
```

Arguments:

quality — The minimum item quality to use for the loot method. This is set to 2 — Uncommon items by default. (number)

- ■ 2 — Uncommon
- ■ 3 — Rare
- ■ 4 — Epic
- ■ 5 — Legendary
- ■ 6 — Artifact

SetMacroItem

Sets a macro to use a specific item and target for visual updates. This function can be used to provide dynamic feedback for macros.

```
SetMacroItem(macroIndex or "macroName", item [,"target"])
```

Arguments:

macroIndex or macroName

- macroIndex — The index of a macro. (number)

- macroName — The name of a macro. (string)

item — The name of the item to use for the macro. (string)

target (optional) — The unit ID to use for the macro distance checking. (unitid)

Example:

```
-- Create a macro and note the index (19--36 are the character ↵
specific indices)
-- Target a friendly item that you can bandage
-- Set the first argument to the macro index
-- Set the second argument to the name of a a bandage you have ↵
in your inventory
SetMacroItem(19, "Heavy Runecloth Bandage", "target")


-- The given macro on your action bars should now use the bandage range
-- in order to indicate whether the macro is "in range"
```

SetMacroSpell

Sets the spell and target unit used to update a macro's icon and range indicator.

```
SetMacroSpell(macro or "name", "spell" [,"target"])
```

Arguments:

macro or name

- macro — The macro index to change. (number)

- name — The name of the macro to change. (string)

spell — The spell to use as the macro icon. (string)

target — The target to use when judging if the unit is in range of the spell. (unitid)

SetMapToCurrentZone

Sets the world map to the player's current zone. This event causes WORLD_MAP_ UPDATE to fire when the current zone is different from the one being displayed.

SetMapZoom

Sets the world map to a specific continent or zone within that continent.

```
SetMapZoom(continentIndex [,zoneIndex])
```

Arguments:

continentIndex — Content index identifier. Use GetMapContinents() for a list. 0 and -1 are valid inputs for Azeroth and the cosmic map, respectively. (number)

zoneIndex — Optional argument to display a specific zone within a continent. Use GetMapZones(continentIndex) for a list. (number)

Example:

```
-- show the cosmic map
SetMapZoom( -1 )
-- show both the azeroth continents
SetMapZoom( 0 )
-- show the outland continent
SetMapZoom( 3 )
-- show dun morogh
SetMapZoom( 2, 7)
```

SetModifiedClick

Sets a modified click for a given action. This function is used for actions such as auto-loot to specify which modified right-click will auto-loot.

```
SetModifiedClick("action", "binding")
```

Arguments:

action — The action to set. (string)

binding — The modified click to set. (string)

SetMouselookOverrideBinding

Overrides the default mouselook bindings to perform another binding with the mouse buttons.

```
SetMouselookOverrideBinding("key", "binding" or nil)
```

Arguments:

key — The mouselook key to override. (string)

- ▪ BUTTON1 — Override the left mouse button.
- ▪ BUTTON2 — Override the right mouse button.

binding — The binding to perform instead of mouselooking, or nil to clear the override. (string)

Example:

```
-- Uses the 'z' button to activate mouselook instead of the ↵
mouse buttons,
-- and the mouse buttons to move forward and backward instead ↵
of mouselooking.
-- Credits to slouken for this code.
CreateFrame("Button", "MouselookButton")
MouselookButton:RegisterForClicks("AnyUp", "AnyDown")
MouselookButton:SetScript("OnClick", function (self, button, down)
  if ( down ) then
MouselookStart()
  else
MouselookStop()
  end
end)
SetOverrideBindingClick(MouselookButton, nil, "Z", "MouselookButton")
SetMouselookOverrideBinding("BUTTON1", "MOVEFORWARD")
SetMouselookOverrideBinding("BUTTON2", "MOVEBACKWARD")
```

SetMultisampleFormat

Sets the client's multi-sampling format.

```
SetMultisampleFormat(index)
```

Argument:

index — The multi-sampling format's index. (number)

Note: See GetMultisampleFormats() for details about each index.

SetOverrideBinding

Sets an override binding to the given command. Override bindings are temporary. The bound key will revert to its normal setting once the override is removed. Priority overrides work the same way but will revert to the previous override binding (if present) rather than the base binding for the key.

You can remove all the bindings for a given owner using ClearOverrideBindings.

```
SetOverrideBinding(owner, isPriority, "key", "command")
```

Arguments:

owner — The frame responsible for setting the override. (table)

isPriority — Indicates this is a priority override binding. (boolean)

key — The key to bind to the command (for example, CTRL-2). (string)

command — The binding command to execute or nil to remove the override binding. (string)

SetOverrideBindingClick

Sets an override binding that acts like a mouse click on a button. An override binding is a temporary key or click binding that can be used to override the default bindings. The bound key will revert to its normal setting once the override has been removed.

```
SetOverrideBindingClick(owner, isPriority, "key", "buttonName" ↵
[, "mouseClick"])
```

Arguments:

owner — The frame responsible for setting the override. (table)

isPriority — Indicates that this is a priority override binding. (boolean)

key — The key to bind to the button (for example, CTRL-2). (string)

buttonName — The name of the button to which the key will be bound, or nil to remove the override binding. (string)

mouseClick (optional) — The mouse button sent to the button's OnClick handler. (string)

SetOverrideBindingItem

Sets an override binding to use a specific item. An override binding is a temporary key or click binding that can be used to override the default bindings. The bound key will revert to its normal setting once the override has been removed.

```
SetOverrideBindingItem(owner, isPriority, "KEY", "itemname")
```

Arguments:

owner — The frame responsible for setting the override. (table)

isPriority — Indicates that this is a priority override binding. (boolean)

key — The key to bind to the button (for example, CTRL-2). (string)

itemName — The name of the item to use when the binding is triggered. (string)

SetOverrideBindingMacro

Sets an override binding to a specific macro. Override bindings are temporary. The bound key will revert to its normal setting once the override is removed. Priority overrides work the same way but will revert to the previous override binding (if present) rather than the base binding for the key.

You can remove all the bindings for a given owner using ClearOverrideBindings.

```
SetOverrideBindingMacro(owner, isPriority, "key", "macroName" ↵
or macroIndex)
```

Arguments:

owner — The frame responsible for setting the override. (table)

isPriority — Indicates that this is a priority override binding. (boolean)

key — The key to bind to the command (for example, CTRL-2). (string)

macroIndex or macroName

- macroIndex — The index of a macro to set for the override binding, or nil to remove the binding. (number)

- macroName — The name of a macro to set for the override binding, or nil to remove the binding. (string)

SetOverrideBindingSpell

Set an override binding to a specific spell. Override bindings are temporary. The bound key will revert to its normal setting once the override is removed. Priority overrides work the same way but will revert to the previous override binding (if present) rather than the base binding for the key.

You can remove all the bindings for a given owner using ClearOverrideBindings.

```
SetOverrideBindingSpell(owner, isPriority, "key", "spellname")
```

Arguments:

owner — The frame responsible for setting the override. (table)

isPriority — Indicates that this is a priority override binding. (boolean)

key — The key to bind to the command (for example, CTRL-2). (string)

spellname — The spell to cast or nil to remove the override binding. (string)

Example:

```
-- Set up Shift-2 to cast Prayer of Mending as an override binding
-- owned by PlayerFrame
SetOverrideBindingSpell(PlayerFrame, 1, "SHIFT-2", "Prayer of
Mending")

-- Clear PlayerFrame's override bindings
ClearOverrideBindings(PlayerFrame)
```

SetPVP

Enables/Disables PvP for the player.

```
SetPVP(state)
```

Argument:

state — 1 to enable PvP, nil to disable. (1nil)

SetPartyAssignment

Assigns a party role (maintank, mainassist) to a player or unit.

```
SetPartyAssignment("role", "unit" or "name" [,exact])
```

Arguments:

role — The role to assign to the given party member. (string)

- ▪ maintank
- ▪ mainassist

unit or name

unit — The unit ID to assign a role. (unitid)

name — The name of the player to assign a role. (string)

exact — When using the name argument, a value of 1 here will only match the name exactly; otherwise it will match the closest name. (1nil)

Note: This function is protected and cannot be called via addons.

SetPetStablePaperdoll

Sets the given model to the currently selected stabled pet's model.

```
SetPetStablePaperdoll(model)
```

Argument:

model — A model frame. (table)

Example:

```
-- Open the character window, and the pet stable before running ↵
this code
-- Changes the character model to the pet model
SetPetStablePaperdoll(CharacterModelFrame)
```

SetPortraitTexture

Sets a portrait texture based on a unit's model.

```
SetPortraitTexture(texture, "unit")
```

Arguments:

texture — The texture object to set. (table)

unit — The unit to use for the portrait texture. (unitid)

SetPortraitToTexture

Sets a portrait to a given texture. This function is used to set a portrait to a static texture. If the texture is square, it is altered so it can fit the circular portrait textures.

```
SetPortraitToTexture("frameName", "texturePath")
```

Arguments:

frameName — The global name of the portrait texture to be altered. (string)

texturePath — The path to the texture to be used. (string)

Example:

```
-- Change the player portrait to be the same as the keychain portrait
SetPortraitToTexture("PlayerPortrait",
"Interface\\ContainerFrame\\KeyRing-Bag-Icon")

-- Set the player portrait to be the icon for "Staff of Infinite
Mysteries"
SetPortraitToTexture("PlayerPortrait",
"Interface\\Icons\\INV_Weapon_Halberd17")
```

SetRaidRosterSelection

Sets the currently selected raid roster unit. This function is used by the default user interface when moving players between groups in the Raid window.

```
SetRaidRosterSelection(index)
```

Argument:

index — The raid index of the selected unit. This is a value from 1 to GetNumRaidMembers(). (number)

SetRaidSubgroup

Moves a raid member to a non-full raid subgroup.

```
SetRaidSubgroup(index, subgroup)
```

Arguments:

index — The raid index of the player to move. This can be obtained by mousing over the player in the raid frame, and running /run ChatFrame1:AddMessage (GetMouseFocus():GetID()). (number)

subgroup — A non-full raid subgroup (1–8) where the player should be moved. (number)

SetRaidTarget

Sets a raid target marker on the given unit.

```
SetRaidTarget("unit" or "name", index)
```

Arguments:

unit or name

- unit — The unit ID of the unit to mark. (unitId)
- name — The full name of the player to mark. (string)

index — The index of the raid target to place, or 0 to clear. (number)

- 0 — Clear any raid target markers.
- 1 — Star
- 2 — Circle
- 3 — Diamond
- 4 — Triangle
- 5 — Moon
- 6 — Square
- 7 — Cross
- 8 — Skull

SetScreenResolution

Sets the screen resolution to a specified value.

```
SetScreenResolution(index)
```

Argument:

index — The index of the resolution to choose. These values correspond to the returns from GetScreenResolutions(). (number)

Example:

```
-- Print the possible resolutions to ChatFrame1
-- These indices can then be used in SetScreenResolution()
local resolutions = {GetScreenResolutions()}
for idx,resolution in ipairs(resolutions) do
  ChatFrame1:AddMessage("Resolution " .. idx .. ": " .. resolution)
end
```

SetSelectedAuctionItem

Selects a specific item in the auction house.

```
SetSelectedAuctionItem("type", index)
```

Arguments:

type — The type of auction house listing. (string)

- ▪ bidder — Auctions the player has bid on

- ▪ list — Auctions available for purchase

- ▪ owner — Auctions the player has placed

SetSelectedBattlefield

Selects a given battleground instance in the window that appears when talking to a battlemaster NPC or attempting to enter a battleground portal.

```
SetSelectedBattlefield(index)
```

Argument:

index — The instance index to select, or 0 for "First Available." (number)

SetSelectedDisplayChannel

Selects the given display channel for use in other functions.

```
SetSelectedDisplayChannel(index)
```

Argument:

index — The index of the display channel to select. (number)

SetSelectedFaction

Sets the current faction selection.

```
SetSelectedFaction(index)
```

Argument:

index — The index of the faction in the Reputation window. (number)

SetSelectedFriend

Sets the selection in the Friends list.

```
SetSelectedFriend(index)
```

Argument:

index — The index of a friend in the Friends list. (number)

SetSelectedIgnore

Sets the currently selected ignore entry.

```
SetSelectedIgnore(index)
```

Argument:

index — The index in the Ignore list. (number)

SetSelectedMute

Selects the given muted player for use by other functions.

```
SetSelectedMute(index)
```

Argument:

index — The index of the muted player to select. (number)

SetSelectedSkill

Sets the currently selected skill in the Skills window.

```
SetSelectedSkill(index)
```

Argument:

index — The index of a skill in the Skill window, including skill headers. (number)

SetSendMailCOD

Sets the Cash On Delivery cost of a mail being sent; when the recipient receives the mail, he'll be prompted to pay this amount (which will be given to the sender of the message) before accepting any attached items. Only has an effect if one or more item attachments are being sent with the message.

```
SetSendMailCOD(amount)
```

Argument:

amount — The COD cost of the item being sent, in copper. (number)

SetSendMailMoney

Sets the amount of money to send with the next mail message. Opening or closing the Mail window will reset the value to 0. For this function to be useful, you must call it while the Mail window is open. If you try to set the value to more money than you currently have, you will receive a "You don't have enough money" error.

```
success = SetSendMailMoney(amount)
```

Argument:

amount — The amount of money to send, in copper. (number)

Returns:

success — 1 if you have enough money (not including postage), otherwise nil. (1nil)

Example:

```
-- Quickly send money to a specified character (only works while at an
-- open mailbox)
function SendCharacterMoney(name, amount)
  SetSendMailMoney(amount)
  SendMail(name, number/10000 .. " gold attached", "")
end
```

SetSendMailShowing

Controls whether right-clicking an item attaches it to the mail to be sent.

```
SetSendMailShowing(enable)
```

Argument:

enable — If true, enables right-click to attach items to the mail to be sent. (boolean)

SetTaxiBenchmarkMode

Turns on flight path "benchmark" mode. In this mode, other players and creatures are not shown during the flight (to provide a consistent environment between repeated tests) and frame rate statistics are printed to the Chat window at the end of the flight.

SetTaxiMap

Sets a texture to show the appropriate background map image for the flight paths on the current continent.

```
SetTaxiMap(texture)
```

Argument:

texture — The texture to set. (table)

Example:

```
-- Create a frame, and set it to the taxi map
TestFrame = CreateFrame("Frame", "TestFrame", UIParent)
TestFrame:SetHeight(200)
TestFrame:SetWidth(200)
TestFrame:SetPoint("CENTER", UIParent, "CENTER", 0, 0)
TestFrameTexture = TextFrame:CreateTexture("TestFrameTexture",
"BACKGROUND")
TestFrameTexture:SetAllPoints()

SetTaxiMap(TestFrameTexture)
```

SetTerrainMip

Sets the value of the "Terrain Detail Level" slider in the video options.

```
SetTerrainMip(value)
```

Argument:

`terrainDetailLevel` — The value to set for the "Terrain Detail Level" slider in the Video options. This is either 0 or 1. (number)

SetTracking

Enables a tracking skill that identifies units or objects on the minimap. Pass `nil` to track nothing.

```
SetTracking(index)
```

Argument:

`index` — The index of a tracking ability, between 1 and `GetNumTrackingTypes()`, or `nil` to track nothing. (number)

SetTradeMoney

Sets the amount of money to trade in the Trade window, in copper.

```
SetTradeMoney(amount)
```

Argument:

`amount` — The amount of money to trade, in copper. (number)

SetTradeSkillInvSlotFilter

Enables or disables an inventory slot filter in the Tradeskill window.

```
SetTradeSkillInvSlotFilter(index [, enable, exclusive])
```

Arguments:

`index` — The index of an inventory slot filter. (number)

`enable` (optional) — 1 to enable the filter, otherwise `nil`. (1nil)

`exclusive` (optional) — 1 to enable the filter exclusively, otherwise `nil`. (1nil)

SetTradeSkillItemLevelFilter

Filters the Tradeskill window's list by required level of produced items. Limits the list of available recipes returned by other tradeskill functions based on the required level (not item level) of items produced.

```
SetTradeSkillItemLevelFilter(minLevel, maxLevel)
```

Arguments:

`minLevel` — Lowest required level of items to show in filtered Tradeskill list. (number)

`maxLevel` — Highest required level of items to show in filtered Tradeskill list. (number)

SetTradeSkillItemNameFilter

Sets the tradeskill item name filter search string.

```
SetTradeSkillItemNameFilter("text")
```

Argument:

text — The search string. (string)

SetTradeSkillSubClassFilter

Enables or disables a given tradeskill subclass filter.

```
isVisible = SetTradeSkillSubClassFilter(index [, enable, exclusive])
```

Arguments:

index — The index of a return from GetTradeSkillSubClasses(). (number)

enable — 1 to enabled, nil to disable. (1nil)

exclusive — 1 to disable all other filters when enabling this one, otherwise nil. (1nil)

Returns:

isVisible — Whether items corresponding to the filter are visible 1 or not nil. (1nil)

SetTrainerServiceTypeFilter

Sets the state of a filter in the trainer window.

```
SetTrainerServiceTypeFilter("type", status [, exclusive])
```

Arguments:

type — The filter type to query. (string)

- available — Shows skills that you are able to learn

- unavailable — Shows skills that you are unable to learn

- used — Shows skills that you have already learned

status (optional) — The new status of the given filter. (number)

- 0 — Disables the filter

- 1 — Enables the filter

exclusive (optional) — Turns off all other filters, if the filter is being enabled. (number)

- 1 — Turns off all other filters, if filter is being enabled.

Example:

```
-- Turn on the "available" filter
SetTrainerServiceTypeFilter("available", 1)

-- Turn on the "used" filter, and turn off all others
SetTrainerServiceTypeFilter("used", 1, 1)
```

SetTrainerSkillLineFilter

Sets the state of a skill line filter in the trainer UI.

```
SetTrainerSkillLineFilter(index [, status, exclusive])
```

Arguments:

index — The index of a skill line filter. These are any of the major headings at a trainer, such as "Frost," "Fire," and "Arcane," or "Development Skills" and "Recipes." (number)

status (optional) — The new status of the given filter. (number)

- 0 — Disables the filter
- 1 — Enables the filter

exclusive (optional) — Turns off all other filters, if the filter is being enabled. (number)

- 1 — Turns off all other filters, if filter is being enabled

Note: These filters are not displayed in-game, but correspond to the collapsable headings that are shown in the UI.

SetUIVisibility

Changes whether UI rendered models are shown. This function is used to toggle user interface elements that exist in the 3D world, such as health bars and player/npc/guild names (but not the selection circle that appears on the ground below a targeted unit).

```
SetUIVisibility(visible)
```

Argument:

visible — Any true value other than 0 to enable UI visibility. False or nil will disable. (number or boolean)

SetView

Sets the camera view to one of the pre-set views.

```
SetView(index)
```

Argument:

index — Sets the camera view to one of the pre-set views. These views can have been previously saved with the SaveView() function; otherwise the game's default views are used. (number)

SetWatchedFactionIndex

Sets the faction to watch reputation progress for.

```
SetWatchedFactionIndex(index)
```

Argument:

index — The index of the faction to watch. (number)

SetWaterDetail

Sets the value for the water details display.

```
SetWaterDetail(value)
```

Argument:

value — The new value for the water detail level. (number)

SetWhoToUI

Sets a flag that determines how the results of a SendWho() request are delivered.

```
SetWhoToUI(state)
```

Arguments:

state — Determines how results of a SendWho() request should be handled. (number)

- ▪ 0 — Any result sets less than four entries should be sent via CHAT_MSG_ SYSTEM events. In this case, the FriendsFrame will not open. However, if the result set is four entries or larger, then the results will be sent via the WHO_LIST_UPDATE event.

- ▪ 1 — Any result set will be displayed in the FriendsFrame and sent via the WHO_LIST_UPDATE event.

SetWorldDetail

Sets the detail level of the world environment.

```
SetWorldDetail(value)
```

Argument:

value — The detail level to set: 0, 1, or 2. (number)

SetupFullscreenScale

Sizes a frame to take up the entire screen. Sizes the frames differently depending on resolution.

```
SetupFullscreenScale(frame)
```

Argument:

frame — Frame to resize to full screen. (table)

ShowBattlefieldList

Displays the instance list window for a battleground the player is currently queued to enter. This function can be used to select a difference instance of the battleground without needing to re-visit the battlemaster or battleground entrance.

```
ShowBattlefieldList(index)
```

Argument:

index — **The index of the battlefield currently queued for** (number)

ShowBuybackSellCursor

Shows the buyback/sell cursor. This function requires the index of an item slot in the merchant UI and validates to ensure that there is an item for sale or buyback before displaying the cursor. This function is best used in `OnEnter` handlers.

`ShowBuybackSellCursor(index)`

Argument:

`index` — A slot index from the Merchant or Buyback window. `(number)`

ShowCloak

This function enables or disables the showing of a cloak, if equipped, on the player's character. Using this function will only affect the player's appearance, without any effect on stats provided by the item. This setting controls not only whether the cloak is visible to you, but also whether it appears to other players; it does not control the appearance of cloak on characters other than yours.

`ShowCloak(enable)`

Argument:

`enable` — 1 to enable helm display, otherwise `nil`. `(1nil)`

ShowContainerSellCursor

Displays the "sell item" cursor for a given container item.

`ShowContainerSellCursor(index, slot)`

Arguments:

`index` — The index of a container. `(number)`

`slot` — The slot within the given container. `(number)`

ShowFriendNameplates

Enables the display of health nameplates in the game world, for any non-enemy units.

ShowFriends

Requests updated friends information from the server. See also:
`FRIENDLIST_UPDATE`.

ShowHelm

This function enables or disables the showing of headgear, if equipped, on the player's character. Using this function will only affect the player's appearance, without any effect on stats provided by the item. This setting controls not only whether the headgear is visible to you, but also whether it appears to other players; it does not control the appearance of headgear on characters other than yours.

`ShowHelm(show)`

Argument:

`show` — 1 to enable helm display, otherwise `nil`. `(1nil)`

ShowInventorySellCursor

Changes the cursor to the "inventory sell" cursor.

ShowMerchantSellCursor

Shows the merchant "sell item" cursor.

```
ShowMerchantSellCursor(index)
```

ShowMiniWorldMapArrowFrame

Shows or hides the battlefield minimap's player arrow.

```
ShowMiniWorldMapArrowFrame(show)
```

Argument:

show — If the battlefield minimap's player arrow should be shown. (boolean)

Note: This function is an internal/debug function.

ShowNameplates

Turns on showing of nameplates for hostile units.

ShowRepairCursor

Changes the cursor to show the repair cursor. As with the other cursor functions, this only changes the cursor for a frame, unless it is called from an OnEnter handler.

ShowingCloak

Returns whether the "Show Cloak" setting is currently enabled.

```
isShown = ShowingCloak()
```

Returns:

isShown — 1 if the cloak is currently set to be shown, otherwise nil. (1nil)

ShowingHelm

Returns whether the "Show Helm" setting is currently enabled.

```
isShowing = ShowingHelm()
```

Returns:

isShowing — 1 if the helm is currently set to be shown, otherwise nil. (1nil)

SignPetition

Signs the currently offered petition.

SitStandOrDescendStart

This function is called when the player sits, stands, or descends while swimming/flying.

Note: This function is protected and cannot be called via addons

SocketContainerItem

Opens the Gem Socketing UI if the given container slot has a socketable item.

```
SocketContainerItem(index, slot)
```

Arguments:

`index` — Container ID. `(number)`

- ■ `-1` — Standard Bank
- ■ `-2` — Keyring
- ■ `0` — Backpack
- ■ `1` — Bag 1
- ■ `10` — Bank Bag 6
- ■ `11` — Bank Bag 7
- ■ `2` — Bag 2
- ■ `3` — Bag 3
- ■ `4` — Bag 4
- ■ `5` — Bank Bag 1
- ■ `6` — Bank Bag 2
- ■ `7` — Bank Bag 3
- ■ `8` — Bank Bag 4
- ■ `9` — Bank Bag 5

`slot` — Slot within container. `(number)`

SocketInventoryItem

Opens the socketing UI for the given inventory item, if it has sockets.

```
SocketInventoryItem(slot)
```

Argument:

`slot` — An inventory slot ID. `(number)`

SortArenaTeamRoster

Sorts the selected arena team's roster by the given sort type.

```
SortArenaTeamRoster(sortType)
```

Arguments:

`sortType` — The column to sort the roster by. `(string)`

- class — Sorts the roster by class
- name — Sorts the roster by name
- played — Sorts the roster by number of played games
- rating — Sorts the roster by personal rating
- won — Sorts the roster by number of won games

Note: Sorting by the same column more than once toggles ascending/ descending order.

SortAuctionApplySort

Applies the currently configured sort for the given auction type.

```
SortAuctionApplySort("type")
```

Arguments:

type — The auction listing type. (string)

- bidder — Auctions the player has bid on
- list — Auctions available for buying/bidding
- owner — Auctions the player has placed

SortAuctionClearSort

Clears any current sorting rules for the given auction house listing.

```
SortAuctionClearSort("type")
```

Arguments:

type — The auction house listing to clear. (string)

- bidder — Auctions the player has bid on
- list — Auctions avalable for bidding or purchase
- owner — Auctions the player has placed

SortAuctionItems

Sorts the auction house listing.

```
SortAuctionItems("type", "sort")
```

Arguments:

type — The type of auction listing to sort. (string)

- bidder — Auctions the player has bid on
- list — Standard auction house listing
- owner — Auctions the player has placed

sort — The column to use to sort the listing. (string)

- bid — The current bid amount
- duration — The time left in the auction
- level — The minimum required level to use the item, if any
- quality — The item quality/rarity
- status — The status of the auction. This column depends on the listing type. When browsing the auction house, this is the name of the seller or the item. When viewing the list of auctions the player has bid on, this is the bid status. On the listing of auctions the player has placed, this is the name of the current high bidder.

SortAuctionSetSort

Sets the server-side sort to be applied to the items returned by an auction house query.

```
SortAuctionSetSort(type, sort, reversed)
```

Arguments:

type — The auction house listing to edit. (string)

- bidder — Auctions the player has bid on
- list — Auctions avalable for bidding or purchase
- owner — Auctions the player has placed

sort — The sort type you want to apply (string)

- bid — Current bid
- buyout — Current buyout
- buyoutthenbid — Sort first by buyout, then by bid
- duration — Auction time left
- level — Item use level
- name — Item name
- quality — Item quality
- quantity — Item quantity (stack size)
- seller — Auction poster
- status — Whether a bid has been placed on the auction

reversed — True if you want the sort to be an inverse one (Z → A), false if you want it to be normal (A → Z). (boolean)

SortBattlefieldScoreData

Sorts the battlefield data based on a specific sortType. Information about the battlefield-specific custom stats can be retrieved using the `GetBattlefieldStatInfo()` function while in the battlefield. Examples include the "Graveyards Assulted/Defended" and "Towers Assaulted/Defended" data in Alterac Valley.

`SortBattlefieldScoreData(sortType)`

Arguments:

`sortType` — The sort type for the battlefield score data. `(string)`

- `class` — Sorts by class type
- `cp` — Sorts by honor points gained
- `damage` — Sorts by damage done
- `deaths` — Sorts by number of deaths
- `healing` — Sorts by healing done
- `hk` — Sorts by number of honor kills
- `kills` — Sorts by number of kills
- `name` — Sorts by player name
- `stat1` — Battlefield-specific custom stat 1
- `stat2` — Battlefield-specific custom stat 2
- `stat3` — Battlefield-specific custom stat 3
- `stat4` — Battlefield-specific custom stat 4
- `stat5` — Battlefield-specific custom stat 5
- `stat6` — Battlefield-specific custom stat 6
- `stat7` — Battlefield-specific custom stat 7
- `team` — Sorts by team name

SortGuildRoster

Sorts the guild roster.

`SortGuildRoster("type")`

Arguments:

`type` — The type of criteria to sort by. `(string)`

- `class` — Sorts by class name
- `level` — Sorts by character level
- `name` — Sorts by name
- `note` — Sorts by guild note
- `online` — Sorts by last online time
- `rank` — Sorts by guild rank
- `zone` — Sorts by current zone name

SortLFG

Sets the sort type for a Looking For Group query.

`SortLFG(sortType)`

Arguments:

`sortType` — The sort method to be used. `(string)`

- `class` — Sorts results by player class
- `level` — Sorts results by player level
- `name` — Sorts results by player name
- `zone` — Sorts results by current zone

SortWho

Sets the sort method for the "Who" list.

`SortWho(sortType)`

Arguments:

`sortType` — A sort type used to sort the list. `(string)`

- `class` — Sorts by class name
- `guild` — Sorts by guild name
- `level` — Sorts by player level
- `name` — Sorts by player name
- `race` — Sorts by race name
- `zone` — Sorts by current zone name

Sound_GetInputDriverNameByIndex

Returns the name of a given input driver.

`name = Sound_GetInputDriverNameByIndex(index)`

Argument:

`index` — The index of the sound driver. `(number)`

Returns:

`name` — The name of the input driver. `(string)`

Sound_GetNumInputDrivers

Returns the number of sound input drivers in the system.

`num = Sound_GetNumInputDrivers()`

Returns:

`num` — The number of input drivers available on the computer. The sounds inputs are indexed beginning at zero, thus in order to use this function, you will need to loop from `0` to `num-1`. `(number)`

Example:

```
-- Print the sound input drivers to chat
for i=0,Sound_GetNumInputDrivers()-1 do
  ChatFrame1:AddMessage(Sound_GetInputDriverNameByIndex(i))
end
```

Sound_GetNumOutputDrivers

Returns the number of sound output drivers.

```
num = Sound_GetNumOutputDrivers()
```

Returns:

num — The number of sound output drivers. (number)

Sound_GetOutputDriverNameByIndex

Returns the name of an output driver. Returns the name of an output driver. The indices for sound output drivers do not begin at 1 like most API functions; instead they begin at 0.

```
deviceName = Sound_GetOutputDriverNameByIndex(index)
```

Argument:

index — The index of the sound output drive to query. (number)

Returns:

deviceName — The name of the output device. (string)

Example:

```
local numDrivers = Sound_GetNumOutputDrivers()
for i=0,numDrivers-1 do
  ChatFrame1:AddMessage(Sound_GetOutputDriverNameByIndex(i))
end
```

Sound_RestartSoundEngine

Restarts the sound engine.

SpellCanTargetItem

Returns whether the spell on the cursor can target an item or not. Will return nil when no spell is on the cursor.

```
canTarget = SpellCanTargetItem()
```

Returns:

canTarget — 1 if the spell on the cursor can target an item, nil if not. (1nil)

SpellCanTargetUnit

Returns whether the spell currently awaiting a target can target a given unit.

```
canTarget = SpellCanTargetUnit("unit")
```

Argument:

unit — The unit to query. (unitid)

Returns:

canTarget — 1 if the spell currently awaiting targeting can target the given unit. (1nil)

SpellHasRange

Returns whether a given spell has a range restriction.

```
hasRange = SpellHasRange("spellName" or spellId [, "bookType"])
```

Arguments:

spellName or spellId

- spellName — The name of a spell. (string)

- spellId — The spell ID of a spell. (number)

bookType (optional) — The type of spellbook the supplied spell ID is for. (string)

- pet — The pet's spellbook

- spell — The player's spellbook

Returns:

hasRange — 1 if the specified spell has a range restriction, otherwise nil. (1nil)

SpellIsTargeting

Returns whether there is a spell currently awaiting a target.

```
isTargeting = SpellIsTargeting()
```

Returns:

isTargeting — 1 if there is a spell currently awaiting a target, otherwise nil. (1nil)

SpellStopCasting

Stops casting or targeting the current spell.

Note: This function is protected and cannot be called via addons.

SpellStopTargeting

Cancels the spell currently waiting for targeting. The cursor changes to a glowing hand for selecting a spell target in various situations: if auto-self-cast is not enabled and the player has no target and casts a spell that requires one; if auto-self-cast is enabled or the player has targeted herself and casts a spell requiring a different target; or if the player casts a spell that targets an item. This function will cancel the targeting mode so that the user can cast another spell.

SpellTargetItem

Targets a unit with the spell currently awaiting an item target.

```
SpellTargetItem(itemID or "name" or "itemlink")
```

Note: This function is protected and cannot be called via addons.

SpellTargetUnit

Targets a unit with the spell currently awaiting a target.

```
SpellTargetUnit("unit" or "name")
```

Arguments:

unit — The unit ID to target with the spell. (unitid)

name — The full name of the unit to target with the spell. (string)

Note: This function is protected and cannot be called via addons.

SplitContainerItem

Splits an item in a given container, placing the new stack on the cursor.

```
SplitContainerItem(index, slot, amount)
```

Arguments:

index — The index of a container that holds the item to be split. (number)

slot — The slot that contains the item to be split. (number)

amount — The number of items to split from the main stack. (number)

Example:

```
-- Split five stacks from the item in the first backpack slot
SplitContainerItem(0, 1, 5)
```

SplitGuildBankItem

Splits an item in a given tab and slot, placing the new stack on the cursor.

```
SplitGuildBankItem(tab, slot, amount)
```

Arguments:

tab — The index of the tab that holds the item to be split. (number)

slot — The slot that contains the item to be split. (number)

amount — The number of items to split from the main stack. (number)

StablePet

Attempts to put your current pet in the stable.

StartAttack

This function is used by Blizzard code to start an attack on a specific unit.

```
StartAttack("unit" or "name")
```

Arguments:

unit or name

- ■ unit — The unit ID of the player to challenge. (unitId)
- ■ name — The name of the player to challenge. (string)

Note: This function is protected and cannot be called via addons.

StartAuction

Starts a new auction. This function requires an item to be placed using the ClickAuctionSellItem() function. In addition, the player must have enough money to cover the deposit, and the runTime must be a valid time.

```
StartAuction(minBid, buyoutPrice, runTime)
```

Arguments:

minBid — The minimum bid, in copper. (number)

buyoutPrice — The buyout price, in copper. (number)

runTime — The run time of the auction, in minutes. (number)

- ■ 720 — 12 hours
- ■ 1440 — 24 hours
- ■ 2880 — 48 hours

StartDuel

Challenges another player to a duel.

```
StartDuel("unit" or "name", exact)
```

Arguments:

unit or name

- ■ unit — The unit ID of the player to challenge. (unitId)
- ■ name — The name of the player to challenge. (string)

Example:

```
-- Challenge Cladhaire to a duel, with an exact name match
StartDuel("Cladhaire", 1)

-- Challenge unit "target" to a duel
StartDuel("target")
```

StopAttack

Stops auto-attack if active.

StopCinematic

Stops a cinematic that is currently playing.

StopMacro

Stops execution of a running macro.

Note: This function is protected and cannot be called via addons.

StopMusic

Immediately stops the currently played in-game music.

StopTradeSkillRepeat

Cancels a repeating tradeskill.

StrafeLeftStart

Begins strafing to the left.

Note: This function is protected and cannot be called via addons.

StrafeLeftStop

Stops the character from strafing left.

Note: This function is protected and cannot be called via addons.

StrafeRightStart

Begins strafing to the right.

Note: This function is protected and cannot be called via addons.

StrafeRightStop

Stops the player from strafing right.

Note: This function is protected and cannot be called via addons.

strjoin

Joins a list of strings together.

```
text = strjoin(sep, ...)
```

Arguments:

`sep` — The string to join between each two elements. `(string)`

`...` — A list of strings to be joined together. `(string)`

Returns:

`text` — The list of strings joined together with the given separator string. `(string)`

Example:

```
strjoin(",", "alice", "bob", "carol")
-- Returns "alice,bob,carol"

strjoin(" mississippi, ", "one", "two", "three")
-- Returns "one mississippi, two mississippi, three
```

strsplit

Splits a string based on another separator string.

```
... = strsplit(sep, text, limit)
```

Arguments:

sep — The separator string to use. (string)

text — The text to split. (string)

limit — The maximum number of pieces to split the string into. (number)

Returns:

... — A list of strings, split from the text based on the separator string. (string)

Example:

```
-- Split the string "a:b:c:d"
strsplit(":", "a:b:c:d", 2)
-- Returns "a", "b:c:d"

-- Split the string "a::b::c::d"
strsplit("::", "a::b::c::d")
-- Returns "a", "b", "c", "d"
```

strtrim

Trims leading and trailing white space from a string.

```
text = strtrim(str)
```

Argument:

str — The string to trim. (string)

Returns:

text — The string wth any training or leading white space removed. (string)

Example:

```
strtrim("  This is a test   ")
-- Returns "This is a test"
```

Stuck

This function is used by the default user interface to call the "Unstuck" GM functionality.

Note: This function is protected and cannot be called via addons.

SwapRaidSubgroup

Swaps two players between groups in the raid.

```
SwapRaidSubgroup("index1", "index2")
```

Arguments:

index1 — The raid ID of the first unit. (unitid)

index2 — The raid ID of the second unit. (unitid)

TakeInboxItem

Takes an attachment from an inbox item without confirmation.

```
TakeInboxItem(messageIndex, attachIndex)
```

Arguments:

`messageIndex` — The index of the message. (number)

`attachIndex` — The index of the attachment. (number)

TakeInboxMoney

Takes the money from the specified mail in the inbox.

```
TakeInboxMoney(index)
```

Argument:

`index` — The index of the mail in the inbox. (number)

TakeInboxTextItem

Sends a request to the server to retrieve the given message's text item. The text of an in-game mail can be retrieved as a readable "Plain Letter" item to store in the player's bags. This function sends a request to the server to retrieve this item. This causes the standard inventory events to fire as the item is placed into the player's inventory.

```
TakeInboxTextItem(index)
```

Argument:

`index` — The message index of the text item to retrieve. (number)

TakeTaxiNode

Takes the indicated flight path. This function is used when clicking a flight path from a flight master.

```
TakeTaxiNode(slot)
```

Argument:

`slot` — Taxi slot to take (1 to `NumTaxiNodes()`). (number)

TargetLastEnemy

Re-targets the last targeted enemy unit.

```
TargetLastEnemy(action)
```

Note: This function is protected and cannot be called via addons.

TargetLastFriend

Targets the player's last friendly target.

```
TargetLastFriend(action)
```

Note: This function is protected and cannot be called via addons.

TargetLastTarget

Targets the last targeted unit.

Note: This function is protected and cannot be called via addons.

TargetNearestEnemy

Targets the nearest enemy target.

Note: This function is protected and cannot be called via addons.

TargetNearestFriend

Targets the nearest friendly unit.

```
TargetNearestFriend(cycle)
```

Note: This function is protected and cannot be called via addons.

TargetNearestPartyMember

Targets the nearest party member.

```
TargetNearestPartyMember(cycle)
```

Note: This function is protected and cannot be called via addons.

TargetNearestRaidMember

Targets the nearest raid member.

```
TargetNearestRaidMember(cycle)
```

Note: This function is protected and cannot be called via addons.

TargetUnit

Sets the given unit as your target. Passing nil will remove your target. Can only be called from the Blizzard UI.

```
TargetUnit("unit" or "name")
```

Arguments:

unit or name

- unit — The unit ID to target. (unitid)
- name — The name of the player to target. (string)

Note: This function is protected and cannot be called via addons.

TaxiGetDestX

Returns the X coordinate of the destination flight path node. This function is used to draw the lines between nodes.

```
dX = TaxiGetDestX(source, dest)
```

Arguments:

source — The source taxi node. (number)

dest — The destination taxi node. (number)

Returns:

dx — The X coordinate of the destination taxi node relative to the width of the taxi frame. (number)

TaxiGetDestY

Returns the Y coordinate of the destination flight path node. This function is used to draw the lines between nodes.

dY = TaxiGetDestY(source, dest)

Arguments:

source — The source taxi node. (number)

dest — The destination taxi node. (number)

Returns:

dy — The Y coordinate of the destination taxi node relative to the height of the taxi frame. (number)

TaxiGetSrcX

Returns the X coordinate of the source flight path node. This function is used to draw the lines between nodes.

sX = TaxiGetSrcX(source, dest)

Arguments:

source — The source taxi node. (number)

dest — The destination taxi node. (number)

Returns:

sx — The X coordinate of the source taxi node relative to the width of the taxi frame. (number)

TaxiGetSrcY

Returns the Y coordinate of the source flight path node. This function is used to draw the lines between nodes.

sY = TaxiGetSrcY(source, dest)

Arguments:

source — The source taxi node. (number)

dest — The destination taxi node. (number)

Returns:

sY — The Y coordinate of the source taxi node relative to the height of the taxi frame. (number)

TaxiNodeCost

Returns the cost to fly to a given flight point.

```
cost = TaxiNodeCost(slot)
```

Argument:

`slot` — The index of a taxi node. `(number)`

Returns:

`cost` — The cost of flying to the given taxi node, in copper. `(number)`

TaxiNodeGetType

Returns the type of the flight point requested.

```
type = TaxiNodeGetType(slot)
```

Arguments:

`slot` — Taxi node slot on the current Taxi Map. Between `1` and `NumTaxiNodes()`. `(number)`

Returns:

`type` — Type of the taxi node. `(string)`

- ▪ `CURRENT` — Your current location
- ▪ `DISTANT` — Unreachable from your current taxi node
- ▪ `NONE` — Taxi node not currently in use on the map
- ▪ `REACHABLE` — Reachable directly from this node, or through other nodes

TaxiNodeName

Returns the name of a given flight point (for example, "Hellfire Peninsula," "The Dark Portal," "Horde," "Shattrath City," "Terokkar Forest").

```
name = TaxiNodeName(slot)
```

Argument:

`slot` — The index of a taxi node slot. `(number)`

Returns:

`name` — The name of the taxi node. `(string)`

TaxiNodePosition

Returns the position of a flight point in the Taxi window.

```
x, y = TaxiNodePosition(index)
```

Argument:

`index` — The index of the taxi node. `(number)`

Returns:

`x` — The x coordinate of the taxi node in the Taxi window, as a percentage of the width of the frame. `(number)`

`y` — The y coordinate of the taxi node in the Taxi window, as a percentage of the height of the frame. `(number)`

TaxiNodeSetCurrent

Sets the "current" flight path node to a specific index. This function is used to show increasing flight path costs along a route.

```
TaxiNodeSetCurrent(slot)
```

Argument:

slot — The internal index of a flight path node. (number)

ToggleAutoRun

Causes the player to start or stop automatically running. The player will continue running until this function is called again.

Note: This function is protected and cannot be called via addons.

ToggleMouseMove

This function switches between mouse movement mode and normal cursor mode. It does not have any real utility for addons; it's simply a Lua reference to the code that starts your mouse moving when you hold down your left or right mouse button in the 3D world. In order for it to function properly, you must be holding down your mouse button in the world frame anyway. Calling this function while in windowed mode without holding down the mouse button will prevent you from placing your mouse inside the window. Your cursor will disappear until it's toggled back off.

TogglePVP

Enables PvP status for the player if it is currently turned off; if PvP status has been manually enabled, will cause it to be disabled after a 5-minute delay in which no PvP action is taken.

TogglePetAutocast

Enables a pet to automatically cast one of its spells when appropriate if such behavior is currently disabled or vice versa.

```
TogglePetAutocast(index)
```

Arguments:

index — Index of a slot on the pet action bar. (number)

Note: This function is protected and cannot be called via addons.

ToggleRun

Toggles between running and walking.

Note: This function is protected and cannot be called via addons.

ToggleSheath

Sheaths or unsheaths the player's hand-held items.

ToggleSpellAutocast

Turns on automatic casting of a spell from the spellbook if it is turned off, or vice versa. Currently, only pet spells can be autocast.

```
ToggleSpellAutocast(spellId, "bookType")
```

Arguments:

spellId — The index of a spell in the spellbook. (number)

bookType — The type of spellbook. (string)

■ pet — The pet's spellbook

■ spell — The player's spellbook

TradeSkillOnlyShowMakeable

Enables or disables the filter that causes the Tradeskill UI to show only recipes for which the player currently holds materials.

```
TradeSkillOnlyShowMakeable(filter)
```

Argument:

filter — 1 to enable the Have Materials filter, nil to show all recipes. (boolean)

TurnInArenaPetition

Turns in an arena petition.

```
TurnInArenaPetition(teamSize, bgColor.r, bgColor.g, bgColor.b,
iconStyle, iconColor.r, iconColor.g, iconColor.b, borderStyle,
borderColor.r, borderColor.g, borderColor.b)
```

Arguments:

teamSize — The size of the arena team. (number)

■ 2 — 2v2

■ 3 — 3v3

■ 5 — 5v5

bgColor.r — The red component of the background color (0.0–1.0). (number)

bgColor.g — The green component of the background color (0.0–1.0). (number)

bgColor.b — The blue component of the background color (0.0–1.0). (number)

iconStyle — The number of the chosen icon. (number)

iconColor.r — The red component of the icon color (0.0–1.0). (number)

iconColor.g — The green component of the icon color (0.0–1.0). (number)

iconColor.b — The blue component of the icon color (0.0–1.0). (number)

borderStyle — The number of the chosen border style. (number)

borderStyle.r — The red component of the border color (0.0–1.0). (number)

borderStyle.g — The green component of the border color (0.0–1.0). (number)

borderStyle.b — The blue component of the border color (0.0–1.0). (number)

TurnInGuildCharter

Turns in a completed guild charter.

TurnLeftStart

This function is called when the player begins turning left via the "Turn Left" key binding.

Note: This function is protected and cannot be called via addons.

TurnLeftStop

This function is called when the player stops turning left via releasing the "Turn Left" key binding.

Note: This function is protected and cannot be called via addons.

TurnOrActionStart

This function is called when the player right-clicks in the 3D world.

Note: This function is protected and cannot be called via addons.

TurnOrActionStop

This function is called when the player releases a right-click in the 3D world.

Note: This function is protected and cannot be called via addons.

TurnRightStart

This function is called when the player begins turning right via the "Turn Right" key binding.

Note: This function is protected and cannot be called via addons.

TurnRightStop

This function is called when the player stops turning right via releasing the "Turn Right" key binding.

Note: This function is protected and cannot be called via addons.

TutorialsEnabled

Returns whether introductory tutorials will automatically appear in appropriate contexts.

```
enabled = TutorialsEnabled()
```

Returns:

enabled — 1 if tutorials are enabled, otherwise nil. (1nil)

UninviteUnit

Removes the specified unit from the current group.

```
UninviteUnit("unit")
```

Argument:

unit — The name of the unit to un-invite. (string)

Note: Only works if you are the raid/party leader or assistant.

UnitAffectingCombat

Returns whether a unit is currently in combat.

```
inCombat = UnitAffectingCombat("unit")
```

Argument:

unit — The name of the unit to query. (string)

Returns:

inCombat — 1 if the unit is currently involved in combat, otherwise nil. (1nil)

UnitArmor

This function returns the current amount of armor and its breakdown between base armor and positive and negative effects due to buffs and debuffs. Note that this function will normally only return valid numbers for "player" or "pet" (or the player's or pet's name), but can in some circumstances return at least partially valid information for other units (such as a creature on whom a Hunter has cast the Beast Lore spell).

```
base, effectiveArmor, armor, posBuff, negBuff = UnitArmor(unitId or
"unitName")
```

Arguments:

unitId or unitName

- ▪ unitId — The unit ID to query, such as player, target, or raid10. (string)
- ▪ unitName — The exact name of the unit to query. (string)

Returns:

base — The base armor for that unit, not counting buffs but counting armor from equipped items. (number)

effectiveArmor — The effective armor for that unit, counting buffs, debuffs, and base armor from equipped items. (number)

armor — The effective armor for that unit, counting buffs, debuffs and base armor from equipped items. It seems to always mirror the effectiveArmor return from this same function. (number)

posBuff — Any positive armor gained from buffs. (number)

negBuff — Any negative armor lost from debuffs. (number)

UnitAttackBothHands

Returns information about a unit's weapon skill.

```
mainHandAttackBase, mainHandAttackMod, offHandAttackBase,
offHandAttackMod = UnitAttackBothHands("unit")
```

Arguments:

unitId or unitName

- ▪ unitId — The unit ID to query, such as player, target, or raid10. (string)
- ▪ unitName — The exact name of the unit to query. (string)

Returns:

`mainHandAttackBase` — The base weapon skill for the type of weapon equipped in the main hand. `(number)`

`mainHandAttackMod` — Any modifiers to the weapon skill for the type of weapon equipped in the main hand. `(number)`

`offHandHandAttackBase` — The base weapon skill for the type of weapon equipped in the offhand. `(number)`

`offHandAttackMod` — Any modifiers to the weapon skill for the type of weapon equipped in the offhand. `(number)`

Note: This function will only return valid information for "player" or "pet" (or the player's or pet's name).

UnitAttackPower

Returns the unit's melee attack power and modifiers.

```
base, posBuff, negBuff = UnitAttackPower("unit")
```

Arguments:

`unitId` or `unitName`

- `unitId` — The unit ID to query, such as `player`, `target`, or `raid10`. `(string)`
- `unitName` — The exact name of the unit to query. `(string)`

Returns:

`base` — The unit's base attack power. `(number)`

`posBuff` — The total effect of positive buffs to attack power. `(number)`

`negBuff` — The total effect of negative buffs to attack power. `(number)`

Note: This function will only return valid information for "player" or "pet" (or the player's or pet's name).

UnitAttackSpeed

Returns the mainhand and offhand attack speed of the given unit. This measure if affected by haste.

```
speed, offhandSpeed = UnitAttackSpeed("unit")
```

Arguments:

`unitId` or `unitName`

- `unitId` — The unit ID to query, such as `player`, `target`, or `raid10`. `(string)`
- `unitName` — The exact name of the unit to query. `(string)`

Returns:

`speed` — The speed of the mainhand attack. `(number)`

`oddhandSpeed` — The speed of the offhand attack. `(number)`

Note: This function will only return valid information for "player" or "pet" (or the player's or pet's name).

UnitBuff

Returns information about a buff on a given unit or player. Duration and time remaining is only available for buffs cast by the player.

```
name, rank, icon, count, duration, timeLeft  = UnitBuff("unit", index
[,filter])
```

Arguments:

unit or name

- ■ unit — The unit to query. (unitid)

- ■ name — The name of the player to query. (string)

index — Which buff to get information about. (number)

filter — 1 to filter only buffs that can be cast by the player, otherwise nil. (1nil)

Returns:

name — The name of the buff. (string)

rank — The rank of the buff. (string)

icon — The path to the buff's icon texture. (string)

count — The number of stacks of the buff. (number)

duration — The full duration of the buff, in seconds. (number)

timeLeft — The amount of time left on the buff, in seconds. (number)

UnitCanAssist

Returns whether one unit can assist another.

```
canAssist = UnitCanAssist("unit", "otherUnit")
```

Arguments:

unit — The first unit ID to query. (unitid)

otherUnit — The second unit ID to query. (unitid)

Returns:

canAssist — 1 if the first unit can assist the second, otherwise nil. (1nil)

UnitCanAttack

Returns whether one unit can attack another unit.

```
canAttack = UnitCanAttack("unit", "otherUnit")
```

Arguments:

unit — The unit that would be attacking. (unitid)

otherUnit — The unit that would be attacked. (unitid)

Returns:

canAttack — 1 if the first unit can attack the second unit, otherwise nil. (1nil)

UnitCanCooperate

Returns whether the two given units can cooperate with each other. Two units are considered to be able to cooperate with each other if they are of the same faction and are both players.

```
canCooperate = UnitCanCooperate("unit" or "fullName", "otherUnit" or
"fullName")
```

Arguments:

unit or fullName

- unit — The unit ID of the first unit to query. (unitid)

- fullName — The full name of the first unit to query (for people in your own group only). (string)

unit or fullName

- unit — The unit ID of the second unit to query. (unitid)

- fullName — The full name of the second unit to query (for people in your own group only). (string)

Returns:

canCooperate — 1 if the two units can cooperate with each other, otherwise nil. (1nil)

UnitCastingInfo

Returns information about the spell a unit is casting.

```
name, nameSubtext, text, texture, startTime, endTime, isTradeSkill  =
UnitCastingInfo("unit")
```

Arguments:

unit — The unit to query. (unitId)

Returns:

name — The name of the spell being cast. (string)

nameSubtext — The rank of the spell being cast, or other secondary text. (string)

text — The text to be displayed. (string)

texture — The path to the spell icon texture. (string)

startTime — The time the cast was started, in millisecond precision. (number)

endTime — The time the cast will be finished, in millisecond precision. (number)

isTradeSkill — 1 if the spell being cast is a tradeskill, otherwise nil. (1nil)

UnitChannelInfo

Returns information about the spell a unit is channeling.

```
name, nameSubtext, text, texture, startTime, endTime, isTradeSkill =
UnitChannelInfo("unit")
```

Argument:

unit — The unit to query. (unitId)

Returns:

name — The name of the spell being cast. (string)

nameSubtext — The rank of the spell being cast, or other secondary text. (string)

text — The text to be displayed. (string)

texture — The path to the spell icon texture. (string)

startTime — The time the cast was started, in millisecond precision. (number)

endTime — The time the cast will be finished, in millisecond precision. (number)

isTradeSkill — 1 if the spell being cast is a tradeskill, otherwise nil. (1nil)

UnitCharacterPoints

Returns the number of unused talent points and profession slots for the given unit.

```
talentPoints, professionSlots = UnitCharacterPoints("unit")
```

Arguments:

unit — The unit of interest. (unitId)

Returns:

talentPoints — The number of unspent talent points for the unit. (number)

professionSlots — The number of available main profession slots for the unit. (number)

Note: Will only work for the "player" unit; returns 0,0 for everyone else.

UnitClass

Queries a unit's class. Returns the class of the given unit in the current locale, as well as a non-localized token representing the class. The second return can be used to match class names across different localizations of the client (for example, English or German), or to access certain global tables (such as RAID_CLASS_COLORS).

For example, on the deDE (German) client, UnitClass() on a warlock character would return Hexenmeister and WARLOCK.

```
class, fileName = UnitClass("unit")
```

Argument:

unit — The unit to query. (unitId)

Returns:

class — The localized name of the queried unit's class. (string)

fileName — A non-localized token representing the unit's class. (string)

Example:

```
-- Print the name of your target, in their class color
local class, fileName = UnitClass("target")
local color = RAID_CLASS_COLORS[fileName]
ChatFrame1:AddMessage(class, color.r, color.g, color.b)
```

UnitClassification

Returns a classification indicator for the queried unit.

```
classification = UnitClassification("unit")
```

Argument:

unit — Unit to query. (unitID)

Returns:

classification — Classification of the queried unit. (string)

- elite — Elite
- normal — Normal
- rare — Rare
- rareelite — Rare-Elite
- worldboss — World Boss

UnitCreatureFamily

Identifies the subtype for certain types of units. Applicable to beasts of the kinds that can be taken as Hunter pets (for example, cats, bears, and ravagers, but not zhevras, talbuks, and chimaerae) and demons of the types that can be summoned by Warlocks (for example, imps and felguards, but not demons that require enslaving such as infernals and doomguards or world demons such as pit lords and armored voidwalkers); returns nil for all other units.

```
family = UnitCreatureFamily("unit")
```

Argument:

unit — The unit to query. (unitid)

Returns:

family — The creature family of the unit, or nil for inapplicable units. (string)

UnitCreatureType

Identifies the type of a given unit (for example, Humanoid, Beast, Demon, Dragonkin, or Undead). Note that some units have no type (for example, slimes, bugs, most creatures in Ahn'Qiraj).

```
type = UnitCreatureType("unit")
```

Arguments:

unit — The unit to query. (unitid)

Returns:

type — The creature type of the unit, or nil for some units. (string)

UnitDamage

Returns information about a unit's melee damage.

```
minDamage, maxDamage, minOffHandDamage, maxOffHandDamage,
physicalBonusPos, physicalBonusNeg, percent  = UnitDamage("unit")
```

Arguments:

unit — UnitID to get information for. (string)

Returns:

minDamage — The unit's minimum melee damage. (number)

maxDamage — The unit's maximum melee damage. (number)

minOffHandDamage — The unit's minimum offhand melee damage. (number)

maxOffHandDamage — The unit's maximum offhand melee damage. (number)

physicalBonusPos — Positive physical bonus (should be >= 0). (number)

physicalBonusNeg — Negative physical bonus (should be <= 0). (number)

percent — Percentage modifier. Usually 1; 0.9 for warriors in defensive stance. (number)

Note: This function will only return valid information for "player" or "pet" (or the player's or pet's name).

UnitDebuff

Returns information about a debuff on a given unit. If the player was the one who caused the debuff, this function will also return the full duration of the debuff, as well as the time left; this is used by the default user interface to show cooldown timers on debuffs.

```
name, rank, icon, debuffStack, debuffType, duration, timeLeft =
UnitDebuff("unit", index [,dispelOnly])
```

Arguments:

unit — The unit to query. (unitId)

index — The buff index to query for the given unit. (number)

dispelOnly (optional) — Only shows those debuffs that can be dispelled by the player. (1nil)

- ▪ 1 — Shows only debuffs the player can dispel
- ▪ nil — Shows all debuffs

Returns:

name — The name of the debuff in the current locale. (string)

rank — The rank of the debuff, or the empty string. (number)

icon — The path to the debuff's icon texture. (string)

debuffStack — The amount of times the given debuff has stacked, or how many charges are left. (number)

debuffType — The type of the debuff if specified, or nil. (string)

- ▪ 1 — Magic
- ▪ 2 — Poison
- ▪ 3 — Disease
- ▪ 4 — Curse

duration — The full duration of the debuff, in seconds. (number)

timeLeft — The amount of time left on the debuff, in seconds. (number)

Example:

```
-- Query the first debuff on "player"
local name, rank, icon, count, debuffType, duration, timeLeft = ↵
UnitDebuff("player", 1)
if name then
  ChatFrame1:AddMessage("Found a debuff: " .. name)
end


-- Query the first debuff on "target" that can be dispelled by the
player
local name, rank, icon, count, debuffType, duration, timeLeft = ↵
UnitDebuff("player", 1, 1)
if name then
  ChatFrame1:AddMessage(debuffType .. " found: " .. name)
end
```

UnitDefense

Returns the unit's defense statistics.

```
base, modifier = UnitDefense("unit")
```

Argument:

unit — The unit ID to query. (unitid)

Returns:

base — Base defense. (number)

modifier — Defense modifier from gear and buffs. (number)

UnitExists

Returns whether a given unit exists.

```
exists = UnitExists("unit")
```

Arguments:

unit or name

- ▪ unit — The unit to query. (unitid)
- ▪ name — The full name of a unit to query. (string)

Returns:

exists — 1 if the unit exists, otherwise nil. (1nil)

UnitFactionGroup

Gives information about the unit's allegiance in English and the game's current locale. Note that this function concerns Alliance versus Horde alignment only, not the individual races or neutral groups one can earn reputation with. Returns nil when not available.

```
factionEnglish, factionLocale = UnitFactionGroup("unit" or "name")
```

Arguments:

unit or fullname

- ▪ unit — The unit to query. (unitId)
- ▪ fullname — The full name of the unit to query. (string)

Returns:

factionEnglish — English faction name (Horde/Alliance) of the unit. (string)

factionLocale — Localized name of the faction. (string)

UnitHasRelicSlot

Returns whether the unit's ranged slot should be displayed as a Relic slot. Only valid for "player" and a unit being inspected.

```
hasRelic = UnitHasRelicSlot("unit" or "name")
```

Arguments:

unit or name

- unit — The unit ID to query. (unitid)
- name — The name of the player to query. (string)

Returns:

hasRelic — 1 if the unit has a relic slot, nil if not. (1nil)

UnitHealth

Returns the current health value for a given unit. Actual health points are only returned for the player and associated units (party or raid members and their pets); for NPCs and players not in the player's group, this function returns a number between 0 and 100, indicating a percentage of actual health.

```
health = UnitHealthMax("unit" or "name")
```

Arguments:

unit or name

- unit — The unit to query. (unitId)
- name — The name of the player to query. (string)

Returns:

health — The current health of the unit, a number between 0 and the value returned by UnitHealthMax for the same unit. (number)

UnitHealthMax

Returns the maximum health value for a given unit. Actual health points are only returned for the player and associated units (party or raid members and their pets); for NPCs and players not in the player's group, this function always returns 100 (indicating that the return of UnitHealth is a percentage of actual health).

```
maxValue  = UnitHealthMax("unit" or "name")
```

Arguments:

unit or name

- unit — The unit to query. (unitId)
- name — The name of the player to query. (string)

Returns:

maxValue — The maximum health value for the given unit. (number)

UnitInBattleground

Returns whether a unit is in the player's battleground.

```
raidNum = UnitInBattleground("unit")
```

Argument:

unit — The unit ID to query. (unitid)

Returns:

raidNum — The raid index of the unit in your battleground, or nil. (number)

UnitInParty

Returns whether a given unit is in the player's party. This function always returns 1 for the player unit. If the player has a pet, it is not considered part of the party.

```
inParty = UnitInParty("unit")
```

Argument:

unit — The unit to query for party membership. (unitId)

Returns:

inParty — 1 if the unit is in the player's party, otherwise nil. (1nil)

UnitInRaid

Returns whether the unit specified is in your raid group.

```
inRaid  = UnitInRaid("unit")
```

Argument:

unit — The unit ID of the unit to query. (unitid)

Returns:

inRaid — Will return 1 if the unit is in your raid group, otherwise nil. (number)

UnitIsAFK

Query a unit's AFK status.

```
isAFK = UnitIsAFK("unit" or "name")
```

Arguments:

unit or fullname

- unit — The unit to query. (unitId)
- fullname — The full name of the unit to query. (string)

Returns:

isAFK — 1 if the given unit is AFK, otherwise nil. (1nil)

UnitIsCharmed

Returns whether a unit or player is currently charmed. A charm is typically in the form of Mind Cotrol, causing normally friendly units to become hostile.

```
isCharmed = UnitIsCharmed("unit" or "name")
```

Arguments:

unit or fullname

- ▪ unit — The unit to query. (unitId)
- ▪ fullname — The full name of the unit to query. (string)

Returns:

isCharmed — 1 if the given unit is charmed, otherwise nil. (1nil)

UnitIsConnected

Returns whether the given unit or player is connected to the game server (that is, not Offline).

```
isConnected = UnitIsConnected("unit" or "name")
```

Arguments:

unit or name

- ▪ unit — The unit ID to query. (unitid)
- ▪ name — The name of a player to query. (string)

Returns:

isConnected — 1 if the player is connected, otherwise nil. (1nil)

UnitIsCorpse

Returns whether the given unit is a corpse.

```
isCorpse = UnitIsCorpse("unit")
```

Arguments:

unit — The unit to query. (unitid)

Returns:

isCorpse — 1 if the unit is a corpse, otherwise nil. (1nil)

UnitIsDND

Returns whether a unit is flagged "Do Not Disturb."

```
isDND = UnitIsDND("unit")
```

Argument:

unit — The unit to query. (unitid)

Returns:

isDND — 1 if the unit is flagged "Do Not Disturb," otherwise nil. (1nil)

UnitIsDead

Returns whether the given unit is dead. This function will only return 1 while the unit is dead and has not yet released her spirit to the graveyard. When the unit becomes a ghost, she is no longer dead and the UnitIsGhost() function must be used.

```
isDead = UnitIsDead("unit")
```

Argument:

unit — A unit ID to query. (unitId)

Returns:

isDead — 1 if the unit is dead, otherwise nil. (1nil)

Example:

```
-- Scan your party or raid and count how many people are dead
local maxNum = GetNumRaidMembers()
local unitType = "raid"
if maxNum <= 0 then
  maxNum = GetNumPartyMembers()
  unitType = "party"
end

if maxNum > 0 then
  local deadCount = 0
  for i=1,maxNum do
    if UnitIsDead(unitType .. i) then
      deadCount = deadCount + 1
    end
  end

  ChatFrame1:AddMessage("There are " .. deadCount .. " people dead in ↵
your " .. unitType)
else
  ChatFrame1:AddMessage("You are not in a party or raid")
end
```

UnitIsDeadOrGhost

Returns whether the given player is either dead or a ghost.

```
isDeadOrGhost = UnitIsDeadOrGhost("unit" or "fullname")
```

Arguments:

unit or fullname

- unit — The unit to query. (unitid)

- fullname — The full name of the player to query. (string)

Returns:

isDeadOrGhost — 1 if the player is dead or a ghost, otherwise nil. (1nil)

UnitIsEnemy

Returns true or false depending on whether the specified units are enemies or not.

```
isEnemy = UnitIsEnemy("unit", "otherUnit")
```

Arguments:

unit — Unit ID of the first target. (string)

otherUnit — Unit ID of the second target. (string)

Returns:

isEnemy — true if the specified units are enemies, otherwise false. (boolean)

UnitIsFeignDeath

Returns whether a given unit is feigning death. This function only works for units in the player's party or raid.

```
isFeign = UnitIsFeignDeath("unit")
```

Argument:

unit — The unit to query. (unitid)

Returns:

isFeign — 1 if the unit is feigning death, otherwise nil. (1nil)

UnitIsFriend

Returns whether two units are friendly.

```
isFriend = UnitIsFriend("unit", "otherUnit")
```

Arguments:

unit — The first unit to query. (unitid)

otherUnit — The second unit to query. (unitid)

Returns:

isFriends — 1 if the two units are friends, otherwise nil. (1nil)

UnitIsGhost

Returns whether a unit or player is currently a ghost.

```
isGhost = UnitIsGhost("unit" or "name")
```

Arguments:

unit or fullname

- ▪ unit — The unit to query. (unitId)
- ▪ fullname — The full name of the unit to query. (string)

Returns:

isGhost — 1 if the given unit is a ghost, otherwise nil. (1nil)

UnitIsInMyGuild

Returns whether a given unit or player is in the player's guild.

`inGuild = UnitIsInMyGuild("unit" or "name")`

Arguments:

unit or name

- ■ unit — The unit ID to query. (unitId)
- ■ name — The name of the player to query. (string)

Returns:

inGuild — 1 if the unit is in the player's guild, otherwise nil. (1nil)

UnitIsPVP

Returns whether a unit is "flagged" for player-versus-player combat. Units with PvP status enabled can be attacked by players of the opposing faction; attacking a PvP-flagged unit will cause the attacker to also become PvP-flagged.

`isPVP = UnitIsPVP("unit" or "name")`

Arguments:

unit or name

- ■ unit — The unit ID to query. (unitId)
- ■ name — The name of the player to query. (string)

Returns:

isPVP — 1 if the unit is PvP enabled, otherwise nil. (1nil)

UnitIsPVPFreeForAll

Returns whether the unit is flagged for free-for-all PvP (that is, can attack or be attacked by any player who is also so flagged), such as in a World Arena.

`isFreeForAll = UnitIsPVPFreeForAll("unit")`

Argument:

unit — The unit ID of the unit to query. (unitid)

Returns:

isFreeForAll — Whether the unit is flagged for free-for-all PvP. (boolean)

UnitIsPVPSanctuary

Returns 1 if the unit in question is in a "sanctuary" area in which no player-versus-player combat is possible, otherwise nil.

`state = UnitIsPVPSanctuary("unit")`

Argument:

unit — The name of the unit to query. (string)

Returns:

state — 1 if the unit is in a PvP Sanctuary, otherwise nil. (1nil)

UnitIsPartyLeader

Returns 1 if the specified unit is the leader of the player's party.

```
leader = UnitIsPartyLeader("unit" or "name")
```

Arguments:

unit or name

- ▪ unit — The unit to query. (unitId)
- ▪ name — The full name of the unit to query. (string)

Returns:

leader — 1 if the unit is the party leader, otherwise nil. (1nil)

UnitIsPlayer

Returns whether a given unit is the player's unit.

```
isPlayer = UnitIsPlayer("unit")
```

Argument:

unit — The unit to query. (unitid)

Returns:

isPlayer — 1 if the unit is the player, otherwise nil. (1nil)

UnitIsPlusMob

Returns whether the given unit is an elite mob.

```
isPlus = UnitIsPlusMob("unit")
```

Argument:

unit — The unit to query. (unitid)

Returns:

isPlus — 1 if the unit is an elite mob, otherwise nil. (1nil)

UnitIsPossessed

Returns whether the given unit is possessed (through Mind Control or a similar ability). Unlike UnitIsCharmed, only returns whether the unit is possessed by another player.

```
isPossessed = UnitIsPossessed("unit" or "fullName")
```

Arguments:

unit or fullName

- ▪ unit — The unit to query. (unitid)
- ▪ fullName — The name of the unit to query. (string)

Returns:

isPossessed — 1 if the given unit is possessed, otherwise nil. (1nil)

UnitIsRaidOfficer

Returns whether the given unit is a raid assistant in the raid.

isOfficer = UnitIsRaidOfficer("unit" or "fullName")

Arguments:

unit or fullName

- ▪ unit — The unit to query. (unitid)
- ▪ fullName — The full name of the unit to query. (string)

Returns:

isOfficer — 1 if the given unit is an officer in the raid, otherwise nil. (1nil)

UnitIsSameServer

Returns whether two units are from the same server (only meaningful in cross-server battlegrounds).

isSame = UnitIsSameServer("unit" or "unitName", "otherUnit" or "otherUnitName")

Arguments:

unit or unitName

- ▪ unit — The first unit to query. (unitid)
- ▪ unitName — The name of the first unit to query. (string)

otherUnit or otherUnitName

- ▪ otherUnit — The second unit to query. (unitid)
- ▪ otherUnitName — The name of the second unit to query. (string)

Returns:

isSame — 1 if the two units are from the same server, otherwise nil. (1nil)

Note: Results are not accurate if UnitExists() does not resolve for both units.

UnitIsSilenced

Returns whether the player is silenced on the specified voice channel.

silenced = UnitIsSilenced(name", "channel")

Arguments:

name — The name of the player to query. (string)

channel — Channel to query for voice status. (string)

Returns:

silenced — 1 if the unit is silenced on this channel, nil if not. (1nil)

Note: This function does not take a unit ID, only unit names.

UnitIsTalking

Returns 1 if the unit is currently talking, otherwise `nil`.

```
state = UnitIsTalking("name")
```

Argument:

`name` — The name of the unit in question. (`string`)

Returns:

`state` — 1 if the unit is currently talking, otherwise nil. (`1nil`)

Note: Despite the "unit" in its name, this function seems only to work with player names as the argument.

UnitIsTapped

Returns whether a unit is "tapped" by anyone, not necessarily the player or his group. (Experience and loot rewards for killing a unit are available only to the player or group who first damaged the unit; once a player has thus established his claim on the unit, it is considered "tapped.")

```
isTapped = UnitIsTapped("unit")
```

Arguments:

`unit` — The unit ID to query. (`unitId`)

UnitIsTappedByPlayer

Returns whether a unit is tapped by the player or his group. (Experience and loot rewards for killing a unit are available only to the player or group who first damaged the unit; once a player has thus established his claim on the unit, it is considered "tapped.")

```
isTapped = UnitIsTappedByPlayer("unit")
```

Argument:

`unit` — The unit to be queried. (`string`)

Returns:

`isTapped` — 1 if the unit is tapped by the player, otherwise `nil`. (`1nil`)

UnitIsTrivial

Returns whether the given unit is trivial (that is, so far below the player's level that killing it will not reward experience). This is used by the default user interface to color UI elements relating to such units as gray.

```
isTrivial = UnitIsTrivial("unit")
```

Argument:

`unit` — The unit ID to query. (`unitid`)

Returns:

`isTrivial` — 1 if the unit is considered trivial, otherwise `nil`. (`1nil`)

UnitIsUnit

Returns whether two unit IDs refer to the same actual character. This can be useful when dealing with composite unit IDs such as `raid12targettarget`, to determine if that unit is the same as another meaningful unit ID, such as `target` or `player`.

```
isSame  = UnitIsUnit("unit", "otherUnit")
```

Arguments:

`unit` — The first unit ID to compare. (`unitId`)

`otherUnit` — The second unit ID to compare. (`unitId`)

Returns:

`isSame` — Returns `1` if the units refer to the same character, otherwise `nil`. (`1nil`)

Example:

```
-- See if raid12targettarget is the same as the target unit
local isSame = UnitIsUnit("raid12targettarget", "target")
```

UnitIsVisible

Returns whether the given unit is visible (in the player's area of interest).

```
isVisible = UnitIsVisible("unit")
```

Argument:

`unit` — The unit ID to query. (`unitid`)

Returns:

`isVisible` — `1` if the unit is visible, otherwise `nil`. (`1nil`)

UnitLevel

Returns the level of a given unit.

```
level = UnitLevel("unit")
```

Arguments:

`unit` — The unit ID to query. (`unitid`)

Returns:

`level` — The level of the unit. If the level is unknown (owing to it being too high), this will return -1. (`number`)

UnitMana

Returns the current mana, rage, energy, or focus points of the given unit. (See `UnitPowerType` to find out how this value should be presented in the UI.) If the unit does not exist, returns nil.

```
mana = UnitMana("unit")
```

Argument:

`unit` — The unit of interest. (`unitId`)

Returns:

`mana` — The unit's current mana points. (`unitId`)

Example:

```
-- Print your targets remaining mana percentage
local percent = 100 * UnitMana("target")/UnitManaMax("target")
DEFAULT_CHAT_FRAME:AddMessage(format("Target has %f%% mana", percent))
```

UnitManaMax

Returns the maximum mana, rage, energy, or focus that a given unit can have. (See `UnitPowerType` to find out how this value should be presented in the UI.)

```
maxValue = UnitManaMax("unit" or "name")
```

Arguments:

unit or name

- unit — The unit to query. (unitid)

- name — The name of the player, the player's pet, or a member of the player's party or raid. (string)

Returns:

maxValue — The maximum amount of mana (or other power) the unit can have. (number)

UnitName

Returns the name of a given unit.

```
name, serverName = UnitName("unit")
```

Argument:

unit — The unit ID to query. (unitid)

Returns:

name — The name of the unit. (string)

servername — The name of the unit's server. This is used in cross-realm battle-grounds to display names. (string)

UnitOnTaxi

Returns whether a given unit is on a flight path. Only valid for "player" and other units in your area of interest.

```
onTaxi = UnitOnTaxi("unit")
```

Argument:

unit — The unit to query. (string)

Returns:

onTaxi — 1 if the unit is on a taxi, otherwise nil. (1nil)

UnitPVPName

Returns the name of the unit with the unit's title prepended to it. (Once titles could only be earned through PvP combat; this function still applies to the newer titles that can be earned through other means.)

```
name = UnitPVPName("unit")
```

Argument:

unit — The unit ID to query. (unitid)

Returns:

name — The name of the unit with the unit's title prepended to it. (string)

UnitPVPRank

The PvP rank system is no longer used; this function always returns 0, even for players who've kept the title of their highest achieved rank from the old system.

```
rank = UnitPVPRank("unit")
```

Argument:

unit — The unit to query. (unitid)

Returns:

rank — The numeric PvP rank of the unit, or 0 for no rank. (number)

UnitPlayerControlled

Returns whether the given unit is a player-controlled character (which includes pets, Mind Control targets, and the like, in addition to player characters).

```
isPlayer = UnitPlayerControlled("unit")
```

Argument:

unit — The unit to query. (unitid)

Returns:

isPlayer — 1 if the unit is a player-controlled character, otherwise nil. (1nil)

UnitPlayerOrPetInParty

This function will tell you if the unit in question is a player in your party or a pet belonging to a player in your party. Note that this function will always return nil when queried with player, pet, the player's or player's pet names since these units are not considered part of the party.

```
inParty = UnitPlayerOrPetInParty("unitId" or "unitName")
```

Arguments:

unitId or unitName

- unitId — The unit ID of the unit you're trying to query, like party1, raid10pet, or PlayerName-target. (string)
- unitName — The full name of the unit you're trying to query. Capitalization is not important. (string)

Returns:

inParty — 1 if the unit, player, or pet is in the party, otherwise nil. (1nil)

UnitPlayerOrPetInRaid

This function will tell you if the unit in question is a player in your raid or a pet belonging to a player in your raid.

```
inRaid = UnitPlayerOrPetInRaid("unit")
```

Argument:

unit — The unit to query. (unitid)

UnitPowerType

Returns the power type (energy, mana, rage, or focus) of the given unit.

```
powerType = UnitPowerType("unit")
```

Argument:

unit — The unit to query. (unitid)

Returns:

powerType — A number indicating what power type the unit has. (number)

- 1 — Mana
- 2 — Rage
- 3 — Focus
- 4 — Energy

UnitRace

Retrieves the unit's race. Returns the race of the given unit in the current locale, as well as a non-localized token representing the race (which often matches the English name, but is not guaranteed to be the same; for example, BloodElf for Blood Elf or Scourge for Undead). The second return can be used to match race names between different localizations of the client (for example, English or German), or for looking up race-specific resources such as textures or sounds (for example, the default interface uses it to determine which background image to show in the Dressing Room UI).

For example, on the deDE (German) client, UnitRace() on a night elf character would return Nachtelf and NightElf.

```
race, fileName = UnitRace(unit or name)
```

Arguments:

unit or name

- unit — The unit ID to query. (unitid)
- name — The name of the player to query. (string)

Returns:

race — The localized name of the queried unit's race. (string)

fileName — The non-localized name of the queried unit's race, as used in the various artwork files. (string)

UnitRangedAttack

Returns a unit's ranged weapon skill.

rangedAttackBase, rangedAttackMod = UnitRangedAttack("unit")

Argument:

unit — The unit to query. (unitid)

Returns:

rangedAttackBase — The base-ranged weapon skill. (number)

rangedAttackMod — Any modifiers to the base-ranged weapon skill. (number)

Note: This function will only return valid information for "player" (or the player's name).

UnitRangedAttackPower

Returns a unit's ranged attack power and bonuses.

base, posBuff, negBuff = UnitRangedAttackPower("unit")

Argument:

unit — The unit to query. Only "player" and "pet" or their equivalents are valid (unitid)

Returns:

base — Base-ranged attack power. (number)

posBuff — Positive buffs to ranged attack power. (number)

negBuff — Negative buffs to ranged attack power. (number)

Note: This function will only return valid information for "player" (or the player's name).

UnitRangedDamage

Returns information about a unit's range attack damage and speed. Returns detailed information on the attack speed, minimum damage, maximum damage, bonuses, and modifiers for a unit's ranged attacks.

rangedAttackSpeed, minDamage, maxDamage, physicalBonusPos, physicalBonusNeg, percent = UnitRangedDamage("unit")

Argument:

unit — The unit to query. (unitid)

Returns:

rangedAttackSpeed — The speed of the unit's ranged attack, or 0 if no ranged weapon is equipped. (number)

minDamage — The minimum base damage per attack. (number)

maxDamage — The maximum base damage per attack. (number)

physicalBonusPos — The amount of bonus physical damage; includes Spell Damage bonuses. (number)

physicalBonusNeg — The amount of negative modifiers to physical damage. (number)

percent — A percentage modifier, represented as decimal 0 to 1. (number)

Note: This function will only return valid information for "player" (or the player's name).

UnitReaction

Returns the reaction of one unit with regard to another as a number. This value can be used with the UnitReactionColor global table to return the color that indicates a given reaction.

```
reaction = UnitReaction("unit", "otherUnit")
```

Arguments:

unit — The source unit ID. (unitid)

otherUnit — The destination unit ID. (unitid)

Returns:

reaction — The reaction of the source unit with regard to the destination unit. This reaction corresponds directly to faction level. (number)

- 1 — Hated
- 2 — Hostile
- 3 — Unfriendly
- 4 — Neutral
- 5 — Friendly
- 6 — Honored
- 7 — Revered
- 8 — Exalted

UnitResistance

Returns resistance information for a specific resistance for a unit ID. Returns 0,0,0,0 for non-existing or disallowed units. The index 1 indicates physical resistance, but this value is currently not used in-game.

```
base, resistance, positive, negative  = UnitResistance("unit",
resistanceIndex)
```

Arguments:

`unit` — The unit ID to query. `(string)`

`resistanceIndex` — Resistance to get data on. `(number)`

- ■ `1` — Physical
- ■ `2` — Fire
- ■ `3` — Nature
- ■ `4` — Frost
- ■ `5` — Shadow
- ■ `6` — Arcane

Returns:

`base` — Base resistance value, for players their racial modifier. `(number)`

`resistance` — Current resistance with all modifiers applied. `(number)`

`positive` — Positive resistance modifiers. `(number)`

`negative` — Negative resistance modifiers. `(number)`

Note: This function will only return valid information for "player" or "pet" (or the player's or pet's name).

UnitSex

Returns the gender of the given unit or player.

```
gender  = UnitSex("unit" or "name")
```

Arguments:

`unit` — The unit ID to query. `(unitId)`

`name` — The name of a player to query. `(string)`

Returns:

`gender` — The gender of the unit or player. `(number)`

- ■ `1` — Unspecified
- ■ `2` — Male
- ■ `3` — Female

UnitStat

Returns information about a given character statistic (intellect, stamina, and so on).

```
stat, effectiveStat, posBuff, negBuff  = UnitStat("unit", statIndex)
```

Arguments:

unit — The unit ID to query. (unitid)

statIndex — The index of the stat to query. (number)

- 1 — Strength
- 2 — Agility
- 3 — Stamina
- 4 — Intellect
- 5 — Spirit

Returns:

stat — The current value of the stat. (number)

effectiveStat — The effective value of the stat (unused). (number)

posBuff — The value of any positive buffs for the given stat. (number)

negBuff — The value of any negative buffs for the given stat. (number)

Note: This function will only return valid information for "player" or "pet" (or the player's or pet's name).

UnitXP

Returns the amount of experience points that the unit currently has.

```
currXP = UnitXP("unit" or "name")
```

Arguments:

unit — The unit ID to query. (unitid)

name — The full name of the character to query. (string)

Returns:

currXP — The amount of experience the unit currently has. (number)

Note: The only unit ID that returns a value other than 0 is "player." To query the pet's experience points, use GetPetExperience() instead of this function.

UnitXPMax

Returns the total amount of XP required to get to the next level.

```
playerMaxXP = UnitXPMax( unit )
```

Argument:

unit — The name of the unit to query. (string)

Returns:

`playerMaxXP` — The total amount of XP required to the next level. `(number)`

Note: Only works on "player," or on "target" if the player targets herself.

UnstablePet

Removes the pet from a given stable slot, making it the active pet. If you have an active pet, this will put it into the stable.

`UnstablePet(slot)`

Argument:

`slot` — The pet stable slot. `(number)`

UpdateAddOnCPUUsage

Scans through the profiling data and updates the per-addon statistics.

Note: CPU profiling must be enabled by setting the CVar `scriptProfile` to 1 in order for related functions to return meaningful results.

UpdateAddOnMemoryUsage

Updates the addon memory usage information.

UpdateGMTicket

Updates the current GM Ticket with the appropriate text.

`UpdateGMTicket("type", "text")`

Arguments:

`type` — Specific GM Ticket Type from the available list. `(string)`

`text` — Updated GM Ticket text. `(string)`

Note: This function is protected and cannot be called via addons.

UpdateMapHighlight

Returns information about the texture used to highlight individual zones on the world map as they are moused over.

```
name, fileName, texCoordX, texCoordY, textureX, textureY,
scrollChildX, scrollChildY = UpdateMapHighlight(x, y)
```

Arguments:

`x` — The X position of the cursor, as a proportion of the WorldMapDetailFrame's width. `(number)`

`y` — The Y position of the cursor, as a proportion of the WorldMapDetailFrame's height. `(number)`

Returns:

name — The name of the zone being highlighted. (string)

fileName — The filename to use for the highlight texture. (string)

texCoordX — The right texCoord value for the highlight texture. (number)

texCoordY — The bottom texCoord value for the highlight texture. (number)

textureX — The width of the texture as a proportion of the WorldMapDetailFrame's width. (number)

textureY — The height of the texture as a proportion of the WorldMapDetailFrame's height. (number)

scrollChildX — The X coordinate for the TOPLEFT anchor point of the texture, as a proportion of the WorldMapDetailFrame's width. (number)

scrollChildY — The X coordinate for the TOPLEFT anchor point of the texture, as a proportion of the WorldMapDetailFrame's width. (number)

UpdateSpells

Queries the server for current information on the contents of the spellbook. The SPELLS_CHANGED event fires when the information becomes available to the client.

UseAction

Uses the given action button slot, optionally on a given target, with a specific type of button click.

```
UseAction(slot, [, target] [, button])
```

Note: This function is protected and cannot be called via addons.

UseContainerItem

Performs the effect of right-clicking an item in one's bags. For items with a "Use" effect (food, mounts, and so on), this function is forbidden against use by third-party addons, as using such items amounts to casting a spell; addons can use macros or secure templates to provide access to such items.

Third-party addons are still allowed to call this function in other conditions. If the item identified by index and slot can be equipped, calling this function attempts to do so. If the Bank, Guild Bank, Send Mail window, or Trade window is open, calling this function attempts to place the item into said window. If none of said windows are open and the item is not usable, calling this function is allowed, but it does nothing.

```
UseContainerItem(index, slot[, target])
```

Arguments:

index — The container that contains the item. (number)

slot — The slot that contains the item. (number)

target (optional) — The target that the item should be used on. (string)

Note: This function is protected and must be called in response to a hardware event.

Example:

```
-- Use the first item in your backpack on your pet
UseContainerItem(0, 1, "pet")
```

UseInventoryItem

Uses an item from the player's inventory.

```
UseInventoryItem(slot)
```

Argument:

slot — An inventory slot ID. (number)

Note: This function is protected and cannot be called via addons.

UseItemByName

Uses an item, optionally on a specified target.

```
UseItemByName("name", "target")
```

Arguments:

name — The name of the item to use. (string)

target — The unit to use as the target of the item, if applicable. (unitId)

Note: This function is protected and cannot be called via addons.

UseSoulstone

This function causes you to use a Warlock's Soulstone or a Shaman's Reincarnation spell when you die. This function can only be used when the Soulstone has been placed on you prior to dying, not to place the Soulstone after dying.

VoiceChat_GetCurrentMicrophoneSignalLevel

Returns the current volume level of the microphone signal.

```
volume = VoiceChat_GetCurrentMicrophoneSignalLevel()
```

Returns:

volume — The current volume level of the microphone signal. (number)

VoiceChat_IsPlayingLoopbackSound

Returns whether the loopback sound is currently being played.

```
isPlaying = VoiceChat_IsPlayingLoopbackSound()
```

Argument:

isPlaying — 1 if the loopback sound is currently being played, otherwise nil. (number)

VoiceChat_IsRecordingLoopbackSound

Returns whether the player is recording a voice sample. The voice chat options window includes a feature to record a sample sound to verify that your equipment is working properly. While a sound sample is being recorded, this function will return 1. Otherwise it returns 0.

```
isRecording  = VoiceChat_IsRecordingLoopbackSound()
```

Returns:

isRecording — 1 if the player is recording a voice sample, otherwise 0. (number)

Example:

```
-- Print a message indicating your recording status
local insertString = ""
if VoiceChat_IsRecordingLoopbackSound() == 0 then
  insertString = "not "
end
DEFAULT_CHAT_FRAME:AddMessage("You are "..insertString.."currently
recording a ↵
sound sample.")
```

VoiceChat_PlayLoopbackSound

Plays a previously recorded loopback sound. This function is used by the default user interface to allow the player to test the voice recording subsystem. A recording of a specified length is recorded using VoiceChat_RecordLoopbackSound(). This recording can be played back using this function. See also: VoiceChat_RecordLoopbackSound().

VoiceChat_RecordLoopbackSound

Records a short voice recording for testing purposes. This is used in the voice chat system to test the microphone input. The recorded sound can later be played back with VoiceChat_PlayLoopbackSound().

VoiceChat_RecordLoopbackSound(seconds)

Argument:

seconds — The amount of time to record (in seconds). (number)

VoiceChat_StopPlayingLoopbackSound

Stops the current playback of the loopback sound.

VoiceChat_StopRecordingLoopbackSound

Stops the recording of the loopback sounds.

VoiceEnumerateCaptureDevices

Returns the name of a voice capture device.

deviceName = VoiceEnumerateCaptureDevices(deviceIndex)

Argument:

deviceIndex — The index of the capture device. (number)

Returns:

deviceName — The name of the voice capture device. (string)

VoiceEnumerateOutputDevices

Returns the name of a given voice output device.

```
device = VoiceEnumerateOutputDevices(index)
```

Argument:

`index` — The index of an output device. `(number)`

Returns:

`device` — The name of the output device. `(string)`

VoiceGetCurrentCaptureDevice

Returns the index of the current voice capture device.

```
index = VoiceGetCurrentCaptureDevice()
```

Returns:

`index` — The index of the current voice capture device. `(number)`

VoiceGetCurrentOutputDevice

Returns the index of the current voice output device.

Returns:

`index` — The index of the current voice output device. `(number)`

VoiceIsDisabledByClient

Returns whether the voice chat system is disabled for hardware reasons.

```
isDisabled = VoiceIsDisabledByClient()
```

Returns:

`isDisabled` — 1 if the voice system is disabled, otherwise nil. `(1nil)`

VoiceSelectCaptureDevice

Selects a voice capture device.

```
VoiceSelectCaptureDevice(deviceName)
```

Argument:

`deviceName` — The name of a voice capture device. This can be obtained using `VoiceEnumerateCaptureDevices()`. `(string)`

VoiceSelectOutputDevice

Sets the voice chat output device. This name is dependent on your systems and drivers, and should be obtained from `VoiceEnumerateOutputDevice(index)`.

```
VoiceSelectOutputDevice("deviceName")
```

Arguments:

`deviceName` — The name of the device, as returned from `VoiceEnumerateOutputDevices(index)`. `(string)`

WithdrawGuildBankMoney

Attempts to withdraw an amount of money from the guild bank. Does nothing on failure.

```
WithdrawGuildBankMoney(money)
```

Argument:

money — Money to withdraw, in copper. (number)

# CHAPTER 29

API Categories

Finding the right function to accomplish a specific task in World of Warcraft can be difficult, because there are over a thousand API functions that could be used. This chapter provides a categorized listing of these functions to make it easier to determine which is the correct function. Some functions appear in more than one category, when necessary.

Action

`ActionHasRange` — Returns whether an action has a range restriction.

`CastPetAction` — Casts a pet action on a specific target.

`GetActionAutocast` — Returns information about autocast actions.

`GetActionCooldown` — Returns cooldown information about a given action slot.

`GetActionCount` — Returns the number of uses remaining for the given action slot.

`GetActionInfo` — Returns information about a given action bar slot.

`GetActionText` — Returns the label for a given action slot.

`GetActionTexture` — Returns the texture for the given action slot.

`GetPetActionCooldown` — Returns cooldown information about a given pet action slot.

`GetPetActionInfo` — Returns information about a pet action.

`GetPetActionsUsable` — Returns whether the pet's actions are usable.

`HasAction` — Returns a flag if an action slot is occupied.

`IsActionInRange` — Returns whether the action is in range of the current target.

`IsAttackAction` — Returns whether the given action flashes when engaged in melee auto-attacking.

IsAutoRepeatAction — Checks if an action is an auto-repeat action (for example, Auto Shot).

IsConsumableAction — Returns 1 if the action ID contains a consumable, otherwise nil.

IsCurrentAction — Returns whether a specific action is currently being cast or awaiting targeting.

IsEquippedAction — Returns whether an action slot contains an equipped item.

IsStackableAction — Returns whether a given action slot contains a stackable action.

IsUsableAction — Returns whether the action is usable.

PickupAction — Picks up an action bar slot and holds it on the cursor.

PickupPetAction — Picks up the pet action in the given slot and places it under the cursor.

PlaceAction — Places the action held on the cursor in a specified action bar slot.

SetActionBarToggles — Configures the display of the additional ActionBars.

TogglePetAutocast — Toggles autocast for a pet action.

UseAction — Optionally, uses the given action button slot on a given target, with a specific type of button click.

Actionbar

ChangeActionBarPage — Changes the current action bar page.

GetActionBarPage — Returns the current action bar page.

GetActionBarToggles — Returns the current visibility settings for the four secondary action bars.

GetBonusBarOffset — Returns the bar offset for the bonus bar.

IsPossessBarVisible — Returns whether the PossessBar should be visible.

Addon

DisableAddOn — Disables an addon by name or index.

DisableAllAddOns — Flags all addons as disabled for the current character.

EnableAddOn — Enables an addon for the current character.

EnableAllAddOns — Enables all addons for the current character (takes effect at the next UI load).

GetAddOnDependencies — Gets all dependencies of the queried addon. Returns nil if no dependencies are listed.

GetAddOnInfo — Returns information about an addon in the client's addon list.

GetAddOnMetadata — Returns the value of certain fields in an addon's TOC file.

GetNumAddOns — Returns the number of addons in the addon listing.

IsAddOnLoadOnDemand — Returns whether a given addon can be loaded on demand.

IsAddOnLoaded — Queries if an addon is loaded (running).

LoadAddOn — Loads an addon manually if it is Load on Demand. Will also load the dependencies of an addon.

`ResetDisabledAddOns` — Resets the enabled status of addons before the change is committed via a reload.

`SendAddonMessage` — Sends a chat-like message to players that will not show up in their chat windows by default.

Arena

`AcceptArenaTeam` — Accepts an invitation to join an arena team.

`ArenaTeamDisband` — Disbands an arena team.

`ArenaTeamInviteByName` — Invites a player to join one of the player's arena teams.

`ArenaTeamLeave` — Leaves an arena team.

`ArenaTeamRoster` — Queries the server for roster information about an arena team.

`ArenaTeamSetLeaderByName` — Promotes an arena team member to team leader.

`ArenaTeamUninviteByName` — Uninvites a player from an arena team.

`CloseArenaTeamRoster` — Closes the Arena Team Roster frame.

`DeclineArenaTeam` — Declines an arena team invitation.

`GetArenaCurrency` — Returns the number of available arena currency points.

`GetArenaTeam` — Returns information about one of the player's arena teams.

`GetArenaTeamRosterInfo` — Returns information about an arena team member.

`GetArenaTeamRosterSelection` — Returns the currently selected arena team member for a given team.

`GetArenaTeamRosterShowOffline` — Returns whether the "Show Offline Members" filter for arena teams is enabled.

`GetCurrentArenaSeason` — Returns the current arena season.

`GetNumArenaTeamMembers` — Returns the number of members in a given arena team.

`IsActiveBattlefieldArena` — Returns whether the current battlefield is an arena match.

`IsArenaTeamCaptain` — Returns whether the player is the team captain for a given arena team.

`IsBattlefieldArena` — Returns whether the NPC the player is interacting with can queue for arenas.

`SetArenaTeamRosterSelection` — Selects a specific member from an arena team roster.

`SetArenaTeamRosterShowOffline` — Enables or disables the showing of offline arena team members.

`SortArenaTeamRoster` — Sorts the selected arena team's roster by the given sort type.

`TurnInArenaPetition` — Turns in an arena petition.

Auction

`CalculateAuctionDeposit` — Returns the cost of an auction house deposit for a given runtime.

`CanSendAuctionQuery` — Returns whether the player can perform a given auction house query.

`CancelAuction` — Cancels an auction that has been placed by the player.

`ClickAuctionSellItemButton` — Causes the item currently being held by the cursor to be placed in the Auction House "Create Auction" item slot.

`CloseAuctionHouse` — Closes the auction house UI and stops all data retrieval.

`GetAuctionHouseDepositRate` — Returns the current auction house deposit rate.

`GetAuctionInvTypes` — Returns a list of the inventory subtypes for a given auction house item subclass.

`GetAuctionItemClasses` — Returns a list of top-level item classes used to categorize auction items (for example, Weapons, Armor, Container, Consumable, Trade Goods, and so on).

`GetAuctionItemInfo` — Returns information about an item up for auction.

`GetAuctionItemLink` — Returns an item link for a given auction item.

`GetAuctionItemSubClasses` — Returns a list of subclasses that are valid for a specific auction item class (for example, One-Handed Axes, Two-Handed Axes, Bows, Guns under Weapons; Miscellaneous, Cloth, Leather and others under Amor, and so on).

`GetAuctionItemTimeLeft` — Returns the time left for a given auction listing.

`GetAuctionSellItemInfo` — Returns information about the item being placed on auction.

`GetAuctionSort` — Returns information about the way the auction house listings are currently being sorted.

`GetBidderAuctionItems` — Retrieves bidding data for items on which you are bidding.

`GetInboxInvoiceInfo` — Returns information about an auction house invoice.

`GetNumAuctionItems` — Returns the number of auction items for a given type of listing.

`GetOwnerAuctionItems` — Queries the server for a page of self-posted auctions.

`GetSelectedAuctionItem` — Returns the index of the currently selected auction house item.

`IsAuctionSortReversed` — Returns whether a column in the auction house interface is reverse sorted or not.

`PlaceAuctionBid` — Places a bid on an auction item.

`QueryAuctionItems` — Queries the auction house's listings for the attributes specified.

`SetSelectedAuctionItem` — Selects a specific item in the auction house.

`SortAuctionApplySort` — Applies the currently configured sort for the given auction type.

`SortAuctionClearSort` — Clears any current sorting rules for the given auction house listing.

`SortAuctionItems` — Sorts the auction house listing.

`SortAuctionSetSort` — Sets the server-side sort to be applied to the items returned by an Auction House Query.

`StartAuction` — Starts a new auction.

Bank

BankButtonIDToInvSlotID — Returns an inventory slot ID mapped from a bank location.

CloseBankFrame — Closes the bank frame.

GetBankSlotCost — Returns the cost of a bank slot.

GetNumBankSlots — Returns information about purchased bank bag slots.

PurchaseSlot — Purchases a bank slot without confirmation.

Battlefield

AcceptAreaSpiritHeal — Notifies the server that you are ready to accept the periodic area resurrection from a battleground spirit healer.

AcceptBattlefieldPort — Accepts the offered teleport to a battleground, or leaves the queue for a given battleground.

CanJoinBattlefieldAsGroup — Returns whether the currently displayed battlefield supports joining as a group.

CancelAreaSpiritHeal — Cancels resurrection if one is pending from a battleground spirit healer.

CheckSpiritHealerDist — Returns whether the player is in range of a spirit healer.

CloseBattlefield — Closes the battlefield selection UI.

GetAreaSpiritHealerTime — Returns the amount of time until a nearby battleground spirit healer resurrects all players in its area.

GetBattlefieldEstimatedWaitTime — Returns the estimated wait time on a battleground or arena queue.

GetBattlefieldFlagPosition — Returns positioning information on the given flag.

GetBattlefieldInfo — Returns information about a battleground when speaking to a battle-master NPC or attempting to enter a battleground instance portal.

GetBattlefieldInstanceExpiration — When a battleground match is over, returns the amount of time remaining before the instance is closed and all players are returned to the locations from which they entered it.

GetBattlefieldInstanceInfo — Returns a numeric ID for a battleground instance listed in the battleground instance selection window.

GetBattlefieldInstanceRunTime — Returns how long the current battleground instance has been running, in milliseconds.

GetBattlefieldMapIconScale — Returns the scale of the battleground map icons.

GetBattlefieldPortExpiration — Returns the time left on a battleground or arena invitation.

GetBattlefieldPosition — Returns information on the queried player's position in a battleground.

GetBattlefieldScore — Returns information about a specific line in the battleground or arena score list.

GetBattlefieldStatData — Returns battleground-specific statistics for a given player.

`GetBattlefieldStatInfo` — Retrieves a list of custom scoreboard columns inside a battleground.

`GetBattlefieldStatus` — Returns information about an active or queued battleground instance.

`GetBattlefieldTeamInfo` — Returns info about teams and their ratings in a rated arena match.

`GetBattlefieldTimeWaited` — Returns the amount of time the player has queued for the given battleground, in milliseconds.

`GetBattlefieldWinner` — Returns the winner of the current battleground or arena match.

`GetNumBattlefieldFlagPositions` — Returns the number of battlefield flags in the current zone.

`GetNumBattlefieldPositions` — Returns the number of team members currently on the battlefield.

`GetNumBattlefieldScores` — Returns the number of scores available in the current battlefield.

`GetNumBattlefieldStats` — Returns the number of battlefield specific columns to be displayed in the final score frame.

`GetNumBattlefields` — Returns the number of available battlefields.

`GetSelectedBattlefield` — Returns the currently selected battlefield index.

`IsActiveBattlefieldArena` — Returns whether the current battlefield is an arena match.

`IsBattlefieldArena` — Returns whether the NPC the player is interacting with can queue for arenas.

`IsRealPartyLeader` — Returns whether the player is the leader of their "real party".

`JoinBattlefield` — Queues for a specific battlefield, optionally as a group.

`LeaveBattlefield` — Exits the current battleground.

`ReportPlayerIsPVPAFK` — Reports a player or unit as AFK in a PvP battleground.

`RequestBattlefieldPositions` — Requests new battlefield position information from the server.

`RequestBattlefieldScoreData` — Requests the latest battlefield score from the server. The score is not directly returned by the function call; it'll dispatch the `UPDATE_BATTLEFIELD_SCORE` event instead.

`SetBattlefieldScoreFaction` — Sets the faction of the battlefield scoreboard.

`SetSelectedBattlefield` — Selects a given battlefield in the battlemaster window.

`ShowBattlefieldList` — Displays the battlefield list window for a previously queued battlefield.

`SortBattlefieldScoreData` — Sorts the battlefield data based on a specific sortType.

`UnitInBattleground` — Returns whether a unit is in the player's battleground.

Binding

ClearOverrideBindings — Clears all override bindings for a given owner.

GetBinding — Returns information about a key binding.

GetBindingAction — Returns the action associated with the given key.

GetBindingByKey — Returns the actions bound to a specific key combination.

GetBindingKey — Returns the key combinations for a given binding command.

GetCurrentBindingSet — Returns the type of key bindings in use.

GetNumBindings — Returns the number of key binding actions listed in the Key Bindings window.

LoadBindings — Loads a set of key bindings.

RunBinding — Runs a key binding by name.

SaveBindings — Saves the current key bindings set to disk.

SetBinding — Sets a key combination to a given binding.

SetBindingClick — Set a key binding directly to a Button object.

SetBindingItem — Binds a specific key to a specific item. Hitting that key after calling this function causes the item to be used or activated.

SetBindingMacro — Assign a key binding to a specific macro.

SetBindingSpell — Binds a spell directly to a key combination.

SetMouselookOverrideBinding — Overrides the default mouselook bindings to perform another binding with the mouse buttons.

SetOverrideBinding — Set an override binding to the given command.

SetOverrideBindingClick — Sets an override binding that acts like a mouse click on a button.

SetOverrideBindingItem — Sets an override binding to use a specific item.

SetOverrideBindingMacro — Sets an override binding to a specific macro.

SetOverrideBindingSpell — Set an override binding to a specific spell.

Buff

CancelPlayerBuff — Cancels one of the player's buffs by name or index.

GetPlayerBuff — Returns information about the player's buffs.

GetPlayerBuffApplications — Returns the number of applications (stacks) for a given buff on the player.

GetPlayerBuffDispelType — Returns the dispel type of a given buff.

GetPlayerBuffName — Returns information about a buff on the player.

GetPlayerBuffTexture — Returns the texture for a given buff on the player.

GetPlayerBuffTimeLeft — Returns the time left on the selected buff on the player.

GetWeaponEnchantInfo — Returns information about temporary item enchants on the player's weapons.

UnitBuff — Returns information about a buff on a given unit or player.

UnitDebuff — Returns information about a debuff on a given unit.

Camera

`CameraOrSelectOrMoveStart` — Called when left-clicking in the 3-D world.

`CameraOrSelectOrMoveStop` — Ends a left-click in the 3-D world.

`CameraZoomIn` — Zooms the camera in a specified distance.

`CameraZoomOut` — Zooms the camera out.

`FlipCameraYaw` — Rotates the camera around the player.

`IsMouselooking` — Returns whether mouselook mode is active.

`MouselookStop` — Disables mouselook mode, where cursor movement rotates camera.

`MoveViewDownStart` — Begins rotating the camera downward.

`MoveViewInStop` — Stops zooming camera after `MoveViewInStart()` has been called.

`MoveViewLeftStart` — Begins rotating camera to the left.

`MoveViewLeftStop` — Stops rotating camera to the left.

`MoveViewOutStart` — Begins zooming the camera out.

`MoveViewRightStart` — Starts your camera orbiting around you to the right (counterclockwise).

`MoveViewRightStop` — Begins rotating camera to the right.

`MoveViewUpStart` — Begins rotating the camera upward.

`MoveViewUpStop` — Stops rotating the camera upward.

`NextView` — Changes the camera view to the next predefined camera angle.

`PitchDownStop` — Stops pitching the camera.

`PrevView` — Changes the camera view to the previous predefined camera angle.

`ResetView` — Resets the given viewmode and switches to that viewmode.

`SaveView` — Saves the current camera view to one of the stored camera positions.

`SetView` — Sets the camera view to one of the pre-set views.

Channel

`AddChatWindowChannel` — Maps a channel in a specific chat frame to a numeric index.

`ChannelBan` — Bans a player from a given chat channel.

`ChannelInvite` — Invites a player to a given channel.

`ChannelKick` — Kicks a player from the given channel.

`ChannelModerator` — Grants a player moderator status on the given channel.

`ChannelMute` — Turns off the specified player's ability to speak in the channel.

`ChannelSilenceAll` — Removes both voice and chat permissions for the given player in the specified channel.

`ChannelSilenceVoice` — Silences the given character for voice chat on the channel. Can only be done as a raid/party/bg leader or assistant.

`ChannelToggleAnnouncements` — Toggles channel announcements for a given channel.

`ChannelUnSilenceAll` — Unsilences a player for chat and voice on a given channel.

`ChannelUnSilenceVoice` — Unsilences a player on a given channel.

ChannelUnban — Unbans a player from a given channel.

ChannelUnmoderator — Revokes moderator status from a given player on a specific channel.

ChannelUnmute — Unmutes the specified player on that channel.

ChannelVoiceOff — Disables voice chat in the given channel.

ChannelVoiceOn — Enables voice chat in the given channel.

CollapseChannelHeader — Collapses a channel header in the chat channel listing.

DisplayChannelOwner — Fires a CHANNEL_OWNER event for the given channel.

DisplayChannelVoiceOff — Disables voice chat in a given channel.

DisplayChannelVoiceOn — Enables voice chat in a given channel.

EnumerateServerChannels — Returns the available server channel names.

ExpandChannelHeader — Collapses a channel header in the chat channel listing.

GetActiveVoiceChannel — Returns the currently active voice channel.

GetChannelDisplayInfo — Returns information about a given chat channel.

GetChannelList — Returns the list of channels to which the player currently belongs.

GetChannelName — Returns information about a given chat channel.

GetChannelRosterInfo — Returns information about a user in a given channel.

GetChatWindowChannels — Returns a list of all channels in which a given chat window is interested.

GetNumChannelMembers — Returns the number of members in a specific chat channel.

GetNumDisplayChannels — Returns the number of channels in the channel display.

GetSelectedDisplayChannel — Returns the channel ID of the selected channel in the "Chat" interface.

IsDisplayChannelModerator — Returns whether the player is a moderator of the currently selected display channel in the Chat tab.

IsDisplayChannelOwner — Returns whether the player is the owner of the currently displayed channel.

IsSilenced — Returns whether the given unit is silenced for Voice Chat on a channel.

JoinChannelByName — Joins the given chat channel. Deprecated; see JoinPermanentChannel.

JoinPermanentChannel — Joins a channel, saving any relevant settings in chat-cache.txt.

JoinTemporaryChannel — Joins a channel.

LeaveChannelByName — Leaves a channel by name.

ListChannelByName — Prints the members of a channel to ChatFrame1.

ListChannels — Prints a list of the channels to which the player currently belongs to DEFAULT_CHAT_FRAME.

RemoveChatWindowChannel — Removes a chat channel from the given chat window .

SetActiveVoiceChannel — Sets the currently active voice channel.

SetActiveVoiceChannelBySessionID — Sets the currently active voice chat channel.

SetChannelOwner — Gives channel ownership to another player.

SetChannelPassword — Sets a password on a custom chat channel.

SetSelectedDisplayChannel — Selects the given display channel for use in other functions.

Chat

AddChatWindowChannel — Maps a channel in a specific chat frame to a numeric index.

AddChatWindowMessages — Sets a chat frame to receive and show messages of the given message group.

CanComplainChat — Returns whether a given chat line can be reported.

ChangeChatColor — Changes the color of a message type in the chat windows.

ComplainChat — Files a complaint about a given chat message.

GetChatTypeIndex — Converts a chat type string to a numeric chat type index.

GetChatWindowChannels — Returns a list of all channels in which a given chat window is interested.

GetChatWindowInfo — Retrieves information about a specific chat window.

GetChatWindowMessages — Returns a list of message events (leaving the CHAT_MSG_ part out) for which a given chat frame is registered.

GetLanguageByIndex — Returns the localized name of the language identified by the index being queried.

GetNumLaguages — Returns the number of languages the player is capable of speaking.

IsIgnored — Returns whether you are ignoring a specific unit.

LoggingChat — Toggles logging of chat to Logs/WowChatLog.txt.

LoggingCombat — Toggles logging of combat events to Logs/WoWCombatLog.txt.

RemoveChatWindowChannel — Removes a chat channel from the given chat window.

RemoveChatWindowMessages — Hides a group of messages from a chat frame.

ResetChatColors — Resets the colors of the chat channels back to default.

ResetChatWindows — Resets the chat windows to hardcoded defaults.

SendChatMessage — Sends a chat message.

SetChatWindowAlpha — Sets the value of the chat window alpha in chat-cache.txt.

SetChatWindowColor — Sets the value of the chat window color in chat-cache.txt.

SetChatWindowDocked — Sets the value of the docked setting for the given chat window in chat-cache.txt.

SetChatWindowLocked — Locks a chat window so it can't be dragged or resized.

SetChatWindowName — Sets the name for a chat window in chat-cache.txt.

SetChatWindowShown — Sets if a chat window is shown in chat-cache.txt.

SetChatWindowSize — Sets the value of chat the window's font size in chat-cache.txt.

China

GetBillingTimeRested — Returns the number of minutes offline required for full experience.

NoPlayTime — Returns whether the player is out of playtime.

PartialPlayTime — Returns whether the character gains partial xp or not.

Client

CancelLogout — Cancels a pending logout.

ForceLogout — Forces the client to log out.

ForceQuit — Immediately exits World of Warcraft.

GetAccountExpansionLevel — Returns the expansion level of the player's account.

GetBuildInfo — Returns the version information about the client.

GetExistingLocales — Returns the locale packs currently available to the client.

GetLocale — Returns the four-character locale code indicating what language the client uses.

IsLinuxClient — Returns whether the game client is running on Linux.

IsMacClient — Returns whether the running client is a Mac.

IsWindowsClient — Checks if the client's OS is Windows.

Logout — Logs out of the current character, taking you back to the character selection screen.

Quit — Quits the game normally.

SetEuropeanNumbers — Enables using comma as the decimal separator.

Combat

AttackTarget — Enables melee auto-attacking against the currently selected target.

LoggingCombat — Toggles combat logging to Logs/WoWCombatLog.txt.

StartAttack — Used by Blizzard code to start an attack on a specific unit.

StopAttack — Stops auto-attack if active.

UnitAffectingCombat — Returns whether a unit is currently in combat.

Complaint

CanComplainChat — Returns whether a given chat line can be reported.

CanComplainInboxItem — Queries an inbox mail item for complain status. This determines if you can report this mail as spam. Returns 1 if you can, nil otherwise. This function only works at the mailbox, and will return nil for anyone on your friends list.

ComplainChat — Files a complaint about a given chat message.

ComplainInboxItem — Reports an inbox item as spam.

ReportPlayerIsPVPAFK — Reports a player or unit as AFK in a PvP battleground.

Container

ContainerIDToInventoryID — Returns the inventoryId that corresponds to a given containerId.

GetBagName — Returns the name of a bag.

GetContainerItemCooldown — Returns information about the cooldown for an item in one of your bags.

GetContainerItemDurability — Returns durability information for an item in one of your bags.

GetContainerItemInfo — Returns information about an item in a container.

GetContainerItemLink — Returns the item link of the item at a specific position in the player's bags or bank.

GetContainerNumSlots — Returns the number of slots for a given container.

PickupBagFromSlot — Picks up a bag from an inventory slot or bank bag slot and holds it on the cursor.

PickupContainerItem — Picks up an item from a container and holds it on the cursor.

PutItemInBackpack — Puts the currently held item into the first open slot in the player's backpack.

PutItemInBag — Attempts to place an item under the cursor inside the specified bag.

SplitContainerItem — Splits an item in a given container, placing the new stack on the cursor.

UseContainerItem — Uses an item from one of your containers, optionally on a target.

Craft

BindEnchant — Confirms enchanting an item when it would cause the item to become soulbound.

CloseCraft — Closes the craft frame.

CollapseCraftSkillLine — Collapses a skill line in the craft frame.

CraftIsEnchanting — Returns whether the current craft window is the enchanting window.

CraftIsPetTraining — Returns whether the open craft window is the pet training window.

CraftOnlyShowMakeable — Enables or disables the "Have Materials" filter in the craft UI.

DoCraft — Performs the selected craft skill.

ExpandCraftSkillLine — Expands a craft skill line header.

GetCraftButtonToken — Returns the global string token for the craft button in the craft UI.

GetCraftCooldown — Returns the amount of time left on a craft skill cooldown.

GetCraftDescription — Returns a short description of what a specified craft does.

GetCraftDisplaySkillLine — Returns information about the currently open craft (Enchanting or Beast Training).

GetCraftFilter — Returns whether a given craft filter is enabled.

GetCraftIcon — Returns the texture of a selected craft to be shown in the craft UI.

GetCraftInfo — Returns information about a given craft recipe or skill (Enchanting, or Pet Training).

GetCraftItemLink — Returns an item link for a craft skill item.

GetCraftItemNameFilter — Returns the value of the craft UI item name filter.

GetCraftName — Returns the name of the current craft that the player has open. If no craft is open, will return the first profession found in the spellbook (even professions that use the TradeSkill API instead of the Craft API).

GetCraftNumMade — Returns the number of items crafted for a given recipe.

GetCraftNumReagents — Returns the number of reagents that are required for the given recipe.

GetCraftReagentInfo — Returns information about a craft skill reagent.

GetCraftReagentItemLink — Returns an item link for a specific craft skill reagent.

GetCraftRecipeLink — Retrieves the recipe link for a given craft skill. The tooltip for this item link shows required reagents and description.

GetCraftSelectionIndex — Returns the index of the currently selected craft item.

GetCraftSkillLine — Returns the name of the currently (or last) open craft skill window.

GetCraftSlots — Returns a list of item slot types for which crafted items can be made.

GetCraftSpellFocus — Returns a list of required items for a craft skill (for example, Enchanting rods).

GetNumCrafts — Returns the number of items in the crafting window.

ReplaceEnchant — Confirms replacing an existing enchant.

SelectCraft — Selects a given item for the active craft (used by Enchanting and Pet Training).

SetCraftFilter — Sets a specific craft filter as active.

SetCraftItemNameFilter — Sets the craft UI item name filter search string.

Cursor

AddTradeMoney — Adds the money currently on the cursor to the trade window.

AutoEquipCursorItem — Tries to equip the item currently held on the cursor.

ClearCursor — Removes whatever is currently attached to the cursor.

ClickAuctionSellItemButton — Causes the item currently being held by the cursor to be placed in the Auction House "Create Auction" item slot.

ClickSendMailItemButton — Causes the item currently being held by the cursor to be placed in the "Mailbox Send" item slot.

ClickSocketButton — Picks up or places a gem in the Item Socketing UI.

ClickTargetTradeButton — Simulates clicking on a specific slot in the target trade window.

ClickTradeButton — Clicks a specific trade window button.

`CursorCanGoInSlot` — Returns whether the item on the cursor can be placed in the given slot.

`CursorHasItem` — Indicates if the cursor is currently holding an item.

`CursorHasMacro` — Returns whether the cursor currently holds a macro.

`CursorHasMoney` — Returns whether the cursor is currently holding money.

`CursorHasSpell` — Returns whether the cursor currently holds a spell.

`DeleteCursorItem` — Confirms deletion of the item currently held on the cursor.

`DropCursorMoney` — Drops the money currently held to the cursor, returning it to where it was taken from.

`DropItemOnUnit` — Drops the currently held item on a specific unit.

`EquipCursorItem` — Attempts to equip the item held on the cursor into a specific inventory slot.

`GetCursorInfo` — Returns information about the object currently held by the cursor.

`GetCursorMoney` — Returns the amount of money currently held by the cursor, in copper.

`GetCursorPosition` — Returns the coordinate position of the cursor on screen.

`GetMouseFocus` — Returns the frame that is currently under the mouse, and has mouse input enabled.

`HideRepairCursor` — Stops displaying the item repair cursor.

`PickupAction` — Picks up an action bar slot and holds it on the cursor.

`PickupBagFromSlot` — Picks up a bag from an inventory slot or bank bag slot and holds it on the cursor.

`PickupContainerItem` — Picks up an item from a container and holds it on the cursor.

`PickupGuildBankItem` — Picks up an item from the guild bank and holds it on the cursor.

`PickupGuildBankMoney` — Withdraws money from the guild bank, placing it on the cursor.

`PickupInventoryItem` — Picks an inventory item up and holds it on the cursor.

`PickupItem` — Picks up an item by name or ID and holds it on the cursor.

`PickupMacro` — Simulates picking up a macro from the macro window, placing it on the cursor.

`PickupMerchantItem` — Picks up an item from the merchant window, holding it on the cursor.

`PickupPetAction` — Picks up the pet action in the given slot and places it under the cursor.

`PickupPlayerMoney` — Picks up money from the player's inventory and holds it on the cursor.

`PickupSpell` — Picks up a spell from the spellbook, placing it on the cursor.

`PickupStablePet` — Picks up a stabled pet and holds it on the cursor.

`PlaceAction` — Places the action held on the cursor in a specified action bar slot.

`PutItemInBackpack` — Puts the currently held item into the first open slot in the player's backpack.

`PutItemInBag` — Attempts to place an item under the cursor inside the specified bag.

ResetCursor — Resets the mouse cursor to the default glove pointer.

SetCursor — Sets the cursor image.

ShowBuybackSellCursor — Shows the buyback/sell cursor.

ShowContainerSellCursor — Displays the "sell item" cursor for a given container item.

ShowInventorySellCursor — Changes the cursor to the "inventory sell" cursor.

ShowMerchantSellCursor — Shows the merchant "sell item" cursor.

ShowRepairCursor — Changes the cursor to show the repair cursor.

SplitContainerItem — Splits an item in a given container, placing the new stack on the cursor.

SplitGuildBankItem — Splits an item in a given tab and slot, placing the new stack on the cursor.

CVar

GetCVar — Returns the value of a stored configuration variable.

GetCVarDefault — Query the default value for a given CVar. Will cause an error if CVar does not exist.

RegisterCVar — Registers a configuration variable to be saved.

SetCVar — Sets the value of a configuration variable in config.wtf.

Debug

FrameXML_Debug — Enables or disables verbose XML logging.

debugprofilestart — Starts and resets the high-resolution debug timer.

debugprofilestop — Returns the value of the running debug profile timer.

debugstack — Returns information about the current function call stack.

geterrorhandler — Returns a reference to the current error handler.

issecure — Returns whether the current execution path is secure.

issecurevariable — Returns whether a variable is secure and, if not, what addon tainted the variable.

seterrorhandler — Sets the default error handler to a specific function.

Faction

CollapseFactionHeader — Collapses a given faction header.

ExpandFactionHeader — Expands a given faction header.

FactionToggleAtWar — Toggles the "at war" status toward a specific faction.

GetFactionInfo — Returns information about a specified faction index.

GetNumFactions — Returns the number of factions the player has encountered.

GetSelectedFaction — Returns the currently selected faction index.

GetWatchedFactionInfo — Returns information about the faction currently being watched.

IsFactionInactive — Returns whether a faction is flagged as "inactive".

SetFactionActive — Sets a faction as the active faction.

SetFactionInactive — Flags a faction as inactive.

SetSelectedFaction — Sets the current faction selection.

SetWatchedFactionIndex — Sets the faction on which to watch for reputation progress.

GM Survey

GMSurveyAnswerSubmit — Submits an answer to a GM survey question.

GMSurveyCommentSubmit — Submits a comment to the current GM survey.

GMSurveyQuestion — Returns the text of a specific question from a GM survey.

GMSurveySubmit — Submits the current GM survey.

GM Ticket

DeleteGMTicket — Abandons the currently pending GM ticket.

GetGMTicket — Requests a GM ticket update from the server.

GetGMTicketCategories — Returns a list of available GM ticket categories.

NewGMTicket — Opens a new GM support ticket.

UpdateGMTicket — Updates the current GM ticket with the appropriate text.

Guild

AcceptGuild — Accept an invitation to join a guild.

BuyGuildCharter — Purchases a guild charter with a given name.

CanEditGuildInfo — Returns whether the player can edit the guild information.

CanEditMOTD — Returns whether the player can edit the guild MOTD.

CanEditOfficerNote — Returns whether the player can edit officer notes.

CanEditPublicNote — Returns whether the player can edit public notes.

CanGuildDemote — Returns whether the player can demote lower-ranked guild members.

CanGuildInvite — Returns whether the player can invite members to their guild.

CanGuildPromote — Returns whether the player has the ability to promote other players within the guild.

CanGuildRemove — Returns whether the player can remove a member from their guild.

CanViewOfficerNote — Returns whether the player can view officer notes.

CloseGuildRegistrar — Closes the guild registrar frame.

CloseGuildRoster — Closes the Guild Roster UI frame.

CloseTabardCreation — Closes the tabard creation window.

DeclineGuild — Declines an offered guild invitation.

GetGuildCharterCost — Returns the cost of a guild charter.

GetGuildEventInfo — Returns information on the guild log.

GetGuildInfo — Retrieves information about a player's guild.

GetGuildInfoText — Returns the information text for the player's guild.

GetGuildRecruitmentMode — Returns the current guild recruitment mode.

GetGuildRosterInfo — Returns information about the selected player in your guild roster.

GetGuildRosterLastOnline — Returns the amount of time since a guild member has been seen online.

GetGuildRosterMOTD — Returns the Message of the Day for your guild.

GetGuildRosterSelection — Returns the raid roster index of your currently selected guild member.

GetGuildRosterShowOffline — Returns whether the "Show Offline" setting is enabled in the Guild tab.

GetGuildTabardFileNames — Returns the filenames of the textures that comprise the player's guild tabard.

GetNumGuildEvents — Returns the number of available guild events for the guild log.

GetNumGuildMembers — Returns the number of members in the player's guild.

GetTabardCreationCost — Returns the cost to create a guild tabard.

GuildControlAddRank — Adds a new rank to the player's guild.

GuildControlDelRank — Deletes a guild rank.

GuildControlGetNumRanks — Returns the number of guild ranks in the guild including the guild master.

GuildControlGetRankFlags — Returns a list of permission flags for a guild rank.

GuildControlGetRankName — Returns the name of the given guild rank.

GuildControlSaveRank — Saves the settings for a guild rank.

GuildControlSetRank — Sets the current rank in the guild control window.

GuildControlSetRankFlag — Sets the current rank permission to enabled or disabled.

GuildDemote — Demotes a guild member by one guild rank.

GuildDisband — Disbands your guild without confirmation. Can only be done by the guild leader.

GuildInfo — Queries the server for the player's guild information.

GuildInvite — Invites a player to your guild.

GuildLeave — Causes the player to leave their current guild without confirmation.

GuildPromote — Promotes a given player to the next-highest guild rank.

GuildRoster — Initiates a guild roster update.

GuildRosterSetOfficerNote — Sets an officer note for a guild member.

GuildRosterSetPublicNote — Sets the public note of a guild member.

GuildSetLeader — Promotes the specified player to be the new guild leader.

GuildSetMOTD — Sets the guild Message of the Day.

GuildUninvite — Uninvites a player from the guild.

IsGuildLeader — Returns whether the current player is guild leader.

IsInGuild — Returns whether the player is in a guild.

QueryGuildEventLog — Queries the server for the guild event log.

SaveGuildRoster — Saves the guild roster, GuildRoster.txt, in the Logs folder.

SetGuildInfoText — Sets the guild information text.

SetGuildRecruitmentMode — Enables or disables auto-joining of the guild recruitment channel.

SetGuildRosterSelection — Sets the selection in the guild roster.

SetGuildRosterShowOffline — Sets the value for the "Show Offline" guild setting.

SortGuildRoster — Sorts the guild roster.

TurnInGuildCharter — Turns in a completed guild charter.

UnitIsInMyGuild — Returns whether a given unit or player is in the player's guild.

Guild Bank

AutoStoreGuildBankItem — Withdraws an item from the guild bank, automatically storing it in your inventory.

BuyGuildBankTab — Purchases the next available guild bank tab, without confirmation.

CanWithdrawGuildBankMoney — Returns whether the player can withdraw money from the guild bank.

CloseGuildBankFrame — Closes the guild bank frame.

DepositGuildBankMoney — Deposits money into the guild bank.

GetCurrentGuildBankTab — Returns the currently selected guild bank tab.

GetGuildBankItemInfo — Returns information about the guild bank item in a given slot.

GetGuildBankItemLink — Returns the item link of the item at a specific position in the guild bank.

GetGuildBankMoney — Returns the amount of money available in the guild bank, in copper.

GetGuildBankMoneyTransaction — Returns information from guild bank money log.

GetGuildBankTabCost — Returns the cost of the next available guild bank tab.

GetGuildBankTabInfo — Returns information about a given guild bank tab.

GetGuildBankTabPermissions — Returns the permissions the currently selected guild rank has for a given guild bank tab.

GetGuildBankTransaction — Returns information about a specific guild bank item transaction.

GetGuildBankWithdrawLimit — Returns the guild bank gold withdraw limit for the current rank being viewed in the guild control pane.

GetGuildBankWithdrawMoney — Returns the amount of gold the player can withdraw from the bank daily.

GetNumGuildBankMoneyTransactions — Returns the number of guild bank money transactions available for the money log.

GetNumGuildBankTabs — Gives the number of purchased tabs for the guild bank.

GetNumGuildBankTransactions — Returns the number of transactions for the specified guild bank tab.

PickupGuildBankItem — Picks up an item from the guild bank and holds it on the cursor.

PickupGuildBankMoney — Withdraws money from the guild bank, placing it on the cursor.

QueryGuildBankLog — Queries server for a guild bank log for a specific tab.

QueryGuildBankTab — Queries server for the contents of the specified guild bank tab.

SetCurrentGuildBankTab — Sets the currently selected guild bank tab.

SetGuildBankTabInfo — Sets the name and icon for a guild bank tab.

SetGuildBankTabPermissions — Enables or disables a specific guild bank tab permission.

SetGuildBankTabWithdraw — Sets the number of withdrawals allowed for the currently selected guild rank, on the given guild bank tab.

SetGuildBankWithdrawLimit — Sets the amount of withdrawals allowed for the selected guild rank.

SplitGuildBankItem — Splits an item in a given tab and slot, placing the new stack on the cursor.

WithdrawGuildBankMoney — Attempts to withdraw an amount of money in coppers from the guild bank. Does nothing on failure.

Inspect

CanInspect — Returns if the given unit can be inspected.

ClearInspectPlayer — Clears the data for the currently inspected player.

GetInspectArenaTeamData — Returns information about an inspect target's arena team.

GetInspectHonorData — Returns honor information about an inspect target.

HasInspectHonorData — Returns whether the client has honor data for the currently inspected player.

NotifyInspect — Queries the server for an inspected unit's talent information.

RequestInspectHonorData — Requests honor data for the currently inspected target.

Instance

CanShowResetInstances — Returns whether the player can reset instances.

GetCurrentDungeonDifficulty — Returns the current dungeon difficulty level.

GetDefaultDungeonDifficulty — Returns the default dungeon difficulty level for the player.

GetInstanceBootTimeRemaining — Returns the amount of time left until the player is removed from the current instance.

GetInstanceDifficulty — Returns your group's dungeon difficulty setting.

GetNumSavedInstances — Returns the number of instances to which the player is saved.

GetSavedInstanceInfo — Returns information on a specific instance to which the character is saved.

IsInInstance — Returns whether the player is currently in an instance and, if so, what type.

ResetInstances — Resets all nonsaved instances.

SetDungeonDifficulty — Sets the dungeon difficulty mode.

Inventory

BankButtonIDToInvSlotID — Returns inventory slot ID mapped from a bank location.

CancelPendingEquip — Cancels a pending equip action.

GetInventoryAlertStatus — Returns the durability level of a given inventory slot.

GetInventoryItemBroken — Returns whether the given inventory item is broken.

GetInventoryItemCooldown — Returns cooldown information about a current inventory item.

GetInventoryItemCount — Returns the number of items stacked in an inventory slot.

GetInventoryItemDurability — Returns the durability stats for a given item.

GetInventoryItemLink — Returns an item link for an inventory item.

GetInventoryItemQuality — Returns the quality level of a given inventory item.

GetInventoryItemTexture — Returns the item texture for a specific inventory item.

GetInventorySlotInfo — Returns information about an inventory slot.

IsEquippedItem — Returns whether the supplied item is currently equipped by the player.

IsEquippedItemType — Returns whether an item type is currently equipped.

IsInventoryItemLocked — Returns whether the given inventory slot is locked.

KeyRingButtonIDToInvSlotID — Converts a key ring slotID to an inventory slotID.

PickupInventoryItem — Picks an inventory item up and holds it on the cursor.

UseInventoryItem — Uses an item from the player's inventory.

Item

AutoEquipCursorItem — Tries to equip the item currently held on the cursor.

CancelItemTempEnchantment — Cancels a temporary item enchant.

CursorHasItem — Indicates if the cursor is currently holding an item.

DeleteCursorItem — Confirms deletion of the item currently held on the cursor.

DropItemOnUnit — Drops the currently held item on a specific unit.

EquipCursorItem — Attempts to equip the item held on the cursor into a specific inventory slot.

EquipItemByName — Equips an item by name, item link, or item ID.

EquipPendingItem — Confirms equipping a pending bind-on-equip item.

GetAbandonQuestItems — Returns any items that would be destroyed by confirming abandoning the current quest.

GetContainerItemCooldown — Returns information about the cooldown for an item in one of your bags.

GetContainerItemDurability — Returns durability information for an item in one of your bags.

GetContainerItemInfo — Returns information about an item in a container.

GetGuildBankItemInfo — Returns information about guild bank items in a given slot.

GetInventoryItemBroken — Returns whether the given inventory item is broken.

GetInventoryItemCooldown — Returns cooldown information about a current inventory item.

GetInventoryItemCount — Returns the number of items stacked in an inventory slot.

GetInventoryItemDurability — Returns the durability stats for a given item.

GetInventoryItemQuality — Returns the quality level of a given inventory item.

GetInventoryItemTexture — Returns the item texture for a specific inventory item.

GetItemCooldown — Returns cooldown information about a given item.

GetItemCount — Returns the number of a given item the player has in possession (possibly including bank).

GetItemGem — Returns the name and link for a gem in a specific item socket.

GetItemInfo — Returns information about an item by name, link, or ID.

GetItemQualityColor — Returns the red, green, and blue components of the color for the given item quality index. Also returns a hex representation of the same color.

GetItemSpell — Returns information about the spell cast when using a given item.

IsConsumableItem — Returns whether a given item is consumable.

IsCurrentItem — Returns true if the item is being used and nothing if it is not.

IsEquippableItem — Returns whether a given item is equippable.

IsEquippedItem — Returns whether supplied item is currently equipped by the player.

IsEquippedItemType — Returns whether an item type is currently equipped.

IsHarmfulItem — Returns whether an item is harmful (hostile to your target).

IsHelpfulItem — Returns whether the item is helpful.

IsItemInRange — Returns whether a usable item is in range of a given unit.

IsUsableItem — Determine the usability of an item.

ItemHasRange — Returns whether the item has a range for use.

PickupContainerItem — Picks up an item from a container and holds it on the cursor.

PickupGuildBankItem — Picks up item from the guild bank and holds it on the cursor.

PickupInventoryItem — Picks an inventory item up and holds it on the cursor.

PickupItem — Picks up an item by name or ID and holds it on the cursor.

PutItemInBackpack — Puts the currently held item into the first open slot in the player's backpack.

PutItemInBag — Attempts to place an item under the cursor inside the specified bag.

RepairAllItems — Attempts to repair all items. Requires the player to be at a merchant that repairs. Passing 1 to the function will attempt to make use of guild bank money for repairs.

SpellCanTargetItem — Returns whether the spell on the cursor can target an item or not. Will return nil when no spell is on the cursor.

SpellTargetItem — Targets an item with the spell currently awaiting targeting.

SplitContainerItem — Splits an item in a given container, placing the new stack on the cursor.

SplitGuildBankItem — Splits an item in a given tab and slot, placing the new stack on the cursor.

UseContainerItem — Use an item from one of your containers, optionally on a target.

UseInventoryItem — Uses an item from the player's inventory.

UseItemByName — Uses an item, optionally on a specified target.

Itemlink

GetAuctionItemLink — Returns an item link for a given auction item.

GetBuybackItemLink — Returns the item link for an item in the buyback window.

GetContainerItemLink — Returns the item link of the item at a specific position in the player's bags or bank.

GetCraftItemLink — Returns an item link for a craft skill item.

GetCraftNumMade — Returns the number of items crafted for a given recipe.

GetCraftNumReagents — Returns number of reagents required for the given recipe.

GetCraftReagentItemLink — Returns an item link for a specific craft skill reagent.

GetCraftRecipeLink — Retrieves the recipe link for a given craft skill. The tooltip for this item link shows required reagents and description.

GetCursorInfo — Returns information about the object currently held by the cursor.

GetExistingSocketLink — Returns an item link for a socketed gem.

GetGuildBankItemLink — Returns the item link of the item at a specific position in the guild bank.

GetGuildBankTransaction — Returns information about a specific guild bank item transaction.

GetInboxItemLink — Returns the item link to the specified attachment.

GetInventoryItemLink — Returns an item link for an inventory item.

GetItemGem — Returns the name and link for a gem in a specific item socket.

GetItemInfo — Returns information about an item by name, link, or ID.

GetLootRollItemLink — Returns an item link for the specified item.

GetLootSlotLink — Returns an item link for a given loot window slot.

GetMacroItem — Returns information about a macro if its next action is to use an item.

GetMerchantItemLink — Returns the full link of the item in question, or nil if the index is out of range.

GetNewSocketLink — Returns an item link for a gem to be socketed.

GetQuestItemLink — Returns an item link for a quest item (reward or requirement).

GetQuestLogItemLink — Returns the item link of a specific item in the quest log reward or progress frame.

GetSendMailItemLink — Returns an item link for an item in the send mail window.

GetTradePlayerItemLink — Returns a link for an item offered by the player in the trade window.

GetTradeSkillItemLink — Returns an item link for the given tradeskill item.

GetTradeSkillReagentItemLink — Returns the item link for a tradeskill's reagent.

GetTradeSkillRecipeLink — Returns an item link for a tradeskill recipe.

GetTradeTargetItemLink — Returns an item link for an item being offered by the target in a trade.

GetTrainerServiceItemLink — Returns an item link for a given trainer service item.

Itemtext

CloseItemText — Closes the item text display frame.

ItemTextGetCreator — Gets the creator of the text currently being viewed. Used for books, parchments, and the like.

ItemTextGetItem — Returns the name of the currently viewed ItemText item.

ItemTextGetMaterial — Returns the texture for the current book/parchment being displayed in the ItemTextFrame. A return value of nil means parchment is being used.

ItemTextGetPage — Returns the page number of the currently item text.

ItemTextGetText — Returns the test associated with the open item.

ItemTextHasNextPage — Determines if the currently open book has another page following the current one.

ItemTextNextPage — Asks the game to move the currently open book, or other readable object, to the next page of text.

ItemTextPrevPage — Asks the game to move the currently open book, or other readable object, to the previous page of text.

KnowledgeBase

KBArticle_BeginLoading — Requests specific knowledge base article from server.

KBArticle_GetData — Returns information about last requested knowledge base article.

KBArticle_IsLoaded — Returns whether the requested knowledge base article has been loaded.

KBQuery_BeginLoading — Queries the knowledge base server for articles.

KBQuery_GetArticleHeaderCount — Returns the number of articles on the current knowledge base search result page.

KBQuery_GetArticleHeaderData — Returns information about an article returned in a knowledge base query.

KBQuery_GetTotalArticleCount — Returns the total number of articles returned for the given query.

KBQuery_IsLoaded — Returns whether knowledge base query was loaded successfully.

KBSetup_BeginLoading — Loads a maximum number of "Top Issues" from a given page.

KBSetup_GetArticleHeaderCount — Returns the number of "Top Issues" articles on the current page.

KBSetup_GetArticleHeaderData — Returns header information about a "Top Issue" article.

KBSetup_GetCategoryCount — Returns the number of available knowledge base categories.

KBSetup_GetCategoryData — Returns information about a knowledge base category.

KBSetup_GetLanguageCount — Returns the number of available knowledge base languages.

KBSetup_GetLanguageData — Returns information about a given knowledge base language.

KBSetup_GetSubCategoryCount — Returns the number of available subcategories for a given category.

KBSetup_GetSubCategoryData — Returns information about a knowledge base subcategory.

KBSetup_GetTotalArticleCount — Returns the number of "Top Issues" articles.

KBSetup_IsLoaded — Returns whether the knowledge base setup has loaded successfully.

KBSystem_GetMOTD — Returns the current knowledge base MOTD.

KBSystem_GetServerNotice — Returns the text of the knowledge base server system notice.

KBSystem_GetServerStatus — Returns knowledge base server system status message.

Keyboard

GetCurrentKeyBoardFocus — Returns the frame that currently has the keyboard focus.

IsAltKeyDown — Returns whether an Alt key on the keyboard is held down.

IsControlKeyDown — Returns whether a Control key on the keyboard is held down.

IsLeftAltKeyDown — Returns whether the left Alt key is currently held down.

IsLeftControlKeyDown — Returns whether the left Control key is held down.

IsLeftShiftKeyDown — Returns whether the left Shift key on the keyboard is held down.

IsModifierKeyDown — Returns whether a modifier key is held down.

IsRightAltKeyDown — Returns whether the right Alt key is currently held down.

IsRightControlKeyDown — Returns whether the right Control key on the keyboard is held down.

IsRightShiftKeyDown — Returns whether the right Shift key on the keyboard is held down.

IsShiftKeyDown — Returns whether a Shift key on the keyboard is held down.

Looking For Group/Looking For More

AcceptLFGMatch — Accepts a proposed LFG match.

CanSendLFGQuery — Returns whether the player can submit an LFG/LFM request for the given type and index.

CancelPendingLFG — Removes the player from all open LookingForGroup queues.

ClearLFGAutojoin — Clears the auto-join functionality in the LFG tool.

ClearLFMAutofill — Stops LFM interface from auto-adding members to your group.

ClearLookingForGroup — Clears the player from any LFG/LFM listings or requests.

ClearLookingForMore — Clears all active LFM requests, removing the player from the LFG queue.

GetLFGPartyResults — Returns information about a party member in the LFG results.

GetLFGResults — Returns information about a specific line of an LFM/LFG query.

GetLFGStatusText — Returns information on your current Looking For Group status.

GetLFGTypeEntries — Returns the valid entries of a specific type in the LFG system.

GetLFGTypes — Returns the type of possible LFG queries.

GetLookingForGroup — Retrieves information about the player's LFG status.

GetNumLFGResults — Returns the number of results from an LFG query.

IsInLFGQueue — Returns whether the player is currently in the LFG queue.

LFGQuery — Sends a Looking for Group request, optionally filtered by class.

SetLFGAutojoin — Enables auto-join in the LFG system.

SetLFGComment — Adds a comment to your listing in the LFG system.

SetLFGType — Sets a filter for the LFG system in a specific slot.

SetLFMAutofill — Turns on the auto-fill option in the Looking For More interface.

SetLFMType — Sets the type of the current LFM request.

SetLookingForGroup — Sets one of the three Looking for Group slots.

SetLookingForMore — Starts looking for more members for the given activity type and index.

SortLFG — Sets the sort type for a Looking for Group query.

Loot

CloseLoot — Closes the loot window.

ConfirmLootRoll — Confirms a loot roll for a given item that will be bound to your character if you win the roll.

ConfirmLootSlot — Confirms the looting of a bind-on-pickup item.

GetAutoLootDefault — Returns whether auto-loot is enabled.

GetLootMethod — Retrieves information about the group's loot setting.

GetLootRollItemInfo — Returns information about the specified item to roll on.

GetLootRollItemLink — Returns an item link for the specified item.

GetLootRollTimeLeft — Returns the amount of time left on the given loot roll, in milliseconds.

GetLootSlotInfo — Returns the information for a loot slot item.

GetLootSlotLink — Returns an item link for a given loot window slot.

GetLootThreshold — Returns the current loot threshold setting.

GetMasterLootCandidate — Returns information about a given loot candidate.

GetNumLootItems — Returns the number of items available to be looted.

IsFishingLoot — Returns whether the currently displayed loot is fishing loot.

LootSlot — Attempts to loot the item in the specified slot.

LootSlotIsCoin — Returns whether a given loot slot contains coins.

LootSlotIsItem — Returns whether a given loot slot contains an item.

RollOnLoot — Performs a type of roll (pass/need/greed) on a given loot.

SetAutoLootDefault — Enables or disables auto-looting.

SetLootMethod — Sets the loot method when in a group or party. Requires leader.

SetLootPortrait — Sets a texture to the current loot portrait.

SetLootThreshold — Sets the loot threshold to a specific item quality.

Mac

IsMacClient — Returns whether the running client is a Mac.

MovieRecording_Cancel — Cancels a currently recording video.

MovieRecording_DataRate — Returns the data rate required per second for recording video.

MovieRecording_DeleteMovie — Deletes a movie currently pending compression.

MovieRecording_GetAspectRatio — Returns the aspect ratio used in any movie recordings.

MovieRecording_GetMovieFullPath — Returns the full path of the movie currently being recorded or compressed.

MovieRecording_GetProgress — Returns information about the movie that is currently being compressed.

MovieRecording_GetTime — Returns the amount of time since the last video recording operation was started.

MovieRecording_GetViewportWidth — Queries the current width of the game's viewport.

`MovieRecording_IsCodecSupported` — Returns whether a given video recording codec is supported by the client.

`MovieRecording_IsCompressing` — Returns whether the client is currently compressing a recording.

`MovieRecording_IsRecording` — Returns whether the client is currently recording a movie.

`MovieRecording_IsSupported` — Returns whether movie recording is supported by client.

`MovieRecording_MaxLength` — Returns the maximum length of a recorded video.

`MovieRecording_QueueMovieToCompress` — Adds a movie to the compression queue, starting immediately if the queue is empty.

`MovieRecording_Search↵UncompressedMovie` — Enables or disables a search for uncompressed movies.

`MovieRecording_Toggle` — Begins recording a new video, or stops the currently recording video.

`MovieRecording_ToggleGUI` — Toggles recording of the user interface when recording a video.

`MusicPlayer_BackTrack` — Goes back a track in iTunes.

`MusicPlayer_NextTrack` — Goes to the next track in iTunes.

`MusicPlayer_PlayPause` — Plays or pauses playback in iTunes.

`MusicPlayer_VolumeDown` — Turns the volume down in iTunes.

`MusicPlayer_VolumeUp` — Turns the volume up in iTunes.

Macro

`CreateMacro` — Creates a new macro.

`CursorHasMacro` — Returns whether the cursor currently holds a macro.

`DeleteMacro` — Deletes a macro by ID.

`EditMacro` — Edit Macro command/button.

`GetMacroBody` — Returns the body of a given macro index.

`GetMacroIconInfo` — Returns the texture for a given macro icon index.

`GetMacroIndexByName` — Converts a macro name to macro index.

`GetMacroInfo` — Returns name, texture, and body of a given macro.

`GetMacroItem` — Returns information about a macro, if its next action is to use an item.

`GetMacroItemIconInfo` — Returns the texture for macro item icons.

`GetMacroSpell` — Returns the spell a given macro is set to cast.

`GetNumMacroIcons` — Returns the number of available macro icons.

`GetNumMacroItemIcons` — Returns the number of available macro item icons.

`GetNumMacros` — Returns the number of macros the player has stored.

`GetRunningMacro` — Returns the index of the currently running macro.

`GetRunningMacroButton` — Returns the mouse button that was used to activate the running macro.

`PickupMacro` — Simulates picking up a macro from macro window and placing it on cursor.

RunMacro — Runs a macro by name or index, as if it had been clicked with a specified button.

RunMacroText — Runs a macro string, as if it had been clicked with a specified button.

SecureCmdOptionParse — Parses a secure command (macro, slash command) into an action and possible target.

SetMacroItem — Sets a macro to use a specific item and target for visual updates.

SetMacroSpell — Sets the spell and target unit used to update a macro's icon and range indicator.

StopMacro — Stops execution of a running macro.

Mail

CanComplainInboxItem — Query an inbox mail item for complain status. This determines if you can report this mail as spam. Returns 1 if you can, nil otherwise. This function only works at the mailbox, and will return nil for anyone on your friends list.

CheckInbox — Requests the player's mailbox information from the server.

ClearSendMail — Clears the send mail window, removing all items, money, and text.

ClickSendMailItemButton — Causes the item currently being held by the cursor to be placed in the mailbox send item slot.

CloseMail — Closes the mail window.

ComplainInboxItem — Reports an inbox item as spam.

DeleteInboxItem — Deletes the given mail from your inbox.

GetInboxHeaderInfo — Returns information on an inbox item.

GetInboxInvoiceInfo — Returns information about an auction house invoice.

GetInboxItem — Returns information about an item attached to a received mail.

GetInboxItemLink — Returns the item link to the specified attachment.

GetInboxNumItems — Returns the number of mail items currently in your inbox.

GetInboxText — Returns information about the text of an inbox message.

GetLatestThreeSenders — Returns names of last three senders of unchecked mail.

GetNumPackages — Returns the number of packages.

GetNumStationeries — Returns the number of available stationeries.

GetPackageInfo — Returns information on the given package. Does not seem implemented by Blizzard, index 1 always returns a "Test Package".

GetSelectedStationeryTexture — Returns the currently selected stationery texture.

GetSendMailCOD — Determines the amount of gold in the COD mail entry when sending a mil item.

GetSendMailItem — Returns information on an item slot in the send mail frame.

GetSendMailItemLink — Returns an item link for an item in the send mail window.

GetSendMailMoney — Returns the amount of money that will be sent with your next mail message.

GetSendMailPrice — Returns the cost associated with sending an in-game mail message.

GetStationeryInfo — Returns information about a given stationery.

HasNewMail — Returns whether the player has new mail.

InboxItemCanDelete — Returns whether an inbox item can be deleted.

ReturnInboxItem — Returns the given inbox item to its sender.

SelectPackage — Not yet implemented.

SelectStationery — Selects a given stationery for usage when sending mail.

SendMail — Sends mail to a player.

SetSendMailCOD — Sets the COD cost of mail being sent.

SetSendMailMoney — Sets the amount of money to send with the next mail message.

SetSendMailShowing — Controls whether right-clicking an item attaches it to the mail to be sent.

TakeInboxItem — Takes an attachment from an inbox item without confirmation.

TakeInboxMoney — Takes the money from the specified mail in the inbox.

TakeInboxTextItem — Sends request to the server to retrieve given message's text item.

Map

GetCorpseMapPosition — Returns the position of the player's corpse on the world map.

GetCurrentMapContinent — Returns the current map continent.

GetCurrentMapZone — Returns number of the zone currently shown on the world map.

GetDeathReleasePosition — Returns the location of the graveyard where your spirit will appear when it is released from your body.

GetMapContinents — Returns a list of the map continents.

GetMapInfo — Returns the map information about the current world map texture.

GetMapLandmarkInfo — Returns information about a map landmark.

GetMapOverlayInfo — Returns information about a world map overlay.

GetMapZones — Returns the map zones for a given continent.

GetNumMapLandmarks — Returns the number of points of interest on the world map.

GetNumMapOverlays — Returns the number of overlays for the current world map.

GetPlayerMapPosition — Returns a unit's position on the current map zoom.

GetWorldLocMapPosition — Converts one position to another, but actual use is unknown.

ProcessMapClick — Possibly changes the WorldMap based on a mouse click.

SetMapToCurrentZone — Sets the world map to the player's current zone.

SetMapZoom — Sets the world map to a specific continent or zone within that continent.

UpdateMapHighlight — Returns information about the texture used to highlight subregions of the world map.

Merchant

`BuybackItem` — Purchases an item from the buyback tab.

`CanMerchantRepair` — Returns whether the open merchant can repair equipment.

`CloseMerchant` — Closes the open merchant window.

`GetArenaCurrency` — Returns the number of available arena currency points.

`GetBuybackItemInfo` — Returns information about an item in the merchant buyback window.

`GetBuybackItemLink` — Returns the item link for an item in the buyback window.

`GetMerchantItemCostItem` — Returns information about an item used as currency to purchase another item (such as battleground rewards).

`GetMerchantItemInfo` — Returns information about an item available at a merchant.

`GetMerchantItemLink` — Returns the full link of the item in question, or `nil` if the index is out of range.

`GetMerchantItemMaxStack` — Determines how many of a merchant's item you can purchase in one transaction.

`GetMerchantNumItems` — Returns the total number of items a merchant has to sell.

`GetNumBuybackItems` — Returns the number of items available on the buyback tab.

`GetRepairAllCost` — Returns the cost to repair all damaged items.

`InRepairMode` — Returns whether the player is currently in "item repair mode".

`PickupMerchantItem` — Picks up an item from the merchant window, holding it on the cursor.

`RepairAllItems` — Attempts to repair all items. Requires the player to be at a merchant that repairs. Passing 1 to the function will attempt to make use of guild bank money for repairs.

Miscellaneous

`CheckBinderDist` — Returns whether the player is in range of an NPC that can bind their hearthstone.

`ConfirmBindOnUse` — Confirms the "Bind on Use" dialog when using a new item.

`ConfirmSummon` — Accepts a summon spell.

`DeclineResurrect` — Declines a resurrection spell.

`FlagTutorial` — Flags a tutorial step as already viewed so it doesn't appear again.

`GetDefaultLanguage` — Returns the default language that the character speaks.

`GetMirrorTimerInfo` — Returns information about a mirror timer bar.

`GetMirrorTimerProgress` — Returns the progress of a mirror timer (breath, exhaustion, and so on).

`GetPossessInfo` — Returns information about the spells in the possess bar.

`GetReleaseTimeRemaining` — Returns the amount of time left until the player is automatically released from their body.

GetSummonConfirmAreaName — Returns the destination area of a pending summon spell.

GetSummonConfirmSummoner — Returns the name of the player who has summoned you, so it can be displayed in the confirmation dialog.

GetSummonConfirmTimeLeft — Returns time left in seconds until summon cancels. Will return 0 with no summon dialog up.

InitWorldMapPing — Resets the position of the ping frame (WorldMapPing) on the WorldMap. There is no real reason to use this.

RegisterForSave — Registers a variable to be saved between sessions.

RegisterForSavePerCharacter — Registers a variable to be saved between sessions on a per-character basis.

RequestTimePlayed — Queries server for amount of time played on a given character.

ResurrectHasSickness — Determines if using a spirit healer to resurrect will give you resurrection sickness.

Screenshot — Takes a screenshot, displaying a message when done.

SetBagPortraitTexture — Sets texture to circular rendering of specified bag's icon.

SetInventoryPortraitTexture — Sets a portrait texture using an inventory item.

SetPortraitTexture — Sets a portrait texture based on a unit's model.

SetPortraitToTexture — Sets a portrait to a given texture.

TutorialsEnabled — Returns the status of the tutorials, if they are enabled or not.

Modified Clicks

GetModifiedClick — Returns the modifiers set (for example, CTRL-SHIFT) for the given modified click.

GetModifiedClickAction — Returns the token/name for a modified click action.

GetNumModifiedClickActions — Returns number of registered modified click actions.

IsModifiedClick — Determines if the modifiers specified in the click-type were held down while the button click occurred.

SetModifiedClick — Sets a modified click for a given action.

Money

AddTradeMoney — Adds the money currently on the cursor to the trade window.

CanWithdrawGuildBankMoney — Returns whether the player can withdraw money from the guild bank.

CursorHasMoney — Returns whether the cursor is currently holding money.

DepositGuildBankMoney — Deposits money into the guild bank.

DropCursorMoney — Drops the money currently held to the cursor, returning it to where it was taken from.

GetCoinIcon — Returns a texture path for an icon depending on the amount passed.

GetCursorMoney — Returns the amount of money currently held by the cursor, in copper.

GetMoney — Returns the amount of money the player currently possesses.

GetPlayerTradeMoney — Returns the amount of money the player deposited in an open trade window.

GetQuestLogRequiredMoney — Returns amount of money required for selected quest.

GetQuestLogRewardMoney — Returns amount of money rewarded on quest completion.

GetTargetTradeMoney — Returns the amount of money the target has placed in the trade window.

PickupGuildBankMoney — Withdraws money from the guild bank, placing it on cursor.

PickupPlayerMoney — Picks up money from player's inventory and holds it on the cursor.

SetSendMailMoney — Sets the amount of money to send with the next mail message.

SetTradeMoney — Sets the amount of money to trade in the trade window, in copper.

WithdrawGuildBankMoney — Attempts to withdraw an amount of money in coppers from the guild bank. Does nothing on failure.

Movement

AscendStop — Called when the player releases the binding for Jump.

DescendStop — Called when the player releases the sit/descend key (while swimming or flying).

FollowUnit — Follows a specified player.

JumpOrAscendStart — Called when the player presses the Jump key, which is also used to ascend when on a flying mount.

MouselookStart — Enables mouselook mode, where cursor movement rotates camera.

MoveAndSteerStart — Called when the player begins moving and steering at the same time (via the "Move and Steer" key binding).

MoveAndSteerStop — Called when the player exits move and steer mode.

MoveBackwardStart — Called when the player begins moving backward via the "Move Backward" key binding.

MoveBackwardStop — Called when the player stops moving backward.

MoveForwardStart — Called when the player begins moving forward via the "Move Forward" key binding.

MoveForwardStop — Called when the player stops moving forward.

PitchUpStop — Stops pitching the camera after PitchUpStart() has been called.

SitStandOrDescendStart — Called when the player sits, stands, or descends while swimming or flying.

StrafeLeftStart — Makes the character start strafing left.

StrafeLeftStop — Stops the character from strafing left.

StrafeRightStart — Begins strafing to the right.

StrafeRightStop — Stops the player from strafing right.

ToggleAutoRun — Turns on auto-run.

ToggleMouseMove — Toggles mouse movement.

ToggleRun — Toggles between running and walking.

TurnLeftStart — This function is called when the player begins turning via the "Turn Left" key binding.

TurnLeftStop — Called when the player stops turning left.

TurnOrActionStart — Called when the player right-clicks in the 3-D world.

TurnOrActionStop — Called when the player releases a right-click in the 3-D world.

TurnRightStart — Called when the player begins a right turn via "Turn Right" key binding.

TurnRightStop — Called when the player stops turning right.

NPC

CloseGossip — Closes the gossip window.

GetGossipActiveQuests — Returns a list of the available quests during a gossip interaction.

GetGossipAvailableQuests — Gets a list of all available quests of the active gossip frame.

GetGossipOptions — Returns the available gossip options for a given NPC.

GetGossipText — Returns text displayed when initially conversing with an NPC.

GetGreetingText — Returns the greeting text displayed for quest NPCs with multiple quests.

GetNumGossipActiveQuests — Returns the number of currently active quests in the gossip window.

GetNumGossipAvailableQuests — Returns the number of available quests in the gossip window.

GetNumGossipOptions — Returns the number of options in the current gossip frame.

SelectGossipOption — Selects an option in the NPC dialog (gossip) window.

Party

AcceptGroup — Accepts an invitation to a party.

ClearPartyAssignment — Clears a specified assignment (main tank, main assist) for the specified unit, or all raid members if not specified.

ConfirmReadyCheck — Sends your ready status to the raid leader when asked for a ready check.

ConvertToRaid — Converts a party to a raid. Does nothing if not in a party or not the party leader.

DeclineGroup — Declines a group invitation.

DoReadyCheck — Perform a ready check.

GetNumPartyMembers — Returns the number of players in your party.

GetPartyAssignment — Returns whether a player is assigned a specific role (maintank, mainassist).

GetPartyLeaderIndex — Returns the index of the current party leader.

GetPartyMember — Returns whether a given party index is exists in the player's party.

GetRealNumPartyMembers — Returns the number of members in the player's "real" non-battleground party.

InviteUnit — Invites a player or unit to the player's party.

IsPartyLeader — Returns whether a unit is the current party leader.

IsRealPartyLeader — Returns whether the player is the leader of his "real party".

LeaveParty — Call this function to leave the current party or raid.

PromoteToLeader — Promotes a player to party/raid leader.

QuestLogPushQuest — Shares currently selected quest with other party members.

SetPartyAssignment — Assigns a party role (maintank, mainassist) to a player or unit.

TargetNearestPartyMember — Targets the nearest party member.

UninviteUnit — Removes the specified unit from the current group.

UnitInParty — Returns whether a given unit is in the player's party.

UnitIsPartyLeader — Returns 1 if specified unit is the leader of the player's party.

UnitPlayerOrPetInParty — Tells you if the unit in question is in your party.

Pet

BuyStableSlot — Purchases the next available stable slot, without confirmation.

CastPetAction — Casts a pet action on a specific target.

CheckPetUntrainerDist — Returns whether the player is in range of a Pet Trainer.

ClickStablePet — Simulates a click on the given stable pet index.

ClosePetStables — Closes the Pet Stable UI window.

ConfirmPetUnlearn — Confirms unlearning a pet's skills.

CraftIsPetTraining — Returns whether open craft window is pet training window.

DisableSpellAutocast — Disables autocast for a given pet spell.

GetNextStableSlotCost — Returns the cost of the next available stable slot.

GetNumStablePets — Returns the number of stabled pets.

GetNumStableSlots — Returns the number of stable slots the player has purchased.

GetPetActionCooldown — Returns cooldown information about a given pet action slot.

GetPetActionInfo — Returns information about a pet action.

GetPetActionsUsable — Returns whether the pet's actions are usable.

GetPetExperience — Returns pet's current experience and amount required to level.

GetPetFoodTypes — Returns a list of strings enumerating the food types your current pet can eat.

GetPetHappiness — Returns information about the player's pet's happiness.

GetPetIcon — Returns the icon the player's pet would have if stabled.

GetPetLoyalty — Returns the loyalty level for the player's pet.

GetPetTimeRemaining — Returns the time till despawn of a temporary pet such as shadow friend and mages' water elemental.

GetPetTrainingPoints — Returns training point information for your pet.

GetSelectedStablePet — Returns the index of the currently selected stabled pet.

GetStablePetFoodTypes — Returns the types of food that a stabled pet will eat.

GetStablePetInfo — Returns information about a currently stabled pet.

HasPetSpells — Returns whether the player's current active pet has spells or not.

HasPetUI — Returns whether the client should show the pet UI.

IsPetAttackActive — Returns whether the pet's attack action is currently active.

PetAbandon — Releases the player's current pet back into freedom.

PetAggressiveMode — Sets your pet to aggressive mode.

PetAttack — Instructs your pet to attack your current target. Requires a keypress.

PetCanBeAbandoned — Returns whether the player's pet can be abandoned.

PetCanBeRenamed — Returns whether the currently controlled pet can be renamed.

PetDefensiveMode — Sets the pet into defensive mode, only attacking when the player or itself is attacked.

PetDismiss — Dismisses the currently controlled pet.

PetFollow — Sets the pet into "Follow" mode.

PetHasActionBar — Returns whether the player's current pet has an action bar.

PetPassiveMode — Sets the pet into passive mode.

PetRename — Renames the currently controlled pet.

PetStopAttack — Stops your pet from auto-attacking.

PetWait — Orders the player's pet into "Stay" mode.

PickupPetAction — Picks up pet action in given slot and places it under the cursor.

PickupStablePet — Picks up a stabled pet and holds it on the cursor.

SetPetStablePaperdoll — Sets given model to currently selected stabled pet's model.

StablePet — Attempts to put your current pet in the stable.

TogglePetAutocast — Toggles autocast for a pet action.

UnitPlayerOrPetInParty — Tells you if the unit in question is in your party.

UnstablePet — Unstables the pet in a given stable slot.

Petition

BuyGuildCharter — Purchases a guild charter with a given name.

BuyPetition — Purchases a petition (used for arena charters).

CanSignPetition — Returns whether the player can sign the currently offered petition.

ClosePetition — Close the petition window.

ClosePetitionVendor — Closes the petition vendor window.

GetGuildCharterCost — Returns the cost of a guild charter.

GetNumPetitionNames — Returns the number of people who have signed the open petition.

GetPetitionInfo — Returns information about the currently open petition.

GetPetitionItemInfo — Returns information about a given petition to create an arena team.

GetPetitionNameInfo — Returns the name of the player who has signed a given petition slot.

HasFilledPetition — Returns whether the player has a completed petition.

OfferPetition — Requests a signature from the targeted player.

RenamePetition — Renames the open petition.

SignPetition — Signs the currently offered petition.

Stuck — Calls the anti-unstuck routine.

TurnInArenaPetition — Turns in an arena petition.

TurnInGuildCharter — Turns in a completed guild charter.

TurnInPetition — Deprecated.

Player

AcceptDuel — Accepts a proposed duel.

AcceptResurrect — Accepts a pending resurrection spell.

AcceptXPLoss — Confirms the loss of 25 percent durability when resurrecting at the spirit healer, without confirmation.

CancelDuel — Cancels a proposed duel, or declines a duel that has been offered.

ConfirmBinder — Confirms a new hearthstone location.

Dismount — Dismounts the player.

DoEmote — Executes a preset emote, with optional target.

FollowUnit — Follows a specified player.

GetBindLocation — Returns the value of the hearthstone bind location.

GetComboPoints — Returns the number of combo points the player has.

GetCorpseRecoveryDelay — Returns the amount of time left until the player can recover his/her corpse.

GetCurrentTitle — Returns the currently selected player title.

GetDeathReleasePosition — Returns the location of the graveyard where your spirit will appear when it is released from your body.

GetNumTitles — Returns the number of available player titles.

GetResSicknessDuration — Returns the duration of resurrection sickness at the player's current level.

GetRestState — Returns the player's current rest state.

GetTimeToWellRested — Returns the amount of time until the player's character is well rested.

GetTitleName — Retrieves a title string from a title ID.

GetXPExhaustion — Returns the amount of rested experience the player has earned.

GuildLeave — Causes the player to leave their current guild without confirmation.

HasFullControl — Returns whether the player has full control over his/her characters.

HasKey — Returns whether the player currently has a key.

HasNewMail — Returns whether the player has new mail.

HasSoulstone — Returns whether the player has a soulstone resurrection available.

HasWandEquipped — Returns whether the player has a wand equipped.

IsFalling — Returns whether the player is falling.

IsFlyableArea — Returns whether the player's current location is a flyable area.

IsFlying — Returns whether the player is currently flying.

IsGuildLeader — Returns whether the current player is guild leader.

IsInGuild — Returns whether the player is in a guild.

IsInInstance — Returns whether the player is currently in an instance and, if so, what type.

IsInLFGQueue — Returns whether the player is currently in the LFG queue.

IsIndoors — Returns whether the player is currently indoors.

IsMounted — Returns whether your character is mounted.

IsOutOfBounds — Returns whether player is currently outside the bounds of the world.

IsOutdoors — Returns whether the player is currently outdoors.

IsRaidLeader — Returns whether the player is the leader of his/her current raid.

IsRaidOfficer — Returns whether the player is a Raid Officer or not.

IsRealPartyLeader — Returns whether the player is the leader of his/her "real party".

IsRealRaidLeader — Returns whether the player is the leader of his non-battle-ground raid party.

IsResting — Returns the player's resting status.

IsStealthed — Returns whether the player is currently stealthed.

IsSwimming — Returns whether the player is currently swimming.

IsTitleKnown — Returns whether a given title is known (available) to the player.

OffhandHasWeapon — Determines whether the player has a weapon in the off-hand slot.

OpeningCinematic — Displays the player's race's opening cinematic.

PlayerHasSpells — Returns whether the player has any spells. Effectively, always returns 1 for all characters.

RepopMe — Releases your spirit and sends you to the graveyard when dead.

ResurrectHasTimer — Returns whether the player must wait to accept the pending resurrection spell.

RetrieveCorpse — Confirms resurrection by returning to the player's corpse.

SetCurrentTitle — Sets the player's title.

ToggleSheath — Sheaths or unsheaths the player's handheld items.

UseSoulstone — Causes you to use a Warlock's Soulstone or a Shaman's Resurrection spell when you die.

Profiling

GetAddOnCPUUsage — Returns the amount of CPU time used by the given addon, in milliseconds.

GetAddOnMemoryUsage — Returns the amount of memory used by a given addon.

GetEventCPUUsage — Returns information about the CPU usage of events.

GetFrameCPUUsage — Gets CPU time used and the number of function calls for a frame and optionally its children

GetFramerate — Returns the current graphical frame rate.

GetFunctionCPUUsage — Returns CPU usage information about a function.

GetNetStats — Returns the game's network statistics.

GetScriptCPUUsage — Returns the total time used by the scripting subsystem.

ResetCPUUsage — Resets the current CPU usage statistics.

UpdateAddOnCPUUsage — Scans through profiling data and update per-addon statistics.

UpdateAddOnMemoryUsage — Updates the addon memory usage information.

PvP

GetHonorCurrency — Returns the number of honor points available to purchase rewards.

GetPVPDesired — Returns whether the player has manually toggled the PvP flag on.

GetPVPLifetimeStats — Returns lifetime honorable kills and the highest PvP rank the player has attained.

GetPVPRankInfo — Returns information about a given PvP rank index.

GetPVPRankProgress — Returns information about the player's PvP progress.

GetPVPSessionStats — Returns the PvP stats for the current session.

GetPVPTimer — Returns the amount of time until the player's PvP flag expires.

GetPVPYesterdayStats — Returns the player's PVP stats from yesterday.

GetZonePVPInfo — Returns PvP information about the current zone.

IsSubZonePVPPOI — Returns whether the current subzone is a PvP point of interest.

SetPVP — Enables/Disables PvP for the player.

TogglePVP — Toggles the player's PvP state.

UnitIsPVPFreeForAll — Returns whether the unit is flagged for free-for-all PvP, such as in a world arena.

UnitIsPVPSanctuary — Returns 1 if the unit in question is in PvP sanctuary, nil otherwise.

UnitPVPName — Returns the name of the unit with the selected PVvP title prepended to it.

UnitPVPRank — Returns a unit's PvP rank as a number.

Quest

AbandonQuest — Confirms abandoning a quest in your log.

AcceptQuest — Accepts the quest that is currently displayed.

AddQuestWatch — Adds a quest to the quest tracker.

CloseQuest — Closes the open quest frame.

CollapseQuestHeader — Collapses a header in the quest log.

CompleteQuest — Completes the current quest in a questgiver dialog.

ConfirmAcceptQuest — Confirms accepting a quest someone in your group is starting.

DeclineQuest — Declines a quest.

ExpandQuestHeader — Expands a quest header in the quest log.

GetAbandonQuestItems — Returns any items that would be destroyed by confirming abandoning the current quest.

GetAbandonQuestName — Returns the name of the quest being abandoned.

GetActiveTitle — Returns the name of an active quest in the QuestFrame.

GetAvailableTitle — Queries the title of the selected available quest at a quest NPC.

GetDailyQuestsCompleted — Returns the number of daily quests the player already completed today.

GetGossipActiveQuests — Returns a list of the available quests during a gossip interaction.

GetGossipAvailableQuests — Gets a list of all available quests of the active gossip frame.

GetGreetingText — Returns the greeting text displayed for quest NPCs with multiple quests.

GetMaxDailyQuests — Returns the maximum number of daily quests that can be completed each day.

GetNumActiveQuests — Returns the number of currently active quests by this player for this NPC.

GetNumAvailableQuests — Returns the number of available quests at the current NPC.

GetNumGossipActiveQuests — Returns the number of currently active quests in the gossip window.

GetNumGossipAvailableQuests — Returns the number of available quests in the gossip window.

GetNumQuestChoices — Returns the number of quest choices the current NPC has available.

GetNumQuestItems — Returns number of items necessary to complete active quest.

GetNumQuestLeaderBoards — Returns number of quest objectives for a given quest.

GetNumQuestLogChoices — Returns number of reward choices for the currently selected quest in the quest log.

GetNumQuestLogEntries — Returns the number of quest log entries.

GetNumQuestLogRewards — Returns the count of the rewards for a particular quest.

GetNumQuestRewards — Returns the number of quest rewards for completing a quest.

`GetNumQuestWatches` — Returns the number of quests currently marked for objective watching.

`GetObjectiveText` — Returns the objective text for the currently displayed quest.

`GetProgressText` — Returns the quest progress text given by an NPC.

`GetQuestBackgroundMaterial` — Returns the background material for a given quest.

`GetQuestGreenRange` — Returns the "green" range for quests.

`GetQuestIndexForTimer` — Returns the quest log quest index for the given timer in the QuestTimer frame.

`GetQuestIndexForWatch` — Returns index in the quest log of a currently watched quest.

`GetQuestItemInfo` — Returns basic information about the quest items for the quest currently shown in the gossip window.

`GetQuestItemLink` — Returns an item link for a quest item (reward or requirement).

`GetQuestLogChoiceInfo` — Returns information about an item available as a quest reward choice.

`GetQuestLogGroupNum` — Returns the suggested group size to complete the currently selected quest.

`GetQuestLogItemLink` — Returns the item link of a specific item in the quest log reward or progress frame.

`GetQuestLogLeaderBoard` — Returns information about tracked quest objectives.

`GetQuestLogPushable` — Determines if the currently selected quest can be shared with your party members.

`GetQuestLogQuestText` — Retrieves the text fields for the quest log details panel of the currently active quest.

`GetQuestLogRequiredMoney` — Returns the amount of money required for a selected quest.

`GetQuestLogRewardHonor` — Returns the amount of honor rewarded for completing the currently selected quest in the quest log.

`GetQuestLogRewardInfo` — Returns information about a quest reward.

`GetQuestLogRewardMoney` — Returns the amount of money rewarded on quest completion.

`GetQuestLogRewardSpell` — Returns information about a quest reward spell.

`GetQuestLogSelection` — Returns the index of the currently selected quest in the quest log.

`GetQuestLogTimeLeft` — Returns the amount of time left on the current timed quest.

`GetQuestLogTitle` — Returns information about a quest in your quest log.

`GetQuestMoneyToGet` — Returns the amount of money required for the currently displayed quest in the gossip frame.

`GetQuestResetTime` — Returns the amount of time until daily quests reset.

`GetQuestReward` — Selects an offered quest reward without confirmation.

`GetQuestText` — Returns the text for the currently displayed quest.

`GetQuestTimers` — Returns a list of the remaining time of all active quest timers.

GetRewardHonor — Returns the amount of reward honor for the displayed quest.

GetRewardMoney — Returns the amount of money rewarded for the quest that is currently being viewed.

GetRewardSpell — Returns information about a spell quest reward.

GetRewardText — Returns the reward text of the quest at the quest completion frame.

GetSuggestedGroupNum — Returns the size of the suggested group for the currently displayed quest.

GetTitleText — Returns the title text for the currently displayed quest.

IsActiveQuestTrivial — Returns whether an active quest in the QuestFrame is considered trivial.

IsAvailableQuestTrivial — Returns the trivial state for the quests available at a quest NPC.

IsCurrentQuestFailed — Queries the failed state for the currently selected quest.

IsQuestCompletable — Returns whether the currently viewed quest is able to be completed.

IsQuestWatched — Returns whether a given quest is currently being watched.

IsUnitOnQuest — Checks if a specified unit is on a quest from the player's quest log.

QuestChooseRewardError — Triggers the client's error when the player hasn't chosen a quest reward from the available choices.

QuestLogPushQuest — Shares currently selected quest with other party members.

RemoveQuestWatch — Stops tracking objectives for a quest in the quest log.

SelectActiveQuest — Selects an active quest in the QuestLog frame.

SelectAvailableQuest — Selects an available quest from the given NPC.

SelectGossipActiveQuest — Selects an active quest in the gossip dialog.

SelectGossipAvailableQuest — Selects the specified quest on the gossip frame for further processing.

SelectQuestLogEntry — Selects a quest from the quest log as the currently active quest to be shown in the details panel.

SetAbandonQuest — Marks the currently selected quest to be abandoned.

Raid

ClearPartyAssignment — Clears a specified assignment (main tank, main assist) for the specified unit, or all raid members if not specified.

ConfirmReadyCheck — Sends your ready status to the raid leader when asked for a ready check.

ConvertToRaid — Converts a party to a raid. Does nothing if not in a party or not the party leader.

DemoteAssistant — Demotes the given player from raid assistant status.

DoReadyCheck — Performs a ready check.

GetNumRaidMembers — Returns the number of members of the player's raid.

GetRaidRosterInfo — Returns information about a member of the player's raid.

GetRaidRosterSelection — Returns the index of the raid member currently selected by the mouse.

GetRaidTargetIndex — Returns the raid target on the given unit.

GetRealNumRaidMembers — Returns the number of members in the player's "real" non-battleground raid group.

GiveMasterLoot — Awards the given loot to the specified candidate.

InviteUnit — Invites a player or unit to the player's party.

IsRaidLeader — Returns whether the player is the leader of his current raid.

IsRaidOfficer — Returns whether the player is a Raid Officer or not.

IsRealPartyLeader — Returns whether the player is the leader of his/her "real party".

IsRealRaidLeader — Returns whether the player is the leader of his/her non-battleground raid party.

PromoteToAssistant — Promotes a player or unit to raid assistant.

RequestRaidInfo — Requests raid information from the server.

SetPartyAssignment — Assigns a party role (maintank, mainassist) to a player or unit.

SetRaidRosterSelection — Sets the currently selected raid roster unit.

SetRaidSubgroup — Moves a raid member to a nonfull raid subgroup.

SetRaidTarget — Sets a raid target marker on the given unit.

SwapRaidSubgroup — Swaps two players between groups in the raid.

UninviteUnit — Removes the specified unit from the current group.

UnitInRaid — Returns whether the unit specified is in your raid group.

UnitIsPartyLeader — Returns 1 if the specified unit is the leader of the player's party.

UnitIsRaidOfficer — Returns whether the given unit is an officer in the raid.

UnitPlayerOrPetInRaid — Returns whether a given unit ID is a member of a player's raid.

Skill

AbandonSkill — Confirms abandoning a skill.

CollapseSkillHeader — Collapses a skill header in the Skills window.

ExpandSkillHeader — Expands a skill header in the Skills window.

GetNumSkillLines — Returns the number of skills to be listed in the Skills window.

GetSelectedSkill — Returns the currently selected skill index, as listed in Skills window.

GetSkillLineInfo — Returns information about a given skill line.

SetSelectedSkill — Sets the currently selected skill in the Skills window.

Social

AddFriend — Adds a player or unit to the friends list.

AddIgnore — Adds a player or unit to the ignore list.

AddOrDelIgnore — Adds or removes a player from the ignore list.

DelIgnore — Removes a player from your ignore list.

GetFriendInfo — Returns information about someone on the player's friends list.

GetIgnoreName — Returns the name of the specified ignored person.

GetNumFriends — Returns the number of friends on the player's friends list.

GetNumIgnores — Returns the number of people currently on the player's ignore list.

GetNumWhoResults — Returns the number of results from a who request.

GetSelectedFriend — Returns the friend index of the friend you have selected.

GetSelectedIgnore — Returns the currently selected index in the ignore listing.

GetWhoInfo — Returns information about a specific index of a who request's results.

RemoveFriend — Removes a friend from your friends list.

SendWho — Sends a who request to the server.

SetSelectedFriend — Sets the selection in the friends list.

SetSelectedIgnore — Sets the currently selected ignore entry.

SetWhoToUI — Sets a flag that determines how results of a SendWho() request are delivered.

ShowFriends — Requests updated friends information from the server.

SortWho — Sets the sort method for the who list.

Socket

AcceptSockets — Accepts the current socketed gems without confirmation.

ClickSocketButton — Picks up or places a gem in the Item Socketing UI.

CloseSocketInfo — Closes the socket frame.

GetExistingSocketInfo — Returns information about the jewel in a given socket for the item in the socketing UI.

GetExistingSocketLink — Returns an item link for a socketed gem.

GetItemGem — Returns the name and link for a gem in a specific item socket.

GetNewSocketInfo — Returns information about a gem that would be socketed.

GetNewSocketLink — Returns an item link for a gem to be socketed.

GetNumSockets — Returns the number of sockets in the open item.

GetSocketItemInfo — Returns information about an item currently open in the socketing UI.

GetSocketTypes — Returns the color of a given gem socket in the socketing UI.

SocketContainerItem — Opens the Gem Socketing UI if the given container slot has a socketable item.

SocketInventoryItem — Opens the socketing UI for the given inventory item, if it has sockets.

Sound

PlayMusic — Plays a music file.

PlaySound — Plays one of the built-in interface sounds (found in Sound\interface within the WoW MPQ files).

PlaySoundFile — Plays a specified sound file.

Sound_GetInputDriverNameByIndex — Returns the name of a given input driver.

Sound_GetNumInputDrivers — Returns number of sound input drivers in the system.

Sound_GetNumOutputDrivers — Returns the number of sound output drivers.

Sound_GetOutputDriverNameByIndex — Returns the name of an output driver.

Sound_RestartSoundEngine — Restarts the sound engine.

StopMusic — Immediately stops the currently played in-game music.

VoiceEnumerateCaptureDevices — Returns the name of a voice capture device.

VoiceEnumerateOutputDevices — Returns the name of a given voice output device.

VoiceGetCurrentCaptureDevice — Returns index of current voice capture device.

VoiceGetCurrentOutputDevice — Returns index of current voice output device.

VoiceSelectCaptureDevice — Selects a voice capture device.

VoiceSelectOutputDevice — Sets the voice chat output device.

Spell

CastSpell — Casts a spell.

CastSpellByName — Casts a spell by name.

ClickSpellByName — Casts a spell, either on your current target or the given target.

CursorHasSpell — Returns whether the cursor currently holds a spell.

DisableSpellAutocast — Disables autocast for a given pet spell.

EnableSpellAutocast — Enables autocast for a given pet spell.

GetItemSpell — Returns information about the spell cast when using a given item.

GetQuestLogRewardSpell — Returns information about a quest reward spell.

GetRewardSpell — Returns information about a spell quest reward.

GetSpellAutocast — Returns whether a spell can be autocasted and is currently being autocast.

GetSpellCooldown — Returns cooldown information about a given spell.

GetSpellCount — Returns the number of times a spell with a reagent can be cast.

GetSpellName — Returns the name and subtext of a given spell ID.

GetSpellTexture — Returns the texture path for a given spell.

HasPetSpells — Returns whether the player's current active pet has spells or not.

IsAttackSpell — Returns whether a given spell is an attack spell.

IsAutoRepeatSpell — Returns whether the given spell is an auto-repeat spell.

IsConsumableSpell — Returns whether a spell requires a consumable reagent.

IsCurrentSpell — Returns whether a given spell is currently being cast or awaiting targeting.

IsHarmfulSpell — Returns whether a given spell is harmful.

IsHelpfulSpell — Returns whether a given spell is helpful.

IsPassiveSpell — Returns whether a given spell is passive (that is, cannot be cast).

IsSelectedSpell — Returns whether a specific spell is currently selected in the spellbook.

IsSpellInRange — Returns whether a spell is in range of a given unit.

IsUsableSpell — Returns whether a given spell is usable or cannot be used due to lack of mana.

PickupSpell — Picks up a spell from the spellbook, placing it on the cursor.

SpellCanTargetItem — Returns whether the spell on the cursor can target an item or not.

SpellCanTargetUnit — Returns whether the spell currently awaiting a target can target a given unit.

SpellHasRange — Returns whether a given spell has a range restriction.

SpellIsTargeting — Returns whether there is a spell currently awaiting a target.

SpellStopCasting — Stops casting or targeting the current spell.

SpellStopTargeting — Cancels the spell currently waiting for targeting.

SpellTargetItem — Targets an item with the spell currently awaiting targeting.

SpellTargetUnit — Targets a unit with the spell currently awaiting a target.

ToggleSpellAutocast — Toggles a spellbook spell as autocast.

UnitCastingInfo — Returns information about the spell a unit is casting.

UpdateSpells — Updates the spells in the player's spellbook.

Stance

CancelShapeshiftForm — Cancels the current shapeshift form.

CastShapeshiftForm — Casts a shapeshift form by index.

GetNumShapeshiftForms — Returns number of available shapeshift forms for a player.

GetShapeshiftForm — Returns the current shapeshift form index.

GetShapeshiftFormCooldown — Returns cooldown information about a given shapeshift slot.

GetShapeshiftFormInfo — Returns information about a shapeshift form.

Stats

GetAttackPowerForStat — Calculates the amount of attack power that your current character would gain from having the given value for the specified stat.

GetBlockChance — Returns your block percentage.

GetCombatRating — Returns the amount of rating a player has for a given rating stat.

GetCombatRatingBonus — Returns the percentage bonus for a given combat rating.

GetCritChance — Returns the player's percent melee critical strike chance.

GetCritChanceFromAgility — Returns the amount of critical strike chance given by the agility stat.

GetDamageBonusStat — Returns the index of the stat that provides the most (not necessarily the only) bonus melee damage when increased for the player's class. Currently this is either 1 (Strength) or 2 (Agility).

GetDodgeChance — Returns the amount of dodge change the player has, as a percentage.

GetExpertise — Returns the amount of expertise the player currently has.

GetExpertisePercent — Returns the reduced chance to be dodged or parried as a result of the expertise rating.

GetManaRegen — Returns the mana regeneration statistics for the player. Return values are in mana per second.

GetParryChance — Returns the player's percentage parry chance.

GetRangedCritChance — Returns the player's ranged critical strike chance.

GetShieldBlock — Returns the amount of damage stopped by a successful block.

GetSpellBonusDamage — Returns the spell damage bonus for a given school.

GetSpellBonusHealing — Queries player's bonus healing from equipment.

GetSpellCritChance — Returns the amount of crit chance for a given spell school.

GetSpellCritChanceFromIntellect — Returns the percent chance to crit granted by Intellect.

GetSpellPenetration — Returns the amount of spell penetration the player currently has.

GetUnitHealthModifier — Returns the health modifier for a pet. Used to modify the amount of health a pet gains from +stamina.

GetUnitHealthRegenRateFromSpirit — Returns the amount of health gained per second while not in combat, as a result of spirit.

GetUnitManaRegenRateFromSpirit — Returns the mana regeneration rate per second the unit has from the spirit stat.

GetUnitPowerModifier — Returns the power modifier for a pet. Used to modify the amount of mana a pet gains from +intellect.

UnitArmor — Returns the current amount of armor and its breakdown between base armor and positive and negative additions due to buffs and debuffs.

UnitAttackBothHands — Returns information about a unit's weapon skill.

UnitAttackPower — Returns the unit's melee attack power and modifiers.

UnitAttackSpeed — Returns the mainhand and offhand attack speed of the given unit.

UnitDamage — Unit damage returns information about your current damage stats.

UnitDefense — Returns the units defense statistics.

UnitHealth — Returns the amount of health the unit has.

UnitHealthMax — Returns the maximum health value for a given unit.

UnitMana — Returns the current mana points of the given unit.

UnitManaMax — Returns the maximum mana or other power that a given unit can have.

UnitRangedAttack — Returns a unit's ranged weapon skill.

UnitRangedAttackPower — Returns a unit's ranged attack power and bonuses.

UnitRangedDamage — Returns information about a unit's range attack damage and speed.

UnitResistance — Returns resistance information for a specific resistance for a unit ID.

UnitStat — Returns information about a given character statistic (intellect, stamina, and so on).

Talent

CheckTalentMasterDist — Returns whether the player is in range of a talent trainer.

ConfirmTalentWipe — Confirms the player unlearning all talents.

GetNumTalentTabs — Returns the number of talent tabs for the player, or the currently inspected unit.

GetNumTalents — Returns the number of talent spell options in a given tab.

GetTalentInfo — Returns information about the talents of the player, or the currently inspected player.

GetTalentPrereqs — Returns the prerequisites for a given talent.

GetTalentTabInfo — Returns information about the specified talent tree from either the player or the unit that is being inspected.

IsTalentTrainer — Always returns 1.

LearnTalent — Learns the selected talent in the selected talent tree.

Target

ClearFocus — Clears the player's focus unit.

ClearTarget — Clears the player's current target.

FocusUnit — Sets the given unit as your focus target. Passing nil will clear your focus. Can only be called by the blizzard UI.

SpellCanTargetUnit — Returns whether the spell currently awaiting a target can target a given unit.

SpellTargetUnit — Targets a unit with the spell currently awaiting a target.

TargetLastEnemy — Retargets the last targeted enemy unit.

TargetLastFriend — Retargets the last targeted friend.

TargetLastTarget — Targets the last targeted unit.

TargetNearestEnemy — Targets the nearest enemy unit.

TargetNearestFriend — Targets the nearest friendly unit.

TargetNearestPartyMember — Targets the nearest party member.

TargetNearestRaidMember — Targets the nearest raid member.

TargetUnit — Sets the given unit as your target. Passing nil will remove your target. Can only be called from the blizzard UI.

Taxi

CloseTaxiMap — Closes the taxi (flight master) map.

GetNumRoutes — Returns the number of routes available from a given taxi node.

GetTaxiBenchmarkMode — Returns whether taxi benchmark mode is enabled.

NumTaxiNodes — Returns the current number of taxi nodes defined.

SetTaxiBenchmarkMode — Turns on flight path "benchmark" mode.

SetTaxiMap — Sets a texture to the TaxiMap texture.

TakeTaxiNode — Take the indicated flight path. This function is used when clicking a flight path from a flight master.

TaxiGetDestX — Returns x coordinate of destination taxi node, relative to taxi frame.

TaxiGetDestY — Returns y coordinate of destination taxi node, relative to taxi frame.

TaxiGetSrcX — Returns x coordinate of source taxi node, relative to taxi frame.

TaxiGetSrcY — Returns y coordinate of source taxi node, relative to taxi frame.

TaxiNodeCost — Returns the cost to fly to a given taxi node.

TaxiNodeGetType — Returns the type of the taxi node slot requested.

TaxiNodeName — Returns the name of a given taxi node slot.

TaxiNodePosition — Returns the position of a taxi node in the taxi window.

TaxiNodeSetCurrent — Sets the current flight path node to a specific index.

UnitOnTaxi — Returns whether a given unit is on a taxi.

Tracking

GetNumTrackingTypes — Returns the number of available tracking types.

GetTrackingInfo — Returns information about a given tracking option.

GetTrackingTexture — Returns the texture of the active tracking buff, if one is active.

SetTracking — Set minimap tracking to the given index between 1 and GetNumTrackingTypes(). Pass nil to track nothing.

Trade

AcceptTrade — Accepts a proposed trade.

AddTradeMoney — Adds the money currently on the cursor to the trade window.

BeginTrade — Accept a trade request from someone.

CancelTrade — Cancels an active trade.

CancelTradeAccept — Cancels trade currently pending accepting by the other party.

ClickTargetTradeButton — Simulates clicking on a specific slot in the target trade window.

ClickTradeButton — Clicks a specific trade window button.

CloseTrade — Closes the trade window.

GetPlayerTradeMoney — Returns the amount of money the player deposited in an open trade window.

GetTargetTradeMoney — Returns the amount of money the target has placed in the trade window.

GetTradePlayerItemLink — Returns a link for an item offered by the player in the trade window.

GetTradeTargetItemInfo — Returns information about an item in the trade window.

GetTradeTargetItemLink — Returns an item link for an item being offered by the target in a trade.

InitiateTrade — Initiates a trade with a given unit.

ReplaceTradeEnchant — Confirms the replacement of an existing enchant being applied in the trade window.

SetTradeMoney — Sets the amount of money to trade in the trade window, in copper.

Tradeskill

CloseTradeSkill — Closes the tradeskill window, if it is open.

CollapseTradeSkillSubClass — Collapses a specified index in the TradeSkill UI.

DoTradeSkill — Casts a tradeskill, optionally multiple times.

ExpandTradeSkillSubClass — Expands a tradeskill subclass in the tradeskill window.

GetFirstTradeSkill — Returns the index of the first tradeskill recipe, as opposed to tradeskill headers.

GetNumTradeSkills — Returns the number of available tradeskill items and headers.

GetTradeSkillCooldown — Returns the cooldown for a given tradeskill.

GetTradeSkillIcon — Returns the inventory icon for the tradeskill item at the index being queried.

GetTradeSkillInfo — Returns information about the recipes of the currently selected tradeskill.

GetTradeSkillInvSlotFilter — Returns whether a given tradeskill inventory slot filter is enabled.

GetTradeSkillInvSlots — Returns a list of inventory slots for which the current tradeskill can craft.

GetTradeSkillItemLevelFilter — Returns the current values for the tradeskill item level filter.

GetTradeSkillItemLink — Returns an item link for the given tradeskill item.

GetTradeSkillItemNameFilter — Returns the text of the tradeskill item name filter.

GetTradeSkillItemStats — Returns information about a given tradeskill item.

GetTradeSkillLine — Returns level information about the active tradeskill line.

GetTradeSkillNumMade — Returns the number of items possibly created when crafting a tradeskill recipe.

GetTradeSkillNumReagents — Returns the number of reagents required for a tradeskill recipe.

GetTradeSkillReagentInfo — Returns information about a tradeskill recipe's reagent.

GetTradeSkillReagentItemLink — Returns the item link for a tradeskill's reagent.

GetTradeSkillRecipeLink — Returns an item link for a tradeskill recipe.

GetTradeSkillSelectionIndex — Returns the index of the currently selected line in the tradeskill window.

GetTradeSkillSubClassFilter — Returns whether a given tradeskill filter is enabled.

GetTradeSkillSubClasses — Returns a list of tradeskill subclasses.

GetTradeSkillTools — Returns required tradeskill tools for a given tradeskill recipe.

GetTradeskillRepeatCount — Returns the number of times the current tradeskill recipe will repeat.

IsTradeskillTrainer — Returns whether the currently open training window is a tradeskill trainer.

IsTrainerServiceTradeSkill — Returns whether the given trainer service is a tradeskill recipe.

SelectTradeSkill — Sets the currently selected tradeskill item.

SetTradeSkillInvSlotFilter — Enables or disables an inventory slot filter in the tradeskill window.

SetTradeSkillItemLevelFilter — Filters the tradeskill window's list by required level of produced items.

SetTradeSkillItemNameFilter — Sets the tradeskill item name filter search string.

SetTradeSkillSubClassFilter — Enables or disables given tradeskill subclass filter.

StopTradeSkillRepeat — Cancels a repeating tradeskill.

TradeSkillOnlyShowMakeable — Enables or disables the "Have Materials" tradeskill filter.

Trainer

BuyTrainerService — Purchases a service available at a trainer.

CheckPetUntrainerDist — Returns whether the player is in range of a pet trainer.

CheckTalentMasterDist — Returns whether the player is in range of a talent trainer.

CloseTrainer — Closes the trainer window.

CollapseTrainerSkillLine — Collapses the given skill line in the class trainer frame.

ExpandTrainerSkillLine — Expands a skill line in the trainer window.

GetNumTrainerServices — Returns the number of available trainer services.

GetTrainerGreetingText — Returns greeting text for currently (or last) open trainer.

GetTrainerSelectionIndex — Returns currently selected index in trainer window.

GetTrainerServiceAbilityReq — Retrieves information about abilities that are required to train a specific skill.

GetTrainerServiceCost — Returns the cost of a given trainer service.

GetTrainerServiceDescription — Returns the description of a given trainer service (spell, tradeskill, and so on).

GetTrainerServiceIcon — Returns the icon for a given trainer service (spell or skill).

GetTrainerServiceInfo — Returns information about a service in the trainer window.

GetTrainerServiceItemLink — Returns an item link for a given trainer service item.

GetTrainerServiceLevelReq — Returns the level requirement for a trainer service.

GetTrainerServiceNumAbilityReq — Returns the number of ability requirements to learn a given spell.

GetTrainerServiceSkillLine — Returns the name of the given skill line.

GetTrainerServiceSkillReq — Returns skill requirement for a given trainer service.

GetTrainerServiceTypeFilter — Queries the enabled state of a filter in the trainer window.

GetTrainerSkillLineFilter — Returns whether a trainer skill line filter is enabled.

GetTrainerSkillLines — Returns the spell schools available at a given trainer.

IsTalentTrainer — Always returns 1.

IsTrainerServiceLearnSpell — Returns whether the given trainer service teaches a spell.

IsTrainerServiceSkillStep — Returns whether the given trainer service is a skill step, rather than a recipe.

IsTrainerServiceTradeSkill — Returns whether the given trainer service is a tradeskill recipe.

OpenTrainer — Closes the trainer window if it is open, otherwise appears to do nothing.

SelectTrainerService — Selects the given trainer service in the class trainer frame.

SetTrainerServiceTypeFilter — Sets the state of a filter in the trainer window.

SetTrainerSkillLineFilter — Sets the state of a skill line filter in the trainer UI.

UI

CheckReadyCheckTime — Unknown, called by UIParent's OnUpdate handler.

ClearTutorials — Clears any already displayed tutorials so they are displayed again.

ConsoleExec — Runs a console command.

GetGameTime — Returns the current in-game time.

GetNetStats — Returns the game's network statistics.

GetNumSpellTabs — Returns the number of spell tabs the player has available.

GetNumWorldStateUI — Returns the number of world state lines (Arathi Basin Points, Black Morass Portals, and so on).

GetSpellTabInfo — Returns information about a tab in the spellbook.

GetWorldStateUIInfo — Returns information about a WorldState UI element.

HideFriendNameplates — Hides friendly nameplates.

HideNameplates — Hides nameplates for hostile units.

InCinematic — Returns whether the character is viewing a cinematic.

InCombatLockdown — Queries the game client to see if the user interface is currently in protected lockdown mode.

NotWhileDeadError — Fires a UI_ERROR_MESSAGE event, with the argument ERR_PLAYER_DEAD.

ReloadUI — Reloads the user interface.

ResetTutorials — Resets tutorials from the beginning.

SetUIVisibility — Changes whether UI rendered models are shown.

SetupFullscreenScale — Sizes a frame to take up the entire screen. Sizes the frames differently depending on resolution. Never returns a meaningful value.

ShowCloak — Enables or disables the showing of the cloak on the player's character.

ShowFriendNameplates — Enables friendly character nameplates.

ShowHelm — Enables or disables the display of the player's helm.

ShowMiniWorldMapArrowFrame — Shows or hides battlefield minimap's player arrow.

ShowNameplates — Turns on showing of nameplates for hostile units.

ShowingCloak — Returns whether the Show Cloak setting is currently checked.

ShowingHelm — Returns whether the helm is currently being shown.

StopCinematic — Stops a cinematic that is currently playing.

Unit

AssistUnit — Assists a player by unit or name.

CanInspect — Returns if the given unit can be inspected.

CheckInteractDistance — Returns whether the player is close enough to interact with a unit.

DropItemOnUnit — Drops the currently held item on a specific unit.

GetBattlefieldPosition — Returns information on the queried player's position in a battleground.

GetMuteStatus — Returns whether the given player or unit ID is muted.

GetUnitHealthModifier — Returns the health modifier for a pet. Used to modify the amount of health a pet gains from +stamina.

GetUnitManaRegenRateFromSpirit — Returns the mana regeneration rate per second the unit has from the spirit stat.

GetUnitPowerModifier — Returns the power modifier for a pet. Used to modify the amount of mana a pet gains from +intellect.

IsIgnored — Returns whether you are ignoring a specific unit.

IsIgnoredOrMuted — Returns a true value if the queried unit is currently ignored or muted by the player.

IsMuted — Returns the mute status for a given player.

`IsUnitOnQuest` — Checks if a specified unit is on a quest from the player's quest log.

`PromoteToAssistant` — Promotes a player or unit to raid assistant.

`StartDuel` — Challenges another player to a duel.

`UnitAffectingCombat` — Returns whether a unit is currently in combat.

`UnitArmor` — Returns the current amount of armor and its breakdown between base armor and positive and negative additions due to buffs and debuffs.

`UnitAttackBothHands` — Returns information about a unit's weapon skill.

`UnitAttackPower` — Returns the unit's melee attack power and modifiers.

`UnitAttackSpeed` — Returns the mainhand and offhand attack speed of the given unit.

`UnitBuff` — Returns information about a buff on a given unit or player.

`UnitCanAssist` — Returns whether one unit can assist another.

`UnitCanAttack` — Returns whether one unit can attack another unit.

`UnitCanCooperate` — Returns whether two given units can cooperate with each other.

`UnitCastingInfo` — Returns information about the spell a unit is casting.

`UnitChannelInfo` — Returns information about the spell a unit is channeling.

`UnitCharacterPoints` — Returns the number of unused talent points and profession slots for the given unit.

`UnitClass` — Queries a unit's class.

`UnitClassification` — Returns a classification indicator for the queried unit.

`UnitCreatureFamily` — Returns the creature family of the given unit.

`UnitCreatureType` — Returns the creature type of a given unit.

`UnitDamage` — Returns information about your current damage stats.

`UnitDebuff` — Returns information about a debuff on a given unit.

`UnitDefense` — Returns the units defense statistics.

`UnitExists` — Returns whether a given unit exists.

`UnitFactionGroup` — Gives information about the unit's faction in English and the game locale. Returns `nil` when not available.

`UnitHasRelicSlot` — Returns whether the queried unit has a relic slot.

`UnitHealth` — Returns the amount of health the unit has.

`UnitHealthMax` — Returns the maximum health value for a given unit.

`UnitInBattleground` — Returns whether a unit is in the player's battleground.

`UnitInParty` — Returns whether a given unit is in the player's party.

`UnitInRaid` — Returns whether the unit specified is in your raid group.

`UnitIsAFK` — Query a unit's AFK status.

`UnitIsCharmed` — Returns whether a unit or player is currently charmed.

`UnitIsConnected` — Returns whether a given unit or player is connected (that is, not offline).

`UnitIsCorpse` — Returns whether the given unit is a corpse.

`UnitIsDND` — Returns whether a unit is flagged DND.

`UnitIsDead` — Returns whether the given unit is dead.

`UnitIsDeadOrGhost` — Returns whether the given player is either dead or a ghost.

`UnitIsEnemy` — Returns `true` or `false` depending on whether the specified units are enemies.

`UnitIsFeignDeath` — Returns whether a given unit is feigning death.

`UnitIsFriend` — Returns whether two units are friendly.

`UnitIsGhost` — Returns whether a unit or player is currently a ghost.

`UnitIsInMyGuild` — Returns whether a given unit or player is in the player's guild.

`UnitIsPVP` — Returns whether a unit is PvP enabled.

`UnitIsPVPFreeForAll` — Returns whether the unit is flagged for free-for-all PvP, such as in a world arena.

`UnitIsPVPSanctuary` — Returns 1 if unit in question is in PvP sanctuary, `nil` otherwise.

`UnitIsPartyLeader` — Returns 1 if the specified unit is the leader of the player's party.

`UnitIsPlayer` — Returns whether a given unit is the player's unit.

`UnitIsPlusMob` — Returns whether the given unit is an elite mob.

`UnitIsPossessed` — Returns whether the given unit is possessed (through mind control, for example).

`UnitIsRaidOfficer` — Returns whether the given unit is an officer in the raid.

`UnitIsSameServer` — Returns whether two units are from the same server.

`UnitIsSilenced` — Returns whether a player is silenced on a specified voice channel.

`UnitIsTalking` — Returns 1 if the unit is currently talking, or `nil` otherwise.

`UnitIsTapped` — Returns whether a unit is tapped by anyone (not necessarily the player).

`UnitIsTappedByPlayer` — Returns whether a unit is tapped by the player or his group.

`UnitIsTrivial` — Returns whether the given unit is trivial.

`UnitIsUnit` — Returns whether two unit IDs refer to the same actual character.

`UnitIsVisible` — Returns whether a given unit is visible (in the player's area of interest).

`UnitLevel` — Returns the level of a given unit.

`UnitMana` — Returns the current mana points of the given unit.

`UnitManaMax` — Returns the maximum mana or other power that a given unit can have.

`UnitName` — Returns the name of a given unit.

`UnitOnTaxi` — Returns whether a given unit is on a taxi.

`UnitPVPName` — Returns the name of the unit with the selected PvP title prepended to it.

`UnitPVPRank` — Returns a unit's PvP rank as a number.

`UnitPlayerControlled` — Returns whether a given unit is a player-controlled character.

`UnitPlayerOrPetInParty` — Tells you if the unit in question is in your party.

`UnitPlayerOrPetInRaid` — Returns whether a given unit ID is a member of the player's raid.

`UnitPowerType` — Returns the power type (energy, mana, rage) of the given unit.

`UnitRace` — Retrieves the unit's race.

`UnitRangedAttack` — Returns a unit's ranged weapon skill.

`UnitRangedAttackPower` — Returns a unit's ranged attack power and bonuses.

`UnitRangedDamage` — Returns information about a unit's range attack damage and speed.

`UnitReaction` — Returns the reaction of one unit with regards to another, as a number.

`UnitResistance` — Returns resistance information for a specific resistance for a unit ID. Returns `0,0,0,0` for nonexistent or disallowed units.

`UnitSex` — Returns the gender of the given unit or player.

`UnitStat` — Returns information about a given character statistic (intellect, stamina, and so on).

`UnitXP` — Returns the amount of experience that the unit currently has.

`UnitXPMax` — Returns the total amount of XP required to get to the next level.

Utility

`CreateFont` — Creates a new font object.

`CreateFrame` — Creates a new frame object dynamically.

`EnumerateFrames` — Returns the next frame following the frame passed, or `nil` if no more frames exist.

`GetCurrentKeyBoardFocus` — Returns the frame that currently has the keyboard focus.

`GetFramesRegisteredForEvent` — Returns all frames registered for a given event.

`GetMouseButtonClicked` — Returns which mouse button triggered the current click.

`GetMouseButtonName` — Converts a mouse button number to a mouse button name.

`GetMouseFocus` — Returns the frame that is currently under the mouse, and has mouse input enabled.

`GetNumFrames` — Returns the number of created frame objects (and derivatives).

`GetRealmName` — Returns the name of the player's realm (server name).

`GetText` — Returns a formatted string from GlobalStrings.

`GetTime` — Returns a number representing the current time, with millisecond precision.

`IsLoggedIn` — Returns whether the `PLAYER_LOGIN` event has already fired.

`IsMouseButtonDown` — Returns whether the given mouse button is held down.

`RandomRoll` — Rolls a random number between min and max.

`RunScript` — Runs a string as a Lua script.

`gcinfo` — Returns the total addon memory usage in kilobytes.

`getglobal` — Returns a global variable with a given name.

`hooksecurefunc` — Adds a function to be called after the original secure function.

`issecure` — Returns whether the current execution path is secure.

`issecurevariable` — Returns whether a variable is secure and, if not, what addon tainted the variable.

`setglobal` — Sets a global variable to a specified value.

`strjoin` — Joins a list of strings together.

`strsplit` — Splits a string based on another separator string.

`strtrim` — Trims leading and trailing whitespace from a string.

Video

GetBaseMip — Returns the level of texture resolution rendered by the client.

GetCurrentMultisampleFormat — Returns the index of the currently selected multisample format.

GetCurrentResolution — Returns the index of the current resolution.

GetFarclip — Returns the value of the "Terrain Distance" video option.

GetFramerate — Returns the current graphical frame rate.

GetGamma — Returns the gamma value for the game client.

GetMultisampleFormats — Returns the available multisample formats.

GetRefreshRates — Returns a list of all available refresh rates for the current system.

GetScreenHeight — Returns the current screen height. This value is affected by scale. To get the true screen height in pixels, divide by GetScreenHeightScale().

GetScreenResolutions — Returns the available screen resolutions.

GetScreenWidth — Queries the width of the screen.

GetTerrainMip — Returns value of "Terrain Detail Level" slider in video options.

GetVideoCaps — Returns information about the video subsystem.

GetWaterDetail — Returns the current value of the water detail option.

GetWorldDetail — Returns the level of rendered world detail in the client.

RestartGx — Restart the client's graphic subsystem.

RestoreVideoDefaults — Restores all video settings to default values and reloads the user interface.

SetBaseMip — Sets the level of texture resolution rendered by the client.

SetFarclip — Sets the value of the "Terrain Distance" slider in the video options.

SetGamma — Sets the Gamma value for the video system.

SetMultisampleFormat — Sets the client's multisampling format.

SetScreenResolution — Sets the screen resolution to a specified value.

SetTerrainMip — Sets value of "Terrain Detail Level" slider in video options.

SetWaterDetail — Sets the value for the water details display.

SetWorldDetail — Sets the detail level of the world environment.

Voice

AddMute — Mutes a player in voice chat.

AddOrDelMute — Adds or removes a player/unit from the voice mute list.

ChannelSilenceAll — Removes both voice and chat permissions for the given player in the specified channel.

ChannelUnmute — Unmutes the specified player on that channel.

ChannelVoiceOff — Disables voice chat in the given channel.

ChannelVoiceOn — Enables voice chat in the given channel.

DelMute — Removes a voice mute for a given player.

DisplayChannelVoiceOff — Disables voice chat in a given channel.

DisplayChannelVoiceOn — Enables voice chat in a given channel.

`GetActiveVoiceChannel` — Returns the currently active voice channel.

`GetMuteName` — Gets the name of a character on the player's mute list.

`GetMuteStatus` — Returns whether the given player or unit ID is muted.

`GetNumMutes` — Returns the number of characters on the player's mute list.

`GetNumVoiceSessionMembersBy↩SessionID` — Returns the number of members in a voice channel.

`GetNumVoiceSessions` — Returns the number of voice sessions the player is in.

`GetSelectedMute` — Returns the index of the selected muted player in the muted list.

`GetVoiceCurrentSessionID` — Returns an identifier for your current voice session.

`GetVoiceSessionInfo` — Returns information about a given voice session.

`GetVoiceSessionMemberInfoBy↩SessionID` — Returns information about a member of a given voice session.

`GetVoiceStatus` — Returns the voice enabled status of the queried player.

`IsIgnoredOrMuted` — Returns a true value if the queried unit is currently ignored or muted by the player.

`IsMuted` — Returns the mute status for a given player.

`IsSilenced` — Returns whether the given unit is silenced for voice chat on a channel.

`IsVoiceChatAllowed` — Returns whether the current client/account is allowed to use the voice chat feature.

`IsVoiceChatEnabled` — Returns whether the voice chat system is enabled.

`SetActiveVoiceChannel` — Sets the currently active voice channel.

`SetActiveVoiceChannelBySessionID` — Sets the currently active voice chat channel.

`SetSelectedMute` — Selects the given muted player for use by other functions.

`UnitIsSilenced` — Returns whether player is silenced on a specified voice channel.

`VoiceChat_GetCurrentMicrophone↩SignalLevel` — Returns the current volume level of the microphone signal.

`VoiceChat_IsPlayingLoopbackSound` — Returns whether the loopsound sound is currently being played.

`VoiceChat_IsRecordingLoopbackSound` — Returns whether the player is recording a voice sample.

`VoiceChat_PlayLoopbackSound` — Plays a previously recorded loopback sound.

`VoiceChat_RecordLoopbackSound` — Records a short voice recording for testing purposes.

`VoiceChat_StopPlayingLoopbackSound` — Stops the current playback of the loopback sound.

`VoiceChat_StopRecordingLoopback↩Sound` — Stops recording of loopback sounds.

`VoiceEnumerateCaptureDevices` — Returns the name of a voice capture device.

`VoiceEnumerateOutputDevices` — Returns the name of a given voice output device.

`VoiceGetCurrentCaptureDevice` — Returns index of current voice capture device.

`VoiceGetCurrentOutputDevice` — Returns index of current voice output device.

VoiceIsDisabledByClient — Returns whether the voice chat system is disabled due to hardware reasons.

VoicePushToTalkStart — Used internally to start talking when push-to-talk is active in voice chat.

VoicePushToTalkStop — Used internally to stop talking when push-to-talk is active in voice chat.

VoiceSelectCaptureDevice — Selects a voice capture device.

VoiceSelectOutputDevice — Sets the voice chat output device.

Zone

GetMinimapZoneText — Returns the zone text for use on the Minimap.

GetRealZoneText — When in an instance, returns the real name of the instance, not the name in the Minimap.

GetSubZoneText — Returns the subzone text of the player's current zone.

GetZonePVPInfo — Returns PvP information about the current zone.

GetZoneText — Returns the name of the current zone.

IsSubZonePVPPOI — Returns whether the current subzone is a PvP point of interest.

Events Reference

World of Warcraft's user interface makes extensive use of event-based programming, allowing bits of code to respond to only those events that are relevant. There are more than 400 events, and while only a fraction of them will be used by the average addon, this chapter details each event, including a description of the arguments that are sent with the event.

ACTIONBAR_HIDEGRID

Fires when you remove an item or a spell from the cursor. The grid referred to is the outline for empty action bar slots.

ACTIONBAR_PAGE_CHANGED

Fires when the action bar page has been changed. Commonly used to redraw the action bars.

ACTIONBAR_SHOWGRID

Fires when you pick up an item or a spell. It triggers the display of the outline surrounding empty bar slots.

ACTIONBAR_SLOT_CHANGED

Fires whenever an action bar slot changes in any way. This includes when the slot's contents change or when it needs to be redrawn for cosmetic reasons.

Arguments:

1 - slot — Action ID of the slot that needs to be updated or 0 if all slots need to be updated. (number)

ACTIONBAR_UPDATE_COOLDOWN

Fires when a cooldown on an action button begins or ends.

ACTIONBAR_UPDATE_STATE

Fires when a skill usage starts or stops. Is used in the default UI to show what spell or skill is currently in use.

ACTIONBAR_UPDATE_USABLE

Fires when a skill or spell on the action bar becomes usable or unusable. Is used by the default UI to discolor unusable skills.

ADDON_ACTION_BLOCKED

Fires when an unofficial addon attempts to use a portion of the API that has been restricted.

ADDON_ACTION_FORBIDDEN

Fires when an unofficial addon attempts to use a portion of the API that is blocked from usage. It is worth remembering that if your addon triggers this message, the user will be told that he should disable your addon by name.

Arguments:

> 1 - culprit — Name of the addon that called the forbidden function. (string)

ADDON_LOADED

Fires when an addon is loaded. Will fire once per addon loaded. It is safe to assume that the saved variables for that addon are available at this point.

Arguments:

> 1 - name — Name of the addon that has been loaded. (string)

AREA_SPIRIT_HEALER_IN_RANGE

Fires when a player enters into the range of a spirit healer that will automatically resurrect the player.

AREA_SPIRIT_HEALER_OUT_OF_RANGE

Fires when a player leaves the area of effect of a spirit healer that will automatically resurrect you.

ARENA_SEASON_WORLD_STATE

Fires when the arena season changes.

ARENA_TEAM_INVITE_REQUEST

Fires when a player is invited to join an arena team.

Arguments:

> 1 - source — Name of the player that invited you to join a team. (string)
>
> 2 - team — Name of the team that you have been invited to join. (string)

ARENA_TEAM_ROSTER_UPDATE

Fires when an arena team detail page is opened or needs to be updated.

Argument:

> 1 - unknown — Appears to be a boolean value to determine if updated information is available. (boolean)

ARENA_TEAM_UPDATE

Fires when you join or leave an arena team.

AUCTION_BIDDER_LIST_UPDATE

Fires when the Bids tab on the Auction House frame is shown or needs to be updated.

AUCTION_HOUSE_CLOSED

Fires when the auction house is closed.

AUCTION_HOUSE_SHOW

Fires when the auction house is opened

AUCTION_ITEM_LIST_UPDATE

Fires when the auction listing has new or updated information available; usually the result of a sort or search on the auction house.

AUCTION_OWNED_LIST_UPDATE

Fires when you're at the auction house and either you look at the Auctions tab or the information on that tab needs to be updated. Is triggered when you sort or page the listing.

AUTOEQUIP_BIND_CONFIRM

Fires when the game attempts to auto equip an item that is bind on equip.
Argument:

> 1 - `slot` — Slot of the item that you are attempting to equip. (`number`)

AUTOFOLLOW_BEGIN

Fires when you start following another character.
Argument:

> 1 - `following` — Unit that you are following. (`number`)

AUTOFOLLOW_END

Fires when you stop following another player.

BAG_CLOSED

Fires when a bag frame is closed.
Argument:

> 1 - `bagID` — ID of the bag that closed. (`number`)

BAG_OPEN

Fires when a bag frame opens.
Argument:

> 1 - `bagID` — ID of the bag that opened. (`number`)

BAG_UPDATE

Fires when the contents of a bag change. This includes using an item, obtaining an item, selling an item, moving an item, and so on.
Argument:

> 1 - `bagID` — ID of the bag that is receiving an update. (`number`)

BAG_UPDATE_COOLDOWN

Fires when a slot in a container has a cooldown that needs updating.

BANKFRAME_CLOSED

Fires when you close your bank. Normally triggers the bank frame closing.

BANKFRAME_OPENED

Fires when you open your bank.

BATTLEFIELDS_CLOSED

Fires when the battlefield or arena frame closes.

BATTLEFIELDS_SHOW

Fires when the battlefield or arena frames show.

BILLING_NAG_DIALOG

Fires when the billing nag dialog shows.

Argument:

> 1 - `remaining` — Number of minutes until your play time runs out. (number)

BIND_ENCHANT

Fires when applying an enchantment to an item that will cause it to become soul-bound.

CANCEL_LOOT_ROLL

Fires when you cancel a roll on an item.

Argument:

> 1 - `rollID` — ID of the roll that was canceled. (number)

CANCEL_SUMMON

Fires when a summon attempt is canceled.

CHANNEL_COUNT_UPDATE

Fires when a voice channel's member number changes.

Arguments:

> 1 - `id` — ID of the chat channel that's getting updated. (number)
>
> 2 - `count` — Number of members in the channel. (number)

CHANNEL_FLAGS_UPDATED

Fires when there is new information available from `GetChannelDisplayInfo`.

Argument:

> 1 - `id` — ID of the channel that has updated data. (number)

CHANNEL_INVITE_REQUEST

Fires when a player is invited into a chat channel.

Arguments:

> 1 - `channelName` — Name of the channel you have been invited to. (string)
>
> 2 - `inviterName` — Name of the character that invited you. (string)

CHANNEL_PASSWORD_REQUEST

Fires when you attempt to join a password-protected channel.

Argument:

> 1 - `channelName` — Name of the channel you are attempting to join. (string)

CHANNEL_ROSTER_UPDATE

Fires when information about the channel changes. Will also fire when the members in a channel change.

Argument:

    1 - `id` — ID of the channel that has updated information. (`number`)

CHANNEL_UI_UPDATE
Fires when the actively displayed channel changes.

CHANNEL_VOICE_UPDATE
Fires when a player in a channel starts or stops talking.
Arguments:

    1 - `id` — ID of the speaker who has changed. (`number`)

    2 - `enabled` — If voice chat is enabled. (`boolean`)

    3 - `active` — If the player is speaking at this moment. (`boolean`)

CHARACTER_POINTS_CHANGED
Fires when the amount of available talent points changes.
Arguments:

    1 - `count` — Number of talent points gained or lost. Positive numbers are gains; negative numbers are expenditures. (`number`)

    2 - `levels` — Number of levels gained in association with this change. Is 0 if there is no level change. (`number`)

CHAT_MSG_ADDON
Fires when a message from `SendAddonMessage` is received
Arguments:

    1 - `prefix` — Prefix declared from `SendAddonMessage`. (`string`)

    2 - `message` — Message from `SendAddonMessage`. (`string`)

    3 - `channel` — Message channel used for this message. Possible values are PARTY, RAID, GUILD, BATTLEGROUND, or WHISPER. (`string`)

    4 - `sender` — Username of the sender. (`string`)

CHAT_MSG_AFK
Fires when an automatic response is received upon attempting to whisper to a player who is Away From Keyboard.
Arguments:

    1 - `message` — Response message. If the AFK user provided a message ("/afk eating dinner," for example), this argument will contain that message ("eating dinner"); otherwise, it'll be the standard "Away From Keyboard". (`string`)

    2 - `sender` — Name of the player on whose behalf the response was made. (`string`)

CHAT_MSG_BATTLEGROUND
Fires when a message is received on the battleground channel.
Arguments:

    1 - `message` — The text of the message. (`string`)

    2 - `sender` — Name of the player who sent the message. (`string`)

    3 - `language` — Language (for example, Common, Orcish, Demonic) the message is in. (`string`)

6 - `flag` — A flag indicating the status or confirming the identity of the sender. Possible values are "AFK", "DND", or "GM". (string)

7 - `worldChannelNumber` — Unused for this event; always 0. (number)

8 - `channelNumber` — Unused for this event; always 0. (number)

10 - `instanceID` — Unused for this event; always 0. (number)

11 - `msgID` — A number identifying this chat message (used for allowing the player to report a message as spam). (number)

CHAT_MSG_BATTLEGROUND_LEADER

Fires when a message is received from the battleground leader.

Arguments:

1 - `message` — The text of the message. (string)

2 - `sender` — Name of the player who sent the message. (string)

3 - `language` — Language (Common, Orcish, Demonic, for instance) the message is in. (string)

6 - `flag` — A flag indicating the status or confirming the identity of the sender. Possible values are "AFK", "DND", or "GM". (string)

7 - `worldChannelNumber` — Unused for this event; always 0. (number)

8 - `channelNumber` — Unused for this event; always 0. (number)

10 - `instanceID` — Unused for this event; always 0. (number)

11 - `msgID` — A number identifying this chat message (used for allowing the player to report a message as spam). (number)

CHAT_MSG_BG_SYSTEM_ALLIANCE

Fires when an Alliance-specific event happens inside a battleground.

Arguments:

1 - `message` — The text of the message. (string)

7 - `worldChannelNumber` — Unused for this event; always 0. (number)

8 - `channelNumber` — Unused for this event; always 0. (number)

10 - `instanceID` — Unused for this event; always 0. (number)

11 - `msgID` — A number identifying this chat message (used for allowing the player to report a message as spam). (number)

CHAT_MSG_BG_SYSTEM_HORDE

Fires when a Horde-specific event happens inside a battleground.

Arguments:

1 - `message` — The text of the message. (string)

7 - `worldChannelNumber` — Unused for this event; always 0. (number)

8 - `channelNumber` — Unused for this event; always 0. (number)

10 - `instanceID` — Unused for this event; always 0. (number)

11 - `msgID` — A number identifying this chat message (used for allowing the player to report a message as spam). (number)

CHAT_MSG_BG_SYSTEM_NEUTRAL

Fires when an event not specific to either side happens inside a battleground. Also fires for certain zone and world messages (for example, warning upon entering Zul'Gurub, announcement of happenings in the Ahn'Qiraj opening world event, and so on).

Arguments:

> 1 - message — The text of the message. (string)
> 7 - worldChannelNumber — Unused for this event; always 0. (number)
> 8 - channelNumber — Unused for this event; always 0. (number)
> 10 - instanceID — Unused for this event; always 0. (number)
> 11 - msgID — A number identifying this chat message (used for allowing the player to report a message as spam). (number)

CHAT_MSG_CHANNEL

Fires when a message is received on a numbered chat channel (a zone channel such as General or Trade, a server channel such as GuildRecruitment or WorldDefense, or a player-created custom channel, for example).

Arguments:

> 1 - message — The text of the message. (string)
> 2 - sender — Name of the player who sent the message. (string)
> 4 - channelString — Full name of the chat channel on which the message was received, including number ("1. General - Shattrath City", for instance). (string)
> 6 - flag — A flag indicating the status or confirming the identity of the sender. Possible values are "AFK", "DND", or "GM". (string)
> 7 - worldChannelNumber — Numeric ID of the channel if it is a system channel (General, Trade, and so on). Always 0 for custom channels. (number)
> 8 - channelNumber — Numeric ID of the channel. (number)
> 9 - channelName — Full name of the channel, not including number (for example, "General - Shattrath City"). (string)
> 10 - instanceID — If the channel is specific to an instance of a zone (for example, a battleground instance such as "Warsong Gulch 13"), a number that can be used to identify that instance; otherwise 0. (Currently unused.) (number)
> 11 - msgID — A number identifying this chat message (used for allowing the player to report a message as spam). (number)

CHAT_MSG_CHANNEL_JOIN

Fires when another player joins a chat channel you are in. (Note: When you join or leave a channel, CHAT_MSG_CHANNEL_NOTICE is used instead.)

Arguments:

> 2 - sender — Name of the player who joined the channel. (string)
> 4 - channelString — Full name of the chat channel on which the message was received, including number (for example, "1. General - Shattrath City"). (string)
> 7 - worldChannelNumber — Numeric ID of the channel if it is a system channel (General, Trade, and so on). Always 0 for custom channels. (number)
> 8 - channelNumber — Numeric ID of the channel. (number)
> 9 - channelName — Full name of the channel, not including number (for example "General - Shattrath City"). (string)

10 - `instanceID` — If the channel is specific to an instance of a zone (for example, a battleground instance such as "Warsong Gulch 13"), a number that can be used to identify that instance; otherwise 0. (Currently unused.) (number)

11 - `msgID` — A number identifying this chat message (used for allowing the player to report a message as spam). (number)

CHAT_MSG_CHANNEL_LEAVE

Fires when another player leaves a channel you are in. (Note: When you join or leave a channel, `CHAT_MSG_CHANNEL_NOTICE` is used instead.)

Arguments:

2 - `sender` — Name of the player who left the channel. (string)

4 - `channelString` — Full name of the chat channel on which the message was received, including number (for example, `"1. General - Shattrath City"`). (string)

7 - `worldChannelNumber` — Numeric ID of the channel if it is a system channel (General, Trade, and so on). Always 0 for custom channels. (number)

8 - `channelNumber` — Numeric ID of the channel. (number)

9 - `channelName` — Full name of the channel, not including number (for example "General - Shattrath City"). (string)

10 - `instanceID` — If the channel is specific to an instance of a zone (for example, a battleground instance such as "Warsong Gulch 13"), a number that can be used to identify that instance; otherwise 0. (Currently unused.) (number)

11 - `msgID` — A number identifying this chat message (used for allowing the player to report a message as spam). (number)

CHAT_MSG_CHANNEL_LIST

Fires in response to a channel list query (for example, `/chatlist`). If there are many players in a channel, this event will fire several times to list all players.

Arguments:

1 - `message` — The text of the message: a comma-separated list of players. (string)

4 - `channelString` — Full name of the chat channel on which the message was received, including number (for example, `"1. General - Shattrath City"`). (string)

7 - `worldChannelNumber` — Numeric ID of the channel if it is a system channel (General, Trade, and so on). Always 0 for custom channels. (number)

8 - `channelNumber` — Numeric ID of the channel. (number)

9 - `channelName` — Full name of the channel, not including number (for example "General - Shattrath City"). (string)

10 - `instanceID` — If the channel is specific to an instance of a zone (for example, a battleground instance such as "Warsong Gulch 13"), a number that can be used to identify that instance; otherwise 0. (Currently unused.) (number)

11 - `msgID` — A number identifying this chat message (used for allowing the player to report a message as spam). (number)

CHAT_MSG_CHANNEL_NOTICE

Fires when certain activities happen on a numbered chat channel, such as when you join or leave a channel; a zone-specific channel (for example, LocalDefense) changes as you move from one zone to another, or you attempt to join or speak in a channel in which you're not allowed.

Arguments:

1 - `message` — A nonlocalized token representing one of the standard notice messages. A localized message for display can be found by looking up a global variable whose name is the token preceded by "CHAT_" and followed by "_NOTICE" and supplying it as the first argument to `string.format` to insert the channel name appropriately. (string)

Example:

```
string.format(getglobal("CHAT"..arg1.."Notice"), ↵
arg4)-- produces something like:
 -- "[5. GoblinGossip] You do not have permission ↵
to speak."
```

4 - `channelString` — Full name of the chat channel to which the notice pertains, including number (for example, `"1. General - Shattrath City"`). (string)

7 - `worldChannelNumber` — Numeric ID of the channel if it is a system channel (General, Trade, and so on). Always 0 for custom channels. (number)

8 - `channelNumber` — Numeric ID of the channel. (number)

9 - `channelName` — Full name of the channel, not including number (for example "General - Shattrath City"). (string)

10 - `instanceID` — If the channel is specific to an instance of a zone (for example, a battleground instance such as "Warsong Gulch 13"), a that can be used to identify that instance; otherwise 0. (Currently unused.) (number)

11 - `msgID` — A number identifying this chat message (used for allowing the player to report a message as spam). (number)

CHAT_MSG_CHANNEL_NOTICE_USER

Fires when certain activities pertaining to one or more specific users happen on a numbered chat channel, such as a user turning voice chat on, a moderator kicking or banning another user from the channel, or a user becoming the channel owner.

Arguments:

1 - `message` — A nonlocalized token representing one of the standard notice messages. A localized message for display can be found by looking up a global variable whose name is the token preceded by CHAT_ and followed by _NOTICE and supplying it as the first argument to `string.format` to insert the channel name and pertinent player names appropriately. (string)

Example:

```
string.format(getglobal("CHAT"..arg1.."NOTICE"), ↵
arg4, arg2, arg5)
-- produces something like:
-- "[5. GoblinGossip] Player Cladhaire kicked by Gazmik."
```

2 - `sender` — Name of the first (or only) user to whom this notice pertains. (`string`)

4 - `channelString` — Full name of the chat channel on which the message was received, including number (for example, `"1. General - Shattrath City"`). (`string`)

5 - `target` — Name of the second player to whom this notice pertains (for example, "Gazmik" in the preceding example). (`string`)

7 - `worldChannelNumber` — Numeric ID of the channel if it is a system channel (General, Trade, and so on). Always 0 for custom channels. (`number`)

8 - `channelNumber` — Numeric ID of the channel. (`number`)

9 - `channelName` — Full name of the channel, not including number (for example "General - Shattrath City"). (`string`)

10 - `instanceID` — If the channel is specific to an instance of a zone (for example, a battleground instance such as "Warsong Gulch 13"), a number that can be used to identify that instance; otherwise 0. (Currently unused.) (`number`)

11 - `msgID` — A number identifying this chat message (used for allowing the player to report a message as spam). (`number`)

CHAT_MSG_COMBAT_CREATURE_VS_CREATURE_HITS
Fires when one creature hits another creature.
Arguments:

1 - `message` — The text of the message. (`string`)

7 - `worldChannelNumber` — Unused for this event; always 0. (`number`)

8 - `channelNumber` — Unused for this event; always 0. (`number`)

10 - `instanceID` — Unused for this event; always 0. (`number`)

11 - `msgID` — A number identifying this chat message (used for allowing the player to report a message as spam). (`number`)

CHAT_MSG_COMBAT_CREATURE_VS_CREATURE_MISSES
Fires when one creature misses another creature in combat.
Arguments:

1 - `message` — The text of the message. (`string`)

7 - `worldChannelNumber` — Unused for this event; always 0. (`number`)

8 - `channelNumber` — Unused for this event; always 0. (`number`)

10 - `instanceID` — Unused for this event; always 0. (`number`)

11 - `msgID` — A number identifying this chat message (used for allowing the player to report a message as spam). (`number`)

CHAT_MSG_COMBAT_CREATURE_VS_PARTY_HITS
Fires when a create hits a party member.
Arguments:

1 - `message` — The text of the message. (`string`)

7 - `worldChannelNumber` — Unused for this event; always 0. (`number`)

8 - `channelNumber` — Unused for this event; always 0. (`number`)

10 - `instanceID` — Unused for this event; always 0. (`number`)

11 - `msgID` — A number identifying this chat message (used for allowing the player to report a message as spam). (`number`)

CHAT_MSG_COMBAT_CREATURE_VS_PARTY_MISSES

Fires when a creature misses a party member.

Arguments:

1 - message — The text of the message. (string)

7 - worldChannelNumber — Unused for this event; always 0. (number)

8 - channelNumber — Unused for this event; always 0. (number)

10 - instanceID — Unused for this event; always 0. (number)

11 - msgID — A number identifying this chat message (used for allowing the player to report a message as spam). (number)

CHAT_MSG_COMBAT_CREATURE_VS_SELF_HITS

Fires when a creature hits you.

Arguments:

1 - message — The text of the message. (string)

7 - worldChannelNumber — Unused for this event; always 0. (number)

8 - channelNumber — Unused for this event; always 0. (number)

10 - instanceID — Unused for this event; always 0. (number)

11 - msgID — A number identifying this chat message (used for allowing the player to report a message as spam). (number)

CHAT_MSG_COMBAT_CREATURE_VS_SELF_MISSES

Fires when a creature misses you.

Arguments:

1 - message — The text of the message. (string)

7 - worldChannelNumber — Unused for this event; always 0. (number)

8 - channelNumber — Unused for this event; always 0. (number)

10 - instanceID — Unused for this event; always 0. (number)

11 - msgID — A number identifying this chat message (used for allowing the player to report a message as spam). (number)

CHAT_MSG_COMBAT_FACTION_CHANGE

Fires when you gain or lose faction by killing a creature.

Arguments:

1 - message — The text of the message. (string)

7 - worldChannelNumber — Unused for this event; always 0. (number)

8 - channelNumber — Unused for this event; always 0. (number)

10 - instanceID — Unused for this event; always 0. (number)

11 - msgID — A number identifying this chat message (used for allowing the player to report a message as spam). (number)

CHAT_MSG_COMBAT_FRIENDLYPLAYER_HITS

Fires whenever a friendly player hits a target in combat.

Arguments:

1 - message — The text of the message. (string)

7 - worldChannelNumber — Unused for this event; always 0. (number)

8 - channelNumber — Unused for this event; always 0. (number)

10 - instanceID — Unused for this event; always 0. (number)

11 - `msgID` — A number identifying this chat message (used for allowing the player to report a message as spam). (number)

CHAT_MSG_COMBAT_FRIENDLYPLAYER_MISSES
Fires whenever a friendly player misses in combat.
Arguments:

    1 - `message` — The text of the message. (string)

    7 - `worldChannelNumber` — Unused for this event; always 0. (number)

    8 - `channelNumber` — Unused for this event; always 0. (number)

    10 - `instanceID` — Unused for this event; always 0. (number)

    11 - `msgID` — A number identifying this chat message (used for allowing the player to report a message as spam). (number)

CHAT_MSG_COMBAT_FRIENDLY_DEATH
Fires whenever a friendly player dies.
Arguments:

    1 - `message` — The text of the message. (string)

    7 - `worldChannelNumber` — Unused for this event; always 0. (number)

    8 - `channelNumber` — Unused for this event; always 0. (number)

    10 - `instanceID` — Unused for this event; always 0. (number)

    11 - `msgID` — A number identifying this chat message (used for allowing the player to report a message as spam). (number)

CHAT_MSG_COMBAT_HONOR_GAIN
Fires whenever a player gains honor.
Arguments:

    1 - `message` — The text of the message. (string)

    7 - `worldChannelNumber` — Unused for this event; always 0. (number)

    8 - `channelNumber` — Unused for this event; always 0. (number)

    10 - `instanceID` — Unused for this event; always 0. (number)

    11 - `msgID` — A number identifying this chat message (used for allowing the player to report a message as spam). (number)

CHAT_MSG_COMBAT_HOSTILEPLAYER_HITS
Fires when a hostile player hits in combat.
Arguments:

    1 - `message` — The text of the message. (string)

    7 - `worldChannelNumber` — Unused for this event; always 0. (number)

    8 - `channelNumber` — Unused for this event; always 0. (number)

    10 - `instanceID` — Unused for this event; always 0. (number)

    11 - `msgID` — A number identifying this chat message (used for allowing the player to report a message as spam). (number)

CHAT_MSG_COMBAT_HOSTILEPLAYER_MISSES
Fires when a hostile player misses in combat.
Arguments:

    1 - `message` — The text of the message. (string)

    7 - `worldChannelNumber` — Unused for this event; always 0. (number)

8 - channelNumber — Unused for this event; always 0. (number)

10 - instanceID — Unused for this event; always 0. (number)

11 - msgID — A number identifying this chat message (used for allowing the player to report a message as spam). (number)

CHAT_MSG_COMBAT_HOSTILE_DEATH

Fires when a hostile player dies.

Arguments:

1 - message — The text of the message. (string)

7 - worldChannelNumber — Unused for this event; always 0. (number)

8 - channelNumber — Unused for this event; always 0. (number)

10 - instanceID — Unused for this event; always 0. (number)

11 - msgID — A number identifying this chat message (used for allowing the player to report a message as spam). (number)

CHAT_MSG_COMBAT_MISC_INFO

Fires for miscellaneous combat log messages: when you suffer durability loss upon death, when you dismiss your pet (or a nearby player dismisses hers), and so on.

Arguments:

1 - message — The text of the message. (string)

7 - worldChannelNumber — Unused for this event; always 0. (number)

8 - channelNumber — Unused for this event; always 0. (number)

10 - instanceID — Unused for this event; always 0. (number)

11 - msgID — A number identifying this chat message (used for allowing the player to report a message as spam). (number)

CHAT_MSG_COMBAT_PARTY_HITS

Fires when a party member hits in combat.

Arguments:

1 - message — The text of the message. (string)

7 - worldChannelNumber — Unused for this event; always 0. (number)

8 - channelNumber — Unused for this event; always 0. (number)

10 - instanceID — Unused for this event; always 0. (number)

11 - msgID — A number identifying this chat message (used for allowing the player to report a message as spam). (number)

CHAT_MSG_COMBAT_PARTY_MISSES

Fires when a party member misses.

Arguments:

1 - message — The text of the message. (string)

7 - worldChannelNumber — Unused for this event; always 0. (number)

8 - channelNumber — Unused for this event; always 0. (number)

10 - instanceID — Unused for this event; always 0. (number)

11 - msgID — A number identifying this chat message (used for allowing the player to report a message as spam). (number)

CHAT_MSG_COMBAT_PET_HITS

Fires when a pet hits in combat.

Arguments:

    1 - message — The text of the message. (string)

    7 - worldChannelNumber — Unused for this event; always 0. (number)

    8 - channelNumber — Unused for this event; always 0. (number)

    10 - instanceID — Unused for this event; always 0. (number)

    11 - msgID — A number identifying this chat message (used for allowing the player to report a message as spam). (number)

CHAT_MSG_COMBAT_PET_MISSES

Fires when a pet misses in combat.

Arguments:

    1 - message — The text of the message. (string)

    7 - worldChannelNumber — Unused for this event; always 0. (number)

    8 - channelNumber — Unused for this event; always 0. (number)

    10 - instanceID — Unused for this event; always 0. (number)

    11 - msgID — A number identifying this chat message (used for allowing the player to report a message as spam). (number)

CHAT_MSG_COMBAT_SELF_HITS

Fires when you hit in combat.

Arguments:

    1 - message — The text of the message. (string)

    7 - worldChannelNumber — Unused for this event; always 0. (number)

    8 - channelNumber — Unused for this event; always 0. (number)

    10 - instanceID — Unused for this event; always 0. (number)

    11 - msgID — A number identifying this chat message (used for allowing the player to report a message as spam). (number)

CHAT_MSG_COMBAT_SELF_MISSES

Fires when you miss in combat.

Arguments:

    1 - message — The text of the message. (string)

    7 - worldChannelNumber — Unused for this event; always 0. (number)

    8 - channelNumber — Unused for this event; always 0. (number)

    10 - instanceID — Unused for this event; always 0. (number)

    11 - msgID — A number identifying this chat message (used for allowing the player to report a message as spam). (number)

CHAT_MSG_COMBAT_XP_GAIN

Fires when you gain experience points from killing a creature in combat, completing a quest, exploring a new area, and so on.

Arguments:

    1 - message — The text of the message. (string)

    7 - worldChannelNumber — Unused for this event; always 0. (number)

    8 - channelNumber — Unused for this event; always 0. (number)

10 - `instanceID` — Unused for this event; always 0. (number)

11 - `msgID` — A number identifying this chat message (used for allowing the player to report a message as spam). (number)

CHAT_MSG_DND

Fires when an automatic response is received upon attempting to whisper to a player who has set their status to Do Not Disturb.

Arguments:

1 - `message` — The text of the message. If the DND user provided a message (for example, `/dnd raiding Hogger`), this argument will contain that message ("raiding Hogger"); otherwise, it'll be the standard "Do not Disturb". (string)

2 - `sender` — Name of the player on whose behalf the response was sent. (string)

7 - `worldChannelNumber` — Unused for this event; always 0. (number)

8 - `channelNumber` — Unused for this event; always 0. (number)

10 - `instanceID` — Unused for this event; always 0. (number)

11 - `msgID` — A number identifying this chat message (used for allowing the player to report a message as spam). (number)

CHAT_MSG_EMOTE

Fires when you receive a custom emote message from yourself or another player, such as one sent by using the `/emote`, `/me`, `/em`, or `/e` commands; not one of the standard emotes such as `/dance`, `/wave`, or `/silly`.

Arguments:

1 - `message` — The text of the message (does not include the sender's name). (string)

2 - `sender` — Name of the player who sent the message. (string)

6 - `flag` — A flag indicating the status or confirming the identity of the sender. Possible values are `"AFK"`, `"DND"`, or `"GM"`. (string)

7 - `worldChannelNumber` — Unused for this event; always 0. (number)

8 - `channelNumber` — Unused for this event; always 0. (number)

10 - `instanceID` — Unused for this event; always 0. (number)

11 - `msgID` — A number identifying this chat message (used for allowing the player to report a message as spam). (number)

CHAT_MSG_GUILD

Fires when you receive a message in guild chat.

Arguments:

1 - `message` — The text of the message (does not include the sender's name). (string)

2 - `sender` — Name of the player who sent the message. (string)

3 - `language` — Language (for example, Common, Orcish, Demonic) the message is in. (string)

6 - `flag` — A flag indicating the status or confirming the identity of the sender. Possible values are `"AFK"`, `"DND"`, or `"GM"`. (string)

7 - `worldChannelNumber` — Unused for this event; always 0. (number)

8 - channelNumber — Unused for this event; always 0. (number)

10 - instanceID — Unused for this event; always 0. (number)

11 - msgID — A number identifying this chat message (used for allowing the player to report a message as spam). (number)

CHAT_MSG_IGNORED

Fires when an automatic response is received upon attempting to whisper to a player who has put you on their ignore list.

Arguments:

1 - message — The text of the message (does not include the sender's name). (string)

2 - sender — Name of the player who sent the message. (string)

7 - worldChannelNumber — Unused for this event; always 0. (number)

8 - channelNumber — Unused for this event; always 0. (number)

10 - instanceID — Unused for this event; always 0. (number)

11 - msgID — A number identifying this chat message (used for allowing the player to report a message as spam). (number)

CHAT_MSG_LOOT

Fires when a player loots, creates, or otherwise receives an item.

Arguments:

1 - message — The text of the message. (string)

7 - worldChannelNumber — Unused for this event; always 0. (number)

8 - channelNumber — Unused for this event; always 0. (number)

10 - instanceID — Unused for this event; always 0. (number)

11 - msgID — A number identifying this chat message (used for allowing the player to report a message as spam). (number)

CHAT_MSG_MONEY

Fires when a player loots money or receives a share of money looted by a group member.

Arguments:

1 - message — The text of the message. (string)

7 - worldChannelNumber — Unused for this event; always 0. (number)

8 - channelNumber — Unused for this event; always 0. (number)

10 - instanceID — Unused for this event; always 0. (number)

11 - msgID — A number identifying this chat message (used for allowing the player to report a message as spam). (number)

CHAT_MSG_MONSTER_EMOTE

Fires when a creature or NPC does an emote.

Arguments:

1 - message — The text of the message. This may be a format string to be used with string.format (for inserting the second and possibly also fifth arguments at appropriate places in the text). (string)

2 - sender — Name of the NPC who sent the message. (string)

5 - `target` — Name of the player or other entity to whom the emote refers. (`string`)

7 - `worldChannelNumber` — Unused for this event; always 0. (`number`)

8 - `channelNumber` — Unused for this event; always 0. (`number`)

10 - `instanceID` — Unused for this event; always 0. (`number`)

11 - `msgID` — A number identifying this chat message (used for allowing the player to report a message as spam). (`number`)

CHAT_MSG_MONSTER_SAY

Fires when a creature or NPC says something (visible only to players nearby).

Arguments:

1 - `message` — The text of the message. (`string`)

2 - `sender` — Name of the NPC who sent the message. (`string`)

3 - `language` — Language (for example, Common, Orcish, Demonic) the message is in, or `nil` for universally understandable messages. (`string`)

5 - `target` — If present, name of the player or other entity who triggered the message. (`string`)

7 - `worldChannelNumber` — Unused for this event; always 0. (`number`)

8 - `channelNumber` — Unused for this event; always 0. (`number`)

10 - `instanceID` — Unused for this event; always 0. (`number`)

11 - `msgID` — A number identifying this chat message (used for allowing the player to report a message as spam). (`number`)

CHAT_MSG_MONSTER_WHISPER

Fires when a creature or NPC whispers something to you.

Arguments:

1 - `message` — The text of the message. (`string`)

2 - `sender` — Name of the NPC who sent the message. (`string`)

3 - `language` — Language (for example, Common, Orcish, Demonic) the message is in, or `nil` for universally understandable messages. (`string`)

5 - `target` — Name of the player to whom the whisper is directed (you). (`string`)

7 - `worldChannelNumber` — Unused for this event; always 0. (`number`)

8 - `channelNumber` — Unused for this event; always 0. (`number`)

10 - `instanceID` — Unused for this event; always 0. (`number`)

11 - `msgID` — A number identifying this chat message (used for allowing the player to report a message as spam). (`number`)

CHAT_MSG_MONSTER_YELL

Fires when a creature or NPC yells something (visible to a wide area or the entire zone).

Arguments:

1 - `message` — The text of the message. (`string`)

2 - `sender` — Name of the NPC who sent the message. (`string`)

3 - `language` — Language (for example, Common, Orcish, Demonic) the message is in, or `nil` for universally understandable messages. (`string`)

5 - `target` — If present, name of the player or other entity who triggered the message. (`string`)

7 - `worldChannelNumber` — Unused for this event; always 0. (`number`)

8 - `channelNumber` — Unused for this event; always 0. (`number`)

10 - `instanceID` — Unused for this event; always 0. (`number`)

11 - `msgID` — A number identifying this chat message (used for allowing the player to report a message as spam). (`number`)

CHAT_MSG_OFFICER

Fires when a message is received in guild officer chat.

Arguments:

1 - `message` — The text of the message. (`string`)

2 - `sender` — Name of the player who sent the message. (`string`)

3 - `language` — Language (for example, Common, Orcish, Demonic) the message is in. (`string`)

6 - `flag` — A flag indicating the status or confirming the identity of the sender. Possible values are `"AFK"`, `"DND"`, or `"GM"`. (`string`)

7 - `worldChannelNumber` — Unused for this event; always 0. (`number`)

8 - `channelNumber` — Unused for this event; always 0. (`number`)

10 - `instanceID` — Unused for this event; always 0. (`number`)

11 - `msgID` — A number identifying this chat message (used for allowing the player to report a message as spam). (`number`)

CHAT_MSG_PARTY

Fires when you receive a message in party chat.

Arguments:

1 - `message` — The text of the message. (`string`)

2 - `sender` — Name of the player who sent the message. (`string`)

3 - `language` — Language (for example, Common, Orcish, Demonic) the message is in. (`string`)

6 - `flag` — A flag indicating the status or confirming the identity of the sender. Possible values are `"AFK"`, `"DND"`, or `"GM"`. (`string`)

7 - `worldChannelNumber` — Unused for this event; always 0. (`number`)

8 - `channelNumber` — Unused for this event; always 0. (`number`)

10 - `instanceID` — Unused for this event; always 0. (`number`)

11 - `msgID` — A number identifying this chat message (used for allowing the player to report a message as spam). (`number`)

CHAT_MSG_RAID

Fires when you receive a message in raid chat.

Arguments:

1 - `message` — The text of the message. (`string`)

2 - `sender` — Name of the player who sent the message. (`string`)

3 - `language` — Language (for example, Common, Orcish, Demonic) the message is in. (`string`)

6 - `flag` — A flag indicating the status or confirming the identity of the sender. Possible values are `"AFK"`, `"DND"`, or `"GM"`. (`string`)

7 - `worldChannelNumber` — Unused for this event; always 0. `(number)`

8 - `channelNumber` — Unused for this event; always 0. `(number)`

10 - `instanceID` — Unused for this event; always 0. `(number)`

11 - `msgID` — A number identifying this chat message (used for allowing the player to report a message as spam). `(number)`

CHAT_MSG_RAID_BOSS_EMOTE

Fires when a raid boss does an emote.

Arguments:

1 - `message` — The text of the message. This may be a format string to be used with `string.format` (for inserting the second and possibly also fifth arguments at appropriate places in the text). `(string)`

2 - `sender` — Name of the NPC who sent the message. `(string)`

5 - `target` — Name of the player or other entity who triggered the emote or to whom it refers. `(string)`

7 - `worldChannelNumber` — Unused for this event; always 0. `(number)`

8 - `channelNumber` — Unused for this event; always 0. `(number)`

10 - `instanceID` — Unused for this event; always 0. `(number)`

11 - `msgID` — A number identifying this chat message (used for allowing the player to report a message as spam). `(number)`

CHAT_MSG_RAID_LEADER

Fires when a message is sent by the raid leader.

Arguments:

1 - `message` — The text of the message. `(string)`

2 - `sender` — Name of the player who sent the message. `(string)`

3 - `language` — Language (for example, Common, Orcish, Demonic) the message is in. `(string)`

6 - `flag` — A flag indicating the status or confirming the identity of the sender. Possible values are `"AFK"`, `"DND"`, or `"GM"`. `(string)`

7 - `worldChannelNumber` — Unused for this event; always 0. `(number)`

8 - `channelNumber` — Unused for this event; always 0. `(number)`

10 - `instanceID` — Unused for this event; always 0. `(number)`

11 - `msgID` — A number identifying this chat message (used for allowing the player to report a message as spam). `(number)`

CHAT_MSG_RAID_WARNING

Fires when a warning message (normally printed in large text in the center of the screen) is sent by the raid leader or a raid officer.

Arguments:

1 - `message` — The text of the message. `(string)`

2 - `sender` — Name of the player who sent the message. `(string)`

3 - `language` — Language (for example, Common, Orcish, Demonic) the message is in. `(string)`

6 - `flag` — A flag indicating the status or confirming the identity of the sender. Possible values are `"AFK"`, `"DND"`, or `"GM"`. `(string)`

7 - `worldChannelNumber` — Unused for this event; always 0. `(number)`

8 - channelNumber — Unused for this event; always 0. (number)

10 - instanceID — Unused for this event; always 0. (number)

11 - msgID — A number identifying this chat message (used for allowing the player to report a message as spam). (number)

CHAT_MSG_SAY

Fires when a message from a nearby player (and visible only to other nearby players) is received.

Arguments:

1 - message — The text of the message. (string)

2 - sender — Name of the player who sent the message. (string)

3 - language — Language (for example, Common, Orcish, Demonic) the message is in. (string)

6 - flag — A flag indicating the status or confirming the identity of the sender. Possible values are "AFK", "DND", or "GM". (string)

7 - worldChannelNumber — Unused for this event; always 0. (number)

8 - channelNumber — Unused for this event; always 0. (number)

10 - instanceID — Unused for this event; always 0. (number)

11 - msgID — A number identifying this chat message (used for allowing the player to report a message as spam). (number)

CHAT_MSG_SKILL

Fires when skill-related messages (for example, "Your skill in Unarmed has increased to 131") are received.

Arguments:

1 - message — The text of the message. (string)

7 - worldChannelNumber — Unused for this event; always 0. (number)

8 - channelNumber — Unused for this event; always 0. (number)

10 - instanceID — Unused for this event; always 0. (number)

11 - msgID — A number identifying this chat message (used for allowing the player to report a message as spam). (number)

CHAT_MSG_SPELL_AURA_GONE_OTHER

Fires when a buff or debuff fades from a creature, NPC, or player other than yourself or a party member.

Arguments:

1 - message — The text of the message. (string)

7 - worldChannelNumber — Unused for this event; always 0. (number)

8 - channelNumber — Unused for this event; always 0. (number)

10 - instanceID — Unused for this event; always 0. (number)

11 - msgID — A number identifying this chat message (used for allowing the player to report a message as spam). (number)

CHAT_MSG_SPELL_AURA_GONE_PARTY

Fires when a buff or debuff fades from a party member.

Arguments:

> 1 - `message` — The text of the message. (`string`)
> 7 - `worldChannelNumber` — Unused for this event; always 0. (`number`)
> 8 - `channelNumber` — Unused for this event; always 0. (`number`)
> 10 - `instanceID` — Unused for this event; always 0. (`number`)
> 11 - `msgID` — A number identifying this chat message (used for allowing the player to report a message as spam). (`number`)

CHAT_MSG_SPELL_AURA_GONE_SELF

Fires when a buff or debuff fades from the player.

Arguments:

> 1 - `message` — The text of the message. (`string`)
> 7 - `worldChannelNumber` — Unused for this event; always 0. (`number`)
> 8 - `channelNumber` — Unused for this event; always 0. (`number`)
> 10 - `instanceID` — Unused for this event; always 0. (`number`)
> 11 - `msgID` — A number identifying this chat message (used for allowing the player to report a message as spam). (`number`)

CHAT_MSG_SPELL_BREAK_AURA

Fires when an aura is broken.

Arguments:

> 1 - `message` — The text of the message. (`string`)
> 7 - `worldChannelNumber` — Unused for this event; always 0. (`number`)
> 8 - `channelNumber` — Unused for this event; always 0. (`number`)
> 10 - `instanceID` — Unused for this event; always 0. (`number`)
> 11 - `msgID` — A number identifying this chat message (used for allowing the player to report a message as spam). (`number`)

CHAT_MSG_SPELL_CREATURE_VS_CREATURE_BUFF

Fires when a creature begins and finishes casting a beneficial spell on another creature.

Arguments:

> 1 - `message` — The text of the message. (`string`)
> 7 - `worldChannelNumber` — Unused for this event; always 0. (`number`)
> 8 - `channelNumber` — Unused for this event; always 0. (`number`)
> 10 - `instanceID` — Unused for this event; always 0. (`number`)
> 11 - `msgID` — A number identifying this chat message (used for allowing the player to report a message as spam). (`number`)

CHAT_MSG_SPELL_CREATURE_VS_CREATURE_DAMAGE

Fires when a creature starts to cast or stops casting a harmful spell against another creature.

Arguments:

> 1 - `message` — The text of the message. (`string`)
> 7 - `worldChannelNumber` — Unused for this event; always 0. (`number`)
> 8 - `channelNumber` — Unused for this event; always 0. (`number`)

> 10 - `instanceID` — Unused for this event; always 0. (number)
>
> 11 - `msgID` — A number identifying this chat message (used for allowing the player to report a message as spam). (number)

CHAT_MSG_SPELL_CREATURE_VS_PARTY_BUFF

Fires when a creature starts to or stops a cast of a beneficial spell on a party member.
Arguments:

> 1 - `message` — The text of the message. (string)
>
> 7 - `worldChannelNumber` — Unused for this event; always 0. (number)
>
> 8 - `channelNumber` — Unused for this event; always 0. (number)
>
> 10 - `instanceID` — Unused for this event; always 0. (number)
>
> 11 - `msgID` — A number identifying this chat message (used for allowing the player to report a message as spam). (number)

CHAT_MSG_SPELL_CREATURE_VS_PARTY_DAMAGE

Fires when a creature starts or stops casting a harmful spell on a party member.
Arguments:

> 1 - `message` — The text of the message. (string)
>
> 7 - `worldChannelNumber` — Unused for this event; always 0. (number)
>
> 8 - `channelNumber` — Unused for this event; always 0. (number)
>
> 10 - `instanceID` — Unused for this event; always 0. (number)
>
> 11 - `msgID` — A number identifying this chat message (used for allowing the player to report a message as spam). (number)

CHAT_MSG_SPELL_CREATURE_VS_SELF_BUFF

Fires when a creature starts or stops casting a beneficial spell on you.
Arguments:

> 1 - `message` — The text of the message. (string)
>
> 7 - `worldChannelNumber` — Unused for this event; always 0. (number)
>
> 8 - `channelNumber` — Unused for this event; always 0. (number)
>
> 10 - `instanceID` — Unused for this event; always 0. (number)
>
> 11 - `msgID` — A number identifying this chat message (used for allowing the player to report a message as spam). (number)

CHAT_MSG_SPELL_CREATURE_VS_SELF_DAMAGE

Fires when a creature starts or stops casting a harmful spell against you.
Arguments:

> 1 - `message` — The text of the message. (string)
>
> 7 - `worldChannelNumber` — Unused for this event; always 0. (number)
>
> 8 - `channelNumber` — Unused for this event; always 0. (number)
>
> 10 - `instanceID` — Unused for this event; always 0. (number)
>
> 11 - `msgID` — A number identifying this chat message (used for allowing the player to report a message as spam). (number)

CHAT_MSG_SPELL_DAMAGESHIELDS_ON_OTHERS

Fires when a damage shield on someone other than you deals damage.

Arguments:

1 - `message` — The text of the message. (string)

7 - `worldChannelNumber` — Unused for this event; always 0. (number)

8 - `channelNumber` — Unused for this event; always 0. (number)

10 - `instanceID` — Unused for this event; always 0. (number)

11 - `msgID` — A number identifying this chat message (used for allowing the player to report a message as spam). (number)

CHAT_MSG_SPELL_DAMAGESHIELDS_ON_SELF
Fires when a damage shield on you deals damage.
Arguments:

1 - `message` — The text of the message. (string)

7 - `worldChannelNumber` — Unused for this event; always 0. (number)

8 - `channelNumber` — Unused for this event; always 0. (number)

10 - `instanceID` — Unused for this event; always 0. (number)

11 - `msgID` — A number identifying this chat message (used for allowing the player to report a message as spam). (number)

CHAT_MSG_SPELL_FAILED_LOCALPLAYER
Fires when a spell fails to complete successfully.
Arguments:

1 - `message` — The text of the message. (string)

7 - `worldChannelNumber` — Unused for this event; always 0. (number)

8 - `channelNumber` — Unused for this event; always 0. (number)

10 - `instanceID` — Unused for this event; always 0. (number)

11 - `msgID` — A number identifying this chat message (used for allowing the player to report a message as spam). (number)

CHAT_MSG_SPELL_FRIENDLYPLAYER_BUFF
Fires when a friendly player begins or stops casting a beneficial spell.
Arguments:

1 - `message` — The text of the message. (string)

7 - `worldChannelNumber` — Unused for this event; always 0. (number)

8 - `channelNumber` — Unused for this event; always 0. (number)

10 - `instanceID` — Unused for this event; always 0. (number)

11 - `msgID` — A number identifying this chat message (used for allowing the player to report a message as spam). (number)

CHAT_MSG_SPELL_FRIENDLYPLAYER_DAMAGE
Fires when a friendly player begins or stops casting a harmful spell.
Arguments:

1 - `message` — The text of the message. (string)

7 - `worldChannelNumber` — Unused for this event; always 0. (number)

8 - `channelNumber` — Unused for this event; always 0. (number)

10 - `instanceID` — Unused for this event; always 0. (number)

11 - `msgID` — A number identifying this chat message (used for allowing the player to report a message as spam). (number)

CHAT_MSG_SPELL_HOSTILEPLAYER_BUFF
Fires when a hostile player starts or stops casting a beneficial spell.
Arguments:

1 - `message` — The text of the message. (`string`)

7 - `worldChannelNumber` — Unused for this event; always 0. (`number`)

8 - `channelNumber` — Unused for this event; always 0. (`number`)

10 - `instanceID` — Unused for this event; always 0. (`number`)

11 - `msgID` — A number identifying this chat message (used for allowing the player to report a message as spam). (`number`)

CHAT_MSG_SPELL_HOSTILEPLAYER_DAMAGE
Fires when a hostile player begins or ends casting a harmful spell.
Arguments:

1 - `message` — The text of the message. (`string`)

7 - `worldChannelNumber` — Unused for this event; always 0. (`number`)

8 - `channelNumber` — Unused for this event; always 0. (`number`)

10 - `instanceID` — Unused for this event; always 0. (`number`)

11 - `msgID` — A number identifying this chat message (used for allowing the player to report a message as spam). (`number`)

CHAT_MSG_SPELL_ITEM_ENCHANTMENTS
Fires when an enchantment is cast on a item.
Arguments:

1 - `message` — The text of the message. (`string`)

7 - `worldChannelNumber` — Unused for this event; always 0. (`number`)

8 - `channelNumber` — Unused for this event; always 0. (`number`)

10 - `instanceID` — Unused for this event; always 0. (`number`)

11 - `msgID` — A number identifying this chat message (used for allowing the player to report a message as spam). (`number`)

CHAT_MSG_SPELL_PARTY_BUFF
Fires when a party member starts or stops casting a beneficial spell.
Arguments:

1 - `message` — The text of the message. (`string`)

7 - `worldChannelNumber` — Unused for this event; always 0. (`number`)

8 - `channelNumber` — Unused for this event; always 0. (`number`)

10 - `instanceID` — Unused for this event; always 0. (`number`)

11 - `msgID` — A number identifying this chat message (used for allowing the player to report a message as spam). (`number`)

CHAT_MSG_SPELL_PARTY_DAMAGE
Fires when a party member starts or stops casting a harmful spell.
Arguments:

1 - `message` — The text of the message. (`string`)

7 - `worldChannelNumber` — Unused for this event; always 0. (`number`)

8 - `channelNumber` — Unused for this event; always 0. (`number`)

10 - `instanceID` — Unused for this event; always 0. (`number`)

    11 - `msgID` — A number identifying this chat message (used for allowing the player to report a message as spam). (`number`)

CHAT_MSG_SPELL_PERIODIC_CREATURE_BUFFS

Fires when a creature gains a single-step beneficial spell.

Arguments:

    1 - `message` — The text of the message. (`string`)

    7 - `worldChannelNumber` — Unused for this event; always 0. (`number`)

    8 - `channelNumber` — Unused for this event; always 0. (`number`)

    10 - `instanceID` — Unused for this event; always 0. (`number`)

    11 - `msgID` — A number identifying this chat message (used for allowing the player to report a message as spam). (`number`)

CHAT_MSG_SPELL_PERIODIC_CREATURE_DAMAGE

Fires when a creature is affected by a periodic harmful spell or ongoing effect.

Arguments:

    1 - `message` — The text of the message. (`string`)

    7 - `worldChannelNumber` — Unused for this event; always 0. (`number`)

    8 - `channelNumber` — Unused for this event; always 0. (`number`)

    10 - `instanceID` — Unused for this event; always 0. (`number`)

    11 - `msgID` — A number identifying this chat message (used for allowing the player to report a message as spam). (`number`)

CHAT_MSG_SPELL_PERIODIC_FRIENDLYPLAYER_BUFFS

Fires when a friendly player gains a buff or is affected by an ongoing beneficial effect.

Arguments:

    1 - `message` — The text of the message. (`string`)

    7 - `worldChannelNumber` — Unused for this event; always 0. (`number`)

    8 - `channelNumber` — Unused for this event; always 0. (`number`)

    10 - `instanceID` — Unused for this event; always 0. (`number`)

    11 - `msgID` — A number identifying this chat message (used for allowing the player to report a message as spam). (`number`)

CHAT_MSG_SPELL_PERIODIC_FRIENDLYPLAYER_DAMAGE

Fires when a friendly player is affected by an instant or ongoing damage effect.

Arguments:

    1 - `message` — The text of the message. (`string`)

    7 - `worldChannelNumber` — Unused for this event; always 0. (`number`)

    8 - `channelNumber` — Unused for this event; always 0. (`number`)

    10 - `instanceID` — Unused for this event; always 0. (`number`)

    11 - `msgID` — A number identifying this chat message (used for allowing the player to report a message as spam). (`number`)

CHAT_MSG_SPELL_PERIODIC_HOSTILEPLAYER_BUFFS

Fires when a hostile player is affected by an instant cast or ongoing beneficial effect.

Arguments:

    1 - `message` — The text of the message. (`string`)

    7 - `worldChannelNumber` — Unused for this event; always 0. (`number`)

8 - `channelNumber` — Unused for this event; always 0. (number)

10 - `instanceID` — Unused for this event; always 0. (number)

11 - `msgID` — A number identifying this chat message (used for allowing the player to report a message as spam). (number)

CHAT_MSG_SPELL_PERIODIC_HOSTILEPLAYER_DAMAGE

Fires when a hostile player is affected by an instant or ongoing damaging effect.
Arguments:

1 - `message` — The text of the message. (string)

7 - `worldChannelNumber` — Unused for this event; always 0. (number)

8 - `channelNumber` — Unused for this event; always 0. (number)

10 - `instanceID` — Unused for this event; always 0. (number)

11 - `msgID` — A number identifying this chat message (used for allowing the player to report a message as spam). (number)

CHAT_MSG_SPELL_PERIODIC_PARTY_BUFFS

Fires when a party member is affected by an instant or ongoing beneficial effect.
Arguments:

1 - `message` — The text of the message. (string)

7 - `worldChannelNumber` — Unused for this event; always 0. (number)

8 - `channelNumber` — Unused for this event; always 0. (number)

10 - `instanceID` — Unused for this event; always 0. (number)

11 - `msgID` — A number identifying this chat message (used for allowing the player to report a message as spam). (number)

CHAT_MSG_SPELL_PERIODIC_PARTY_DAMAGE

Fires when a party member is affected by an instant or ongoing harmful spell or effect.
Arguments:

1 - `message` — The text of the message. (string)

7 - `worldChannelNumber` — Unused for this event; always 0. (number)

8 - `channelNumber` — Unused for this event; always 0. (number)

10 - `instanceID` — Unused for this event; always 0. (number)

11 - `msgID` — A number identifying this chat message (used for allowing the player to report a message as spam). (number)

CHAT_MSG_SPELL_PERIODIC_SELF_BUFFS

Fires when you gain or are affected by an instant cast or ongoing beneficial spell or effect.
Arguments:

1 - `message` — The text of the message. (string)

7 - `worldChannelNumber` — Unused for this event; always 0. (number)

8 - `channelNumber` — Unused for this event; always 0. (number)

10 - `instanceID` — Unused for this event; always 0. (number)

11 - `msgID` — A number identifying this chat message (used for allowing the player to report a message as spam). (number)

CHAT_MSG_SPELL_PERIODIC_SELF_DAMAGE

Fires when you gain or are affected by an instant or ongoing spell or effect.

Arguments:

1 - message — The text of the message. (string)

7 - worldChannelNumber — Unused for this event; always 0. (number)

8 - channelNumber — Unused for this event; always 0. (number)

10 - instanceID — Unused for this event; always 0. (number)

11 - msgID — A number identifying this chat message (used for allowing the player to report a message as spam). (number)

CHAT_MSG_SPELL_PET_BUFF

Fires when your pet casts a beneficial spell.

Arguments:

1 - message — The text of the message. (string)

7 - worldChannelNumber — Unused for this event; always 0. (number)

8 - channelNumber — Unused for this event; always 0. (number)

10 - instanceID — Unused for this event; always 0. (number)

11 - msgID — A number identifying this chat message (used for allowing the player to report a message as spam). (number)

CHAT_MSG_SPELL_PET_DAMAGE

Fires when your pet casts a harmful spell.

Arguments:

1 - message — The text of the message. (string)

7 - worldChannelNumber — Unused for this event; always 0. (number)

8 - channelNumber — Unused for this event; always 0. (number)

10 - instanceID — Unused for this event; always 0. (number)

11 - msgID — A number identifying this chat message (used for allowing the player to report a message as spam). (number)

CHAT_MSG_SPELL_SELF_BUFF

Fires when you start and stop casting a beneficial spell.

Arguments:

1 - message — The text of the message. (string)

7 - worldChannelNumber — Unused for this event; always 0. (number)

8 - channelNumber — Unused for this event; always 0. (number)

10 - instanceID — Unused for this event; always 0. (number)

11 - msgID — A number identifying this chat message (used for allowing the player to report a message as spam). (number)

CHAT_MSG_SPELL_SELF_DAMAGE

Fires when you start and stop casting a damaging spell.

Arguments:

1 - message — The text of the message. (string)

7 - worldChannelNumber — Unused for this event; always 0. (number)

8 - channelNumber — Unused for this event; always 0. (number)

10 - `instanceID` — Unused for this event; always 0. (`number`)

11 - `msgID` — A number identifying this chat message (used for allowing the player to report a message as spam). (`number`)

CHAT_MSG_SPELL_TRADESKILLS

Fires when you perform or a nearby player performs a tradeskill action.

Arguments:

1 - `message` — The text of the message. (`string`)

7 - `worldChannelNumber` — Unused for this event; always 0. (`number`)

8 - `channelNumber` — Unused for this event; always 0. (`number`)

10 - `instanceID` — Unused for this event; always 0. (`number`)

11 - `msgID` — A number identifying this chat message (used for allowing the player to report a message as spam). (`number`)

CHAT_MSG_SYSTEM

Fires when you receive a system message (examples: noting your AFK or DND status, indicating that a friend or guild member has come online or gone offline, a welcome message upon logging into the game, and so forth).

Argument:

1 - `message` — The text of the message. (`string`)

NOTE Many standard system message patterns can be found as localized format strings in `FrameXML\GlobalStrings.lua`. The message is already localized/formatted when it appears in this event, but referring to the original format strings can be useful if you want to parse variables from a standard message format.

CHAT_MSG_TEXT_EMOTE

Fires when a standard emote (for example, `/dance`, `/wave`, or `/silly`) is performed.

Arguments:

1 - `message` — The text of the emote message (for example, "Gazmik waves at Cladhaire"). (`string`)

2 - `sender` — Name of the player who sent the message. (`string`)

7 - `worldChannelNumber` — Unused for this event; always 0. (`number`)

8 - `channelNumber` — Unused for this event; always 0. (`number`)

10 - `instanceID` — Unused for this event; always 0. (`number`)

11 - `msgID` — A number identifying this chat message (used for allowing the player to report a message as spam). (`number`)

CHAT_MSG_WHISPER

Fires when you receive a whispered message from another player.

Arguments:

1 - `message` — The text of the message. (`string`)

2 - `sender` — Name of the player who sent the message. (`string`)

6 - `flag` — A flag indicating the status or confirming the identity of the sender. Possible values are `"AFK"`, `"DND"`, or `"GM"`. (string)

7 - `worldChannelNumber` — Unused for this event; always 0. (number)

8 - `channelNumber` — Unused for this event; always 0. (number)

10 - `instanceID` — Unused for this event; always 0. (number)

11 - `msgID` — A number identifying this chat message (used for allowing the player to report a message as spam). (number)

CHAT_MSG_WHISPER_INFORM

Fires when you send a whispered message to another player.

Arguments:

1 - `message` — The text of the message. (string)

2 - `sender` — Name of the player who sent the message. (string)

7 - `worldChannelNumber` — Unused for this event; always 0. (number)

8 - `channelNumber` — Unused for this event; always 0. (number)

10 - `instanceID` — Unused for this event; always 0. (number)

11 - `msgID` — A number identifying this chat message (used for allowing the player to report a message as spam). (number)

CHAT_MSG_YELL

Fires when the player yells or receives a message yelled by another player (visible to players in a wide area).

Arguments:

1 - `message` — The text of the message. (string)

2 - `sender` — Name of the player who sent the message. (string)

3 - `language` — Language (for example, Common, Orcish, Demonic) the message is in. (string)

6 - `flag` — A flag indicating the status or confirming the identity of the sender. Possible values are `"AFK"`, `"DND"`, or `"GM"`. (string)

7 - `worldChannelNumber` — Unused for this event; always 0. (number)

8 - `channelNumber` — Unused for this event; always 0. (number)

10 - `instanceID` — Unused for this event; always 0. (number)

11 - `msgID` — A number identifying this chat message (used for allowing the player to report a message as spam). (number)

CINEMATIC_START

Fires when the introductory cinematic for new characters starts.

CINEMATIC_STOP

Fires when the introductory cinematic for new characters stops.

CLOSE_INBOX_ITEM

Fires when you take an item from a mail.

Argument:

1 - `id` — ID of the mail slot from which you took the item. (number)

CLOSE_TABARD_FRAME
Fires (twice) when you close the tabard design window.

CLOSE_WORLD_MAP
Should fire when the world map is close, however, it doesn't appear to fire.

COMBAT_RATING_UPDATE
Fires when the player's combat statistics (as seen in the Character window) have changed.

COMBAT_TEXT_UPDATE
Fires when the client receives a message that can be displayed by the standard UI's floating combat text feature.

Arguments:

1 - `type` — The type of the combat message. Possible values: (string)

"ABSORB"	"DODGE"	"PARRY"
"AURA_END"	"ENERGY"	"PERIODIC_HEAL"
"AURA_END_HARMFUL"	"FACTION"	"RAGE"
"AURA_START"	"FOCUS"	"RESIST"
"AURA_START_HARMFUL"	"HEAL"	"SPELL_ABSORBED"
"BLOCK"	"HEAL_CRIT"	"SPELL_ACTIVE"
"COMBO_POINTS"	"HONOR_GAINED"	"SPELL_DAMAGE"
"DAMAGE"	"MANA"	"SPELL_RESISTED"
"DAMAGE_CRIT"	"MISS"	

2 - `desc1` — This field varies depending on the type of message. See Table 30-1 for details.

3 - `desc2` — This field varies depending on the type of message. See Table 30-1 for details.

Table 30-1: COMBAT_TEXT_UDPATE Description Arguments

TYPE	DESC1	DESC2
Damage	Amount Taken	nil
Power Gains and Honor Gains	Amount Gained	nil
Heals	Healer's Name	Amount Healed
Auras	Aura's Name	nil
Partial Absorptions	Amount Taken	Amount Absorbed
Full Absorptions	nil	nil
Faction Gain	Faction Name	Amount Gained
Spell Activation	Spell Name	nil

CONFIRM_BINDER
Fires when you attempt to bind your Hearthstone at an innkeeper NPC.

Argument:

    1 - newHome — New location to which your Hearthstone will be bound. (string)

CONFIRM_LOOT_ROLL

Fires when you attempt to roll on an item that is bind on pickup.

Arguments:

    1 - id — Slot ID that you're rolling for (number)

    2 - rolltype — Number representing the type of roll. (number)

- 0 — Pass

- 1 — Need

- 2 — Greed

CONFIRM_PET_UNLEARN

Fires when asking a Pet Trainer NPC to reset your (Hunter) pet's skills and training points.

Argument:

    1 - cost — Amount in copper that the untraining costs. (number)

CONFIRM_SUMMON

Fires when a summon is attempted on your character.

CONFIRM_TALENT_WIPE

Fires when you attempt to unlearn your talents.

Argument:

    1 - cost — The amount in copper that it will cost you to untrain your talents. (number)

CONFIRM_XP_LOSS

Fires when you attempt to resurrect at a graveyard Spirit Healer and will incur a cost (resurrection sickness) to do so. (Resurrecting at a graveyard formerly caused the player to lose experience points, but no longer does.)

CORPSE_IN_INSTANCE

Fires when you approach an entrance to the instance in which your corpse was left when you died.

CORPSE_IN_RANGE

Fires when you are close enough to your corpse to resurrect.

CORPSE_OUT_OF_RANGE

Fires when you leave the range around your corpse in which you can resurrect.

CRAFT_CLOSE

Fires when the craft frame closes. This is the frame used for Enchanting and Beast Training.

CRAFT_SHOW

Fires when the craft frame shows. This is the frame used for Beast Training and Enchanting.

CRAFT_UPDATE
Fires when the craft frame needs to be redrawn due to data update.

CURRENT_SPELL_CAST_CHANGED
Fires when a spell cast starts or stops.

CURSOR_UPDATE
Fires anytime the cursor changes.

CVAR_UPDATE
Fires when a client variable has been updated (though its value might not have changed).
Arguments:
> 1 - name — Name of the CVar that was updated. (string)
>
> 2 - value — Updated value assigned to the CVar. Note: For boolean values this is a string of 0 or 1. (string)

DELETE_ITEM_CONFIRM
Fires when you attempt to delete an item.
Arguments:
> 1 - itemName — Name of the item you are attempting to delete. (string)
>
> 2 - itemQuality — Numeric index representing the items quality. (number)

DISABLE_TAXI_BENCHMARK
Fires when a taxi benchmarking session is over.

DISPLAY_SIZE_CHANGED
Fires when the game resolution changes.

DUEL_FINISHED
Fires when a duel is finished.

DUEL_INBOUNDS
Fires when you are out of bounds of the duel area and then reenter bounds.

DUEL_OUTOFBOUNDS
Fires when you leave the duel area.

DUEL_REQUESTED
Fired when you are challenged to a duel. Does not fire when you challenge others to a duel.
Argument:
> 1 - challenger — The challenger's username. (string)

ENABLE_TAXI_BENCHMARK
Fires when a taxi benchmarking session is enabled.

EQUIP_BIND_CONFIRM
Fires when you attempt to equip a Bind on Equip item.
Argument:
> 1 - slot — Slot you are equipping into. (number)

FRIENDLIST_UPDATE

Fires when the content of the friends list has been updated.

GMSURVEY_DISPLAY

Fires when you are chosen to participate in a GM survey.

GOSSIP_CLOSED

Fires when the gossip frame is closed. (Still fires if the default UI skips display of the gossip frame in cases where it contains only one option.)

GOSSIP_CONFIRM

Fires when you need to confirm a gossip option other than binding to an inn.

Arguments:

1 - index — Numeric index of the gossip option you're confirming. (number)

2 - message — Message to display for the confirmation. (string)

3 - cost — The cost of the action you're confirming. Will be 0 if there is no cost. (number)

GOSSIP_CONFIRM_CANCEL

Fires when an attempt to confirm a gossip action gets canceled.

GOSSIP_ENTER_CODE

Fires when you attempt a gossip action that needs a code entered to complete (such as when redeeming a "loot card" from the WoW Trading Card Game or for a special Blizzard event).

Argument:

1 - id — ID of the gossip action you are attempting. (number)

GOSSIP_SHOW

Fires when the gossip window shows.

GUILDBANKBAGSLOTS_CHANGED

Fires when the contents of the guild bank have been updated.

GUILDBANKFRAME_CLOSED

Fires when the guild bank frame closes.

GUILDBANKFRAME_OPENED

Fires when the guild bank is opened.

GUILDBANKLOG_UPDATE

Fires when either the Log or the Money Log is shown.

GUILDBANK_ITEM_LOCK_CHANGED

Fires when you start or stop dragging an item in the guild bank.

GUILDBANK_UPDATE_MONEY

Fires when the amount of gold in the guild bank changes.

GUILDBANK_UPDATE_TABS

Fires when the number, names, icons, or settings of guild bank tabs have been updated.

GUILDBANK_UPDATE_WITHDRAWMONEY

Fires when the amount of money you can withdraw from the guild changes. (Includes changes due to deposits.)

GUILDTABARD_UPDATE

Fires when your guild's tabard changes.

GUILD_EVENT_LOG_UPDATE

Fires when you view the guild event log. Does not fire when updates to it happen.

GUILD_INVITE_CANCEL

Fires when you turn down a guild invitation.

GUILD_INVITE_REQUEST

Fires when your character is invited into a guild.

Arguments:

> 1 - from — Username of the player who invited you to their guild. (string)
>
> 2 - guildname — Name of the guild to which you are being invited. (string)

GUILD_MOTD

Fires when the guild message changes.

Argument:

> 1 - message — New guild message. (string)

GUILD_REGISTRAR_CLOSED

Fires twice when the guild registrar frame closes.

GUILD_REGISTRAR_SHOW

Fires when the guild registrar frame is shown.

GUILD_ROSTER_UPDATE

Fires when an update is available to the guild roster.

Argument:

> 1 - update — Happens whether or not the guild roster actually changes. Typically indicates if a player has joined or left your guild. (boolean)

HONOR_CURRENCY_UPDATE

Fires when your honor points update.

IGNORELIST_UPDATE

Fires twice whenever you edit your ignore list.

INSPECT_HONOR_UPDATE

Fires when you are inspecting another player and view their honor points.

INSPECT_TALENT_READY

Fires when you attempt to inspect another player and can view their talents.

INSTANCE_BOOT_START

Fires to indicate the player will soon be removed from the current instance (for example, if you leave a party while still in that party's dungeon instance). The amount of time remaining before that happens can be found by calling GetInstanceBootTimeRemaining.

INSTANCE_BOOT_STOP
Fires to indicate the player is no longer due to be removed from the current instance (for example, if you rejoin the party who owns the instance).

ITEM_LOCK_CHANGED
Fires when an item gets dragged or moved inside your inventory.
Arguments:

   1 - `bagID` — The bag ID that the slot is in. `(number)`

   2 - `slotID` — Slot ID whose lock is changing. `(number)`

ITEM_PUSH
Fires when you gain an item.
Arguments:

   1 - `bagID` — ID of the bag that the item is going into. `(number)`

   2 - `icon` — The icon file for the item being received. `(string)`

ITEM_TEXT_BEGIN
Fires when you examine an item like a book that displays a text screen.

ITEM_TEXT_CLOSED
Fires when the item text frame closes.

ITEM_TEXT_READY
Fires when you read an item like a book that has text. Also fires when you change pages.

ITEM_TEXT_TRANSLATION
Fires when an item text's translation amounts change.
Argument:

   1 - `maxvalue` — Max value. `(number)`

KNOWLEDGE_BASE_ARTICLE_LOAD_FAILURE
Fires when an article in the knowledge base fails to load.

KNOWLEDGE_BASE_ARTICLE_LOAD_SUCCESS
Fires when a knowledge base article successfully loads.

KNOWLEDGE_BASE_QUERY_LOAD_FAILURE
Fires when a knowledge base query fails due to load.

KNOWLEDGE_BASE_QUERY_LOAD_SUCCESS
Fires when a knowledge base query succeeds.

KNOWLEDGE_BASE_SERVER_MESSAGE
Fires when the knowledge base receives a new server message.

KNOWLEDGE_BASE_SETUP_LOAD_FAILURE
Fires if the knowledge base fails to load.

KNOWLEDGE_BASE_SETUP_LOAD_SUCCESS
Fires when the top issues load successfully.

KNOWLEDGE_BASE_SYSTEM_MOTD_UPDATED
Fires when the Knowledge Base MOTD changes.

KNOWN_TITLES_UPDATE
Fires when the number of titles available to the player changes.

LANGUAGE_LIST_CHANGED
Fires when the list of known languages changes.

LEARNED_SPELL_IN_TAB
Fires when a spell is learned inside of a given spell book tab.
Argument:
> 1 - `tabID` — ID of the tab that has the updated item. (`number`)

LFG_MATCH_CANCEL
Fires when a looking for group match is canceled.

LFG_MATCH_REQUEST
Fires when you have been matched to a group.
Argument:
> 1 - `matchedFor` — The reason you have been matched to a group. (`string`)

LFG_PENDING_CANCEL
Fires when you indicate that you are looking for a group to be matched with.

LFG_PENDING_REQUEST
Fires when you are attempting to be matched to a group.

LFG_UPDATE
Fires when the list of matching people gets updated.

LOCALPLAYER_PET_RENAMED
Fires when a hunter renames his pet.

LOGOUT_CANCEL
Is fired when a logout request is aborted.

LOOT_BIND_CONFIRM
Fired when a character attempts to loot an item that is bind on pickup.
Argument:
> 1 - `slotID` — ID of the loot slot in question. (`number`)

LOOT_CLOSED
Fired when the loot frame is closed.

LOOT_OPENED
Fires when the loot frame opens.
Argument:
> 1 - `autoLoot` — Specifies whether loot should be automatically picked up.
> (`boolean`)

LOOT_SLOT_CLEARED
Fires when you loot an item.
Argument:
> 1 - `slotID` — Numeric ID of the slot that was looted. (`number`)

MACRO_ACTION_BLOCKED

Fires when a macro attempts to do a blocked action.

MACRO_ACTION_FORBIDDEN

Fires when a macro attempts to do a forbidden action.

MAIL_CLOSED

Fires when the mailbox is closed.

MAIL_FAILED

Fires when a mail fails to send (for example, if the recipient is invalid).

MAIL_INBOX_UPDATE

Fires when the mailbox listing updates. Fires when you first open the mail box, or when you open and delete mail.

MAIL_SEND_INFO_UPDATE

Fires when you place an attachment in one of the mail item slots.

MAIL_SEND_SUCCESS

Fires when a mail is sent successfully.

MAIL_SHOW

Fires when the mailbox is opened.

MEETINGSTONE_CHANGED

Fires when new information is available for the Looking For Group interface. (The LFG UI takes over a function previously used by Meeting Stone world objects; this event has no relation to the current use of Meeting Stones.)

MERCHANT_CLOSED

Fires when you close a merchant window.

MERCHANT_SHOW

Fires when you open a merchant window.

MERCHANT_UPDATE

Fires when the content of the Merchant UI updates; for example, due to buying an item from or selling an item to the merchant. (Includes all purchases/sales, not just limited-supply items.)

MINIGAME_UPDATE

Triggers an update for the active minigame.

NOTE **Minigame APIs are currently unused and unavailable to third-party addons.**

MINIMAP_PING

Fires when you or a party member clicks the minimap to generate a ping on it.
Arguments:
> 1 - unit — Unit of the player that was the source of said event. (string)
> 2 - x — The x coordinate. 0 is the center point going out to .5 to the right and
> -.5 to the left. (number)
> 3 - y — The y coordinate. 0 is the center point going out to .5 to the top and
> -.5 to the bottom. (number)

MINIMAP_UPDATE_TRACKING

Fires when you change what you are tracking.

MINIMAP_UPDATE_ZOOM

Fires when the internal zoom level of the minimap changes — that is, upon entering an area where the minimap uses a different scale than the area you were in (major cities, buildings/caves, or the outdoor world, for instance), not upon manually zooming in or out on the minimap.

MIRROR_TIMER_PAUSE

Pauses a given mirror timer.

Argument:

1 - duration — How long the timers should be paused. (number)

MIRROR_TIMER_START

Fires when a new mirror time starts.

Arguments:

1 - name — Name of the timer that is starting. (string)

2 - value — The current value of the timer. (number)

3 - maxvalue — Max value of the timer. (number)

4 - step — Step that the value moves. (number)

5 - pause — Signifies whether the timer is paused. (number)

6 - label — Label for the timer. (string)

MIRROR_TIMER_STOP

Fires when a mirror timer stops.

Argument:

1 - name — Name associated with the timer that stopped. (string)

MODIFIER_STATE_CHANGED

Fires when a modifier key is pressed or released.

Arguments:

1 - key — Name of the key that you pressed. Possible values are LSHIFT, RSHIFT, LCTRL, RCTRL, LALT, and RALT. (string)

2 - state — State the key has entered. 1 means that the key has been pressed. 0 means that the key has been released. (number)

MOVIE_COMPRESSING_PROGRESS

Fires when video compression starts.

NOTE Currently, movie recording APIs are only functional on the Mac OS X client.

MOVIE_RECORDING_PROGRESS

Fires when movie recording starts.

MOVIE_UNCOMPRESSED_MOVIE

Fires when binding the "Compress Movies" is used.

Argument:

    1 - `filename` — Filename of the movie to compress. (`string`)

MUTELIST_UPDATE
Fires twice when a muted player leaves or joins a channel.

NEW_AUCTION_UPDATE
Fires whenever an item is placed in the Auction Item slot in the auction house. Also fires when the item is removed.

NEW_TITLE_EARNED
Fires when a new title becomes available to the player.

Argument:

    1 - `title` — Name of the title. (`string`)

OLD_TITLE_LOST
Fires when a title is lost and is no longer available.

Argument:

    1 - `title` — Name of the title you've lost. (`string`)

OPEN_MASTER_LOOT_LIST
Fires when the master loot list is opened.

OPEN_TABARD_FRAME
Fires when the create guild frame shows.

PARTY_INVITE_CANCEL
Should fire when an incoming party invite is canceled server side.

PARTY_INVITE_REQUEST
Fires when you are invited to a party.

Argument:

    1 - `sender` — Name of the player who sent the invite. (`string`)

PARTY_LEADER_CHANGED
Fires when the party leader changes or when you invite someone into your party.

PARTY_LOOT_METHOD_CHANGED
Fires when the loot method changes (or initially set upon forming a group).

PARTY_MEMBERS_CHANGED
Fires whenever you invite a member, a person declines an invitation, a member joins the group, a member leaves, or when the leader changes.

PARTY_MEMBER_DISABLE
Fires when a party member's offline state changes.

Argument:

    1 - `id` — The party ID of the disabled player. (`number`)

PARTY_MEMBER_ENABLE
Fires when a party member is enabled.

Argument:

1 - `id` — ID of the affected party member. (number)

PETITION_CLOSED

Fires when a guild or arena charter closes.

PETITION_SHOW

Fires when a guild or arena charter is presented to you.

PETITION_VENDOR_CLOSED

Fires when you close the Arena Registrar frame. In-game this is shown by visiting the Arena Organizer.

PETITION_VENDOR_SHOW

Fires when you open the Arena Registrar frame. In-game this is shown by visiting the Arena Organizer.

PETITION_VENDOR_UPDATE

Fires when the Arena Registrar frame updates. In-game this is shown by visiting the Arena Organizer.

PET_ATTACK_START

Fires when your pet enters combat.

PET_ATTACK_STOP

Fires when your pet leaves combat.

PET_BAR_HIDEGRID

Fires when you stop dragging a pet skill on or off of the their action bar.

PET_BAR_SHOWGRID

Fires when you start dragging a pet skill onto or off of the pet action bar.

PET_BAR_UPDATE

Fires when you summon or dismiss a pet. Fires when the bar changes.

PET_BAR_UPDATE_COOLDOWN

Fires when a pet skill's cooldown changes.

PET_DISMISS_START

Fires when a pet is dismissed; only applies to pets dismissible by the `PetDismiss` function (Warlock minions, Mind Control targets, quest or other special pets, and so on, but not Hunter pets).

PET_STABLE_CLOSED

Fires twice when the pet stable frame closes.

PET_STABLE_SHOW

Fires when the pet stable frame shows.

PET_STABLE_UPDATE

Fires when you swap pets around or buy a pet slot. However, this event appears to be deprecated and no longer fires.

PET_STABLE_UPDATE_PAPERDOLL

Fires when you select another one of your pets in the stable. However, this appears depreciated and does not fire.

PET_UI_CLOSE

Fires when the Pet tab on the Character frame closes. However, this appears to be deprecated and does not fire.

PET_UI_UPDATE

Fires when the Pet tab on the Character frame needs to be updated. However, this appears to be deprecated and doesn't fire.

PLAYERBANKBAGSLOTS_CHANGED

Fires when you buy a bank bag slot.

PLAYERBANKSLOTS_CHANGED

Fires when the content of a bank slot changes.

Argument:

> 1 - slotID — Slot ID that changes. 1-28 are the bank slots. 29-35 are the bank bags. (number)

PLAYER_ALIVE

Fires when a player releases her spirit after death or if she accepts a resurrection before releasing.

PLAYER_AURAS_CHANGED

Fires when you receive or lose a buff or debuff.

PLAYER_CAMPING

Fires when you attempt to log out while not in an area that provides Rest state.

PLAYER_COMBO_POINTS

Fires whenever your combo points change.

PLAYER_CONTROL_GAINED

Fires when you gain control of your character; such as when a fear effect wears off or a taxi flight ends.

PLAYER_CONTROL_LOST

Fires when you lose control of your character (for example, when suffering a fear effect, under Mind Control, or taking a taxi flight).

PLAYER_DAMAGE_DONE_MODS

Fires when an effect changes the spell damage your character does. This does not fire for physical damage modifiers (that is, it fires for applying Wizard Oil, not for applying Rockbiter Weapon).

Argument:

> 1 - unit — Is always "player". (string)

PLAYER_DEAD

Fires when the player dies.

PLAYER_ENTERING_WORLD

Fires when the player enters the world for the first time, or whenever a loading screen is shown.

PLAYER_ENTER_COMBAT

Fires whenever the player enters combat.

PLAYER_FARSIGHT_FOCUS_CHANGED
Fires whenever a change in the focus of your view ends. Examples include Eye of Kilrogg, Eyes of the Beast, Eagle Eye, and other similar spells and effects.

PLAYER_FLAGS_CHANGED
Fires whenever a unit's flags change due to events like going or coming back from AFK status.
Argument:

> 1 - unitID — Unit of the affected player. (string)

PLAYER_FOCUS_CHANGED
Fires whenever your target focus has changed.

PLAYER_GUILD_UPDATE
Fires when something about a characters position in a guild changes.
Argument:

> 1 - unitID — Unit of the player effect. Most of the time this will be player, however sometimes it will be nil. (string)

PLAYER_LEAVE_COMBAT
Fires when a player leaves combat.

PLAYER_LEAVING_WORLD
Fires when a player is logging out or leaving one continent or instance for another.

PLAYER_LEVEL_UP
Fires whenever you level up.
Arguments:

> 1 - level — New player level. More accurate than UnitLevel at that time. (string)
>
> 2 - hp — Hit points gained. (number)
>
> 3 - mp — Mana points gained. (number)
>
> 4 - talentPoints — Talent points gained. (number)
>
> 5 - strength — Strength points gained. (number)
>
> 6 - agility — Agility points gained. (number)
>
> 7 - stamina — Stamina points gained. (number)
>
> 8 - intellect — Intellect points gained. (number)
>
> 9 - spirit — Spirit points gained. (number)

PLAYER_LOGIN
Fires only the first time a player enters the game.

PLAYER_LOGOUT
Fires when the player is actually leaving the game.

PLAYER_MONEY
Fires whenever the player gains or loses money.

PLAYER_PVP_KILLS_CHANGED
Fires whenever a player kills another player in a PvP battle.

PLAYER_PVP_RANK_CHANGED

Fires whenever your PvP rank has changed.

PLAYER_QUITING

Fires when you type **/quit**.

PLAYER_REGEN_DISABLED

Fires when normal health regeneration is stopped upon entering combat.

PLAYER_REGEN_ENABLED

Fires when normal health regeneration is resumed upon leaving combat.

PLAYER_SKINNED

Fires when the insignia from your corpse is taken in a battleground.

PLAYER_TARGET_CHANGED

Fires when you target someone new.

PLAYER_TRADE_MONEY

Fires whenever the money on the trade frame gets updated.

PLAYER_UNGHOST

Fires when the player resurrects after returning to her corpse as a ghost.

PLAYER_UPDATE_RESTING

Fires when the player enters or leaves a place where they can gain Rest status.

PLAYER_XP_UPDATE

Fires whenever the player's current total of experience points changes.

PLAYTIME_CHANGED

Fires in relation to total play time limits enforced in certain locales.

QUEST_ACCEPT_CONFIRM

Fires when certain types of quests (for example, escort quests) are accepted by another person in the player's group.

> **Arguments:**
>> 1 - name — Name of the user who started the quest. (string)
>> 2 - quest — Name of the quest that was started. (string)

QUEST_COMPLETE

Fires when you are turning in a completed quest.

QUEST_DETAIL

Fires when the quest detail frame displays.

QUEST_FINISHED

Fires when the quest frame is closed.

QUEST_GREETING

Fires when a quest NPC offers or accepts more than one quest.

QUEST_ITEM_UPDATE

Fires when quest item info is updated. However, this event doesn't seem to fire and may be deprecated.

QUEST_LOG_UPDATE

Fires when new information is available for the Quest Log.

QUEST_PROGRESS

Fires when you talk to a quest NPC about a quest you have not yet completed.

QUEST_WATCH_UPDATE

Fires when a quest's goals are updated.

Argument:

> 1 - questID — ID of the quest that got updated. (number)

RAID_INSTANCE_WELCOME

Fires when you enter an instance that has a reset timer.

Arguments:

> 1 - name — Name of the instance you're entering. (string)
>
> 2 - ttl — The time till the instance resets, in seconds. (number)

RAID_ROSTER_UPDATE

Fires when the raid roster changes. This occurs when a raid is formed, disbanded, gains a new member, loses a member, or changes loot rules, or when raid members are rearranged.

RAID_TARGET_UPDATE

Fires when a raid target icon is altered.

READY_CHECK

Fires when a ready check is triggered.

Argument:

> 1 - name — Username of the person who triggered the ready check. (string)

REPLACE_ENCHANT

Fires when you attempt to replace an enchant on an item with another.

Arguments:

> 1 - current — Name of the current enchant. (string)
>
> 2 - new — Name of the proposed enchant. (string)

RESURRECT_REQUEST

Fires when someone attempts to resurrect you.

Argument:

> 1 - name — Name of the user who is attempting to resurrect you. (string)

SCREENSHOT_FAILED

Fires if a screenshot attempt fails for whatever reason.

SCREENSHOT_SUCCEEDED

Fires when a screenshot is successfully taken.

SEND_MAIL_COD_CHANGED

Fires when you change the COD amount on an outgoing mail.

SEND_MAIL_MONEY_CHANGED

Fires when the money sent on a mail item changes.

SHOW_COMPARE_TOOLTIP

Should fire to trigger the compare tooltip, however, it doesn't seem to fire.

SKILL_LINES_CHANGED

Fires when you gain a skill or train to a higher rank in a profession.

SOCKET_INFO_CLOSE

Fires when you close the socket info window.

SOCKET_INFO_UPDATE

Fires when the socket info window opens. Also fires when you add or remove a gem, or when you click Socket Gems.

SPELLS_CHANGED

Fires when the contents of your spellbook change, either graphically (for example, swapping your main hand weapon, which changes the icon of the Attack spell) or actual contents (learning a new spell). Also fires upon opening the Spellbook UI.

SPELL_UPDATE_COOLDOWN

Fires when a spell cooldown starts.

SPELL_UPDATE_USABLE

Fires when your ability to use spells changes. Examples would include the short cooldown between skill usages.

START_AUTOREPEAT_SPELL

Fires when you start an action that automatically repeats itself, such as a "Shoot".

START_LOOT_ROLL

Fires when a new group loot roll is started.

Arguments:

> 1 - `id` — ID for this roll. (number)
>
> 2 - `time` — How long the roll will last. (number)

START_MINIGAME

Fires when a minigame starts.

NOTE Minigame APIs are currently unused and unavailable to third-party addons.

STOP_AUTOREPEAT_SPELL

Fires when you cancel an action that automatically repeats itself, such as a "Shoot".

SYSMSG

Fires when a system message needs to be displayed. (Used for certain messages appearing by default in the UIErrorsFrame at the top center of the screen, not for system messages in the chat window.)

Arguments:

> 1 - `message` — Message that needs to be displayed. (string)
>
> 2 - `red` — Red value for the message, between 0 and 1. (number)
>
> 3 - `green` — The green value for the message, between 0 and 1. (number)
>
> 4 - `blue` — The blue value for the message, between 0 and 1. (number)

TABARD_CANSAVE_CHANGED
Fires when the tabard is savable.

TABARD_SAVE_PENDING
Fires when there is a tabard save in progress.

TAXIMAP_CLOSED
Fires when you close the taxi frame.

TAXIMAP_OPENED
Fires when the taxi frame is opened.

TIME_PLAYED_MSG
Fires when the user requests the amount of time played, normally via **/played**.
Arguments:

> 1 - total — The amount of time played total, in seconds. (number)
>
> 2 - level — The amount of time played this level, in seconds. (number)

TRADE_ACCEPT_UPDATE
Fires when the accepted status on either side changes during a trade.
Arguments:

> 1 - player — Your accepted status. 1 for yes, 0 for no. (number)
>
> 2 - target — Your target's accepted status. 1 for yes, 0 for no. (number)

TRADE_CLOSED
Fires when the trade frame hides.

TRADE_MONEY_CHANGED
Fires when your trade target changes the amount of money they are offering you in a trade.

TRADE_PLAYER_ITEM_CHANGED
Fires when you change one of your trade item slots. Your trade target does not trigger this event.
Argument:

> 1 - slotID — Slot ID of the item you are trading (1-7). (number)

TRADE_REPLACE_ENCHANT
Fires if a trade based enchant will replace a current enchantment.
Arguments:

> 1 - current — The current item enchant. (string)
>
> 2 - new — Name of the new proposed item enchant. (string)

TRADE_REQUEST
Currently unused; was used in earlier versions of the game to ask the player for confirmation before showing a trade window offered by another player.

TRADE_REQUEST_CANCEL
Fires when a trade has been canceled without being completed.

TRADE_SHOW
Fires when the trade frame is shown.

TRADE_SKILL_CLOSE

Fires when the trade skill frame is closed.

TRADE_SKILL_SHOW

Fired when the trade skill frame is shown.

TRADE_SKILL_UPDATE

Fires when your trade skill list needs to be updated; this includes learning a new skill, showing the trade skill frame, and toggling a header.

TRADE_TARGET_ITEM_CHANGED

Fires when the contents of the other player's item slots in the trade window change.
Argument:

> 1 - slotID — Slot's ID that changed (1-7). (number)

TRADE_UPDATE

Should be firing when the frame needs to be redrawn, however it does not seem to fire and may be deprecated.

TRAINER_CLOSED

Fires when the class or profession trainer frame closes.

TRAINER_SHOW

Fires when the class or profession trainer frame shows.

TRAINER_UPDATE

Fires when the skill list at the class trainer needs updating. This includes when the frame opens, filter is changed, skills are learned, and headers are being toggled.

TUTORIAL_TRIGGER

Fires when the tutorial/tips are shown. Will not fire if tutorials are turned off.
Argument:

> 1 - id — ID for the tutorial that needs to show. Valid values are between 1 and 51. (number)

UI_ERROR_MESSAGE

Fires when a game error message (for example, "You cannot attack that target," "Your pet is dead," "Your inventory is full," and so on; does not include scripting error messages) occurs and should be displayed in the UI.
Argument:

> 1 - message — Message that's to be displayed. (string)

UI_INFO_MESSAGE

Fires when an informative message (for example, "No fish are hooked" or the message that appears upon trying to enter a raid instance for which you don't meet the requirements) needs to be displayed in the UI.
Argument:

> 1 - message — Message that needs to be displayed. (string)

UNIT_ATTACK

Fires when a unit's weapon changes.

Argument:

> 1 - unitID — Unit that was affected. (string)

UNIT_ATTACK_POWER

Fires when a unit's attack power changes.

Argument:

> 1 - unitID — Unit that was affected. (string)

UNIT_ATTACK_SPEED

Fires when a unit's attack speed is changed.

Argument:

> 1 - unitID — Unit that was affected. (string)

UNIT_AURA

Fires when a unit loses or gains a buff or debuff.

Argument:

> 1 - unitID — Unit that was affected. (string)

UNIT_CLASSIFICATION_CHANGED

Fires when a unit changes classification, such as to elite.

Argument:

> 1 - unitID — Unit that was affected. (string)

UNIT_COMBAT

Fires when a unit takes damage during combat.

Arguments:

> 1 - unitID — Unit that was affected. (string)
>
> 2 - action — The action type that happened, such as WOUND, DODGE, HEAL. (string)
>
> 3 - descriptor — A descriptor that describes the action, such as CRITICAL, CRUSHING. (string)
>
> 4 - damage — The amount of damage or healing received. (number)
>
> 5 - damageType — The type of damage dealt. Is 0 (physical) for healing. (number)

UNIT_DAMAGE

Fires when a unit's weapon damage changes.

Argument:

> 1 - unitID — Unit that was affected. (string)

UNIT_DEFENSE

Fires when a unit's defense changes.

Argument:

> 1 - unitID — Unit that was affected. (string)

UNIT_DISPLAYPOWER

Fires when the type of power your character has changes; for example, a druid shapeshifting causing his mana bar to be replaced by a rage or energy bar.
   Argument:

   1 - unitID — Unit that was affected. (string)

UNIT_ENERGY

Fires when a unit's energy level changes.
   Argument:

   1 - unitID — Unit that was affected. (string)

UNIT_FACTION

Fires when a unit's PvP status changes.
   Argument:

   1 - unitID — Unit that was affected. (string)

UNIT_FLAGS

Fires during combat, when a unit has a status change. Flags include effects such as stunned, in combat, and fleeing.
   Argument:

   1 - unitID — Unit that was affected. (string)

UNIT_FOCUS

Fires when a unit's focus level (the power type used by Hunter pets) changes.
   Argument:

   1 - unitID — Unit that was affected. (string)

UNIT_HAPPINESS

Fires when pet happiness changes.

UNIT_HEALTH

Fires whenever a unit's health changes.
   Argument:

   1 - unitID — Unit that was affected. (string)

UNIT_INVENTORY_CHANGED

Fires whenever an equipped item changes.
   Argument:

   1 - unitID — Unit that was affected. (string)

UNIT_LEVEL

Fires when a unit's level changes.
   Argument:

   1 - unitID — Unit that was affected. (string)

UNIT_LOYALTY

Fires when your pet's loyalty changes.

UNIT_MANA

Fires when a unit's mana level changes.
Argument:

> 1 - unitID — Unit that was affected. (string)

UNIT_MAXENERGY

Fires when a unit's maximum energy levels change.
Argument:

> 1 - unitID — Unit that was affected. (string)

UNIT_MAXFOCUS

Fires when a unit's maximum focus changes.
Argument:

> 1 - unitID — Unit that was affected. (string)

UNIT_MAXHAPPINESS

Fires when a unit's maximum happiness changes. Currently unused (happiness for Hunter pets is not treated as a power type in the current version of the client, though it was once defined as such).
Argument:

> 1 - unitID — Unit that was affected. (string)

UNIT_MAXHEALTH

Fires when a unit's maximum health changes.
Argument:

> 1 - unitID — Unit that was affected. (string)

UNIT_MAXMANA

Fires when a unit's maximum mana changes.
Argument:

> 1 - unitID — Unit that was affected. (string)

UNIT_MAXRAGE

Fires when a unit's maximum rage changes.
Argument:

> 1 - unitID — Unit that was affected. (string)

UNIT_MODEL_CHANGED

Fires when a unit's model changes; can be due to shapeshifting, being affected by Polymorph or a similar spell, or by equipping weapons or armor.
Argument:

> 1 - unitID — Unit that was affected. (string)

UNIT_NAME_UPDATE

Fires when a unit's name is changed or announced.

Argument:

> 1 - unitID — Unit that was affected. (string)

UNIT_PET

Fires when a unit changes its pet, including loss or gain.
Argument:

> 1 - unitID — Unit that was affected. (string)

UNIT_PET_EXPERIENCE

Fires when a unit's pet gains or loses experience points.

UNIT_PET_TRAINING_POINTS

Fires when a unit's pet's training points change.

UNIT_PORTRAIT_UPDATE

Fires when a unit's portrait changes; can be due to shapeshifting, being affected by Polymorph or a similar spell, or by equipping weapons or armor. Also fires when a unit's portrait changes from a generic image for their race and gender to a specific image based on the unit's model.
Argument:

> 1 - unitID — Unit that was affected. (string)

UNIT_QUEST_LOG_CHANGED

Fires when a unit's Quest Log changes.
Argument:

> 1 - unitID — Unit that was affected. (string)

UNIT_RAGE

Fires when a unit's rage changes.
Argument:

> 1 - unitID — Unit that was affected. (string)

UNIT_RANGEDDAMAGE

Fires when a unit's range damage changes.
Argument:

> 1 - unitID — Unit that was affected. (string)

UNIT_RANGED_ATTACK_POWER

Fires when a unit's ranged attack power changes.
Argument:

> 1 - unitID — Unit that was affected. (string)

UNIT_RESISTANCES

Fires when a unit's resistances change.
Argument:

> 1 - unitID — Unit that was affected. (string)

UNIT_SPELLCAST_CHANNEL_START

Fires when a unit starts channeling a spell.

Arguments:

    1 - `unitID` — Unit casting. (`string`)

    2 - `spell` — Name of the spell being cast. (`string`)

    3 - `rank` — Rank of the spell being cast. (`string`)

UNIT_SPELLCAST_CHANNEL_STOP

Fires when a spell that's being channeled stops.

Arguments:

    1 - `unitID` — Unit that was casting. (`string`)

    2 - `spell` — Name of the spell whose cast ended. (`string`)

    3 - `rank` — Rank of the spell whose cast ended. (`string`)

UNIT_SPELLCAST_CHANNEL_UPDATE

Fires when a channel spell gets interrupted or delayed.

Arguments:

    1 - `unitID` — Unit casting. (`string`)

    2 - `spell` — Name of the spell being cast. (`string`)

    3 - `rank` — Rank of the spell being cast. (`string`)

UNIT_SPELLCAST_DELAYED

Fires when a regular spell cast is delayed.

Arguments:

    1 - `unitID` — Unit casting. (`string`)

    2 - `spell` — Name of the spell being cast. (`string`)

    3 - `rank` — Rank of the spell being cast. (`string`)

UNIT_SPELLCAST_FAILED

Fires when a spell cast fails.

Arguments:

    1 - `unitID` — Unit casting. (`string`)

    2 - `spell` — Name of the spell being cast. (`string`)

    3 - `rank` — Rank of the spell being cast. (`string`)

UNIT_SPELLCAST_FAILED_QUIET

Fires when a spell cast fails.

Arguments:

    1 - `unitID` — Unit casting. (`string`)

    2 - `spell` — Name of the spell being cast. (`string`)

    3 - `rank` — Rank of the spell being cast. (`string`)

UNIT_SPELLCAST_INTERRUPTED

Fires when a spell cast is interrupted.

Arguments:

1 - unitID — Unit casting. (string)

2 - spell — Name of the spell being cast. (string)

3 - rank — Rank of the spell being cast. (string)

UNIT_SPELLCAST_SENT

Fires when a spell cast attempt is started. Only fires for spells cast by the player.

Arguments:

1 - unitID — Unit casting. (string)

2 - spell — Name of the spell being cast. (string)

3 - rank — Rank of the spell being cast. (string)

4 - target — Name of the target of your spell. (string)

UNIT_SPELLCAST_START

Fires when you start casting a spell.

Arguments:

1 - unitID — Unit casting. (string)

2 - spell — Name of the spell being cast. (string)

3 - rank — Rank of the spell being cast. (string)

UNIT_SPELLCAST_STOP

Fires when a unit's spell cast stops.

Arguments:

1 - unitID — Unit casting. (string)

2 - spell — Name of the spell being cast. (string)

3 - rank — Rank of the spell being cast. (string)

UNIT_SPELLCAST_SUCCEEDED

Fires when a unit's spellcast succeeds.

Arguments:

1 - unitID — Unit casting. (string)

2 - spell — Name of the spell being cast. (string)

3 - rank — Rank of the spell being cast. (string)

UNIT_STATS

Fires when a unit's stats change.

Argument:

1 - unitID — Unit affected by the event. (string)

UNIT_TARGET

Fires when a unit's target changes.

Argument:

1 - unitID — Unit affected by the event. (string)

UPDATE_BATTLEFIELD_SCORE

Fires when a new battleground score is available.

UPDATE_BATTLEFIELD_STATUS

Fires when your status in a battleground or its queue changes.

UPDATE_BINDINGS

Fires when a key binding is made or unbound.

UPDATE_BONUS_ACTIONBAR

Fires when the bonus action bar needs an update.

UPDATE_CHAT_COLOR

Fires when you change one of the color filters on the chat frame.

Arguments:

    1 - `type` — Filter that you're changing. (`string`)

    2 - `red` — Red in the color. The value is between 0 (none) and 1 (full). (`number`)

    3 - `green` — The green in the color. The value is between 0 (none) and 1 (full). (`number`)

    4 - `blue` — The blue in the color. The value is between 0 (none) and 1 (full). (`number`)

UPDATE_CHAT_WINDOWS

Fires during loading, indicating that information about the configuration of chat windows is available.

UPDATE_EXHAUSTION

Fires when your rest status (which determines the amount of experience points earned from killing creatures) changes.

UPDATE_FACTION

Fires when you gain or lose reputation with a faction or discover a new faction.

UPDATE_FLOATING_CHAT_WINDOWS

Fires during loading, indicating that information about the configuration of certain chat windows is available.

UPDATE_GM_STATUS

Fires when you enter or exit the section of the UI that allows you to submit GM tickets.

Argument:

    1 - `available` — Is 1 if filing GM tickets is allowed, 0 otherwise. (`number`)

UPDATE_INSTANCE_INFO

Fires when updated raid info is available.

UPDATE_INVENTORY_ALERTS

Fires if an item's durability status changes.

UPDATE_LFG

Fires when query results are available.

UPDATE_LFG_LIST

Fires when query results are available.

UPDATE_LFG_TYPES

Fires when the types of groups available changes.

UPDATE_MACROS

Fires when your macro selection changes, a new macro is created, or a macro is deleted.

UPDATE_MASTER_LOOT_LIST

Fires when new information is available for the master loot list.

UPDATE_MOUSEOVER_UNIT

Fires whenever you mouse over any player or nonplayer character.

UPDATE_PENDING_MAIL

Fires when your amount of new mail has changed.

UPDATE_SHAPESHIFT_FORM

Fires when the player enters or leaves a state considered a shapeshift by game mechanics (which includes states other than Druid shapeshifting, such as Warrior stances, Rogue and Druid Cat Form stealth, and Priests' Shadowform; but excludes some abilities normally shown on the shapeshift action bar such as Paladin auras).

UPDATE_SHAPESHIFT_FORMS

Fires when the player learns (or unlearns) an ability normally shown on the shapeshift action bar (which includes abilities other than Druid shapeshifting, such as Paladin auras and Warrior stances).

UPDATE_STEALTH

Fires when you enter or leave stealth mode.

UPDATE_TICKET

Fires when the status of an active GM ticket changes.

UPDATE_TRADESKILL_RECAST

Fires when a single tradeskill item from a batch tradeskill creation finishes.

UPDATE_WORLD_STATES

Fires from within a battlefield when a score changing event occurs.

USE_BIND_CONFIRM

Fires when using an item will cause it to bind to you.

VARIABLES_LOADED

Fires during loading, indicating that the values of saved variables used by the default UI have been initialized. Addon-specific saved variables may not have been initialized when this event fires; addon authors should monitor the ADDON_LOADED event for confirmation of when their variables are loaded.

VOICE_CHAT_ENABLED_UPDATE

Fires when the voice chat feature is enabled or disabled (for the local client).

VOICE_LEFT_SESSION

Fires periodically when in a voice channel.

VOICE_PLATE_START

Fires when a channel member starts to talk in voice chat.

Arguments:

    1 - name — Username of the player who's talking. (string)

    2 - unit — Unit ID of the player who's talking (for example, party1). (string)

VOICE_PLATE_STOP

Fires when a player in a voice channel is done talking.

> 1 - `name` — Username of the player who's talking. (`string`)
>
> 2 - `unit` — Unit ID of the player who's talking (for example, party1). (`string`)

VOICE_PUSH_TO_TALK_START

Fires when you push the button to start talking.

VOICE_PUSH_TO_TALK_STOP

Fires when the player releases the talk button.

VOICE_START

Fires when a player starts talking in voice chat.

Argument:

> 1 - `unit` — Unit of the player that's talking (for example, party1. (`string`)

VOICE_STATUS_UPDATE

Fires whenever a party member changes their voice status. Also fires when their settings or privileges change.

VOICE_STOP

Fires when another player stops talking in voice chat.

Argument:

> 1 - `unit` — Unit of the player that's talking (for example, party1. (`string`)

WHO_LIST_UPDATE

Fires when new info is available in response to a who query.

WORLD_MAP_UPDATE

Fires when the world map needs an update — when it is shown or hidden, or the player moves to a different zone.

ZONE_CHANGED

Fires when the player moves from one area to another (including from one subzone to another, or even when moving between areas that have the same name), but only if `ZONE_CHANGED_INDOORS` and `ZONE_CHANGED_NEW_AREA` do not fire.

ZONE_CHANGED_INDOORS

Fires when the player moves from one area to another and the "is indoors/outdoors" flag (which restricts the use of certain abilities including mounts) may have changed.

ZONE_CHANGED_NEW_AREA

Fires when the player moves from one major zone (for example, Elwynn Forest, Durotar, Shattrath City, or Netherstorm) to another, including upon entering or leaving an instance.

# CHAPTER 31

Widget Reference

Most addons require frames to operate, either for event registration and dispatch or to display some custom user interface element. Once these frames are created (either through XML or using the API function `CreateFrame()`), they may need to be manipulated. World of Warcraft provides an expansive interface to frames in its Widget API.

Widget API

UIObject

UIObject is an abstract UI object type that can't actually be created. It serves as a base for all other UI objects, implementing methods that are common to all UI elements. The UIObject methods follow:

- `UIObject:GetName()` — Returns the name of the object.
- `UIObject:GetObjectType()` — Returns the type of the object (`Frame`, `Button`, and so on).
- `UIObject:IsObjectType(type)` — Returns whether the object is of the given type (`Frame`, `Button`, and so on).

FontInstance

FontInstance is an abstract UI object type; that can't actually be created. It serves as a base for other font-related objects, grouping together methods that are common to all font derivatives. FontInstance inherits all methods from UIObject, in addition to the following:

- `FontInstance:GetFont()` — Returns the font details of the font instance (`fontName`, `fontHeight`, `fontFlags`)

- `FontInstance:GetFontObject()` — Returns the font object used by the font, if present. See SetFontObject.

- `FontInstance:GetJustifyH()` — Returns the horizontal justification of the text in the FontInstance.

- `FontInstance:GetJustifyV()` — Returns font's vertical justification.

- `FontInstance:GetShadowColor()` — Returns the color of the font's text shadow (`red`, `green`, `blue`, `alpha`). `FontInstance:GetShadowOffset()` — Returns the font's shadow offset (`x`, `y`).

- `FontInstance:GetSpacing()` — Returns the font's spacing.

- `FontInstance:GetTextColor()` — Returns the default text color for the FontInstance (`r`, `g`, `b`, `a`).

- `FontInstance:SetFont(filename, fontHeight[, flags])` — Sets the font of the font object.

- `FontInstance:SetFontObject(font or "font" or nil)` — Sets a font object to be used as the current font.

- `FontInstance:SetJustifyH↵("justify")` — Sets the horizontal justification. (`"LEFT"`, `"CENTER"`, `"MIDDLE"`, `"RIGHT"`).

- `FontInstance:SetJustifyV↵("justify")` — Sets the vertical justification. (`"TOP"`, `"CENTER"`, `"MIDDLE"`, `"BOTTOM"`).

- `FontInstance:SetShadowColor(red, green, blue [, alpha])` — Sets the color of the font's shadow.

- `FontInstance:SetShadowOffset(x, y)` — Sets the distance to offset the shadow of the text.

- `FontInstance:SetSpacing(spacing)` — Sets the spacing of the font.

- `FontInstance:SetTextColor()` — Sets the primary (text) color.

Region

Region is an abstract UI object type that can't actually be created. It serves as a base for UI Objects, grouping together methods related to the size, location, and visibility of a UIObject. This is not a "Region" that can be returned using `Frame:GetRegions()`. Region inherits all methods from UIObject, in addition to the following:

- `Region:CanChangeProtectedState()` — Returns whether or not a frame can make a protected change. This is true when the frame is not secure or the player isn't in combat.

- `Region:ClearAllPoints()` — Clear all anchor points for the given region. Note: This function cannot be called during combat lockdown.

- `Region:GetBottom()` — Returns the distance in pixels from the top of the screen to the bottom of the region.

- `Region:GetCenter()` — Returns the screen coordinates of the region's center (x, y).

- `Region:GetHeight()` — Returns the height of the region.

- `Region:GetLeft()` — Returns the distance in pixels between the left edge of the screen and the left edge of the region.

- `Region:GetNumPoints()` — Returns the number of anchor points set for the frame.

- `Region:GetParent()` — Returns the region's parent object.

- `Region:GetPoint(index)` — Returns the specified anchor point for the frame (`point, relativeTo, relativePoint, offsetX, offsetY`). The index must be a number from 1 to `frame:GetNumPoints()`.

- `Region:GetRect()` — Returns the rectangle position and size for the region (`left, right, width, height`).

- `Region:GetRight()` — Returns the distance in pixels between the left edge of the screen and the right edge of the Region.

- `Region:GetTop()` — Returns the distance in pixels between the top of the screen and the top of the region.

- `Region:GetWidth()` — Returns the width of the region.

- `Region:IsProtected()` — Indicates that insecure code cannot call protected methods of this region during combat.

- `Region:SetAllPoints(region or "regionName")` — Sets all anchors of this region to match the given region's. Note: This function cannot be called during combat lockdown.

- `Region:SetHeight(height)` — Sets the height of this region to the given value. Setting the height to `0` will cause it to be determined by the region's anchors instead. Note: This function cannot be called during combat lockdown.

- `Region:SetParent(region or "regionName")` — Sets the parent of this region to the given region. Note: This function cannot be called during combat lockdown.

- `Region:SetPoint("point" [, region [, "relativePoint"]] [, offsetX, offsetY])` — Sets a given anchor point on this region. This function has several optional parameters, all with default values. `region` is by default the parent object; `"relativePoint"` is by default the same as `"point'"`; `offsetX` and `offsetY` both default to `0`. Note: This function cannot be called during combat lockdown. Example:

```
local frame = CreateFrame("Frame", "TestFrame");
local background = frame:CreateTexture("TestFrameBackground", ↵
"BACKGROUND");
background:SetTexture(1, 1, 1, 0.25);
```

```
frame:SetParent(UIParent);

-- Position the frame's background in the frame
background:SetPoint("TOPLEFT");
background:SetPoint("BOTTOMRIGHT");

-- Set the top left corner 5px to the right and 15px above ↵
UIParent's top left corner
frame:SetPoint("TOPLEFT", 5, 15);

-- Set the bottom edge to be 10px below WorldFrame's center
frame:SetPoint("BOTTOM", WorldFrame, "CENTER", 0, -10);

-- Set the right edge to be 20px to the left of WorldFrame's right edge
frame:SetPoint("RIGHT", WorldFrame, -20, 0);
```

■ `Region:SetWidth(width)` — Sets the width of this region to the given value. Setting the width to `0` will cause it to be determined by the region's anchors instead. Note: This function cannot be called during combat lockdown.

VisibleRegion

VisibleRegion is an abstract UI object type that can't actually be created. It serves as a base or any UI object that can be made visible. VisibleRegion inherits all methods from UIObject and Region, in addition to the following:

■ `VisibleRegion:GetAlpha()` — Returns the current alpha value for the region.

■ `VisibleRegion:Hide()` — Hides the region. Note: This function cannot be called during combat lockdown.

■ `VisibleRegion:IsShown()` — Returns if the region is shown.

■ `VisibleRegion:IsVisible()` — Returns if the region, its parent, its parent's parent, and so on are all shown.

■ `VisibleRegion:SetAlpha(alpha)` — Sets the alpha value.

■ `VisibleRegion:Show()` — Shows the region. Note: This function cannot be called during combat lockdown.

LayeredRegion

LayeredRegion is an abstract UI object type that can't actually be created. If serves as a base for the UI objects that are displayed on the screen but may not be full-fledged frames (such as Texture and FontString). LayeredRegion inherits all methods from UIObject, Region, and VisibleRegion, in addition to the following:

■ `LayeredRegion:GetDrawLayer()` — Returns this layered region's draw layer (for example, BACKGROUND and ARTWORK).

- LayeredRegion:SetDrawLayer↵("layer") — Sets this layered region's draw layer to the given value (for example, "BACKGROUND" and "ARTWORK").

- LayeredRegion:SetVertexColor([r][, g][, b][, alpha]) — Sets the color tint of this layered region to the given percentage values (0.0-1.0), modifying the original texture.

Font

Font objects are used to group the attribute of a font (such as the font file, height, border) together into an object that can be set as the font object for another UI element. If the font object is later altered, the change will immediately propagate down to the elements using the given Font object. Font inherits all methods from UIObject and FontInstance, in addition to the following:

- Font:CopyFontObject(font) — Copies the settings from the specified font. The font can be specified by a direct object reference or the name of an object/template.

- Font:GetAlpha() — Returns the alpha value for the Font (from 0 to 1).

- Font:SetAlpha(alpha) — Sets the alpha value for the Font (from 0 to 1).

Texture

A Texture object is used to display a graphic within the game client. Textures must belong to a frame, but can be anchored independently of the parent frame. Texture inherits all methods from UIObject, Region, LayeredRegion, and VisibleRegion, in addition to the following:

- Texture:GetBlendMode() — Returns the blend mode of the texture. This is equivalent to the XML attribute "alphaMode."

- Texture:GetTexCoord() or ULx, ULy, LLx, LLy, URx, URy, LRx, LRy = Texture:GetTexCoord() — Returns the current TexCoord setting for the texture (minX, maxX, minY, maxY).

- Texture:GetTexCoordModifiesRect() — Returns whether or not TexCoords modify the size of the texture. If, for example, the texture's dimensions were 100x100 px (with no TexCoords set), and the TexCoords were then set to (0, 0.5, 0, 0.5), the texture's size would change to 50x50 px.

- Texture:GetTexture() — Returns the path of the current texture file.

- Texture:GetVertexColor() — Returns the vertex color of the texture (red, green, blue, alpha).

- Texture:IsDesaturated() — Returns if the texture is currently desaturated.

- Texture:SetBlendMode("mode") — Sets the blend mode of the texture.

- ▪ `Texture:SetDesaturated()` — Sets whether or not the function should be displayed with no saturation. This function returns `1` if the graphic card supports desaturation; otherwise, it returns `nil`. In this case, the developer can manually use `SetVertexColor()` to accomplish similar results. Returns: `supported`.

- ▪ `Texture:SetGradient("orientation", minR, minG, minB, maxR, maxG, maxB)` — Sets a gradient for the texture.

- ▪ `Texture:SetGradientAlpha("orientation", minR, minG, minB, minA, maxR, maxG, maxB, maxA)` — Sets a gradient for the texture, with alpha values.

- ▪ `Texture:SetTexCoord(minX, maxX, minY, maxY)` or `SetTexCoord(ULx, ULy, LLx, LLy, URx, URy, LRx, LRy)` — Sets the corner coordinates for the texture display.

- ▪ `Texture:SetTexCoordModifies↵Rect(flag)` — Sets whether or not the TexCoords for the texture modified the size of the texture.

- ▪ `Texture:SetTexture(texture or "texture" or nil)` — Sets the texture to be displayed on a texture object.

FontString

A FontString object is used to display text within the game client. FontStrings must belong to a frame, but can be anchored independently of the parent frame. FontString inherits all methods from UIObject, FontInstance, Region, VisibleRegion and LayeredRegion, in addition to the following:

- ▪ `FontString:CanNonSpaceWrap()` — Returns whether the font string will wrap text in the middle of a word.

- ▪ `FontString:GetStringHeight()` — Returns the height of the text displayed on the font string.

- ▪ `FontString:GetStringWidth()` — Returns the width of the text displayed on the font string.

- ▪ `FontString:GetText()` — Returns the text currently set in the font string widget.

- ▪ `FontString:SetAlphaGradient(start, length)` — Fades the font string text out with an alpha gradient, returning `1` if successful and `nil` otherwise.

- ▪ `FontString:SetFormattedText(format, ...)` — Sets the text of the font string widget using the defined format rules. This is equivalent to `:SetText(string.format(format, ...))`, but does not create a throwaway Lua string and, as such, is better on memory churn.

- ▪ `FontString:SetNonSpaceWrap(flag)` — Sets whether the font string will wrap text in the middle of a word.

- ▪ `FontString:SetText("text")` — Sets the text to be displayed in the font string.

- ▪ `FontString:SetTextHeight↵(pixelHeight)` — Scales the rendered text to the specified height. Note: this may distort the text. Use `SetFont` to render the text at a different size.

Frame

The Frame type is the basis for all graphics and text displayed in WoW. Frames consist of a number of draw layers that can contain Textures and FontStrings. The Frame type also serves as the basis for all concrete UI widgets.

- Frame:AllowAttributeChanges() — Temporarily allows insecure code to modify attributes on the Frame during combat. The permission is rescinded at the next OnUpdate. Note: This function cannot be called during combat lockdown.

- Frame:CreateFontString(name[, layer[, inherits]]) — Creates a new FontString for the Frame on the given layer, optionally inheriting from a template. The layer can be one of BACKGROUND, BORDER, ARTWORK (default), OVERLAY, or HIGHLIGHT.

- Frame:CreateTexture(name[, layer[, inherits]]) — Creates a new texture for the frame on the given layer, optionally inheriting from a template. The layer can be one of BACKGROUND, BORDER, ARTWORK (default), OVERLAY, or HIGHLIGHT.

- Frame:CreateTitleRegion() — Creates a title region for the frame. A title region is automatically set to allow moving the frame by clicking on the title region.

- Frame:DisableDrawLayer(layer) — Disables rendering of the frame's specified layer. The layer can be one of BACKGROUND, BORDER, ARTWORK (default), OVERLAY, or HIGHLIGHT.

- Frame:EnableDrawLayer(layer) — Enables rendering of the frame's specified layer. The layer can be one of BACKGROUND, BORDER, ARTWORK (default), OVERLAY, or HIGHLIGHT.

- Frame:EnableKeyboard(flag) — Enables or disables keyboard interactivity. Note: This function cannot be called during combat lockdown.

- Frame:EnableMouse(flag) — Enables or disables mouse interactivity. Note: This function cannot be called during combat lockdown.

- Frame:EnableMouseWheel(flag) — Enables or disables mouse wheel interactivity. Note: This function cannot be called during combat lockdown.

- Frame:GetAttribute("name") — Returns the name attribute.

- Frame:GetBackdrop() — Returns the backdrop information for the frame. If the frame has a backdrop, a table definition is returned, otherwise nil.

- Frame:GetBackdropBorderColor() — Returns the frame's backdrop border color (red, green, blue, alpha).

- Frame:GetBackdropColor() — Returns the frame's backdrop color (red, green, blue, alpha).

- Frame:GetBoundsRect() — Returns the frame's boundaries (x, y, width, height).

- Frame:GetChildren() — Returns the list of child frames. Example:

```
-- Function to iterate through a frame's children
local function iterateChildren(...)
  for i=1,select("#",...) do
```

```
    local child = select(i,...)
      -- process child
  end
end
```

```
iterateChildren(frame:GetChildren())
```

- `Frame:GetClampRectInsets()` — Returns the rect insets for the clampedto-screen system.

- `Frame:GetEffectiveAlpha()` — Returns the frame's effective alpha. This is equivalent to `frame:GetAlpha()` * ↵frame:GetParent():GetEffective↵Alpha().

- `Frame:GetEffectiveScale()` — Returns the frame's effective scale. This is equivalent to `frame:GetScale()` * ↵frame:GetParent():GetEffective↵Scale().

- `Frame:GetFrameLevel()` — Returns the current frame level.

- `Frame:GetFrameStrata()` — Returns the current frame strata.

- `Frame:GetFrameType()` — Returns the type of frame as a string. This has the same return value as `GetObjectType`.

- `Frame:GetHitRectInsets()` — Returns the inserts for the frame's hit rect (`left`, `right`, `top`, `bottom`). The values given are distances in pixels from the edge toward the center of the frame. Negative values indicate the hit rect extends beyond the actual frame on that edge.

- `Frame:GetID()` — Returns the frame's numeric identifier.

- `Frame:GetMaxResize()` — Returns the maximum resize width and height (x, y).

- `Frame:GetMinResize()` — Returns the minimum resize height and width (x, y).

- `Frame:GetNumChildren()` — Returns the number of children this frame has.

- `Frame:GetNumRegions()` — Returns the number of regions belonging to this frame.

- `Frame:GetRegions()` — Returns the regions (font strings, textures) that belong to this frame.

- `Frame:GetScale()` — Returns the scale of the frame.

- `Frame:GetScript("type")` — Returns the widget handler for `"type"`.

- `Frame:GetTitleRegion()` — Returns the `TitleRegion` object for the frame.

- `Frame:HasScript("type")` — Returns whether or not the frame has the widget handler `"type "`. Note that this is not whether a handler has been set for that particular widget event, but whether the frame type supports that event. Check the return of `GetScript` to check if a handler has been set.

- `Frame:HookScript("type", function)` — Securely hooks a widget handler script.

- `Frame:IsClampedToScreen()` — Returns whether or not the frame is clamped to the screen.

- `Frame:IsEventRegistered("event")` — Returns whether or not the frame is registered for the given event.

- `Frame:IsFrameType(type)` — Returns whether or not the frame is of the given type.

- `Frame:IsKeyboardEnabled()` — Returns whether or not the frame is keyboard enabled.

- `Frame:IsMouseEnabled()` — Returns whether or not the frame is mouse enabled.

- `Frame:IsMouseWheelEnabled()` — Returns whether or not the frame is mouse wheel enabled.

- `Frame:IsMovable()` — Returns whether or not the frame is movable.

- `Frame:IsResizable()` — Returns whether or not the frame is resizable.

- `Frame:IsToplevel()` — Returns whether or not the frame is at the top level.

- `Frame:IsUserPlaced()` — Returns whether or not the frame is flagged as "user placed."

- `Frame:Lower()` — Lowers the frame's frameLevel. Note: This function cannot be called during combat lockdown.

- `Frame:Raise()` — Raises the frame's frameLevel. Note: This function cannot be called during combat lockdown.

- `Frame:RegisterAllEvents()` — Registers the frame for all events.

- `Frame:RegisterEvent("event")` — Registers the frame for an event.

- `Frame:RegisterForDrag(...)` — Registers the frame for dragging via specific mouse buttons. Valid mouse buttons are LeftButton, RightButton, MiddleButton, Button4, and Button5.

- `Frame:SetAttribute("name", value)` — Sets an attribute on the given frame. Note: This function cannot be called during combat lockdown.

- `Frame:SetBackdrop({bgFile = "bgFile", edgeFile = "edgeFile", tile = false, tileSize = 0, edgeSize = 32, insets = { left = 0, right = 0, top = 0, bottom = 0 }})` — Sets a frame's backdrop as defined by a table. This function accepts the return from the `Frame:GetBackdrop()` function.

- `Frame:SetBackdropBorderColor(red, green, blue [, alpha])` — Sets the color of the frame's backdrop border.

- `Frame:SetBackdropColor(red, green, blue [, alpha])` — Sets the backdrop color for the frame.

- `Frame:SetClampRectInsets(left, right, top, bottom)` — Sets the clamp rect insets for the frame, so a portion of it could move off screen.

- `Frame:SetClampedToScreen(flag)` — Sets whether or not the frame should be clamped to the screen.

- `Frame:SetFrameLevel(level)` — Sets the frame level of the frame. Note: This function cannot be called during combat lockdown.

- `Frame:SetFrameStrata(strata)` — Sets the frame's frame strata. Note: This function cannot be called during combat lockdown.

- `Frame:SetHitRectInsets(left, right, top, bottom)` — Sets the frame's HitRectInsets, which define where the mouse can interact with the frame. Note: This function cannot be called during combat lockdown.

- `Frame:SetID(ID)` — Sets the numeric identifier for the frame. Note: This function cannot be called during combat lockdown.

- `Frame:SetMaxResize(maxWidth, maxHeight)` — Sets the maximum resize limits for the frame.

- `Frame:SetMinResize(minWidth, minHeight)` — Sets the minimum resize limits for the frame.

- `Frame:SetMovable(flag)` — Sets whether or not the frame is movable.

- `Frame:SetResizable(flag)` — Sets whether or not the frame is resizable.

- `Frame:SetScale(scale)` — Sets the scale of the frame. Note: This function cannot be called during combat lockdown.

- `Frame:SetScript("type", function)` — Sets a function to call for the given widget handler on this frame. Example:

```
-- Set PlayerFrame's <PostClick>
local function PostClick(self, button)
  ChatFrame1:AddMessage("Stop touching me!!!")
end
PlayerFrame:SetScript("PostClick", PostClick)
```

- `Frame:SetToplevel(flag)` — Sets whether or not the frame should raise itself to the top frame level when clicked. Note: This function cannot be called during combat lockdown.

- `Frame:SetUserPlaced(flag)` — Flags the frame as user placed or not. A user-placed frame has its position stored and restored during the login process.

- `Frame:StartMoving()` — Starts moving the frame.

- `Frame:StartSizing()` — Starts resizing the frame.

- `Frame:StopMovingOrSizing()` — Stops the frame from being moved or resized, and saves the position in `layout-cache.txt`.

- `Frame:UnregisterAllEvents()` — Unregisters all events for the frame.

- `Frame:UnregisterEvent("event")` — Unregisters the frame for the given event.

The following handlers are available for Frame: `OnAttributeChanged`, `OnChar`, `OnDragStart`, `OnDragStop`, `OnEnter`, `OnEvent`, `OnHide`, `OnKeyDown`, `OnKeyUp`, `OnLeave`, `OnLoad`, `OnMouseDown`, `OnMouseUp`, `OnMouseWheel`, `OnReceiveDrag`, `OnShow`, `OnSizeChanged`, `OnUpdate`.

GameTooltip

A GameTooltip object is used to display mouseover tooltips throughout the user interface. In addition to basic text display, the GameTooltip has a number of methods that fill the tooltip with information that is not available elsewhere in the API. GameTooltips inherits all methods from UIObject, Region, VisibleRegion and Frame, in addition to the following:

- GameTooltip:AddDoubleLine("textLeft", "textRight" [, rL, gL, bL [, rR, gR, bR]]) — Adds a line to the tooltip with both a left and a right component. Each text string can be colored individually.

- GameTooltip:AddFontStrings(leftstring, rightstring) — Adds font strings to the tooltip, dynamically expanding the number of lines.

- GameTooltip:AddLine(text [, red, green, blue [, wrapFlag]]) — Adds a line to the tooltip with optional color. Setting wrapFlag to 1 will allow the line of text to wrap within the tooltip. This function will add the line to the tooltip, but will not resize it to fit. You can call GameTooltip:Show() to properly resize the tooltip.

- GameTooltip:AddTexture↵("texturePath") — Adds a texture to the beginning of the last tooltip line added. Example:

```
-- Run this when mousing over somethign that displays
-- the tooltip.  It will add the texture of your first
-- spell tab to the tooltip.
local name,texture = GetSpellTabInfo(2)
GameTooltip:AddTexture(texture)
```

- GameTooltip:AppendText("text") — Adds text to the first line of the tooltip.

- GameTooltip:ClearLines() — Clears the lines of the tooltip. This function clears the left lines, but only hides the right lines. To ensure the tooltip is entirely clear, you would have to manually clear those lines.

- GameTooltip:FadeOut() — Causes the tooltip to begin fading out.

- GameTooltip:GetAnchorType() — Returns the current anchor type. Valid values are ANCHOR_TOPRIGHT, ANCHOR_RIGHT, ANCHOR_BOTTOMRIGHT, ANCHOR_TOPLEFT, ANCHOR_LEFT, ANCHOR_BOTTOMLEFT, ANCHOR_CURSOR, ANCHOR_PRESERVE, ANCHOR_NONE.

- GameTooltip:GetItem() — Returns the name and the link of the item being displayed in the tooltip (name, link).

- GameTooltip:GetOwner() — Returns the owner of the tooltip.

- GameTooltip:GetSpell() — Returns the name and rank of the spell currently being displayed (name, rank).

- GameTooltip:GetUnit() — Returns the unit for which the tooltip is currently displaying information (unitName, unitId).

- GameTooltip:IsOwned(frame) — Returns whether or not the tooltip is owned by the given frame.

- GameTooltip:IsUnit("unit") — Returns whether or not the tooltip is currently displaying the given unit's information.

- GameTooltip:NumLines() — Returns the number of lines in the tooltip object.

- GameTooltip:SetAction(slot) — Sets the GameTooltip to show the statistics for the action at the given slot.

- `GameTooltip:SetAnchorType("anchorType"[, xOffset][, yOffset])` — Changes the anchor point for the tooltip relative to its owner, optionally with offsets. See `GameTooltip:SetOwner()` for valid anchor types.

- `GameTooltip:SetAuctionItem("type", index)` — Sets the tooltip to the specified index in the specified auction house listing. Type can be either `list` or `bidder` or `owner`.

- `GameTooltip:SetAuctionSellItem()` — Sets the tooltip for the item currently set to be auctioned.

- `GameTooltip:SetBagItem(bag,item)` — Sets the `GameTooltip` to show the item from the given bag and slot.

- `GameTooltip:SetBuybackItem(slot)` — Sets the tooltip to the specified merchant buyback item. Slot must be within 1 to `GetNumBuybackItems()`.

- `GameTooltip:SetCraftItem(craft↵Index, reagentIndex)` — Displays the item tooltip of the given craft item's reagent. Uses the last-opened craft to decide what items to display. Errors if no craft has been opened, or if the passed indices are invalid for that craft.

- `GameTooltip:SetCraftSpell↵(craftIndex)` — Displays the spell tooltip that will be the result of making this craft item. Uses the last-opened craft to decide what items to display. Errors if no craft has been opened, or if the passed index is invalid for that craft.

- `GameTooltip:SetExistingSocket↵Gem(gemIndex [, toDestroy])` — Displays the item tooltip of the given gem already socketed in a socket in the gem socketing frame. Passing the `toDestroy` parameter changes the tooltip to notify the player that the given gem will be destroyed when socketing the new gem.

- `GameTooltip:SetGuildBankItem(tab, itemIndex)` — Displays the item tooltip for the given guild bank tab and item index. The guild bank has to be opened and the given tab selected this session for this method to work.

- `GameTooltip:SetHyperlink(itemLink)` — Sets the `GameTooltip` to show the item indicated by the `itemLink`. Calling too many items that have not been seen on the server yet will disconnect you.

- `GameTooltip:SetHyperlink↵CompareItem("itemLink" [, index])` — Displays the item tooltip for the item currently equipped in the same slot as the given item link. Returns `1` if the action succeeds, `nil` otherwise. An optional index can be passed to display the item tooltip for slot types with more than one item (that is, trinkets, rings, and one-handed weapons).

- `GameTooltip:SetInboxItem↵(messageIndex, attachmentIndex)` — Sets the tooltip of the specified inbox item of the specified mail message.

- `GameTooltip:SetInventoryItem(unit, slot [, nameOnly])` — Sets the tooltip to the specified slot on the specified unit. This function will only work for player characters of the same faction, as the players are close enough to inspect. If `nameOnly` is given, it will omit the stats when presenting the tooltip.

- `GameTooltip:SetLootItem(index)` — Sets the `GameTooltip` to show the item at the given index.

- `GameTooltip:SetLootRollItem(id)` — Sets the tooltip for the selected loot roll item.

- `GameTooltip:SetMerchantCost↵Item(merchantIndex, itemCostIndex)` — Sets the tooltip for the item cost of a specific item. This function only works for those merchant items that require other items (instead of gold) to purchase, such as Badges of Justice for the purchase of heroic rewards from G'eras in Shattrath.

- `GameTooltip:SetMerchantItem(index)` — Sets the tooltip to the specified merchant's item index. Index must be within 1 to `GetMerchantNumItems()`.

- `GameTooltip:SetMinimumWidth(width[, force])` — Sets the minimum width of the tooltip to the given value. The width is not affected until the `:Show()` method is called. Without the `force` parameter set, the tooltip's width is only affected when text lines wrap because they are too long.

- `GameTooltip:SetOwner(frame [, "anchorType"][, xOffset][, yOffset])` — Sets the owner of the tooltip, modifying parent and anchor points. The `anchorType` argument can be the following values:

  - `ANCHOR_TOPRIGHT` — Aligns bottom right of tooltip with top right of the owner.

  - `ANCHOR_RIGHT` — Aligns bottom left of tooltip with top right of the owner.

  - `ANCHOR_TOPLEFT` — Aligns bottom left of tooltip with top left of the owner.

  - `ANCHOR_LEFT` — Aligns the bottom right of the tooltip with the top left of the owner.

  - `ANCHOR_BOTTOMLEFT` — Aligns top right of tooltip with bottom left of the owner.

  - `ANCHOR_CURSOR` — Anchors tooltip to the cursor (offsets do not apply for this).

  - `ANCHOR_PRESERVE` — preserves the current anchors.

  - `ANCHOR_NONE` — Removes all anchors. May have strange side effects if the tooltip was shown when `:SetOwner()` was called.

- `GameTooltip:SetPadding(amount)` — Sets the padding on the right side of the tooltip. This is used by the default user interface to make space for the close button on the ItemRef tooltip.

- `GameTooltip:SetPetAction(slot)` — Sets the `GameTooltip` to show the statistics for the given pet action slot.

- `GameTooltip:SetPlayerBuff(buff↵Index)` — Sets the tooltip to the description of the specified buffIndex.

- `GameTooltip:SetPossession(slot)` — Displays the tooltip for the possession bar slots.

- `GameTooltip:SetQuestItem("type", index)` — Displays the item tooltip for the given type and index.

- `GameTooltip:SetQuestLogItem(index)` — Sets the tooltip to a quest log item reward by index.

- `GameTooltip:SetQuestLogRewardSpell()` — Displays the spell tooltip of the spell you will receive when completing the selected quest in the quest log.

■ GameTooltip:SetQuestRewardSpell() — Displays the spell tooltip of the spell you will receive when completing the currently active quest at a quest NPC.

■ GameTooltip:SetSendMailItem(index) — Sets the GameTooltip to the item at the given attachment index in the send mail interface.

■ GameTooltip:SetShapeshift(index) — Displays the spell tooltip for the shapeshift spell with the given index.

■ GameTooltip:SetSocketGem(gemIndex) — Displays the item tooltip of the given gem to be socketed in a socket in the gem socketing frame.

■ GameTooltip:SetSocketedItem() — Displays the item tooltip for the item currently being socketed with gems.

■ GameTooltip:SetSpell(spellID, ↵bookType) — Sets the GameTooltip to show a spell from the spellbook.

■ GameTooltip:SetTalent(tabIndex, talentIndex [,isInspect]) — Sets the tooltip description for the specified talent. If isInspect is specified, it will instead show the talent description of the unit being inspected.

■ GameTooltip:SetText(text) — Sets the tooltip to read just the text sent to this function. Any lines already present will be removed.

■ GameTooltip:SetTracking() — Sets the tooltip to a description of the current tracking type or "Click to choose tracking type" if no tracking type is selected.

■ GameTooltip:SetTradePlayerItem↵(itemIndex) — Displays the item tooltip for the given item index in your trade. This method is used for items to be traded away by the player when the trade is accepted. See GameTooltip: SetTradeTargetItem() for items to be received from the trade.

■ GameTooltip:SetTradeSkillItem(tradeskillIndex[, reagentIndex]) — Displays the given tradeskill item in the tooltip, or optionally a reagent of the given tradeskill item instead.

■ GameTooltip:SetTradeTargetItem↵(itemIndex) — Displays the item tooltip for the given item index in your trade. This method is used for items to be given to the player when the trade is accepted. See GameTooltip:SetTradePlayerItem() for items to be traded away by the player.

■ GameTooltip:SetTrainerService↵(index) — Sets the tooltip for a trainable spell at a trainer.

■ GameTooltip:SetUnit("unit" or "unitName") — Displays the mouseover tooltip for the given unit in this tooltip.

■ GameTooltip:SetUnitBuff("unit", buffIndex [, castFilter]) — Sets this tooltip to show the given unit and buff index's buff name and description, optionally filtered to only show buffs you can cast.

■ GameTooltip:SetUnitDebuff("unit", debuffIndex[, dispelFilter]) — Sets this tooltip to show the given unit and debuff index's debuff name and description, optionally filtered to only show buffs you can dispel.

The following handlers are available for `GameTooltip`: `OnAttributeChanged`, `OnChar`, `OnDragStart`, `OnDragStop`, `OnEnter`, `OnEvent`, `OnHide`, `OnKeyDown`, `OnKeyUp`, `OnLeave`, `OnLoad`, `OnMouseDown`, `OnMouseUp`, `OnMouseWheel`, `OnReceiveDrag`, `OnShow`, `OnSizeChanged`, `OnTooltipAddMoney`, `OnTooltipCleared`, `OnTooltipSetDefaultAnchor`, `OnTooltipSetItem`, `OnTooltipSetSpell`, `OnTooltipSetUnit`, `OnUpdate`.

EditBox

The EditBox widget is used to allow user input via the keyboard, in a standard edit box. EditBox inherits all methods from UIObject, FontInstance, Region, VisibleRegion, and Frame, in addition to the following:

- `EditBox:AddHistoryLine("text")` — Adds a line of text to an edit box's history. This history is browseable on many edit boxes using up and down. On the Chat-FrameEditBox it's done via alt-up and alt-down.

- `EditBox:ClearFocus()` — Clears the input focus from an edit box. After this function is called, the edit box in question will no longer receive keypresses.

- `EditBox:GetAltArrowKeyMode()` — Returns the arrow key mode state. If 1, it means you must use alt+arrow to navigate the edit box; otherwise, arrow keys will navigate it normally. The chat frame edit box is set to 1 by default.

- `EditBox:GetBlinkSpeed()` — Returns the cursor's blink speed.

- `EditBox:GetCursorPosition()` — Returns the current cursor position inside a given edit box. The index starts at 0 at the front of the line.

- `EditBox:GetHistoryLines()` — Returns the max number of history lines.

- `EditBox:GetInputLanguage()` — Returns the current input language charset selected.

- `EditBox:GetMaxBytes()` — Returns the maximum number of bytes allowed in the edit box. Note: WoW uses multibyte Unicode (UTF-8) so the number of characters is not the same as the number of bytes.

- `EditBox:GetMaxLetters()` — Returns the maximum number of letters you can enter into an `EditBox`.

- `EditBox:GetNumLetters()` — Returns the number of letters in the `EditBox`.

- `EditBox:GetNumber()` — Returns the contents of the `EditBox` converted to a number. This is equivalent to a `tonumber()` call on the text.

- `EditBox:GetText()` — Retrieves the text stored in the `EditBox`.

- `EditBox:GetTextInsets()` — Returns the distance between the edges of the `EditBox` and the text inside it (`left`, `right`, `top`, `bottom`).

- `EditBox:HasFocus()` — Returns whether the `EditBox` has the keyboard cursor focus.

- `EditBox:HighlightText([start [,end]])` — Highlights the selected text in the `EditBox`.

- `EditBox:Insert(text)` — Inserts text into the `EditBox` at the current cursor position.

- `EditBox:IsAutoFocus()` — Returns `true` if the `EditBox` will automatically grab keyboard focus when it is shown.

- `EditBox:IsInIMECompositionMode()` — Returns whether the `EditBox` is in IME composition mode. Will only return `true` for certain international clients.

- `EditBox:IsMultiLine()` — Returns whether the `EditBox` uses more than one line of text.

- `EditBox:IsNumeric()` — Returns whether the `EditBox` is in numeric mode. See `SetNumeric`.

- `EditBox:IsPassword()` — Returns whether the `EditBox` is in password mode.

- `EditBox:SetAltArrowKeyMode(flag)` — Sets the `EditBox` to ignore arrow keys unless you hold Alt. The flag must be `false` (not `nil`) to turn off this mode.

- `EditBox:SetAutoFocus(flag)` — Sets whether or not the `EditBox` will automatically acquire cursor focus.

- `EditBox:SetBlinkSpeed(speed)` — Sets the blink rate for the cursor. The speed parameter indicates how long the blinking text cursor stays in one state; if `speed` is set to `1.0`, it will toggle between being shown and hidden once every second.

- `EditBox:SetCursorPosition(position)` — Sets the cursor position in the `EditBox`. Position `0` places the cursor before the first character in the `EditBox`.

- `EditBox:SetFocus()` — Gives the `EditBox` keyboard cursor focus.

- `EditBox:SetHistoryLines(numLines)` — Sets the number of history lines to store for the `EditBox`.

- `EditBox:SetMaxBytes(max)` — Sets the maximum number of bytes to display in the `EditBox`.

- `EditBox:SetMaxLetters(max)` — Sets the maximum number of letters allowed in the `EditBox`.

- `EditBox:SetMultiLine(flag)` — Sets the `EditBox` to use multiple lines of text. Note: flag must be `false` (not `nil`) to set the `EditBox` to single-line mode.

- `EditBox:SetNumber(number)` — Sets the contents of the `EditBox` to the specified number.

- `EditBox:SetNumeric(flag)` — Sets whether the `EditBox` should only accept numbers. Note: flag must be `false`, not `nil`, to turn off numeric mode.

- `EditBox:SetPassword(flag)` — Sets the `EditBox` into password mode, masking all input. The flag must be `false` (not `nil`) to clear this mode.

- `EditBox:SetText(text)` — Sets the contents of the `EditBox` to text. This fires the `OnTextChanged` handler.

- `EditBox:SetTextInsets(left, right, top, bottom)` — Sets the padding between the edges of the `EditBox` and its text.

- `EditBox:ToggleInputLanguage()` — Toggles the input language for the `EditBox`. This is only valid for international clients with multiple input methods.

Handlers

The following handlers are available for `EditBox`: `OnAttributeChanged`, `OnChar`, `OnCharComposition`, `OnCursorChanged`, `OnDragStart`, `OnDragStop`, `OnEditFocusGained`, `OnEditFocusLost`, `OnEnter`, `OnEnterPressed`, `OnEscapePressed`, `OnEvent`, `OnHide`, `OnInputLanguageChanged`, `OnKeyDown`, `OnKeyUp`, `OnLeave`, `OnLoad`, `OnMouseDown`, `OnMouseUp`, `OnMouseWheel`, `OnReceiveDrag`, `OnShow`, `OnSizeChanged`, `OnSpacePressed`, `OnTabPressed`, `OnTextChanged`, `OnTextSet`, `OnUpdate`.

Slider

Slider widgets allow the user to select a numeric value by moving a drag handler on a fixed bar. Slider inherits all methods from UIObject, Region, VisibleRegion, and Frame, in addition to the following:

- `Slider:GetMinMaxValues()` — Returns the minimum and maximum values for the slider.
- `Slider:GetOrientation()` — Returns the orientation of the slider (`VERTICAL` or `HORIZONTAL`).
- `Slider:GetThumbTexture()` — Returns the thumb texture for the slider.
- `Slider:GetValue()` — Returns the current value of the slider.
- `Slider:GetValueStep()` — Returns the current step value for the slider.
- `Slider:SetMinMaxValues(min, max)` — Sets the minimum and maximum values for the slider.
- `Slider:SetOrientation("orientation")` — Sets the orientation of the slider (`VERTICAL` or `HORIZONTAL`).
- `Slider:SetThumbTexture(texture or "texture")` — Sets the thumb texture for the slider.
- `Slider:SetValue(value)` — Sets the value of the slider.
- `Slider:SetValueStep(value)` — Sets the step value for the slider. This value can be used to better control what minimum incremental step the slider uses when dragging the handle.

The following handlers are available for Slider: `OnAttributeChanged`, `OnChar`, `OnDragStart`, `OnDragStop`, `OnEnter`, `OnEvent`, `OnHide`, `OnKeyDown`, `OnKeyUp`, `OnLeave`, `OnLoad`, `OnMouseDown`, `OnMouseUp`, `OnMouseWheel`, `OnReceiveDrag`, `OnShow`, `OnSizeChanged`, `OnUpdate`, `OnValueChanged`.

Model

The Model widget is used to display 3-D models in the user interface. Model inherits all methods from UIObject, Region, VisibleRegion, and Frame, in addition to the following:

- `Model:AdvanceTime()` — Advances to the next animation frame for the model.
- `Model:ClearFog()` — Disables fog display for the model.

- `Model:ClearModel()` — Removes the current mesh from the model object.

- `Model:GetFacing()` — Gets the current rotation angle of the model in radians.

- `Model:GetFogColor()` — Returns the current fog color for the model (r, g, b, a).

- `Model:GetFogFar()` — Returns the far clipping distance for the model's fog. This determines how far from the camera the fog ends.

- `Model:GetFogNear()` — Returns the near clipping distance for the model's fog. This determines how close to the camera the fog begins.

- `Model:GetLight()` — Returns information about the light source used when rendering the model. The results are compatible with the `:SetLight()` method.

- `Model:GetModel()` — Returns the file name currently used by the model.

- `Model:GetModelScale()` — Returns the scale of the mesh displayed by the model.

- `Model:GetPosition()` — Returns the position of the mesh displayed by the model object (x, y, z).

- `Model:ReplaceIconTexture(path)` — Sets the icon texture path used by the model. Only affects models that use icons (for example, the animation model when an item goes into a bag).

- `Model:SetCamera(index)` — Sets the pre-defined camera view for the model. The index can be 0 for a facial view, 1 for a full frontal view, or any other number to allow the camera to move freely.

- `Model:SetFacing(facing)` — Gets the current rotation angle of the model in radians.

- `Model:SetFogColor(r, g, b[, a])` — Sets the fog color and enables fog display for the model.

- `Model:SetFogFar(value)` — Sets the far clipping distance for the model's fog. This sets how far from the camera the fog ends.

- `Model:SetFogNear(value)` — Sets the near clipping distance for the model's fog. This sets how close to the camera the fog begins.

- `Model:SetLight(enabled[, omni, dirX, dirY, dirZ, ambIntensity[, ambR, ambG, ambB], dirIntensity[, dirR, dirG, dirB]])` — Sets the origin of the light source for rendering of the model.

- `Model:SetModel(filename)` — Sets the model to the specified file.

- `Model:SetModelScale(scale)` — Sets the scale of the mesh displayed by the model.

- `Model:SetPosition(x, y, z)` — Sets the position of the mesh displayed by the model.

- `Model:SetSequence(sequence)` — Sets the model to use the specified animation sequence. Exact behavior depends on the model.

- `Model:SetSequenceTime(sequence, time)` — Sets the animation sequence and time index for the model.

The following handlers are available for Model: `OnAnimFinished`, `OnAttribut-eChanged`, `OnChar`, `OnDragStart`, `OnDragStop`, `OnEnter`, `OnEvent`, `OnHide`, `OnKeyDown`, `OnKeyUp`, `OnLeave`, `OnLoad`, `OnMouseDown`, `OnMouseUp`, `OnMouseWheel`, `OnReceiveDrag`, `OnShow`, `OnSizeChanged`, `OnUpdate`, `OnUpdateModel`.

MessageFrame

MessagesFrames are used to display a static number of messages, with new messages replacing older ones. This frame type does not allow scrolling. MessageFrame inherits all methods from UIObject, FontInstance, Region, VisibleRegion, and Frame, in addition to the following:

- `MessageFrame:AddMessage(message [, r, g, b])` — Adds a message to this message frame, optionally with specified colors.
- `MessageFrame:Clear()` — Clears all messages from the message frame.
- `MessageFrame:GetFadeDuration()` — Returns the current fade duration for the message frame.
- `MessageFrame:GetFading()` — Returns 1 when the messages in the message frame are set to fade out after a certain amount of time, `nil` otherwise.
- `MessageFrame:GetInsertMode()` — Returns where messages are inserted for this message frame (that is, `TOP` or `BOTTOM`).
- `MessageFrame:GetTimeVisible()` — Returns the time in seconds that a message sent to this message frame will stay visible before starting to fade.
- `MessageFrame:SetFadeDuration↵(seconds)` — Sets the amount of time before a new message will fade out.
- `MessageFrame:SetFading(flag)` — Enables or disables message fading for the message frame. To disable fading, you can do `MessageFrame:SetFading (false)` or `MessageFrame:SetFading(nil)` or `MessageFrame:SetFading(0)`, but `MessageFrame:SetFading()` does not disable it.
- `MessageFrame:SetInsertMode↵(position)` — Sets the insertion mode for new messages in the frame (`TOP` or `BOTTOM`).
- `MessageFrame:SetTimeVisible↵(seconds)` — Sets the amount of time that individual messages will remain visible.

The following handlers are available for MessageFrame: `OnAttributeChanged`, `OnChar`, `OnDragStart`, `OnDragStop`, `OnEnter`, `OnEvent`, `OnHide`, `OnKeyDown`, `OnKeyUp`, `OnLeave`, `OnLoad`, `OnMouseDown`, `OnMouseUp`, `OnMouseWheel`, `OnReceiveDrag`, `OnShow`, `OnSizeChanged`, `OnUpdate`.

Cooldown

A Cooldown object is used to display a circular countdown (or countup) timer, such as those on the default action buttons, or buffs and debuffs on the target frame. Cooldown inherits all methods from UIObject, Region, VisibleRegion, and Frame, in addition to the following:

■ Cooldown:SetCooldown(start, duration) — Sets up the parameters for a cooldown model. The start value indicates the time when the cooldown began (your system time in seconds) and duration is how long the cooldown lasts.

■ Cooldown:SetReverse(flag) — Sets the cooldown model to be animated in reverse.

The following handlers are available for Cooldown: OnAttributeChanged, OnChar, OnDragStart, OnDragStop, OnEnter, OnEvent, OnHide, OnKeyDown, OnKeyUp, OnLeave, OnLoad, OnMouseDown, OnMouseUp, OnMouseWheel, OnReceiveDrag, OnShow, OnSizeChanged, OnUpdate.

ScrollFrame

ScrollFrame widgets are used to enclose another frame and clip the display to a specific size. The viewport can then be scrolled to display the different portions of the enclosed clip. ScrollFrame inherits all methods from UIObject, Region, VisibleRegion, and Frame, in addition to the following:

■ ScrollFrame:GetHorizontalScroll() — Returns the current horizontal scroll offset.

■ ScrollFrame:GetHorizontal↵ScrollRange() — Returns the maximum horizontal scroll offset.

■ ScrollFrame:GetScrollChild() — Returns the scroll child frame.

■ ScrollFrame:GetVerticalScroll() — Returns the current vertical scroll offset.

■ ScrollFrame:GetVerticalScrollRange() — Returns the maximum vertical scroll offset.

■ ScrollFrame:SetHorizontal↵Scroll(offset) — Sets the horizontal scroll offset. Note: This function cannot be called during combat lockdown if the scroll child is a protected widget.

■ ScrollFrame:SetScrollChild(frame) — Sets the scroll child for the scroll frame. Note: This function cannot be called during combat lockdown if the scroll child is a protected widget.

■ ScrollFrame:SetVerticalScroll↵(offset) — Sets the vertical scroll for the frame. Note: This function cannot be called during combat lockdown if the scroll child is a protected widget.

■ ScrollFrame:UpdateScrollChildRect() — Updates the rect information for the scroll child. This should be called when the contents of the scroll child change.

The following handlers are available for ScrollFrame: OnAttributeChanged, OnChar, OnDragStart, OnDragStop, OnEnter, OnEvent, OnHide, OnHorizontalScroll, OnKeyDown, OnKeyUp, OnLeave, OnLoad, OnMouseDown, OnMouseUp, OnMouseWheel, OnReceiveDrag, OnScrollRangeChanged, OnShow, OnSizeChanged, OnUpdate, OnVerticalScroll.

ColorSelect

The ColorSelect widget gives the user a way to select colors from a color wheel, or other type of color selector. ColorSelect inherits all methods from UIObject, Region, VisibleRegion, and Frame, in addition to the following:

- ColorSelect:GetColorHSV() — Returns the hue, saturation, and value of the currently selected color (hue, saturation, value).

- ColorSelect:GetColorRGB() — Returns the component colors of the currently selected color (red, green, blue).

- ColorSelect:GetColorValueTexture() — Returns the texture used to display the color value in the color select widget.

- ColorSelect:GetColorValueThumb↵Texture() — Returns the texture used for the color value thumb in the color select widget.

- ColorSelect:GetColorWheelTexture() — Returns the texture used for the color wheel on the given color select widget.

- ColorSelect:GetColorWheelThumb↵Texture() — Returns the thumb texture for the color select widget.

- ColorSelect:SetColorHSV(hue, saturation, value) — Sets the color of the color select widget using hue, saturation, and value.

- ColorSelect:SetColorRGB(red, blue, green [, alpha]) — Sets the selected color for the given color select widget with an RGB value.

- ColorSelect:SetColorValue↵Texture(texture or nil) — Sets the texture of the opacity selector.

- ColorSelect:SetColorValue↵ThumbTexture(texture or "texture") — Sets the texture of the "Value Thumb", which is the two arrows that show you where your brightness is set.

- ColorSelect:SetColorWheel↵Texture(texture) — Allows you to set the texture of the color wheel.

- ColorSelect:SetColorWheel↵ThumbTexture(texture or "texture" or nil) — Allows you to set the texture of the color wheel thumb, which is the little circle that shows you where on the color wheel you have currently selected.

The following handlers are available for ColorSelect: OnAttributeChanged, OnChar, OnColorSelect, OnDragStart, OnDragStop, OnEnter, OnEvent, OnHide, OnKeyDown, OnKeyUp, OnLeave, OnLoad, OnMouseDown, OnMouseUp, OnMouseWheel, OnReceiveDrag, OnShow, OnSizeChanged, OnUpdate.

Minimap

The Minimap widget type is used to create the minimap object that is displayed in the default user interface. The game only supports one minimap object at a time; attempts to create a new one will cause the old one to stop working. Minimap inherits all methods from UIObject, Region, VisibleRegion, and Frame, in addition to the following:

- `Minimap:GetPingPosition()` — Returns the coordinates of the last ping on the minimap (relative to the center) (x, y).

- `Minimap:GetZoom()` — Returns the current zoom level for the minimap.

- `Minimap:GetZoomLevels()` — Returns the highest zoom level you are allowed to use for `Minimap:SetZoom`.

- `Minimap:PingLocation(x, y)` — Pings the minimap at the given coordinate (relative to the center).

- `Minimap:SetArrowModel("file")` — Sets the model of the minimap arrow.

- `Minimap:SetBlipTexture("file")` — Sets the texture of the minimap blips.

- `Minimap:SetIconTexture(path)` — Sets the texture for the minimap icons.

- `Minimap:SetMaskTexture("file")` — Sets the texture with which to mask the minimap texture. Although you can change the mask texture to something other than a circle, the minimap arrows will continue to be rendered in a circle.

- `Minimap:SetPlayerModel("file")` — Sets the model of the player on the minimap.

- `Minimap:SetZoom(zoom)` — Sets the minimap zoom.

The following handlers are available for Minimap: `OnAttributeChanged`, `OnChar`, `OnDragStart`, `OnDragStop`, `OnEnter`, `OnEvent`, `OnHide`, `OnKeyDown`, `OnKeyUp`, `OnLeave`, `OnLoad`, `OnMouseDown`, `OnMouseUp`, `OnMouseWheel`, `OnReceiveDrag`, `OnShow`, `OnSizeChanged`, `OnUpdate`.

SimpleHTML

SimpleHTML widgets can be used to display formatted text using a very simple HTML-like markup language. SimpleHTML inherits all methods from UIObject, Region, VisibleRegion, and Frame, in addition to the following:

- `SimpleHTML:GetFont(["element"])` — Returns the font information for the frame. This function optionally takes the name of a SimpleHTML element (such as <p> or <h1>), and gets the attribute for that element only (`font`, `height`, ...).

- `SimpleHTML:GetFontObject`↵(["element") — Returns the font object for the frame. This function optionally takes the name of a SimpleHTML element (such as <p> or <h1>), and gets the attribute for that element only.

- `SimpleHTML:GetHyperlinkFormat()` — Returns the hyperlink format for the framer.

- `SimpleHTML:GetJustifyH`↵(["element"]) — Returns the horizontal alignment of the frame. This function optionally takes the name of a SimpleHTML element (such as <p> or <h1>), and gets the attribute for that element only.

- `SimpleHTML:GetJustifyV↵(["element"])` — Returns the vertical alignment of the font. This function optionally takes the name of a SimpleHTML element (such as `<p>` or `<h1>`), and gets the attribute for that element only.

- `SimpleHTML:GetShadowColor↵([element])` — Returns the shadow color for the font (`red`, `green`, `blue`, `alpha`). This function optionally takes the name of a SimpleHTML element (such as `<p>` or `<h1>`), and gets the attribute for that element only.

- `SimpleHTML:GetShadowOffset↵(["element"])` — Returns the shadow offset for the font (`x`, `y`). This function optionally takes the name of a SimpleHTML element (such as `<p>` or `<h1>`), and gets the attribute for that element only.

- `SimpleHTML:GetSpacing(["element"])` — Returns the line spacing of the font. This function optionally takes the name of a SimpleHTML element (such as `<p>` or `<h1>`), and gets the attribute for that element only.

- `SimpleHTML:GetTextColor↵(["element"])` — Returns the color of the font (`red`, `green`, `blue`, `alpha`). This function optionally takes the name of a SimpleHTML element (such as `<p>` or `<h1>`), and gets the attribute for that element only.

- `SimpleHTML:SetFont(["element"], "font", fontHeight [, flags])` — Sets the font file, height, and flags to be used. This function optionally takes the name of a SimpleHTML element (such as `<p>` or `<h1>`), and sets the attribute for that element only.

- `SimpleHTML:SetFontObject↵(["element"], font or "font" or nil)` — Sets the font object to be used. This function optionally takes the name of a SimpleHTML element (such as `<p>` or `<h1>`), and sets the attribute for that element only.

- `SimpleHTML:SetHyperlinkFormat↵("format")` — Sets the format to use for hyperlinks in the frame. The default is `"|H%s|h%s|h"`, where the first `%s` is the data in the hyperlink, and the second `%s` is the text to be displayed.

- `SimpleHTML:SetJustifyH(["element"], "justify")` — Sets the horizontal alignment for the font. This function optionally takes the name of a SimpleHTML element (such as `<p>` or `<h1>`), and sets the attribute for that element only.

- `SimpleHTML:SetJustifyV(["element"], "justify")` — Sets the vertical alignment of the font. This function optionally takes the name of a SimpleHTML element (such as `<p>` or `<h1>`), and sets the attribute for that element only.

- `SimpleHTML:SetShadowColor([element,] red, green, blue [, alpha])` — Sets the color of the font's shadow. This function optionally takes the name of a SimpleHTML element (such as `<p>` or `<h1>`), and sets the attribute for that element only.

- `SimpleHTML:SetShadowOffset↵([element], x, y)` — Sets the offset for the font's shadow. This function optionally takes the name of a SimpleHTML element (such as `<p>` or `<h1>`), and sets the attribute for that element only.

- `SimpleHTML:SetSpacing(["element"], spacing)` — Sets the spacing between lines in the display. This function optionally takes the name of a SimpleHTML element (such as `<p>` or `<h1>`), and sets the attribute for that element only.

- `SimpleHTML:SetText("text")` — Sets the text of the SimpleHTML frame.

- `SimpleHTML:SetTextColor(["element"], red, green, blue [, alpha])` — Sets the text color (optionally for a given SimpleHTML element such as `<p>`, `<h1>`, and so on).

The following handlers are available for SimpleHTML: `OnAttributeChanged`, `OnChar`, `OnDragStart`, `OnDragStop`, `OnEnter`, `OnEvent`, `OnHide`, `OnHyperlinkClick`, `OnHyperlinkEnter`, `OnHyperlinkLeave`, `OnKeyDown`, `OnKeyUp`, `OnLeave`, `OnLoad`, `OnMouseDown`, `OnMouseUp`, `OnMouseWheel`, `OnReceiveDrag`, `OnShow`, `OnSizeChanged`, `OnUpdate`.

ScrollingMessageFrame

ScrollingMessageFrames display messages sequentially, with the ability to scroll back through the buffer to review previous messages. The default ChatFrames are ScrollingMessageFrames. ScrollingMessageFrame inherits all methods from UIObject, FontInstance, Region, VisibleRegion, and Frame, in addition to the following:

- `ScrollingMessageFrame:`↵AddMessage(text [, red, green, blue [, id]]) — Adds a message to the frame.

- `ScrollingMessageFrame:AtBottom()` — Returns whether or not the message frame is scrolled all the way to the bottom.

- `ScrollingMessageFrame:AtTop()` — Returns whether or not the message frame is scrolled all the way to the top.

- `ScrollingMessageFrame:Clear()` — Clears the message frame.

- `ScrollingMessageFrame:`↵GetCurrentLine() — Returns the last line that was added to the frame.

- `ScrollingMessageFrame:`↵GetCurrentScroll() — Gets the current scroll offset for the frame.

- `ScrollingMessageFrame:`↵GetFadeDuration() — Returns the fade duration for the text.

- `ScrollingMessageFrame:GetFading()` — Returns if text fading is enabled for the frame.

- `ScrollingMessageFrame:`↵GetInsertMode() — Returns the insert mode for the scrolling frame (TOP or BOTTOM).

- `ScrollingMessageFrame:`↵GetMaxLines() — Returns the maximum number of lines in the message frame.

- `ScrollingMessageFrame:`↵GetNumLinesDisplayed() — Returns the number of lines displayed in the message frame.

- `ScrollingMessageFrame:`↵GetNumMessages() — Returns the number of messages in the message frame.

- `ScrollingMessageFrame:`↵GetTimeVisible() — Returns the amount of time that messages are displayed.

- `ScrollingMessageFrame:PageDown()` — Scrolls down a page in the message frame.

- `ScrollingMessageFrame:PageUp()` — Scrolls up a page in the message frame.

- `ScrollingMessageFrame:ScrollDown()` — Scrolls down in the message frame.

- `ScrollingMessageFrame:`↪ScrollToBottom() — Scrolls to the bottom of the message frame.

- `ScrollingMessageFrame:`↪ScrollToTop() — Scrolls to the top of the message frame.

- `ScrollingMessageFrame:ScrollUp()` — Scrolls up in the message frame.

- `ScrollingMessageFrame:`↪SetFadeDuration(seconds) — Sets the fade duration for the frame.

- `ScrollingMessageFrame:`↪SetFading(enabled) — Sets whether or not text fades after a period of time.

- `ScrollingMessageFrame:`↪SetInsertMode("TOP" or "BOTTOM") — Sets the insert mode for the message frame.

- `ScrollingMessageFrame:`↪SetMaxLines(maxLines) — Sets the maximum number of lines to be kept in the frame.

- `ScrollingMessageFrame:`↪SetScrollOffset() — Sets the current scroll offset.

- `ScrollingMessageFrame:`↪SetTimeVisible(seconds) — Sets the visible time for messages.

- `ScrollingMessageFrame:Update`↪ColorByID(id, red, green, blue) — Updates the color for a specific message `id`. This message ID is the same ID that can be specified in the `AddMessage()` method.

The following handlers are available for ScrollingMessageFrame: `OnAttributeChanged`, `OnChar`, `OnDragStart`, `OnDragStop`, `OnEnter`, `OnEvent`, `OnHide`, `OnHyperlinkClick`, `OnHyperlinkEnter`, `OnHyperlinkLeave`, `OnKeyDown`, `OnKeyUp`, `OnLeave`, `OnLoad`, `OnMessageScrollChanged`, `OnMouseDown`, `OnMouseUp`, `OnMouseWheel`, `OnReceiveDrag`, `OnShow`, `OnSizeChanged`, `OnUpdate`.

StatusBar

StatusBars are used to display information using simple textured progress bars. StatusBar inherits all methods from UIObject, Region, VisibleRegion, and Frame, in addition to the following:

- `StatusBar:GetMinMaxValues()` — Returns the minimum and maximum values of the status bar.

- `StatusBar:GetOrientation()` — Returns the current orientation of the status bar (`HORIZONTAL` or `VERTICAL`).

- `StatusBar:GetStatusBarColor()` — Returns the current color of the status bar texture (`red`, `green`, `blue`, `alpha`.).

- StatusBar:GetStatusBarTexture() — Returns the current status bar texture.

- StatusBar:GetValue() — Gets the current value of the status bar.

- StatusBar:SetMinMaxValues(min, max) — Sets the minimum and maximum values for the status bar.

- StatusBar:SetOrientation↵("orientation") — Sets the orientation of the status bar (HORIZONTAL or VERTICAL).

- StatusBar:SetStatusBarColor(red, green, blue [, alpha]) — Sets the color of the status bar texture. This is equivalent to a :SetVertexColor call on the status bar's texture.

- StatusBar:SetStatusBarTexture↵(texture or "texture" [, "layer"]) — Sets the status bar texture.

- StatusBar:SetValue(value) — Sets the current value of the status bar.

The following handlers are available for StatusBar: OnAttributeChanged, OnChar, OnDragStart, OnDragStop, OnEnter, OnEvent, OnHide, OnKeyDown, OnKeyUp, OnLeave, OnLoad, OnMouseDown, OnMouseUp, OnMouseWheel, OnReceiveDrag, OnShow, OnSizeChanged, OnUpdate, OnValueChanged.

Button

The Button type is used to create widgets that can respond to mouse clicks. Button inherits all methods from UIObject, Region, VisibleRegion, and Frame, in addition to the following:

- Button:Click(mouseButton, down) — Simulates a click on the given button. The mouseButton and down parameters are passed to the PreClick, OnClick, and PostClick handlers.

- Button:Disable() — Disables the button so it cannot be clicked. This function may change the visual state of the button if DisabledTexture, DisabledTextColor or DisabledFontObject are set.

- Button:Enable() — Enables the button for clicks. This may change the appearance of the button depending on the various textures specified.

- Button:GetButtonState() — Returns the buton's current state: NORMAL, PUSHED, or DISABLED.

- Button:GetDisabledFontObject() — Returns the Font object used when the button is in the DISABLED state.

- Button:GetDisabledTextColor() — Returns the text color for the button's disabled-mode text (red, blue, green, alpha).

- Button:GetDisabledTexture() — Returns the texture object that is displayed when the button is in the DISABLED state.

- Button:GetFont() — Returns the font currently used for display on the button (filename, fontHeight, ...). The ... is a list containing any number of OUTLINE, THICKOUTLINE, or MONOCHROME.

- Button:GetFontString() — Returns the FontString object that is used for the button's label.

- Button:GetHighlightFontObject() — Returns the font object used for the button's highlight text.

- Button:GetHighlightTextColor() — Returns the color of the button's highlight text color (red, green, blue, alpha).

- Button:GetHighlightTexture() — Returns the texture object that is displayed when the button is highlighted.

- Button:GetNormalTexture() — Returns the texture object that is displayed when the button is in its normal state.

- Button:GetPushedTextOffset() — Returns the text offset for when the button is in the PUSHED state (x, y).

- Button:GetPushedTexture() — Returns the texture that is displayed when the button is in the PUSHED state.

- Button:GetText() — Returns the text of the button's label.

- Button:GetTextColor() — Returns the color of the button's normal text object (red, blue, green, alpha).

- Button:GetTextFontObject() — Returns the font object that is used when the button is in the NORMAL state.

- Button:GetTextHeight() — Returns the height of the button's text.

- Button:GetTextWidth() — Returns the width of the button's label.

- Button:IsEnabled() — Returns if the button is enabled.

- Button:LockHighlight() — Locks the button's highlight state so it is always drawn as highlighted.

- Button:RegisterForClicks(...) — Registers a button to receive mouse clicks. A button is registered for LeftButtonUp by default.

- Button:SetButtonState("state", lock) — Sets a button's state, optionally locking it into that state.

- Button:SetDisabledFontObject(font) — Sets the font object to be used when the button is disabled.

- Button:SetDisabledTextColor(red, green, blue [, alpha]) — Sets the color of the button's text when the button is disabled.

- Button:SetDisabledTexture(texture) — Sets the texture to be used when the button is disabled. This function takes either a texture object or a path to a texture.

- Button:SetFont("font", fontHeight, ...) — Sets the font for a given button.

- Button:SetFontString(fontstring) — Sets the button's label FontString.

- Button:SetFormattedText(fmt, ...) — Sets the button's label, using a format string and arguments. This prevents a new text string from being allocated, saving memory if the text is frequently changed to a new string.

- Button:SetHighlightFontObject↵(font) — Sets the font object to be used for the button's highlight text.

- Button:SetHighlightTextColor(red, green, blue [, alpha) — Sets the color of the button's highlight text.

- Button:SetHighlightTexture(texture or "texture" [, "blendmode") — Sets the highlight texture and blend mode for the button. This function takes either a texture object or a path to a texture. The blend mode can be one of the following values: DISABLE (the texture is drawn entirely opaque with no alpha blending), BLEND (the image should be drawn on top of the current one, using the alpha channel if present)), ALPHAKEY (draw the image on top of the current one using 1-bit alpha), ADD (use additive blending when drawing the texture, MOD (use modulating blending when drawing the texture).

- Button:SetNormalTexture(texture) — Sets a button's normal texture. This function takes either a texture object or a path to a texture.

- Button:SetPushedTextOffset(x, y) — Sets the offset for the button's label when the button is pushed. This gives the button depth when being clicked. In the default interface templates, this matches the offset in the pushed texture.

- Button:SetPushedTexture(texture) — Sets the texture to be used when the button is in the PUSHED state. This function takes either a texture object or a path to a texture.

- Button:SetText("text") — Sets the text to be displayed on the button's label.

- Button:SetTextColor(red, blue, green, alpha) — Sets the color for the button's normal text.

- Button:SetTextFontObject(font) — Sets the font object to use when the button is in the NORMAL state.

- Button:UnlockHighlight() — Unlocks the button's highlight state, so it operates normally.

The following handlers are available for Button: OnAttributeChanged, OnChar, OnClick, OnDoubleClick, OnDragStart, OnDragStop, OnEnter, OnEvent, OnHide, OnKeyDown, OnKeyUp, OnLeave, OnLoad, OnMouseDown, OnMouseUp, OnMouseWheel, OnReceiveDrag, OnShow, OnSizeChanged, OnUpdate, PostClick, PreClick.

PlayerModel

The PlayerModel type is used to display the 3-D model of a character in the user interface. PlayerModel inherits all methods from UIObject, Region, VisibleRegion, Frame, and Model, in addition to the following:

- PlayerModel:RefreshUnit() — Refreshes the model given its current unit. If you change targets (and the model's unit is set to "target"), for instance, use this function to update to the new target's model.

▪ `PlayerModel:SetRotation(angle)` — Sets the rotation angle (in radians) of the mesh displayed in the model.

▪ `PlayerModel:SetUnit(unitId)` — Sets the model to display the given unit.

The following handlers are available for PlayerModel: `OnAnimFinished`, `OnAttributeChanged`, `OnChar`, `OnDragStart`, `OnDragStop`, `OnEnter`, `OnEvent`, `OnHide`, `OnKeyDown`, `OnKeyUp`, `OnLeave`, `OnLoad`, `OnMouseDown`, `OnMouseUp`, `OnMouseWheel`, `OnReceiveDrag`, `OnShow`, `OnSizeChanged`, `OnUpdate`, `OnUpdateModel`.

CheckButton

CheckButtons are an extension of buttons that add a CHECKED state. This is used for radio buttons and checkboxes in the default user interface. CheckButton inherits all methods from UIObject, Region, VisibleRegion, Frame, and Button, in addition to the following:

▪ `CheckButton:GetChecked()` — Returns if the button is checked.

▪ `CheckButton:GetCheckedTexture()` — Returns the texture that is displayed when thebutton is checked.

▪ `CheckButton:GetDisabledChecked↵Texture()` — Returns the `DisabledChecked` texture for the button.

▪ `CheckButton:SetChecked(checked)` — Sets the checked state of a button.

▪ `CheckButton:SetCheckedTexture↵(texture or "texture")` — Sets the texture to be displayed when the button is checked. This function takes either a texture object or a path to a texture.

▪ `CheckButton:SetDisabledCheckedTexture(texture or "texture")` — Sets the texture to be displayed when the button is disabled and checked. This function takes either a texture object or a path to a texture.

The following handlers are available for CheckButton: `OnAttributeChanged`, `OnChar`, `OnClick`, `OnDoubleClick`, `OnDragStart`, `OnDragStop`, `OnEnter`, `OnEvent`, `OnHide`, `OnKeyDown`, `OnKeyUp`, `OnLeave`, `OnLoad`, `OnMouseDown`, `OnMouseUp`, `OnMouseWheel`, `OnReceiveDrag`, `OnShow`, `OnSizeChanged`, `OnUpdate`, `PostClick`, `PreClick`.

TabardModel

The TabardModel type is used to display the 3-D model of a tabard in the user interface. TabardModel inherits all methods from UIObject, Region, VisibleRegion, Frame, Model, and PlayerModel, in addition to the following:

▪ `TabardModel:CanSaveTabardNow()` — Returns whether or not the tabard can be saved.

▪ `TabardModel:CycleVariation↵(variationIndex, delta)` — Cycles through a tabard model's variations by delta. The variationIndex can be:

  ▪ 1 — Icon
  ▪ 2 — Icon color

- 3 — Border
- 4 — Border color
- 5 — Background color

- `TabardModel:GetLowerBackground↵FileName()` — Returns the path to the lower background texture file.
- `TabardModel:GetLowerEmblemFile↵Name()` — Returns the path to the lower emblem texture file.
- `TabardModel:GetLowerEmblem↵Texture(texture)` — Returns the lower emblem texture.
- `TabardModel:GetUpperBackground↵FileName()` — Returns the path to the upper background texture file.
- `TabardModel:GetUpperEmblemFile↵Name()` — Returns the path to the upper emblem texture file.
- `TabardModel:GetUpperEmblem↵Texture(texture)` — Returns the upper emblem texture.
- `TabardModel:InitializeTabard↵Colors()` — Initializes the tabard's color options.
- `TabardModel:Save()` — Saves the designed tabard.

The following handlers are available for TabardModel: `OnAnimFinished`, `OnAttributeChanged`, `OnChar`, `OnDragStart`, `OnDragStop`, `OnEnter`, `OnEvent`, `OnHide`, `OnKeyDown`, `OnKeyUp`, `OnLeave`, `OnLoad`, `OnMouseDown`, `OnMouseUp`, `OnMouseWheel`, `OnReceiveDrag`, `OnShow`, `OnSizeChanged`, `OnUpdate`, `OnUpdateModel`.

DressUpModel

The DressUpModel type is used to display the 3-D model of a character and allow items to be added to the mode to see how they will look on a given character. DressUpModel inherits all methods from UIObject, Region, VisibleRegion, Frame, Model, and Player-Model, in addition to the following:

- `DressUpModel:Dress()` — Sets the model to reflect the character's current inventory.
- `DressUpModel:TryOn(item)` — Adds an item (ID, string, or link) to the model.
- `DressUpModel:Undress()` — Sets the model to reflect the character without inventory.

The following handlers are available for DressUpModel: `OnAnimFinished`, `OnAttributeChanged`, `OnChar`, `OnDragStart`, `OnDragStop`, `OnEnter`, `OnEvent`, `OnHide`, `OnKeyDown`, `OnKeyUp`, `OnLeave`, `OnLoad`, `OnMouseDown`, `OnMouseUp`, `OnMouseWheel`, `OnReceiveDrag`, `OnShow`, `OnSizeChanged`, `OnUpdate`, `OnUpdateModel`.

Handler Listing

Each type of widget has several script handlers that can be used to respond to user interaction and other widget events. The following is a listing of the different handlers that are available.

- **OnAnimFinished** — Fires when the model's animation finishes. OnAnimFinished will only fire for models that do not repeat their animation. This is used, for example, by bag slots to animate items being "pushed" into a bag when you buy an item at a merchant.

  Argument:
  self — The frame object for which this handler was called.

- **OnAttributeChanged** — Sets an arbitrary, named, taintless value on a frame. Attributes are used by the secure template system. They allow addons to configure the behavior of action buttons, unit frames, and other protected frames in ways specifically set forth by the templates' code. Because you cannot call SetAttribute in combat, your addon cannot make intelligent, reactive decisions on what action to take for you. See Chapter 17 for more information.

  Arguments:
  self — The frame object for which this handler was called.
  name — The name of the attribute. (string)
  value — The new value of the attribute. (any)

  Example:

  ```
  -- Create an action button that uses action slot 2 on-- right click,
  otherwise 1
  CreateFrame("CheckButton", "MyButton", UIParent, ↵
  "ActionBarButtonTemplate")
  MyButton:SetPoint("CENTER")
  MyButton:SetAttribute("type", "action")
  MyButton:SetAttribute("*action2", 2)
  MyButton:SetAttribute("action", 1)
  ```

- **OnChar** — Fires when a text character is received by a frame. Rather than tracking individual key presses, this event only fires when some text character results. For example, on Windows computers, holding Alt while you type 233 on the number pad will enter the character é once you let go of Alt. OnChar receives that character.

  - Except for edit boxes, OnChar will only fire if the frame is at least at the "DIALOG" strata. See EnableKeyboard.
  - WoW uses UTF-8 Unicode so the length of the string may be more than 1.

  Arguments:
  self — The frame object for which this handler was called.
  text — The character entered (multibyte) (string)

- **OnCharComposition** — Fires when an EditBox's input composition mode changes. This handler will only fire in international clients that can use IME composition.

Argument:
self — The frame object for which this handler was called.

▪ OnClick — Fires in response to a click on the button. By default, a button only accepts "up" clicks from the left mouse button. You can use the RegisterForClicks method to enable other buttons and receive click events on mouse down as well as mouse up. Note: if you move the mouse away from the button before releasing it, the *Click handlers will not fire an "up" click event (though OnMouseUp still will). See also: Click, PreClick, PostClick.

Arguments:
self — The frame object for which this handler was called.
button — The name of the mouse button that clicked the frame. (string)

- ▪ LeftButton

- ▪ RightButton

- ▪ MiddleButton

- ▪ Button4

- ▪ Button5

- ▪ Remapped button *(see Chapter 25)*

down — Indicates that the click was triggered by mouse down. (boolean)

Example:

```
-- This sample illustrates the timing of the various
-- mouse events when clicking a button.
local b = CreateFrame("Button", nil, UIParent, ↵
"UIPanelButtonTemplate2")
b:SetPoint("CENTER")
b:RegisterForClicks("AnyUp", "AnyDown")
local upDown = { [false] = "Up", [true] = "Down" }
local function show(text, color)
   DEFAULT_CHAT_FRAME:AddMessage(text, color, color, color)
end
local color
b:SetScript("OnMouseDown", function(self, button)
   color = .60
   show(format("OnMouseDown: %s", button), color, ↵
color, color)
end)
b:SetScript("OnMouseUp", function(self, button)
   color = .60
   show(format("OnMouseUp: %s", button), color, color, color)
end)
b:SetScript("OnClick", function(self, button, down)
   color = color + 0.1
   show(format("OnClick: %s %s", button, ↵
upDown[down]), color, color, color)
end)
```

```
b:SetScript("PreClick", function(self, button, down)
  color = color + 0.1
  show(format("PreClick: %s %s", button, ↵
upDown[down]), color, color, color)
end)
b:SetScript("PostClick", function(self, button,down)
  color = color + 0.1
  show(format("PostClick: %s %s", button, ↵
upDown[down]), color, color, color)
end)
```

▪ OnColorSelect — Fires for a ColorSelect frame when you choose a color.

Arguments:
self — The frame object for which this handler was called.
r — The red component of the selected color (0 to 1). (number)
g — The green component of the selected color (0 to 1). (number)
b — The blue component of the selected color (0 to 1). (number)

▪ OnCursorChanged — Fires for edit boxes when the position of the cursor changes. All measurements are in pixels. The x and y positions are relative to the top-left corner of the edit box (0, 0). Also fires with the most recent parameters when the edit box gains or loses focus.

Arguments:
self — The frame object for which this handler was called.
x — The horizontal position of the cursor. (number)
y — The vertical position of the cursor. (number)
width — The width of the cursor. (number)
height — The height of the cursor and, by extension, the height of a line of text. (number)

▪ OnDoubleClick — Fires when the user double-clicks the button. The cutoff time between clicks for it to be counted as a double-click is 0.3 seconds. Anything slower will trigger two OnClicks.

Arguments:
self — The frame object for which this handler was called.
button — The mouse button that double-clicked the frame. (string)

  ▪ LeftButton

  ▪ RightButton

  ▪ MiddleButton

  ▪ Button4

  ▪ Button5

▪ OnDragStart — Fires when the user starts moving the mouse after clicking down on the frame. See also: OnDragStop, OnReceiveDrag, RegisterForDrag

Arguments:
self — The frame object for which this handler was called.
button — The name of the mouse button that dragged the frame. (string)

- LeftButton

- RightButton

- MiddleButton

- Button4

- Button5

Example:

```
-- This example illustrates the various handlers
--involved in dragging. Dragging to or from either
-- button will display messages detailing the process.
local nextNum = 1
local last
local handlers = {
  "OnMouseDown", "OnMouseUp", "OnDragStart", ↵
"OnDragStop", "OnReceiveDrag"
}
local function CreateButton()
  local curNum = nextNum
  local b = CreateFrame("Button", "Test"..curNum, ↵
UIParent, "UIPanelButtonTemplate2")
  if curNum == 1 then
    b:SetPoint("CENTER")
  else
    b:SetPoint("LEFT", last, "RIGHT", 5, 0)
  end
  b:SetText(curNum)
  b:RegisterForDrag("LeftButton", "RightButton")

  for _, handler in ipairs(handlers) do
    b:SetScript(handler, function(self, button)
      button = button and ", "..button or ""
      DEFAULT_CHAT_FRAME:AddMessage(format("%s: ↵
%d%s", handler, curNum, button))
    end)
  end

  nextNum = nextNum + 1
  last = b
end
CreateButton()
CreateButton()
```

- OnDragStop — Fires when you release the mouse button after beginning a drag on the frame. See also: OnDragStart, OnReceiveDrag

Argument:
self — The frame object for which this handler was called.

- OnEditFocusGained — Fires when an edit box receives keyboard focus.

Argument:

self — The frame object for which this handler was called.

■ OnEditFocusLost — Fires for an edit box when it loses keyboard focus.

Argument:

self — The frame object for which this handler was called.

■ OnEnter — Fires whenever the cursor becomes focused on a frame. The motion parameter is only true if the OnEnter was triggered by actual mouse movement. Other situations can cause OnEnter as well, such as a frame being shown under the cursor.

Argument:

self — The frame object for which this handler was called.
motion — Indicates whether the leave occurred due to mouse movement or not. (boolean)

■ OnEnterPressed — Fires for a currently focused edit box when you press the Enter key.

Argument:

self — The frame object for which this handler was called.

■ OnEscapePressed — Fires for a currently focused edit box when you press the Escape key.

Argument:

self — The frame object for which this handler was called.

■ OnEvent — Fires on each frame that is registered for a given event. The event reference contains details of each event that can be passed to this handler. See also: RegisterEvent and the event reference

Arguments:

self — The frame object for which this handler was called.
event — The API event to be processed. (string)
... — Arguments specific to the event. (any)

■ OnHide — Fires when the frame is hidden. OnHide occurs whether the frame was hidden directly or via its parent.

Argument:

self — The frame object for which this handler was called.

■ OnHorizontalScroll — Fires whenever a scroll frame changes its horizontal scroll offset. See also: SetHorizontalScroll, OnVerticalScroll, SetVerticalScroll

Arguments:

self — The frame object for which this handler was called.
offset — The offset in pixels that the frame has scrolled horizontally. (number)

■ OnHyperlinkClick — Fires for a SimpleHTML or ScrollingMessageFrame when you click a hyperlink in it.

Arguments:

`self` — The frame object for which this handler was called.

`linkData` — The interior portion of the link (for example, `"item:1234:0:0:0:0:0:0:0"`). (string)

`link` — The full hyperlink (for example, `"|Hplayer:Cogwheel:24|h[Cogwheel]|h"`). (string)

`button` — The mouse button used to click the link. (string)

- ▪ `LeftButton`

- ▪ `RightButton`

- ▪ `MiddleButton`

- ▪ `Button4`

- ▪ `Button5`

Example:

```
-- Print information about a clicked hyperlink
local someMessageFrame = WowLuaFrameOutput
someMessageFrame:SetScript("OnHyperlinkClick", ↵
function(self, linkData, link, button)
     self:AddMessage(format("You clicked on %s ↵
with %s", link, button))
end)
```

- ▪ `OnHyperlinkEnter` — Fires for a `SimpleHTML` or `ScrollingMessageFrame` when your mouse enters a hyperlink in it. See also: `OnHyperLinkClick`, `OnHyperlinkLeave`

Arguments:

`self` — The frame object for which this handler was called.

`linkData` — The interior portion of the link (for example, `"item:1234:0:0:0:0:0:0:0"`). (string)

`link` — The full hyperlink (for example, `"|Hplayer:Cogwheel:24|h[Cogwheel]|h"`). (string)

Example:

```
-- Prints data about the hyperlink you enter in the ↵
default chat frame
DEFAULT_CHAT_FRAME:SetScript("OnHyperlinkEnter", ↵
function(self, linkData, link)
  local color = link:match("|c%x%x%x%x%x%x%x%x") or ""
  self:AddMessage("linkData: "..linkData)
  self:AddMessage(format("link: %s%s", color, ↵
link:gsub("|","||")))
end)
```

- ▪ `OnHyperlinkLeave` — Fires for a `SimpleHTML` or `ScrollingMessageFrame` when your mouse leaves a hyperlink in it. See also: `OnHyperLinkClick`, `OnHyperlinkEnter`

Arguments:

`self` — The frame object for which this handler was called.

`linkData` — The interior portion of the link (for example, `"item:1234:0:0:0:0:0:0:0"`). (string)

`link` — The full hyperlink (for example, `"|Hplayer:Cogwheel:24|h[Cogwheel]|h"`). (string)

Example

```
-- Prints data about the hyperlink you leave in the ↵
default chat frame
DEFAULT_CHAT_FRAME:SetScript("OnHyperlinkLeave", ↵
function(self, linkData, link)
  local color = link:match("|c%x%x%x%x%x%x%x%x") or ""
  self:AddMessage("linkData: "..linkData)
  self:AddMessage(format("link: %s%s", color, ↵
link:gsub("|","||")))
end)
```

▪ `OnInputLanguageChanged` — Fires when the input language for the edit box changes. This is only valid for international clients that allow multiple input languages.

Arguments:

`self` — The frame object for which this handler was called.

`language` — The new input language for the EditBox. (string)

▪ `OnKeyDown` — Fires when the frame receives a "down" key press. Only the currently focused, keyboard-enabled frame will receive this event. See also: `OnKeyUp`, `EnableKeyboard`

Arguments:

`self` — The frame object for which this handler was called.

`key` — The key that was pressed. (string)

▪ `OnKeyUp` — Fires when the frame receives an "up" key press. Only the currently focused, keyboard-enabled frame will receive this event. See also: `OnKeyDown`, `EnableKeyboard`

Arguments:

`self` — The frame object for which this handler was called.

`key` — The key that was pressed. (string)

▪ `OnLeave` — Fires whenever the cursor is no longer focused on a frame. The `motion` parameter is only `true` if the `OnLeave` was triggered by actual mouse movement. Other situations can cause `OnLeave` as well, such as a frame hiding or being covered up by another mouse-enabled frame.

Arguments:

`self` — The frame object for which this handler was called.

`motion` — Indicates whether the leave occurred due to mouse movement or not. (boolean)

■ OnLoad — Fires when a frame is first created. This is only applicable to frames instantiated from XML templates. Frames created with CreateFrame will have already run their OnLoad scripts by the time the function returns.

Argument:
self — The frame object for which this handler was called.

■ OnMessageScrollChanged — Fires when the scrolling message frame's scroll range changes (for example, after adding a new message).

Argument:
self — The frame object for which this handler was called.

■ OnMouseDown — Fires when a mouse button is pressed down while the mouse-enabled frame has mouse focus. See also: OnMouseUp, OnClick

Arguments:
self — The frame object for which this handler was called.
button — The mouse button clicking the frame. (string)

- ■ LeftButton

- ■ RightButton

- ■ MiddleButton

- ■ Button4

- ■ Button5

■ OnMouseUp — Fires when the mouse button is released after clicking on a frame. This event will always fire for the frame that received the initial click, even if you move the mouse away from that frame. If OnDragStart occurs before the user releases the mouse button, OnMouseUp will not fire. See also: OnClick

Arguments:
self — The frame object for which this handler was called.
button — The mouse button clicking the frame. (string)

- ■ LeftButton

- ■ RightButton

- ■ MiddleButton

- ■ Button4

- ■ Button5

■ OnMouseWheel — Fires for a mouse wheel-enabled frame when the user rolls the mouse wheel while over the frame.

Arguments:
self — The frame object for which this handler was called.
delta — Indicates one "notch" in a particular direction: 1 for up, -1 for down. (number)

Example:

```
-- Print the mousewheel delta for a button
CreateFrame("Frame", "test", UIParent, ↵
"UIPanelButtonTemplate2")
test:SetPoint("CENTER")
test:EnableMouseWheel(true)
test:SetScript("OnMouseWheel", function(self, delta)
    DEFAULT_CHAT_FRAME:AddMessage(delta)
end)
```

▪ OnReceiveDrag — Fires when you release the mouse button over a frame after starting a drag. See also: OnDragStart, OnDragStop

Argument:
self — The frame object for which this handler was called.

▪ OnScrollRangeChanged — Fires whenever the scroll range of a scroll frame changes. The extents are the distance you would have to scroll in the given axis to be fully scrolled. In other words, if the top-left corner of the scroll frame is visible, the scroll values are (0, 0). When you scroll all the way to the bottom-right, the scroll values are (xExtent, yExtent). For example, xExtent is equivalent to: max(scrollChildWidth - scrollFrameWidth, 0). See also: UpdateScrollChildRect

Arguments:
self — The frame object for which this handler was called.
xExtent — The horizontal scroll extent. (number)
yExtent — The vertical scroll extent. (number)

Example:

```
-- Set the min and max values of a scroll bar (Slider) ↵
based on the scroll range
scrollFrame:SetScript("OnScrollRangeChanged", ↵
function(self, x, y)
  verticalScrollBar:SetMinMaxValues(0, y)
end)
```

▪ OnShow — Fires whenever a frame becomes visible after being not visible. Fires whenever the frames Visibility status (retrieved by Frame:IsVisible()) changes from hidden to shown. This can be triggered by Region:Show() being called on the frame itself, or by Region:Show() being called on an ancestor. This handler does NOT fire if the frame was already visible.

Argument:
self — The frame object for which this handler was called.

▪ OnSizeChanged — Fires whenever a frame's size changes.

Arguments:
self — The frame object for which this handler was called.
width — The new width of the frame. (number)

height — The new height of the frame. (number)

■ OnSpacePressed — Fires for a currently focused edit box when you press the Space key.

Argument:
self — The frame object for which this handler was called.

■ OnTabPressed — Fires for a currently focused edit box when you press Tab. This is useful for switching fields on a frame with many text inputs.

Argument:
self — The frame object for which this handler was called.

■ OnTextChanged — Fires whenever text in an edit box changes. This change can be caused by typing or calling SetText on the frame. In the latter case, OnTextChanged will fire twice. If SetText does not actually change the text, the handler will not fire.

Argument:
self — The frame object for which this handler was called.

OnTextSet — Fires for an edit box when its text is set via SetText.

Argument:
self — The frame object for which this handler was called.

■ OnTooltipAddMoney — Fires when a tooltip needs to add a money line and at every subsequent tooltip update. Note: this is only fired by the game engine when one of the Set* functions sets the tooltip to something that should display money (for example, an item while a vendor window is open). There is no corresponding widget API.

Arguments:
self — The frame object for which this handler was called.
amount — The amount of money (in copper) that was added to the tooltip. (number)

Example:

```
-- Display the amount of copper that is added to the ↵
tooltip
GameTooltip:HookScript("OnTooltipAddMoney", ↵
function(self, amount)
     DEFAULT_CHAT_FRAME:AddMessage(format("Money: ↵
%d", amount))
end)
```

■ OnTooltipCleared — Fires whenever the tooltip's lines are cleared. This can be triggered by hiding the tooltip or calling GameTooltip:ClearLines.

Argument:
self — The frame object for which this handler was called.

■ OnTooltipSetDefaultAnchor — Fired by C code when the tooltip needs to set its anchor to the default position. For example, mousing over a unit in the world frame.

Argument:
self — The frame object for which this handler was called.

■ OnTooltipSetItem — Fires in response to a corresponding SetItem call. Note: This handler does not pass the item as a parameter. This handler can fire more than once per tooltip, as information is retrieved from the server. This process is complete when Tooltip:GetItem() returns non-nil. See GetItem

Argument:
self — The frame object for which this handler was called.

■ OnTooltipSetSpell — Fires in response to a corresponding SetSpell call. Note: This handler does not pass the spell as a parameter. See GetSpell

Argument:
self — The frame object for which this handler was called.

■ OnTooltipSetUnit — Fires in response to a corresponding SetUnit call. Note: This handler does not pass the unit as a parameter. See GetUnit

Argument:
self — The frame object for which this handler was called.

■ OnUpdate — Fires once for every visible frame each time the UI is rendered. This handler is often used for timers or tasks that must run continuously without interfering with gameplay. The rate OnUpdate is fired is exactly the same as your frame rate.

Arguments:
self — The frame object for which this handler was called.
elapsed — The number of seconds (fractional) since the last call to OnUpdate. (number)

■ OnUpdateModel — Fires whenever a model changes or animates.

Arguments:
self — The frame object for which this handler was called.

■ OnValueChanged — This handler fires whenever the value of a Slider or StatusBar changes. See also: SetValue

Arguments:
self — The frame object for which this handler was called.
value — The new value for the frame. (number)

Example:

```
-- Use a slider to move a frame across the center of ↵
the screen
local button = CreateFrame("Button", nil, UIParent, ↵
"UIPanelButtonTemplate2")
local slider = CreateFrame("Slider", nil, UIParent, ↵
"OptionsSliderTemplate")
slider:SetPoint("CENTER", 0, -60)
slider:SetWidth(400)
slider:SetMinMaxValues(-200, 200)
slider:SetValueStep(1)
slider:SetScript("OnValueChanged", function(self, value)
      button:SetPoint("CENTER", value, 0)
end)
slider:SetValue(0)
```

▪ OnVerticalScroll — Fires whenever a scroll frame changes its vertical scroll offset. See also: SetVerticalScroll, OnHorizontalScroll, SetHorizontalScroll

Arguments:
self — The frame object for which this handler was called.
offset — The offset in pixels that the frame has scrolled vertically. (number)

▪ PostClick — Fires immediately after OnClick with the same parameters. This handler is useful for processing clicks on a button without interfering with handlers inherited from a secure template. See also: OnClick, PreClick

Arguments:
self — The frame object for which this handler was called.
button — The name of the mouse button that clicked the frame. (string)

   ▪ LeftButton

   ▪ RightButton

   ▪ MiddleButton

   ▪ Button4

   ▪ Button5

   ▪ Remapped button (See Chapter 25)

down — Indicates that the click was triggered by mouse down. (boolean)

▪ PreClick — Fires immediately before OnClick with the same parameters. This handler is useful for processing clicks on a button without interfering with handlers inherited from a secure template. See also: OnClick, Click, PostClick

Arguments:
self — The frame object for which this handler was called.
button — The name of the mouse button that clicked the frame. (string)

   ▪ LeftButton

   ▪ RightButton

   ▪ MiddleButton

- Button4

- Button5

- Remapped button *(See Chapter 25)*

down — Indicates that the click was triggered by mouse down. (boolean)

Example:

```
<!--
Outside of combat, change the button's spell based on ↵
the class you
are targeting.
-->

<PreClick>
  if InCombatLockdown() then
    return
  end

  local class = select(2, UnitClass("target"))
  local spell
  if class == "WARRIOR" then
    spell = "Blessing of Kings"
  elseif class == "ROGUE" then
    spell = "Blessing of Might"
  else
    spell = "Blessing of Wisdom"
  end

  self:SetAttribute("spell", spell)
</PreClick>
:1234:0:0:0:0:0:0:0"). (string)
```

link — The full hyperlink (for example, "|Hplayer:Cogwheel:24|h[Cog-wheel]|h"). (string)

Example

```
-- Prints data about the hyperlink you leave in the i
default chat frame
DEFAULT_CHAT_FRAME:SetScript("OnHyperlinkLeave", i
function(self, linkData, link)
  local color = link:match("|c%x%x%x%x%x%x%x%x") or ""
  self:AddMessage("linkData: "..linkData)
  self:AddMessage(format("link: %s%s", color, i
link:gsub("|","||")))
end)
```

- OnInputLanguageChanged — Fires when the input language for the edit box changes. This is only valid for international clients that allow multiple input languages.

Arguments:

self — The frame object for which this handler was called.

language — The new input language for the EditBox. (string)

■ OnKeyDown — Fires when the frame receives a "down" key press. Only the currently focused, keyboard-enabled frame will receive this event. See also: OnKeyUp, EnableKeyboard

Arguments:

self — The frame object for which this handler was called.

key — The key that was pressed. (string)

■ OnKeyUp — Fires when the frame receives an "up" key press. Only the currently focused, keyboard-enabled frame will receive this event. See also: OnKeyDown, EnableKeyboard

Arguments:

self — The frame object for which this handler was called.

key — The key that was pressed. (string)

■ OnLeave — Fires whenever the cursor is no longer focused on a frame. The motion parameter is only true if the OnLeave was triggered by actual mouse movement. Other situations can cause OnLeave as well, such as a frame hiding or being covered up by another mouse-enabled frame.

Arguments:

self — The frame object for which this handler was called.

motion — Indicates whether the leave occurred due to mouse movement or not. (boolean)

■ OnLoad — Fires when a frame is first created. This is only applicable to frames instantiated from XML templates. Frames created with CreateFrame will have already run their OnLoad scripts by the time the function returns.

Argument:

self — The frame object for which this handler was called.

■ OnMessageScrollChanged — Fires when the scrolling message frame's scroll range changes (for example, after adding a new message).

Argument:

self — The frame object for which this handler was called.

■ OnMouseDown — Fires when a mouse button is pressed down while the mouse-enabled frame has mouse focus. See also: OnMouseUp, OnClick

Arguments:

self — The frame object for which this handler was called.

button — The mouse button clicking the frame. (string)

  ■ LeftButton

  ■ RightButton

  ■ MiddleButton

- ▪ Button4

- ▪ Button5

- ▪ OnMouseUp — Fires when the mouse button is released after clicking on a frame. This event will always fire for the frame that received the initial click, even if you move the mouse away from that frame. If OnDragStart occurs before the user releases the mouse button, OnMouseUp will not fire. See also: OnClick

    Arguments:
    self — The frame object for which this handler was called.
    button — The mouse button clicking the frame. (string)

    - ▪ LeftButton

    - ▪ RightButton

    - ▪ MiddleButton

    - ▪ Button4

    - ▪ Button5

- ▪ OnMouseWheel — Fires for a mouse wheel-enabled frame when the user rolls the mouse wheel while over the frame.

    Arguments:
    self — The frame object for which this handler was called.
    delta — Indicates one "notch" in a particular direction: 1 for up, -1 for down. (number)

    Example:

    ```
    -- Print the mousewheel delta for a button
    CreateFrame("Frame", "test", UIParent, i
    "UIPanelButtonTemplate2")
    test:SetPoint("CENTER")
    test:EnableMouseWheel(true)
    test:SetScript("OnMouseWheel", function(self, delta)
        DEFAULT_CHAT_FRAME:AddMessage(delta)
    end)
    ```

- ▪ OnReceiveDrag — Fires when you release the mouse button over a frame after starting a drag. See also: OnDragStart, OnDragStop

    Argument:
    self — The frame object for which this handler was called.

- ▪ OnScrollRangeChanged — Fires whenever the scroll range of a scroll frame changes. The extents are the distance you would have to scroll in the given axis to be fully scrolled. In other words, if the top-left corner of the scroll frame is visible, the scroll values are (0, 0). When you scroll all the way to the bottom-right, the scroll values are (xExtent, yExtent). For example, xExtent is equivalent to: max(scrollChildWidth - scrollFrameWidth, 0). See also: UpdateScrollChildRect

Arguments:

self — The frame object for which this handler was called.

xExtent — The horizontal scroll extent. (number)

yExtent — The vertical scroll extent. (number)

Example:

```
-- Set the min and max values of a scroll bar (Slider) i
based on the scroll range
scrollFrame:SetScript("OnScrollRangeChanged", i
function(self, x, y)
  verticalScrollBar:SetMinMaxValues(0, y)
end)
```

▪ OnShow — Fires whenever a frame becomes visible after being not visible. Fires whenever the frames Visibility status (retrieved by Frame:IsVisible()) changes from hidden to shown. This can be triggered by Region:Show() being called on the frame itself, or by Region:Show() being called on an ancestor. This handler does NOT fire if the frame was already visible.

Argument:

self — The frame object for which this handler was called.

▪ OnSizeChanged — Fires whenever a frame's size changes.

Arguments:

self — The frame object for which this handler was called.

width — The new width of the frame. (number)

height — The new height of the frame. (number)

▪ OnSpacePressed — Fires for a currently focused edit box when you press the Space key.

Argument:

self — The frame object for which this handler was called.

▪ OnTabPressed — Fires for a currently focused edit box when you press Tab. This is useful for switching fields on a frame with many text inputs.

Argument:

self — The frame object for which this handler was called.

▪ OnTextChanged — Fires whenever text in an edit box changes. This change can be caused by typing or calling SetText on the frame. In the latter case, OnTextChanged will fire twice. If SetText does not actually change the text, the handler will not fire.

Argument:

self — The frame object for which this handler was called.

OnTextSet — Fires for an edit box when its text is set via SetText.

Argument:

self — The frame object for which this handler was called.

■ `OnTooltipAddMoney` — Fires when a tooltip needs to add a money line and at every subsequent tooltip update. Note: this is only fired by the game engine when one of the `Set*` functions sets the tooltip to something that should display money (for example, an item while a vendor window is open). There is no corresponding widget API.

Arguments:

`self` — The frame object for which this handler was called.

`amount` — The amount of money (in copper) that was added to the tooltip. (number)

Example:

```
-- Display the amount of copper that is added to the i
tooltip
GameTooltip:HookScript("OnTooltipAddMoney", i
function(self, amount)
     DEFAULT_CHAT_FRAME:AddMessage(format("Money: i
%d", amount))
end)
```

■ `OnTooltipCleared` — Fires whenever the tooltip's lines are cleared. This can be triggered by hiding the tooltip or calling `GameTooltip:ClearLines`.

Argument:

`self` — The frame object for which this handler was called.

■ `OnTooltipSetDefaultAnchor` — Fired by C code when the tooltip needs to set its anchor to the default position. For example, mousing over a unit in the world frame.

Argument:

`self` — The frame object for which this handler was called.

■ `OnTooltipSetItem` — Fires in response to a corresponding `SetItem` call. Note: This handler does not pass the item as a parameter. This handler can fire more than once per tooltip, as information is retrieved from the server. This process is complete when `Tooltip:GetItem()` returns non-nil. See `GetItem`

Argument:

`self` — The frame object for which this handler was called.

■ `OnTooltipSetSpell` — Fires in response to a corresponding `SetSpell` call. Note: This handler does not pass the spell as a parameter. See `GetSpell`

Argument:

`self` — The frame object for which this handler was called.

■ `OnTooltipSetUnit` — Fires in response to a corresponding `SetUnit` call. Note: This handler does not pass the unit as a parameter. See `GetUnit`
Argument:

`self` — The frame object for which this handler was called.

- ▪ OnUpdate — Fires once for every visible frame each time the UI is rendered. This handler is often used for timers or tasks that must run continuously without interfering with gameplay. The rate OnUpdate is fired is exactly the same as your frame rate.

Arguments:
self — The frame object for which this handler was called.
elapsed — The number of seconds (fractional) since the last call to OnUpdate. (number)

- ▪ OnUpdateModel — Fires whenever a model changes or animates.

Arguments:
self — The frame object for which this handler was called.

- ▪ OnValueChanged — This handler fires whenever the value of a Slider or StatusBar changes. See also: SetValue

Arguments:
self — The frame object for which this handler was called.
value — The new value for the frame. (number)

Example:

```
-- Use a slider to move a frame across the center of i
the screen
local button = CreateFrame("Button", nil, UIParent, i
"UIPanelButtonTemplate2")
local slider = CreateFrame("Slider", nil, UIParent, i
"OptionsSliderTemplate")
slider:SetPoint("CENTER", 0, -60)
slider:SetWidth(400)
slider:SetMinMaxValues(-200, 200)
slider:SetValueStep(1)
slider:SetScript("OnValueChanged", function(self, value)
     button:SetPoint("CENTER", value, 0)
end)
slider:SetValue(0)
```

- ▪ OnVerticalScroll — Fires whenever a scroll frame changes its vertical scroll offset. See also: SetVerticalScroll, OnHorizontalScroll, SetHorizontalScroll

Arguments:
self — The frame object for which this handler was called.
offset — The offset in pixels that the frame has scrolled vertically. (number)

- ▪ PostClick — Fires immediately after OnClick with the same parameters. This handler is useful for processing clicks on a button without interfering with handlers inherited from a secure template. See also: OnClick, PreClick

Arguments:
self — The frame object for which this handler was called.
button — The name of the mouse button that clicked the frame. (string)

  - ▪ LeftButton

- ▪ RightButton

- ▪ MiddleButton

- ▪ Button4

- ▪ Button5

- ▪ Remapped button *(See Chapter 25)*

down — Indicates that the click was triggered by mouse down. (boolean)

- ▪ PreClick — Fires immediately before OnClick with the same parameters. This handler is useful for processing clicks on a button without interfering with handlers inherited from a secure template. See also: OnClick, Click, PostClick

Arguments:

self — The frame object for which this handler was called.

button — The name of the mouse button that clicked the frame. (string)

- ▪ LeftButton

- ▪ RightButton

- ▪ MiddleButton

- ▪ Button4

- ▪ Button5

- ▪ Remapped button *(See Chapter 25)*

down — Indicates that the click was triggered by mouse down. (boolean)

Example:

```
<!--
Outside of combat, change the button's spell based on i
the class you
are targeting.
-->

<PreClick>
  if InCombatLockdown() then
    return
  end

  local class = select(2, UnitClass("target"))
  local spell
  if class == "WARRIOR" then
    spell = "Blessing of Kings"
  elseif class == "ROGUE" then
    spell = "Blessing of Might"
  else
    spell = "Blessing of Wisdom"
  end

  self:SetAttribute("spell", spell)
</PreClick>
```

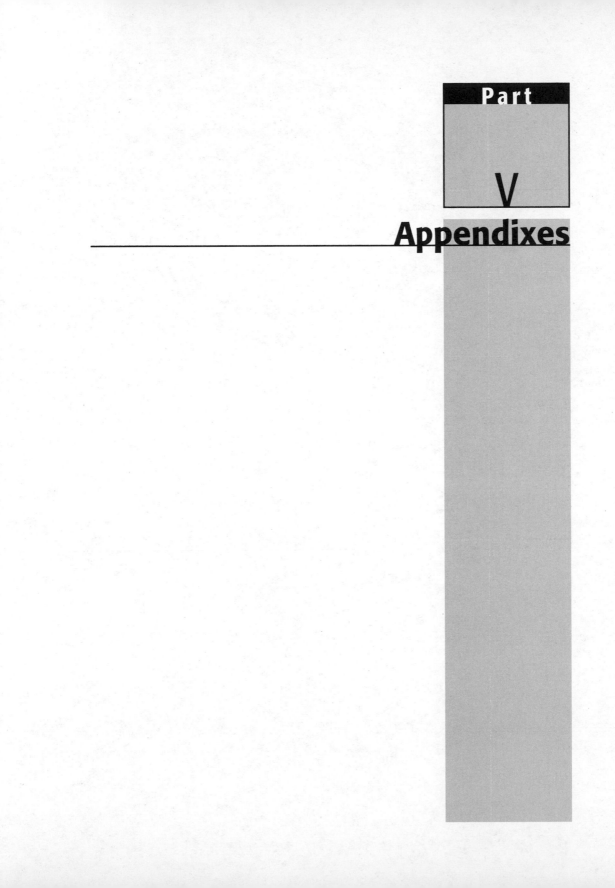

Part

V

Appendixes

Distributing Your Addon

James Whitehead II

Through the course of this book you've learned how to extend the default user interface and to create new custom addons. The next step in your journey is finding a place to host and promote your addon so other users can find it. This appendix covers the various options available for addon writers who want to distribute their work.

Hosting Websites

The actual business of hosting an addon is relatively simple. You could put it up on some free file-sharing website or even post it on your own personal webspace, but, in time, you may find yourself being overwhelmed with no way to easily track bug reports and feature requests. While the two can be mutually exclusive, this section presents a number of options that include some manner of bug/feature tracking along with hosting facilities.

Google Code — http://code.google.com/hosting

In March of 2007, Google launched a new application designed to support open source project development. Google Code Project Hosting (`http://code.google.com/hosting`) offers a version control system using Subversion, also known as SVN (detailed in Appendix B) and includes a powerful issue tracking system. Although relatively new to the open source hosting game, it's already got quite a following.

Project Creation

Creating a new project is a relatively simple process of choosing a name, creating a summary and description for the new project, and setting any number of metadata labels that will be used to categorize the project. An addon for World of Warcraft might include "World of Warcraft," "Addon," "Lua," "XML," and "WoW" as labels. Finally, you must choose a license for your project from a limited list.

All projects hosted on Google Code must be open source, and further must have an open source license. As a result, there are only eight choices for the licensing of your addon. Open source and software licensing topics are beyond the scope of this book, but you may find some useful information at `www.wikipedia.org/wiki/Open_source_license`.

Group Management

Anyone with a Google account can be given access to work on your project as either an administrator or a project member. Project members have limited access to the issue tracker and the capability to commit code to your source repository (where your actual addon code is stored). Adding a user is a simple matter of putting another's name in an edit box and clicking Submit. The new member is sent an email informing him of the change and providing him with information about the project.

Issue Tracking

The issue tracking system uses the metadata concept quite heavily, giving you flexibility over what different statuses and responses can be selected for a set of issues. The system will email the poster and anyone else who is signed up for notification anytime the status of an issue changes or more information is provided.

The issue tracking system does not allow anonymous users to add issues to the tracker.

Documentation

Each project created on Google Code has an attached wiki that can be used for posting news, documentation, release notes, or for allowing the development group to easily collaborate. The wiki is stored within the version control system and, as a result, can be edited via the web or through the source directly.

The wiki uses a specific markup that is different from the MediaWiki standard that has emerged, but it's relatively easy to adapt.

File Hosting

File hosting at Google Code is no-frills; it simply allows you to upload a file (up to 20 MB) with a one-line summary and metadata using labels.

Currently, a quota on each project's file downloads section allows only 100 MB, but this quota can be extended by contacting Google Code's support group.

Sourceforge — http://sourceforge.net

Created in November 1999, Sourceforge (http://sourceforge.net) was the first large-scale collaborative open source software project hosting website. Initially, it offered version control using CVS, and systems for documentation, project management, and issue tracking. Over the past eight years it has matured into a professional-scale software development system used by thousands of open source projects.

Project Creation

Creating a project at Sourceforge tends to take much longer than the alternatives, in that it typically takes 15 to 30 minutes to complete. You are guided through each step of the process with extensive documentation and help to ensure you make the correct choices for your project. Sourceforge only provides hosting to open source projects, so you must choose a compatible license for your work. After you've chosen the category for your project and provided descriptions and other information, your new project is submitted for approval.

The approval process can take anywhere from a few hours to a few days, but this quality-control process ensures that the information for your project is accurate and that the project will be properly categorized in the software listing.

Group Management

The administrative interface for Sourceforge is immense, giving the project administrator control over exactly what permissions each user has in the project and what information is displayed to the public.

Project members can be given access to the version control system and the issue tracker separately, and there are fine-grained controls for the documentation section, news, screenshots, and each individual portion of the site. A user must have a valid Sourceforge account to participate in a project.

Issue Tracking

The issue tracking system (called Tracker) separates bugs from feature requests, and also allows you to track incoming code patches as well as support requests from clients. It is relatively straightforward and allows the user to attach files that may better describe the support issue.

The system enables you to run reports on the Tracker, giving you statistics about how long it took to resolve the average issue in your project.

Documentation

Sourceforge has a comprehensive documentation manager that enables you to group and classify documents as you add them.

A document can consist of basic HTML markup pasted into an edit box, or a simple uploaded text file. The format is somewhat limiting, but the flexibility of HTML lets you to link between documents and throughout the project.

Community

Sourceforge allows you to host a limited number of mailing lists for your project, so your developers can have discussion on one mailing list while users submit questions and comments via another list. Each list can be displayed and linked directly from the project webpage.

File Hosting

The file release section of Sourceforge is well known due to the large number of projects that are hosted there. When you visit a project's webpage, you are given the option of downloading one of a number of packages that might have been defined for your project. If you want to offer two versions of your addon — one that is basic and another that is enhanced — you can create different packages inside the actual addon project.

Once the user has selected a package, he is given a list of versions and files that he can download directly. These file releases can have release notes attached to them.

WoWInterface — http://www.wowinterface.com

The folks at WoWInterface (`www.wowinterface.com`) have been involved in the MMORPG (massively multiplayer online role-playing games) community since Everquest was initially released, and their World of Warcraft site brings years of experience working with authors to the table. WoWInterface offers a range of features that are specifically designed for addon authors, including a version control system, feature and issues tracker, community forums, and per-project comments.

Project Creation

There are two ways to create a project at WoWInterface: Upload an existing addon or request a new project for development purposes.

Each addon project requires a description, screenshot, and other basic information. All addons go through a manual approval process to ensure there are no copyright or license violations, and that the addon listed is what's actually available for download.

Group Management

At the moment, an addon is owned by a specific user, but the user can have a team of developers who have access to the version control system. Permissions can be granted for a specific directory, or the SVN as a whole.

Issue Tracking

Each author can create a portal to be used for issue and feature request tracking on a per-addon basis. Each section of the portal has a separate RSS feed so both users and developers can keep track of the current issues list. Because WoWInterface caters only to World of Warcraft addons, the issue tracker's options are extremely focused and pertinent.

Documentation

Each author portal can house any number of webpages with static content. These are useful for introductions or other documentation for addons. There is also a frequently asked questions (FAQ) application that allows authors to easily add questions and answers for each of their individual projects.

Community

WoWInterface offers different forums for basic conversation, interface help, and requests, as well as more focused topics for existing addons and programming topics. In addition, each addon has a comments section that can be used for discussions about the addon.

File Hosting

Almost every feature of WoWInterface is focused around the file hosting. Each addon page offers a simple download button alongside links to the issues tracker, author portal, and installation instructions. Each file can have up to five screenshots and captions showcasing features of the addon.

If the addon has a Subversion system associated with it, the author can publish new versions (and development versions) to the website directly, without having to manually zip and package the addon. A development version available for download is listed on the addon page.

Curse — http://curse.com

Curse (http://curse.com) was initially started as a simple site that provided addon downloads, but it has grown into a full-blown massively multiplayer online (MMO) portal that still offers addon hosting and downloads. Although the site's focus is now split across multiple games, it still is a useful resource for WoW addons.

Project Creation

Uploading a new addon requires some basic data entry — including name, summary, description, and tags — that can be used to categorize your addon. Downloads can be flagged as development versions so users can download them for testing.

Group Management

Any number of authors can be added to an addon project, each having full control over the comments, tickets, and files available for download. This is a simple matter of going into addon setup and adding the user as a new author.

Issue Tracking

Each addon has a comments section that can be used for basic discussion, but the author can also activate a tickets system that can be used for issue tracking and feature requests.

The ticket system enables you to create individual components for larger addon packages so tickets can be for a specific portion of an addon.

Documentation

Curse doesn't have any specific places for addon documentation other than its main wiki. Each addon has a section for changelog and description, but you can link to the wiki pages from them.

Community

Other than the file comments, there isn't a very large user community at Curse. The forums are somewhat active, but they tend to be focused on the larger scope of MMORPGs.

File Hosting

An addon can have different versions of the same file, and they're all available through an easy two-click download system (first you select the file then the server that you'd like to download the file from). Uploading a new file is a matter of adding a changelog and altering the description, then uploading the actual packaged file.

IncGamers — http://wowui.incgamers.com

Formerly known as ui.worldofwar.net, IncGamers (`http://wowui.incgamers.com`) recently revamped its site to be more of an overall portal for various computer games (including StarCraft II, Diablo II, and other Blizzard enterprises). The WoW interface portion of the site remains very specific and offers a number of features that help addon authors.

Project Creation

Uploading a new addon is a simple process. First you upload the `.zip` file, and it tries to automatically determine certain information about the addon (such as the title and description) from your Table of contents file. Filling in any other details, the process is quick to complete.

Group Management

There is currently no way to share an addon project among multiple authors.

Issue Tracking

The only issue tracking system on IncGamers is the comments that are available for each addon.

Documentation

There is no separate way to host documentation on IncGamers.

Community

There is an active forum community on IncGamers but no real separation between the different major topics.

File Hosting

The file hosting on IncGamers is simple, enabling you to host both release and beta versions of your addons, and allowing the users to choose between them when downloading.

WowAce — http://www.wowace.com

Initially started as a community of developers using the Ace addon framework for World of Warcraft, the WowAce community has turned into a hub of addon development. Unlike some of the other hosting options, WowAce runs entirely off a central Subversion Repository (see Appendix B). As a result, it currently lacks any real project management, but provides an easy way to make your addon available to thousands of users through the WowAceUpdater.

Project Creation

There are no real "projects" on the WowAce SVN, but each project can create its own directories in the repository, pages on the wiki, and can have bug and issue tracking set up through the Jira system that WowAce runs. The first step to getting developer access to the SVN is reading the rules page and following the procedure for getting an account: www.wowace.com/wiki/SVN_Rules.

Group Management

There is no group management available on WowAce because the entire repository is open to the entire community. If a valid reason is given, you may be able to obtain a restricted directory, although this is discouraged.

Issue Tracking

Issue tracking is handled using the Atlassian Jira software. The process is relatively straightforward and individual projects can be created. The software is extremely professional and easy to use once you're familiar with the interface. A user must have an account (separate from the SVN and forum accounts) to post new issues or feature requests.

Documentation

Much like the community SVN, there is a single community wiki that can be used to document your addons online. New addons that are committed to the SVN automatically have an addon page created with basic information (pulled from the table of contents file). There is also automatic addon documentation that can be accomplished using a markup called Autodoc. More information can be found at `www.wowace.com/wiki/Autodoc_Format`.

Community

The WowAce forums at `www.wowace.com/forums` are very active but tend towards the discussion of Ace-based addons, although other discussions are certainly allowed. While the login/password is the same as your wiki login, a separate password is required for the SVN and issue tracker.

File Hosting

Any addon that resides in the `trunk` section of the repository is zipped up every 20 minutes and posted to `files.wowace.com`, where users can download it. This addon listing is used by a number of automatic downloaders, so new users are exposed to your addons very quickly. For this reason, it may be a good idea to keep your addon in the `branches` section of the repository until it's fully developed.

Personal Web Hosting

Of course, instead of using an existing website, you could choose to host your files on your own, but each of the preceding sites has taken time to create systems that are suited to the needs of addon authors. In addition, each of those sites is relatively well known in the addon community, ensuring users are comfortable downloading your addons.

If you choose to host your own files, you may want to consider adding the following:

- Forums for users to discuss your addons. It's a very happy day when your users step in and help support each other.

- Issue tracking system that allows you to keep a to-do list of bugs to fix and features to consider for later versions.

A mailing list or some other way for users to subscribe to be notified of future updates.

Tracking History Using Version Control Systems

James Whitehead II

A recent trend in addon development has been to track the history of development using version control systems. In short, each time the developer commits a set of changes to the system, a snapshot is taken that allows comparisons between snapshots. This means when a bug creeps into an addon, the history can be examined to determine exactly how and when the change made it into the software.

The most prevalent version control software in use in the addon community is currently Subversion, designed as a replacement for the older CVS version control software. This appendix explores the different aspects and commands of Subversion so you will be more familiar with some of the terminology. If you end up using Subversion (called SVN for short) in one of your projects, you should also consult the official documentation at `http://svnbook.red-bean.com`.

Subversion Terminology

A list of terms that you will encounter when working with the Subversion software follows:

- repository — The actual central location that houses the version control system (often shortened to repo). This is typically a remote location and can be of the form `http://some-host/repository/address` or `svn://some-host/repository/address`. There is typically one repository per project (or addon), although this requirement is not hard and fast.

- commit — A developer can make as many changes to his local code as he'd like, but each time he pushes a change back to the central repository, it is called a commit. A commit must include log messages explaining the changes that are being committed. Commits aren't expected every single time you save the file on your local machine, but rather at relevant stopping points (when you've fixed a specific bug, added a specific feature, and so on).

- checkout — A user or developer can download the current state of a given repository by checking it out. This downloads the current files as well as some basic history information. Typically, any user can check out a repository, but only developers can commit

- working copy — The local copy that one obtains when checking out a Subversion repository.

- diff — A file showing the differences between two versions of a given file or two different states of a repository.

A Subversion repository is just a sequence of directories and files with some extra metadata stored for versioning. The typical repository has the following subdirectories at the root level:

- trunk — The main development directory. This typically represents the bleeding edge of development and should be used with care. It's generally meant for developers and testers only.

- branches — Used when there are multiple versions of software being worked on at the same time. For example, if you're still providing support for some stable version of your addon, you might make a branch to keep it separate from your trunk development.

- tags — Tags are typically synonymous with releases, allowing you to see the state of the source code at the point you released a version to the public.

Obtaining Subversion

Subversion can be downloaded for your platform from the main Subversion website at `http://subversion.tigris.org/project_packages.html`. Binaries exist for both Mac OS X and Windows machines and, in most cases, come with a simple installer. Once installed, you can test that your system works properly by running the `svn` command in a terminal or command window:

```
> svn
Type 'svn help' for usage
```

If you see some other message, the command may not be in your path and you'll have to do a bit more experimentation. Several good guides to installing and using Subversion on any system are linked directly from the main Subversion website.

Subversion Command Primer

This section details the major Subversion commands you will use in the course of daily development. As always, more detail is available using the svn help command, or in the official documentation.

svn checkout <url> [path]

Checking out a Subversion repository is a matter of calling the svn checkout command with the URL of the repository. By default, a folder is created with the same name you are checking out, but you can specify a path argument to use a different folder name instead. The following command checks out the code for TomTom (one of my addons) into the folder trunk at your current location:

```
svn checkout svn://svn.wowinterface.com/TomTom-7032/trunk
```

Here's a command that checks out the repository into a folder called TomTom in your current directory:

```
svn checkout svn://svn.wowinterface.com/TomTom-7032/trunk TomTom
```

The following command checks out the repository into the folder c:\Subversion\TomTom on your computer:

```
svn checkout svn://svn.wowinterface.com/TomTom-7032/trunk ↵
c:\Subversion\TomTom
```

svn update [path]

The update command is used to update a working copy by contacting the central server and downloading any changes that have been made since the last update. By default, it updates whatever directory you are currently in (assuming it's a working copy).

If the current directory is a working copy, the following command updates it to the latest revision:

```
svn update
```

This command updates the working copy in c:\Subversion\TomTom to the latest revision:

```
svn update c:\Subversion\TomTom
```

svn commit [path]

The commit command is used when you have changes that need to be pushed to a central repository. On most systems, your default text editor will be opened and you'll be prompted for a commit message. Simply save the file in the text editor and the commit will begin.

You may be prompted for a username or password if this is your first commit. Whichever service runs your repository should be able to provide you with this information. As usual, this command assumes the current directory is a working copy, but a specific path can be specified.

svn log [path]

The `log` command can be used to give a history of log messages for a working copy. By default, it uses the current directory, but you can specify a path to check.

svn diff [path]

The `diff` command will print a listing of the differences between the code in your working copy, versus the last commit to the repository. This is a handy way to check what changes you've made to the file before commiting.

Creating a Local Repository

Even if you choose not to use an external Subversion service, you can create repositories locally on your machine using the `svnadmin` command. The command takes a path that will serve as the destination of the repository on the file system. The following command creates a new repository in the `C:\Subversion\MyAddon` folder that can then be used to check out and commit, assuming the `c:\Subversion` directory already exists:

```
svnadmin create c:\Subversion\MyAddon
```

Instead of using the `http://` or `svn://` type of URL, you use `file://`. To check out this repository, use the following command:

```
svn checkout file:///c:/Subversion/MyAddon
```

You can now use this new URL to store your history. That allows you a nice and easy way to keep version history locally. If you happen to delete your code or make some other destructive change, at least the effect is limited.

Best Practices

Matthew Orlando

Throughout this book the authors have made an effort to present code that follows patterns to make your programming life easier. However, not all of these ideas can be passed on implicitly. This appendix presents generally accepted practices that will empower you to be more effective at writing addons. These tips will help you produce addons more quickly, write better-performing code, and make your code itself more readable to others (and to you if you are away from a project for more than a few weeks).

Be aware that many people follow their own, more extensive sets of rules. To some extent, "best practice" is as much a case of personal preference as it is absolute commandments. We have done our best to pick the most widely applicable, least controversial ideals for inclusion here. However, you should always defer to your better judgment. If a solution that goes against these ideas presents itself to you, and either you can't think of an alternative or the alternatives are cumbersome and awkward, by all means, use what works.

General Programming

Certain practices are applicable to nearly every programming language in existence. These are not so much technical as they are conceptual; the intent is to help you think about a problem in ways that make it easier to solve. If you have had any formal training in programming, you will most likely be familiar with the suggestions presented here.

Use Meaningful Variable Names

If you've ever taken algebra or higher math, you know how difficult it can be to swim in a sea of seemingly random letters and numbers. It takes weeks of practice and memorization to fully understand and appreciate the mish-mash of variables, coefficients, and operators necessary to describe various constructs. This difficulty is no different and, in fact, is multiplied in programming.

Often, a new programmer will use short, abbreviated variable names to save time typing. At first the variables might seem self-evident, but that's only an illusion — an illusion that quickly goes away. Take the following two functions, for example:

```
function ic(i)
  local a = 0
  for j = 0, 4 do
    for k = 1, ns(j) do
      local l = il(j, k)
      if l and i == tn(sm(l, "item:(%d+):")) then
        a = a + sl(2, ii(j, k))
      end
    end
  end
  return a
end

function GetBagItemCount(itemID)
  local count = 0
  for bag = 0, 4 do
    for slot = 1, GetContainerNumSlots(bag) do
      local link = GetContainerItemLink(bag, slot)
      if link and itemID == tonumber(strmatch(link, "item:(%d+):")) then
        count = count + select(2, GetContainerItemInfo(bag, slot))
      end
    end
  end
  return count
end
```

Someone unfamiliar with your code (including yourself after some time away — we cannot reiterate this enough) would have to spend an unfortunate amount of time deciphering the first example. Even if you can follow the logic, there is absolutely no indication of what it does on a conceptual level. The only way to figure that out would be to research what the functions ns, il, tn, sm, sl, and ii do, all the while praying that they're not implemented in the same manner. You literally have to rename things in your mind to understand their behavior.

On the other hand, the code in the second example clearly spells out exactly what it does. The functions it calls describe what they do and the returns are placed into variables that describe what they represent. Even without looking at any of the code, the name of the function itself gives you an idea of its behavior. The time you spend at the front end typing the longer names more than pays off in the long run.

It *is* possible to be concise and clear at the same time. Rather than typing out the full description of something, you can use straightforward abbreviations. For example, you can use `desc` instead of `description`, `tbl` instead of `table`, `numSlots` instead of `numberOfSlots`, and so on.

Variable Naming Exceptions

As with algebra, there are certain well-known, single-letter variables that are used throughout the software industry. Some of them, in fact, are borrowed directly from algebra. Table C-1 lists some of the more common terse variables and their uses. If you decide to use these, make sure they are unique to the context — that is, the most important piece of data of its kind. For example, if you use `t` as a time value, it should usually be the most important time value in the function. You can get a bit more flexibility by numbering them (`t1`, `t2`) but it's best to limit how far you take it.

Table C-1: Common Single-Letter Variables

VARIABLE	USES
n	A number or count of something. Should be the most important count in its context.
t	A time or table value. Should be fundamental to the context (for example, a sort function could use `t` for the table it is sorting).
r, g, b, a	Color values. Red, green, blue, and alpha, respectively.
x, y	Screen coordinates. Horizontal and vertical, respectively.
i, j*	Numerical `for` loop index: `for i = 1, 10 do`
k, v*	Associative index and value in `for` loop: `for k, v in pairs(someTable) do`

_ (underscore)	Throwaway value. Something you don't actually plan to use:
	`local var1, var2, _, _, var3 = ↵`
	`someFunc()`

* In nested loops, it is usually better to use descriptive names to avoid confusion.

Use Constants Instead of 'Magic Numbers'

Programs often require some arbitrary number to control their behavior. The number of items that will fit in a list, a time limit for some complex operation, and the default number of buttons on an action bar are all numbers that could potentially be used in many places throughout your code. Rather than *hard coding* these numbers each place they occur in your code, store them in variables and use the variables in the code.

By doing this, you only have to make one change to affect every location the number appears in your code. The more occurrences of the number, the more time (and potential for error) you save. As with meaningful variable names, using constants gives significance to an otherwise random-looking number.

Convention dictates that you use all capital letters when naming your constants (such as NUM_ACTIONBAR_BUTTONS). This makes them easily identifiable in your source code, adding to readability. It is also a good idea to define all related constants in one location, usually near the top of the file where they are used. If they are scattered throughout your source code, you will needlessly waste time searching for the one you want to change.

Be sure you don't go overboard, though. If the number itself is fundamental to the problem you are solving, go ahead and use it literally. For example, the expression for calculating the circumference of a circle given its radius is $2\pi r$. If you need to make an area function, go ahead and use the 2 as-is (you'll obviously want to use a constant for the value of π, which WoW provides in PI).

Reorganize for Easier Maintenance

Code can sometimes become unwieldy. This occurs in a few different ways, but there are some things you can do to help.

Rework Repetitive Code

You may be working on some bit of functionality and find yourself repeating essentially the same lines of code over and over with only minor differences. Consider creating a function that takes a few parameters and does all of the steps each repetitive part of your original code would do. This will save you from many copy/paste errors as well as allow you to more easily add new occurrences of the same sort of functionality. You did something like this creating buff and debuff frames in Chapter 15; the processes are nearly identical.

Lua gives you even more of an edge with its tables. For more than a few repetitions, it might make more sense to define all your parameters in a list and then call the function in a for loop. For example, say you have a function, CreateTexture, which takes three parameters: name, id, and filename. If you have four textures, you could create a table and for loop like the following (notice how the numerical index is used to generate an ID for the texture):

```
local textures = {
  { name = "Picture of me",
    file = "Interface\\AddOns\\MyMod\\Images\\me.tga"
  },
  { name = "Picture of Ziggart",
    file = "Interface\\AddOns\\MyMod\\Images\\ziggart.tga"
  },
  { name = "Frame Background",
    file = "Interface\\AddOns\\MyMod\\Images\\bg.tga"
  },
```

```
  { name = "Some other texture",
    file = "Interface\\AddOns\\MyMod\\Images\\other.tga"
  },
}

for id, entry in ipairs(textures) do
  MyAddon.CreateTexture(entry.name, id, entry.file)
end
```

Now if you want to add a new texture, you can just create a new entry in the table. If you insert one in the middle, the rest will automatically have the correct IDs. Tables are also more recognizable as a data structure, so they make more sense semantically than calling `CreateTexture` four times with the various parameters.

Break Apart Long Functions

There is an upper limit to the number of words on a line of text or in a paragraph before our brains have trouble absorbing the information. In a similar fashion, functions that drag on and on over multiple screens become hard to follow. If you have a really long function that does a number of different tasks, you might want to break it apart into smaller functions that are called by one "master." A fairly common rule of thumb is to keep functions down to one screen of code or less.

Use Consistent Programming Style

Much of programming is a matter of personal style and preference. From indentation format to variable names, you can make many choices that affect the overall look and feel of your code. By remaining consistent in these choices, you will serve yourself in the long run. Following are some examples of choices you will have to make for yourself. Obviously, we could never hope to create a complete list, but this provides a good sample to get you thinking.

- **Naming conventions** — Do you begin all your functions with capital or lowercase letters? Do your variables use underscores or mid-caps (`numSlots` versus `num_slots`)? Do all functions follow a specific grammar (`Verb`, `VerbNoun`, and so on)?

- **Whitespace** — How many blank lines do you have between functions? Do you use tabs or spaces for indenting? How wide should indents be? Do you split long statements into multiple lines?

- **Organization** — Do you split your source into multiple files by functionality? Are your functions mostly local or do you use a namespace table? If you're using a table, do you use method syntax or simple indexing (`MyMod:function` versus `MyMod.function`)?

- **Comment format** — Do all of your functions have descriptions of their parameters and effects? Do you include a copyright notice at the beginning of your files? Do you use inline comments to describe complex algorithms?

Lua Tips

The Lua language is deceptive. On the surface it displays a clean, consistent syntax with intuitive keywords, and it has enough in common with other languages that experienced programmers can get the hang of it quite easily. However, to use Lua to its fullest extent takes a bit of creative thinking. Many of its features are unique (or at least rare) and certain idioms are downright foreign to programmers from other languages (let alone people new to programming in general). To help you in this regard, this section presents some tips that apply to Lua in general: some idiomatic concepts that will help you take full advantage of its features, and various optimizations to help you tune the performance of your addons.

Use Local Variables

As you may remember from Part I, variables are always global unless defined with the `local` keyword. Global variables, while suitable for many purposes, have a couple of important caveats. Each time you reference a global variable, Lua has to do a table lookup on the global environment (`_G`) with the name of said variable. Locals, on the other hand, are stored in a location of memory determined when the code is compiled. In fact, their names are irrelevant and inaccessible during runtime.

Additionally, each global variable has the potential for conflict. For instance, your addon might define a `print` function to help you display text to the chat window. However, as such a common name, there is always the possibility that it will overwrite a `print` function created by some other addon. If the two use different parameters, have different effects, and so on, your new function would break the existing addon (or vice versa depending on which loads first). One obvious solution would be to give the function a more unique name, perhaps tacking your addon name to the beginning, but that would unnecessarily add to your typing requirements. It would also add information to your code that provides no meaningful advantage to understanding the logic, potentially making it harder to follow.

For these reasons, use locals for every variable or function that does not need to be referenced outside of a given scope (whether it's the file, a function, or even within an `if` block). Also, if you have a legitimate global but performance is an issue, create a local copy. For example, if your addon needs to use `string.find` several times per frame, add the following line to the beginning (you can name it anything you want, perhaps `strfind`).

```
local string_find = string.find
```

Notice that this doesn't call `string.find` (as shown by the lack of parentheses), but merely copies the function reference to the new local variable. By using `string_find` throughout the file, you will save two table lookups on each call (`_G@@rastring@@rafind`). These savings can add up quite quickly for addons that do a lot of data processing each frame.

Minimize Garbage

Lua is a garbage-collected language. Every so often, it will go through all the objects in its memory and remove anything that is no longer being referenced. Say you have a function that creates a table when it runs. After that function exits there are no references to that table, so it will be collected later.

The Lua runtime is very fast by virtual machine standards. It outperforms many other common scripting languages in various tasks. However, nothing in the world is free — especially in computing. Every time you call your function, it creates a new table. Depending on how much information you pack into it, how often you call the function, and a few other factors, collecting this garbage can make a noticeable dent in WoW's performance.

The three main garbage-collected objects that you will encounter are tables, strings, and closures. Tables are definitely the most frequently abused objects. Strings are less obvious but can be just as frequent. Each unique string is a collectable object. Once there are no more variables set to a particular string, that string can be collected. Finally, each time you create a new function it makes a closure that includes the function itself and references to any upvalues.

Just like waste in real life, you should make an effort to reduce, reuse, and recycle. This will help prevent the garbage collection cycle from getting out of hand.

However, don't go overboard trying to wipe out every trace of garbage creation from your addon. If you have a situation where you only rarely need to create a new table, string, or closure, go ahead. Sometimes simplicity should take priority over efficiency, especially when the garbage does not have a substantial impact on performance.

It should also be noted that some of these techniques may actually take longer to run than the avoided garbage collection operation. Unfortunately, there is no sure way to know if this will be the case. It depends entirely on how much data is being used and what kind of processing is going on. If you start out using one technique and find that some areas need optimization, try it the other way.

How to Reduce Garbage

The most obvious way to improve your addon's garbage situation is not to create any in the first place.

Use Multiple Returns and Variable Arguments Instead of Tables

In many cases, your first instinct might be to use tables, being Lua's only true data structure. If you come to Lua from another programming language, you are probably used to dealing with structures, arrays, and such when you want to operate on a set of data. Sometimes, however, tables are unnecessary and even wasteful.

If a function needs to return a set of data, it is usually best to return multiple values unless the fundamental purpose of the function is to return some sort of table. This way, the calling function has complete control over how to treat the data. It can pack the returns into a table for later use, pass them to another function for further processing, or simply store them in local variables, as needed.

You have seen plenty of examples of multiple returns thanks to their extensive use in WoW's API. However, most of those functions return a fixed number of values. To pass an arbitrary amount of data to a calling function, you must use some form of recursion, which is explored a little later in this appendix.

Receiving arguments, both fixed and variable, has been covered fairly extensively in this book. The next section shows a way to operate on every value passed through the vararg (. . .) and return the modified values without using any intermediary.

Avoid Creating Unnecessary Strings

Try to steer clear of building strings piece by piece, adding new elements one by one. If possible, store each element in a variable and then put them all together in one mass concatenation. For example, say you are building a string such as `"123g 45s 67c"`. You may be tempted to break it down as follows:

```
money = gold.."g "

money = money..silver.."s "

money = money..copper.."c"
```

In this example, each line creates an entirely new string. Once the third line executes, the first two strings that were created are now garbage and can be collected. You can prevent this by building the entire string in one statement. Each of the following lines achieves the same result:

```
money = gold.."g "..silver.."s "..copper.."c"

money = strconcat(gold, "g ", silver, "s ", copper, "c")

money = string.format("%dg %ds %dc", gold, silver, copper)
```

In each case, only one string results from the operation, reducing the amount of garbage. The third line actually has a slight advantage over the other two. In the interest of simplicity, we neglected to mention that even the `"g"`, `"s"`, and `"c"` strings themselves are collectable objects once the function ends. This means that the original example actually contains five entirely wasted strings. In the `string.format` example, though, there's only one: `"%dg %ds %dc"`.

NOTE The function `strconcat` is actually specific to WoW. However, its behavior is fundamental enough that it is appropriate for this section. It is simply a function version of the concatenation operator (. .). `strconcat`'s main advantage over . . is that it can take a variable number of items to concatenate — something you will see in the next example.

SETFORMATTEDTEXT

Another WoW-specific tip that belongs here is the use of `SetFormattedText`. Suppose you intend to do something like the following after the code in the Money example.

```
text:SetText(money)
```

In this case, you can reduce created garbage further still and get a slight performance improvement by combining the `string.format` example and the `SetFormattedText` function.

```
text:SetFormattedText("%dg %ds %dc", gold, silver, copper)
```

The only garbage you create now is the formatting string. The `SetFormattedText` method does not generate the final string in the Lua environment at all. It exists entirely in the UI engine.

There are also some situations where a more garbage-friendly solution is not immediately apparent. Building a string in a loop, for instance, does not lend itself to the preceding approach. Consider the following loop (and forgive the contrived example):

```
local sequence = ""
for i = 1, 10 do
  sequence = sequence..i
end
```

The price you pay for its simplicity is that every single time through the loop creates a brand new string. After the next loop, the previous string is made obsolete. In addition to creating garbage, the Lua interpreter must copy the existing string data each time through, which also takes extra CPU time. One apparent solution to the garbage string problem is to use a table to store each new addition to the string and then call `table.concat`. But that still creates a garbage string for each element as well as generating an extraneous table.

Luckily, there's another trick using variable arguments and multiple returns. This time you add recursion to the mix:

```
local function MakeSequence(n, ...)
  if n > 1 then
    return MakeSequence(n - 1, n, ...)
  else
    return n, ...
  end
end

local sequence = strconcat(MakeSequence(10))
```

If you haven't had much experience with recursive functions, it may be hard to understand how this works. Let's run through the execution of `MakeSequence`.

1. `MakeSequence` is called with a single argument of `10`.

2. Because n is more than `1`, you call `MakeSequence` with the arguments `9` (n - 1) and `10` (n). . . . is empty so nothing else is passed this time around.

3. You are now one level deeper in recursion. n is `9` and . . . contains one argument, `10`. Again, because n is more than `1`, you call `MakeSequence` with the arguments `8` (n - 1), `9` (n), and `10` (. . .).

4. Recursion continues in this manner until the arguments to `MakeSequence` are n: `1` and . . .: `2, 3, 4, 5, 6, 7, 8, 9, 10`.

5. n has finally reached `1`, so you return the entire sequence from 1 to 10. This is passed back down through each level of recursion until it reaches the original call.

Or to put it more concisely:

```
MakeSequence(10)
  MakeSequence(9, 10)
      [Repetitive lines omitted]
              MakeSequence(2, 3, 4, 5, 6, 7, 8, 9, 10)
                MakeSequence(1, 2, 3, 4, 5, 6, 7, 8, 9, 10)
                return 1, 2, 3, 4, 5, 6, 7, 8, 9, 10
              return 1, 2, 3, 4, 5, 6, 7, 8, 9, 10
      [Repetitive lines omitted]
  return 1, 2, 3, 4, 5, 6, 7, 8, 9, 10
return 1, 2, 3, 4, 5, 6, 7, 8, 9, 10
```

Once the final call to `MakeSequence` returns, the values are passed to `strconcat`, which joins them all together as in the previous money example. In this way, you take advantage of Lua's stack to store each step of the process. Because items on the stack cease to exist as soon as the function ends, none of the data you pass back and forth needs to be collected.

TAIL CALLS

You may have noticed that all the `return`s in the previous diagram are identical. In reality, Lua processes the recursive function a bit differently than presented. Take a look at the line where you call `MakeSequence` inside itself. Because you are simply returning the results to the previous level without making any modifications, Lua uses a technique called a *tail call*.

Normally, when you call a function, the parameters are *pushed* onto the stack along with the location in your program to which the function should return. Then control is passed to the function being called. When that function finishes, it returns to the location you pushed originally.

In a tail call situation, on the other hand, the return location is omitted. Instead, the original return location in the *current* level of the call stack is used. When your deeper

TAIL CALLS *(continued)*

`MakeSequence` **call returns, it goes to the location of the very first call. Here is a more realistic diagram to illustrate what's actually going on:**

```
MakeSequence(10)
MakeSequence(9, 10)
    [Repetitive lines omitted]
MakeSequence(2, 3, 4, 5, 6, 7, 8, 9, 10)
MakeSequence(1, 2, 3, 4, 5, 6, 7, 8, 9, 10)
return 1, 2, 3, 4, 5, 6, 7, 8, 9, 10
```

To reiterate, tail calls are used only when you do not do anything to the values being returned by the function you call. That means you must use a `return` **statement in conjunction with the call. Even if the function you are calling does not return any values, as in the following example, Lua has no way to know this for certain at compile time.**

```
function foo()
    -- Do stuff without returning anything
end

function bar()
    foo()
end
```

When `bar` **calls** `foo`**, there is a hidden operation of discarding any values returned by** `foo` **that break your chance to use tail recursion. Changing the line inside** `bar` **to the following is all you need to fix it:**

```
return foo()
```

Tail call recursion also prevents a stack overflow, which you might expect if you have had prior programming experience. Because the recursion does not actually create a new level on the stack, the depth is limited to the maximum number of addressable parameters (around two billion in most Lua distributions). Chances are, your computer will run out of memory before you reach the limit.

Obviously, each unique problem requires slightly different logic. Let's look at another example to help you think recursively.

Many addons define their own `print` functions to make text output simpler. It also helps debugging because you can do unit testing outside the game with a Lua interpreter and leave the code unmodified to test it in-game. Most first attempts look something like the following (notice the similarity to the original sequence example):

```
local function print(...)
  local output = ""
  local n = select("#", ...)

  for i = 1, n do
```

```
      output = output..tostring(select(i, ...))
      if i < n then
        output = output..", "
      end
  end

  DEFAULT_CHAT_FRAME:AddMessage(output)
end
```

In this function you have two main problems to solve:

1. Each parameter must be converted into a string because concatenation does not automatically convert anything but numbers to strings.

2. The various parameters must be joined together with commas in between each entry.

You can handle the first problem with a dedicated function to convert all its parameters to strings and return the lot of them:

```
local function toManyStrings(...)
  if select("#", ...) > 0 then
    return tostring((...)), toManyStrings(select(2, ...))
  end
end
```

When `toManyStrings` is called with more than one argument, it returns its first argument converted to a string plus the `toManyStrings`ed versions of the rest of its arguments. Again, because you are not modifying the results of the inner call to `toManyStrings`, Lua will use a tail call so you don't have to worry about the number of arguments.

The second problem has already been solved for you. WoW comes with a function called `strjoin` that works a bit like `strconcat`, taking a variable number of arguments and putting them together. However, the first parameter to `strjoin` is a separator that is placed in between each element of the concatenation. For example, `strjoin(" sep ", "hello", "middle", "goodbye")` returns the string `"hello sep middle sep goodbye"`. Putting these two solutions together, your print function now becomes much simpler and produces far less garbage.

```
local function print(...)
  DEFAULT_CHAT_FRAME:AddMessage(strjoin(", ", toManyStrings(...)))
end
```

Reuse Objects

Reusing objects is easy to do, but the need and manner to do so may not be immediately apparent. Consider the following function, which hides a number of predefined frames:

```
local function HideFrames()
  local frames = {
    PlayerFrame,
```

```
        TargetFrame,
        MinimapCluster,
    }

    for _, frame in ipairs(frames) do
        frame:Hide()
    end
end
```

It may be immediately apparent to you that each time you call this function it recreates the `frames` table. After the function exits, `frames` goes out of scope and becomes collectable. The solution is simply to move the table to the same scope as `HideFrames`:

```
local frames = {
    PlayerFrame,
    TargetFrame,
    MinimapCluster,
}

local function HideFrames()
    for _, frame in ipairs(frames) do
        frame:Hide()
    end
end
```

The reference to the table will now persist as long as the scope it shares with `HideFrames` exists.

There *is* a tradeoff made using this technique. By defining the `frames` table at the file level, the memory is consumed at load time. With the previous listing, we defer creation of the table until it's actually needed. However, this tradeoff is easily dismissed in nearly every situation. Once the memory is allocated, it is completely free. Without garbage collection to worry about, it uses absolutely no processor time to remain in existence. Furthermore, `HideFrames` operates more quickly because the original version always creates the table even if it has already been used.

In the same way, you should not be creating functions inside other functions — "`function() end`" is to functions what "`{ }`" is to tables — unless you have a specific need for a new closure.

This technique can also extend to strings. Using string constants in a higher scope prevents them from being collected (think the `"g "`, `"s "`, and `"c"` strings from the previous section). Unlike tables and functions, strings are not created anew every time the code runs. There is not as much of a benefit to reusing them, but it still can save a few steps in the garbage collection. The performance advantage depends heavily on how many strings you use and the time between using them.

Recycle Tables

Tables are the only mutable garbage-collected objects in Lua. Unlike strings and functions, you can directly manipulate the contents of tables. This unique characteristic allows you to empty individual tables and reuse them.

There are a few ways to accomplish table recycling. In fact, some addon authors have created libraries for just this purpose. The simplest method uses a table to store the empty tables, a function to get an empty table, and another function to recycle an unneeded table. Following is one possible implementation:

```
local freeTables = {}

function GetTable()
  return table.remove(freeTables) or {}
end

function RecycleTable(t)
  for key in pairs(t) do
    t[key] = nil
  end
  table.insert(freeTables, t)
end
```

Whenever you want a new table, you call `GetTable`. This function attempts to remove a recycled table from `freeTables`. A new one will be created for you if the table is empty. Once you're done with the table, you call `RecycleTable` to empty it and place it back into `freeTables`.

The major disadvantage of table recycling is that it puts you, the programmer, back in charge of handling memory allocation and deallocation, essentially taking on the role of garbage collector. In fact, some programmers believe this completely defeats the purpose of using a garbage-collected language in the first place. However, in time-critical tasks where you need to use (and discard) many small tables, the performance gains cannot be ignored. It is up to you to strike the appropriate balance between performance and clarity.

Other Fine-tuning Optimizations

The next few tips offer slight performance improvements for various situations. For the most part, Lua is fast enough to let you organize your addon's logic as intuitively as possible. However, there may be times when you need to squeeze out every last ounce of CPU power.

Check Expected Conditions First

When Lua processes a chain of `if...elseif` statements, it goes through one by one until it finds a condition that evaluates to true — or it runs into the `end`. If the chain is long enough, careful ordering can provide a substantial speed improvement. Most of the time when creating such statements, you will have some idea of which conditions are most likely. Take advantage of this foreknowledge to place the most likely conditions earlier in the chain, as in the following pseudo code:

```
if likely condition then
  do stuff
elseif less likely condition then
```

```
  do other stuff
elseif equally likely condition then
  do yet some more stuff
elseif unlikely condition then
  more stuff goes here
end
```

Even if you do not know beforehand what conditions will be most likely, some simple profiling tests can help figure that out for you. For instance, you could maintain counters for each clause that increment whenever they execute. Then you could create a function to print out the stats. Most of the time, such optimization is unnecessary. If you're doing anything in `OnUpdate` or some other extremely frequent code path, though, it may just be worth the research. (Remember to remove said counters for the release version of your mod because incrementing them has its own performance impact.)

Exploit Shortcut Evaluation

In a similar vein, you can use a feature of Lua (and other programming languages) called *shortcut evaluation* to optimize the conditionals themselves. Consider the expression `a or b`. The `or` operator evaluates to `true` if either `a` or `b` evaluates to `true`. Once Lua knows that `a` is `true`, there is no reason to evaluate `b`. Similarly, as soon as it's known that `c` is `false` in the expression `c and d`, the entire expression is known to be `false`.

Any time you have a complex condition with several clauses, you should try to put the most likely and/or fastest-to-evaluate clauses first. In pseudo code, this would look something like the following.

```
if likely condition or less likely condition then
  do stuff
elseif fast condition and slow condition then
  do stuff
end
```

NOTE This section describes the *logical* result of the evaluation of boolean expressions. As discussed in Chapter 2, the actual results of the `and` **and** `or` operators are one of the two operands depending on whether the first one is interpreted as `true` **(anything but** `false` **or** `nil`**) or** `false`/`nil` — **the** `return table.remove(freeTables) or {}` **statement from the preceding** `GetTable` **function, for example.**

Use Tables as a Logic Structure

Sometimes you will have a long chain of `if`...`elseif` where each clause compares the same variable to some constant. The prime example in addon programming is an `OnEvent` script. Consider the following:

```
if event == "SOME_EVENT" then
  -- do stuff
```

```
elseif event == "ANOTHER_EVENT" then
  -- do stuff
elseif event == "THIRD_EVENT" then
  -- do stuff
elseif event == "FOURTH_EVENT" then
  -- do stuff
end
```

You can use a table in a manner similar to the "Rework Repetitive Code" section earlier in this appendix. Instead of the if statement, you fill a table with functions indexed by the name of the event:

```
local eventHandlers = {
  ["SOME_EVENT"] = function(frame, namedArgument)
    -- do stuff
  end,
  ["ANOTHER_EVENT"] = function(frame, namedArgument1, namedArgument2)
    -- do stuff
  end,
  ["THIRD_EVENT"] = function(frame)
    -- do stuff
  end,
  ["FOURTH_EVENT"] = function()
    -- do stuff
  end
}
```

Now the OnEvent script can be simplified to four lines (or one if you are careful about what events you register):

```
function MyEventHandler(frame, event, ...)
  local handler = eventHandlers[event]
  if handler then
    handler(frame, ...)
  end
end
```

This technique affords a few advantages:

- The underlying architecture of the table lookup usually executes more quickly than a string of if...elseif clauses, especially with a large number of entries.

- Each event handler is a separate entity. Defining separate functions for each one adds a level of context that can make the code easier to follow.

- Parameters can be adjusted to suit the event. As demonstrated in the preceding example, you can give names to the individual elements of . . . that would normally be accessed via select or creating new local variables in each if/elseif clause. You can even eliminate parameters altogether if they are irrelevant to the given event.

▪ As with the textures example earlier, you can use the table keys for the actual registering and unregistering of the events:

```
for event in pairs(eventHandlers) do
  someFrame:RegisterEvent(event)
end
```

The WoW Environment

The last part of this appendix deals specifically with constructs and procedures unique to World of Warcraft.

Use What You're Given

By now, it should be second nature to look for APIs and widget methods to help with your day-to-day tasks. However, many other built-in features go neglected. For instance, authors often write their own functions to convert the returns from `UnitName` into `"name"` or `"name-realm"` to indicate cross-realm players. Granted, this is a rather trivial task, but WoW already provides such a function at the end of `FrameXML\UnitFrame.lua`.

Obviously, we do not expect you to familiarize yourself with the entirety of FrameXML code as you're starting out, but it is always a good idea to look in files that may be related to your addon, both to see how things are done in the default UI and to find functions to take advantage of yourself. For example, if you are writing an alternative quest frame, you should look over `QuestFrame.lua` and `QuestFrame.xml` before you begin work on your addon.

`GetBagItemCount` from the beginning of this appendix could actually be improved slightly. Rather than `for bag = 0, 4 do`, where 4 is a prime example of a magic number, you can define a constant for the number of bags. However, Blizzard has saved you the trouble. Near the top of `FrameXML\ContainerFrame.lua` is the constant `NUM_BAG_FRAMES`, which represents the number of bags besides the backpack. Using the Blizzard-defined constant adds a bit of future-proofing to your code. If they ever increase the number of bags a player can carry, they will bump `NUM_BAG_FRAMES` to the new count and your function will be instantly compatible.

Localize with Global Strings

Virtually every display string in the UI is stored in a constant in `FrameXML\GlobalStrings.lua`. This file is translated to every language WoW supports. By using the constants in this file for various aspects of your addon, you will be automatically localizing certain parts of it, which is of great benefit to your international users.

Error messages, button text, combat log strings, and many others are there for the taking. Many common terms such as "Yes," "No," and "Okay," are easy enough to recognize. You will also see strings for the various races, genders, classes, and other commonly used terms. Whenever you are looking into localization for your addon, open `GlobalStrings.lua` and do a preliminary search for the terms you want.

Even if you do not see the exact phrase you're looking for, the search may still help. If you are trying to do localization yourself, you may be able to figure out the basic structure of the phrase in the target language but not how some particular term translates. You can find `GlobalStrings.lua` from other locales on some addon sites and compare the phrases to come up with the missing term.

Avoid Deprecated Systems

The World of Warcraft UI code has gone through many evolutionary changes as new needs for the game and from the addon community have come to light. New systems are constantly being added and tweaked to take better advantage of Lua design patterns, improve efficiency, and implement new game features. Unfortunately, the time invested in the older systems is significant enough that many of them are still around in some form or another. Through the patch cycle, though, the default UI is being slowly reworked to use the newer methods and, at some point in time, the old ways may no longer be supported.

Throughout this book we have purposefully omitted coverage of these past practices. If you use the code for the default UI or other addons as research material for your own addon, translate any usage of the constructs discussed in the following sections into the newer method.

NOTE Rather than listing all deprecated systems in this section, specific events, APIs, and so forth that should no longer be used are marked as deprecated in their reference entries (see Part IV).

Global Widget Handler Arguments

The widget handler system you saw in Chapter 11 is new as of patch 2.0. Instead of calling your handler with a `self` parameter and other related data (`button` for `OnClick`, `event` and ... for `OnEvent`, and so on), the old system used a global variable called `this` and several global argument variables (`arg1`, `arg2`, and so on). There were a few problems with this approach. Using global variables for a parameterized system does not make much sense conceptually, not to mention their impact on performance. Also, the generic `argn` variables go against the very first pointer in this appendix. The only way for you to know the meaning of the argument when reading old code is to look at a reference for the given handler or hope you can infer its meaning from what the code does with it.

Following are two somewhat useless functions to illustrate the difference. If you use `SetScript` to assign them to an `OnHyperlinkClick` script, they will function identically.

```
function MyAddon_OnHyperlinkClick()
  if arg3 = "LeftButton" then
    this.link = arg1
    print("You clicked on "..arg2)
  end
```

```
end

function MyAddon_OnHyperlinkClick(self, link, text, button)
  if button = "LeftButton" then
    self.link = link
    print("You clicked on "..text)
  end
end
```

As you can see, `this` corresponds to `self`, `arg1` corresponds to `link`, `arg2` corresponds to `text`, and `arg3` corresponds to `button`. With the exception of `OnEvent`, `this` and `arg1`-`argn` will always match the parameter list of the given handler. In this way, you can use the widget handler reference in Chapter 30 to determine the meanings of the global arguments in any legacy code. The only difference with `OnEvent` is that `event` always had its own global. `arg1`-`argn`, in this case, correspond to the parameters passed through . . . .

SecureStateDriverTemplate

Chapter 26 showed you how to use macro conditionals to drive a state header with `RegisterStateDriver`. Prior to patch 2.1, the only way to achieve a similar effect was by using `SecureStateDriverTemplate`. This template created a driver with states for stance, stealth, action bar page, and modifier keys. In fact, the template that exists for backward compatibility is simply a secure frame that calls `RegisterStateDriver` for each state type in its `OnLoad` script.

At this point, however, there is no compelling reason to use this template. If you only need one particular state type, it will actually hurt performance because the driver will be paying attention to states that are of no interest. In addition, the FrameXML code has a comment saying it's only there for backward compatibility, so there's always the possibility that the template will be removed in a future patch.

bag and slot Attributes on item Type Action Buttons

Another change in 2.1 is the simplification of secure action buttons with a `"type"` attribute of `"item"`. Previously, the `"item"` attribute could only be used to activate an item by name. To use an item in your inventory would require a `"slot"` attribute; to use an item in your bags required `"bag"` and `"slot"` attributes. Now the `"item"` attribute works the same way as the `/use` macro command. It accepts an item name, item ID (in the form `"item:12345"`), slot number, or bag and slot numbers separated by a space (for example, `"3 12"`).

Again, for backward compatibility, the `"bag"` and `"slot"` attributes are still supported. However, you should no longer use them as a comment in `FrameXML\SecureTemplates.lua` demonstrates: "Backward compatibility code, deprecated but still handled *for now*." [Emphasis mine.]

Avoiding Common Mistakes

James Whitehead II

Addon authors can make dozens of common mistakes as they develop their addons. Many of them have been covered throughout the book, but the following deserve to be mentioned here, as well. You may find some similarities between the items listed here and the "best practices" that are covered in Appendix C but, of course, the best way to avoid common mistakes is to use best practices to prevent them in the first place.

Initializing Global Variables

When writing a function, it's easy to accidentally set a global variable instead of a local variable by omitting the `local` keyword. This can be especially problematic when the global is something simple like `color`, which would potentially conflict with another addon. Make sure that you declare variables as locals, unless you have a specific reason to do otherwise.

Adding Files

When World of Warcraft loads, it scans the file system and builds a table of files that can be loaded during that session. If you add files while the game is open, they won't be part of that table and cannot be loaded or recognized by the game. A related common mistake is adding a new file to your addon and the table of contents file without fully exiting the game.

If you add files to the file system, make sure that you fully exit and restart the game so that the changes will be fully registered.

Entering | into the EditBox

Because World of Warcraft uses the | character in its color codes, any that are entered in the edit box are automatically escaped to a double ||. This can be problematic when running Lua scripts with the /script and /run commands. You can substitute the sequence \124 instead of the actual character to get around this limitation.

"Hidden" Frames

In order for a frame to be visible, it must meet the following requirements:

- The frame must have some visual component, such as a texture, backdrop, or text element.
- The frame must not be set as hidden in the XML file, or the frame's :Show() method must have been called to explicitly show the frame.
- Each frame that is a parent of the frame must also be shown. This includes the frame's parent, the parent's parent, and so on.
- The frame must be anchored somewhere within the bounds of the screen.

It's easy to spend time digging through your code only to find later that you've forgotten to place the frame on the screen.

Logs\FrameXML.log

When working on XML, there are two places to check to ensure the file is being parsed and validated properly:

- Load the file in some program that can indicate that the file is well-formed. This could include most web browsers or a more complex XML editor/validator.
- Check the Logs\FrameXML.log file to ensure there weren't any errors parsing the file.

Not Checking API Returns

There are times when the Blizzard API functions may return something other than what you'd expect. For example, there's a small period of time where UnitClass(unit) can return nil when you'd expect a class name to be returned. If you use these function returns in some other computation, such as indexing a table or calling another function, you may get an error somewhere along the line.

In many cases, you can fix the problem by supplying default values in the following way, or by throwing an explicit error with the `error()` function:

```
local class = UnitClass(unit) or "Warrior"
```

Even if the class is wrong, you can be sure you won't have an unexpected error.

Requesting Data Before PLAYER_LOGIN

As stated in the earlier chapters, a number of functions don't return the correct results until the `PLAYER_LOGIN` event has fired. This can be remedied by delaying the call until that point, but you should be aware when getting unexpected results that the information may not be available in the client at that moment.

Multiple Anchor Points

Each frame can have multiple anchor points that help define the placement or size of the frame. When adjusting anchor points, make certain that you've cleared any that should no longer be set. When in doubt, run `:ClearAllPoints()` to ensure that a frame has no anchors before adding your own anchor points.

Utilizing Addon Libraries

James Whitehead II

When a system as incredibly complex as the World of Warcraft API is released, inevitably someone writes an interface that makes it easier for specific uses, or adds certain functionality. True to form, several addon frameworks and libraries have been written for WoW. This appendix explores the creation of libraries and points you toward some existing libraries.

Why a Library?

After writing several addons, you may reach a point where you've written the same basic code block in a few different locations, perhaps even copied and pasted directly from one to the other. When you find yourself in this situation, it can be beneficial to pull the common code out into some sort of library that each addon can use. Take the following function:

```
local function PrintString(fmt, ...)
  local message = fmt
  if select("#", ...) > 0 then
    local txt,err = pcall(string.format, fmt, ...)
    if not msg then
      error("Bad arguments to string.format: " .. tostring(err))
    else
      message = txt
```

```
        end
    end

    ChatFrame1:AddMessage("|cffff1100PrintString:|r " .. ↵
tostring(message))
end
```

This function enables you to print directly to the chat frame while allowing you to use `string.format()` format codes in your text. That means you don't have to type the following each time you want to print a message:

```
local msg = string.format("You have reached your destination %s", destination)
ChatFrame1:AddMessage("|cffff1100PrintString:|r " .. tostring(msg)
```

You can use the following instead:

```
PrintString("You have reached your destination %s", destination)
```

While the gain may seem minimal, using something like this regularly can be a big time saver. Copying and pasting this function into each of your addons is an easy way to reuse your code, but makes it very difficult to maintain. If you find a bug in the function, you need to edit each and every file that defines that function, or you risk running into the bug in another addon.

Creating a library that can be used by your other addons can be a nice way to share code between different addons.

Dependencies versus Embedded Libraries

A library of functions can be written as a dependency, meaning that it's a separate addon that must be downloaded by the user or packaged with the original addon. Alternatively, a library could be written as a small Lua file that is packaged with each addon that uses it. This type of library is called an *embedded* library.

Dependency Libraries

Writing a library that is used as a dependency is easy. Create a new addon with a name that is meaningful (or indicates what the library is used for) and provide a single global table with your functions included. To avoid conflicting with other addons, this table should have a reasonably unique name. The preceding example can be extended by changing it to the following:

```
CladUtils = {}

function CladUtils.PrintString(fmt, ...)
    local message = fmt
    if select("#", ...) > 0 then
```

```
    local txt,err = pcall(string.format, fmt, ...)
    if not msg then
      error("Bad arguments to string.format: " .. tostring(err))
    else
      message = txt
    end
  end

  ChatFrame1:AddMessage("|cffff1100PrintString:|r " ..
tostring(message))
end
```

Now instead of calling a local `PrintString()` function, each addon will package the `CladUtils` addon and call `CladUtils.PrintString()`. This method actually works quite well for a small, focused set of functions used by a single author, but can easily get out of hand when a library becomes popular. Specifically, if the library is packaged with each addon that requires it, users can easily accidentally overwrite the library's files with an older version, removing the bug fixes or changes you may have made in a newer version. Embedded libraries were designed to help alleviate some of these issues.

Embedded Libraries

An embedded library is one that is part of the addon that uses it, rather than standing alone as a separate addon. For this system to work and be robust, each library must have two bits of information:

- Major version — A unique name that indicates the name and version of the library. Two libraries with different major versions will run alongside each other.

- Minor version — A number that indicates the specific version of a given major version. If two libraries have the same major version but different minor versions exist, the older one will be "upgraded" to the newer one using some defined process.

The major version should be updated whenever there is a change to the behavior of the underlying functions or a change to the parameters that is not backwards-compatible with previous versions. The major difference between the two versions is that minor versions can be upgraded without issues, while major versions indicate some change that could break something.

For example, if the `PrintString` function is changed so that it no longer prints to `ChatFrame1`, or an argument is added to the start of the argument list, the major version should be changed to a new one. This way, people who were using the old version can continue to do so without worrying about their addons breaking. If only the minor version were changed, errors would almost certainly occur.

VERSIONING YOUR LIBRARY

The code to manage the versioning of your library can be as simple as a check against the minor version of the existing version, such as:

```
local minor_version = 501
if MyLibraryName and minor_version < MyLibraryName.minor then
    return
end
```

This code would cause the file to stop running after checking the minor version and realizing that it's already out of date. In addition to this simple method, a number of library versioning "stubs" have been created just for this purpose.

Recently, LibStub was created as a cross-community project to standardize the way libraries are registered and accessed by the community. Using LibStub, the preceding code would look like this:

```
local lib = LibStub:NewLibrary("MyLibraryName", 501)

if not lib then
    return
end
```

LibStub keeps a central repository of all libraries and their current major version numbers. When you call `LibStub:NewLibrary()` with your major and minor version, it either returns a table (which is the existing library) or `nil`. If you're given a table, you can simply use that to define your library.

Because you receive a table that is already populated, you may need to clear it or handle other upgrade tasks. For more information, visit `http://www.wowwiki.com/LibStub`.

Library Upgrading

Here's the general process for loading an embedded library:

1. Check to see if a library with the same major version is already loaded.

2. If a version exists, then compare the minor version numbers. If the new library being loaded has a newer minor version, it should replace the old one and upgrade itself.

3. If a version exists but the minor version of the new instance is less than the existing one (meaning this library is older), you can safely return and stop initializing.

4. If the major version does not already exist, the library should be loaded.

Using embedded libraries, multiple copies of the library may be loaded and then thrown away, which can increase load times. This would only happen in the situation that addons loaded in a very specific order that had increasing minor versions of the same library. In addition, the library author needs to be sensitive to the potential upgrade process, and should test the library thoroughly before releasing a minor version update to a library.

Choosing a Library Method

Each library scheme has its own set of benefits and tradeoffs, and no solution has been found that fills everyone's needs sufficiently. If your library is only for personal use, and something you can easily control, then making your library a dependency is a natural choice. If you are using someone else's library, or know that it will be used by other developers, an embedded library gives you much stricter control over what version of a library you are using.

Both methods require discipline on the part of the addon author, making sure they increment the major version and minor version, as required. The library business can be very sticky because someone else's changes can directly affect your addon, but the benefits often outweigh any difficulties you may encounter.

Existing Libraries

Rather than give full detail on a set of existing libraries, including how to use them and what API is available, this section shows you where to find libraries that currently exist and gives you general information about what some of them do.

Ace2

The Ace2 (`http://www.wowwiki.com/Ace2`) suite of libraries was designed to be included as embedded libraries that use each other as dependencies. There are libraries that provide the following functionality:

- AceLibrary — Library versioning and loading.
- AceOO-2.0 — Provides an object-oriented framework for addons to use.
- AceAddon-2.0 — The core of the Ace2 framework, AceAddon-2.0 is the basis for any new addon.
- AceComm-2.0 — Provides an API layer for inter-addon communication using the Blizzard `SendAddonMessage()` function.
- AceConsole-2.0 — Adds slash command functionality to addons as well as providing some helpful slash commands, such as `/reload` to reload the user interface and `/print` to print something to the chat frame.
- AceTab-2.0 — Adds tab completion support for slash commands.
- AceDB-2.0 — Provides a layer on top of the SavedVariables system to include default values and support for nonstandard group settings, such as per-class.
- AceEvent-2.0 — Allows for event registration and handling, along with a system, for scheduling delayed events.
- AceDebug-2.0 — Provides some simple debugging functions to simplify addon debugging.
- AceHook-2.1 — Allows addons to easily hook functions in the default user interface using a system that ensures it's done without interfering with other addons.

- AceLocale-2.2 — Provides some mechanisms for localization of addons.
- AceModuleCore-2.0 — Allows you to separate your addon into multiple modules that can be turned on and off.

For more information on the Ace2 family of libraries, visit `http://www.wowace.com` or `http://www.wowwiki.com/Ace2`.

Chronos

Chronos — `http://www.wowwiki.com/Chronos_(addon)` — is a simple timing library that enables you to schedule tasks to be run in the future, or at some periodic interval. Scheduled tasks can be cancelled ahead of time, and there is API support to determine how much time is left on a given timer.

Dongle

Dongle (`http://www.wowwiki.com/Dongle`) is a collection of functions that should be useful to anyone writing a new addon. Designed to be extremely small without excess functionality, it provides an easy way to register events, schedule tasks, and comes with a database system that makes creating saved variables structures with defaults easy.

Earth

Earth (`http://www.wowwiki.com/Earth`) is a library that is designed to ease the pain of creating and building graphical user interfaces (GUIs) for your addons. The library contains a set of useful templates, as well as functions that can be used to alter templates as you see fit.

Satellite

The Satellite (`http://www.wowwiki.com/Satellite`) library can make creating slash commands for your addon a bit more manageable and consistent. In addition, it allows you to add custom chat types to the chat frame configuration window so they can be turned on/off and colored independently.

Sea

Sea (`http://www.wowwiki.com/Sea`) is a Java-style library of utility functions for writing addons. It consists of the following major sections:

- data — Information tables useful to the game (subsections item and spells).
- IO — Input and output functions.
- lang — Language and localization functions and constants.
- math — Math functions and constants that aren't included in Lua's standard libraries.

- string — String manipulation and formatting functions.
- table — Table manipulation utility functions.
- util — Miscellaneous common utility functions, such as function hooking.
- wow — Utility functions specific to World of Warcraft game objects, such as tooltips.

Telepathy

Telepath (`http://www.wowwiki.com/Telepathy`) is an addon library focused on providing a more consistent API layer that allows inter-addon communication between different players. The `SendAddonMessage()` function is the basis for this communication, and Telepath provides a layer on top of that which makes sending messages and registering listeners easier.

Other Library Resources

There are literally dozens of libraries written for any number of purposes, and most of them are well documented and readily available. The best places to explore for libraries to use are the following:

- `http://www.wowwiki.com/Function_Library`
- `http://wowace.com/wiki/Category:Libraries`

Some of these libraries depend on other libraries (which can get quite messy), but if you're looking for a good existing API for something that you find peculiar in the Blizzard API, they may just have what you're looking for.

Author and Addon Communities

James Whitehead II

Naturally, with so many users downloading addons and developers writing new ones everyday, it's important to have a community for interface customization. This appendix details a few of the prominent addon discussion communities and what they focus on specifically.

Official World of Warcraft Forums

The Blizzard-sponsored WoW forums are extremely active, and we're lucky enough to have Blizzard employees who post somewhat regularly as they make changes to the user interface. As a result, there are stickies that detail the major changes in the last patch, as well as any upcoming changes that have already been announced. This allows authors to plan ahead and discuss potential changes with the community and developers.

These forums are also a nice place to ask for and provide help with addon writing, as well as to announce new projects and seek feedback on existing ones. The Official World of Warcraft forums can be found at `http://forums.worldofwarcraft.com/ board.html?forumId=11114`.

IncGamers UI Customization Forums

Titled the "Unofficial World of Warcraft Forums," the UI Customization forums at IncGamers (`http://wow.incgamers.com/forums/forumdisplay.php?f=107`) provide a forum to generally discuss addons for WoW and another subforum for authors to converse with each other. This splits the forums into a less technical forum for assistance and a highly technical forum for those who need it.

WoWInterface Forums

Because WoWInterface (`http://www.wowinterface.com/forums/index.php`) is dedicated to user interface customization for WoW, it has quite a number of forums dedicated to different topics or modes of conversation. For example, it has its own Chit-Chat forum, along with separate forums for Interface Help and Interface Requests. Authors can discuss their released addons in the Released Interfaces/Scripts forum. In addition, there is a set of six forums that focus on developers helping developers.

There are a number of featured projects and authors on WoWInterface.com, and each of them has their own forum to discuss the addon. This helps both the reader and the developer stay more organized.

In addition, there is an IRC channel sponsored by WoWInterface.com on the `irc.freenode.net` network, in the channel `#wowi-lounge`.

Elitist Jerks

The Elitist Jerks (`http://www.wowinterface.com/forums/index.php?`) is an extremely capable World of Warcraft guild. It hosts a forum specifically for the discussion of user interface and addons that tends to be extremely active with both announcements of new addons and discussion of the uses of existing ones. It may not be the best place to go if you're having difficulty installing or using certain addons, but if you want to propose new addon ideas, or stay on the bleeding edge of what's being created, it may be just what you need.

WowAce Forums

The WowAce forums (`http://www.wowace.com/forums`) are dedicated to the discussion and development of the Ace family of addons. Most of the authors who release their addons via the WowAceUpdater are active on the forums and have posts for supporting and collecting feedback for their addons. The site is separated into developer and users sections to facilitate having a support thread and a very technical discussion thread without causing confusion.

CosmosUI Forums

Cosmos is a packaged set of addons written to use consistent configuration interfaces and to easily interoperate. The CosmosUI Forums (`http://cosmosui.org/forum.php?`) provide user support and allow suggestions, feature requests, and technical discussions about the addons to take place in a controlled environment. The forums have an extremely active user base, and there are quite a number of how-to or tutorial threads that make using Cosmos even easier.

WowProgramming Forums

Meant to allow readers of this book to talk with each other and converse with the authors, a set of forums are available on the book's companion website (http://wowprogramming .com/forums). There you will find other like-minded authors who are working through the same examples and documentation that you are.

We have also registered an IRC channel #wowprogramming on the irc.freenode.net network. Many of the individuals who worked on the book frequent IRC, and you can look to the channel for help and discussion about the contents herein.

Glossary

The whole of this book is extremely technical and can be confusing to even the most seasoned programmer. This glossary is a list of terms that may be unfamiliar to the reader in the context of World of Warcraft.

1nil — An imaginary value type that indicates the value is either the number 1 or the value nil. These types of returns are used frequently throughout the default user interface to indicate the existence (1) or lack of (nil) some setting. It is also used sometimes as a way to know if a called function succeeded or failed.

Alpha — A graphical element's alpha channel defines the level of transparency for that element. The simplest form of alpha values are used throughout the widget system, where any color or frame can be declared partially or wholly transparent (any value 0.0–1.0). Texture files can contain alpha transparency in two forms:

- 1-bit alpha — Each pixel has an on/off switch for alpha, allowing each to be either fully transparent or fully opaque.
- 8-bit alpha — Each pixel can be flagged fully transparent, fully opaque, or any of 253 values in between (because 0 is transparent and 255 is opaque).

Action — A spell, item, or macro that has been placed on one of the game's action buttons.

Action Slot — A number between 1 and 132 that references a specific action. Only the first 120 of those slots are usable by addons; the actions assigned to the last 12 are used by the possession bar and cannot be changed by addons.

Anchor — A way of visually attaching one frame to another. A specific point on frameA is anchored to a point on frameB. Anchors can be used to define positioning as well as size.

Battlefield — A player versus player instance. Currently, the only types of Battlefields are Arenas and Battlegrounds.

Bonus Bar — The shapeshift/stealth/stance bars that are used when a class shapeshifts, stealths, or changes stance.

Button — The only widget (frame) type that can receive mouse click events.

Craft — The user interface used for the Enchanting and Pet Training systems in WoW. Each of the items in the Craft UI can be referred to as a *Craft Skill* or *Craft Recipe*, depending on the context.

Deposit — The amount of money that must be paid to place an item up for auction.

Event — A special type of message that is sent from the game client to anyone who is registered for the given event. These events are used to notify the user interface that something has happened that may require an update of an on-screen element. For example, the UNIT_HEALTH event indicates that the health of a unit of interest has changed, notifying anyone displaying that value to update.

Focus — A secondary target unit that allows the player to view and query information about two units at the same time. This is useful for allowing players that can crowd control to watch their crowd control target while still attacking the primary target.

Frame — An object within WoW that can contain graphics, font strings, and other frames to display graphical elements on screen. Frames can also be used to register for system events and other notifications.

Gossip Frame — The frame that is displayed when first speaking to an NPC. The gossip frame gives basic introductory text and then displays a list of options. This allows a single NPC to act in multiple roles, such as Innkeeper and Merchant.

Header — A heading displayed in one of the listing frames in-game. For example, the Reputation window displays a heading for each grouping of factions so they are better organized.

Hook — A function hook is a method of replacing one function with another, so the new function is called instead of the original.

Inventory — The items a player currently has equipped, or the slots that could be equipped. For the purpose of the WoW API, bags on the player as well as bags in the bank bag spaces are considered equipped.

LFG/LFM — The in-game system that allows players to find other players that are interested in grouping together for a specific purpose (quest, dungeon, and so on). LFG and LFM stand for Looking For Group, and Looking For More, respectively.

NPC — Non Player Character. Any in-game entity that is not player controlled.

Override Binding — A temporary key binding that has priority over other types of key bindings. These are used to allow addons to temporarily override the default game bindings so those key combinations can be re-used.

Petition — An in-game petition used to charter arena teams and guilds.

Query — A request sent to the server to get more information about something. For example, to retrieve the current auction house listing, one must send a query to the auction house.

Quest Frame — The frame that quests are displayed in when interacting with NPCs. This is different from the *Quest Log*.

Quest Log — The frame the player can use to view his currently active quests. This is different from the *Quest Frame*.

Quest Tracker — The in-game quest objective tracker.

Roster — A list of members of a given group. The most prevalent roster types are Arena, Guild, and Raid rosters.

Scale — Each frame in WoW has a scale associated with it. This allows the frame and its children to be shrunk or blown up by the graphics engine on the fly. Scale is inherited from parent to child, so a frame with a scale of 0.5 that is the child of a frame that also has a 0.5 scale will have an *effective scale* of 0.25.

Secure Template — A new system of XML templates introduced during the release of The Burning Crusade. These templates allow the developer to define the behavior of a frame ahead of time and have the frames change dynamically during combat. Secure templates are required whenever the frame is capable of casting spells or targeting units.

Skill — An ability that is known by the player. Skills include language skills, weapon skills, and primary and secondary professions.

Taint — The security system in WoW allowing Blizzard's code to be flagged as secure, capable of actions that addons cannot take. This is accomplished by flagging any non-Blizzard code as "tainted." This taint is used to deny specific actions and to assign blame when an action that requires an untainted path is called from a tainted one.

Target — The player's current target.

Temp Enchantment — A temporary item enchantment, such as Wizard Oil, Rogue poisons, or a Shaman's Rockbiter spell.

Texture — A graphics file that can be loaded by the client. All texture files must be in either the TGA or BLP format and each side must be a power of two. For example, a 128x256 graphic is valid, while a 100x200 graphic is not.

Tradeskill — All of the game's tradeskills, with the exception of Enchanting are displayed in the Tradeskill UI. Each item in the tradeskill window can be referred to as a *Tradeskill* or *Tradeskill Recipe*. Each of the primary and secondary professions, with the exception of Enchanting are tradeskills.

Trainer — Any in-game NPC that can directly teach the player skills or recipes.

Trainer Service — A skill or recipe that can be learned directly from an NPC.

Unit — A special token that refers to a specific player or character within the game. The `player` and `pet` units always refer to the player and his pet, while other units such as `target, focus, raid1`, and `party2target` can change dynamically.

Widget — A specific type of frame that can be created through the WoW API. Example widgets are `StatusBar, Button, EditBox`, and `Slider`.

Index

G